NAVIGATION AFLOAT

A Manual for the Seaman

Navigation Afloat

A Manual for the Seaman

ALTON B MOODY

Captain, U.S. Naval Reserve
Former Chief, Future Applications Satellites,
National Aeronautics and Space Administration
Former Chief, Long Distance Navigation Branch,
Federal Aviation Administration
Former President, U.S. Institute of Navigation
Royal Institute of Navigation Gold Medallist
Thurlow Navigation Award

Foreword by
M. W. Richey, M.B.E.
Director, the Royal Institute of Navigation

VNR VAN NOSTRAND REINHOLD COMPANY
NEW YORK CINCINNATI TORONTO LONDON MELBOURNE

Published by Van Nostrand Reinhold Company
A division of Litton Educational Publishing, Inc.
135 West 50th Street, New York, NY 10020, U.S.A.

Van Nostrand Reinhold Limited
1410 Birchmount Road
Scarborough, Ont. M1P E27, Canada

Library of Congress Cataloging in Publication Data

Moody, Alton B   1911-
   Navigation afloat.

   Bibliography: p.
   Includes index.
   1. Navigation—Handbooks, manuals, etc.
I. Title.
VK555.M62   623.89′02′02   79-22271
ISBN 0-442-25488-1

CONTENTS

CONTENTS

CONTENTS

FOREWORD

M. W. Richey M.B.E.

Director, The Royal Institute of Navigation

Over the centuries manuals, or books of instruction for the seaman, have exercised a considerable influence on the development of navigation. The most vivid example which springs to mind is that of Martin Cortes' *Arte de Navegar* published in Madrid in 1551 which, translated by Richard Eden, formed the basis of Bourne's *A Regiment for the Sea*, which so affected the tardive English school later to assume such significance. But there is no lack of modern examples and any seaman will call to mind works which in their day broke new ground or gave a fresh perspective to the art: Robertson, Lecky, Bowditch, Raper, Dutton to name but a few. The standard texts are regularly up-dated and go into innumerable editions, and they perform a useful and educationally vital function. But there comes a time when a fresh look at the whole subject seems called for. The last thirty years have witnessed a navigation explosion—an expansion of ideas, methods, techniques and concepts—which has transformed the subject.

For the most part this transformation has been provided for in the literature, in scientific papers of one kind and another, many of them published in the journals of the Institutes of Navigation throughout the world; and philosophically in one magisterial work in particular, *The Principles of Navigation* by E. W. Anderson. But there has only been a piecemeal reflection in the manuals of instruction on either side of the Atlantic and it is to fill this gap that the present work has been undertaken.

Captain Moody's qualifications for the task are impressive. A graduate of the U.S. Naval Academy at Annapolis, where he later taught navigation, he joined the Navigational Sciences Division of the U.S. Navy Hydrographic Office (as it was then) in 1946 and was closely involved in a number of the Division's projects, including the design and preparation of the navigation tables H.O.214 and H.O.249. He compiled the *Navigation Dictionary* (H.O.220) and revised and largely rewrote for the U.S. Navy the famous *American Practical Navigator* (Bowditch, H.O.9). Alton Moody was for some years Chief of the Long-distance Navigation Branch of the Federal Aviation Administration and is author of a textbook on air navigation. In addition he was the originator of a satellite navigation system that was narrowly turned down in favour of the Navy Navigation Satellite System (Transit). His work over the years has been recognized by the award of the Royal Institute of Navigation's Gold Medal and the Thurlow Award of the American Institute.

Differences in navigational terminology and in usage of contractions, abbreviations and symbols pose a problem for a book to be published on both sides of the Atlantic. Where terms differ (as *range* and *transit*, or *nun* and *conical*) both have been given in this volume. The matter of conventions is less easily solved and American practice so far as abbreviations and symbols go (such as Lo rather than λ for longitude) has, for the most part, been adhered to in the text whilst the glossary contains both. Again for consistency American chartwork notation, which differs slightly from the British, has been preserved and a note to that effect added where necessary.

London, 1980   M.W.R.

Author's Preface

Navigation in some form is involved in all travel from one place to another, and therefore has been practised from the beginning of time. In its most primitive form it consists of the use of one's senses to guide one's motion toward the desired destination. Those who developed skill in this endeavour established the *art* of navigation. As time progressed and various devices were developed to aid the navigator and make his work more precise, the *science* of navigation evolved. With the emergence of this science, the art of navigation underwent a decline.

The successful navigator of the late twentieth century realizes that both the art and science of navigation have limitations. He relies heavily upon science, while he develops the art needed to apply it intelligently and skilfully.

This book summarizes briefly the knowledge a mariner should have as a point of departure in mastering the subject of navigation afloat, with particular emphasis on its application in the merchant service. Emphasis has been given to modern methods, while not entirely neglecting older methods still in limited use. An extensive bibliography provides information on other sources of information for those who desire to explore navigation and related subjects in greater depth.

The writing of this book was suggested by Michael Richey, Director of the Royal Institute of Navigation, editor of *The Journal of Navigation*, and internationally renowned ocean racing navigator. His guidance and encouragement are acknowledged gratefully. I am indebted to Mr. R. F. Reeves for drawing the numerous diagrams. I am also indebted to my wife Kathryn, who spent many hours alone while the writing was in progress, provided encouragement in the project, and typed the manuscript.

San Diego, California, 1979   ALTON B MOODY

I
Introduction

1. Definition

Navigation is the process of conducting a craft as it moves about its ways. The term *craft*, sometimes used to refer only to small vessels, is in this book used in a general sense to refer to any vessel or vehicle, or, one might say, any object having need to be navigated. Navigation includes, in addition to the application of scientific principles, use of judgment and some skill. It is a dynamic process requiring constant vigilance and an awareness of the situation. However versed a person may be in the science of navigation, and with whatever skill he may apply the principles involved, the final test of his ability as a navigator is whether his craft remains afloat at all times.

The navigator is involved basically in two activities: (1) determining the position of his craft, and (2) establishing the optimum path to reach a desired destination. In engaging in these two activities, he is faced with a number of tasks, such as acquiring information relating to his environment, making observations of various kinds, calculating, plotting, and avoiding collision with fixed or moving objects. He is concerned with direction, distance, speed, time, velocity, and acceleration.

At sea in good weather, navigation can be a somewhat leisurely process, although the prudent navigator does not allow this situation to induce him to relax his vigilance. Demands on his time and skill increase during periods of poor visibility, and reach a maximum when he is entering or leaving a busy harbour in thick weather.

In merchant service operations, scheduling is often an important consideration, but the wise navigator never permits adherence to a schedule to compromise safety. Nothing is quite so disruptive of a schedule as a grounding or a collision.

2. Position Determination

If a craft leaves a known position and moves in a known direction for a known distance, one can determine its new position by extrapolation. The process is called *dead reckoning* (*DR*), and a position determined in this manner is called a *dead-reckoning position* (*DR position*). Distance travelled might be determined by direct measurement or by computation based upon measurement of speed and elapsed time.

In navigation afloat, direction of motion and either distance travelled or speed is generally measured relative to the water through which the vessel travels. The water itself may be in motion over the surface of the Earth. This motion of water may be referred to as *current*, although this term is sometimes restricted in its application to non-tidal flow, to distinguish it from *tidal stream* (p. 203). Navigators often use the term current loosely to refer to the combined effect of actual motion of the water and any effect of wind or other element in altering the direction or speed of the craft.

Occasionally, the expression dead-reckoning position is used to refer to a position determined by allowing for the best estimate of actual motion of the craft over the bottom, following the common practice of air navigators. In navigation afloat, however, this practice of using motion relative to the bottom as the basis of dead reckoning is best used only when motion of the craft relative to the bottom is measured directly, as by a Doppler sonar navigator (p. 540) or inertial navigator (p. 532). When dead reckoning referring to motion relative to the bottom is used, the expression *sea position* (*SP*) or *water position* (*WP*) may be used to refer to a craft's position determined by its motion relative to the water.

Dead reckoning is a simple position-determination method nearly always available in some form. However, because of current and leeway (p. 167), dead-reckoning positions are subject to an uncertainty that increases with elapsed time. Imperfection in measurement of direction and distance travelled add uncertainty that increases with distance travelled. Accordingly, it is generally necessary from time to time to revise a position based upon dead reckoning alone.

This is done by a process known as *position fixing*, or by adjusting a DR position for current, or by some combination of the two.

A position determined by position fixing is called a *fix* if the data upon which it is based are obtained simultaneously or nearly so, or a *running fix* (*R Fix*) if this condition is not met. Position fixing is usually accomplished by making measurements permitting establishment of *position lines* (*PL's*), also called *lines of position* (*LOP's*), on each of which the craft is presumed to be located. The fix is established at the intersection of these position lines. Although two position lines suffice for establishment of a fix, a third line is generally considered desirable as a check. If the three position lines do not meet at one point, the triangle formed is called a *cocked hat*. In this case the fix is generally considered to be that point within the triangle equidistant from the three position lines. A fix might also be obtained by placing the craft at a known position, as alongside a buoy.

Pilotage, or *piloting*, is involved when position is determined relative to established geographical points on earth, generally natural or man-made landmarks or seamarks. *Astronavigation*, also called *celestial navigation*, involves observation of celestial bodies. *Electronic navigation* involves the use of electronics.

Data sufficient for establishment of a fix are not always available, but the navigator may have information permitting improvement of a DR position. This information may be a good estimate of current and other disturbing elements, a lone position line, or position lines of less than desired reliability. Any position, other than a DR position, established under these circumstances, is called an *estimated position* (*EP*). In practice, the designation EP is generally limited to (1) a DR position adjusted for current (in the broad usage of the term), (2) the foot of a perpendicular from a DR position to a lone position line, (3) the foot of a perpendicular from (1) to a lone position line, and (4) a position obtained by radio bearings.

The expression *most probable position* (*MPP*) is sometimes used to designate that point which is judged to represent the most likely position of the craft at any time. The MPP might be a fix, running fix, EP, DR position, or some intermediate position established by weighting all available data.

When a navigator establishes a position, other than by dead reckoning, in which he has confidence, he considers this a 'known position' and starts a new dead reckoning from it. In practice, a new DR is started from a fix or running fix, but generally not from an EP.

3. The Earth

For many purposes of navigation the Earth is considered a sphere, although actually it is flattened somewhat at the poles, and bulges slightly at the equator, giving it the shape of an *oblate spheroid*. If very small deviations from this figure (not including topography) are taken into account, the shape is a *geoid*. These small differences are significant in predicting the orbits of satellites used for position fixing. A number of determinations of size and shape of the Earth have been made, each resulting in a different *reference ellipsoid* (spheroid) which differs slightly because of differences in data and method, but the equatorial radius (a) is about 6,378,135 metres, and the polar radius (b) about 6,356,750.5 metres, giving a *flattening* (f) or *ellipticity* of about 1 part in 298.26: $f = (a-b)/a$.

The Earth rotates on an axis terminating at the North and South *Poles* (P). The intersection of the surface of the Earth, considered a sphere, with a plane through its centre is a *great circle* (GC). Refer to Fig. 101. The great circle midway between the geographical poles of the Earth is the *equator*. Semi-great circles from pole to pole are *meridians* (mer). The intersection of the spherical Earth's surface and any plane not passing through its centre is a *small circle*. Circles parallel to the plane of the equator are *parallels*, or *parallels of latitude*. *Latitude* (L, lat) of a place, designated north or south, from 0° to 90°, is the angular distance, along a meridian, from the equator. Because of the ellipticity of the Earth, the angle between the equator and a line normal to the reference ellipsoid, called *geodetic latitude* or *geographic latitude*, the

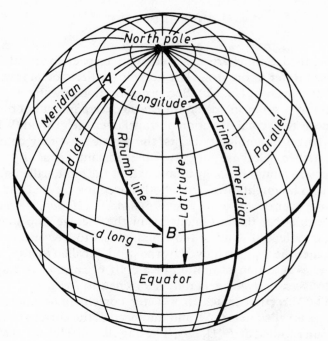

FIG. 101. The Earth.

value used in navigation, is not quite the same as the *geocentric latitude*, the angle between the plane of the equator and a line from a point in the surface of the Earth to the Earth's centre. *Latitude difference* (*d lat*, *l*) is the angular distance, along a meridian, between any two parallels. *Longitude* (λ, *Lo, long*) designated east or west, from 0° to 180°, is the angular distance, along a parallel, between two meridians, one of which is considered the *prime meridian*, or the origin of longitude measurement. By international agreement, the meridian through the Royal Observatory at Greenwich (now a part of the National Maritime Museum), is accepted as the prime meridian. The length of the arc of a parallel between any two meridians is *longitude difference* (*d* λ, *d long*, or *DLo*) if expressed in angular measure, and *departure* (*p*, *dep*) if expressed in linear units. A *rhumb line* maintains a constant angle with respect to all meridians. Thus, a craft maintaining an unchanging true direction of travel follows a rhumb line. An oblique rhumb line traces a spiral called a *loxodrome* on the surface of the Earth.

4. Direction

Several directions are involved with respect to travel of a vessel. Refer to Fig. 102. The horizontal direction of travel is called *course* (*C, Cn, Co*). Because of motion of water and the effect of wind, principally, the *course steered* might not be the same as the actual direction of travel over the ground. When no danger of ambiguity exists, the term course may be used for either. Because of yaw, the instantaneous forward direction along the longitudinal axis of the craft, called *ship's head* (*SH*) might differ from both the course steered and the course over the ground. The term *heading* (*H, hdg*) is used to refer to either the instantaneous or the average ship's head.

The effect of wind in blowing a vessel to leeward, or the distance the vessel is moved by the wind, is called *leeway*. The angular deviation of motion of a craft because of leeway is called *leeway angle*, generally shortened to *leeway*.

The direction in which a water current or tidal stream moves is called its *set* (*S*), and the speed of the current or tidal stream is called *drift* (*D, Dr*). The angular difference between the course steered and the direction of motion of the craft is called *drift angle* (*D, Dr*), designated right (R) or left (L) of the course steered. Note the difference between the convention for current and that for wind. An easterly wind blows from the east toward the west, while an easterly current flows from the west toward the east. The total distance travelled by water over some period of time is referred to as its

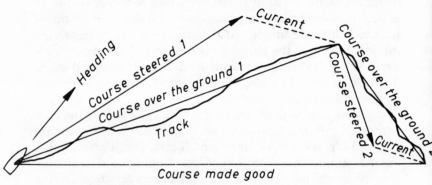

FIG. 102. Directions involved in travel of a vessel.

total drift. Often the total departure from a line extending in the direction of the heading is considered to be the effect of current. Thus, any factor affecting the accuracy of measurement of course steered is included. This procedure is convenient and generally justifiable, for the navigator is usually concerned with the total departure more than with its components. The mean course actually achieved, relative to the surface of the Earth, over a period of time is called the *course made good* (*CMG*). The course may differ from time to time because of changes in current or course steered. Course with respect to the surface of the Earth is called *course over the ground* (*COG*).

A line extending in the direction of a course is called a *course line*, and one extending in the direction of a heading is called a *heading line*. The path followed by a vessel as it moves across the surface of the Earth is called its *track* (*TR*). The track differs from the course line by the fact that the latter extends in one direction only, while the former includes all the deviations and changes from a straight line. Although the track is the actual path followed, the term is sometimes used to refer to the intended future path of the craft, and also to the path of any moving entity, such as a storm centre, and, by extension, to the direction of the path.

The horizontal direction of one point from another is its *bearing* (*B, Bn, brg, brng*). The term is usually used to indicate the direction of an object as observed from one's craft. Bearings, as other directions, are generally expressed as angles from some *reference direction*, or *datum*. The usual reference direction is north, but it is sometimes convenient to use the heading as the reference direction for bearings, which are then called *relative bearings* (*RB*). Directions are usually stated in degrees, in three digits, from 000° at the reference direct on clockwise through 360°. Relative bearings are occasionally stated in degrees right (green) or left (red) of the heading. Approximate relative directions are sometimes expressed in 'points', one point being 1/32 of a circle, or $11\frac{1}{4}$ degrees. Using this system, one might express the relative position of another craft or other object as so many points green or red, or as 'dead ahead' (relative bearing 000°), one-, two-, or three points 'on the bow', 'broad on the bow' (relative bearing 045° or 315°), three-, two-, or one point 'forward of the beam', 'broad on the beam' (relative bearing 090° or 270°), one-, two-, or three point 'abaft the beam', 'broad on the quarter' (relative bearing 135° or 225°), three-, two-, or one point 'on the quarter', or 'dead astern' (relative bearing 180°). Except for 'dead ahead' and 'dead astern' the relative direction starboard or port (sometimes green or red) is stated. The term 'ahead' or 'astern' is sometimes used to indicate a generally forward or after direction. The bearing of an astronomical body is generally called its *azimuth* (Z, Az).

The calculated value of an angle representing a direction generally involves a conversion from the calculated value to a direction on the 000° to 360° scale. To distinguish between the calculated angle and the direction, the navigator adds the word 'angle' to the designation of the calculated value. Thus, one may calculate a *course angle* (C), *heading angle, bearing angle* (B), *azimuth angle* (Z, Az), or *track angle* and convert the values to course, heading, bearing, azimuth, or track.

5. Units of Measurement

Navigators usually express distance (d, dist) travelled in *nautical miles* (M, n $mi.$, NM). This unit differs from the *statute mile* ($mi.$, st $mi.$) of 5,280 feet (1,609.344 metres) used on land; it is very nearly equal to one minute of arc of a great circle of the Earth. This relationship makes the nautical mile a convenient unit because meridians are semi-great circles, and thus the latitude scale of the navigator's chart serves also as a nautical mile scale, although a slightly variable one because of the ellipticity of the Earth. This variable unit is sometimes referred to as a *sea mile* to distinguish it from the true nautical mile. The relationship is particularly fortuitous in the case of Mercator charts (p. 41), those most commonly used by mariners, because their scale varies with latitude. Also, distance and certain astronavigation calculations yield nautical miles (minutes of arc) directly. Because of minor differences in definition and the size and shape of the Earth accepted by different countries, and at different times, a standard *international nautical mile* of 1,852 metres has been established and generally adopted. The *geographical mile* of one minute of arc of the equator is used only for meridional parts (p. 41).

In navigation, distances are usually stated to the nearest 0.1 M. Shorter distances, as from one's craft to a nearby lighthouse, may be expressed in *cables* (*cab*), units of 0.1 M in British terminology, or 720 feet in United States terminology, or metres (m), although feet (ft) or yards (yds) may be encountered occasionally. Depths of water and heights of land and structures above water are generally given in metres, but feet and fathoms are sometimes encountered, particularly on older charts and those produced in the United States. A *fathom* (*fm*) is six feet, or 1.8288 metres.

The unit of speed commonly used by navigation is the *knot* (*K, kn*), defined as one nautical mile per hour. Speed is usually stated to 0.1 knot.

Directions are expressed in degrees, usually to a precision of $0°.1$. Latitude and longitude are usually stated in degrees and minutes of arc, to the nearest $0'.1$.

Navigators express the time of day in four digits without punctuation, starting with 0000 at midnight through 2400. That is, 2400, the end of one day, is 0000, the start of a new day. The first two digits indicate the hour, and the second two the minutes after the hour. Thus, 0423 is 4:23 a.m. and 1623 is 4:23 p.m. They are spoken as 'oh four twenty-three' and 'sixteen twenty-three' respectively. The use of the word 'hours' after the four digits expressing a time has no place in navigation. The nearest minute of time is usually used for indicating positions of the craft, except that when a craft is traversing a busy harbour, where almost continuous position fixing may be needed, half minutes might be used. Timing of celestial observations in astronavigation is usually done to the nearest second, time being expressed in hours, minutes, and seconds, as $18^h 01^m 33^s$.

In recording quantities in which a zero is involved, one should avoid omission of the zero, as a precaution against error. Thus, latitude $18°04'.7$ N. should not be recorded $18°4'.7$ N. (which could erroneously be read $18°47'$ N.). A

23

zero following a whole number should be retained to indicate the degree of precision. Thus, 146.0 M indicates a distance to a precision of 0.1 M, while 146 M indicates a precision of one nautical mile.

In rounding off a quantity, one takes the *nearest* value, anything 4 or less being rounded to the next lower value, and anything 6 or greater being rounded to the next higher value. A value ending in 5 can sometimes be resolved by using an additional place, but if the quantity ends in 5 exactly, it is rounded to the nearest *even* value. Thus, 17°.24 is rounded to 17°.2, 17°.26 is rounded to 17°.3, 17°.251 is rounded to 17°.3, 17°.25 is rounded to 17°.2, and 17°.35 is rounded to 17°.4.

6. Errors

The term *error* may be used to indicate any deviation from the truth. Thus, in navigation, *watch error* (*WE*) is the difference between the correct time and time as indicated by the watch. *Compass error* (*CE*) is the difference between true (geographical) directions and directions as indicated by a magnetic compass. Atmospheric refraction introduces an error in the observation of the altitude of an astronomical body.

A more restrictive meaning of error is considered here. If the watch error is known, a correction can be applied to the *watch time* (*W*) to determine the correct time. Similarly, compass error might be determined and a correction applied to a compass bearing to determine the true bearing. Tables exist for determining the correction to be applied to altitude readings to compensate for atmospheric refraction error. But if the watch is believed to be 12 seconds fast, and in fact is 14 seconds fast, a residual error of 2 seconds fast remains after the correction is applied. Similarly, the compass error might not be known exactly, leaving a residual error. Atmospheric refraction tables are computed for standard atmospheric conditions, which rarely exist in their entirety, resulting in some residual error after the correction is applied. It is these residual errors that are of concern here.

Another source of inaccuracy is the *blunder*, or mistake. If the navigator neglected to apply watch error, compass error, or a correction for atmospheric refraction, or if he used the wrong sign (perhaps adding when he should have subtracted), or if he selected the wrong value from a table of corrections, he would be committing a blunder.

Navigation, involving observations, measurements and calculations, is subject to a great many residual errors. Some of these are inadvertent. Examples have been given, each being the result of lack of knowledge. In some cases these errors might have been reduced by greater care in determination of the corrections to be applied. Other errors are accepted, or even introduced deliberately in the interest of simplicity or the conservation of time. The added accuracy that might be obtained simply does not justify the time and effort involved. Greater safety might be achieved by redundancy. Numerous examples might be cited. The Earth is a geoid (p. 18), but the calculation of directions and distances on such a surface is tedious and time consuming, and there would be little benefit in knowing that the geodetic distance between ports is 2,638.169 miles, while the great-circle distance is 2,639.987 miles, especially if one considers the various adjustments one might be required to make en route to avoid obstructions or to correct for the effects of the winds and currents to be encountered. Sight reduction tables (p. 402) and almanacs (p. 360) could be tabulated to additional decimal places, but this would increase their size and add to the time of computation, and the additional precision would hardly be justified if altitudes could not be measured more accurately than to the nearest half minute of arc. Lengthy calculations to determine the location of the craft an hour previous are of less value than a good approximation of the present position.

In considering safety of navigation, one should understand the difference between accuracy and precision. *Accuracy* relates to conformity to the truth, while *precision* relates to the refinement to which a value is stated. Thus, if the speed of a craft is measured to be 15.4 knots, but is actually 15.7 knots, the measured value is inaccurate by 0.3 knot. But if a navigator wishing to calibrate his log traverses a measured distance (p. 142) of one mile in 3^m48^s, he could calculate his speed to be $60^m \div 3^m8 = 15.789473684$ knots, approximately. The calculation could be carried to additional decimal places, but they would be without significance. In fact, if the elapsed time is accurate to the nearest second, it may be in error by as much as 0^s5, and this magnitude of error in time represents an error of about 0.035 knot in speed at 15.8 knots. Therefore, any digit past the first decimal in speed is questionable, and all those beyond the second digital are meaningless. Further, there may be some slight error in making the reading or detecting the exact moment at which a reading should be made. Even if the time was completely without error, if the uncertainty in the length of the measured distance was one metre, an error would be introduced, for at the speed involved in the example the vessel would travel about eight metres per second. This would introduce an uncertainty of about 0^s125 in the time, or 0.009 knot in the speed. It should be evident that the speed determined in this example is not more reliable than about 0.05 knot, even if the effects of variations in wind and current are not considered.

In general, stating a quantity to a greater precision than accuracy is not justified. However, one is usually justified in retaining one or more additional places during a calculation involving a number of quantities, to avoid a cumulative error from rounding off each quantity. Navigators sometimes retain an additional place in the answer, for consistency and to remind themselves of the need for careful work. Thus, a typical uncertainty in a position obtained by astronavigation is two miles, but a navigator usually records nearly all positions at sea to a precision of $0'.1$ of latitude and longitude.

The term *accuracy*, used without modification with respect to position determination, generally refers to the difference between the stated position of the craft and its actual position. *Repeatable accuracy* refers to the accuracy with which a craft can return to a position previously determined in the same manner. *Relative accuracy* refers to the difference in error of position of two craft using the same means of position determination. Repeatable and relative accuracy are generally greater than absolute accuracy because any error common to both position determinations is not included in the total. *System accuracy* refers to the accuracy of a navigation system exclusive of errors introduced by its users, geodesy, and cartography, and is therefore greater than absolute accuracy.

Several different types of error are encountered in navigation. A *systematic error* is one that follows some law by which it might be predicted. A common systematic error is the *constant error*. If a watch is 20 seconds fast, all readings are 20 seconds fast. Another form of systematic error is the *rate error*. If a watch is set to exactly the correct time at 1200, but gains at the uniform rate of six seconds per day, it will be one second fast at 1600, two seconds fast at 2000, three seconds fast at 2400, etc. If the watch is 20 seconds fast at 1200 and has a uniform rate of gaining six seconds per day, it will be 21 seconds fast at 1600, 22 seconds fast at 2000, etc. Thus, the total systematic error is the sum of the individual components. Other types of systematic error may exist, the error changing other than linearly. An inertial navigator (p. 532) may have an oscillatory rate of 84.4-minute intervals.

The effect of a systematic error can be eliminated by removal, compensation, or correction. A watch indicating an incorrect time can be reset, its rate can be adjusted, or a correction applied to convert its reading to the correct time. A magnetic compass affected by magnetism in the ship's iron can be adjusted by setting up an equal and opposite force, as by small magnets placed in correct positions close to the compass. If a systematic error could be determined exactly and full correction made, it would not affect the result. But the best effort is imperfect. It is difficult to align a direction-measuring instrument exactly with the longitudinal axis of a ship, for example.

Another and often more troublesome error is the *random error*. It is unpredictable as to sign or magnitude. Two people may get a slightly different value if they read the same setting of an instrument. A value of 127.2 in a table might represent any value from 127.15 to 127.25. Plotting on a chart is subject to small errors. Because random errors cannot be predicted or detected, they cannot be removed. However, the probability

27

of a reduction in magnitude can be achieved by averaging a number of readings, where this is possible.

An important point to remember is that the effect of a random error is proportional to the *square* of its magnitude. Suppose a given result is affected by eleven different errors, as follows:

Error: 1 −2   4 −1   0   8   1   0 −5 −3   2

Error^2:   1   4 16   1   0 64   1   0 25   9   4

The sum of the squares is 125. If this is divided by the number of errors, the result is 11.4, called the *mean square*. The square root of 11.4 is 3.4, called the *root mean square* (*RMS*). If the sum of the squares is divided by one less than the number of errors, the result is $125 \div 10 = 12.5$, called the *variance*. The *standard deviation* is the square root of the variance, in this case $\sqrt{12.5} = 3.5$. This is the 68 per cent or one *sigma* (σ) error, meaning that in a large number of errors having a standard deviation of 3.5, 68 per cent would not be greater than this value. The 50 per cent error (about 2/3 sigma) is known as the *probable error*, meaning that an individual error has an equal chance of being greater or less than this amount. In comparing accuracy of navigation methods or systems, one should be careful to make the comparison on the same basis. For example, comparing the probable error of one system with the standard deviation of another would not yield conclusive results. The 95 per cent error (about two sigma) is a value frequently used in navigation.

Random error distribution might best be visualized by means of a diagram, Fig. 103. The central vertical line represents zero error. Magnitude of error is represented horizontally and the probability of an error of any given size is represented vertically. Note that the curve *approaches* the horizontal base, but does not quite touch it. The shaded area indicates the probable error, or 50 per cent of the area under the curve. This diagram is the *Gaussian distribution*. It is also called the *normal distribution*, although not everyone agrees that it is 'normal' in its representation of navigational arrors. Various curves that have been suggested as more

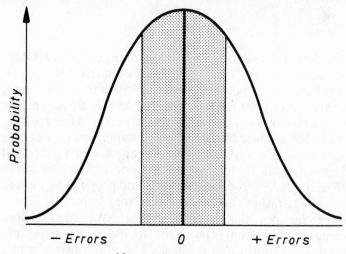

FIG. 103. Normal distribution of random errors.

representative vary principally at the outer edges of the diagram, at the so-called 'tails' of the curve. Although few errors of this magnitude are encountered, and hence the difficulty of establishing the shape of the curve at these tails, these are the errors most dangerous to the safety of a craft, and therefore of concern to navigators.

If a systematic error existed in addition to random errors, the total error would be the sum of the two. Refer to Fig. 104. The random error is of the same shape as before, but is offset from zero by the amount of a constant error.

Errors encountered in navigation may not be pure random or systematic. Atmospheric refraction may be essentially systematic over the short interval of time during which

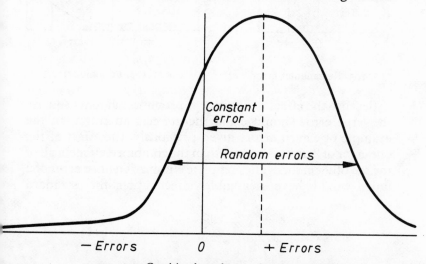

FIG. 104. Combined random and constant errors.

observations are made for an astronavigation fix, but random over long periods. Note, too, that although the normal distribution curve approaches but never quite reaches zero, there are practical limits in some cases. A direction, for example, cannot be more than 180° in error. However, an error of 180° is more likely to occur than one of 90°, or 60°, because a line has two directions 180° apart, and a reciprocal reading is more likely to be made than one differing by 90° or 60°. Reading a reciprocal, though, should properly be classed as a blunder, rather than a random error.

Some random navigational errors have distributions differing greatly from Gaussian. *Rounding-off errors* are rectangular. As indicated previously, a table value of 127.2 might represent any value from 127.15 to 127.25, and the probability of any value within these limits is exactly the same in many tables. This type of error has a *rectangular distribution*, shown in Fig. 105. Its 50 per cent error is one-fourth the tabular interval, or one half the maximum error.

Another type of navigational error, known as a *periodic error*, has a U-shaped distribution curve, as shown in Fig. 106. An example is the heading of a ship that is yawing. The reading tends to be steadiest at the extremity of the yaw, when the error is greatest. An average of the extreme readings is likely to be near the correct average reading.

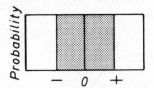

FIG. 105. Rectangular error.   FIG. 106. Periodic error.

Because the effect of an error is proportional to its square, the large error should claim the greatest attention. In the example of eleven errors given previously, the effect of the one error of 8 units is greater than the combined effect of all of the ten other errors. The complete elimination of an error of 2 units would have negligible effect upon the standard deviation, reducing it from 3.54 to 3.48. The error of 8 units is four times as large, but has an effect 16 times as great. If this error were reduced by one half, to 4 units, the standard deviation would be reduced from 3.54 to 2.77, or from 3.5 to 2.8, a 20 per cent reduction.

If the Gaussian distribution curve is steep and narrow, indicating a proportionally large number of small errors, and the offset by a systematic error is large, reduction of the systematic error would well be given higher priority than reduction of random errors.

In the practice of navigation, the navigator seldom consciously analyses the nature of the various errors involved, drawing distribution diagrams or computing standard deviations; nor does he often have the information needed for such an analysis. A consciousness of the types of errors involved and their characteristics, however, is useful and highly practical. For example, the uncertainty of a dead reckoning position increases with time and with distance travelled. Experience will provide a guide as to a reasonable magnitude of the uncertainty under existing conditions of wind, current, sea, equipment, and skill of the helmsman. The wise navigator thinks of a dead reckoning position as a circle, rather than a point, with a *radial error* appropriate to the situation. If his estimate of speed is believed to be less reliable than his estimate of direction of travel, he may think of the area of uncertainty as being an ellipse, with the long axis along his course line. If the speed is more accurate, the long axis is perpendicular to the course line.

Similarly, a position line is considered a band, rather than a line, the width of the band indicating the uncertainty. Where a dead-reckoning position and a single position line are available, the most probable position may be somewhere between the dead-reckoning position and the foot of a perpendicular from that position to the position line, the effect of the error of each being proportional to its square. If the areas of uncertainty of the dead-reckoning position and the position line do not intersect, as shown in Fig. 107, a blunder should be suspected, although one may be in the tail of the distribution curve. Another reading for an additional

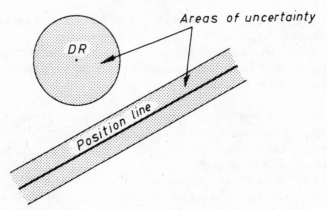

FIG. 107. Non-intersecting areas of uncertainty.

position line, or, better, verification by an independent source, if available, is desirable.

Geometry affects navigational accuracy. Refer to Fig. 108. Two position lines having an *angle of cut* of 90°, meaning that they are mutually perpendicular, have an area of uncertainty that can be considered a rectangle, although the actual shape is a curved area differing somewhat from this figure. In the illustration, the uncertainty of AB is 2 miles, and that of CD is 3 miles. The resulting rectangular uncertainty in the position is represented by the shaded area. The maximum error is 3.6

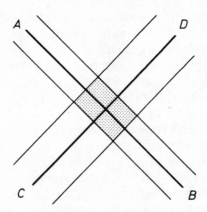

FIG. 108. Area of uncertainty for a 90° angle of cut.

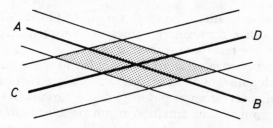

FIG. 109. Area of uncertainty for a 30° angle of cut.

miles. If, however, the angle of cut is 30°, as shown in Fig. 109, the maximum error is 9.7 miles. Thus, where a choice is available, one should select objects providing position lines intersecting at equal angles. A third position line is customarily obtained where possible. It may add little to accuracy, but it provides a valuable check. If three or more bearings have a constant error of the same sign, the correct position is at the point of common intersection found by adjusting each bearing line by the angular error, as shown in Figs. 508 and 509. If the total error of the measured altitude of each of three or more celestial bodies is the same in both magnitude and sign, an adjustment of each position line an equal distance, all toward or all away from the bodies observed, will locate the correct position of the fix, as shown in Figs. 617 and 618. If three objects or bodies observed are within an arc of 180°, and the constant error in bearing or altitude is the only error, the correct position of the fix is *outside the cocked hat*. A constant error in timing celestial observations results in all position lines, and the fix, being displaced in longitude, west of the true position if the time is fast, and east if slow.

Lack of consistency is another means of detecting errors, particularly blunders. If positions are determined frequently, they should form a pattern that is apparent, particularly when the positions are plotted. A sudden, unexplained deviation from the pattern is an indication of possible error. Similarly, differencing in a series of values is a common means of locating errors in tabular or observational data. Thus, if consecutive values of any quantity, at equal intervals, are 12, 15, 19, 21, 33, 27 and 31, it should be readily apparent that 33

33

is an incorrect value. The small variations in the differences between other consecutive values are reasonable, perhaps reflecting the results of rounding off.

With experience, an alert navigator learns what constitutes reasonable values of different quantities, as well as reasonable results of observation or plotting, under various conditions, and by keeping this information in mind is able to detect major errors.

II

The Nautical Chart

---

1. General

The curved surface of the Earth, another astronomical body, or the celestial sphere (p. 281) may be shown with considerable accuracy on the surface of a globe, but a globe is not convenient for most purposes of navigation. A representation, usually on a flat surface, of all or part of the surface of a spheroidal surface such as the Earth, is called a *map*. A map intended primarily for navigation is called a *chart*.

The chart commonly used by mariners is called a *nautical chart*. It depicts water areas, primarily, with adjacent land areas. It has latitude and longitude scales, and shows depths of water, heights of land areas and landmarks, dangers, aids to navigation, magnetic information, various notes, etc. Nautical charts are supplemented by specialized charts intended for some specific purpose, such as *pilot charts* (p. 79), time-zone charts, and star charts.

The nautical chart is one of the oldest and most reliable aids of the navigator. A chart is customarily spread out on a chart table on or near the bridge of a ship, for convenient reference. Plotting instruments should be near at hand, for much of the navigation of a ship consists of plotting directly on the chart. Because a navigator places such dependence upon his charts, both for planning voyages and for navigating his vessel, he should be careful to maintain a suitable selection of appropriate charts, make necessary corrections to them, and safeguard them from damage, mutilation, or loss.

The prudent navigator studies his charts and becomes thoroughly acquainted with them, being careful to note such things as the locations and characteristics of navigational lights, the units of depth and height measurements, dangers, etc.

Although the modern nautical chart is a highly reliable aid, it does have limitations. The chart, of course, is no more reliable than the information used in its production. The date of the survey upon which the chart is based, usually shown in the legend, is some indication. In unfrequented areas, particularly, an old survey may be the best available, and it may not have been accomplished with the thoroughness one might wish. Lines of soundings suggesting that they might have been made by ships during passages of the area, or areas with a scarcity or absence of soundings, for example, may be an indication that uncharted shoals or rocks might exist, particularly if such features abound in adjacent areas. Even in well-surveyed areas, as in busy harbours, undetected isolated obstructions might exist.

Sometimes the problem is with too much, rather than not enough, information. The ever-increasing volume of data becoming available is sometimes greater than can be adequately processed by staffs of limited size. The result is delay in making use of available information, and the ever-present possibility of an important item being overlooked or an error being made in the assimilation of the data.

One should keep in mind, too, that depth of water changes with state of the tide, which is difficult to determine at some distance from the shore. Further, meteorological tides, both positive and negative, of as much as two metres are not uncommon, particularly in a semi-confined area such as the North Sea. Mobile submerged sand dunes are also a problem in some areas. These shifting piles of sand tend to occur in waves perpendicular to lines of soundings, which in turn are generally perpendicular to depth contours (p. 58). Sand waves of as much as five metres in height have been found in the North Sea.

Mammoth tankers, having draughts of 25 metres or more, pose a particular problem. Until recently, depths greater than 20 metres were considered beyond the reach of any vessel, and little effort was made to detect obstructions, including wrecks, at these depths. Also, very large ships change draught appreciably when rolling or pitching: a ship 300 metres long increases draught more than two and half metres in a $1°$ pitch.

Changes in bottom topography and in landmarks, particularly cultural features, might have taken place after the chart was compiled or last corrected. One should be particularly alert to the possibility of silting along the edges of a dredged channel. A good general rule is to consider the charted depth to be accurate only for the middle 80 per cent of the channel.

Charts seldom show all of the soundings or all of other information available to the compiler. This is particularly true on small-scale charts (p. 56). A good general rule is to use the largest-scale chart available.

Although the paper on which charts are printed is selected with care, some uneven expansion with changing weather conditions can be expected.

2. Chart Projections

A sphere or spheroid is said to be *non-developable* because its surface cannot be depicted on a flat surface without distortion. This problem is overcome, in part, by transferring the spherical or spheroidal surface to a *developable* surface, which is then converted to a flat surface. The particular scheme used for any specific map is called a *map projection*, or, if the final product is to be a chart, a *chart projection*. Many such schemes have been devised, but only a very few have been used for navigation, because many projections lack characteristics desirable for this purpose. These desirable characteristics are:

Orthomorphism, meaning that very small shapes are represented correctly.

Conformality, meaning that angles around any point are represented correctly. Because neither orthomorphism nor conformity can exist without the other, these terms can be considered synonymous. Where these properties exist, meridians and parallels cross at right angles, and the scale in every direction about a point is constant.

Scale constancy. A constant scale over an entire chart permits the use of a distance scale on the chart or on a ruler.

Rhumb lines as straight lines. Course lines used by marine

37

craft are nearly always rhumb lines, and so it is convenient to have a chart on which they appear as straight lines.

Great circles as straight lines. For planning long voyages over open water it is desirable to have charts on which great circles appear as straight lines. An arc of a great circle is the shortest distance, across the surface of a sphere, between two points on the sphere. In practice, a ship making a long voyage usually steers a series of rhumb lines that closely approximate a great circle, but the great circle is needed before approximations can be established. The great-circle chart can be used to establish the great circle, or to determine whether a computed one is clear of obstructions.

Unfortunately, no one projection can have all of these characteristics. A straight line, for example, cannot be both a rhumb line and a great circle, unless it is the equator or a meridian. The differences among the various projections are most apparent on charts covering large areas. On charts of a small area, such as a harbour, the differences are virtually indistinguishable, and all of the desirable characteristics can be considered present.

Three developable surfaces are used for chart projections. These are the cylinder (resulting in a *cylindrical projection*), cone (resulting in a *conic projection*), and a plane (resulting in a *zenithal* or *azimuthal projection*). Cylinders and planes can be considered limiting cases of a cone. Projections may also be classed as *equatorial*, *polar*, or *oblique*, depending upon whether the projection is centred at the equator, a pole, or some point or circle other than a pole or the equator.

The network of lines representing parallels and meridians is called a *graticule*. If the parallels and meridians are projected geometrically from the spherical or spheroidal surface to the developable surface, by straight lines from one point (including infinity), a *geometric projection* results. Most maps projections are not geometric, being derived mathematically.

3. Cylindrical Projections

A cylindrical projection can be visualized by imagining a cylinder wrapped around the Earth, tangent along some great circle, usually the equator. If the meridians are projected from the Earth to the cylinder, by projecting lines from the centre of the Earth, they appear as vertical lines, or elements, of the cylinder, as shown in Fig. 201. If the cylinder is cut along a meridian and spread out flat, the meridians appear as parallel vertical lines, as shown in Fig. 202.

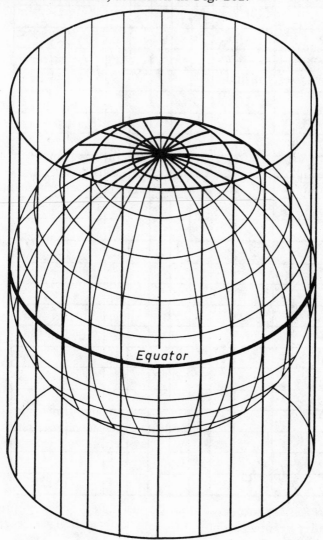

Equator

FIG. 201. Locating meridians on a cylindrical projection.

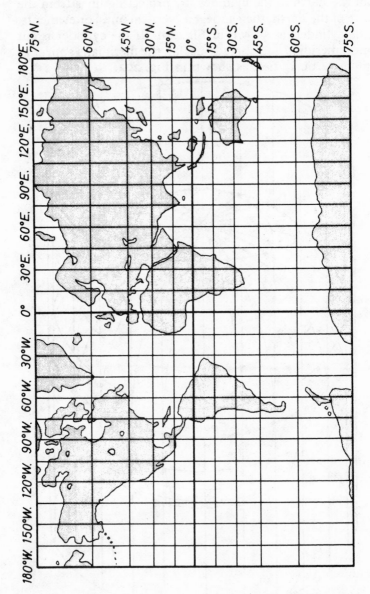

FIG. 202. A Mercator map.

On the Earth the meridians converge towards the poles, as shown in Fig. 201. The distance between any two meridians varies as the cosine of the latitude with a small correction for ellipticity of the Earth. It should be evident, then, that distortion of longitude, as shown on a cylindrical projection, increases from zero at the equator to infinity at the poles.

The various cylindrical projections differ in their schemes for locating the parallels. If the parallels are equally spaced, the same distance apart as the meridians, a *rectangular projection* results. Although easy to construct, this projection has little to recommend it because it is not orthomorphic and the relationship of latitude to longitude becomes increasingly erroneous with increase of latitude. It does, however, have the merit that an entire sphere can be shown on one chart of modest size. For this reason it is sometimes used to show positions of astronomical bodies on the celestial sphere. The coordinates of any body can be taken directly from the chart, making the chart a sort of graphic table.

The cylindrical projection most commonly encountered by navigators is the *Mercator*, shown in Fig. 202. Classed by its characteristics, it is an *equatorial cylindrical orthomorphic projection*. That is, it is a cylindrical projection with the cylinder tangent along the equator, and very small shapes (and all angles) are represented correctly. Orthormorphism is achieved by placing the parallels so that the expansion at any point is the same in both latitude and longitude. This means that the ratio of one minute of latitude at any place to one minute of longitude at the same place is the same on a Mercator chart as on the Earth. On the surface of the Earth the distance between parallels remains almost the same (not exactly the same because of the ellipticity of the Earth), while the meridians converge. On a Mercator chart, the meridians are the same distance apart and the distance between parallels increases. This is accomplished mathematically, the Mercator not being a geometric projection.

The placing of parallels on a Mercator chart is facilitated by means of tables of *meridional parts*, (M, MP, *mer parts*), defined as the length of a meridional arc between the equator and any given parallel on a Mercator chart, expressed in units of one minute of longitude at the equator (a *geographical mile*). Thus, at the equator, where one minute of latitude is equal to one minute of longitude, approximately, one minute of latitude is about one meridional part in length. But at latitude 60°, either north or south, one minute of latitude is about two meridional parts in length. Note the relationship of meridional parts to cosines. The cosine of 60° is 0.5. On a sphere, the length of one minute of longitude at latitude 60° is exactly half the length at the equator, and one minute of latitude is the same as at the equator, or exactly twice the length of one minute of longitude. Therefore, if one minute of longitude is doubled in length so that it is the same length on the chart as at the equator, the length of one minute of latitude must also be doubled if the correct relationship of meridians and parallels is to be maintained. The increasing scale of a Mercator chart is evident in Fig. 202, where each rectangle represents an area 15° each in latitude and longitude. Note the increase in the vertical dimensions with increasing latitude, either north or south. Tables of meridional parts are given in books of nautical tables, or may be computed by the equation given on p. 176.

The Mercator projection thus has the disadvantage of variable scale and a latitude limitation. It cannot be carried to the poles, where the expansion reaches infinity, but near the poles the scale changes so rapidly that the projection is not suitable for navigation, anyway.

The advantages of the Mercator projection, however, so far outweigh the disadvantages that it is used almost universally for nautical charts. Mariners do not usually navigate in areas of such high latitude that the excessive distortion there is a problem.

One of the principal characteristics of the Mercator projection that makes it attractive for marine navigation is the fact that rhumb lines appear on it as straight lines. This makes it convenient both for planning courses and for plotting. Great circles other than the equator and meridians appear as curved lines concave to both the equator and the rhumb lines connecting any two points on the great circle. Refer to Fig. 203, showing a rhumb line connecting points A and B,

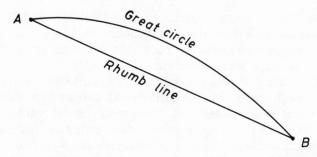

FIG. 203. Relationship of a rhumb line and an arc of a great circle.

both in the northern hemisphere, and part of the great circle through the same points. The great-circle arc appears to be longer than the rhumb line, but is actually shorter on the Earth, the deception being attributable to the increased distortion of the Mercator chart in higher latitudes. Thus, the shortest distance between two points is not the straight line connecting them on a Mercator chart. Bearing lines are arcs of great circles, but over the short distances involved in visual bearings, significant errors are seldom introduced by plotting them as rhumb lines. Radio bearings (p. 486), which may involve greater distances, sometimes require small corrections if they are to be plotted as rhumb lines on a Mercator chart. Position lines based upon observations of astronomical bodies are small circles, but again, over the short distances involved, no significant error is introduced by plotting them as rhumb lines, except when the body is near the zenith (p. 299). Such observations are difficult to make accurately and are usually avoided.

Because the Mercator projection is conformal, the scale in all directions around a point is the same. Otherwise, angles could not be plotted accurately. The latitude scale is used for a mile scale, care being exercised to use that part of the scale at the latitude involved. On the Earth, the length of one minute of latitude increases about one per cent from the equator to the pole, but within the limits of practical navigation, the error involved in using the latitude scale as a mile scale is rarely significant.

Plotting of directions is facilitated by *compass roses* printed on the chart. These are circles graduated in degrees or other circular units. Because the meridians are all shown as parallel lines, use of the same compass rose for measurement of directions anywhere on the chart is valid.

It is occasionally convenient to have a chart based upon the Mercator principle, but with the cylinder rotated 90° so as to be tangent along a meridian. This arrangement results in a *transverse Mercator projection*, also called a *transverse cylindrical orthomorphic projection*, and *Gauss projection*. The advantage of this projection is that it transfers the area of little distortion from the equatorial region to that adjacent to a meridian. The projection is used for charts of polar regions and for star charts extending vertically from pole to pole but of limited extent horizontally.

If the cylinder is tangent to a great circle other than the equator or a meridian, an *oblique Mercator projection* results. It may also be called an *oblique cylindrical orthomorphic projection*. This projection may be used for a chart showing the area adjacent to the arc of a great circle between two widely separated points. Such a chart is useful in air navigation, but is not likely to be encountered in marine navigation.

Both the transverse and oblique Mercator projections have the disadvantage of portraying both meridians and parallels as curved lines.

4. Conic Projections

If the parallels and meridians are transferred from the Earth to a cone or series of cones, a *conic projection* is produced. For a *simple conic projection* the cone may be placed over the earth so as to be tangent along a parallel, the cone's axis coinciding with the polar axis of the Earth. If the meridians are projected geometrically from the surface of the Earth to the cone, they appear as straight lines coinciding with elements of the cone. If the cone is cut along an element and spread out flat, the meridians appear as straight lines converging toward the nearer pole.

The parallel of tangency is called the *standard parallel*. It

44

appears as an arc of a circle with its centre at the point of convergence of the meridians, so that it intersects each meridian at right angles. The scale in longitude increases with distance north or south on either side of the standard parallel. If the projection is orthomorphic, all parallels are arcs of circles, concentric with the standard parallel, and spaced increasingly far apart on either side of the standard parallel, at distances derived mathematically to preserve the same expansion of parallels and meridians at every point. Thus, like the Mercator, a conic orthomorphic projection is not a geometric projection.

The increase of scale with distance from the standard parallel is rapid and of increasing rate. The usefulness of the projection is therefore limited in latitude range, but unlimited in range of longitude. The useful latitude range can be increased by using a secant cone, one that intersects the Earth at two standard parallels, as shown in Fig. 204. The

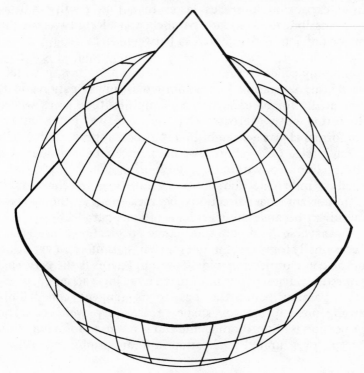

FIG. 204. A secant cone.

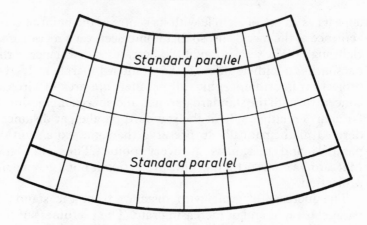

Standard parallel

Standard parallel

FIG. 205. A Lambert conformal map.

area between the two standard parallels is compressed, and the area outside is expanded. Because the distortion resulting from expansion increases faster than that resulting from compression, the standard parallels are selected so that the major portion of the chart lies between them.

The *secant conic orthomorphic projection*, Fig. 205, commonly called the *Lambert conformal projection*, is widely used in air navigation, but has limited use in navigation afloat, principally for nautical charts of high-latitude areas where distortion on a Mercator chart is excessive. On Lambert conformal charts a straight line is a good approximation of a great circle. Over short distances it can be considered a rhumb line also, without excessive error. The latitude scale, used as a mile scale, does not vary greatly over the chart, but it is important that directions be measured at the nearest meridian, because the meridians are not parallel.

Transverse and oblique conic projections are used occasionally for maps, but not for charts. A different variation of the conic projection widely used in atlases is the *polyconic projection*. Distortion is minimized by using a series of cones, each parallel being the base of a tangent cone. This arrangement preserves shapes reasonably well, but the projection is not orthomorphic and is not used for navigation except for a limited application in hydrographic surveying.

5. Zenithal Projections

If the parallels and meridians are transferred directly from the Earth to a plane, eliminating the cutting and flattening, the result is a *zenithal projection*, also called an *azimuthal projection*. Several useful zenithal projections are geometric.

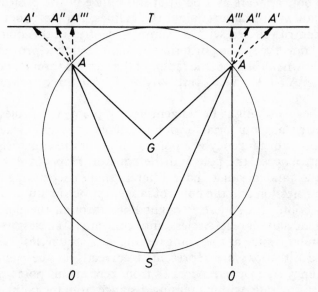

FIG. 206. Geometric zenithal projections.

Refer to Fig. 206. Suppose a plane is placed tangent to the Earth at the North Pole, T. It will then be perpendicular to the polar axis of the Earth. If points on the surface of the Earth are projected by means of lines from the centre of the Earth, G, to the tangent plane, a *gnomonic projection* is produced. Points A, for example, are projected to points A'. If the projecting lines emanate from the surface of the Earth 180° from the point of tangency, or from the South Pole in Fig. 206, a *stereographic projection* is produced. Points A are projected to points A" on the tangent plane. Note that points A" are closer to the point of tangency than points A'. If the origin of the projecting lines is an infinite distance away from the point of tangency, with the projecting lines parallel to the polar axis of the Earth, an *orthographic projection* results.

Points A on the Earth are projected to A''' on the plane, still closer to the point of tangency than in the gnomonic and stereographic projections.

Note that all three of these projections are geometric. In any zenithal projection with the point of tangency at a pole, that pole appears as a point at the centre of the projection. Meridians appear as straight radial lines. Parallels appear as concentric circles with a common centre at the point of tangency, the spacing differing from projection to projection. As shown in Fig. 206, the radius of the parallel through points A, is TA', TA'', TA''', respectively, for the three projections illustrated.

The plane might be tangent at any point, the projection being polar, equatorial, or oblique depending upon whether the point of tangency is a pole, a point on the equator, or a point between the pole and the equator, respectively. The parallels and meridians have different shapes depending upon the projection and the point of tangency, but in any zenithal projection of a sphere, straight lines through the point of tangency are great circles, and concentric circles with a common centre at the point of tangency are circles. Great-circle directions are represented correctly at the point of tangency. Distortion increases from zero at this point, at an increasing rate, with increasing distance from the point. The area of moderate distortion of a geometric zenithal projection can be increased by using an intersecting, rather than a tangent, plane, compressing the area inside the circle of intersection and expanding the area outside this circle, analagous to the procedure used for the Lambert conformal projection.

Fig. 207 illustrates the appearance of a graticule as seen on a gnomonic chart tangent at latitude 30° N. The equator, meridians, and the solid line connecting points A and B are all straight lines. They are all arcs of great circles. The rhumb line from A to B is shown as a broken line. It is the characteristic of showing any great circle as a straight line that makes the gnomonic projection useful for navigation. In fact, gnomonic charts are commonly called *great-circle charts*, their principal use being for drawing great circles between[1]

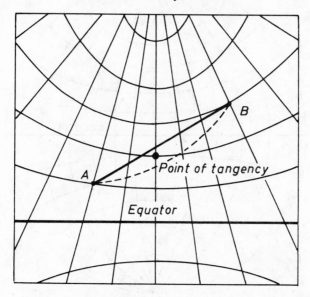

FIG. 207. A gnomonic graticule with point of tangency at latitude 30° N.

points of departure and destinations. The navigator can determine visually whether the route is free from major obstructions, and is otherwise favourable. Points along the great circle, as at intersections with selected meridians, can be plotted on a Mercator chart, using the latitude and longitude coordinates as taken from the great-circle chart. These points can then be connected by rhumb lines to determine the courses and distances for the voyage, as shown in Fig. 412. Although a gnomonic chart is not orthomorphic, its principal disadvantage, a graphical method of determining the great-circle distance and the direction of the line at any point may be explained by notes on the chart. The changing direction of a great circle with respect to meridians, as contrasted with the constant direction of a rhumb line, is illustrated in Fig. 207. An entire hemisphere cannot be shown on a gnomonic chart because the great circle 90° from the point of tangency would be at infinity.

An equatorial stereographic graticule of a hemisphere is

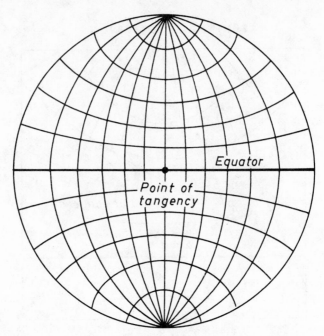

FIG. 208. A stereographic graticule of a hemisphere.

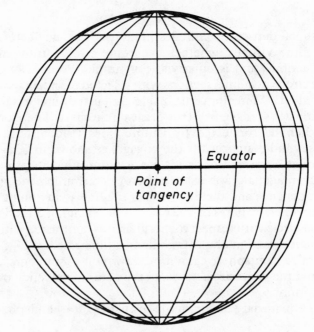

FIG. 209. An orthographic graticule of a hemisphere.

shown in Fig. 208. On this projection, all great circles through the point of tangency, including the equator and the central meridian, appear as straight, radial lines. All other circles appear as circles, although the centre is offset unless it is the point of tangency. This projection is orthomorphic, and the polar stereographic projection is used for charts of polar regions, useful primarily for air navigation. The projection is also used for star charts (p. 334) and for coordinate conversion diagrams and devices sometimes used in astronavigation. The stereographic projection cannot be used to show the entire Earth because the point antipodal to the point of tangency would be a circle of infinite radius with its centre at the point of tangency.

An equatorial orthographic graticule of a hemisphere is shown in Fig. 209. Comparing Figs. 208 and 209, one notes that in both, as in any zenithal projection, straight lines through the point of tangency are great circles. But in the orthographic projection, parallels appear as straight lines and meridians appear as ellipses, spaced more widely at the centre than near the edges, in contrast to the spacing in the stereographic projection. In the oblique orthographic projection both the parallels and the meridians appear as ellipses. The orthographic projection is not orthomorphic, but is useful for star charts and for coordinate conversion diagrams (p. 302) and devices. The orthographic projection can be used for a hemisphere, but with excessive compression near the outer edges.

Fig. 210 shows the graticule of the entire Earth on a *zenithal equidistant projection* tangent at latitude 35° N. This projection, also called *azimuthal equidistant projection*, is neither geometric nor orthomorphic. As in any zenithal projection, radial lines through the point of tangency represent great circles. Equally spaced concentric circles with a common centre at the point of tangency represent distances from this point, with a constant distance scale along the radials. Thus, great-circle directions and distances *from the point of tangency* can be scaled directly from the chart. As an aid to such measurement, the outer circle, representing the point antipodal to the point of tangency, is usually graduated

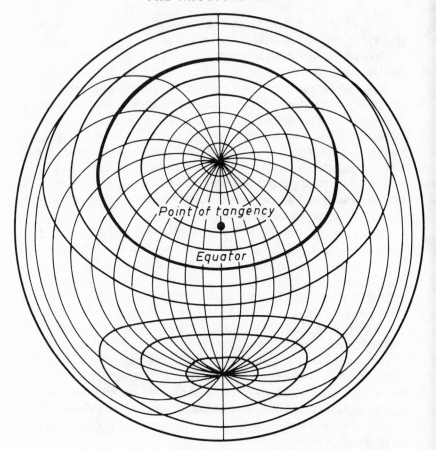

FIG. 210. A zenithal equidistant graticule of the Earth with point of tangency at latitude 35° N.

in degrees, and a distance scale is provided. The use of this projection is primarily in radio communications, although it might be used for radio navigation, for radio waves follow great circles, approximately, or for great-circle sailing. It may also be used for star charts and star finders (p. 341). As shown in Fig. 210, the zenithal equidistant projection can be used to show the entire surface of the Earth, but with excessive distortion near the point antipodal to the point of tangency.

6. Plotting Sheets

For plotting astronavigation position lines and for general navigation plotting at sea, far from coast lines and shoals, one does not need a nautical chart with all the detailed information it provides, nor is such a chart at an appropriate scale always available. A *plotting sheet* or *plotting chart* is quite adequate for the purposes stated, and much cheaper.

Plotting sheets are available from charting agencies and others, in a variety of forms and scales. Generally, a plotting sheet consists of a printed graticule on the Mercator projection, sometimes with a compass rose, and nothing more. Because the latitude-longitude relationship is a function of latitude, a given plotting sheet can be used accurately only for the range of latitude specified, but it is appropriate for use in any longitude. Accordingly, the labels of the parallels are printed, but meridian labels are not. If the parallels are labelled for north latitude, the plotting sheet is inverted for use in south latitude.

A plotting chart is basically a plotting sheet with a limited amount of additional information shown. If the land areas are outlined, the plotting chart may be called an *outline chart*. The positions of certain aids to navigation, particularly radio aids, may be shown. If the plotting of radio bearings is intended, a projection on which great circles appear truly or approximately as straight lines, such as the gnomonic or Lambert conformal, may be used. Because it involves specific geographical locations, a plotting chart is limited to a specific range of both latitude and longitude. Thus, a plotting chart provides more information than a plotting sheet but less than a nautical chart.

A *universal plotting sheet* can be used in any latitude, except at the poles, as well as in any longitude. This is accomplished by printing meridians and only one parallel, or parallels and only one meridian. Additional parallels or meridians are drawn by the user. The parallel-meridian spacing relationship at the mid latitude is used over the entire plotting sheet, thus limiting its useful spread in latitude. For this reason, it is often called a *small-area plotting sheet*. Its principal use is for plotting astronavigation position lines.

A small-area plotting sheet can be constructed easily without the aid of a printed sheet. The process consists simply of drawing horizontal lines, appropriately spaced, to represent parallels, and vertical lines, placed correctly to represent their spacing relative to the parallels. Cosines, or their reciprocal secants, provide a close approximation of this relationship quite adequate for practical navigation.

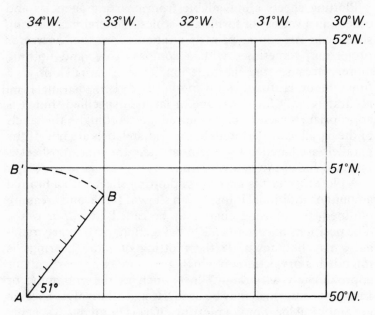

FIG. 211. A small-area plotting sheet.

If it is desired to have the meridians spaced at some convenient interval, a series of vertical lines are drawn at this interval, as shown in Fig. 211. A horizontal line is drawn connecting the lower ends of the meridians. At any convenient point, as at the lower left intersection of a meridian and the parallel, a line is drawn inclined to the *parallel* at an angle equal in degrees to the mid latitude. In Fig. 211 this angle is 51°. The length of the inclined line between any two meridians, AB, is the distance between parallels, AB'. Thus, if the meridians through points A and B

54

are $1°$ apart in longitude, the parallels through points A and B'
are $1°$ apart in latitude. Additional parallels are drawn using
the same spacing. Meridians and parallels are labelled. The
inclined line can be divided into an appropriate number of
equal parts to provide a scale for measuring latitude, miles,
and longitude. Latitude and mile units are measured along the
inclined line. Longitude units are measured horizontally
from the graduation on the inclined line to the appropriate
meridian.

A variation of this procedure is used if it is desired to have
the parallels spaced at some convenient interval. The
parallels are drawn as horizontal lines at this interval. A
meridian is drawn through the left edges of the parallels, and
from a convenient intersection, the inclined line is drawn at
the appropriate angle to the horizontal, and of length equal to
the spacing of the parallels. A second vertical line
representing another meridian is drawn through the outer
end of the inclined line. Additional meridians, as desired, are
drawn, using the spacing established.

Several variations of these procedures may suggest
themselves. The inclined line might be drawn left or right, up
or down. Its origin might be the centre of the plotting sheet,
rather than one corner. One advantage of using the centre is
that a compass rose might be constructed first. If the second
method is used, the central parallel could be drawn through
the centre of the compass rose, and additional parallels drawn
tangent to the circle at the top and bottom. If the inclined line
is drawn from the centre of the compass rose, it will terminate
at the circumference of the circle, and the second meridian is
drawn through the point of intersection of the inclined line
and the circle.

If a larger range of latitude is desired, or if it is desired to
retain a better relationship of latitude to longitude, the secant
of each degree of latitude can be used, or for even greater
accuracy, to allow for the ellipticity of the Earth, meridional
parts can be used. Suppose a plotting sheet is to be
constructed between latitudes $50°$ and $52°$, either north or
south. The secant of $50°30'$ is 1.57, and the secant of $51°30'$ is
1.61. The distance between the parallels of $50°$ and $51°$ is

55

therefore 1.57 times the distance between meridians, and the distance between the parallels of 51° and 52° is 1.61 times the meridional spacing. If meridional parts are used, the meridional distances are 1.57 and 1.60 times the spacing of the meridians, respectively. The meridional-parts values are derived by subtracting the values for consecutive integral degrees (51° minus 50°, 52° minus 51°) and dividing by 60. Alternatively, the meridians can be spaced 60 units apart, using any convenient unit, and the meridional-parts differences used directly, at the same scale, for spacing the parallels.

7. Chart Scale

The ratio of a distance on a chart to the actual distance it represents is the *scale* of the chart. It is commonly expressed as a fraction, when it is called *natural scale*. For example, a chart scale of 1/100,000, usually expressed as 1/100T, means that one unit of distance, such as a centimetre, on the chart represents 100,000 of the same unit of distance on the Earth. This is equivalent to stating that one centimetre represents 0.54 nautical mile. This number is derived by dividing 100,000 by 185,200, the number of centimetres in a nautical mile.

A *large-scale chart* is one covering a small area, and a *small-scale chart* covers a large area. The expressions are relative, a scale of 1/100T being considered large with respect to one of 1/1M (meaning 1/1,000,000), but small when compared with one of 1/25T. The terms *large* and *small* are derived from the scale expressed as a fraction. Thus, if the scale is 1/100T, one centimetre on the chart is 1/100,000, or 0.00001 of the distance it represents. With a scale of 1/1M one centimetre is 0.000001 of the distance it represents, and thus the scale is smaller than 0.00001.

Because of distortion involved in portraying the curved surface of the Earth on flat paper, the scale of a chart is not constant, as evident from variations in the latitude scale. The stated scale of a chart is that of a specific part, such as the mid latitude of a Mercator chart, the standard parallel of a conic chart, or the standard circle or point of tangency of a zenithal chart. Because of the variation of scale over a chart, a graphic mile scale is rarely given for charts of scale smaller than 1/80T unless a variable scale for different latitudes is shown. However, the scale at any given latitude can be determined approximately by measurement, using the latitude scale. Thus, if one centimetre of this scale spans 1.3 nautical miles the scale is $1/(1.3 \times 185,200)$ or $1/240,760$.

Nautical charts may be grouped according to scale in some manner such as the following:

Sailing charts of scale 1/600T or smaller, of broad ocean areas, used principally for planning or showing the progress of a vessel at sea.

General charts of scale 1/150T to 1/600T, used for navigation well offshore, where off-lying dangers are not usually found.

Coast charts of scale 1/50T to 1/150T, for close-in coastal navigation.

Harbour charts of scale larger than 1/50T.

The greatest detail, of course, is shown on charts of the largest scale, with progressively less detail as the scale decreases, until only major features and generalized coast lines are shown on a sailing chart. It is for this reason that the general rule is given that one should use the largest-scale chart available. If this rule is not followed for any reason, one should study the largest-scale chart for applicable information, such as location of obstructions, not shown on the chart in use.

8. Chart Symbols and Abbreviations

Much of the information shown on charts is by symbol or abbreviation, making possible the inclusion of a large amount of information while maintaining an uncluttered appearance. Through the efforts of the International Hydrographic Organization at Monaco, a high degree of standardization on charts produced by various nations has been achieved. However, some differences persist, particularly on older charts. Soundings, for example, are generally shown in metres, or metres and tenths in shallow areas. But the metrication of large numbers of charts is of necessity a slow process, and charts with soundings in fathoms or feet are in use. The unit is displayed prominently on each chart.

The use of colour on charts varies from country to country, and even on different charts produced by the same agency. In general, land areas are given a buff or grey tint, and shallow water a blue tint. Among Admiralty charts a buff land tint indicates a British metric chart. The entire water areas of *bathymetric charts*, which are charts designed to emphasize water depths, are usually tinted in blue, heavier tints being used to indicate greater depths. Symbols indicating the positions of lighted aids to navigation are accompanied by or overprinted with a magenta symbol, and symbols indicating positions of radio transmitters are enclosed by magenta circles.

Land heights are usually shown by *contours*, which are lines connecting points of the same height. Solid lines, broken to accommodate numbers indicating the heights represented, are used where data are adequate for accurate delineation. Lines consisting of a series of dashes indicate approximate locations of contours, called *form lines*. Summits are indicated by dots accompanied by numbers indicating heights. Contours shown in water areas are *depth contours*, or *bathymetric contours*, lines connecting points of equal depth. Individual depths are indicated by numbers. Where insufficient data are available for accurate location of depth contours, these lines are omitted. Only a small percentage of soundings obtained in a thorough survey are shown on the chart, and these are selected with safety in mind, the *least* depth in any vicinity usually being shown.

A complete listing of all symbols and abbreviations shown on Admiralty charts is given in a booklet identified as chart No. 5011. A similar publication relating to United States charts is called chart No. 1. A navigator should be thoroughly conversant with chart symbols, as well as with charts of the area in which his vessel operates. In an emergency there may not be time to acquire information that he should have memorized. Admiralty Sailing Directions, NP 100, *The*

Mariner's Handbook, also contains useful information relating to Admiralty charts.

9. Chart Datums

A *datum* is a base from which something is measured. A *chart datum* is the water level from which depths shown on a chart are measured. (In this usage the plural of datum is *datums*, not *data*.) Because of the fluctuations of water level subject to tides, depths measured at different stages of the tide are converted to depths at the chart datum before they are used on charts.

In the interest of safety, the chart datum selected for a particular area is usually a level below which the tide seldom falls. Because of wide differences in tidal conditions throughout the world, a number of different tidal levels are used. Tides and tidal levels are explained in section 10 of chapter IV (p. 188). The actual chart datum used in an area is often an approximation of the stated level, usually because the datum was selected before sufficient data were available for accurate determination of tide levels, or because tidal heights might have changed since the datum was selected. Thus, Admiralty charts based upon British surveys have usually used a level somewhat lower than mean low water springs unless the daily inequality is large, when an approximation of Indian spring low water has been used. Increasingly, new metric Admiralty charts are using the lowest astronomical tide as a datum. Charts of the United States use mean low water on the Atlantic and Gulf coasts, and mean lower low water on the Pacific coast. Charts based upon foreign surveys usually use the chart datums of those surveys. The chart datum, if known, is stated in the legend.

Small-scale charts may cover areas where several different chart datums are used for large-scale charts, and therefore chart datums of all charts of an area might not be the same. As a general rule, the chart datum of the largest-scale charts of an area is the same as the datum used for tide heights given in tide tables.

The actual water level encountered can be lower than the

chart datum, a fact that should be kept in mind when traversing an area affording little clearance under the keel. A predicted height lower than the datum used for tide tables is indicated in the tables by a negative number. Because of meteorological conditions, primarily, the actual height of the tide at any given time often differs somewhat from the predicted height, being either higher or lower.

Where the tidal range is great, the water can be considerably deeper than shown on the chart, an important consideration when soundings are used to help determine the position of a vessel (p. 255). Also, charted soundings that were obtained by echo sounders (p. 148) are probably the values uncorrected for temperature, pressure, and salinity. Such charted depths are usually shallower than actual depths, again for safety considerations, unless the water is very cold or has a low salt content, as off the mouth of a very large river.

The datum for heights shown on a chart usually differs from the chart datum. Mean high water is the usual datum for heights near the coast, but mean sea level is used frequently as the height datum for more distant features. The datum used for heights is not always stated on the chart.

The shore line shown on charts is usually the line of demarcation between land and water at mean high water. On gently sloping beaches where there is considerable tidal range, the shore line may vary considerably with the state of the tide. On large-scale charts, the low-water line in such cases may be indicated, in addition to the high-water shore line, sometimes with indication of the material (sand, mud, etc.) of the surface that uncovers at low water. The area of intermittent flooding may be given a tint that is a combination of both the land- and shallow-water tints. If the shore is a marsh or is covered with mangrove, the outer edge of vegetation is shown as the shore line, and the inner edge of water is shown as a dashed line, unless it is marked by the symbol of some feature, such as a bluff. The vegetation-covered water area may be given the land tint or combination land-water tint.

Chart datums as discussed thus far are *vertical datums*. *Horizontal datums* are also involved in the construction of charts. An area is surveyed relative to a defined starting point, or origin, called a *control point*. Secondary control points are established relative to the origin, which origin may not be within the area being surveyed. The system of control points based upon a single origin constitutes a horizontal datum, and is given a name indicative of its geographical location, as the 'European Datum' or the 'North American Datum of 1927'. The origin of each horizontal datum has been established independently, based upon its position determined as accurately as possible at the time of its establishment. In extending the survey outward from the origin, surveyors adopt an assumed size and shape of the Earth that seems to best fit the area. As a result of the independent determination of position of each origin, and different assumptions of the figure of the Earth, coordinates of a point as determined relative to different horizontal datums differ slightly. Fortunately, the difference is seldom sufficiently great to be of navigational significance, and boundaries between datums generally occur in locations where such errors as might occur are acceptable, as on the high seas or in sparsely-populated areas. Normally, datum differences are of concern only with respect to such activities as establishment of national boundary markers, firing of long-range missiles, and precise scientific work.

10. Aids to Navigation

The expression *navigational aid* refers to anything that assists the navigator, such as a conspicuous structure on land or in the water, an instrument, an electronic system, a chart or publication, or plotting equipment useful in the process of navigation. A navigational aid involving radio is often called a *navaid*. The more restrictive expression *aid to navigation* refers specifically to a device external to one's craft, constructed and maintained by man to help the navigator fix the position of his craft or avoid danger.

Aids to navigation are generally established and maintained by government agencies or government-chartered institutions, although private aids are permitted for specific purposes. Along most British coasts, aids to navigation are the specific responsibility of Trinity House, which came into being in about 1513 and has had exclusive authority over aids to navigation since 1836. The United States Coast Guard has similar authority in United States waters.

Aids to navigation may be located either on land or in water areas, and may be either lighted or unlighted. They may make their presence known visually, or by sound transmitted through air or water, or by radio. In water areas they may be either floating or fixed in position. A prominent structure on land is a form of *landmark*. The term *seamark*, is applied to aids to navigation, is generally restricted in its application to marks in water areas. The general term *mark* applies to any conspicuous object, structure, or light serving as an indicator for guidance or warning of a craft. An unlighted mark may be called a *daymark*.

Positions of aids to navigation are shown on nautical charts by distinctive symbols, supplemented, as appropriate, by abbreviations and text. The navigator should be familiar with these symbols and the specific part of each symbol that designates the position of the aid to navigation. He should understand, too, that in the case of an anchored aid, the charted position is the position of the anchor, and that the position of the mark at any time may differ somewhat from that position. Large-scale charts show all aids to navigation (except some of the privately-maintained ones), with relatively complete information regarding each. Smaller-scale charts show only the more important aids, with restricted supplementary information. *Admiralty List of Lights*, published by the British Admiralty; *Light Lists*, published by the United States Coast Guard; *Lists of Lights* published by the United States Defense Mapping Agency Hydrographic Topographic Center; and similar publications of other nations give complete information on lighted aids to navigation throughout the world.

Aids to navigation require positive identification. An incorrectly identified mark is a hazard, not an aid, to navigation. Identification is accomplished by position of the mark and its shape, colour, distinctive markings, and sometimes by coded signals. A mark may also display an identifying designation consisting of a number, letters, or some combination of the two. Some marks are equipped with coded signal lights. The lighting equipment normally consists of a light source, an optical system to concentrate the light energy into desired directions (vertically, horizontally, or both), and a means of providing the desired code. Light sources are usually provided by electricity or gas, either acetylene or propane. Some older lights use oil.

Although navigational lights are intended primarily for use during darkness, they are being used increasingly by day, requiring high luminance. Daytime use is principally for inland waterways, leading lights (p. 66), and harbour approach.

The coded signals of a navigational light, called *characteristics*, or *character*, consist of distinctive colours and a sequence of light and dark intervals. The sequence and duration of light and dark intervals is called the *rhythm* of the light. The elapsed time needed to complete a cycle of the characteristics is called the *period* of the light. The following terminology (with chart abbreviations shown in parentheses), illustrated in Fig. 212, indicates the principal light characteristics:

Fixed (F). Emitting a fixed, steady light.

Flashing (Fl). Emitting at regular intervals a single flash, the duration of light being shorter than that of darkness.

Fixed and flashing (F Fl). Emitting a fixed light varied at regular intervals by a single flash of greater brilliance.

Group flashing (Gp Fl). Emitting at regular intervals a group of two or more flashes separated by a dark interval of longer duration, or alternating single and group flashes.

Fixed and group flashing (F Gp Fl). Emitting a fixed light varied at regular intervals by a group of two or more flashes of greater brilliance.

Short-long flashing (S-L Fl). Emitting at regular intervals a group of two flashes, the second being of considerably longer duration than the first.

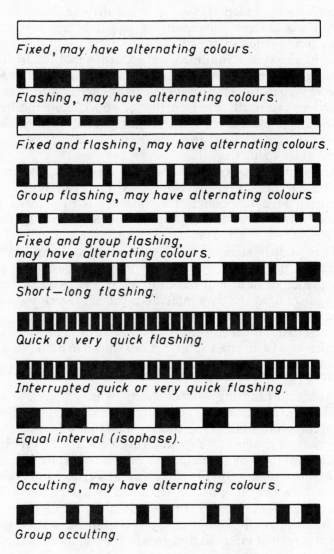

FIG. 212. Navigational light characteristics.

Quick flashing (Qk Fl). Emitting at regular intervals a single flash of short duration at a rate of 50 or more flashes per minute. A distinction may be made between quick flashes of 50 or 60 per minute and very quick flashes of 100 or 120 per minute.

Interrupted quick flashing (I Qk Fl). Emitting at regular intervals a group of quick flashes with the groups separated by a dark interval of longer duration.

Equal interval (E Int) or *isophase (Iso)*. Having light and dark intervals of equal duration.

Occulting (Occ). Emitting a light that is eclipsed at regular intervals, the duration of light being longer than that of darkness.

Group occulting (Gp Occ). Emitting a light that is eclipsed at regular intervals with two or more dark intervals, the dark intervals being of shorter duration than those of light.

Alternating (Alt). Emitting a fixed light that changes colour periodically.

Alternating flashing (Alt Fl). Emitting a flashing light that alternates colours.

Alternating fixed and flashing (Alt F Fl). Emitting a fixed and flashing light of alternating colours.

Alternating group flashing (Alt Gp Fl). Emitting a group flashing light with the groups alternating in colour.

Alternating fixed and group flashing (Alt F Gp Fl). Emitting a fixed and group flashing light alternating in colour.

Alternating occulting (Alt Occ). Emitting an occulting light alternating in colour.

The colours used for navigation lights are white (W), red (R), green (G), and yellow (Y). Yellow was introduced in the IALA buoyage System A, described below, p. 70. If no colour is designated, the light can be assumed to be white if of one colour, and white and red if alternating.

A typical designation of a navigational light, as shown on a large-scale nautical chart is: Alt Gp Fl W R (3) 12 sec 50m 16M '4'. Interpreted, this means that the light exhibits a group of three flashes every 12 seconds, alternate groups being white and red, the light is 50 metres high (usually height above mean high water), has a nominal range (p. 262) of 16 nautical miles, and has a designated identification number 4. On new Admiralty charts 'sec' is shortened to 's' to conserve space.

Some lights have *sectors* (*SEC*) exhibiting lights of different characteristics, or in which the light is obscured. Sectors may indicate areas of dangerous and safe waters. Thus, a red sector in an otherwise white light generally marks an area of shoal water, rocks, or other danger. A boundary of such an area, or a single point or line to be avoided, such as a submarine cable, may be marked by two transit, or range, lights (p. 224), one higher than the other, called *lights in line*. A very narrow light sector, usually flanked by broader sectors of different colours, may be used to mark a channel or a safe route through dangers. Such a light is called a *direction light*, and constitutes a lone *leading light* (*Ldg Lt*). The two marks of a transit, or range, used for this purpose are called *leading marks*, and the lights of leading marks are called *leading lights*. The line indicated by a leading light or lights is called a *leading line*. The use of two leading lights is generally preferable to a lone leading light, where conditions permit the installation of two lights, because there is no possibility of different observers aboard a vessel being in different sectors, and because the two lights provide some indication of the degree of deviation of the vessel from mid channel. All sectors of a sectored light have the same rhythm. The limits of sectors are indicated on nautical charts by pecked (dotted) lines, and the directions *of* the light *from* the craft at the boundaries are stated in degrees true.

Major navigational lights are exhibited from prominent structures called *lighthouses* (*LH, Lt Ho*). They may be located on land or in shoal water. The size and type of structure, and the power of the light, are suited to the importance of the light and its environment. Among the considerations are the background against which it is to be seen, the distance at which it is to be visible in clear weather, the type of soil on which it is to be constructed, and the probability of damage by violent weather or heavy seas. Each lighthouse is given distinctive markings to enhance its conspicuousness and to assist in its identification during daylight.

The most powerful lights, sometimes called *landfall lights*, are placed at points of first contact by observers approaching from the open sea, where they provide a point of transition from deep-water navigation techniques to pilotage. Because of relatively large errors sometimes existing in the former, especially long range of visibility is required of landfall lights, necessitating high powers and high elevations of the lights. These lights generally have simple characteristics, and are usually white, to avoid the reduction in intensity that would accompany use of a colour filter. With continued improvement in the accuracy, reliability, availability, and use of electronic methods of navigation, a reduction in the required range of landfall lights may be possible at some future time. The distance at which lights are visible is discussed in chapter V, section 10 (p. 260).

Modern technology has provided highly efficient lights of such reliability that they can be monitored at a distance, with periodic visits for servicing. Where the amount and complexity of the equipment warrant personal attendance, some of the equipment and personnel are now generally housed in structures separate from the lighthouse, the entire complex being called a *light station*.

The floating equivalent of a lighthouse is a *lightship* (*LS*), or *light vessel* (*LV*). Such vessels are anchored at locations at which a prominent aid to navigation is needed and the construction of a lighthouse would be impracticable or too costly. Daylight identification is enhanced by distinctive painting and the name of the station exhibited in large letters on each side. By night a lightship displays a masthead light and a less brilliant light on the forestay, in addition to the navigational light. The lights by night and the aspect of the ship by day provide an indication of the direction of the current or wind, as a lightship is secured by an anchor, and thus heads into the current or wind. Upon the approach of another vessel that does not seem to be aware of its identity, or upon request, a lightship displays its International Code call letters by signal flags. When underway to or from its station, a lightship displays the International Code signal 'PC' and by night the lights prescribed by the appropriate Rules of the

Road, and does not perform any of the functions of a lightship on station. While a lightship is away from its station, it is replaced by another vessel, which performs the same functions, generally with the same characteristics, but may have a somewhat different appearance and has the word RELIEF painted on its sides instead of the name of the station.

Many earlier lightships have been replaced by large pillar buoys (p. 69). Some lightships have been replaced by lighthouses. More recently, advances in technology have made possible the erection of towers in relatively deep water, and additional lightships have been replaced by such *light towers*.

While any mark serving as a guide or warning may be called a *beacon*, in navigation the term applies specifically to a fixed structure of importance secondary to that of a lighthouse. Such a structure may or may not display a navigational light, an unlighted one sometimes being called a *daybeacon*. Lighted beacons may be used to mark a transit, or range, the beacon nearer the channel being lower than the more distant one. There is no sharp demarcation between lighthouses and lighted beacons, the former displaying more powerful lights than the latter.

The most numerous aid to navigation is the buoy, a minor, floating aid used to mark channels, shoals, and other obstructions, and for various special purposes. A buoy is a minor aid only in the sense that it is essentially a short-distance aid. Buoys are of great importance to the navigator, because of their versatility and extensive use. Failure to sight a buoy when expected may be sufficient reason for anchoring and awaiting better visibility.

The following are the buoy shapes used most commonly:

Can. Having the above-water portion in the shape of a cylinder.

Conical, or *nun*. Having the above-water portion in shape of a cone or truncated cone. The entire buoy may be in the shape of two vertical cones, base to base.

Spherical. Having the above-water portion in the shape of a sphere or part of a sphere.

Spar. Having the shape of a tapered log, anchored so as to float in an approximately vertical position.

Pillar or Large Automatic Navigational Buoy, Lanby. A tall central structure mounted on a broad, flat base, the height of the central structure and the diameter of the base each being typically ten to fifteen metres; or a skeleton buoy.

Skeleton. A small skeleton tower mounted on a float with a curved upper portion.

A buoy may have a navigational light, generally of less power than those of other aids; sound signal; radiobeacon; light- or radar reflector; *topmark* (a distinctive shape attached to the top of a buoy or beacon); or some combination of these additions.

Two systems of buoyage have emerged. The *lateral system* is appropriate for marking channels. The shape, colour, and number of each buoy relates to its position relative to the channel as traversed in a specified direction, generally inbound from the open sea. In contrast, the *cardinal system* places and identifies buoys relative to the nearest danger, thus being appropriate for an area having numerous rocks, shoals, and islands, and for isolated dangers in the open sea.

An international conference in 1889 recommended that in the lateral system buoys on the starboard side of a channel as traversed in an inbound direction be red, and those on the port hand be black. As lights were added, those on the starboard were usually red or white, and those on the port side were green or white. With some variations, most countries outside Europe use this convention. Off coasts of the United States, the 'inbound' direction of channels that roughly parallel the coast is considered to be in a clockwise direction around the country; that is, southward along the Atlantic coast, westward along the Gulf coast, and northward along the Pacific coast. Conical (nun), spar, or skeleton buoys are used for the starboard side and given even numbers increasing from the outward end of the channel. Can, spar, or skeleton buoys with odd numbers increasing from seaward are used for the port side. The memory aid 'Red, Right, Returning—with even numbers' helps one remember the convention.

Unfortunately for uniformity, a League of Nations

subcommittee in 1936 recommended a reversal of the colouring convention established in 1889, suggesting the use of black buoys for the starboard side, and red buoys for the port side. This lateral convention was to be used in conjunction with the cardinal system for isolated dangers, where appropriate, the overall system being designated the *Uniform System*. Another innovation was the extensive use of topmarks. Numbering or lettering of buoys was made optional. The Uniform System was adopted widely in Europe, but with variations to suit local conditions or resulting from differences in interpretation of wording, particularly with reference to topmarks. Another source of confusion has been the meaning of 'inbound', generally taken to mean the direction of the main flood stream. This direction is not always obvious, and in some areas it changes in mid channel, as north of the Isle of Wight. Further, the demarcation between use of the lateral and cardinal system is not always apparent.

In 1976 the International Association of Lighthouse Authorities (IALA) recommended a new buoyage system intended to correct the deficiencies of the Uniform System. The new system, designated simply *System A*, retains the basic features of the Uniform System, but with important simplifications and clarifications. It applies to all fixed and floating marks except lighthouses; transit or range, and other leading lights; very large *sea buoys* exhibiting major lights; and lightships.

A significant change is the adoption of a 'General Direction of Buoyage' for areas where the direction of the main flood stream is not definitely the direction taken by a vessel approaching estuarine waters from seaward. The general direction is clockwise (as in the United States system) around the continent of Europe, interpreted as being in a generally northern direction around the United Kingdom and Ireland. The directions in local areas are to be shown in sailing directions and, where doubt may exist, by a large magenta arrow on appropriate charts.

By day, the significance of any mark of System A depends upon its colour, shape, and topmark. By night, both the colour of a light and its rhythm are significant.

System A provides for five types of marks (buoys or beacons) which may be used in any combination. These are: *Lateral marks.* Starboard hand: green (black in exceptional cases) conical, spar, or pillar buoys, each with a single cone topmark (optional on conical buoy) of the same colour, pointing upward; lights, where fitted, green, any rhythm. Port hand: red can, spar, or pillar buoys, each with a single red cone topmark (optional on can buoy); light, where fitted, red, any rhythm.

Cardinal marks. Black and yellow pillar or spar buoys. Indicated direction is direction of mark relative to point of interest. Each mark surmounted by a topmark consisting of two black cones, one over the other. North mark: black over yellow, cones pointing upward. East mark: black with broad horizontal yellow band, cones base to base. South mark: yellow over black, cones pointing downward. West mark: yellow with broad horizontal black band, cones point to point. Lights: quick flashing or very quick flashing white, uninterrupted for north mark, three flashes in a group for east mark, six flashes in a group followed by a longer flash of at least two seconds duration for south mark, nine flashes in a group for west mark. The periods of the east, south, and west lights are, respectively, 5, 10 and 10 seconds if very quick flashing; and 10, 15 and 15 seconds if quick flashing.

Isolated danger marks, indicating isolated dangers of limited extent, surrounded on all sides by navigable water. Black pillar or spar buoy with one or more broad horizontal red bands, surmounted by topmark consisting of two black spheres, one above the other; light, where fitted, white showing group of two flashes.

Safe water marks, indicating navigable water all around and under the mark (mid-channel buoy). Red and white vertical striped spherical, pillar, or spar buoy with a red sphere topmark; light, where fitted, white isophase, occulting, or one long flash of at least two seconds duration every ten seconds.

Special marks, indicating features not otherwise provided, such as quarantine, spoil ground, deep-draught vessel channel within a laterally-marked channel, etc. Yellow buoy of optional shape not conflicting with regular navigational marks, having an optional topmark consisting of a yellow cross; light, where fitted, yellow and having characteristics not used for white lights.

Greater detail regarding the new system is given in a British Hydrographic Department publication NP 735, *IALA Maritime Buoyage System A* and in a booklet *Seaway Code: A Guide for Small Boat Users* issued by the British Department of Trade. In addition, a new page L 70 to chart No. 5011, also available separately as chartlet No. 5044, gives details of System A as shown on British Admiralty charts, and includes accompanying changes in Admiralty chart symbology. As the system is established in various areas, information will be included in the sailing directions (p. 84) of those areas. One should also be alert to items in *Notices to Mariners* (p. 78) and radio navigational warnings (p. 523) relative to introduction of the new system in various areas.

Establishment of the new system began in 1977 in the English Channel east of the Greenwich meridian, and the North Sea south of latitude 52° 10′ N. Implementation in north-western Europe is scheduled for completion by August 1982, one phase being completed between April and August of each year. One should keep in mind that a large number of charts and publications are involved, and that some time may elapse between implementation in an area and the issuance of new editions reflecting the changes.

Introduction of System A, or a System B for those countries preferring red to starboard for channel markings, is under consideration.

Distinctive sound signals emanating from an identifiable position can serve as a useful navigational aid, particularly in time of restricted visibility. Sound signals intended for this purpose, called *fog signals*, are usually associated with an aid to navigation. However, the position of the source of the sound signal may not coincide with its associated visual or radio aid to navigation. Any appropriate sound source might serve the purpose of a fog signal. A variety is used to assist in identification. The principal sound sources in use are:

Bell. Sound is produced by the striking of the metal bell

by a suitable hammer.

Gong. Similar to a bell, but several are used in combination, each having a different tone.

Whistle. Sound is produced by the emission of compressed air or steam through a circular slot into a cylindrical chamber.

Siren. Sound is produced by rotation of a disc or cup-shaped rotor operated by electricity, compressed air, or steam.

Diaphone. Sound is produced by means of a slotted reciprocating piston operated by compressed air. Two separate tones may be sounded sequentially, the second being of a lower pitch than the first.

Reed horn. Sound is produced by the vibration of a steel reed operated by compressed air.

Diaphragm horn. Sound is produced by vibration of a disc diaphragm operated by electricity, compressed air, or steam. Two or three tones may be sounded simultaneously, producing a chime.

A *distance-finding station*, identified on the chart by the letters 'D F S' transmits simultaneous radio and sound signals. The difference in travel time of the two signals is used to determine distance between the source of the sound signal and the user, as explained in chapter V, section 13 (p. 273).

The positions of radiobeacons (p. 484) and other radio stations useful in aiding the process of fixing the positions of vessels are shown on nautical charts and accompanied by appropriate lettering to indicate the type of facility, as R Bn for a radiobeacon and Ra for a radar station (p. 499).

A limited number of aids to navigation intended primarily for use by aircraft are shown and properly identified on nautical charts. Those shown are considered useful by mariners.

Several precautions should be observed in the use of aids to navigation. When using a floating aid to assist in fixing the position of his craft, the navigator should remember that the charted position of each such aid is the position of its anchor, and that the mark changes position as it swings about its anchor with changes of current or wind. Also, there is a possibility that a floating aid may drag anchor, or be capsized, sunk, or carried away in a storm or by ice. The assigned position of a lightship or especially important buoy is indicated by a small *station buoy* which serves as a marker if the aid is off station or missing.

Most sound signals are operated electrically or by compressed gas. However, buoy sound signals powered by wave action on the buoy still exist in some areas of the world. In calm seas, buoy motion may be inadequate to sound the signal. A fog signal may not be sounded because there is no fog at its location while undetected fog does exist a short distance away. Fog signals may be heard at varying distances in different directions and under different atmospheric conditions.

Because of the high reliability needed for navigational lights, stand-by power sources and lamps are generally provided, with equipment for automatic switching in case of failure. Nevertheless, mechanical or electrical failure may extinguish a light or silence a sound signal. In some areas, particularly where ice is a problem, buoys are removed during certain seasons. The published dates that the buoys are scheduled to be on station are subject to modification because of local conditions at a particular time.

Notices to Mariners and radio navigational warnings may warn of casualties, but one should remember that a time lag of variable duration exists between the time of a casualty and dissemination of information relating to it. In contrast, notice of a *planned* change in an aid to navigation is generally given in advance of the change.

Another type of caution relates to the observation and identification of lights. The distance at which a light can be seen varies considerably with changes in atmospheric conditions. One should be particularly alert to the possibility of a fog bank at a light, or between the light and one's vessel, even though visibility may otherwise be good. The distance at which lights can be expected to be seen is discussed at greater length in chapter V, section 10 (p. 260).

A coloured light may not be visible as far as a white light, so that an observer at a distance near the luminous range of a light that has more than one colour may not see all of the colours exhibited. In the case of an alternating light, this may affect the apparent character of the light. Colour confusion, even among those not suffering from defective colour sensing, may be the result of atmospheric conditions. As an example, a white light observed through haze may have a reddish hue. Accuracy of colour perception is enhanced in some areas by the use of blue-green light for green lights, bluish-white light for white lights (to enhance the distinction between white and yellow lights), and somewhat orange lights for red lights. At short distances, in clear weather, a powerful light may appear to have a continuous faint light during nominal dark periods. Light energy is concentrated into a narrow horizontal band, usually 15° in vertical extent for buoys. In heavy weather the tilt of a buoy might cause this band to be moved out of range of visibility. If a light is not sighted when expected, one should consider the possibility of its having been extinguished, perhaps intentionally. Finally, the positions of navigational lights, as given in light lists, are approximate only, intended to assist in the locations of the lights on charts, not for coordinates to be used in fixing the position of a craft.

11. Landmarks

Many prominent features, in addition to aids in navigation, are useful to the navigator, and are shown on nautical charts. Landmarks may be either natural or man-made. The only requirements for navigation are that they be visible to the eye or to radar, their identification be established accurately, and that their positions be known.

A natural landmark might be a mountain peak, a prominent outcropping, a promontory, a conspicuous clump of trees, or any other feature that is sufficiently distinctive to permit identification. Any prominent structure might be useful as a man-made landmark. The amount of detail regarding landmarks shown on a chart depends upon the scale of the chart and the information available to the charting agency.

Natural landmarks, if of small extent, may be shown by symbol. Ground elevations may be shown in a variety of ways. Contours are generally used, where appropriate, and where sufficient information is available. Form lines may be used to indicate relative steepness and height where the data available are not in sufficient detail to permit drawing of accurate contours. Elevations of form lines are not given. A steep slope is sometimes indicated by short lines, called *hachures*, extending in the direction of the slope. *Spot elevations* above mean high water, usually in metres, may be given for summits or tops of other landmarks.

Terms describing man-made landmarks, as given on nautical charts, are generally understandable without need for clarification. However, an explanation of some terms may be helpful. The term *building* or *house* is used when the entire structure, rather than some prominent feature of it, is the landmark. A *dome* is a rounded structure constituting the entire or major portion of the roof of a building, while a small dome-shaped tower rising above the roof of a building is called a *cupola*. A *stack* is a tall smokestack more prominent than any buildings that may be associated with it, while the term *chimney* is used to indicate a prominent smokestack rising from a building of greater prominence. Similarly, a *flagpole* stands by itself, while a *flagstaff* rises from a building. An entire city may be shown by streets, crosshatching, an area of different colour or shade, or symbol, depending upon the size of the area, its prominence, and the scale of the chart. Highways and railroads may also be shown.

Positive identification is essential if a landmark is to be used for navigation. Incorrect identification can be disastrous. When aids to navigation are established, care is taken to make each one distinctive enough to minimize the possibility of its being mistaken for another aid in the vicinity. This is not the case, of course, with other landmarks. It is not unusual for two or more features to appear the same if one looks only at the general appearance. This is particularly true of natural landmarks. One should look for specific, unique, identifying features that make a landmark different from all others within reasonable distance. This precaution is particularly true when making landfall. One should keep in mind, too, that the appearance of a landmark may change with distance as well as with a change in the direction from which it is observed. As shown in Fig. 532, an apparent summit nearby may mask a higher one beyond. An apparent tangent of a point of land may not be the one shown on the chart if a low, sandy spit extends seaward from higher ground. Faulty identification is not limited to natural landmarks. Towers, spires, stacks, tanks and domes are particularly susceptible to misidentification. Caution and careful attention to detail, when identifying landmarks, are marks of a good navigator.

12. Miscellaneous Data

Although the principal function of charts is to provide graphical representation of navigable areas, showing depths, heights, positions of landmarks and aids to navigation, characteristics of navigational lights, etc., they contain other information useful to the navigator. Examples are compass roses and data on currents, tide rips, and measured distances (p. 142).

Magnetic information is given in a variety of ways. On large-scale charts the local variation is given in the centre of each compass rose, usually to the nearest 15′, with the annual change to the nearest 1′. A compass rose oriented to magnetic north may be shown inside a true compass rose. On small-scale charts variation is shown by isogonic lines (p. 95). On insets the variation may be given by note, as is information of magnetic anomalies (p. 104).

Notes appearing on charts should be read carefully, for they usually convey important information that cannot readily be shown graphically. The title box generally contains information on the chart projection, scale, horizontal and vertical datums (p. 59), units of depth and height measurements, and source and date of the data from which the chart was constructed. Additional information relating to the chart itself, such as the identity of the charting agency, chart number, edition, the date to which it has been corrected, and numbers of adjoining charts, is given in the margins.

Notes on the chart itself, in contrast to those in the margins or the legend, are of particular importance. Examples are information on *controlling depth* (the minimum depth in a channel and its approaches, indicating the maximum draught of vessels that can use the area), isolated dangers, restrictions, anchorages, and dumping grounds.

Not all available pertinent information is shown on charts. Additional information is given in the applicable volume of sailing directions (p. 84).

13. Chart and Publication Correction

Changes in aids to navigation, landmarks, depths of water, and even the locations of shore lines, take place continually, seemingly at an ever-increasing rate. Nautical charts, sailing directions, light lists, and lists of radio signals need correction promptly as these changes occur, if they are to serve the navigator faithfully. When purchasing a chart or one of the publications with perishable information, one should determine the date to which it has been corrected. The correction date of charts is usually indicated in the margin. Any changes announced after that date are the responsibility of the user. Mariners themselves are important sources of information needed to correct charts and publications. Any discrepancy or missing data available to the mariner should be promptly reported to the publishing agency. Instructions for reporting are given in British Admiralty sailing directions, NP 100, *The Mariner's Handbook*, and in United States Defense Mapping Agency Hydrographic Topographic Center Pub. No. 606, *Guide to Marine Observing and Reporting*.

Applicable changes to charts and publications are tabulated in a publication called *Notices to Mariners*, issued weekly by the British Admiralty, the United States Defense Mapping Agency Hydrographic Topographic Center, each United States Coast Guard District, and by appropriate agencies of other nations. One should consult the notice issued by the country publishing the charts used. In addition, the more important changes and navigational warnings are broadcast daily and printed in a publication called *Daily*

Memorandum. The schedules of these broadcasts are given in British Admiralty Publication NP 275(5), *Admiralty List of Radio Signals,* volume V, 'Navigation Aids' and in the United States Defense Mapping Agency Hydrographic Topographic Center Publication 117, *Radio Navigational Aids.*

Because of the large number of corrections, and the danger of neglect or error in making the corrections, efforts have been made to ease the burden on the crews of seagoing vessels. Some large steamship companies and other organizations have established shore-based units that review all changes and provide each vessel leaving port with those changes applicable to it. The United States Defense Mapping Agency Hydrographic Topographic Center has pioneered the use of pressure-sensitive blocks that can be applied directly to a chart in such a manner as not to interfere with the use of parallel rulers or with folding a chart. One can reasonably expect further innovations in chart and publication correction as the magnitude of the task continues to increase.

Generally, the issuance of a new edition of a chart is a signal that older editions should be retired from service, for the preparation of a new edition frequently indicates changes too extensive or inappropriate for adequate dissemination in the usual manner.

14. Pilot Charts

Information gleaned from numerous ship's logs and other sources over a period of more than a century is presented, mainly in graphical form, on a series of *pilot charts* for different seasons in various parts of the world. Several different types of information are presented. Meterological information includes such items as prevailing winds; percentage of gales, calms, and fog; and lines of equal air temperature and atmospheric pressure. Oceanographic information includes data on ocean currents, water temperature, icebergs, and ice fields. Magnetic information includes isogonic lines (p. 95) and annual change of variation (p. 101). Miscellaneous information includes recommended routes for both power and sailing vessels and a variety of other useful information. Pilot charts are not intended for plotting the dead-reckoning track or fixing the position of a vessel at sea, but for reference. As such, they serve a useful function in making available to the mariner a summary, in convenient form, of the accumulated experience and research of many persons over the years.

15. Chart Usage

To be of maximum benefit to the user, charts should be thoroughly understood, corrected promptly when changes are announced, used and stored properly, and safeguarded adequately.

A navigator should study his charts thoroughly *before* use, particularly large-scale charts of areas where manoeuvring room is limited. If time is taken for this activity during passage through such an area, the safety of the vessel may be jeopardized. Before the passage, the navigator should be certain that he understands the various symbols shown, the datums and units used for indicating depths of water, latitude and longitude scales, and the significance of any notes appearing on the charts. He should acquaint himself with the aids to navigation and other landmarks and seamarks available for fixing the position of his craft, noting particularly the presence of useful transits, or ranges (p. 224), and suitable indicators of turning points in channels. He may want to draw arcs of circles of visibility (p. 260), for his height of eye, around symbols of navigational lights, and perhaps clearing sounding lines (p. 255) by coloured pencil. Perhaps he would like to add useful notes on his own without cluttering the chart too much or obscuring printed information. He should check to be certain that chart correction is up-to-date, and that permanent corrections have been made in ink, to prevent their inadvertent erasure when the chart is cleaned after use.

Charts should be stowed flat with minimum folding, and indexed to afford ready access. The navigator should be sure that he knows the locations of charts that will be needed for the next part of his voyage. When use of a chart is completed, it should be stored carefully in its place.

In use, a chart should be spread out flat on the chart desk or table, and properly secured to prevent slippage during use or damage or loss by being blown or knocked off the surface where it is to be used. During use, a chart should be protected from water and other liquids that might cause uneven expansion and attendant distortion. If a chart should become wet, distortion can be minimized by ironing it with a warm iron until it is dry. It should be borne in mind that expansion of a chart also takes place when one that has been stowed in a dry place encounters moist air. With an increase of relative humidity from 30 per cent to 90 per cent, a distance on the chart increases approximately 1 per cent. This should not cause error if distance measurements are made by means of scales printed on the chart itself, unless the expansion is unequal in different directions.

In plotting on his chart, a navigator should avoid marking the chart with sufficient pressure to leave indentations in the surface. He should avoid lines longer than necessary, and should label lines and points, as appropriate, promptly, to avoid mistakes. At the conclusion of a voyage, the charts used during that passage should be cleaned with a soft eraser, to avoid damage to the charts or obliteration of printed information. Markings left on a chart may cause confusion and error when the chart is used again. However, if the voyage has been marked by any incident, such as a grounding or collision, that might result in the navigator or master being questioned, erasure should be delayed until there is no further reasonable probability that a review of the charts will be needed. With proper care, a chart can be used many times.

Provision should be made for adequate lighting of a chart during use at night, without interfering with the night vision of bridge personnel. This precaution is particularly important in the case of a person whose duties require that he both refer to a chart and keep a lookout for lights and any unlighted objects. One of the most effective means of providing suitable illumination is by means of a light *beneath* the chart, with a translucent glass or plastic surface between the light and the chart. Suitable material of this type, when properly installed as the top of a plotting desk or table, makes an excellent surface for spreading out a chart on which plotting is to be done.

If underlighting is not available, a red light above the chart produces minimum interference with the night vision of a person. However, any coloured light causes the appearance of a chart to change, and some colours either to disappear or to appear as different colours. Before permanently installing any lighting system, one should experiment with it to be certain that it will provide the desired illumination with a minimum of undesirable effects.

Charts have become so reliable that one might not expect to find imperfections in them. Although errors are rare, they do occur. One should be alert to such errors, and if one is found, it should be verified carefully and then reported promptly to the producer of the chart, as explained in section 13 of this chapter.

16. Chart Sources

Most maritime nations produce and distribute nautical charts, in varying degrees of completeness. Only a small number of nations attempt to maintain essentially complete coverage of navigable waters throughout the world. In the United Kingdom such coverage is provided by the Hydrographic Department of the Ministry of Defence. The United States provides similar coverage, most of its nautical charts being produced by the Defense Mapping Agency Hydrographic Topographic Center (foreign areas) and the National Ocean Survey, National Oceanic and Atmospheric Administration (domestic waters). Actual distribution of charts is principally through agents located in principal ports throughout the world. Each agent maintains a catalogue of the charts available.

The primary source of data used in the production of charts is the hydrographic survey, but many sources contribute to the operation, including the users of charts, who report many details that are helpful to the chartmaker. Because of the magnitude of the task, problems encountered in surveying the territorial waters of foreign nations, and the unnecessary duplication of effort this would involve, there is a free exchange of information among the various maritime nations of the world. Much of this cooperative effort and a high degree of standardization in the production of charts have been brought about through the efforts of the International Hydrographic Organization at Monaco. More than forty nations are members of this organization.

The exchange of information has been so successful that it has created another problem: the assimilation of all of the data available. Two approaches to the solution of this problem have been pursued. One has been the simplification of charts by elimination of information of questionable value to the mariner, and adopting styles permitting automated production. This effort is producing a more readable, and possibly more useful, chart. The second approach has been an increase in the cooperative effort by the exchange of 'repromats', making possible the reproduction by one nation of charts drafted by another nation, or to permit chart reproduction by facsimile.

In 1967, the International Hydrographic Bureau (assumed into the International Hydrographic Organization in 1970) established a Commission to study the practicability of a series of international charts, each nation producing charts of its own waters and granting other member nations the right to print in facsimile all charts of the series. Subsequently, the Commission decided to confine the initial effort to charts of two scales, one at 1/10M for general ocean navigation, and a second at 1/3.5M for offshore navigation. Each series would be on a common longitude scale, with a standard overlap, so that all charts of the series, at the same latitude, could be joined together. Detailed specifications were adopted.

Various problems associated with an international cooperative charting effort have been encountered. As acceptable solutions to these are found, duplication of effort can be expected to decrease. The attendant increase in standardization and decrease in cost of chart production should benefit the chart user and contribute to maritime safety.

III

Dead-Reckoning
and Pilotage Equipment

1. Charts

Navigators make extensive use of charts, which supply a wealth of information in convenient form. Charts should be selected with care, an adequate number of the latest editions of reliable charts on the most suitable scales being obtained to help ensure safe navigation. Unneeded charts add to the cost of equipping a vessel, increase the stowage space and indexing required for ready access, and augment the task of correcting the charts to keep them current. An uncorrected chart is a potential hazard.

Thorough knowledge of chart symbology and familiarity with details of the charts in use are essential to safe navigation. One should be aware, too, of chart limitations, including the fact that not all data available to charting agencies are displayed. A mariner can help improve chart usefulness by reporting errors and changes that come to his attention, and by making known his requirements and desires.

2. Publications

A number of publications are available to assist the navigator. Among the most useful are *Notices to Mariners*, *Daily Memorandum*, sailing directions, light lists, tide and tidal stream (tidal current) tables, lists of radio navigational signals, books of nautical tables, almanacs, and sight-reduction tables. Additionally, a navigation dictionary and a large number of manuals and books related to particular phases of navigation, or related subjects, are available. Appendix A lists a number of these publications.

PUBLICATIONS

Sailing directions, also called *pilots*, are books of descriptive material, in narrative style, of coastal and offshore features, aids to navigation, facilities, and other pertinent information supplementing data shown on nautical charts. Volume NP 100 of the British Admiralty sailing directions, called *The Mariner's Handbook*, contains a wealth of useful information of a general nature such as instructions on the use and limitations of Admiralty charts. Many of the British publications useful to the navigator are published by the Hydrographic Department of the Ministry of Defence, H.M. Stationery Office, the Department of Trade, Royal Greenwich Observatory, British Standards Institution, and the Royal Institute of Navigation. Prominent among United States sources are the Defense Mapping Agency Hydrographic Topographic Center; National Ocean Survey, National Oceanic and Atmospheric Administration, and National Weather Service; United States Government Printing Office; United States Coast Guard; and United States Naval Observatory. Many of the government publications can be obtained from authorized sales agents in principal ports throughout the world. Useful non-governmental publications are available from the International Hydrographic Organization at Monaco and from private publishers and book stores.

A number of periodicals print timely articles on subjects of interest in navigators. Among the more notable of such periodicals are *The Journal of Navigation*, published by the Royal Institute of Navigation, London; *Navigation, Journal of The Institute of Navigation*, Washington; *Navigation*, published by The Australian Institute of Navigation, Sydney; *Navigation, Revue Technique de Navigation Maritime Aérienne et Spatiale*, published by the Institut Français de Navigation, Paris; *The International Hydrographic Review*, published by the International Hydrographic Organization, Monaco; *United States Naval Institute Proceedings*, Annapolis; *The Nautical Magazine*, Glasgow; *The American Neptune*, Salem; and *The Mariner's Mirror*, published by the Society for Nautical Research at the National Maritime Museum, Greenwich, England.

3. Plotting Equipment

Adequate facilities should be available for plotting. The *chart desk* or *chart table* should be of convenient height and should be properly illuminated to provide sufficient light for plotting and chart reading but not so as to interfere with night vision of bridge personnel not involved in chart work. Red light should be avoided if charts with red symbols, lines, or lettering are used. It is desirable to have a chart desk of sufficient size to accommodate the largest charts that will be used, with minimum folding of the charts. In small vessels this is not always practicable, but one should not compromise the size of the chart desk without good cause. Masking or other suitable tape is prefarable to thumbtacks for securing a chart or plotting sheet to the chart-desk top, because tape interferes less with use of plotting equipment, is less likely to become detached, and does not leave holes in the desk top.

Provision should be made for secure stowage of all loose items of equipment to prevent inaccessibility, damage, or loss, especially in heavy weather.

Medium-soft pencils should be used, so that lines and labels are easily visible without smudging, and erasable without leaving indentations in the chart, which might be used again. Several well-sharpened pencils should be kept on hand, with provision for resharpening as necessary or desirable. Erasers should be soft so as to remove pencil marks without damaging the chart or plotting sheet.

Plotting involves drawing of lines, transferring lines parallel to themselves, drawing lines perpendicular to other lines, measuring direction, measuring or plotting angles, and measuring distances.

A *straight-edge* is used as a guide for drawing straight lines. Rather than using a simple ruler for this purpose, a navigator usually uses a device having additional features.

Parallel rulers consist of two rulers connected in such a manner that when one is held firm against the chart, the other can be moved parallel to itself so that a line can be drawn parallel to another line. In this manner the device can be 'walked' from any part of a chart or plotting sheet to any other part. Parallel rulers can also be used for drawing a line in a desired direction on a Mercator chart if a compass rose (p. 43) is available on the chart, by aligning one ruler with the desired direction, as indicated by the compass rose, and then transferring this direction to the point through which the line is to be drawn. The reverse process is used for measuring the direction of a line or the direction between two points on the chart or plotting sheet. In another form, the device consists of a single ruler with two or more connected rollers, or one long roller, so that the device can be moved parallel to itself across the chart. This form of the device is somewhat easier to use than the double-ruler type, but is constrained to movement in a straight line only, and must be secured adequately when not in use to avoid its rolling off the chart table. Some skill and care are needed with either form of parallel rulers to prevent slippage, which would destroy the parallelism, during transfer.

Draughtmen's triangles can also be used as straight-edges or, in combination, for transferring lines parallel to themselves, by sliding one along the edge of another. A right triangle, when used with another straight-edge, is also a convenient means of drawing a line perpendicular to another line or direction.

A simple protractor, preferably a large, clear, plastic one, is useful in measuring directions by alignment with a printed meridian or parallel. However, a direction might be needed at any point on a chart or plotting sheet. Therefore, a protractor is of somewhat limited use. For this reason, directions are more commonly measured by means of a compass rose and parallel rulers or by a different type of device.

A plotter is a device combining a protractor with one or more straight-edges, so that a straight line in any desired direction can be drawn at any point on the chart or plotting sheet, or the direction of a line measured, without the aid of a compass rose. Plotters take many forms, some with movable arms and some with one or more fixed straight-edges. The most desirable is a matter of personal preference. A station pointer, or three-arm protractor, is a form of plotter having a protractor and three arms, one fixed and the other two rotatable to provide means for measurement of angles. The

87

principal use of this device is for fixing the position of a vessel by means of horizontal angles between landmarks, as observed aboard the vessel (p. 231).

A *draughting machine* is a mechanical device that can be clamped securely to the chart desk and has a protractor, one or more straight-edges, and a parallel-motion mechanism. The protractor can be oriented to true north by alignment with a printed meridian or parallel, and clamped in this orientation. Thereafter, any direction indicated by the protractor is a true direction. Several straight-edges of varying length are usually provided, and these can be interchanged without disturbing the orientation of the protractor. Some models provide means for mounting a second straight-edge perpendicular to the first. Such a device thus has provision for drawing straight lines, transferring a line parallel to itself, drawing a line perpendicular to another line or direction, and measuring direction.

Distances and coordinates on a chart or plotting sheet are measured by means of *dividers*, a device consisting, in simple form, of two legs pivoted at one end and pointed at the other. The legs can be spread to the distance to be measured and then transferred to any other place on the chart or plotting sheet. The pivot should have enough friction to prevent slippage during transfer, but not so much that it interferes with easy manipulation with one hand. Dividers with relatively long legs are preferable, to permit measurement of long distances, but the legs should not be so long that the device is cumbersome to use. The legs should be of equal length and should close evenly, to permit measurement of very short distances. *Beam dividers*, consisting of a bar and movable legs that can be clamped in position along the bar, are sometimes useful for measurement of long distances.

Compasses are a device similar to dividers, but with one of the legs having a device for holding a pen, pencil, or graphite 'lead' at one end, instead of a point. Compasses can be used for measuring distance, but the more common use is for drawing circles for small-circle position lines (p. 224) or to indicate the limit of visibility of a navigational light. *Beam compasses* are similar to beam dividers, but with provision for drawing circles.

Proportional dividers have points at both ends of the legs, and an adjustable pivot between the ends. The device is sometimes useful when transferring a distance or coordinate to a chart or plotting sheet of different scale, or for use with time–distance relationships.

Spacing dividers are a device having a number of legs that maintain equal separation intervals as the legs are separated. The device is useful for laying off equal-distance intervals along a line, as in plotting a line of soundings (p. 257).

4. Direction

Navigators generally express direction as an angle between a line extending in some reference direction and a line extending in the direction to be designated. The primary function of a *compass* is to locate a reference direction. Having done this, it then provides means for indicating other directions. Compasses in general use by mariners are of two types: magnetic and gyro.

Magnetic compasses depend upon the magnetic field of the Earth for their directional property. The reference direction indicated by a magnetic compass is called *compass north*, which usually differs somewhat from *magnetic north* because of local magnetic disturbances in the vicinity of the compass.

Gyro compasses depend upon the rotation of the Earth and the force of gravity for their directional property. The reference direction indicated by a gyro compass is *gyro north*, which is usually a close approximation of *true north*, the northerly direction along a geographical meridian.

Gyro compasses are now used extensively for guiding vessels of all types except small craft and ship's boats, the latter using a small magnetic compass called a *boat compass*. Increasingly, yachts are using some modern, light, compact version of gyro compass. Although in many modern vessels the magnetic compass has become a stand-by instrument, it should not be neglected, and no wise navigator will fail to understand its operation and use, for in the event of failure of his gyro compasses, through loss of power or otherwise, the safety of his vessel might depend upon the condition of a magnetic compass and the ability of the crew to use it.

5. Magnetism

Although a recognition of the existence of magnetism extends back at least to the seventh century BC, man's knowledge of this phemonenon is still far from complete. However, a general understanding of the subject is available and useful to the mariner who would gain maximum benefit from his magnetic compass.

Magnetism is the ability to attract certain kinds of material, notably iron and ferrous alloys containing nickel and cobalt. An object having this ability is called a *magnet*. Magnetism can be either permanent or temporary. A piece of metal that retains the ability to attract other magnetic material is called a *permanent magnet*. If it gradually loses its magnetism over a relatively long period of time, it is sometimes said to have *subpermanent magnetism*. A form of magnetite, a ferrous oxide ore, has magnetic properties naturally as it occurs in nature. It is thus a *natural magnet*, the *lodestone* that mystified ancients who encountered it. Magnetism is also associated with electric currents.

The space in which magnetism exists is called a *magnetic field*. The magnetism existing in an object only when it is in the presence of a strong magnetic field is called *induced magnetism*, and the process of thus inducing magnetism is called *magnetic induction*. When the strength of a magnetic field is changed, the effect on magnetic material in its presence lags behind the change in the strength of the field, an effect called *hysteresis*. Some ferrous material, called 'hard iron', accepts magnetism grudgingly, but retains a high percentage of the magnetism thus acquired. This type of material is suitable for permanent magnets. The opposite condition—ready acceptance but low *retentivity* of magnetism—exists in 'soft iron'. In this application, 'hard' and 'soft' apply only to magnetic properties of the material, and not to metallurgical properties.

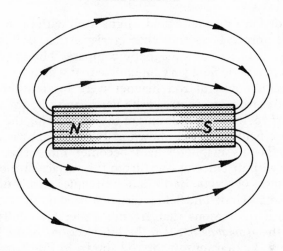

FIG. 301. Magnetic lines of force.

A magnetic field is visualized as consisting of a number of closed *magnetic lines of force*, as shown in Fig. 301. Relative strength of field is indicated by spacing of the lines, closer spacing indicating a stronger field.

A magnet has two *magnetic poles (P)* at which the attraction is concentrated. The lines of force emanate from the *north* pole and enter the *south* pole. For convenience, the north pole of a magnet is called the *red* pole, and the south pole is designated the *blue* pole. The ends of permanent magnets are sometimes painted red and blue to indicate polarity.

Like magnetic poles repel one another and unlike poles attract. The product of the distance between two magnetic poles and the average strength of the poles is called *magnetic moment*. The average magnetic moment per unit volume is called the *intensity of magnetization (M)*. The intensity of magnetization of a uniform magnetic field is called *magnetic field intensity (H)*. *Magnetic flux (ϕ)* is the magnetic flow in a magnetic circuit. *Magnetic flux density (B)* is the ratio of magnetic flux in a cross section to the area of the cross section. *Susceptibility (χ)* is the ratio M/H, and *permeability (μ)* is the ratio B/H, or $1 + \chi$.

A permanent magnet in the shape of a rod, if freely

suspended in a magnetic field, aligns itself with the magnetic lines of force. It is this characteristic that provides the directive property of a magnetic compass. The Earth has a natural magnetic field very much like that which would exist if a small, powerful rod magnet were located about 342 kilometres from the centre of the Earth, and tilted some $11°.5$ with respect to the Earth's axis of rotation, giving the Earth's magnetic field the shape shown in Fig. 302, approximately.

The Earth's magnetic field becomes more regular but weaker with distance upward from the surface of the Earth. At distances of several Earth radii it becomes greatly distorted by the solar wind. The field is also distorted on the surface of the Earth for reasons that are not understood fully. As a result, the *geomagnetic poles*, the intersections of the Earth's surface and extensions of the rod shown in Fig. 302, do not coincide with either the geographical or *magnetic poles (P)*, the north magnetic pole being located in the vicinity of Prince of Wales Island in northern Canada, and the south magnetic pole being located in the vicinity of Wilkes Land in Antarctica, offset considerably from the antipode of the north magnetic pole.

Note that the lines of force of the Earth's magnetic field emanate from the *southern* pole of the fictitious rod magnet, and enter the *northern* pole. Thus, the *north* geomagnetic and magnetic poles have *south* magnetism and vice versa—one reason for the red-blue designation of magnetic poles.

Lines of force of the Earth's magnetic field are parallel to the Earth's surface along an irregular line called the *magnetic equator*, roughly midway between the Earth's magnetic poles. At all other places, the lines of force are inclined to the horizontal. The angle between the horizontal plane and a line of force is called *magnetic dip (I)*, or *magnetic inclination*. The Earth's magnetic poles are those poorly-defined points at which magnetic dip is $90°$. The *magnetic latitude* of a place is the angle of which the tangent is half that of the magnetic dip of the place.

The *total intensity (F)* of the Earth's magnetic field at any point is the strength of the field along the line of force through the point. The *horizontal intensity (H)* is the horizontal

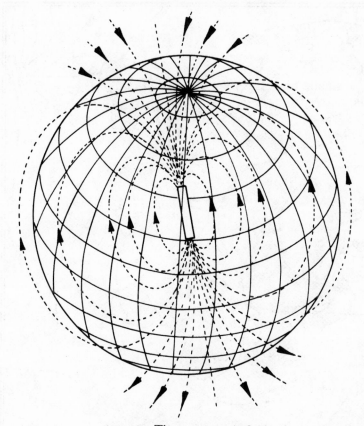

FIG. 302. The geomagnetic field.

component of the total intensity. Along the magnetic equator, H and F are the same, but H decreases with increased magnetic latitude, becoming zero at the magnetic poles. Because the magnets of a compass at rest are constrained to remain in the horizontal, the directive force of the compass is related to H. It is for this reason that magnetic compasses become erratic in high magnetic latitudes, where H is weak. The component of H along a geographic meridian is called the *north component* (X), and along a parallel the *east component* (Y). The *vertical intensity* (Z) is the vertical component of total intensity.

93

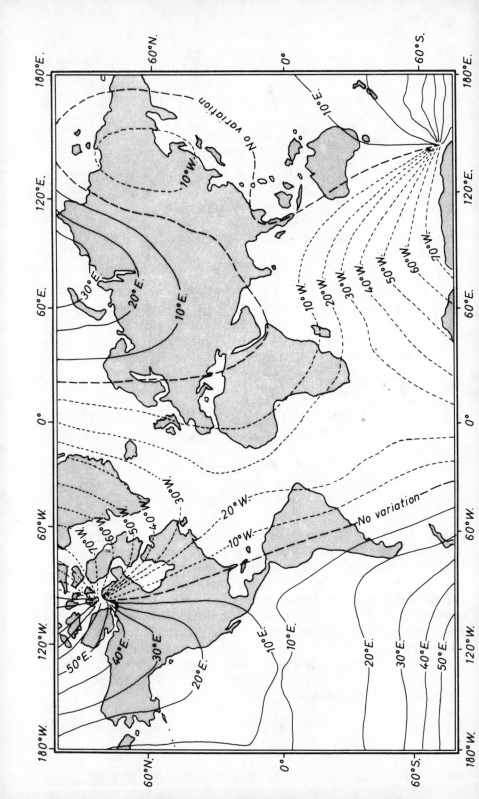

The horizontal component of a line of force of the Earth's field is called a *magnetic meridian*. Although magnetic meridians bear some resemblance to geographic meridians, they are not semi-great circles, as are *geomagnetic meridians* connecting the geomagnetic poles, but irregular lines connecting the north and south magnetic poles of the Earth. Rarely does part of a magnetic meridian lie in a geographic meridian. In most places the two form an angle called *variation* (*V*, *var*), or *magnetic declination*. A simplified chart of variation is shown in Fig. 303. The lines connecting points of equal magnetic variation, as shown, are called *isogonic lines*. These are *not* magnetic meridians. A line connecting points of no variation is called an *agonic line*. Variation is discussed in more detail in section 8 of this chapter.

The magnetic field of the Earth is neither uniform nor static. The lack of uniformity is evident in Fig. 303. Changes are of three general types:

Diurnal change is that somewhat regular change that occurs on a daily cycle. It is attributed to fluctuating electric currents in the upper atmosphere because of ultraviolet radiation from the Sun, principally, and the Moon to a much lesser extent. The magnitude of the diurnal change varies with latitude, season, and sunspot cycle. To the navigator, the effect of principal interest is the change of variation. In general, the north-seeking ends of compass magnets are deflected *away* from the Sun, moving toward the west in the morning and the east in the afternoon, 'noon' in this case being the time when the Sun is on the geomagnetic meridian. Near the Earth's magnetic poles, which move within an elliptical area approximately 50 miles long, oriented in a generally north–south direction, the diurnal change in variation sometimes reaches a magnitude of several degrees. Elsewhere it is much less. The average daily fluctuation at London is about $0.^{\circ}1$ at the time of sunspot minimum, and about twice this amount at sunspot maximum.

Secular change is a very slow, progressive change occurring over a very long period of time. It, too, seems to be cyclical, although one cycle has not occurred over the four centuries during which it has been observed. In 1580, variation at

London was nearly 11° E. In subsequent years it decreased to zero and then increased in a westerly direction until it reached a maximum of 24° W. in 1820. Since then it has decreased, now being only about one third of this maximum. The greatest known secular change rate in variation, other than in polar areas, is in the vicinity of Malagasy Republic, where variation is changing at the rate of about 0°.25 per year. All well-known centres of large secular change seem to be drifting westward slowly.

The third type of change occurs during magnetic storms, called *sudden ionospheric disturbances* (*SID*). These begin about a day after solar flares occur on the Sun. They cause disruption of short-wave radio communications, increased auroral activity, and erratic fluctuations of a magnetic compass. The change in magnetic variation might reach a magnitude of several degrees in latitudes frequented by ships of the merchant service. The most intense period lasts for as long as half a day, after which the disturbance dies out gradually until normal conditions are restored about two days after the storm began.

6. Magnetic Compass

Modern magnetic compasses for use at sea are available in a variety of sizes and styles, but all are expected to meet certain requirements:

Directive element. One or more magnets are mounted so as to be free to align themselves with the horizontal component of the Earth's magnetic field. Several short rod magnets, kept parallel by the method of mounting, are usually considered preferable to a single magnet, although single ring magnets are used in some compasses. Compass magnets are generally made of an alloy of iron, nickel, and cobalt with high magnetic retentivity.

Direction indication. The directive element of a compass is attached to a thin circular disk called a *compass card*, on which various directions are indicated. North on the compass card is aligned with the north-seeking or red ends of the compass magnets. Compass-card graduations nearly always consist primarily of 360 evenly-spaced marks around the periphery, labelled at intervals in degrees from 0° at north clockwise through 360°. An older compass card, graduated from 0° to 90° in opposite directions from both north and south, might occasionally be encountered. Compass cards often have auxiliary graduations in *compass points*, once the primary or only graduations. There are 32 compass points, each of $11\frac{1}{4}$ degrees. These are named, in clockwise order from north: north, north by east, north-north-east, north-east by north, north-east, north-east by east, east-north-east, east by north, east, and so on through the remaining three quadrants. Naming compass directions in order is called *boxing the compass*. Mariners of bygone days prided themselves on their ability to box the compass to quarter points—128 in all. Modern compass cards may have 32-point graduations, but generally have fewer, only the cardinal and intercardinal graduations being common. A typical compass card is shown in Fig. 304. The direction of the heading is indicated by a reference mark, called a *lubber line*, on the compass mounting, the compass-card graduation aligned with the lubber line being the heading. Other graduations indicate other directions, as bearings of objects. Some small compasses are

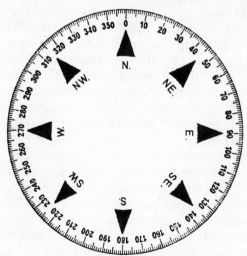

FIG. 304. A compass card.

provided with compass cards in the form of a vertical cylinder. These compasses are intended to be read from the after *side*, instead of the top, with the graduations indicating the directions on the opposite side of the card. A cylindrical compass card is shown in Fig. 305, indicating a heading of 155°.

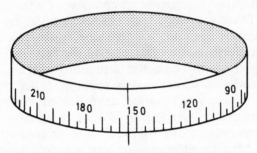

FIG. 305. A cylindrical compass card.

Mounting. The directive element and card are mounted so as to be free to seek magnetic north with minimum error from friction. For this purpose, the magnet-card assembly may be carefully balanced on a hard sharply-pointed spindle seated in a jewelled bearing.

Oscillation damping. A compass as described thus far would be subject to excessive oscillations imparted to it by motions of the vessel and other disturbances. These oscillations are minimized by mounting the directive element and compass card in a bowl filled with liquid, either a methanol and water solution or a refined petroleum product, either of which will not freeze at temperatures to which the compass is likely to be subjected. The liquid also reduces the weight of the magnet–card assembly on the spindle, thus further reducing friction, and helps keep the magnet–card assembly horizontal. Provision is made for expansion and contraction of the liquid with changes of temperature, to prevent damage and the formation of bubbles within the liquid. The top of the bowl of a top-reading compass is of glass to permit viewing the compass card. Some compasses have hemispherical tops to provide magnification of the card and to reduce eddy currents in the liquid.

Horizontal mounting. If the compass is not horizontal, errors in reading can be made, and the disturbing effects of magnetic influences within the craft are changed, thus introducing unwanted deflection of the compass card. In addition to the effect of the liquid in helping keep the magnet–card assembly horizontal, it is desirable to keep the compass bowl in a horizontal position.

Neutralization of local magnetic influences. The magnetic material of a craft, and electric currents in the vicinity of the compass, cause deflection of the directive element. These disturbing forces are reduced to a minimum by mounting the compass in a stand or other receptacle called a *binnacle*, which is provided with means for setting up equal and opposite forces, as nearly as practicable. The means of doing so is discussed in sections 11 and 12 of this chapter. The binnacle itself, in common with parts of the compass other than the directive element, is made of non-magnetic material.

Illumination. If a compass is to be used in an unlighted or dimly lighted position during darkness, some means of illumination is generally provided.

Proper installation of a magnetic compass is important. A location on the centre line of the vessel is desirable, to enhance the symmetrical effect of the craft's magnetic material. Such a location is not always practical for the intended use of the compass. Freedom from magnetic influences of moving magnetic material, such as cranes, and from strong direct-current electric currents is desirable. If the compass is to be used for measuring bearings of various objects, a location free from obstructions in the relative directions to be observed should be selected, or a portable hand-held *bearing compass* used. Some compasses are mounted in an exposed location above the wheel house, to provide a favourable position magnetically and an obstructed view, with a periscope arrangement to permit reading the compass by the conning officer and helmsman below. One magnetic compass, located in a favourable position and accurately calibrated, is designed the *standard compass*. A compass used for steering a vessel is termed a *steering compass*. Whatever the location, the lubber line should be carefully aligned with the longitudinal axis of the craft, so that compass headings will be indicated correctly.

The installation having been made, the crew then has the responsibility of keeping the compass ready for use when needed. A properly-installed magnetic compass is a dependable instrument requiring very little maintenance. It is for this reason, in part, that the device tends to be neglected. The little maintenance recommended by the manufacturer should be understood and given. Beyond this, those concerned should understand the operation and vagaries of the magnetic compass. Its deviation (section 9) on various headings should be determined from time to time and checked periodically, especially upon a major change of magnetic latitude or after a craft has been on essentially the same heading for a long period of time (as when laid up for a period), structural changes in the craft have been made, a cargo of magnetic material has been taken aboard or discharged, riding out heavy seas, grounding, collision, being struck by a projectile, or the craft has been struck by lightning. All of these events can produce changes in the magnetic field in the vicinity of the compass, thus affecting deviation.

One should be careful, too, of small magnetic influences in the immediate vicinity of the compass. A changed position of a crane, a pocket-knife or ring of keys in the pocket of the helmsman or other person near the compass, a steel tool or electric equipment placed near the compass, and even nylon clothing can change deviation. Understanding and vigilance are essential if one is to obtain the reliable operation a magnetic compass is capable of delivering.

Certain auxiliary equipment is desirable. A hood may be placed over a steering compass to prevent its illumination from disturbing the night vision of bridge personnel other than the helmsman. A cover is desirable to protect an exposed compass from weather when not in use. If the compass is to be used for measuring bearings or azimuths (p. 299), a device to facilitate the measurement is desirable. For flat top-reading compasses this device may be in the form of a ring that fits over the compass, provided with suitable sighting vanes, the capability of being rotated to any desired direction, and provision for reading the compass direction in which the vanes are oriented. Some magnetic compasses are provided with electrical pick-offs permitting readings of the compass to be duplicated by a *compass repeater* in a remote location. Repeaters are more common with gyro compasses than with magnetic compasses.

7. Compass Error

A direction is designated as true, magnetic, or compass as the reference direction is true, magnetic, or compass north. Thus, the same *direction*, such as a heading or bearing, may have different numerical designations depending upon the reference direction. When it is desirable to designate the reference direction, the letter T, M, or C is appended to the number indicating the direction, to identify the reference direction as true, magnetic, or compass, respectively. Thus, C 048 T indicates a true course of 048°, H 157 M indicates a magnetic heading of 157°, and B 322 C indicates a compass bearing of 322°. Alternatively, the reference direction might be given as a prefix, as TC 048, MH 157, or CB 322.

The angle between true and magnetic meridians is called *variation* (V, *var*), and the angle between a magnetic meridian and the north–south axis of a magnetic compass card is called *deviation* (D, *dev*). Each is designated east (E., +) or west (W., −) to indicate whether the effect rotates the compass card clockwise or anticlockwise. Fig. 306 shows the orientation of a compass card with respect to magnetic and true compass roses if variation is 8° W. and deviation is 3° E. As indicated, all magnetic designations of direction are 8° *greater* than *true* designations of the same directions. Also, all compass designations are 3° *less* than *magnetic* designations, and 5° *greater* than *true* designations. *Compass error* (*CE*) is the algebraic sum of variation and deviation, in this case 8° W. − 3° E. = 5° W., or −8 + 3 = −5.

A navigator should be able to interconvert true, magnetic, and compass designations of a direction quickly and accurately. The use of an incorrect sign could be disastrous.

Certain conventions are used to simplify the process and help the navigator avoid error. Both variation and deviation are thought of as errors. Thus, a magnetic designation of a direction has one error (variation) and a compass designation has one error (deviation) with respect to magnetic, and two errors (deviation and variation) with respect to true. The process of applying corrections to remove errors, when converting a compass designation to magnetic or true, or magnetic to true, is said to be *correcting*. Conversion in the opposite direction is called *uncorrecting*.

A memory aid that might prove useful is the expression *correcting add east*, meaning that when correcting, an easterly error is added. It follows that westerly errors would then be subtracted. In the illustration shown in Fig. 306, if a compass bearing is $244°$, the magnetic bearing is $244° + 3° = 247°$, and the true bearing is $247° - 8° = 239°$, or $244° - 5° = 239°$. The statement 'correcting add east' might be remembered more readily if one makes an easily-remembered sentence using the initial letters C, A, E. 'Come at Eight' will do.

Another way of avoiding a blunder is to arrange the various elements of the problem as follows:

$$\longleftarrow \text{W.} \quad + \quad \text{E.} \longrightarrow$$
$$\text{C} \qquad \text{D} \qquad \text{M} \qquad \text{V} \qquad \text{T}$$
$$244° \quad 3° \text{ E.} \quad 247° \quad 8° \text{ W.} \quad 239°$$

The letters C, D, M, V, T refer to compass, deviation, magnetic, variation, and true, respectively. The order might be remembered more readily if, again, one combines them in a sentence. One often used is 'can dead men vote twice?' The designation above letters indicates merely that in going from C to M to T one adds if the error is easterly, and that going from T to M to C one adds if the error is westerly. The designation has no reference to direction on the Earth, but the direction to draw and label the arrows should be evident if one remembers that east is towards the right, and west towards the left, when the top of a chart is north, the usual orientation.

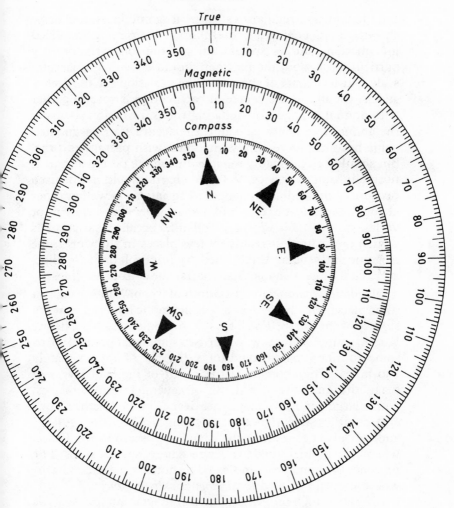

FIG. 306. Orientation of compass card when variation is 8° W. and deviation is 3° E.

8. Variation

Because variation is the angle between true and magnetic meridians, its magnitude is a function of location, and therefore can be shown on charts. Fig. 303 is an *isomagnetic chart* showing *isogonic lines*, or lines connecting points of equal magnetic variation. On small-scale charts such as

Fig. 303 small irregularities in the isogonic lines cannot be shown. Such charts are useful for obtaining generalized information, but for specific information on variation at a particular location, the mariner should consult the largest-scale nautical chart of the area. The variation for the area is stated, usually in the centre of each compass rose, together with annual change, for updating the information. Because the annual rate is not constant, the accuracy of an updated value becomes increasingly uncertain with passage of time, but should be reasonably reliable during the period a chart is normally kept in service. Very old charts should not be used because of unpredicted changes in variation, as well as other changes. Even at the epoch of a chart, the values shown for variation are not completely reliable because variation is actually measured at relatively few places in the world, the isogonic lines being established by interpolation. Smaller-scale charts, as many coastal charts, show isogonic lines.

Magnetic anomalies in the pattern of isogonic lines occur in some places because of deposits of magnetic material near the surface of the Earth. The largest known anomaly is located at Kursk, south of Moscow, where two somewhat parallel strips some 40 miles apart extend for a distance of approximately 150 miles. The anomaly is the result of inclined layers of magnetite-quartzite at a depth of several hundred metres, with a large deposit of magnetite deeper in the Earth. As one crosses either strip, the variation changes nearly 180°. A large anomaly also occurs near the island of Jussarö in the Baltic, where it has contributed to the wreckage of several ships. The presence of anomalies is indicated by notes on nautical charts, where they are termed *local magnetic disturbances*.

In polar regions, where grid navigation (p. 594) is commonly practised, *grid variation (GV)*, or *grivation*, may be shown. This is the angle between the grid and magnetic meridians through a place. Lines connecting points of equal grid variation are called isogrivs.

9. Deviation

Deviation is the angle between a magnetic meridian and the north–south axis of a magnetic compass card. Unlike variation, deviation varies with the heading of the craft.

The directive element of a magnetic compass tends to align itself with the magnetic field in which it is located. This field consists of the magnetic field of the Earth, modified by any local magnetic influences. It is the modification of the Earth's field that causes deviation, by deflecting the north–south axis of the compass card.

The magnetic field of a wooden sailing vessel without machinery may be quite simple or virtually nonexistent, in contrast with the highly complex field of a modern steel ship. The magnetic field of each ship is unique, being the result of the design of the craft, the material used in its construction, the method and length of time of construction, the magnetic heading on which the vessel was constructed, the history of the vessel after launch, and whether it was given magnetic treatment to alter its magnetic characteristics. The field also varies with the heading of the vessel and the magnetic latitude of its location. Further, the effect of a vessel's magnetic field in causing deviation varies with position of the compass in the craft. A general understanding of the types and locations of local magnetic fields within a vessel can help a navigator understand his magnetic compasses and their sometimes seemingly erratic behaviour.

The material used in the construction of a vessel is seldom selected with a view to its influence upon a magnetic compass. The steel of a typical vessel consists of varying degrees of magnetic 'hardness' (p. 90). For simplification, 'hard iron' is understood to be all metal having any degree of permanent magnetism, and 'soft iron' that which has only induced magnetism resulting from its position in the Earth's magnetic field.

The construction process contributes to the acquisition of permanent magnetism. That part of a vessel toward the blue pole of the Earth (located in the northern hemisphere) acquires red magnetism, and the opposite part acquires blue magnetism. Consider the situation of a vessel constructed on a heading of magnetic north in Scotland, where the magnetic dip is about 70°. The lower and forward portions of the craft acquire red magnetism, while the upper and after portions acquire blue magnetism. If the heading during construction at the same location were magnetic west, the lower starboard section would acquire red magnetism and the upper port section would acquire blue magnetism. If the construction heading were not a cardinal direction, the permanent magnetic field of the vessel would be more complex, but could be visualized by remembering that red magnetism would be acquired in the lower portion of the vessel towards magnetic north, and blue magnetism would be acquired in the upper portion toward magnetic south.

After launch of the vessel, the permanent magnetism decreases if the vessel is placed on a magnetic heading different from that during construction of the hull. The change is relatively rapid during the first few days, the rate of change decreasing gradually. The permanent magnetism tends to change to suit the new heading, the effect becoming stronger with longer time on the heading. Sudden changes, both in strength and polarity, may occur if the vessel is subjected to a strong field of direct current electricity, as during magnetic treatment for degaussing (section 12) or if the vessel is struck by lightning, or if the vessel is subject to shock, as in fighting heavy seas or being struck by or striking some object. After any experience that might alter the magnetic characteristics of a vessel, the deviation of its magnetic compasses should be checked, and if significant changes are noted, a new compass adjustment (section 11) should be performed. Because of the gradual change in ship's magnetism after it is disturbed, the new adjustment should be delayed several days to avoid *Gaussin error*, the deviation caused by transient induced magnetism after removal of the inducting force.

The effect of permanent magnetism on a magnetic compass depends upon the position of the compass relative to the red and blue poles of the vessel, both with respect to direction and distance, as well as upon the strength of the poles. If a pole is in line with the north–south axis of a compass, the only effect is to augment or weaken the field of the Earth, thus strengthening or weakening the directive force. If a pole is to one side of the north–south axis, it establishes a *magnetic couple*, attracting one end of the directive element and repelling the other end, thus causing its rotation. If two poles, one red and the other blue, are on the same side of the compass, they tend to cancel one another. But if the poles are on opposite sides of the compass, both tend to cause deviation in the same direction.

The effect of soft iron differs somewhat from that of hard iron, in that the magnetism of soft iron changes with orientation of the vessel. As with permanent magnetism, the red pole is in that part of the vessel facing the blue pole of the Earth, and the blue pole is in the opposite part of the craft, but as the orientation of the vessel changes as it rolls, pitches, or changes heading or trim, the poles move to accommodate the new orientation. The positions of the poles of induced magnetism also change with a change in magnetic latitude, and the strength changes with changes in the strength of the Earth's field.

In general, induced magnetism can be considered as being concentrated in two rods, one horizontal and in a magnetic north–south direction, and the other vertical. The northern end of the horizontal rod has red magnetism and the southern end has blue magnetism. In north magnetic latitude the red end of the vertical rod is down, and in south magnetic latitude the red end is up. The total effect of the vertical soft iron of a conventional vessel is that of a vertical rod on the centre line of the vessel. If the compass is in the upper part of the vessel, it is affected principally by the upper pole of the rod, blue in the northern magnetic hemisphere and red in the southern, and increasing in strength as magnetic latitude increases. If the compass is well forward in the vessel, the pole is likely to be aft of the compass. If the vessel is on a heading of magnetic north or south, the pole augments or weakens the directive force, but if the vessel is on a heading of magnetic east or west, the pole deflects the compass magnets, causing deviation. If the compass is not on the longitudinal axis through the pole, this relationship is somewhat different.

If the horizontal soft iron is symmetrical with respect to the compass, as for a compass location on the centre line of a conventional vessel, it strengthens or weakens the directive force but does not cause deviation if the vessel is on a cardinal heading with respect to magnetic north. Maximum deviation from symmetrical horizontal soft iron occurs on compass intercardinal headings. The effect of asymmetrically-arranged horizontal soft iron in producing deviation is 'maximum on compass cardinal headings. Asymmetrical horizontal soft iron can also produce a constant component of deviation on all headings if the compass is located off the longitudinal axis of the vessel's horizontal soft iron.

Although the total magnetic field in the vicinity of a compass is quite complex, and changes as the vessel's position and orientation change, it can be visualized in simple form as consisting of the resultant effect of the Earth's magnetic field, the permanent magnetism of the vessel, and the induced magnetism in symmetrical and assymmetrical horizontal and vertical soft iron. The effect of the magnetism within the craft is to either augment or weaken the directive force of the magnetic compass or to cause deviation by deflection of the directive element of the compass. Although the strengthening or weakening of the directive force of a magnetic compass does not itself cause deviation, it may affect the magnitude of deviation resulting from a deflecting force.

Deviation on various headings is shown in a *deviation table* recorded on a *deviation card*, also called a *compass correction card* (section 13). Deviation on any heading can change, sometimes in a very short period of time, if the craft's magnetism is altered, or if magnetic material is introduced or removed from the vicinity of the compass. For this reason, it is good practice to check the deviation frequently when convenient opportunities present themselves. This can be done by comparing the compass reading with the magnetic designation of the same direction. The magnetic designation can be determined in a number of ways, as explained in section 10.

10. Compass Correction

The basic principle of *compass correction* is to establish, at a magnetic compass, magnetic fields of the same kinds of magnetism, permanent or induced, and of equal strength but opposite polarity to those fields resulting from magnetic influences other than that of the Earth. *Compass adjustment* (section 11) is the neutralization of a craft's magnetic field at a magnetic compass. *Compass compensation* (section 12) is the neutralization of the magnetic field, at a compass, established by a vessel's degaussing system (p. 124). The expressions *correction*, *adjustment*, and *compensation* are sometimes used interchangeably.

One of the purposes of compass correction is to reduce deviation. If it were possible to neutralize completely the disturbing magnetic fields, all deviation would be eliminated. Because of the complex nature of these fields, a small amount of *residual deviation* generally remains after compass correction.

A second purpose of compass correction is to restore the corrective force of the compass. Some of the magnetic influences in the vicinity of a compass either weaken or augment the Earth's field. In an extreme situation, the disturbing field is stronger than the Earth's field, resulting in the compass being oriented primarily to the disturbing field, making some compass headings unattainable. The effect of a disturbing field in producing deviation varies with the craft's heading and with the magnetic latitude, changes in either resulting in changes in relative strengths of the components making up the disturbing field.

A third purpose of compass correction is to minimize the change in the deviating effect as the vessel heels and the trim is changed, as during rolling and pitching. At these times a change occurs in the strengths and positions of the components of the field relative to the compass.

Research has been directed toward the design of a compartment free from disturbing magnetic influences. The development of transmitting compasses, permitting greater choice of compass location within a vessel, has encouraged such research. However, even if a magnetic compass is located in such a compartment, one would be unwise to assume that no compass correction is needed.

Although compass correction is normally the work of a

professional, knowledge of the basic principles involved is useful to the navigator.

Because of the impractibility of locating and neutralizing each magnetic pole within a vessel, the magnetic field of the vessel is considered to consist of a number of components, or parameters, as follows:

Permanent magnetism. *Parameter P*, the fore-and-aft component, positive if the equivalent pole forward of the compass is blue, and negative if red.

Parameter Q, the athwartship component, positive if the equivalent pole to starboard is blue, and negative if red.

Parameter R, the vertical component, positive if the equivalent pole below the compass is blue, and negative if red.

Induced magnetism, consisting of a number of hypothetical slender rods of soft iron. Each end of a rod is positive if forward, to starboard, or below the compass.

Rods a, b, c each has one end level with the compass in line with its fore-and-aft axis, either forward or aft of the compass. The a rod extends in a fore-and-aft direction, the b rod in an athwartship direction, and the c rod in a vertical direction.

Rods d, e, f each has one end level with the compass in line with its athwartship axis, either to starboard or port of the compass. The d rod extends in a fore-and-aft direction, the e rod in an athwartship direction, and the f rod in a vertical direction.

Rods g, h, k each has one end in line with the vertical axis of the compass, either above or below it. The g rod extends in a fore-and-aft direction, the h rod in an athwartship direction, and the k rod in a vertical direction.

Deviation from different sources may have different characteristics. Whatever the source or combination of sources, a component of deviation having unique characteristics is called a *coefficient*. Six principal coefficients are identified:

A. Constant deviation, being equal on all headings. It is caused by asymmetrical arrangement of the various individual sources of deviation. An offset lubber line may cause an *apparent* constant coefficient.

B. Semi-circular deviation proportional to the sine of the compass heading, increasing from zero on north or south headings to maximum on east and west headings. *Semicircular deviation* changes sign in opposite semi-circles. It is caused by permanent magnetism and by induced magnetism in asymmetrical vertical soft iron.

C. Semi-circular deviation proportional to the cosine of the compass heading, increasing from zero on east or west headings to maximum on north and south headings.

D. Quadrantal deviation proportional to the sine of the sum of the compass and magnetic headings, increasing from zero on cardinal headings to maximum on intercardinal headings. *Quadrantal deviation* changes sign in adjacent quadrants, being the same in opposite quadrants. It is caused by induced magnetism in horizontal soft iron.

E. Quadrantal deviation proportional to the cosine of the sum of the compass and magnetic headings, increasing from zero on intercardinal headings to maximum on cardinal headings.

J. Change of deviation for a heeled vessel on compass heading north or south.

An aditional coefficient *I* is sometimes identified as the change of deviation as a vessel pitches. For marine craft this coefficient is usually small, and no separate provision is made for neutralizing it.

A knowledge of the magnitude and sign of each coefficient is useful in understanding the magnetic properties of the vessel and providing optimum compass correction. The determination of these quantities and their study constitutes *deviation analysis*. Deviation is first recorded on each cardinal and intercardinal heading *by the compass being analysed*. It is considered positive $(+)$ if easterly and negative $(-)$ if westerly. The approximate value of each coefficient is:

A. The mean deviation on all headings.

B. The mean deviation on headings 090° and 270°, with the sign at 270° reversed.

C. The mean deviation on headings 000° and 180°, with the sign at 180° reversed.

D. The mean of deviation on intercardinal headings, with the signs at headings 135° and 315° reversed.

E. The mean of deviation on cardinal headings, with the signs at 090° and 270° reversed.

J. The change of deviation for a heel of 1° with the vessel heading 000° by compass, considered positive (+) if the north end of the compass card is deflected toward the low side and negative (−) if it is deflected toward the high side.

Compass correction consists of placing the vessel on various *magnetic* headings, noting the deviation, and placing suitable correctors in positions to remove or reduce the deviation. Magnetic headings can be determined in a number of ways:

Gyro compass. The heading of the vessel by magnetic compass is compared with the heading by gyro compass. Any gyro error (p. 133) is applied to the reading of the gyro compass to obtain the true heading. Variation is then applied to obtain the magnetic heading. The difference between this value and the conpass heading is the deviation on that heading. Thus, if the heading by magnetic compass is 088° in an area where the variation is 8° W., and at the same instant the heading by a gyro compass with a gyro error of 1° E. is 081°, the true heading is 081° + 1° E. = 082°, and the magnetic heading is 082° + 8° W. = 090°. The deviation is 090° − 088° = 2° E. Using the convention shown in section 7 of this chapter:

$$\longleftarrow \text{W.} \quad + \quad \text{E.} \longrightarrow$$

C	D	M	V	T
088°	2° E.	090°	8° W.	082°

A similar convention could have been used to apply gyro error. GE:

$$\longleftarrow \text{W.} \quad + \quad \text{E.} \longrightarrow$$

G	GE	T
081°	1° E.	082°

Comparison with a gyro compass should preferably be made after the vessel has been on the same heading for several hours, to avoid temporary alteration of gyro error, and gyro error should be verified.

Another magnetic compass. Heading comparison is made as

with a gyro compass. Deviation of the second compass is applied to the reading of that compass to obtain magnetic heading. The difference between this heading and the reading of the compass being checked is the deviation. If the heading by the second compass is 139°, and it has a deviation on this heading of 4°W., the magnetic heading is 135°. If at the same time the heading by the first compass is 136°, the deviation of that compass is 1° W. The deviation of the second compass, of course, must be known accurately.

Bearing. If the vessel is at a known position, the true direction of a landmark or seamark can be determined from the chart, the variation applied to obtain the magnetic bearing, and this bearing compared with the bearing as indicated by compass. If a magnetic compass rose is printed on the chart, the magnetic bearing can be obtained directly by measurement. If the position of the vessel is in doubt, a close approximation of the magnetic bearing can be obtained by averaging the compass bearings at equal intervals of heading. Intervals of 30° are usually adequate for this purpose. The deviation obtained by comparing magnetic and compass bearings is for the heading of the craft at the time of observation. The object sighted should preferably be at a distance of several miles from the craft, to avoid magnification of small errors in its position, the position of the vessel, or in plotting. A transit, or range (p. 224), either natural or man-made, provides a convenient and accurate direction to use.

As an example of the method, if it is desired to place the craft on heading magnetic west, and the true bearing of a distant mark is 141° in an area where the variation is 14° E., the magnetic bearing is 141° − 14° = 127°. When the craft is on magnetic west, the relative bearing is 127° + 360° − 270° = 217°, or 143° red. When the craft is at the known position and the relative bearing is 217° (143° red), the deviation is the difference between the compass heading and the desired magnetic heading (in this case 270°). If the bearing is to be observed by another magnetic compass or by gyro compass or repeater, the true bearing is converted to the equivalent bearing by the instrument to be used for the observation.

Because of the need to be at a specific position when readings are taken, and possible manoeuvring restrictions, this method is more time consuming and less convenient than others.

Azimuth. The method is similar to that of using a bearing or transit (range), with the calculated azimuth of an astronomical body (p. 299) used in place of the bearing. This method gives greater freedom to manoeuver because the azimuth does not change appreciably over the area normally used for compass correction. The azimuth does change with time, however, and the advance preparation of a *curve of magnetic azimuths* is desirable. During the process of compass correction and swinging ship (section 13) it is necessary to have accurate time available and to record the time as well as other data at each observation, to permit checking of results later. If an astronomical body low in the sky in an easterly or westerly direction is selected (usually the Sun during early morning or late afternoon), the azimuth changes slowly with both change of position of the craft and time. The curve of magnetic azimuths is prepared by computing the azimuth at intervals, applying variation to determine the equivalent magnetic directions, and plotting these values *vs.* time at a convenient scale on coordinate paper. For a body low in the eastern or western sky an interval of 20 minutes is convenient. If the Moon is used, its change in declination (p. 294) and the difference between its rate of motion and $15°$ per hour should be taken into account.

If compass headings are used for swinging ship, the use of bearings of a distant mark or transit (range) or magnetic azimuths is somewhat simplified. Another method is to place a good magnetic compass without correctors at a magnetically undisturbed position ashore at some mark easily recognized from the craft. At suitable signals, preferably by radio communication, simultaneous bearings are observed aboard the craft and at the shore station, each observing the other. The reciprocal of the bearing ashore is the magnetic bearing of the shore station from the craft, without significant error in most cases, and the difference between this value and the bearing observed aboard the craft is the deviation for the heading of the craft at the time of observation.

11. Compass Adjustment

No separate correction is made for coefficient A. Its presence can be detected by adding algebraically the deviation on headings at equal intervals, and dividing the sum by the number of headings. If the result is not zero, the accuracy of compass alignment with the longitudinal axis of the vessel should be checked, and any error in the alignment corrected by rotating the binnacle.

Semi-circular deviation caused by permanent magnetism in the vessel is removed by small permanent B and C magnets placed near the compass. Many binnacles provide a number of tubes below the compass for inserting the magnets. The deviation from permanent magnetism being semi-circular, with maximum values on the cardinal headings, the magnets are inserted when the vessel is on magnetic cardinal headings, the athwartship magnets being inserted while on a north or south heading, and the fore-and-aft magnets being inserted while on an east or west heading. The number of magnets to use, and the direction of the poles, can be determined easily by trial and error. The ends of the magnets are usually painted red and blue, or at least one end is painted, to facilitate placing of the magnets. In some binnacles, provision is made for raising and lowering the trays, or for rotating them in a scissor-like fashion so as to change the angle between them. The purpose of either arrangement is to provide a fine adjustment for precise removal of deviation. While compass adjusting, one should be careful to keep unused magnets at sufficient distance to avoid noticeable effect upon the compass.

Quadrantal deviation resulting from induced magnetism in symmetrical horizontal soft iron is removed by placing two spheres of soft iron on opposite sides of the compass. Provision is generally made for changing the distance between the spheres and the compass, and for replacing the spheres with others of a different size. These spheres remove coefficient D. Sometimes provision is made for slewing one or both of the spheres to correct for coefficient E, caused by induced magnetism in asymmetrical horizontal soft iron, but deviation from this source is usually small enough to be ignored. These spheres are known as *quadrantal correctors*. From time to time they should be tested to determine whether they have acquired permanent magnetism. This test can be made by rotating the spheres, one at a time, through 180° without changing their positions with respect to the compass, or the true heading of the craft. If the compass heading changes, permanent magnetism has been acquired. It can usually be removed by placing the blue pole toward the north and tapping the sphere lightly with a hammer. If this is not effective, the sphere should be removed, heated to a dull red, allowed to cool slowly, and replaced in its proper position.

Quadrantal deviation caused by induced magnetism in vertical soft iron is removed by placing a bar of soft iron, called a *Flinders bar*, in a vertical position near the compass. In determining the length of the Flinders bar to use, one should take into account the vessel's *shielding factor* (λ), the proportion of the strength of the Earth's magnetic field available at a magnetic compass. Typically, it varies from about 0.7 to 1.0. Binnacles of large compasses generally provide a vertical tube for insertion of the bar. The strength of the field established by the bar can be changed by varying its length, pieces of several different lengths being provided. Non-magnetic 'spacers' are available for occupying the remaining space in the tube, below the bar. Other methods that might be used for changing the strength of the field are to provide means for varying the distance between the bar and the compass, and to keep the length and distance constant but vary the number of rods. The Flinders bar is placed on the opposite side of the compass from the effective pole of the vertical soft iron. If the compass is on the centre line, in a relatively high exposed position in the forward part of a vessel, the Flinders bar is usually placed on the forward side of the compass, with its top even with or slightly higher than the compass.

The effective pole of magnetism induced in vertical soft iron generally being forward or aft of the compass, the deviation from this source is maximum on headings magnetic east and west, decreasing to a minimum or zero on headings magnetic north and south. The B coefficient also being maximum on headings east and west, one is faced with the problem of what part of the deviation on these headings should be removed by the B permanent magnets and what part by the Flinders bar. The ideal would be to correct the compass on the magnetic equator, where there is no vertical component of the Earth's field, removing all of the deviation by B magnets; then to proceed to a position of high magnetic latitude and use a Flinders bar sufficient to remove all of the deviation noted on compass headings east and west.

This solution seldom being practicable, one generally must resort to some other method. A professional compass adjuster can usually make a good estimate of the amount and position of Flinders bar needed. Similar installations in other vessels of comparable construction may furnish a useful guide. If the vessel is to be used in an area of little change of magnetic latitude, a Flinders bar may not be used, all of the deviation on cardinal headings being removed by permanent magnets.

With any installation, one should be alert to a change of deviation on easterly or westerly headings after a substantial change of magnetic latitude. If such a change is noted, the rule suggested by Lord Kelvin (Sir William Thompson) is a good one to use if no specific method of separating the two effects is available. Lord Kelvin's suggestion for removing deviation observed on headings of magnetic east and west, after adjustment of a magnetic compass, is to use the fore-and-aft B permanent magnets when the vessel enters an area of weaker vertical field (lower magnetic latitude) and to use the Flinders bar when the vessel enters an area of stronger vertical field (higher magnetic latitude). After several such changes, the correct amount of Flinders bar should be established. It should not be changed subsequently unless the compass location is changed or the vessel undergoes structural or other change affecting its magnetic characteristics.

A Flinders bar, like the quadrantal correctors, can acquire some degree of permanent magnetism. One should be careful to insert it gently in its tube, and avoid striking it against a bulkhead, stanchion, etc. while transporting it. It can be tested for permanent magnetism by reversing its ends in its tube while the vessel is on an easterly or westerly heading, and noting any change in deviation. On any heading it can be removed from its tube and held in a horizontal position in a generally east–west orientation with one end near the compass, and then reversing the ends and noting any change in deviation. If permanent magnetism has been acquired, it might be removed by holding the blue pole toward magnetic north and tapping the bar lightly with a hammer. If this does not produce satisfactory results, the bar should be heated to a dull red, allowed to cool slowly, and returned gently to its place in its tube.

When a vessel heels, the magnetic field of the craft changes relative to a magnetic compass, introducing a change in deviation called *heeling error* (*HE*). Poles of permanent magnetism change their position relative to the compass. For example, a pole directly below a compass when the vessel is on an even keel causes no deviation, but when the vessel rolls, the pole moves from side to side, causing the compass to oscillate. When a vessel changes trim or heels, horizontal soft iron acquires a vertical component, and vertical soft iron acquires a horizontal component.

The change in induced magnetism usually produces a greater effect than the relocation of poles of permanent magnetism relative to the compass. Because most of the soft iron is usually lower than the compass, the most effective means of removing deviation introduced when the vessel leaves its even-keel orientation would be to place the correct amount of soft iron in an appropriate position and orientation *above* the compass. Because this approach is generally not practicable, the rule of setting up an equal but opposite force of the same kind is violated by placing a permanent magnet, called a *heeling magnet*, in a tube directly below the compass when the craft is on an even keel. Because induced magnetism is being neutralized by permanent magnetism, the position of the magnet may need to be changed with a change of magnetic latitude, being lowered with a decrease in magnetic latitude, and inverted upon crossing the magnetic equator.

The usual procedure is to put the craft on a heading of

magnetic north or south, list it, and use a heeling magnet to remove all of the change in deviation. Alternatively, if the vessel is rolling moderately while on a northerly or southerly heading, the position of the heeling magnet is adjusted until oscillation of the compass is minimum. The normal orientation of a heeling magnet is with the red end uppermost in north magnetic latitude.

Because of the positions of the soft iron quadrantal correctors and Flinders bar relative to the permanent magnets of the compass, and the B and C magnets used in compass correction, some of the magnetism induced in the soft iron is from these sources, thus reducing to some extent their effectiveness. For this reason, it is good practice to place the soft iron correctors and the heeling magnet before inserting B and C magnets.

A complete compass adjustment is normally performed by a professional, but in an emergency, it may have to be done by the ship's company. Certain preliminary steps should precede the actual correction. Careful planning should include the selection of a favourable time and location where adequate manoeuvring space and the necessary aids are available, and the operation will not interfere with or be impeded by other craft. The magnetic variation of the area should be noted and any necessary updating made. If azimuths of astronomical bodies are to be used as a reference, a clear day and the availability of an astronomical body low in the eastern or western sky are desirable. The necessary calculations, preparation of work forms and diagrams, and the instruction of personnel who will participate should all be accomplished before the adjustment process begins.

The trim and any list of the vessel should be checked. The position of the compass in the binnacle should be noted. If the compass heading changes as the heeling magnet is moved up or down in its tube under the compass, the compass is not centred in the binnacle, and a suitable adjustment should be made. The compass itself should be free from bubbles, and properly mounted in its gimbals, without play.

The accuracy with which the lubber line is aligned with the longitudinal axis of the craft can be checked by sighting on the jackstaff or other object on the centre line of the craft if the compass is located on the centre line. For other compasses, a batten can be erected at a distance from the centre line equal to the offset of the compass. Any error found should be corrected by rotation of the compass.

The magnetic environment of the compass to be corrected and any other magnetic compass to be used as a reference should be checked carefully. Any movable equipment of magnetic material, such as boat davits, should be secured in its normal position at sea. If wires for carrying direct-current electricity are near the compass, the wires should be twisted and the electricity turned on or off in accordance with the normal condition while underway. No tools, metal cans, portable electric equipment, metal coat hangers, keys, pocket knives, or other possible source of deviation should be permitted near the compass.

The magnets to be used in the adjustment should be readily available but at such distance as not to deflect the compass, until inserted in the binnacle. The binnacle itself should be checked for condition and freedom of motion of movable parts. The quadrantal correctors and Flinders bar should be tested for permanent magnetism, and any necessary correction made. These soft iron correctors should then be put in place, using the best information available. If they have been used previously, they should remain as before unless one has better information on their size and location. If the installation is a new one, the quadrantal correctors should be placed at the centres of their tracks and the Flinders bar length determined by estimate. The heeling magnet should be in its tube below the compass in the same position as before. If no heeling magnet was used and no reliable information on its correct position is available, it should be placed at the bottom of its tube with the red end uppermost in the northern hemisphere.

All necessary preparations having been made and any corrections performed, the craft proceeds to the area selected, and the actual compass adjustment is started. During the process, turns are made slowly and the vessel is permitted to settle on each new magnetic heading for several minutes before a reading is taken. One should use great care in keeping the vessel steady on each desired magnetic heading. In rough seas good compass adjustment is difficult.

The various steps in compass adjustment should be performed in the following order:

1. Put the craft on heading magnetic east and place a sufficient number of permanent magnets in the fore-and-aft tubes to bring the compass and magnetic headings into agreement. All coefficient B deviation on this heading has then been removed. If a choice is available, use magnets in pairs, as far below the compass as possible. All magnets should have the red ends in the same direction, either forward or aft. If the magnets are placed in the wrong orientation, the deviation increases, thus indicating the error. If no provision is made for a fine adjustment, the deviation should be reduced to the smallest amount possible.

2. Put the craft on heading magnetic south and repeat the process of step *1*, using the athwartship magnets to correct for coefficient C.

3. Put the craft on heading magnetic west and adjust the fore-and-aft B correctors to remove *half* the deviation observed.

4. Put the craft on heading magnetic north and adjust the athwartship C correctors to remove *half* the deviation observed.

5. Put the craft on heading magnetic north-east and move the quadrantal correctors toward or away from the compass, keeping them equal distances from the compass, to remove all deviation on this heading, thus correcting for coefficient D.

6. Put the craft on heading magnetic south-east and remove half the deviation ovserved, by adjusting the positions of the quadrantal correctors, again keeping them equal distances from the compass.

7. If provision is available for listing the craft, put it on heading magnetic north or south, list the craft, and remove all *change* in deviation by adjusting the heeling magnet in its tube, thus correcting for coefficient $\mathcal{J}$. If the craft is rolling while on heading magnetic north or south, it need not be listed, the position of the heeling magnet being

adjusted to minimize the oscillation of the compass.

An alternative procedure is to use *any* cardinal heading to start the process, making turns in either direction until the craft has been placed on all four cardinal headings, altering the procedure as appropriate. Similarly, any intercardinal heading can be used for step 5, followed by either adjacent intercardinal heading for step 6.

A simple, relatively quick method of approximate compass adjustment can be accomplished by means of a device known as a *deflector*. The function of this device is to determine those settings of the *B* and *C* correctors and the quadrantal correctors that will result in the directive force of the compass being the same on all cardinal headings. The device is seldom used on vessels of the Royal Navy or by American seamen.

The form of deflector most frequently used on board British merchant vessels was designed by Lord Kelvin. It consists principally of two permanent bar magnets hinged at one end like the legs of a pair of dividers, with opposite poles at the hinge. The separation of the unhinged ends can be controlled by means of a thumbscrew. A scale indicates the amount of separation. Compass adjustment is accomplished in five steps, as follows:

1. The craft is put on heading *compass* north by the compass to be adjusted. The heading by a second compass is noted, and the craft is steered by this second compass, keeping the heading constant. The deflector is mounted vertically over the centre of the compass to be adjusted, with the blue pole of the unhinged end of one deflector magnet toward the north side of the compass. The deflector is then rotated through 170°, and the separation of the unhinged ends of the deflector is adjusted until the deflection of the compass card is 90°. The reading of the deflector separation is recorded, and the deflector is removed.

2. The craft is put on heading compass east, and the procedure of step 1 is repeated.

3. The craft is put on heading compass south, and the deflector reading is noted when the compass card has been deflected 90°. The deflector separation is then adjusted to the position midway between this reading and that on heading compass north, and the fore-and-aft corrector magnets are adjusted to restore the deflection to 90°. The deflector is then removed.

4. The craft is put on heading compass west and the procedure of step *3* is repeated with respect to heading compass east, but using the athwartship corrector magnets. The deflector is *not* removed.

5. The craft is kept on the same heading as in step *4* and the deflector is set to the mid position between the final settings in steps *3* and *4*. The quadrantal correctors are then adjusted to bring the deflection to 90°. The deflector is removed.

As with the method given previously, any cardinal heading can be used to start the adjustment, and turns can be made in either direction, altering the procedure as appropriate.

While the deflector method is noted for its simplicity and conservation of time, it is not as thorough as the method described earlier, and it is accurate only to about 2° to 3°. It does not correct for coefficients A or J, and does not determine the amount of Flinders bar needed.

When the compass adjustment, by any method, has been completed, all correctors should be secured and a record made of the number, size, and position of each. The ship is then swung and a deviation table prepared (section 13).

If the maximum deviation after adjustment is more than a small number of degrees, or if deviation changes erratically on successive headings, an analysis of the various coefficients might prove helpful, but the best procedure is to seek the services of a professional compass adjuster at the first convenient opportunity.

12. Compass Compensation

The total magnetic field at any point is the vector sum of all individual fields existing at that point. In the vicinity of a vessel having a magnetic field, the field resulting from the Earth's magnetism alone is altered. This principle is utilized in warfare by means of mines and torpedoes that are responsive to changes in a magnetic field.

Some protection against such devices is afforded by neutralizing, as far as practicable, the magnetic field of the craft. A vessel to be given such protection passes over a device that measures the change in the Earth's magnetic field during passage, and a trace is made of the measurement. This trace, called the vessel's *magnetic signature*, is unique for each vessel.

The vessel may then be given magnetic treatment to give it magnetic characteristics largely offsetting the influence of the Earth's field on the vessel. The treatment consists of subjecting it to fields of direct-current electricity of strength and position appropriate to the vessel's magnetic signature, electric cables being temporarily placed properly to attain the desired results. If practicable, all magnetic compasses and Flinders bars should be removed from a vessel before it is given magnetic treatment. Quadrantal correctors and permanent magnets used in compass correction are little affected by magnetic treatment, and need not be removed. Magnetic treatment alters a vessel's magnetic characteristics, necessitating new compass correction.

More complete protection is accomplished by providing a vessel, whether or not it has been given magnetic treatment, with a system of permanently-installed direct-current coils constituting a *degaussing (DG)* system, the term 'degaussing' being derived from 'gauss', a unit used for indicating the strength of a magnetic field. The vertical component of the ship's field is opposed by a horizontal cable, called the *main coil*, or *M coil*, completely encircling the vessel horizontally near the water line. Additional horizontal *forecastle (F)* and *quarterdeck (Q) coils* may be placed around the forward and after parts of the weather deck. These two coils may be combined and installed in two parts, further designated *I* and *P* to indicated induced and permanent, the types of magnetism each opposes. The longitudinal horizontal field of the vessel may be opposed by a *longitudinal coil*, or *L coil*, consisting of a series of vertical coils placed athwartship. Similarly, the athwartship horizontal field may be opposed by an *athwartship coil*, or *A coil*, placed vertically in the fore-and-aft direction.

When a degaussing system is energized, the magnetic field in the vicinity of a magnetic compass is altered, resulting in a change of deviation. This condition is offset, as far as practicable, by means of small coils attached to the binnacle in such manner as to neutralize the effects of the three parts of the degaussing system. A *heeling coil* surrounds the binnacle at about the level of the compass card. Two vertical coils or sets of coils 90° apart offset the effect of the L and A coils. The installation of these coils and the adjustment of direct current in each, called *compass compensation*, is normally accomplished by shipyard personnel immediately following installation of the degaussing system. The navigator should obtain complete information on the electrical properties of the degaussing system and compensating coils. The degaussing and compensating coils are interconnected in such manner that a change in one is accompanied by a corresponding change in the other. The degaussing compensation should take place after compass adjustment. Normally, the compensation need not be changed unless a change is made in the degaussing system or in the position or size of the quadrantal correctors or in the amount of Flinders bar. However, if a significant change in deviation is noted, the installation should be checked for a possible ground caused by moisture.

Because compensation to offset the deviating effects of a degaussing system is not likely to be perfect, the ship should be swung and a deviation table made out with the system turned off, and repeated with the system turned on.

13. Deviation Table

An important step following compass correction, either compass adjustment or compass compensation, is *swinging ship*. This consists of placing the craft on successive magnetic headings at equal intervals and noting the deviation on each heading. Heading intervals of 15° are desirable but if the deviation is small and time is limited, larger intervals can be used and intermediate values determined by interpolation. If the deviation is small, compass headings can be used without introduction of significant error. If the vessel has a degaussing system (section 12), the first swing is made with the system turned off. The system is then energized and the process repeated.

Following each swing a *deviation table* is prepared showing deviation on each heading. The table is recorded on a *deviation card*, also called a *compass correction card*. It is customary in this table to list deviation for various *magnetic* headings. If the deviation is small and changes slowly with change of heading, the table can be entered with either magnetic or compass heading without significant error, but if the deviation is large, care should be used in extracting information, for the deviation on a given compass heading may be quite different from that on the magnetic heading having the same numerical value. Under such conditions, if the deviation cannot be reduced by effective compass correction, one might consider preparation of separate deviation tables for magnetic and compass heading entries.

Mag. hdg	Dev	Mag. hdg	Dev.
000°	1°.0 W.	180°	1°.0 E.
015°	1°.5 W.	195°	1°.5 E.
030°	2°.0 W.	210°	2°.5 E.
045°	2°.0 W.	225°	3°.0 E.
060°	2°.5 W.	240°	2°.5 E.
075°	2°.0 W.	255°	2°.0 E.
090°	1°.5 W.	270°	1°.5 E.
105°	1°.0 W.	285°	1°.0 E.
120°	0°.5 W.	300°	0°.5 E.
135°	0°.5 W.	315°	0°.0
150°	0°.0	330°	0°.5 W.
165°	0°.5 E.	345°	1°.0 W.

FIG. 307. A deviation table.

A typical deviation table is shown in Fig. 307. Note that deviation is given to the nearest 0°.5, a common practice. In using any deviation table, one should keep always in mind that the table is entered with the *heading* of a vessel. In correcting a compass *bearing*, one enters the table with heading, extracts deviation, and applies it to the bearing.

Various graphical forms of deviation table have been devised, the best known being called *Napier diagram*.

The deviation card is a good place to record essential information regarding the various correctors used in compass adjustment, date of the most recent compass adjustment, by whom performed, and any other useful information regarding the compass, with its identity.

The card should be protected in some manner as by mounting it on a board and covering it with clear shellac, or posting it under glass in the vicinity of the compass to which it applies. This precaution is particularly applicable for a compass in an exposed position. A second copy should be posted in the chart house.

14. Gyro Compass

In all but the smallest vessels, the gyro compass has almost universally replaced the magnetic compass as the primary direction-indicating instrument. Several advantages have contributed to this change. The gyro compass is not affected by magnetism, and hence eliminates the need for magnetic compass correction, swinging ship, and applying variation and deviation. Selection of location within a vessel is less critical. The gyro compass can be used in the vicinities of the magnetic poles of the Earth, where the magnetic compass is unreliable or useless. The small error that may be present is constant on all headings, thus being easy to apply accurately. Having a strong directive force, a gyro compass can be used as the source of directional information for various auxiliaries such as compass repeaters, gyro pilots, and mechanical dead-reckoning equipment.

These advantages are obtained at the cost of some disadvantages. The gyro compass has numerous moving parts requiring some maintenance and having the possibility of failure. A constant source of electric power is needed. When started after having been turned off or after a power failure, a gyro compass requires a settling period that may be as long as four hours. It is subject to certain errors (section 15) that require understanding and correction. The directive force decreases with higher geographic latitude, becoming totally absent at the geographical poles. Finally, the price of a gyro compass is likely to exceed that of a comparable magnetic compass.

Early gyro compasses were heavy and bulky, limiting their use to large vessels. Over the years since their development began simultaneously in Europe and America in the early twentieth century, gyro compasses have increased in reliability and accuracy, and have decreased in size and weight, a great variety now being available to meet the various needs of marine craft.

The operation of a gyro compass depends upon four phenomena. These are gyroscopic inertia, gyroscopic precession, gravity, and rotation of the Earth.

A simple form of *gyroscope* (*gyro*) consists of a rotating mass mounted in gimbals giving it three degrees of freedom, or motion about two axes perpendicular to the *spin axis* and to each other. These two additional axes are called the *torque axis* and the *precession axis*. A perfect gyroscope, free from all external forces, continues to maintain its spin axis in the same direction *in space*. This phenomenon is called *gyroscopic inertia*. Thus, if the spin axis is pointed toward a star, the axis follows the star as it appears to move across the sky while the Earth rotates on its axis, and therefore changes direction and inclination relative to the Earth's surface. This was the phenomenon used by Leon Foucault, French physicist, in 1851 to demonstrate the rotation of the Earth. It was he who gave the name 'gyroscope', from the Greek words *gyros*, 'turn', and *skopein*, 'to view', to the device so-called.

As stated, the spin axis of a perfect gyroscope continues to point in the same direction in space *if it is not subjected to an external force*. If such a force is applied, the direction of motion of the spin axis is in a direction 90° to the direction of application of the force, in the direction of spin. This phenomenon is called *gyroscopic precession*. Refer to Fig. 308. The rotor is rotating in a clockwise direction. If a force is applied that would cause the spin axis to tilt upward if the rotor were not spinning, the motion is in a direction 90° ahead, or to the right.

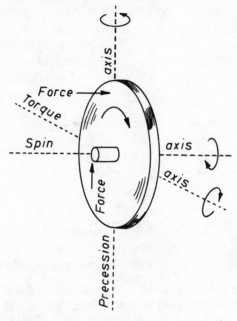

FIG. 308. Gyroscopic precession.

Gravity and the rotation of the Earth are utilized, with gyroscopic inertia and gyroscopic precession, to give a gyroscope north-seeking characteristics and thus make of it the principal element of a gyro compass.

The requirements of a gyro compass are that it have one or more gyroscopes mounted in such manner that an identifiable axis (the spin axis if a single gyroscope constitutes the directive element) seeks the geographic meridian, with means for damping the oscillations on each side of the meridian; provision for mounting a compass card, keeping it level, and correcting errors inherent in the compass design; suitable housing for the various parts; and a constant source of electric power.

A gyroscope is given meridian-seeking characteristics by mounting it in such manner that when the spin axis tilts as the Earth rotates, a force is applied, causing precession toward the meridian. A simple way of producing this force is by making the mounting pendulous by the addition of a small weight below the rotor. Another way is by providing inter-connecting reservoirs containing a liquid that flows from one to the other as the axis tilts. With either design, the axis would follow an ellipse centred on the meridian, as shown in Fig. 309, if there were no means of damping its motion,

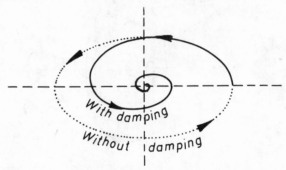

FIG. 309. Precession of a gyro compass axis toward the meridian.

completing one cycle in 84.4 minutes. This interval is the period of a pendulum having a length equal to the radius of the Earth. A device having this period is said to be Schuler tuned, after Dr. Maximilian Schuler, a German professor who first identified it in 1908, as described in a paper by him published in 1923. If a gyro compass is given an 84.4 minute period, it is not disturbed by accelerations over the surface of the Earth. If the application of force causing precession is offset slightly from the meridian, the axis spirals toward the meridian, and comes to rest there (subject to certain errors discussed in section 15), as shown by the solid spiral in Fig. 309.

Details of construction, operation, and maintenance of a particular gyro compass are given in an instruction manual provided by the manufacturer. A wise navigator becomes familiar with the information contained in the manuals for instruments aboard his craft.

15. Gyro Compass Errors

Although gyro compasses are not affected by magnetism, they are subject to certain errors. Correction of these errors can be fully automatic by means of proper design and electrical inputs from suitable sensors and a computer, partly automatic with a requirement for manual setting of adjustments for latitude and speed, or entirely manual by means of tables or graphs of corrections. Compass designs vary considerably depending upon cost and intended use. The instruction manual provided with each instrument indicates any need for manual adjustments or application of corrections. If the navigator has occasion to go into high latitudes, typically beyond 70°, he should prepare in advance by giving careful attention to instructions for the use of his gyro compass in such areas.

The error most likely to require manual adjustment relates to the course and speed of the vessel at various latitudes. If correction is not made automatically, the approximate latitude and speed need to be inserted manually by means of appropriate controls. Course information is derived directly from the compass itself.

The Earth rotates on its axis at the rate of $15°.041$ per hour, approximately, or 902.46 minutes of arc. Without this rotation, a gyro compass would have no meridian-seeking properties, and would be useful as a compass only if it could be pointed in the desired direction. A *directional gyro* compass of this kind, although not perfectly free from drift, does have some uses, particularly in polar regions and in aircraft. But the marine gyro compass in its usual operating mode depends upon meridian-seeking capabilities for its usefulness.

In terms of knots, the speed of rotation of the Earth decreases from maximum at the equator to zero at the poles, being equal to $902.46 \cos L$, approximately. If a gyro compass is at rest on the surface of the Earth, its speed relative to the Earth's axis is that of the Earth's rotation alone. But if the compass is installed aboard a craft that is under way over the surface of the Earth, the total velocity is the vector sum of the velocity of the Earth and that of the craft. The velocity of the craft can be resolved into east–west and north–south components. The east–west component is equal to $S \sin C$, and the north–south component is equal to $S \cos C$, where S is the speed in knots, and C is the course.

The east–west component serves only to increase or decrease the total speed, but the north–south component changes not only the speed, but also the direction of the total velocity vector, as shown in Fig. 310. In the illustration, vector AB represents the Earth's velocity of rotation, BC the

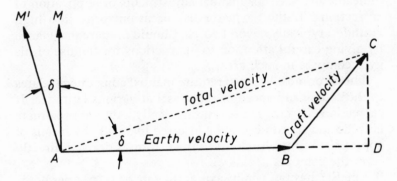

FIG. 310. Latitude and velocity error of gyro compass.

craft's velocity over the surface of the Earth (exaggerated for purposes of illustration), and AC the total velocity. Also, BD is the east–west component and DC the north–south component of craft velocity. The true meridian is represented by AM, and the perpendicular to AC by AM′. A gyro compass, unless corrected, reacts to the total speed vector and seeks the false meridian AM′.

The tangent of the angle between true and false meridians, δ, is DC/AD, or

$$\tan \delta = \frac{S \cos C}{902.46 \cos L + S \sin C}.$$

Except in high latitudes, the term S sin C is small enough relative to the Earth's velocity, at speeds of marine craft, that it can be ignored. For small angles, the tangent of an angle can be considered the angle itself, in radians. Thus, for practical purposes at latitudes usually frequented by marine craft, the equation can be stated:

$$\delta = \frac{57.3 \; S \cos C}{902.46 \cos L} = \frac{S \cos C}{15.75 \cos L} = 0.0635 \; S \cos C \sec L.$$

For a ship steaming at 18 knots on course 020° at latitude 50° N., the latitude, course, and speed error is:

$$\delta = 0.0635 \times 18 \times 0.93969 \times 1.55572 = 1\overset{\circ}{.}67.$$

If the craft's course has a northerly component, as in this example, the gyro compass settles to the west of north, giving it a westerly error. For a course with a southerly component, the error is easterly.

A change in course or speed resulting in an acceleration in the north–south component of the craft's velocity introduces an additional temporary error if the gyro compass is not accurately Schuler tuned.

If a gyro compass has a damping system consisting of reservoirs of liquid, the compass settles at some point east of the meridian in north latitude and west of the meridian in south latitude. The error increases with latitude, and is corrected mechanically or combined with the latitude and velocity correction. One means of correction is by offsetting the lubber line. Consequently, one should be careful to avoid upsetting the correction if a check on the position of the lubber line indicates a possible error.

As a vessel rolls, the vertical axis of a gyro compass oscillates in an attempt to align itself with the apparent vertical, resulting in precession and possible mechanical rotation. This error is maximum on intercardinal headings, and changes direction in adjacent quadrants. A properly designed compass provides correction for this error.

Correction of all error in the reading of a gyro compass is seldom perfect. The angle between the geographic meridian and the north–south axis of a gyro compass is called *gyro error* (*GE*). If the axis is offset towards the east, the gyro error is designated east, or plus; and if towards the west, it is designated west, or minus. For a properly designed compass, adequately corrected, the gyro error is usually less than 1°, except in high latitudes, and can be ignored for ordinary purposes of navigation. However, it should be checked frequently, for an undetected error can prove disastrous. An error can be introduced by malfunction or interruption of electric power.

Frequent checks, as each half-hour, with another compass should reveal any significant change in gyro error. However, an accurate determination of gyro error is made by comparing a true direction with the same direction as measured by gyro compass. Any of the methods described in section 10 can be adapted by omitting use of variation. That is, deviation is the difference between *magnetic* and *magnetic compass* directions, while gyro error is the difference between *true* and *gyro compass* directions. It is good practice to determine gyro error at least twice daily and at any time when a change in gyro error is suspected. One should be particularly alert to possible change in gyro error when there are frequent changes in course or speed, as when a vessel is entering or leaving port. Transits, or ranges (p. 224), both natural and man-made, are especially useful for this purpose.

Gyro error, like deviation and variation, is applied by adding an easterly or plus error to a gyro direction to obtain the equivalent true direction. From this relationship— 'correcting add east'—all other situations can be derived. Unlike deviation and variation, uncorrected gyro error is approximately the same on all headings.

16. Compass Repeaters

A typical gyro compass provides a transmission system for remote indication of gyro heading. Some magnetic compasses also have transmission systems. A *transmitting compass* can be located in a favourable position that might not be otherwise suitable for the intended use of the compass.

A compass provided with remote indicators is called a *master compass*, and its remote indicators are called *compass repeaters*. The number of repeaters that can be driven by one master compass is a function of the power provided to the transmission system.

Typically, a master compass and its repeaters are self-synchronous, so that after a shut-down of the master compass or the temporary loss of power, the repeaters synchronize themselves automatically with the master. However, in some installations the repeaters respond only to *changes* in indications of the master compass, so that an interruption of power between the master and its repeaters may result in error in the synchronization. Ships have grounded far from their supposed positions because of the failure of the crews to check the synchronization or compare compass indications at frequent intervals.

A compass repeater can be mounted anywhere in a vessel, and need not be horizontal unless its intended use dictate such an orientation. Thus, a repeater used as a heading indicator or as an essential element of a course recorder (p. 154) can be mounted vertically on a bulkhead, while a repeater intended for measuring bearings or azimuths needs to be horizontal. Other applications of transmitted indications of master compasses are to provide heading information for autopilots (p. 153) and track plotters (p. 154). The same information is provided to true-motion radar (p. 495) and to direction-stabilized radar. In naval vessels certain fire control equipment requires heading inputs provided by a transmitting compass.

17. Pelorus

A *pelorus* has aptly been called a 'dumb compass'. It resembles a compass, but, in its simplest form, is without a directive element. It consists essentially of a suitably-mounted *pelorus card*, resembling a compass card, and a sighting device, usually consisting of a pair of vanes on opposite ends of a bar pivoted at the centre of the pelorus card. The pelorus card can be rotated so as to bring any desired graduation in line with a lubber line scribed in the forward part of the mount and aligned with the longitudinal axis of the craft.

A pelorus, also called a *bearing plate*, is a cheap device used for measuring bearings and azimuths. Customarily, one is mounted on each wing of the bridge. If zero is set at the lubber line, relative bearings (p. 21) and relative azimuths are measured. If the heading is set at the lubber line, the measured bearings and azimuths are true, magnetic, compass, gyro, or grid depending upon the heading used to set the device, *provided the actual heading of the craft is the same as the set heading at the time of observation.* This can be assured by the helmsman calling out a prearranged signal when the heading is within an agreed limit of error, as half a degree. Alternatively, the observer can call out when he makes an observation, and the helmsman can note the heading at that moment. If the heading is to the *right* of the heading on the pelorus, the difference is *added* to the pelorus reading, and if *left*, the difference is *subtracted*. Thus, if the pelorus is set to a heading of 090°, and the actual heading is 088° at the time of observation, 2° is subtracted from the observed reading, so that if a bearing of 134° is observed, the correct bearing is 132°.

A typical modern pelorus is provided with a prism to permit simultaneous observation of the pelorus card and the object being sighted. Some peloruses are provided with telescopes for greater observational accuracy. A compass repeater may be mounted in place of the dumb pelorus card, providing means for observing compass or gyro directions without setting of a pelorus card. A telescope mounted over a compass repeater may be self-synchronous, so that it remains synchronized with the repeater, rather than turning with the vessel. A telescope mounted over a pelorus, compass repeater, or compass for observing bearings is sometimes called an *alidade*.

18. Speed and Distance Travelled

Dead reckoning requires the ability to determine the distance travelled or the speed (and time interval) as well as the direction of travel. Distance of travel and speed are related through the time interval, distance travelled being equal to speed multiplied by time interval, or $D = S \times t$, where D is distance travelled, S is speed, and t is the time interval. If speed is given in knots and t in hours, distance is in nautical miles. If any two of these quantities are known, the third can be found by a simple calculation. Speed–time–distance tables are available in most books of nautical tables, to eliminate the need for calculation. Tables are also available to indicate the speed involved for different times needed to travel some established distance, usually one nautical mile. Slide rules and calculators are also used for solution of speed–time–distance problems. The experienced navigator generally becomes adept at solving many of the problems of this type by mental arithmetic.

The principal problem involved in measuring speed or distance travelled is the separation of the motion of the craft from the motion of the medium in which it moves—water in the case of marine craft. Over the years, a number of different methods have been used to determine speed or distance travelled. Three basic approaches have been used. These involve measurement of distance, speed, or acceleration. A device used for measurement of distance travelled or speed is called a *log*.

Distance is determined in one of three ways. If the positions of the craft at two different times are established by accurate position fixing, the distance between fixes is the distance travelled. Knowing the times at which the craft occupied the two positions, and knowing the distance, one can determine the average *speed made good* (*SMG*) relative to the surface of the Earth.

The second way of determining distance travelled is by direct linear measure. One might do this in shallow water by means of a *ground log*. A weight is attached to a line and thrown overboard. When the weight reaches the bottom and a sufficient amount of line is paid out so that the line is nearly horizontal, time measurement is started, and the amount of additional line paid out in some interval of time is measured. This method, like that of measuring the distance between fixes, provides an indication of distance over the ground, but is of limited application and is rarely used. The *chip log* uses the same principle but determines speed by a device that remains essentially stationary in the water, thus giving a measure of speed relative to the water, not to the ground. A *Dutchman's log* accomplished the same purpose by measurement of the time interval for a floating object to be passed by a known length of the vessel. It has been held by some that logs involving an object *dead* in the water are the origin of the expression *dead* reckoning.

The third way of determining distance is by towing an object provided with a propeller-like rotor that is turned by the relative flow of water past it as the vessel moves forward. The number of turns is measured and converted, by suitable calibration, to distance. This device is called a *taffrail log*, deriving its name from the rail at the stern of a vessel, where it is usually secured. The dial or gauge indicating distance may be at the rotor, requiring the device to be hauled aboard periodically for reading, but more often is at the taffrail. In some installations the indications are transmitted electrically to the bridge. A log of this type is subject to inaccuracies and possible damage if it encounters seaweed, refuse, ice, or other obstructions. The towing line should be sufficiently long or otherwise streamed in such manner that the rotor is clear of disturbed water in the wake of the vessel. A taffrail log, now seldom used except in some slow-moving vessels, is usually streamed as one takes departure upon clearing a harbour at the start of a voyage, and is hauled aboard as the vessel approaches the entrance to the harbour of destination. This type log measures distance through the water, not over the ground.

Speed is the quantity most often measured by modern logs. Various ways of doing this have been devised.

A commonly-used method of measuring speed through the water is by means of dynamic pressure exerted by water as a vessel moves through it. One type of log using this principle is called a *Pitot-static log*. A *Pitot tube* is a double tube, the inner one open at the forward end and the outer one having openings along its sides. A *rodmeter*, consisting principally of a Pitot tube, projects somewhat less than a metre below the hull of the vessel, into relatively undisturbed water. As the vessel moves through the water, dynamic pressure by the water is exerted on the open end of the inner tube, in addition to static pressure, while the outer tube is subjected to static pressure only. The difference between the two is the dynamic pressure. Speed of the vessel is directly proportional to the square root of the dynamic pressure, and is shown on a dial or gauge aboard the vessel. It may also be transmitted to various parts of the vessel to serve as an input to other equipment such as gyro compasses and mechanical dead-reckoning equipment (p. 154). A Pitot-static log may also have means of indicating distance travelled.

The accuracy of a Pitot-static log is affected slightly by changing density of sea water, and, to a greater extent, by fouling by foreign matter or mechanical failure, but the error of a properly-operating log should be considerably less than 0.1 knot at normal operating speeds. The error increases at slow speeds, less than about 5 knots, and also at speeds in excess of about 40 knots. In shallow water the projecting rodmeter is vulnerable to mechanical damage by impact with the bottom, and to fouling by mud. Provision is made for retracting the rodmeter into the vessel.

The dynamic pressure principle is also used in logs other than those using a Pitot tube. A log generally called a *speedometer*, popular among yachtsmen, uses a small strut extending through the hull. The force of dynamic water-pressure on the strut is transmitted mechanically, hydraulically, or electrically to a suitable dial, where it is displayed as speed. The strut is raked aft to avoid accumulation of debris. A log of this type is cheaper but not as accurate as a Pitot-static log.

A speed-measuring device that has become increasingly popular as it has been improved in recent years is called an *electromagnetic (E M) log*, the rodmeter of which is illustrated in Fig. 311. This log operates on the principle of electromagnetic induction used in electric generators. The rodmeter is a streamlined, flat, ellipsoidal housing attached to the outer end of a strut projecting vertically from the bottom of the hull. A coil is mounted vertically inside the housing. An electric current through the coil produces a horizontal magnetic field around the housing. As the vessel moves through the water, movement of the magnetic field relative to the water produces a voltage in the water. This voltage is linearly proportional to the speed of relative water flow, and

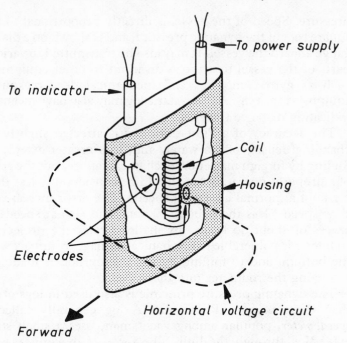

FIG. 311. Rodmeter of electromagnetic log.

therefore a measure of the speed of the vessel through the water. The voltage generated in the water is picked up by a pair of athwartship electrodes mounted on the outside of the housing, and is transmitted to suitable indicators within the vessel. The speed and distance thus measured may be further transmitted to various parts of the vessel, as needed. If a second pair of electrodes is mounted in the longitudinal axis, lateral speed through the water—leeway—can be measured, but accurate calibration of this speed is difficult and time consuming. A modern EM log is accurate within about 0.1 knot.

The principal advantages of an EM log are linear output throughout its operating range (typically 0 to 40 knots), high sensitivity, calibration stability over a long period of time, and relative freedom from fouling. The log, however, is expensive. The EM log is widely used in naval vessels and increasingly so in ships of the merchant service.

Another method of measuring speed through the water is by means of a rodmeter having a small propeller that is rotated by the relative flow of water as the vessel moves. This device, called an *impeller-type log*, differs from a taffrail log not only by being mounted in a rodmeter extending about six decimetres below the hull, but also by the fact that the rotation of the propeller generates an electric current, the frequency of which is directly proportional to the speed of the vessel. Speed and distance may be transmitted to various locations within the vessel, as needed. The impeller-type log has an accuracy of about 0.15 knot through a range of about 0.25 knot to 25 knots. It is cheaper than an EM log, but is subject to fouling.

Speed through the water is also determined by calibrating the propeller shaft revolution rate. The shaft rate is measured by means of a *tachometer*, or the number of revolutions is counted by means of an *engine revolution counter*. This method has the advantage of requiring a minimum of equipment, but is accurate only to about one knot, the accuracy being affected by the draft and trim of the vessel, the amount of rolling and pitching, and the condition of the hull with respect to fouling.

A method of speed measurement used by some deep submergence vessels and geophysical survey vessels, principally, uses beams of acoustic energy directed downward from the vessel, at an angle to the vertical. The ultrasonic signals are reflected back by the ocean floor in water not deeper than about 400 metres, or by water reverberation in deeper water. If the vessel has a component of motion in the direction of a beam, the frequency of the return signal differs from that of the outgoing signal because of the Doppler effect (p. 470), the difference being proportional to the speed over the ground if reflections are from the ocean bottom, or relative to the water if return is by water reverberation. This device, called a *Doppler sonar navigator*, is discussed in more detail in section 3 of chapter XI.

Doppler radar logs similar to those used in aircraft have been developed for use, primarily, in high-speed hydrofoil and air-cushion craft. The speed thus measured is relative to the water. A *laser log*, using the same Doppler principle, has been used experimentally. A *laser* (acronym for *l*ight *a*mplification by *s*timulated *e*mission of *r*adiation) is a device for producing a narrow, intense beam of light amplified and focused by an appropriate input signal. A somewhat different use of the Doppler principle is discussed in section 15 chapter X.

Acceleration is measured by means of an *inertial navigator* (p. 532). Speed is determined by integration of acceleration, and distance travelled by a second integration. Use of inertial navigators in marine craft is limited primarily to special-purpose applications.

Calibration of logs is necessary after installation and after any significant change that would affect the accuracy. In addition, the navigator should be alert to any indication of error, which should be apparent from inconsistency with other data. Traditionally, speed of a vessel has been determined by means of a *measured distance*. At convenient locations relatively free from cross currents of wind and water, distances of exactly one nautical mile or other distance stated on the chart are measured along the beach, to an accuracy generally better than one metre. Each end is marked by a transit, or range (p. 224). The locations of these markers are shown on nautical charts. The course to steer, which must be perpendicular to the transits (ranges) for accurate results, is also shown. The vessel makes several runs in each direction, steadying on the desired heading and speed well before reaching the first marker, and keeping both heading and speed as constant as practicable during the run. Speed is determined by reference to a table, or calculated from the relationship $S = D/t$. If the distance is exactly one mile, and time interval is measure in seconds, $S = 3600/t$. Thus, if a vessel covers a measured distance of one mile in 3 minutes 45 seconds, or 225 seconds, the speed is $3600/225 = 16.0$ knots exactly. Distances other than measured ones can be used, of course, but scaling distance from a chart is ordinarily not sufficiently accurate for log calibration.

Speed can also be determined electronically. Two methods are used. In one, an electronic positioning system of sufficient accuracy for survey purposes (p. 516) is used to determine positions at the start and finish of runs of 10 to 20 minutes, measured as exactly as practicable. The distance between positions is determined and the speed is calculated. The effects of wind and current, if constant during the runs, are eliminated by making runs in opposite directions. Accuracy of position scaled from a chart overprinted with a lattice of position lines of the electronic aid used is not sufficiently accurate for purposes of determining speed for calibration of logs. Positions should be calculated.

The second method is more accurate, and provides an accurate method of eliminating the effects of wind and current, assuming only that these are the same both at the vessel and at the position of the other object. The 'other object' is another vessel of similar characteristics and draught or a drifting buoy having a draught about the same as that of the vessel. Absence of wind is ideal, but light wind should not introduce serious error. Radar or, preferably, a more accurate system for measuring distance, is used. After steadying on a course and speed either directly toward or away from the other object, the vessel maintains this heading and speed while it travels some convenient distance, such as five miles. The time and distance at the start and finish of the run are measured carefully, and from these data the speed is calculated. The effects of wind and current are largely eliminated by having the other object drifting, its movement over the bottom being assumed to be the same as that of the vessel.

In any method, measurement of the time interval to better than one second is desirable. At 18 knots, for example, an error of one second in time of travelling a measured mile introduces an error in speed determination of 0.09 knot.

19. Distance Off

Knowledge of the distance between a vessel and an identifiable, charted object can be useful in fixing the position of the vessel (p. 224).

One method of measuring distance off is by means of a

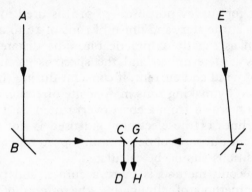

FIG. 312. Range finder principle.

device known as a *range finder*, but which might more appropriately be called a *distance finder*. The principle of the range finder is illustrated in Fig. 312. Line ABCD represents a ray of light from an object being observed, the ray being reflected at B and C to an eyepiece at D. Another ray, EFGH, from the same object, is similarly reflected at F and G to H, within the same eyepiece as D. One ray is from the upper part of the object, and the other from the lower part. Note that AB and EF are not parallel. The reflector at F is rotatable about an axis perpendicular to the plane of the illustration. If the reflector at F is rotated until rays AB and EF are parallel, the object might appear as in Fig. 313a. When the reflector at F is rotated, the upper part of the image moves. When it is

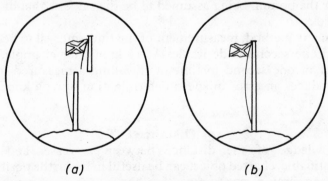

(a)   *(b)*

FIG. 313. Range finder view, a. incorrect distance setting, b. correct distance setting.

brought into coincidence with the lower part of the image, as in Fig. 313b, a scale indicates the angle through which the reflector has been turned. The angle varies with distance of the object, and the scale is graduated in metres or other linear unit. Accuracy of measurement increases with greater length BF, called the *base line*. In actual construction, a range finder differs somewhat from that shown in Fig. 312. Prisms are generally used at B, C, F, and G. Instead of a rotatable reflector at F, a wedge may be used between F and G, with provision for moving it back and forth to vary the distance setting, the scale indicating the position of the wedge.

A range finder measures the angle *at the object* subtended by the base line of the range finder. A *stadimeter*, a small hand-held instrument, measures the angle *at the observer* subtended by an object. As with a range finder, the scale of a stadimeter is graduated in linear units. Knowledge of the height, or other dimension, of the object is required. Stadimeters are used principally aboard naval vessels, as an aid in station keeping when vessels are proceeding in formation.

Distance off can be measured acoustically by means of *sonar*, an acronym for *so*und *n*avigation *a*nd *r*anging. This device transmits a sonic or ultrasonic signal through the water. Any obstruction in the path of the signal scatters the energy of the signal, some of it returning to the vessel as an echo. This return signal is received and amplified. The elapsed time between transmission of the signal and return of the echo is a measure of the distance off. A form of sonar in wide use aboard various types of vessels is the echo sounder (p. 148) used to measure vertical distance off, or depth. Use of sonar for measuring horizontal distance off is limited primarily to naval vessels and fishermen.

Other means of measuring distance off are by radar (p. 494), sextant angle (p. 274), and distance-finding station (p. 273).

20. Depth

From a small craft in shallow water the depth can be determined by means of an oar or pole. Traditionally, however, the common method of *sounding*, or measuring depth, has been by means of a weight attached to a line. Such a device is called a *sounding lead*, or simply a *lead*, from the substance usually used for the weight. *Lead lines* of different lengths are available for attachment to leads. A 20-metre line is adequate for most purpose, although lines as long as 50 metres are used for casting by hand. A *deep-sea lead* (dĭpsey lĕd) having a line of 200 metres or more has been used, but has largely fallen into disuse since echo sounders have come into general use. A *hand lead* is typically of three to six kilograms, while a deep-sea lead may weigh 12 to 45 kilograms.

Various *marks* are placed on a lead line to indicate depth. Different systems of marks have been used. The system introduced by the British Hydrographer of the Navy as part of metrication is as follows:

Metres	Mark
1, 11, 21	one strip of leather
2, 12, 22	two strips of leather
3, 13, 23	blue bunting
4, 14, 24	green and white bunting
5, 15, 25	white bunting
6, 16, 26	green bunting
7, 17, 27	red bunting
8, 18, 28	blue and white bunting
9, 19, 29	red and white bunting
10	leather with a hole in it
20	leather with a hole in it and 2 strips of leather
30	leather with a hole in it and 3 strips of leather
40	leather with a hole in it and 4 strips of leather
50	leather with a hole in it and 5 strips of leather
each 0.2	piece of mackerel line

Before metrication, lead lines were commonly marked in fathoms (p. 23), but occasionally in feet if the use of the line was to be restricted to shallow water. The system commonly used for marking in fathoms is as follows:

Fathoms	Mark
2	two strips of leather
3, 13	three strips of leather
5, 15	white cloth (usually cotton)
7, 17	red cloth (usually wool)
10	leather with hole in it
20	short line with two knots
25, 35, 45, etc.	short line with one knot
30	short line with three knots
40	short line with four knots
50	short line with five knots

One should be sure of the units and system of marks on the lead line before using it. It may be well to have at least one line marked in each system as long as both metres and fathoms (or feet) are used on charts for indicating depth of water. If this is done, each line should be identified clearly, to avoid error. Marks should be placed on a lead line when it is wet, for the wet and dry lengths may differ. A depth corresponding to one of the marks is reported 'by the mark . . . (depth)', and one between marks as 'deep . . . (depth)'.

A lead may have a hollow recess in its bottom, for *arming*. This consists of placing tallow or other substance in the recess, so that a sample of the material forming the ocean floor, called a *bottom sample*, can be obtained. In some areas charts show the nature of the bottom, so that a bottom sample can be useful in fixing the position of a vessel.

Use of a lead for measurement of a depth of more than about 10 to 15 metres, depending upon the speed of the vessel and the skill of the leadsman, requires slowing or stopping the vessel. To avoid this requirement, Lord Kelvin invented the *sounding machine*. This device has a means of measuring depth independent of the amount of line paid out, as by pressure. This method of depth measurement is subject to several errors and is seldom encountered on modern vessels.

The usual method of depth measurement is by means of an

echo sounder, a form of sonar. A great variety of instrumentation is available, and the navigator should study the descriptive material furnished with his equipment, to become thoroughly informed of its operation, capability, and limitations.

An echo sounder converts electrical energy into acoustic energy by means of a *transducer* mounted at the bottom of the vessel. The *sonic* signal (within audible range) produced in earlier versions had been largely replaced by higher-frequency *ultrasonic* signals (above audible range) to reduce the interference from noise, which may originate internally from mechanical or electrical sources, or externally from aeration or water reverberations.

The acoustic signal travels to the ocean floor, where it is reflected. The returning *echo* is received by the transducer or a hydrophone, converted to electrical energy, and displayed as depth, the depth being directly proportional to elapsed time from transmission of signal to return of echo. Depth is displayed as a flash of light on an appropriate circular scale, on a cathode ray tube (p. 477), digitally, or as a trace producing a *bottom profile*, as shown in Fig. 314. The trace is produced by a stylus moving across a moving paper and marking each sounding as it is measured, thus permitting visual correlation of individual soundings. With a smooth bottom the width of the trace is dictated by the pulse length, but with a rough

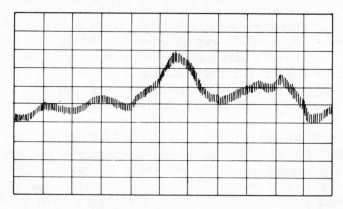

FIG. 314. A bottom profile.

bottom, the trace is wider because of multiple echoes. Readings may be in metres, fathoms, or feet. Several different scales may be available for use in water of different depths. If the depth of water is greater than the maximum depth of the scale in use, a sounding may be indicated at a depth equal to the actual depth minus the maximum scale reading or some multiple of it.

Most echo sounders use a very short burst, or pulse, of acoustic energy ranging in length from a fraction of a millisecond to 100 or more milliseconds, depending upon the instrument and the depth scale used. A relatively new type of echo sounder uses a longer pulse and compares the received echo waveform with a replica of the transmitted waveform, producing an output pulse when the two waveforms match. Equipment using this replica correlation approach reduces error from noise, which is particularly troublesome with digital read-out, and eliminates the need for manual gain or threshold adjustment needed in other equipment to cope with changing conditions.

An echo sounder provides a convenient means for measuring depth continuously, in any depth within the range of the equipment. However, it is subject to certain errors and limitations which should be understood if one is to obtain maximum benefit from the equipment. It is subject to mechanical or electrical malfunction and failure, of course, and is dependent upon a continuous source of electrical power. For these reasons, a vessel should not be without a sounding lead, both for calibration and checking of the accuracy of the echo sounder, and for use in an emergency.

The accuracy of depth indications of an echo sounder is dependent upon the speed of sound in water, and this speed varies with temperature, pressure, and salinity of the water. By international agreement, a speed of 1,500 metres per second is used for calibrating echo sounders. In very cold or fresh water the actual depth is a little *less* than that indicated by an echo sounder. Before agreement was reached on a speed of 1,500 metres per second, some surveys were made using a speed somewhat slower, thus providing a margin of safety. At depths comparable to the draughts of vessels, any error in depth measurement resulting from non-standard conditions is considerably less than the safety factor normally used to ensure adequate clearance. Depths shown on charts are uncorrected, to permit direct comparison with depths obtained by mariners.

If there is appreciable horizontal distance between the transmitter and the receiver, the indicated depth is greater than actual depth by a maximum value of half the distance between the transmitter and the receiver.

The acoustic signal is transmitted downward in the form of a cone of perhaps 30° to 60° width, so that contact with the bottom directly under the vessel can be maintained when a vessel is rolling or pitching. The echo received from the nearest obstruction is the depth indicated, and so an error results if the distance to a pinnacle, bank, or other obstruction within the cone is less than the depth directly below the vessel. Sometimes, in shallow water, a second return is received from multiple echoes, as from a signal reflected by the bottom back to the surface of the water and again back to the bottom and then to the vessel. Echoes from a discontinuity within the water, as between a layer of fresh water over salt water near the mouth of a large river, may also produce a false reading. Multiple returns may also be received when a layer of soft mud overlies a rocky layer beneath, both surfaces returning echoes. If a thick layer of mud is below the vessel, or aeration is present in the water, the echo may be weak or missing altogether.

A false bottom called a *phantom bottom* may appear because of the presence of a *deep scattering layer*. This is a characteristic feature of some areas, consisting of a concentrated, layered colony of phototrophic zooplankton, tiny marine animals, or deep-sea fish attracted to the plankton. A major member of the deep scattering layer has been identified as a delicate, transparent, free-swimming or floating siphonophore, but shrimp, copepod, and squid have also been found there. These animals, being sensitive to light, dive deeper as the light increases, reaching a depth anywhere from about 200 to more than 700 metres during meridian passage of the Sun on a clear day. By night they may approach close to the surface. Sound scattering by the deep scattering layer is produced by small gas bubbles associated with some members of the colony.

An unwanted signal can sometimes be eliminated by reducing the gain, while a weak or missing signal can sometimes be identified by increasing the gain (amplification of the signal).

In using an echo sounder, one should be careful to ascertain whether the indicated depth is from the bottom of the hull, from the surface of the water, or from some other level. Echo sounders generally have means of adjusting the reference level, to accommodate changes in draught of the vessel.

21. Timepieces

Either time of day or elapsed time during some interval is needed at sea for dead reckoning, adjusting position lines to a common time, timing astronomical observations, and for determining characteristics of navigational lights as an aid to their identification, as well as for regulating daily activities aboard ship. Some form of local time is adequate for many purposes, but time at a reference meridian, usually that of Greenwich, is needed for astronavigation.

Accuracy to the nearest minute is adequate for dead reckoning, but for astronavigation an accuracy of one second or better is needed because each second of error in time introduces an error of a quarter of a minute of longitude in the calculated position of the vessel. Identification of a light by its characteristics requires measurement of a short time *interval* to similar accuracy.

Measurement of time intervals in microseconds or smaller units is involved in some electronic equipment. For other purposes, time measurement is provided by some form of *timepiece*. Traditionally, reference time at sea has been provided by a marine *chronometer* (*chron*), a clock having a nearly uniform *chronometer rate*, sometimes called *daily rate* if expressed in change of error per day. A marine chronometer is customarily kept set to Greenwich mean time (p. 328), approximately, and not reset between servicings at intervals of perhaps two or three years. It is wound at the same time each day, and a record is kept of *chronometer error* (*CE*), the difference between *chronometer time* (*C*) and Greenwich mean time (GMT); chronometer rate, determined by comparison of chronometer error on different days; and the difference of the errors of separate chronometers if more than one is carried. Chronometer error is determined periodically by means of time signals transmitted by radio from stations throughout the world. Details of these broadcasts are given in the British *Admiralty List of Radio Signals*, volume V, 'Navigational Aids', NP 275(5), and in the United States Defense Mapping Agency Hydrographic Topographic Center Publication 117, *Radio Navigational Aids*.

A typical marine chronometer has a half-second beat. With a little practice one can imitate quite accurately this beat, a useful skill in comparing a watch with a chronometer to determine watch error, timing a navigational light to determine its characteristics, or timing an astronomical observation when an assistant is not available.

In the past, ships invariably carried three chronometers, so that an erratic one could be identified. With ready availability of radio time signals throughout the world, and improved accuracy and reliability of timepieces other than the traditional chronometers, modern vessels now generally have only one standard timepiece. Increasingly, ships are using accurate *chronostats*, which are timepieces having compensated balance wheels and movements governed by transistors, or *chronographs*, which provide a graphical record of timed events. Quartz crystal oscillator clocks have been used aboard ship, but some users report that these clocks have been disappointing because of relatively poor stability over long periods of time at sea. Use of caesium clocks aboard ship is a prospect for some applications at sea, but the extreme accuracy of such timepieces is far beyond that needed even for timing astronomical observations. If they come into general use at sea, it will more likely be as the heart of an electronic positioning or collision-avoidance system.

A marine chronometer is kept in its box, stowed so as to minimize shock and large fluctuations of temperature. It is not moved about the ship. Ship's clocks may be used for dead reckoning and pilotage, but *watches* are generally used for timing astronomical observations and navigational lights. *Watch error* (*W E*) is determined by comparison of *watch time* (*W*) with chronometer time, allowing for chronometer error, or directly from time signals. A reasonably steady *watch rate* (*daily rate* if expressed in change of error per day) is desirable, but does not need to be as unwavering as chronometer rate because watch error is customarily determined immediately before or after timing observations, or both.

A watch used for timing astronomical observations, regulating ship's clocks, and general purposes at sea is variously called a *hack watch* (or simply a *hack*), *deck watch*, or *comparing watch*, the last expression applying particularly to a watch compared with a chronometer and later with other timepieces to regulate them relative to the chronometer.

In addition to a reasonably steady, low rate, desirable features of a hack watch are a sweep-second hand, second-setting capability, and a luminous dial to permit reading at night without other lighting. Some navigators prefer a stop watch for timing astronomical observations, and such a watch is useful for timing lights. Some stop watches have two second hands, one of which can be stopped while the other continues to run.

Watches regulated to sidereal time (p. 331) have been produced, but have little to offer for navigation and have not found much favour among mariners.

22. Autopilot

Automatic steering is provided by means of an *autopilot*. This device receives heading inputs from a transmitting compass. Deviation from the desired heading, set by means of a heading selector, actuates the rudder to turn the vessel to recover the desired heading. The device performs quite well in a calm sea, but when the vessel is yawing, especially with a following or quartering sea, manual steering by an experienced helmsman is generally considered to be superior to steering by autopilot.

23. Mechanical Dead-Reckoning Equipment

A number of devices have been produced to perform the dead-reckoning function mechanically. One such device used increasingly in the merchant service is called a *track plotter*. It receives inputs from a master transmitting compass and a log and automatically plots the progress of the vessel. It does this by resolving the heading–distance vector into north–south and east–west components. The north–south component is called *northing* or *southing*, depending upon the direction of progress. Similarly, the east–west component is called *easting* or *westing*, as appropriate. Northing or southing in a given time interval is determined by multiplying distance travelled during the interval by the cosine of the course, and easting or westing by multiplying distance by the sine of the course.

Counters may also be provided for registering latitude and longitude of the present position, if the correct position is inserted at the start of the dead reckoning. Change of latitude, in minutes of arc, is input directly from the north–south component of distance travelled, in miles. *Departure* (*p*, *dep*), the east–west component of distance in miles, is converted to longitude difference by multiplying it by the secant of the latitude.

Over a short interval of time, the length of which is determined by speed of the vessel and scale and size limitations of the scope, a vessel's progress is also displayed by a true-motion radar (p. 495).

As computer and other technology continues to progress, one can reasonably anticipate future availability of electronic equipment for accomplishing the dead-reckoning function, perhaps with automatic provision for allowance for the effects of wind and current.

Some mechanical dead-reckoning equipment now available has provision for tracking other vessels, information useful in avoiding collision, and having additional value to warships. Auxiliary radar equipment for performing this function is also available (p. 648).

A device useful primarily to naval vessels and others having frequent heading changes is called a *course recorder*. It receives inputs from a master transmitting compass and automatically traces a plot of heading *vs*. time on suitably-prepared paper that continuously moves from one roller to another, past a pen controlled by the signals from the transmitting compass. Thus, the device would more appropriately be called a *heading recorder*.

24. Miscellaneous

A permanent record should be kept of data needed for dead reckoning and pilotage, such as courses and speeds ordered, bearings, observed compass errors, and other pertinent information, with the applicable time of each entry. The information should be recorded when received, for later entry in the deck log and for use by the navigator in his dead reckoning, pilotage, and astronavigation. A *navigator's notebook* is used for recording the information as received.

The navigator should be provided with a pair of binoculars to assist in sighting aids to navigation.

He should also have a good flashlight with a red bulb or filter to protect the dark adaption of the eyes of bridge personnel. The flashlight is used for illuminating a watch used for timing navigational lights to determine their characteristics, or sights of astronomical bodies; reading an unlighting pelorus; reading a sextant; and perhaps other functions.

Weather instruments for measuring temperature, barometric pressure, and wind velocity are also useful to a navigator.

IV

Dead Reckoning

Publishers' Note: The chartwork conventions used in this book differ in certain respects from those used in the *Admiralty Manual of Navigation*. Please refer to p. 161 and Appendix D.

1. Definition

Navigation based upon distance and direction travelled from a known position is called *dead reckoning* (*DR*). While this definition, approximating to that adopted by the British Standards Institution, is generally acceptable, some difference of opinion exists in its interpretation. There are two principal points of difference.

The first difference relates to what constitutes a 'known' position. Positions are 'known' with varying degrees of certainty. There is little question when a vessel leaves an anchorage or passes close to an established aid to navigation. At sea, however, the situation is different. There, navigators generally limit a new start of dead reckoning to a fix (p. 226) or running fix (p. 235), the practice used throughout this book. Occasionally, however, a navigator may elect to start a new dead reckoning at other positions in which he has confidence, such as the most probable position (p. 17) based upon a combination of dead reckoning and a lone position line believed to have a high degree of accuracy. The question is one of confidence in the accuracy of what is considered a 'known' position. Even a fix can be of questionable accuracy. Judgment based upon experience is valuable in assessing the reliability of all navigational data. Until the navigator gains adequate experience, he should exercise caution in relying upon information that is not thoroughly authenticated. Whatever the practice, when a position is considered sufficiently accurate to be considered 'known', the previous dead reckoning is abandoned and a new one is started without attempting to bridge the gap, except in surveying operations where it is desired to establish as accurately as possible the actual track followed throughout the operation.

The second difference of opinion regarding dead reckoning relates to whether motion of the water should be taken into account in determining the distance and direction of travel. One of the serious deficiencies of navigation is the lack of reliable, cheap devices for measuring progress of a vessel over the ground. Because of 'current', including leeway and other disturbing factors, the speed and direction of motion made good over the ground are seldom the same as speed through the water and the heading. Traditionally, navigators, especially those of military vessels, have favoured the use of course and speed through the water. However, some navigators, principally in the merchant service, agree with air navigators that motion relative to the ground is the most realistic basis of dead reckoning. This book uses measured speed and direction of motion for dead reckoning, which generally means motion relative to the water. In the absence of measured values, estimates are the only recourse.

A position determined by dead reckoning alone is called a *dead-reckoning position* (*DR position*). When dead reckoning relates to motion relative to the water, a position adjusted for motion of the water is called an *estimated position* (*EP*). When dead reckoning is based upon motion relative to the ground, a position determined by using course and distance relative to the water, without considering motion of the water, may be called a *sea position* (*SP*), an expression suggested by the British Standards Institution, or *water position* (*WP*), analogous to the 'air position' of aviation.

Dead reckoning is useful in providing some indication of position at any time; estimating time of arrival at various points, when aids to navigation can be expected to be sighted, and when sunrise and sunset will occur; identifying landmarks and seamarks; advancing positions and position lines; and in evaluating the accuracy of position-fixing data. Because of the importance of dead reckoning, a complete log should be kept of all courses and speeds and any other data affecting its accuracy.

Dead reckoning is usually accomplished by plotting on the chart or plotting sheet, but in some instances mechanical devices or mathematical solutions, called *sailings* (p. 170) are used.

2. Plotting

Graphical solution of dead-reckoning problems by plotting on the chart in pilotage waters, or plotting sheet on the open sea, is an important function of the navigator. He should therefore master the technique and acquire facility in the use of his plotting equipment. As an example, he should learn to manipulate dividers quickly and accurately with one hand, preferably either hand.

The latitude of a position on the chart is determined by placing one point of the dividers on the position and the other point on the nearest printed parallel, directly above or below the position. The dividers are then moved horizontally to the latitude scale, without changing the spread of the legs, one point being kept on the printed parallel. The latitude of the position is read at the point indicated by the other leg of the dividers. Longitude is determined by a similar process, using the position, the nearest printed meridian, and the longitude scale at the top or bottom of the chart.

The process is reversed for plotting a position of which the coordinates are known. Sometimes it is easier to place a straight-edge horizontally on the chart with one edge along the desired parallel, as indicated by the latitude of the position to be plotted, and, with the dividers set to the increment of longitude from the nearest printed meridian, locate the position on the chart.

Direction can be measured on a chart by means of a protractor, some form of plotter or drafting machine that includes a protractor, or by means of a compass rose (p. 43) printed on the chart. If a protractor or plotter is used, the direction is measured as an angle with respect to one of the printed meridians. If a printed compass rose is used, a straight-edge is placed along an imaginary line extending from the centre of the rose to that peripheral point indicating the desired direction, and then moved parallel to itself until the edge is over the point from which the direction is to be measured. The process is reversed for determination of the direction of a line on the chart. Some charts have both true and magnetic compass roses, permitting the direct measurement of either true or magnetic directions. It is usually good practice to limit measurements to true directions only, for to mix reference directions is to invite error.

Plotting techniques other than those discussed here can be used. With practice, the navigator can develop the technique best suited to his liking and ability.

Distance in nautical miles is customarily measured by means of the latitude scale, the error introduced by considering one minute of latitude equal to one mile seldom being of significance. The distance between two positions on the chart is measured by placing one point of the dividers at each of the positions, and, without changing the spread of the legs, transferring the dividers to the latitude scale. The number of minutes of latitude between the points is the distance in miles. If the distance is too great for the maximum convenient spread of the divider legs, the line is measured in segments. The process is reversed for measuring a given distance.

In measuring distance on a Mercator chart, with its changing latitude scale, one should be careful to use that part of the scale at the same latitude as the positions on the chart. The importance of using the scale at the same latitude as the positions decreases as the scale of the chart increases. For a very large-scale chart, as a typical harbour chart, the scale changes so little that a distance scale applicable to any part of the chart may be printed on the chart. A mile scale of this type placed at the top or bottom of the chart is best avoided as a precaution against using the longitude scale for a mile scale, the two being similar and similarly oriented.

If position relative to some charted point, such as the location of a lighthouse, is known or desired, it can be measured by means of the direction and distance involved.

Procedures for plotting on a chart other than Mercator differ somewhat from those described, but should be apparent from a study of the chart. One should note, particularly, that if the meridians are not parallel to one another, directions should be measured at the printed meridian nearest to the point involved. Direction and distance as measured on a Mercator chart relate to a rhumb line. On some projections they may relate to a great circle or an approximation of it.

Upon leaving a harbour for the open sea, a navigator customarily obtains the best fix obtainable to serve as the origin of his dead reckoning away from land. This process is called *taking departure*. Having done so, he may shift from a chart to a plotting sheet (p. 53). From the fix, called the *point of departure*, he draws a line in the direction of the course, and labels it, as shown in Fig. 401. The label consists

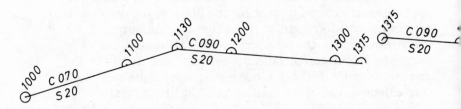

FIG. 401. A DR plot.

of two parts. Above the line he places the letter C followed by three digits indicating the true course in degrees. Below the line, under the course label, he places the letter S followed by one or two digits indicating the speed in knots. Because units of direction and speed are understood, they need not be indicated unless other than conventional units are used. In a plot of a planned voyage, distances, usually to 0.1 mile, between turning points or passage of major landmarks or aids to navigation may be substituted (with the letter D replacing S) for speed, and *estimated time of arrival* (*ETA*) at major points indicated.

Dead-reckoning positions at intervals along the course line

are located and labelled, as shown in Fig. 401. It is good practice to plot a D R position at each hour; at each change of course or speed; and at the time of each fix, running fix, or lone position line. In pilotage waters (p. 221), intervals shorter than an hour might be desirable.

Distance travelled in a given time at a given speed can be determined mathematically, knowing that distance in miles is equal to speed in knots multiplied by time in hours. Distance can also be determined by calculator, slide rule, logarithmic scale, nomograms, or speed-time-distance table printed in some books of nautical tables. At certain speeds mental solutions can be made easily. At a speed of 15 knots, for example, a craft travels one mile in four minutes; at 20 knots it travels one mile in three minutes. At any speed, multiples of six minutes of time are tenths of an hour.

Each line and marked point should be labelled *at the time it is plotted*. To delay or fail to label is to invite error. The plotting conventions used in this book, in wide but not universal use, shorten the labels of certain positions, reducing both the plotting time and clutter. As shown in Fig. 402, a semi-circle is used for a D R position, a square for an

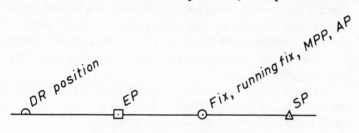

FIG. 402. Position symbology.

estimated position (EP), and a circle for a fix, running fix, most probable position (MPP), assumed position (AP) (p. 404), or any other position for which no separate provision is made. If a distinctive symbol is desired for a sea position (SP), a triangle might be used. A dot accompanies each position symbol to indicate the actual position represented. If these conventions are used, D R, estimated, and sea positions, and fixes (unless there is a possibility of mistaken identity) need be labelled with time only. Any other position indicated by a circle should be labelled with both time and the identity of the position.

A label relating to a line should be placed along the line to which it applies, while a label relating to a point should be placed at an angle to any line in the vicinity. Whenever there is a change of course or speed, or a break in the plot, the DR position at the time of the change should be plotted and labelled, and a new course and speed label shown immediately following the change, to avoid any reasonable doubt of the time of the change. Additions to the plot might be made when they clarify the situation.

The time used in a label is customarily the time kept by the ship, usually some form of zone time (p. 328), but Greenwich mean time (p. 328) is used by some navigators. The kind of time used should be understood clearly by all personnel concerned with the navigation of the vessel. If there is any reasonable room for doubt, an appropriate notation should be made on the chart. When a ship's time is changed, both old and new times should be shown and identified.

It is good practice to plot with a medium-soft pencil, making lines and labels that can be seen easily and yet can be erased without leaving indentations in the chart paper. It is also good practice to limit the plot to those items necessary for clarity of the situation, and to avoid extending lines beyond their utility.

In plotting, it is customary to consider alterations of course and speed as instantaneous changes, the error thus introduced seldom being significant at sea.

3. Current

The term *current* refers to motion of water over the surface of the Earth, including the rivers of water in the ocean (p. 210), wind-induced streams of water (p. 211), and tidal streams (p. 203). In navigation, the term may also be used to refer to the total effect of all factors causing deviation from the heading and speed ordered, such as leeway, errors in heading and speed measurement, erratic steering, and heavy seas, in addition to actual motion of the water.

The *set* (*S*) of a current is the direction *toward which* it moves, opposite to the convention for indicating wind direction. The rate of motion, or speed, of a current is its *drift* (*D*, *Dr*). The expression *total drift* refers to the distance of movement during some stated time interval, as between a fix and some later time. Total drift in miles is equal to rate or drift in knots multiplied by time interval in hours. The angular difference between the course steered and the direction of motion of the craft over the surface of the Earth is called *drift angle* (*D*, *Dr*). It is suffixed R or L to indicate drift right or left of the course steered, respectively.

An estimate of the anticipated set and drift of tidal streams and ocean currents can be determined by reference to tidal stream (current) tables (p. 209); sailing directions; and notes or arrows on nautical charts, tidal stream (current) charts and atlases, or pilot charts. The effect of wind in causing temporary ocean currents is discussed in section 13 of this chapter. The effect of wind in causing leeway is discussed in section 4.

The average current between two fixes can be determined by comparing the later fix with the D R position (the S P if the D R allows for estimated current), at the same time, run forward from the earlier fix. The direction of the second fix from the D R position at the same time is the set of the current. The distance between these two positions is the total drift. The drift in knots is the total drift in miles divided by the time interval in hours. This procedure is illustrated in Fig. 403. The 0900 fix of a vessel is as shown. The course is 275°, and the speed by engine revolution is 11 knots. The D R plot is shown by the solid line. At 1400 a new fix is obtained,

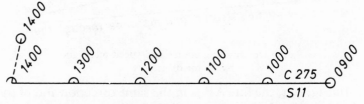

FIG. 403. Determining set and drift of current by concurrent DR position and fix.

as shown. The set of the average current between 0900 and 1400 is 020°, the direction of the broken line between the 1400 DR position and the 1400 fix. The length of this line, 7.5 miles, is the total drift during the five-hour period between the 0900 and 1400 fixes. The average drift of the current during this period is therefore $7.5/5 = 1.5$ knots.

At sea, far from shoal water or other obstructions, a simple DR plot as shown in Fig. 403 is generally adequate. In the vicinity of obstructions, where areas of safe water may be limited, one should be constantly aware of the possibility, and reasonable magnitude, of error in the DR position, and plan the courses accordingly. Safety considerations may dictate frequent plotting of estimated positions making allowance for current, or making an 'estimated reckoning' plot of the course and speed the vessel is thought to be making good over the ground. Every opportunity should be taken to fix the position of the vessel.

The effect of current can conveniently be determined by constructing a *vector diagram*. A *vector* is a straight line oriented to represent direction, and of length to represent magnitude. A vector diagram is a diagram of more than one vector drawn to the same scale and reference direction and in correct position relative to one another. With respect to currents, the vector diagram may be either a speed triangle or a distance triangle, the former being a special case of the latter, using distances in one hour. Both are used in navigation.

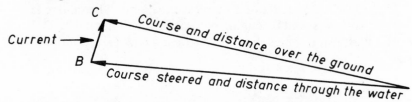

FIG. 404. Determining course and speed made good, by vector diagram.

In Fig. 404, the line AB is in the same direction and of the same length as the line connecting the 0900 fix and the 1400 DR position in Fig. 403, and line BC is the same as the 1400 DR position/1400 fix line. Line AC then represents the course and distance made good over the ground. The speed made good between 0900 and 1400 is the distance AC divided by the time, 5 hours. The vector diagram of Fig. 404, then, is the distance triangle. A speed triangle of the same situation would be similar. Line AB would be drawn to represent the course steered and speed ordered, BC would represent the drift, and AC would represent the course and speed over the ground. A speed triangle is thus a *velocity* (*vel.*) diagram, velocity being a vector quantity representing both speed and direction.

Current vector diagrams have several uses. Fig. 404 illustrates its use in determining estimated course and speed over the ground. If it is desired to make good a given course, the procedure is as shown in Fig. 405. A line AB of indefinite

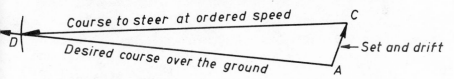

FIG. 405. Determining course to steer to make good a desired course.

length is drawn in the direction of the desired course to be made good over the ground. Line AC is drawn to represent the current velocity. With C as the centre, and a radius equal to the speed to be used, an arc is struck intersecting AB at D. The direction of line CD is the course to steer. If both a given course and given speed are desired to be made good, as when it is desired to arrive at a harbour entrance at the time of a favourable tide, the line AB is drawn as before, but point D is located so that AD is the desired speed to be made good. Vector AC is drawn as before to represent the set and drift of the current. Line CD then represents the course to steer and the speed to use to make good the desired course and speed over the ground.

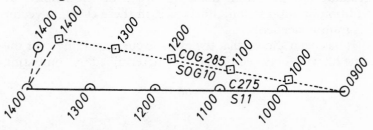

FIG. 406. Dead-reckoning and estimated-position plots.

Usually, the current encountered differs somewhat from that anticipated. In Fig. 406 a vessel is proceeding on course 275° at ordered speed 11 knots, as in Fig. 403. The navigator anticipates a current of 2.0 knots setting 040°, and uses this current to determine, by vector diagram, a *course over the ground (COG)* of 285° and a *speed over the ground (SOG)* of 10.0 knots. At 1400 he obtains a fix. The DR position, EP, and fix at 1400 are shown. A variation of this procedure is shown in Fig. 407. The dead-reckoning plot is carried forward to 1400. From the DR position at each hour a line is drawn in direction 040°, the set of the anticipated current. The EP's are located along these lines at distances equal to total anticipated drift in the elapsed time since 0900. The total actual drift of 7.5 miles at 1.5 knots is shown, as before, by the line *from* the 1400 DR *to* the 1400 fix.

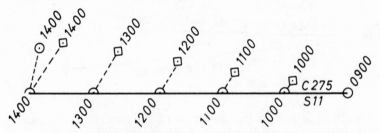

FIG. 407. A dead-reckoning plot with estimated positions.

The vector diagram can be plotted directly on the chart at the DR plot, at a compass rose, or at any convenient place. With practice, one can learn to construct the diagram by dividers and a straight-edge, or protractor and dividers, without actually drawing the extra lines needed, and thus reduce the clutter on the chart. However, one should not sacrifice accuracy or confidence for convenience, especially if one is a beginner. If the set is the same as the course to steer or its reciprocal, the course to steer is the course over the ground, and the speed made good can be determined by addition or subtraction. Therefore, in these cases no vector diagram is needed.

It has been shown that the average current acting over the time interval between fixes can be determined by comparing the DR position and fix at the same time. Neither of these positions is affected by current. Any position that is so affected cannot be used without an inaccurate solution. For this reason, a running fix, an estimated position, or a most probable position involving use of estimated current is not used for determining current.

One should use caution and some restraint in assuming that current determined by comparison of a DR position with a concurrent fix will continue, because of the various sources of error involved, as well as changing conditions, particularly near a coast, where the tidal effect related to various estuaries might be variable. One should be particularly wary of assuming a continuation of the set, especially if the DR position and fix are close together. A small error in either might introduce a large error in the measured set. One should be alert to conditions, noting particularly changes in the tidal cycle, entrances into and exits from established ocean currents, and changes in the wind. Some of these changes can be quite abrupt. As an example, the water of the Gulf Stream off the eastern North American coast is a distinctive blue colour quite different from that of the water on either side, and the edges are so sharply defined that the crossing of the boundary is often quite apparent. On the open sea it is usually best to assume zero current unless one has specific information supporting some other conclusion. This does not mean that one should not be alert to possible current and allow for it when there is justification for doing so. Indeed, one should be alert to possible deviations from a DR plot and make such allowance as the available data dictates. However, rules are no substitute for experience and sound judgment in considerations relating to current.

4. Leeway

The leeward notion of a vessel is called *leeway*. The term is applied, also, to the distance a vessel is moved by the wind over some period of time, the rate of such motion, and the angular deviation from the heading because of wind, although *leeway angle* is used frequently to indicate the angular deviation.

The amount of leeway varies with the type of vessel, its loading, trim, and speed; the depth of water under the keel; the state of the sea; and the speed and the direction of the wind relative to the heading of the vessel. The navigator should learn what he can about the characteristics of his vessel by reference to whatever data might be available, supplemented by his own observations.

The effect of leeway may be considered as a component of current, discussed in section 3, or its effect can be determined separately, by vector diagram, if suitable data are available.

Wind measured aboard a stationary vessel is true wind. If the vessel is underway, the *apparent wind* one measures is a combination of true wind and ship motion. *True wind* is the vector sum of apparent wind and ship velocity, and therefore can be determined by a vector diagram, as shown in Fig. 408.

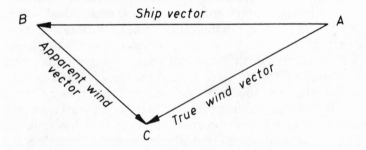

FIG. 408. Determining true wind from apparent wind and vessel motion.

An apparent wind of 10 knots from 40° on the starboard bow is measured aboard a ship on course 280°, speed 20 knots. Line AB is the ship's velocity vector. From B the wind velocity vector is plotted in the apparent direction of motion of the wind (*not* the direction from which it blows). The line AC is the true wind vector. By measurement, the true wind is blowing *toward* 252°, or *from* 072°, at a speed of 14 knots. The apparent wind is always from a direction *forward* of the direction of the true wind, and on the same side of the vessel, when the latter is oblique to the motion of the vessel. The ship velocity vector is motion along the course over the ground, not the heading. Some books of nautical tables provide tabular solutions to the apparent-/true-wind velocity problem.

Wind velocity estimated from appearance of the sea is true wind.

5. Mechanical Dead Reckoning

Although dead reckoning is normally accomplished manually by plotting on a chart or plotting sheet, mechanical devices are available for accomplishing this function. Such equipment is useful, but its limitations should be understood. Any mechanical equipment, however perfect and reliable, is subject to error, malfunction, and failure. Where electric power is involved, interruption of the flow of power results in incorrect output. The importance of having a current dead-reckoning position always available is too great to be entrusted entirely to equipment that may not always provide the needed information accurately. Mechanical dead-reckoning equipment does, however, provide a useful duplication that serves as a safeguard against major mistakes.

Unless the dead-reckoning equipment has provision for making allowance for current and leeway, one is under the necessity of making this allowance separately. If current and leeway are applied manually, either to the equipment or to its output, one should be alert to possible changes in these data.

Only in the case of frequent changes of course or speed is a position by dead-reckoning equipment likely to be more accurate than the corresponding plot by the navigator. Only when virtually continuous fixing capability is available and in use should one consider neglect of one's dead reckoning, and sometimes even then the dead reckoning can serve as a check on major errors and as a back-up in case of failure of the position-fixing capability.

6. Dead Reckoning by Calculation

Dead reckoning involves the determination of position by extrapolation from a 'known' position, using course and distance. The reverse of this problem is the determination of course and distance between positions. The common methods of solving problems of dead reckoning graphically by plotting on a chart or plotting sheet, or by mechanical equipment, are not the only approaches. Mathematical solutions are sometimes desirable. The different methods of solution are, collectively, called the *sailings*. The calculation itself can be carried out in a variety of ways, as by simple arithmetic, logarithms, tables, slide rule, or computer. Graphical solutions other than by plotting on a chart or plotting sheet, either by using any suitable surface or by mechanical device, are also possible.

In the various sailings a number of simplifying assumptions are made to avoid complexity of solution. Examples are the consideration of one minute of latitude as the equivalent of one mile, and the surface of the Earth as a plane, sphere, or spheroid, depending upon the nature of the method. The errors introduced by the simplifying assumptions are generally of no importance in the ordinary practice of navigation. More rigorous solutions can be achieved, if required, by calculation or by reference to appropriate tables found in some books including nautical tables. Methods of calculation are explained in books on geodesy. True directions should be used in calculations. If allowance is made for current and leeway, estimated, rather than dead-reckoning, positions result.

Meridian sailing involves motion along a meridian. The latitude of the destination is the latitide of the point of departure corrected for the number of minutes of latitude (miles) travelled. The longitude of the point of departure and the destination are the same. In the reverse problem, the course is 000° or 180° depending upon whether the destination is north or south of the point of departure. The distance in miles is the latitude difference between the two places.

Parallel sailing involves motion along a parallel of latitude. The longitude difference between two meridians is the same at any latitude if expressed as the arc of a parallel between them. But the distance between meridians when expressed in miles varies from a maximum at the equator to zero at the poles. Tables are available for determining the length of one degree of longitude at various latitudes. In using parallel sailing in the ordinary course of navigation, however, one considers the Earth a sphere and converts distance along a parallel, in miles, to minutes of longitude by the relationship DLo = p sec L; in which DLo is longitude difference; p is the distance between meridians, in miles, called *departure*; and L is latitude. The reverse problem is solved by the equation p = DLo cos L. A suffix E. or W. is added to DLo and p to indicate the direction of travel as course 090° or 270°, respectively.

In *plane sailing*, the Earth's surface is considered to be flat. Various relationships are computed by solving a plane right triangle, as shown in Fig. 409. In the illustration, P_1 is the

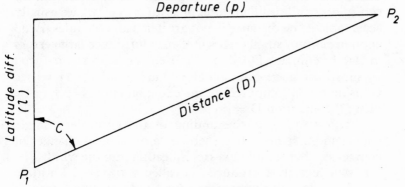

FIG. 409. The plane sailing triangle.

point of departure, P_2 is the destination, and C is the course angle between them. Sides of the triangle are labelled. The relationships among course angle (C), latitude difference (l), distance (D), and departure (p) are as follows:

$$\cos C = l/D,$$
$$\sin C = p/D,$$
$$\tan C = p/l,$$
$$l = D \cos C = p \cot C,$$
$$D = l \sec C = p \csc C,$$
$$p = D \sin C = l \tan C.$$

In the solution of problems of plane sailing, l is labelled N. or S. to indicate whether the parallel of the destination is north or south of the point of departure, and p is labelled E. or W. to indicate whether the meridian of the destination is east or west of the point of departure. In the solution of problems of the sailings, course angle is labelled C and course Cn. In plane sailing, C is converted to Cn by applying C as a correction to 000° (360°) if l is N. and to 180° if l is S. Thus, if C is 23°, Cn is 000° + 23° = 023° if the destination is N. and E. of the point of departure, 180° − 23° = 157° if S. and E., 180° + 23° = 203° if S. and W., and 360° − 23° = 337° if N. and W.

In plane-sailing problems, all quantities except C are in miles (or minutes of latitude). Departure and DLo are interconverted by means of parallel sailing. Errors introduced by considering the· Earth's surface flat and by considering miles and minutes of latitude as equal are usually acceptable if the distance is not greater than 600 miles. As C approaches 90°, small errors in C may introduce large errors in D if the equation $D = l \sec C$ is used. These can be reduced by substituting the equation $D = l \tan C \csc C$ for $D = l \sec C$, using tan C computed by the equation $\tan C = p/l$, or by using the equation $D = p \csc C$.

Traverse sailing is the finding of the equivalent single course and distance when there are a number of changes of course, as when a sailing vessel is beating into the wind. The series of legs thus produced is called a *traverse*. Latitude difference and departure are calculated, or found from a *traverse table*, for each leg and then added algebraically to determine the single equivalent, which can then be used in the plane-sailing equations to determine direction (course) and distance from the point of departure to the destination.

Middle-latitude, Mercator, great-circle, and composite sailings are discussed in the following sections.

7. Middle-Latitude Sailing

As pointed out in section 6, the relationship of departure and longitude difference varies with latitude. Plane sailing provides solutions for departure but leaves unanswered its conversion to longitude difference. *Middle-latitude sailing,* often shortened to *mid-latitude sailing,* provides for the conversion by defining the latitude to be used.

In its simplest form, mid-latitude sailing uses the latitude of the point midway between the point of departure and the destination, conveniently found by adding algebraically half the latitude difference to the latitude of departure. This practice introduces an error because the meridians do not converge at a uniform rate, as do the sides of a plane triangle. Some books of nautical tables provide a correction to be applied to the *middle latitude (Lm)* to produce a corrected mid latitude, or *mean latitude (mL, m lat)* for use in the interconversion of p and DLo. *These tables should be used with caution, or, better, avoided,* for in some instances they introduce more error than they remove. The reason for this is that some of the correction tables attempt to allow for the ellipticity of the Earth, but apply the spheroidal effect to the correction only and not to the basic equations of mid-latitude sailing, resulting in increasing the error in some cases. At best, mid-latitude sailing is an approximation, and if its use is limited to distances not exceeding 600 miles, the approximate results will be adequate for ordinary purposes of navigation, without the application of a correction to Lm. For greater accuracy or longer distances, some method other than mid-latitude sailing should be used.

The equations of mid-latitude sailing are those of plane sailing and parallel sailing. The usual problem solved by mid-latitude sailing is to find the point of arrival if one follows a known course for a known distance from a known point of departure. The applicable equations are:

$$l = D \cos C,$$
$$p = D \sin C,$$
$$D Lo = p \sec Lm.$$

Thus, if a ship leaves a fix at L $43°14\!.7$ N., Lo $37°14\!.1$ W. and steams for 187.9 miles on course 068°, its point of arrival can be determined as follows:

$$l = 187.9 \times 0.37461 = 70.4 \text{ N.} = 1°10\!.4 \text{ N.,}$$
$$p = 187.9 \times 0.92718 = 174.2 \text{ E.}$$

The suffixes N. and E. are determined from the course, 068°, which is taking the vessel to more northerly latitudes and more easterly longitudes. The latitude of the point of arrival, L_2, is found by adding l to L_1, the point of departure:

$$L_2 = L_1 + l = 43°14'.7 \text{ N.} + 1°10'.4 \text{ N.} = 44°25'.1 \text{ N.}$$

The mid latitude, Lm, is then:

$$Lm = L_1 + \tfrac{1}{2}l = 43°14'.7 \text{ N.} + 35'.2 \text{ N.} = 43°49'.9 \text{ N.}$$

Departure can now be converted to DLo:

$$DLo = 174.2 \text{ E.} \times 1.38624 = 241'.5 \text{ E.} = 6°01'.5 \text{ E.}$$

The longitude of the point of arrival, Lo_2, is then found by subtracting DLo from the longitude of the point of departure, Lo_1:

$$Lo_2 = Lo_1 - DLo = 37°14'.1 \text{ W.} - 6°01'.5 \text{ E.} = 31°12'.6 \text{ W.}$$

If one's run takes the vessel across the equator, one need not calculate the two parts (one on each side of the equator) separately, as some books suggest, because errors tend to cancel out. Thus, if L_1 is 1°09'.6 N. and l is 3°26'.3 S., L_2 is 1°09'.6 N. $- 3°26'.3$ S. $= (-)$ 2°16'.7 or 2°16'.7 S., $\tfrac{1}{2}l$ is 1°43'.2 S., and Lm $= 1°09'.6$ N. $- 1°43'.2$ S. $= (-)$ 33'.6 $= 0$ 33'.6 S.

Mid-latitude sailing can also be used to calculate the course and distance between two places of known coordinates. In this case, l, DLo, and Lm can be determined from the coordinates of the two places. From these quantities, p can be calculated, using the equation p = DLo cos Lm. Course angle can then be calculated by the equation tan C = p/l, and distance by the equation D = l sec C = p csc C. Thus, from Portland Harbour, England (L 50°34'.0 N., Lo 2°26'.0 W.) to Le Havre, France (L 49°29'.0 N., Lo 0°07'.0 E.):

$$l = 50°34'.0 \text{ N.} - 49°29'.0 \text{ N.} = 1°05'.0 \text{ S.} = 65'.0 \text{ S.,}$$
$$DLo = 2°26'.0 \text{ W.} + 0°07'.0 \text{ E.} = 2°33'.0 \text{ E.} = 153'.0 \text{ E.,}$$
$$Lm = 50°34'.0 \text{ N.} - 0°32'.5 \text{ S.} = 50°01'.5 \text{ N.,}$$
$$p = 153.0 \times 0.64245 = 98.3,$$
$$\tan C = 98.3/65.0 = 1.51231,$$
$$C = \text{S. } 56°31.5 \text{ E.,}$$
$$Cn = 180° - 56°31'.5 = 123°28'.5 = 123°.5,$$
$$D = 65.0 \times 1.81300 = 117.8M.$$

As in plane sailing, small errors in C may introduce large errors if C is near 90° if the equation D = l sec C is used.

8. Mercator Sailing

The dead-reckoning plot is a graphical solution of *Mercator sailing*. This method eliminates the troublesome problem of determining the correct value to use for mid-latitude sailing, and can be used without distance limitation, if one remembers that the solution is for a rhumb line and that the distance is in units of minutes of latitude. It is somewhat more accurate than plotting because it eliminates the errors associated with measurement on a chart, including the use of averages of the latitude scale. That is, the expansion of the latitude scale is used exactly, within the limits of rounding-off errors and uncertainty of the ellipticity of the Earth, instead of segments of the latitude scale.

Mercator-sailing equations are derived from the triangles shown in Fig. 410. The lower triangle is identical with that of Fig. 409. The longer vertical side of the larger triangle is the *meridional difference* (*m*, *DMP*, *d mer parts*), or the difference in meridional parts (p. 41) of the two places.

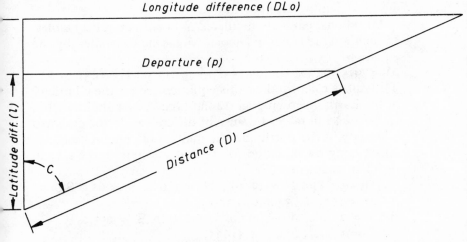

FIG. 410. The Mercator sailing triangle.

The usual problem solved by Mercator sailing is to find the course and distance between two places of known coordinates.

175

The equations are:
$$l = L_1 \sim L_2,$$
$$m = M_1 \sim M_2,$$
$$DLo = Lo_1 \sim Lo_2,$$
$$\tan C = DLo/m,$$
$$D = l \sec C.$$

The symbol $\sim$ means 'algebraic difference', either plus or minus, as appropriate. That is, if two places are on the same side of the equator or both in east longitude or both in west longitude, the smaller value is subtracted from the larger; but if of opposite sign, the two are added. Subscripts 1 and 2 refer to the point of departure and the destination, respectively. If C is near 90°, possible large errors in D can be avoided by using the equation:
$$D = l \tan C \csc C = p \csc C.$$

Other equations that are sometimes useful are:
$$\cos C = l/D,$$
$$\sin C = p/D,$$
$$l = D \cos C = p \cot C,$$
$$p = D \sin C = l \tan C = l \times DLo/m,$$
$$m = DLo \cot C.$$

Meridional parts are tabulated in books of nautical tables. If such a table is not available, M can be calculated by the equation:

$$M = 7915.704 \log \tan (45° + \tfrac{1}{2}L) - 23.013 \sin L - 0.051 \sin^3 L.$$

The values calculated by this equation are for the ellipticity of the Earth given on page 18, and may differ slightly from those found in tables because of differences in the assumed ellipticity of the Earth and the method of computation.

Applying the equations of Mercator sailing to the second problem of section 7:

$$l = 50°34'.0 \text{ N.} - 49°29'.0 \text{ N.} = 1°05'.0 \text{ S.} = 65'.0 \text{ S.,}$$
$$m = 3509.9 - 3409.0 = 100.9,$$
$$DLo = 2°26'.0 \text{ W.} + 0°07'.0 \text{ E.} = 2°33'.0 \text{ E.} = 153'.0 \text{ E.,}$$
$$\tan C = 153.0/100.9 = 1.51635,$$
$$C = \text{S.}56°35'.8\text{E.}$$
$$Cn = 180° - 56°35'.8 = 123°24'.2 = 123°.4,$$
$$D = 65.0 \times 1.81643 = 118.1\text{M.}$$

Over the short distance involved, the differences between the answers obtained by the two methods are minor.

Solutions of problems of the sailings are conveniently solved by means of logarithms (logs). A convenient work form for Mercator-sailing problems follows:

L_1	50°34′.0 N.	M_1	3509.9	Lo_1	2°26′.0 W.
L_2	49°29′.0 N.	M_2	3409.0	Lo_2	0°07′.0 E.
l	1°05′.0 S.	m	100.9	DLo	2°33′.0 E.
l	65′.0 S.			DLo	153′.0 E.

DLo	153′.0 E.	log 2.18469	l sec	0.25922
m	100.9	log(−) 2.00389	log	1.81291
C	S.56°35′.8 E.	l tan 0.18080	log	2.07213
l	65′.0 S.			
D	118.1M			
Cn	123°.4			

In the solution, l tan refers to log tangent, and l sec to log secant. The answers are identical with those of the previous solution.

9. Great-Circle Sailing

For distances of not more than a few hundred miles, great-circle and rhumb-line tracks can be considered identical without serious error, except in very high latitudes. For greater distances, a great-circle track might offer a significant saving in distance, the great-circle track being the shortest of any track between two points on the surface of a sphere. The actual shortest track on the surface of the spheroidal Earth differs slightly from the great-circle track, but its calculation is much more complex, and the difference in distance is too small to be of practical consequence in the ordinary practice of navigation.

Every great circle of a sphere bisects every other great circle, and only one great circle passes through any two points on the surface of the sphere, unless the two points are antipodal, being at opposite ends of a diameter of the sphere, in which case they are connected by an infinite number of great circles. The geographical poles are examples of antipodal points. Except for the equator, each great circle lies half in the northern hemisphere and half in the southern. The point farthest from the equator, in either hemisphere, called the *vertex* (V) is midway between the intersections with the equator. At the vertices the great circle extends in an east-west direction. The direction changes continuously as one proceeds along the great circle until one reaches the intersection with the equator, where its deviation from $090°$–$270°$ reaches a maximum equal to the latitude of the vertex. Any two points at opposite ends of a diameter of the great circle are $180°$ apart in longitude and have the same latitude numerically but on opposite sides of the equator, unless both are on the equator.

On a Mercator chart a great circle, other than a meridian or the equator, appears as a curve symmetrical about the equator. The arc of such a great circle between two points on the same side of the equator is therefore always farther from the equator than the rhumb line connecting the same two points. The separation of the great-circle arc and the rhumb line increases with greater distance between the points, higher latitude, and greater deviation from a north-south direction. For two places on opposite sides of the equator, the direction of curvature of the great circle with respect to the rhumb line reverses at the equator, so that the two might intersect, the point of intersection being at the equator if the two places are equal distances from the equator.

Rhumb-line sailing involves plane trigonometry, while great-circle sailing involves spherical trigonometry. The spherical triangle solved in the latter is illustrated in Fig. 411. Points A and B are two places on the surface of the Earth, and line AVXB is an arc of the great circle through the two places. Point V is the vertex, in this case between A and B, and X is any point on the great circle. Point P is the pole nearer A, the point of departure (also nearer B, the destination, in this case). Then PAM_A is part of the meridian through A, M_AA is the latitude of A, and PA is the co-latitude of A. Similar relationships are shown with respect to points V, X, and B. Angle APB is the longitude difference, DLo, between A and B. If one knows the coordinates of A and B, then sides PA and PB and angle APB are known, and one can solve for angle

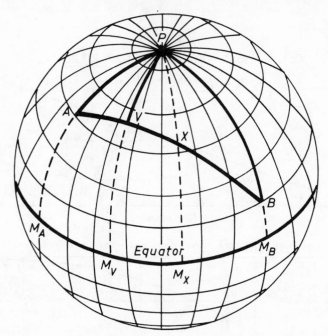

FIG. 411. The navigational triangle of great-circle sailing.

PAB, the initial great-circle course angle, and side AB, the great-circle distance between A and B. If it is of interest, one can also solve for angle PBA, the supplement of the final great-circle course angle.

Great-circle sailing problems can be solved by plotting, by conversion angle, or by calculation (including graphical and mechanical solutions). Calculation involves solution of the spherical triangle APB, called the *navigational triangle* of great-circle sailing.

Mariners usually perform plotting solutions by means of a chart on the gnomonic projection (p. 47). Because this is the principal use of such charts, they are often called *great-circle charts*. The upper part of Fig. 412 is a gnomonic chart of the North Atlantic, with its point of tangency at L 30° N., Lo 30° W. Below this chart is a Mercator chart of approximately the same area. The DR position of a ship as it passes Bishop's Rock Light, about 12 miles to starboard, will be L 49°40′.2 N., Lo 6°27′.4 W. The vessel is bound for Hamilton, Bermuda. From the chart, a point off the entrance

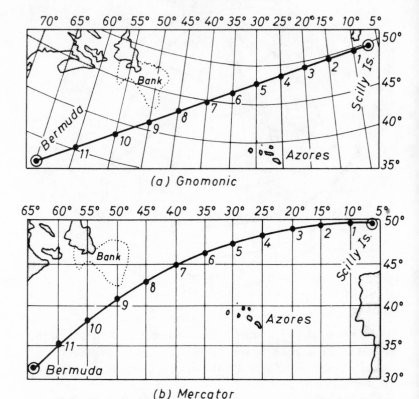

FIG. 412. Transferring points on a great circle from a
gnomonic to a Mercator chart.

of the harbour is selected, and its coordinates are found to be
L 32°19′.0 N., Lo 64°49′.0 W. The two points are plotted on
the gnomonic chart and connected by a straight line, as
shown. This line is the great-circle track between the two
places. The gnomonic projection not being orthomorphic
(p. 37), angles are not represented correctly. However,
gnomonic charts may provide instructions for measuring
both direction and distance. The principal use of the
gnomonic chart, however, is to indicate the great-circle track.
In this instance, the track is seen to pass clear of obstructions.
Points at convenient intervals along the great-circle track, as
at its intersections with meridians at 5° intervals, are located

and their coordinates measured. These points are then plotted on a Mercator chart and connected by straight lines, the rhumb lines to be followed from point to point until the destination is reached. Points 1, 2, 3, etc. on the lower chart of Fig. 412 are the transferred points 1, 2, 3, etc. from the upper chart. The series of rhumb lines is a close approximation of the great circle.

Great-circle tracks and distances between selected ports are shown on pilot charts (p. 79) and on some nautical charts. Recommended tracks are sometimes indicated in sailing directions.

A *conversion angle* is the angle between the great circle and the rhumb line between two points. It is equal, approximately, to half the difference between the initial and final great-circle courses. Books of nautical tables may include a table of conversion angles, usually intended primarily for use in plotting radio bearings (great-circle directions) on Mercator charts. Approximate values of conversion angle can be calculated by the equation:

$$\tan \alpha = \tan \tfrac{1}{2}DLo \, \sin Lm \, \sec \tfrac{1}{2}l,$$

in which α is the conversion angle. This equation is valid only if both places are on the same side of the equator. For small angles, a secant can be considered 1 and a tangent equal to the angle itself, in radians. Therefore, if neither l nor DLo is large (greater than about 15°), the equation can be written:

$$\alpha = \tfrac{1}{2}DLo \, \sin Lm.$$

A graphical solution is shown in Fig. 413. Line AB is drawn of indefinite length. Line AC is laid off at an angle to AB equal to the middle latitude between the point of departure and the destination, and of length $\tfrac{1}{2}DLo$, to any convenient linear scale. The length of CD, the perpendicular from C to AB, to the same linear scale, is the conversion angle. Its sign (whether it should be added to or subtracted from the rhumb-line course) should be apparent if one remembers that the rhumb line is always farther from the nearer pole than the great circle.

The conversion-angle method has several approximations, is increasingly inaccurate with greater difference of latitude or longitude, and provides no indication of the location of the

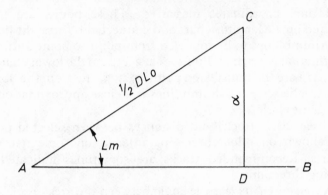

FIG. 413. Graphic determination of conversion angle.

track with respect to land or other possible obstructions, unless the various legs are transferred to a chart, a new solution being made at the end of each leg. The legs are tangents, rather than chords, of the great circle as plotted on a Mercator chart. They can be converted to chords by subtracting from each conversion angle an angle equal to the conversion angle divided by the number of remaining legs.

Any method of solving spherical triangles can be used in great-circle sailing. However, with some methods an answer near 90° might leave reasonable doubt of the quadrant involved. For this reason, equations involving haversines are preferable for those parts of the solution in which such ambiguity might occur. In great-circle sailing, no quantity need be greater than 180°, and haversines increase progressively from 0 at 0° to 1 to 180°.

In the following equations, subscript 1 refers to the point of departure (A), 2 to the destination (B), v to the vertex (V), x to any point on the great circle (X), and vx to the difference between V and X. These points are illustrated in Fig. 411.

Equations for finding the great-circle distance from A to B and the initial great-circle course are:

$$\text{hav } D = DLo \cos L_1 \cos L_2 + \text{hav } l,$$
$$\text{hav } C = \sec L_1 \csc D \left[\text{hav } coL_2 - \text{hav } (D \sim co\, L_1) \right].$$

A work form for solution by logarithms can be arranged

conveniently as shown in the following example, using the coordinates previously given for a point of departure off Bishops's Rock (L $49°40.2$ N., Lo $6°27.4$ W.) to a destination off the entrance to the harbour at Hamilton, Bermuda (L $32°19.0$ N., Lo $64°49.0$ W.).

Lo_1 6 27.4 W.			D 46°00.9	
Lo_2 64 49.0 W.			coL_1 40°19.8	
DLo 58 21.6 W.	l hav 9.37605		D~coL_1 5 41.1	
L_1 49 40.2 N.	l cos 9.81103		l sec 0.18897	
L_2 32 19.0 N.	l cos 9.92691			
	l hav 9.11399			
l 17°21.2 S.		n hav 0.13001		
D 46°00.9		n hav 0.02276		
coL_2 57 41.0		n hav 0.15277	l csc 0.14295	
D~coL_1 5 41.1	n hav 0.23270			
	n hav (−) 0.00246			
	n hav 0.23024		l hav 9.36217	
Cn 270.6		C N. 89°21.6 W.	l hav 9.69409	
D 2760.9 M				

This is a good example of the need for haversines. If C had been found by using a sine or cosine function, reasonable doubt would exist whether Cn should be $270°.6$ or $269°.4$.

In the solution, DLo is the difference between Lo_1 and Lo_2 if both are east or both are west, the sum of Lo_1 and Lo_2 if one is east and the other west and the sum is less than $180°$, and $360°$ minus the sum if the sum exceeds $180°$. The latitude difference, l, is the difference between L_1 and L_2 if both are of the same *name* (N. or S.), or the sum if they are of contrary name. The co-latitude of L_1 is always $90° - L_1$, but coL_2 is $90° - L_2$ if L_2 and L_1 have the same name, and $90° + L_2$ if of contrary name. The quantity D~coL_1 is always the numerical difference between D and coL_1, found by subtracting the smaller from the larger. Distance D is converted to miles by multiplying the number of degrees by 60 and adding the minutes. Course angle C is converted to course Cn by giving it a prefix N. or S. to agree with L_1 and a suffix E. or W. to agree with DLo. Note the difference between this procedure and that used in rhumb-line sailings. In great-circle sailing, the initial course might be northerly (in the northern hemisphere) although the destination is south of the point of departure, as in this example. The letter l preceding a trigonometric function indicates the logarithm of the function, while n indicates the natural function.

If the great-circle track is to be plotted on a Mercator chart or plotting sheet, the coordinates of points along the track are needed. First, the latitude (L_v) and longitude (Lo_v) of the vertex and its distance (D_v) from the point of departure are computed using the equations:

$$\cos L_v = \cos L_1 \sin C,$$
$$\sin D Lo_v = \cos C \csc L_v,$$
$$\sin D_v = \cos L_1 \sin D Lo_v.$$

The solution, continuing the example and convenient work form for logarithmic computation, follows:

L_1	49°40.2 N.	l cos 9.81103		l cos 9.81103
C	N. 89°21.6 W.	l sin 9.99997	l cos 8.04801	
L_v	49°40.4 N.	l cos 9.81100	l csc 0.11784	
Lo_v	7°17.8 W.	D Lo_v 0°50.4 W.	l sin 8.16585	
D_v	0°32.6			l sin 8.16585
D_v	32.6 M			l sin 7.97688

Haversines are not needed because L_v is always of the same name but in higher latitude than L_1, and neither D Lo nor D is greater than 90°. The fact that C is in the NW. quadrant indicates that $D Lo_v$ is toward the west, in this case between the point of departure and the destination. If C had been in the SW. quadrant, the vertex would have been toward the east, beyond the great-circle arc between the point of departure and the destination. In this case one sometimes finds it more convenient to use the vertex in the opposite hemisphere. It has the same latitude, but of opposite name, as the calculated L_v and is 180° in longitude from the calculated vertex. In this example the vertex is very near the point of departure, as one would anticipate from the fact that C is very near 90°.

A convenient method of determining the coordinates of points along the great-circle track is to compute the latitude at which the track crosses meridians at selected values of D Lo from the vertex, using the equation:

$$\tan L_x = \cos D Lo_{vx} \tan L_v.$$

If points are desired in the example at longitudes 20° W., 30° W., 40° W., and 50° W., solution by logarithms can be arranged conveniently as follows:

Lo_v	7°17′.8 W.	7°17′.8 W.	7°17′.8 W.	7°17′.8 W.
Lo_x	20°00′.0 W.	30°00′.0 W.	40°00′.0 W.	50°00′.0 W.
$D Lo_{vx}$	12°42′.2 W.	22°42′.2 W.	32°42′.2 W.	42°42′.2 W.
l cos $D Lo_{vx}$	9.98923	9.96497	9.92504	9.86622
l tan L_v	0.07116	0.07116	0.07116	0.07116
l tan L_x	0.06039	0.03613	9.99620	9.93738
L_x	48°58′.2 N.	47°22′.8 N.	44°45′.0 N.	40°53′.0 N.

It is known that L_x has the same name as L_v because $D Lo_{vx}$ is in each case less than 90°. If $D Lo_{vx}$ is greater than 90°, L_x is on the opposite side of the equator from L_v. It is probable that one would desire a greater number of points along the great-circle track than the limited number shown to illustrate the method of solution. If the vertex is near the mid-point between the point of departure and the destination, the solution for points along the track can be simplified somewhat by using some convenient $D Lo_{vx}$, as each 5°, so that the same solution for L_x can be used for points at the same $D Lo_{vx}$ on opposite sides of the vertex.

If a work form is made out for the entire solution before any values are extracted from the tables, some time can be saved by looking up and recording all values pertaining to any quantity at one opening of the tables. As an example, l cos of L_1 is required in three places, and l sec in one place. Also l cos, l csc, and l tan of L_v are required and can be taken from the tables with one opening. If tables of log secant and log cosecants are not available, log cosines and log sines can be used with negative signs.

If it is desired to calculate the coordinates of points at equal *distances*, or at any given distance, along the great-circle track, the following equations can be used:

$$\sin L_x = L_v \cos D_{vx},$$
$$\sin D Lo_{vx} = \sec L_x \sin D_{vx}.$$

If it is desired to know the longitude at which the great-circle track crosses any given parallel, $D Lo_{vx}$ can be calculated by the equation:

$$\cos D Lo_{vx} = \tan L_x \cot L_v.$$

If, in Fig. 411, the coordinates of an astronomical body equivalent to latitude and longitude on the Earth are substituted for the coordinates of the destination at B, the spherical triangle becomes the *navigational triangle* of astronavigation. Any method of solving the navigational triangle can be used for determining initial great-circle course angle and distance, if certain substitutions are made. Books of tables designed primarily for astronavigation usually explain the use of the tables for great-circle sailing. Books of tabulated solutions (p. 402) involve triple interpolation and are not arranged conveniently for determination of points along the great-circle track. Their principal value is in providing a quick approximate (without interpolation) check on a solution by calculation. In the example given above, the solution by NP 401 (U.S. Pub. No. 229) without interpolation, is Cn 269°.7, D 2759.3M. With triple interpolation the answers are Cn 270°.7, D 2760.9M, almost identical with the solution by calculation.

Solution of great-circle sailing problems, of course, can be made without logarithms or by calculator. A number of graphical solutions have also been devised, and some of them have been mechanized. Answers can also be obtained directly from a globe, using a thread, curved protractor, and dividers. All such solutions are generally of a scale to preclude great accuracy. They do, however, provide answers that might be adequate for the purpose desired. They also provide a check on other solutions, as a safeguard against gross errors.

A great-circle track cannot always be followed in its entirety without encountering some obstruction, such as an island or peninsula, or undesirable area such as a high latitude where ice might be a problem. It is therefore desirable in planning a voyage involving a great-circle track to lay out the entire track in advance, so that any needed alterations can be made with optimum results. If an obstruction is small in extent, as a small islet, it can be avoided by minor alterations of course when in its vicinity. One's vessel might be set to one side by current or leeway so that avoiding action is not needed.

Large obstructions are another matter. The alteration

needed depends upon the situation. Sometimes two great circles afford the best solution. A point off the obstruction is selected to provide safety, and great circles through this point and the point of departure and destination are used. At other times the optimum track might be a series of rhumb lines without regard to great-circle sailing. An example would be a voyage from Southampton to Athens.

A method sometimes employed is to use a great circle for the first and last portions of a voyage, with a rhumb line for the intervening portion. A common form of this is called *composite sailing*, used when the great-circle track from the point of departure to the destination would take the vessel to a higher latitude than desired. The principle is to use the desired limiting latitude as the latitude of the vertex. The track then follows a great circle from the point of departure to the vertex at the limiting latitude, then proceeds along the limiting parallel until it reaches the vertex of a great circle through the destination, and then follows the second great circle to the destination.

Solution of the composite-sailing problem can be obtained easily by means of a gnomonic chart. Calculation can also be used. The equation $\cos D Lo_{vx} = \tan L_x, \cot L_v$, used for determining the longitude of any point on a great circle if the vertex is known, can be used. The latitude of the vertex is the limiting latitude. The latitude of the point of departure is used as L_x to determine the longitude difference between the point of departure and the first vertex, from which the longitude of that vertex can be determined. Similarly, the longitude of the second vertex can be determined by using the latitude of the destination as L_x. The computed $D Lo_{vx}$ is measured *back* from the destination. Solution can then be made by considering the two great-circle arcs as part of the same great circle, using the combined longitude differences, and adding the distance along the limiting parallel, found by parallel sailing.

Composite sailing, of course, can be used only when the vertex lies between the point of departure and the destination.

During a voyage involving great-circle sailing a vessel follows a series of rhumb lines approximating the great circle, as stated previously. The greater the number of points selected along the great circle the nearer the series of course lines approaches the great-circle track, but a greater number of course lines requires more frequent changes of course. If one is steering by magnetic compass, the changes in variation might partly offset the changes in true course, so that fewer magnetic course changes are necessary. Conversely, if both changes are of the same sign, more frequent changes might be needed. In general, successive course changes of about 2° to 5° are desirable.

During a voyage one is likely to find the vessel set laterally off the desired track. Small deviations can be ignored in the prospect that the vessel might later be set in the opposite direction, but if there is a progressive set to one side, the heading should be altered to bring the course line parallel to the desired track, or to a direction to converge gradually until it intersects the desired track some distance ahead, where a further adjustment should be made to bring the two into coincidence. If the next scheduled course change is not far ahead, one might elect to wait and select a somewhat different course for the next leg, or make the change early, heading directly for the next following point, as shown in Fig. 414. If one is set far to one side of the desired track, as during a severe storm, one might consider an entirely new great-circle track from a dead-reckoning position a short distance ahead to the destination.

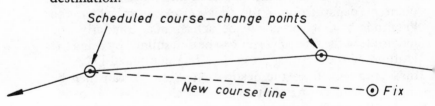

FIG. 414. Course line to intersect future course-change point.

10. Tides

The term *tide* refers to the periodic rise and fall of the surface of the ocean. It is caused primarily by differences in gravitational attractions of various astronomical bodies on the rotating Earth. Sir Isaac Newton's *universal law of gravitation* states that every particle of matter in the universe attracts every other particle with a force directly proportional to the product of the masses of the two particles and inversely proportional to the square of the distance between them. The tide-producing force of any astronomical body on the Earth is directly proportional to its mass and inversely proportional to the *cube* of its distance from the Earth. Consequently, the Moon, because of its proximity to the Earth, is the astronomical body exerting the principal tidal effect upon the Earth. Because of its much greater distance (approximately 150,000,000 kilometres as compared to about 385,000 kilometres for the Moon), the Sun, although many times as massive as the Moon, produces tides only about 46 per cent as high as those caused by the Moon. Astronomical bodies other than the Sun and Moon have a negligible tide-producing effect.

Consider the Earth–Moon system. Although the Moon is generally considered to revolve around the Earth, the two bodies actually revolve around their common centre of mass, which is within the Earth, about three-fourths of the distance from its centre toward the surface facing the Moon. The two bodies are held in orbit by a balance between the *centrifugal force*, tending to cause the bodies to fly apart, and the *centripetal force*, pulling them together. The centripetal force is constant for the entire Earth as one body, being equal to the *average* gravitational force of the Earth–Moon system. The gravitational force between the Earth and the Moon varies over different parts of each body because of the difference in distance at various places. On the Earth, that point at which the Moon is directly overhead is closer to the Moon, by the Earth's radius, than the centre of the Earth, and the antipodal point on the opposite side of the Earth is farther away by about the same distance. The distance between these two points, at opposite ends of a diameter of the Earth, is approximately 12,742 kilometres. It is the difference between the centripetal and gravitational forces at various points on the surface of the Earth that causes the tides. The *gravitational force* between the Earth and Moon, a factor in producing tides, should not be confused with Earth *gravity,* the gravitational force of the Earth and a particle of mass, as modified by centrifugal force resulting from rotation of the Earth.

On the side of the Earth facing the Moon, the gravitational force of the Earth–Moon system is greater than the centripetal force. On the opposite side of the Earth, the centripetal force is greater by about the same amount. Thus, at both of these places the tide-producing effect of the Moon is maximum, and is directed *away* from the centre of the Earth. However, the force is only a small fraction of the Earth's gravity, so that actual lifting of the water upward against gravity is negligible. Along a great circle midway between the two antipodal points of maximum tidal force, the gravitational and centripetal forces are equal, with no tidal force. Between this great circle and the two points of maximum tidal force, the direction of the tidal force has both a vertical and a horizontal component. The vertical component is opposed by the Earth's gravity, but the horizontal component is without opposition, except for frictional effects. It is this horizontal component that produces the tides, by causing the water to move across the surface of the Earth. The moving water itself is referred to as the *tidal stream* or *tidal current,* discussed in section 11, while the change in depth of water as it tends to 'pile up' at the points of maximum tidal force, by moving away from the great circle between them, is the *tide.*

High tide or *high water* (*HW*) occurs when the depth of water is maximum as the result of a *rising tide,* and *low tide* or *low water* (*LW*) occurs at minimum depth as a result of a *falling tide.* The difference in depth between the two is the *range* of the tide. For a moment at either high tide or low tide, there is no change of water level. This condition is called the *stand* of the tide. From either stand the rate of change of water level increases until it reaches a maximum approximately midway between stands, and then decreases until the next stand. The interval between a high tide and the one occurring approximately a day later is called a *tidal day.* A complete set

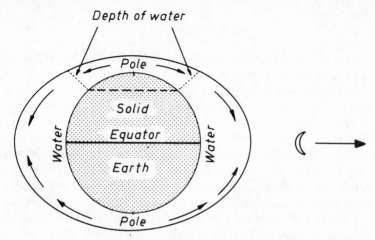

FIG. 415. Tides when the Moon is over the equator.

of tidal conditions occurring between repetitions of some periodic phenomena, such as a tidal day, is called a *tidal cycle*. The condition of the tide at any time is called the *stage* (or *state*) *of the tide*.

Because of the two points of maximum tidal effect on opposite sides of the Earth, there are two high tides and two low tides during each rotation of the Earth with respect to the Moon, a period of about 24 hours 50 minutes. When the Moon is directly over the equator, the two high tides at a place off the equator are approximately equal in height, as shown in Fig. 415. But when the Moon is not in the equatorial plane, the two high tides are of unequal depth, as shown in Fig. 416, the difference being called the *diurnal inequality*, an

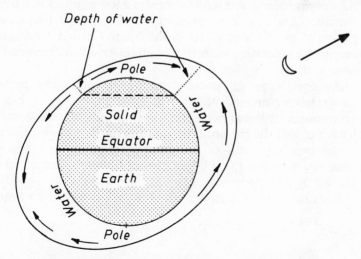

FIG. 416. Tides when the Moon is not over the equator.

expression sometimes used also to indicate the difference in the time interval between successive high and low tides. With diurnal inequality in the heights of tides, there is, during a tidal day, a *higher high water* (*HHW*), *lower high water* (*LHW*), *higher low water* (*HLW*), and *lower low water* (*LLW*).

The Earth–Sun system is similar to the Earth–Moon system, but with lesser tidal effect. The average height of the lunar tide on the open sea is 54 centimetres, as compared with an average solar tide of 25 centimetres. The total tidal effect of the lunar and solar tides is the vector sum of the two, called the *equilibrium tide*. The ideal, as discussed thus far, is modified greatly by the sizes, shapes, depths, and natural periods of oscillation of ocean basins; rotation of the Earth; the positions and shapes of land masses and shoals; meteorological conditions; variations of run-off of land water into estuaries; and tsunamis.

Any basin, whether a lake, bay, or semi-enclosed portion of the ocean, when its water is disturbed, develops free oscillations characteristic of its size, shape, and depth, if the forces responsible for the disturbance are not sustained. Such an oscillation is called a *seiche* (believed to have been derived from the Latin *siccus*, meaning *dry*). The causes are primarily meteorological, but tsunamis and a surge of water from run-off following a heavy rainstorm on land or by release of water forced against a shore by wind can also course seiches to form. The period of a seiche may vary from a few minutes to a large fraction of a day, depending upon the natural oscillation period of the body of water in the basin. Certain conditions may cause a standing wave to remain relatively unchanged for several days.

As the ridge of water forming a high tide moves progressively around the world once in about 24 hours 50 minutes, it behaves essentially as a wave having a wave length of half the circumference of the Earth, or some 20,000 kilometres. This rate of one circumference in 24 hours 50 minutes, or some 1,600 kilometres per hour, is the speed of the wave, not the water.

Because of their long length and period (about 12 hours

25 minutes), *tide waves* (not to be confused with tsunamis and storm waves, popularly but erroneously called *tidal waves*) and seiches are affected by the rotation of the Earth. *Coriolis*, an apparent force acting upon a mass in motion, because of rotation of the Earth, causing deflection to the right in the northern hemisphere and to the left in the southern hemisphere, is the cause of the cyclonic motion of the atmospheric. Coriolis produces a similar effect in the ocean, causing a long-period or standing wave to rotate in an anticlockwise direction in the northern hemisphere and in a clockwise direction in the southern hemisphere. A rotating wave of this type establishes what is called an *amphidromic system* from the Greek *amphi*, meaning *both*, and *dromos*, meaning *running*. At the focal point of such a system, called its *amphidromic point*, the depth of water does not change. *Co-tidal lines*, connecting points of equal stage of the tide, extend outward in a somewhat radial fashion from the amphidromic point and rotate with the wave. Circular or elliptical *co-range lines*, connecting points of equal range of the tide, surround an amphidromic point. Amphidromic systems are present in all large oceanic areas, and amphidromic tendencies are observed even in the North Sea and the Baltic and in other bodies of similar size. The effect is stronger in higher latitudes, because Coriolis is stronger there. Coriolis explains some interesting phenomena. An example is the occurrence of high tides along the southern shore of the Dover Strait at the same time that low tides are occurring along the northern shore. Along the Pacific Coast of the United States tides occur progressively later with increased latitude, being about six to eight hours later at Seattle than at San Diego.

As the tide wave approaches a land mass or a shoal, the wave is modified considerably. On the open sea, the tilt of the sea surface attributable to tidal action is of the order of $0''.016$ when both lunar and solar tides are acting in unison. In contrast, the tilt caused by differences in temperature and density of sea water and atmospheric pressure can be as much as $1''.5$.

At isolated stations on small islands in the open ocean, the tide range approximates the theoretical value of the equilibrium tide. But over broad continental shelves and in the somewhat confined waters of various estuaries the departure from the ideal varies considerably. There are several reasons for this departure from the ideal. When any wave enters shallow water, its height increases because of retardation of the bottom of the wave by friction with the ocean floor and because the energy of the wave is confined into less space. The increase in range is approximately inversely proportional to the fourth root of the water depth. When the natural period of a body of water is identical with the period of the tide, resonance occurs, resulting in increased range of tide. As a tide wave moves up a funnel-shaped estuary, nearly the same volume of water is crowded into a narrower space, resulting in higher high tides. The increase in range produced by this effect is approximately inversely proportional to the square root of the width of the estuary. In areas where the range of the tide is very great, the tilt of the sea surface may approach o.́5 under extreme conditions.

The secondary effect of meteorological conditions and water run-off in inducing seiches has been mentioned. A primary effect is present, also. An onshore wind tends to cause water to move toward land, producing a *meteorological tide* superimposed upon the normal tide. The effect is most pronounced when a strong wind blows toward or up a relatively long estuary for several days, or when two or more wind-induced currents (p. 211) converge, either effect producing abnormally high tides. An offshore wind has the opposite effect of producing lower tides than normal. A severe tropical storm may produce a single surge of water of sufficient height to cause damage when it encounters the shore. A surge of this kind is called a *storm wave, storm surge,* or *storm tide.* Under some conditions negative surges occur. Other causes of meteorological tides are variations from normal atmospheric pressure, sea-water temperature, and salinity; and by heavy, prolonged precipitation, either in an estuary or on land with abnormal run-off into an estuary. Abnormal run-off is particularly effective in causing higher-than-normal tides in tidal rivers. For a stationary low-pressure area the water rises approximately one centimetre for each millibar depression below normal pressure. For a moving low-pressure system the effect is somewhat less, decreasing with higher speed of the low. A higher-than-normal atmospheric pressure is accompanied by a depressed water level at about the same rate. The effect of atmospheric pressure may be altered by Coriolis, as explained in section 13.

Tsunamis have also been mentioned with respect to seiches. Like some meteorological effects and water run-off, tsunamis may have a direct, and occasionally disastrous, effect upon the depth of water. A tsunami is a gravity-wave system formed after a major short-duration disturbance of the surface of the ocean, caused by an earthquake, volcanic or man-induced underwater explosion, bottom slumping, landslide, or large meteorite impact. The principal cause is an earthquake of magnitude greater than 6.5 on the Richter scale, at a depth of not more than 50 kilometres. Not all earthquakes produce tsunamis. A tsunami wave caused by a submarine earthquake is called a *seismic sea wave*.

The origin of a tsunami, the point directly above the disturbance when it is submerged, is called the *epicentre*. A tsunami moves outward from its epicentre in an ever-widening circle, much as the wave system produced when a pebble is dropped into a pond of water. Typically, a tsunami has a wave length in excess of 100 miles and a height of not more than half a metre in deep water. Consequently, its presence at sea is generally not apparent. It moves at a speed that may exceed 500 knots, and has a period of the order of 15 to 20 minutes.

As a tsunami moves outward from its epicentre, it becomes distorted by large-scale variations in depth of water. Its amplitude decreases as its energy is spread over a circle of increasing circumference. When it enters shoal water, it increases in height because its bottom is slowed by friction with the ocean floor and its energy is confined into less space. Extreme heights of the order of 15 to 20 metres have been encountered at the shore line. As a wave of this magnitude moves inland, it may cause extensive property damage and loss of life. The height at any point along a shore depends upon the magnitude and nature of the originating disturbance, the distance the wave has travelled, and the configuration of the ocean floor and shore line.

As a tsunami crosses the coastal shelf, it may trigger a seiche there that gradually decreases over a period of several days. The tsunami itself typically consists of a series of waves that increase in height to a maximum and then gradually decrease over a period of several hours to several days. The imminent approach of a major tsunami wave is heralded by an abnormal receding of the water along the beach as the sea water rushes out to join the oncoming wave.

Strong currents sometimes associated with tsunamis and seiches may be a source of damage to marine craft.

With many factors influencing the tides, and numerous variations in local conditions, it should not be surprising that there is an almost endless variation in the pattern of tides in various places around the world, each place having an essentially unique pattern because of local conditions and the tidal influences to which it responds most readily. In range, the variation is from virtually no tide to tremendous tides of more than 12 metres at Bassin des Mines in the funnel-shaped Bay of Fundy in eastern Canada. Tides are almost as high in the similarly-shaped River Severn, and at Liverpool they approach nine metres. In contrast, the maximum tidal range at Puerto Rico, near an amphidronic point, is only about three centimetres. In the Mediterranean Sea, of the wrong size to be resonant to any astronomical tidal period and with small openings at each end, the range is typically 10 to 15 centimetres. The sequence of high and low tides at a place can be broadly categorized in one of three types, as illustrated in Fig. 417.

Semi-diurnal has two high tides and two low tides each tidal day of about 24 hours 50 minutes, with little diurnal inequality. This type of tide is characteristic of points around the perimeter of the Atlantic Ocean.

Diurnal has one high tide and one low tide each tidal day. Tides of this type occur at a number of isolated locations having favourable conditions, examples being the eastern Baltic, Java Sea, and part of the northern shore of the Gulf of Mexico.

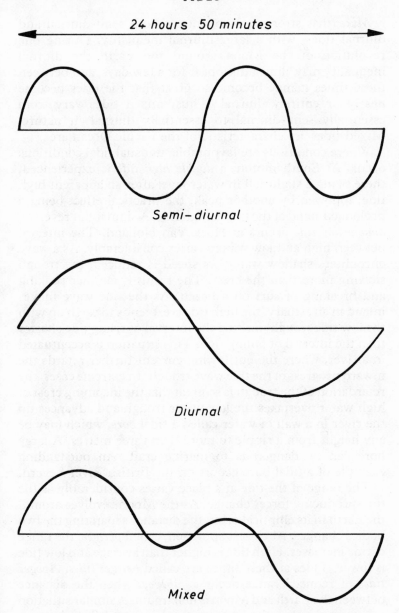

FIG. 417. Characteristics of semi-diurnal, diurnal, and mixed tides.

Mixed has strong components of both semi-diurnal and diurnal tides, with a large diurnal inequality. During one revolution of the Moon around the Earth the diurnal inequality may almost disappear for a few days, and between these times it may become so great that the tides become nearly or entirely diurnal. Thus, mixed tides vary from essentially semi-diurnal to essentially diurnal in nature. Mixed tides are characteristic of the Pacific Ocean area.

Where conditions are favourable, unusual tidal conditions occur. At Southampton, a *double high tide* is experienced, there being a slight fall in water level after an apparent high tide, followed by another peak, the practical effect being a prolonged stand of the tide at high tide. A similar but reversed *double low tide* occurs at Hoek Van Holland. The interval between high and low waters varies considerably. As a wave encounters shallow water, its speed is reduced, the trough slowing more than the crest. The result is familiar peaking and breaking of surf on a beach. As the tide wave moves inland in an estuary, the high tide crest tends to catch up with the low tide trough, making the interval of rising tide shorter than the interval of falling tide. This situation is accentuated in a river, where the outflowing current further retards the inward progress of the tide wave trough. In extreme cases, the retardation of the trough is so great that the incoming crest of high water overtakes the low water trough and advances up the river in a wall of water called a tidal *bore*, which may be any height from a ripple to more than three metres. A large bore can be dangerous to marine craft. An outstanding example of a tidal bore occurs on the British River Severn.

The range of the tide at a place varies considerably as the tide-producing forces change. As the Moon revolves around the Earth in its elliptical orbit, the distance separating the two bodies changes. At closest approach, called *perigee*, the range of tide increases. High tide is higher than average and low tide is lower. Tides at these times are called *perigee tides. Apogee tides* of reduced range occur at *apogee*, when the distance between the Earth and Moon is maximum. A similar situation occurs as the distance between the Earth and Sun changes, but the effect is very much smaller, both because the solar tidal force is less than half that of the lunar tidal force and because the percentage variation of distance is only about one fourth that of the Moon. When the Moon is at *syzygy*, at full or new moon, it is said to be at *opposition* or *conjunction*, respectively. At either of these times the Sun, Moon, and Earth are approximately in line. The lunar and solar tide-producing forces are in phase, resulting in greater range of tide. *Spring tides* occur at syzygy. The name has no relationship to the spring season of the year. At *quadrature*, when the Moon is at first or third quarter, the two tide-producing forces are in opposite phase, and tidal ranges are reduced. *Neap tides* occur at these times. The diurnal inequality changes as the Sun or Moon changes its position relative to the plane of the equator of the Earth, as illustrated in Figs. 415 and 416. *Equatorial tides* of minimum diurnal inequality occur when the Moon is over the equator. *Tropic tides* of maximum diurnal inequality occur when the Moon is at maximum distance north or south of the equator. Similar effects in solar tides are smaller, of course. When two or more conditions causing higher than average high tides occur simultaneously, as when spring and perigee tides occur at the same time, the range of tide is especially great. During *equinoctial tides*, when the Sun is over the equator, the range of spring tides is greater than average, and during *solstitial tides*, when the sun is at maximum distance from the equator, the range of tropic tides is greater than average.

The continual change in the range of tides is attributable, in part, to the fact that the period of change in each factor affecting the range is different. The high waters or low waters of a lunar semi-diurnal tide repeat at intervals of 12 hours 25 minutes, and those of a solar origin at intervals averaging 12 hours. The diurnal components occur at twice these intervals. The interval between successive spring or neap tides is a little less than 15 days, while the interval between successive equatorial or tropic tides is a little less than 14 days. The interval between perigee or apogee tides is a little more than 27 days. The period of change of the Sun's position relative to the equator is half a year, and its distance change interval is one year. At intervals of 18.6 years, called the *nodal period*, the orbit of the Moon returns to the same orientation with respect to the Earth and Sun. The mean value of tidal range at a place is the value determined by averaging the range observed or computed for this 18.6-year period of time. Meteorological factors, run-off, and tsunamis add to the range variations associated with astronomical phenomena.

The Moon being the principal factor in causing tides, the stage of the tide at a place at any time is related to the position of the Moon relative to the place. High water on the open ocean does not occur when the Moon is over the meridian or 180° from it because of rotation of the Earth and the fact that water continues to flow toward a place for some time after meridian passage, just as the temperature continues to rise after the sun crosses the meridian. Along coast lines, particularly in estuaries, the configuration of land further retards the occurrence of high water following passage of the Moon. The interval between passage of the Moon over the meridian of a place, or that 180° away, and the next high tide or low tide at a place is called the *lunitidal interval*, either the *high water lunitidal interval* or the *low water lunitidal interval*. The average at high tides is called *mean high water lunitidal interval* or *establishment*, and the average at low tides is called *mean low water lunitidal interval*. The average high water lunitidal interval at the time of spring tides is called *high water full and change (H W F & C)* or *vulgar establishment*. Where the tide is semi-diurnal, the lunitidal interval is reasonably constant, but where other periods are prominent, the variation in lunitidal interval is greater. Because of local conditions, the lunitidal interval differs considerably from place to place.

The principal effect of the Sun with relation to the time of tide is to cause an offset in the time of any stage of the tide. Thus, if the solar high tide occurs a short time before the lunar high tide, the highest tide occurs earlier than it would if there were no solar effect. *Priming of the tides* is an expression used by some to indicate that high tides occur sooner than they would if produced solely by the Moon, and by others to refer to the effect of the Sun in shortening the mean interval between successive occurrences of any stage of the tide. The opposite effect is called *lagging of the tides*. By the first definition, priming occurs between spring and neap tides, and lagging occurs between neap and spring tides. The opposite is true of the second definition. Some authorities have used the two definitions interchangeably, apparently not noting the inconsistency.

The *height of the tide* at any time is the difference between the depth of water at that time and an established reference level called a *tidal datum*. Tidal datums differ in various areas of the world, the datum selected being an appropriate level near the lowest water that occurs at the place. This means that the water level can be *below* the tidal datum, as indicated by a minus sign. Because the tidal datum is used both for predicted tide levels as given in tide tables (p. 209) and for the chart datum (p. 59) on the largest-scale charts of the area, the depth of water at any time is the depth as shown on the chart plus the height of tide. When the water level is lower than the tidal datum, as indicated by a *negative tide*, the negative value is *subtracted* from the charted depth to determine the depth of water. *Thus the depth of water at a particular time can be less than the charted depth.* Heights are usually reckoned from a different reference level than the tidal datum, some form of high water being used. The height of the high-water reference level above the tidal datum is sometimes called the *rise* of the tide. The various reference levels for tides or heights are as follows:

Lowest low water, the lowest depth occurring at the place, or even a level slightly lower than this.

Lowest astronomical tide (*LAT*), the level of the lowest predicted low water caused by astronomical conditions.

Lowest normal low water, the approximate level of the average monthly low water.

Indian spring low water (*ISLW*), a low level including both spring and tropic effects, being approximately at the level of lower low water at the time of the Moon's maximum distance north or south of the equator. This datum is also called *Indian tide plane* and *harmonic tide plane*.

Mean lower low water springs (*MLLWS*), the average level of the lower of the two low waters at the times of spring tides.

Tropic lower low water (*TcLLW*), the average level of the lower of the two low tides at the time of maximum distance of the Moon north or south of the equator.

Equatorial spring low water (*EqSLW*), the average level of low water at the time of equatorial spring tides.

Mean lower low water (*MLLW*), the average level of lower low water.

Mean low water springs (*MLWS*), the average level of low water at the times of spring tides.

Mean low water (*MLW*), the average of all low tides at a place.

Mean sea level (*MSL*), the average level of the ocean. This level may be used for both depth of water and heights above it in an area where the tide is very small, as in the Baltic and Black Seas. *Half-tide level*, the level midway between mean high water and mean low water, or sometimes the level midway between consecutive high and low waters, may differ somewhat from mean sea level.

Mean high water (*MHW*), the average level of all high tides at a place.

Mean high water springs (*MHWS*), the average level of high water at the times of spring tides.

Mean higher high water (*MHHW*), the average level of higher high water.

Tropic higher high water (*TcHHW*), the average level of the higher of the two high tides at the time of maximum distance of the Moon north or south of the equator.

In the establishment of a reference level, abnormal effects attributable to meteorological conditions, run-off, or tsunamis are discarded. Normally, an established datum is not changed if subsequent observations indicates an error or change in the reference level.

Tides and their associated tidal streams (tidal currents) are of major interest to navigators, as they affect the depth and horizontal motion of the water in which a vessel operates. Depth is a consideration in selecting a safe route and perhaps the time of crossing a shoal. The height of the tide at any time may be significant if one is using soundings to help establish the position of one's craft. Horizontal motion of the water affects the dead reckoning and sometimes the process of position fixing, and may be a consideration in the selection of the time of entering or leaving a harbour, a favourable tidal stream (tidal current) sometimes contributing significantly to energy conservation.

In addition to tides in the water envelope covering some 71 per cent of the area of the world, tides also occur in the solid Earth and in the atmosphere surrounding the Earth, but these Earth and atmosphere tides are not readily apparent and are not a direct concern to the navigator.

11. Tidal Streams

As stated in section 10, water moving across the surface of the Earth in response to tidal forces is called a *tidal stream* or *tidal current*. The direction *toward* which any current flows is called its *set* (*S*), and its rate of motion, or speed, is usually called its *drift* (*D, Dr*). The speed of a tidal stream, however, as a component of the entire current in an area, is usually called its *velocity* (*vel.*) without regard to its direction of flow, being a scalar, rather than a vector, quantity. The maximum velocity of a tidal stream is called its *strength*.

Tidal streams and tides having a common origin, both are periodic and subject to the same cycles. In general, the various terms applied to tides apply with similar significance to tidal streams. Examples are semi-diurnal, diurnal, mixed, diurnal inequality, perigee, apogee, spring, neap, equatorial, tropic, equinoctial, and solstitial.

Tidal streams may be either *reversing* or *rotary*.

A reversing tidal stream flows alternately toward and away from land. While flowing toward land, it is called a *flood stream* or *flood current*, and while flowing away from land it is called an *ebb stream* or *ebb current*. Reversing tidal streams occur principally in estuaries and straits, where the direction of flow is restricted to some degree. As the direction of flow reverses, there is a moment of *slack water* when there is no flow, analogous to the stand of the tide. The velocity gradually increases from zero at slack water to maximum and then decreases to zero again at the next slack water. In general, maximum velocity occurs about midway between slack waters. A wide variation exists in the relationship of the strength of a tidal stream and the range of tide at the same place. Some areas of very great range of tide have relatively weak tidal streams. However, at a particular place the *variation* of strength is about the same as the *variation* of range of tide at the place.

Water flow in relation to a *progressive* wave, as the tide wave proceeding inbound or outbound in an estuary is called, is in the same direction as the wave motion in the crest, and in the opposite direction in the trough, maximum velocity being at the crest and trough, and minimum or no motion occurring approximately midway between the two. Thus, the strength of a tidal stream associated with a progressive tide wave occurs at the times of high tide and low tide, and slack water at about the time of mid tide. For a *standing* wave and a long-period wave exhibiting characteristics similar to those of a standing wave, the situation is different. Minimum flow occurs at the crest and trough, where there is no change in height, and maximum flow occurs approximately midway between the crest and trough. Accordingly, slack water occurs at high tide and at low tide, with strength at about mid tide.

As the actual tide at many places reflects some combination of progressive and standing waves, the time relationship of tides and tidal streams varies considerably from place to place, and from time to time at the same place. Accordingly, it is not wise to infer a given tidal-stream condition from tide predictions. In general, the times of slack water tend to agree closely with the times of high tide and low tide along an open coast, including indentations with wide openings. In relatively large bodies of water connected with the ocean by narrow passages, the maximum velocity of the streams at the entrance may be at the time of high tide or low tide, when the difference in the level of water at opposite ends of the entrance is maximum. At such times the strength of the tidal stream might reach velocities of as much as four or five knots, and where augmented by flow of water from the land, ebb velocities in excess of ten knots sometimes occur. Variation both in time and velocity of the tidal stream at different places within an estuary is extensive. In general, the velocity is greater and slack water occurs later in the principal channel than near the edges.

Tidal streams and their effects are modified by non-tidal flow, the total current at any time and place being the combined effect of all forces causing water flow. In the tidal portion of a river, and for some distance into the ocean, the flow of river water downstream may be the dominant feature. The period of flooding is shortened and the period of ebbing is lengthened. In some cases the flow may continue downstream but with decreased velocity at some periods when a flood stream would normally be expected. In a few places the opposite situation occurs at times because of unique conditions peculiar to those localities.

Where the flow of river water is comparable to or greater than the tidal flow, the water tends to stratify, the fresh river water tending to override the more dense sea water. Where the river flow is very great, fresh surface water may extend some distance seaward from the mouth of the river. A prime example is off the mouth of the Amazon River in South America. When the water in an estuary becomes stratified, the flow of water may vary considerably with depth. The flooding of sea water near the bottom may begin before the fresh surface water of the river ceases to ebb. The difference in time of slack water at the surface and the bottom may be more than an hour. Even though the water may be flowing in the same direction throughout its vertical extent, the velocity of the ebb tends to decrease with depth, while the velocity of the flood is the same or increases with depth. The effect on motion of a vessel might be different from that anticipated by observation of surface conditions only, depending upon its draught and local conditions. Shoaling because of sedimentation is more likely to occur in the tidal portion of a tidal river than in other estuaries. Sediments carried downstream by a river tend to remain suspended until they are eventually carried out to sea, where they may be deposited to form a bar, while sediments brought into the river from the ocean have a greater tendency to be deposited in the river because of the slower velocity of the ebb flow of the salt water. In estuaries where there is little or no river flow the periodic flushing is more efficient in preventing sedimentation because of the nearly equal velocity of the flood and ebb streams.

In a river, the greatest depth and velocity are generally near the middle of the river, where it is relatively straight. In a curve, deeper water and stronger current generally occur near the outer bank of the curve. Along the edges of a river, eddies and countercurrents flowing in the opposite direction to the main stream are not unusual, particularly along the inner portion of a curve in the river.

A *hydraulic stream* is a form of reversing tidal stream occurring in a narrow strait connecting two tidal bodies of water in which the height of water is periodically different because of differences in range and times of corresponding tidal stages. Water flows through the strait from the side of higher water to the side of lower water at a speed varying at about the square root of the difference in height of water. A hydraulic stream is characterized by short periods of weak

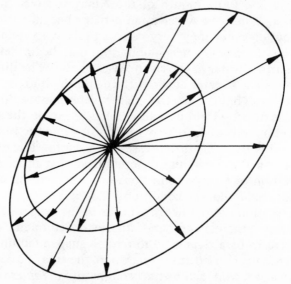

FIG. 418. A rotary tidal stream double ellipse.

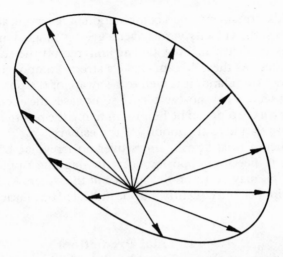

FIG. 419. A rotary tidal stream ellipse in an area of nontidal flow.

flow at slack water, and long periods of near-maximum velocity.

Offshore, where water is less restrained in its flow than in estuaries, the tidal stream is generally rotary because of Coriolis, its set changing progressively through all directions once or twice each tidal day. In general, the rotation is clockwise in the northern hemisphere and anticlockwise in the southern hemisphere. If arrows are drawn to represent, at intervals throughout one rotation, the direction of flow and the velocity of the tidal stream, and the outer ends of the arrows are connected by a curve, the figure approximates an ellipse because of variations in both the direction and velocity. If the curve is continued throughout a tidal day, it is likely to be a double ellipse because of the diurnal inequality, somewhat as shown in Fig. 418. If the rotary tidal stream is superimposed upon a non-tidal current, the shape of the figure representing the total current is also an ellipse, if the non-tidal current is constant, but offset, as shown in Fig. 419. If the non-tidal current is sufficiently strong, the origin of the arrows is *outside* the ellipse.

At sea, the tidal stream is generally weak, seldom exceeding one knot, and usually being much less. Along a coast, where the tidal stream may be a combination of reversing and rotary streams, the velocity varies over a greater range. Particularly strong tidal streams may be encountered off the entrance to estuaries. As these streams have a strong component toward or away from land, it is well to be aware of the possibility of being set toward shoal water. In some cases the encountering of such a current can be helpful in fixing the position of one's vessel relative to the mouth of the estuary.

When a tidal stream flows over an irregular bottom, or when it meets an opposing current, standing ripples, called *tide rips*, may occur on the surface of the water. Areas where tide rips occur frequently may be indicated on nautical charts.

12. Tidal Predictions

Predictions of the times and heights of tides, and the times and strengths of tidal streams, or tidal currents, have been made for various places throughout the world. These predictions are largely empirical, being based upon observations made over a period of time.

The tidal observations at a place are used to establish a number of *harmonic constituents* for that place. Each harmonic constituent is a sine wave representing one element of tide or tidal stream. The constituents reflect changing relative positions of the Earth, Moon, and Sun and the effects of bottom topography in shaping the tides and tidal streams at a place. As many as 55 harmonic constituents are identified for major tide stations. The predicted tide or tidal stream at a place is the sum of all harmonic constituents established for that place.

Because of the various tidal cycles involved, a period of the longest cycle of 18.6 years is desirable to identify completely all harmonic constituents for a place. However, they can be established with reasonable accuracy by observation over a period of one year, and a 29-day period of observation may suffice for establishment of the major constituents. The earliest known recording tide gauge used for providing a continuous record of the height of tide *vs.* time was established about 1850 at London. Previous to that, the height of tide was determined by periodic visual observation of the level of water with respect to a *tide staff*, or *tidepole*.

Tidal predictions are available in *Admiralty Tide Tables* published annually by the British Admiralty, and by separate tide and tidal current (tidal stream) tables published annually by the National Ocean Survey of the National Oceanic and Atmospheric Administration in the United States, as well as by other maritime nations and a number of non-government organizations. In general, tidal prediction tables provide complete information on times and heights of all high and low tides and times of slack waters and maximum velocity (speed) of tidal stream for a number of places called *standard ports* in British publications and *reference stations* in United States publications. For each of a larger number of *secondary ports*, in British tables, tabulations of the four principal harmonic constituents or tidal differences are given, to be applied to the information tabulated for a stated standard port having the same type of tide or tidal stream. Similarly, U.S. tide and tidal current tables give tidal differences for a large number of *subordinate stations*. Tidal prediction publications generally have auxiliary tables and diagrams providing additional useful data, as for determining the height of tide and velocity (speed) of the tidal stream at any time. In addition, tidal-stream charts and atlases are published for a number of major ports. These reflect average conditions which may vary from the detailed information given in the tidal-stream tables for a specific time. A limited amount of tidal information may be given on a nautical chart, and sailing directions usually include general information and warnings relating to specific conditions at various places. If the lunitidal interval (p. 200) of a place is known, it provides means of determining the approximate *times* of tides.

In using tidal predictions, one should remember that, except for very short-term local predictions, they exclude factors that cannot be predicted a long time in advance, such as those attributable to meteorological conditions, abnormal run-off from land, and tsunamis. One should remember, also, that during periods of high atmospheric pressure or strong offshore winds the tide may be lower than normal. Tides in rivers are likely to be higher than predicted after heavy rain or melting snow in the watershed areas result in increased flow in the rivers. The range of tide and strength of tidal streams are generally less along an open coast than in an estuary. Variations over short distances within an estuary, particularly a narrow one of irregular shape and depth, are generally greater than along an open coast or in a large enclosed basin. Tidal streams increase in velocity through restrictions caused by a decrease in width or depth. One should remember, too, that currents other than the tidal stream may be present, particularly offshore, and that the effect upon the position of a vessel is a function of the total resultant current in the area. Within estuaries, however, the tidal stream predictions generally are for the total current to the extent to which it can be predicted a long time in advance. The effect of any current in altering the position of a vessel increases as the speed of the vessel decreases, because of the longer time in which the current acts. In general, tidal predictions, both with respect to tides and tidal streams are less reliable where there is a large diurnal inequality (p. 191) than elsewhere.

13. Ocean Currents

Water in motion across the surface of the Earth is called a *current*, though in British terminology the term is generally restricted in its application to non-tidal flow to distinguish it from tidal streams. The direction *toward* which the water moves is the *set* (S) of the current, and the speed of flow is the *drift* (D, Dr). The large mass of water comprising the Earth's oceans is in continuous motion. Some well-defined streams flow with great persistence, while others are largely seasonal, and still others are temporary during short periods of favourable conditions. Some are relatively shallow, some are of considerable vertical extent, and some are subsurface only. Some are relatively narrow, fast-moving streams and others are broad, slow-moving *drift currents*. Some are warm relative to surrounding water, and some are cold.

This great diversity among ocean currents reflects the variations in cause, location, and topography. Although knowledge of ocean currents is incomplete, several causes of water movement have been identified:

Wind. The major ocean current-producing force is wind as it blows across the surface of the water. A wind continuing at approximately the same speed in nearly the same direction over a long distance (called the *fetch*) for a considerable period of time sets up a current that attains a drift of as much as three per cent, or more, of the wind speed after about 12 hours of continuous wind. A local *wind-induced current* (also called *wind-drift current*) produced by a temporary wind may extend vertically downward for about 100 metres, but more-or-less permanent currents caused by prevailing winds that blow with great persistence in nearly the same direction may have a much greater vertical extent, with a tremendous volume of water being transported.

In shallow water the set of a wind-induced current is nearly the same as the direction of motion of the wind that causes it. Because of Coriolis (p. 193), the flow in deeper water is deflected toward the right in the northern hemisphere and the left in the southern hemisphere. The deflection increases with depth of water, reaching a theoretical maximum of 45° in the deepest portion of the oceans. Because of other modifying factors, such as the shape of the basin, deflections of as much as 60° have been observed. These figures refer to the surface current. Because of internal friction within the water, the deflection increases and the drift decreases, both progressively, with increased depth. A line connecting the outer ends of vectors originating along a vertical line and representing the velocity (set and drift) at various depths forms a curve known as the *Ekman spiral*, Fig. 420, postulated by V. W. Ekman early in the twentieth century. At a depth of about 100 metres the set of the current is opposite to that at the surface, but the drift is only about 4 per cent of the surface rate. The total movement of water in the 100-metre surface layer is 90° to the right of the direction of wind motion in the northern hemisphere, and 90° to the left in the southern hemisphere.

Because of the 90° difference in the direction of wind and water motion, water tends to pile up at the centre of a high-

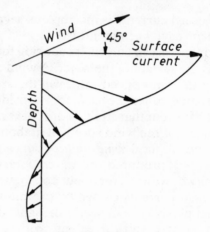

FIG. 420. The Ekman spiral.

pressure area, and move away from the centre of a low-pressure area. In broad ocean areas, where the flow of water is unhampered by land and the depth is sufficient for the full effect, this flow from a low-pressure area to a high-pressure area predominates over the opposite, direct effect of atmospheric pressure in depressing or raising the water level and causing flow in the opposite direction, a condition affecting the height of tide in shallow-water coastal areas. Accordingly, the height of water at the centre of a somewhat permanent high-pressure area such as the mid North Atlantic is about 1.5 metres greater than along the coasts of Europe and North America. In permanent low-pressure areas the height is of the order of 0.5 metre less than in surrounding areas.

Gravity waves. A particle of water in motion because of *gravity waves*, the ordinary wind-induced waves in the ocean, moves in nearly a vertical circle. At the crest of a wave the particle moves in the same direction as the wave. As the crest passes, the motion is downward, then in the direction opposite to wave motion as the trough passes, and finally upward as the next crest approaches. The speed of particle motion is slightly greater at the crest than at the trough. Accordingly, at the end of each cycle it has advanced a short distance in the direction of motion of the waves, as shown,

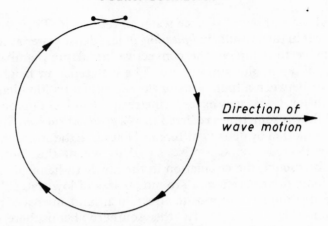

FIG. 421. Motion of a particle of water during passage of a wave.

exaggerated, in Fig. 421. In deep water the *gravity-wave current* thus induced is very weak. But in shallow water as the wave approaches a shore, the circulatory motion becomes elliptical, the horizontal motion predominating. At the end of its travel on a sloping beach a wave breaks and the water rushes up the slope until its energy is dissipated and it is carried back to sea by the force of gravity. If waves strike a beach at an oblique angle, a component of motion parallel to the shore sets up a narrow *longshore current* along the beach. This effect may be diminished somewhat by *refraction* or bending of the waves toward the beach. Ocean waves being caused primarily by wind, *a wave-induced current* can be considered a secondary form of wind-induced current.

Density. The density of sea water varies with temperature, pressure, and salinity. The pressure at any given depth being essentially constant, the principal factors affecting density-induced ocean currents are differences in temperature and salinity. Increased salinity, producing more dense water, may occur in an area of high evaporation, as in the Mediterranean Sea, or in an area of extensive sea-ice formation, as along the Antarctic coast. Decreased salinity may occur in an area of extensive dilution of fresh water flowing from land, as off the mouth of a large river.

As water increases in density, it sinks to the bottom,

resulting in flow of surface water to replace it. This *density current* in turn results in *upwelling* of less dense water at some distance to complete the convective circulation, similar to that of air in the atmosphere. The difference in height of water between a high-density (low-level) and a low-density (high-level) area may exceed a metre in 100 miles. This down-hill flow is sometimes referred to as a *gradient current*. Water set in motion by density difference, like air in the atmosphere, is deflected by Coriolis, so that when the flow is unobstructed, the circulation in the northern hemisphere is cyclonic or anticlockwise around an area of low water (high density) and in the opposite direction around an area of high water (low density). In the southern hemisphere the directions of flow are opposite to those in the northern hemisphere. The flow tends to be along *isopycnic lines*, which are lines connecting points of the same density at the same depth, similar to *geostrophic winds* along isobars in the atmosphere.

Tide. Tidal currents, or streams, affect the flow of water in the oceans as discussed in section 11.

Run-off. Water flowing from rivers into the ocean have a direct effect by its motion, and secondary effect by its influence upon the density of the ocean water, discussed previously.

The various forces at work in the oceans produce a continuous circulation of water, both in the horizontal and in the vertical. Wind being the principal factor in producing the ocean currents, the oceanic flow is related roughly to the pattern of prevailing winds, but with variations attributable primarily to the presence of land obstruction to flow of water.

The general horizontal circulation varies somewhat seasonally, particularly in an area where strong seasonal variations in winds occur. An excellent example is in the monsoon area of the northern Indian Ocean. The principal features of the oceanic circulation during the northern hemisphere winter are shown in Fig. 422. This flow is characterized by subtropical anticyclonic gyres (clockwise in the northern hemisphere and anticlockwise in the southern hemisphere) in the Atlantic, Pacific, and Indian Oceans;

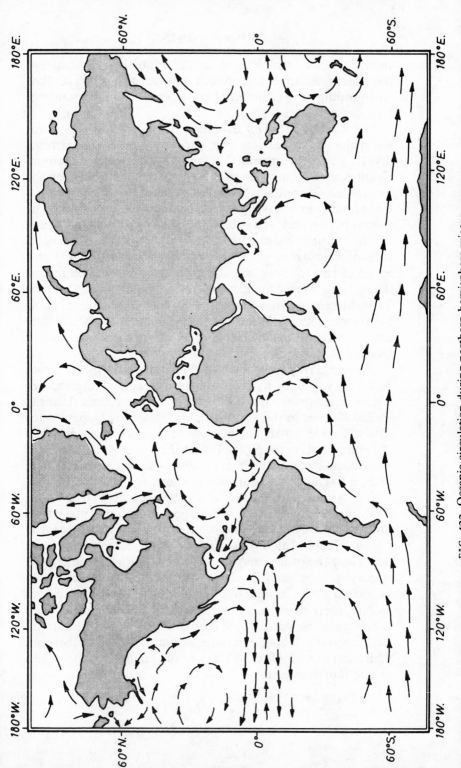

FIG. 422. Oceanic circulation during northern hemisphere winter.

small subpolar cyclonic gyres in higher northerly latitudes of the North Atlantic and North Pacific; and a zonal flow surrounding the Antarctic continent in high southern latitudes.

The *North* and *South Equatorial Currents* flow westward. As major land barriers are encountered, these currents divide, part curving and flowing eastward in an *Equatorial Countercurrent* some 300 to 500 kilometres wide between the Equatorial Currents. The water transport of the Equatorial Countercurrents varies greatly, from one to 60 million cubic metres per second, at a speed of the order of one knot. Much of the return water flows in the *Cromwell Current*, a subsurface current some 300 kilometres wide flowing at a speed of two to three knots at a depth of 100 to 300 metres below the surface, the maximum flow being at 200 metres. This current, with a transport of some 40 million cubic metres per second, is centred on the equator in the Atlantic and Pacific, and somewhat south of the equator in the Indian Ocean.

The western part of each of the subtropical gyres moves poleward in a narrow, deep current of relatively high speed. These currents are the *Gulf Stream* in the North Atlantic, *Brazil Current* in the South Atlantic, *Kuroshio* (Japanese for 'Black Stream', so named because of the dark water of which it is composed) in the North Pacific, *East Australia Current* in the South Pacific, and the *Agulhas Current* in the Indian Ocean. Each of these currents is about 100 kilometres wide and has a maximum speed that may be in excess of four knots. They are relatively deep. While most ocean currents extend downward only about one kilometre, the Gulf Stream is known to extend all the way to the bottom, some 5 kilometres deep, and the others may do so. The result is a tremendous transport of water. The Gulf Stream transport has been estimated to be as much as 100 million cubic metres per second, more than 100 times the combined transport of all of the rivers of the world. If the Kuroshio extends to the bottom, its transport is about the same as that of the Gulf Stream, while that of each of the other currents ranges from one tenth to one fourth as much.

As the currents curve eastward, they spread out and become broad, slow-moving drift currents. The gyres are completed by motion toward the equator. These equatorward currents are broad, typically 500 to 1,000 kilometres across, slow-moving, and not well defined. They are known as the *Canary Current* in the North Atlantic, the *Benguela Current* in the South Atlantic, the *California Current* in the North Pacific, the *Peru* or *Humboldt Current* in the South Pacific, and the *West Australia Current* in the Indian Ocean. The transport of water in one of these currents is typically one tenth to one fourth that of the Gulf Stream or Kuroshio. The marked disparity between the western poleward part of each subtropical gyre and the eastern equatorward part is accounted for by the fact that in the poleward flow the natural circular flow caused by the prevailing winds and land configuration is augmented by an increasing Coriolis effect, so that the two effects tend to reinforce one another; while in the equatorward flow the two forces are in opposition as the Coriolis effect is decreasing.

The subpolar gyres are weaker and transport far less water than the subtropical gyres.

The *Antarctic Circumpolar Current* is unique in that it flows eastward through all longitudes around Antarctica, its only major deflection being in the relatively narrow strait between South America and the northward extension of Antarctica to the south. Although this current is typically 1,000 kilometres wide and flows at a speed of about 0.4 knot, its transport of water is about the same as that of the Gulf Stream or the Kuroshio.

A current of interest primarily because of its great speed is known as a *turbidity current*. When large quantities of sediment become suspended, as by earthquake, the turbid water may become of sufficient density to plunge down a slope under the force of gravity, similar to an avalanche on land. Speeds as high as 60 knots have been reached by such temporary subsurface currents.

The general circulation that has been described has many variations and numerous exceptions associated with local conditions. Well-established currents, particularly those relatively narrow, high-speed ones, are subject to meanders that vary in position and time, and may be accompanied by eddies and countercurrents along their edges. The current data available on nautical charts, pilot charts, and sailing directions and tidal stream (tidal current) tables is a reasonably reliable guide to the currents one might expect at a particular time and place. All such data, however, are averages. The prudent navigator is alert to changes in standard conditions used in predictions, and in the possibility of vagaries that may cause variation from the best-available information.

A navigator's primary interest in ocean currents relates to their effect upon the dead reckoning of his vessel, his speed over the ground being the vector sum of his speed through the water and the horizontal speed of the water over the ground. This problem is discussed in section 3. Indirect effects are also of interest to a navigator. Fog may form when warm, moist air cools as it travels over a cold ocean current. This is called *advection fog* to distinguish it from *radiation fog* that forms over land that cools during the night, lowering the temperature of the air immediately over it. A form of fog called *frost smoke* or *arctic sea smoke* results from apparent steaming of relatively warm water in the presence of much colder air. Warm water has greater evaporation than cold water. The warming of air over a warm current, and the opposite effect over a cold current, affect the air circulation and atmospheric pressure pattern. The effect of ocean currents on climate is apparent in areas where onshore winds reflect the temperature of the water near the coast. Thus, England and southern Alaska, each influenced by a relatively warm ocean current, are warmer than an area at the same latitude but with a cold current offshore, such as Labrador. South-western Iceland has a higher average winter temperature than New York City, although the latter is more than 20° farther south.

The famed mild climate of a narrow strip of coastal land in California, on the west coast of North America, is partly the result of a favourable situation relative to ocean currents. During the summer, breezes from the relatively cool

California Current keep the air temperature down. Additionally, in Southern California, the moist air cools during the night, clouds form, and the surface is shielded from the warming rays of the sun until the clouds dissipate during the late morning or early afternoon. During the winter the California Current is pushed westward by the weak but warm *Davidson Current* flowing northward immediately offshore. Onshore breezes are warmed by the water of this current. As a result, the average temperature varies little between summer and winter, remaining at a pleasant level throughout the year. One additional effect contributes further to this condition. During the spring and early summer, the prevailing wind has a southerly component off Southern California. This produces an offshore transport of water, with its accompanying upwelling of relatively cold water near the shore, resulting in later onset of warm summer weather. The opposite effect occurs in late summer and early fall, again delaying the onset of colder weather. At San Diego, on the southern border of the United States, the average daily high temperature in November is several degrees higher than in June.

In addition to direct meterological effects, ocean currents affect navigation by physically transporting ice to latitudes lower than those in which the ice forms. Icebergs are a menace to shipping in the North Atlantic, being carried southward by the cold *Labrador Current* flowing out of Baffin Bay. Sea ice, but not icebergs, is carried southward through the Bering Strait into the Pacific.

The cold Peru Current, also called the Humboldt Current, flows northward along the western coast of South America. Under the combined influence of offshore winds and Coriolis the current curves westward at about latitude 6° south, and flows toward the Galapagos Islands. Upwelling of even colder water occurs at several locations along the coast, bringing up nutrients for enough plankton to feed one of the world's largest fish populations. Harvesting of great quantities of this seafood is a major industry of Peru. During February and March of each year a tongue of the warm Equatorial Countercurrent setting southward meets the Peru

Current and joins it in its westward flow. This warm tongue is called *El Niño*, 'The Child' after the Christ Child. At intervals of about seven years El Niño becomes much stronger, for reasons not fully understood, forcing its way between the Peru Current and the coast as far south as latitude 12° south. When this occurs, upwelling ceases and the supply of nutrients is cut off, with an accompanying catastrophic destruction of plankton and fish life. Decaying marine organisms release hydrogen sulphide gas that discolours sea water and, when combined with fog, blackens the paint of ships. The normally arid coastal region is drenched by heavy rains, resulting in floods and severe damage to agricultural crops. This disastrous situation is called the *El Niño Effect*.

V
Pilotage

1. Definition
Pilotage, sometimes called *piloting*, is the navigation of a craft relative to geographical points. In a broad sense, it may be considered the same as position fixing, as contrasted with dead reckoning. In general usage, however, the term refers to the entire process of navigating a craft near the shore or other dangers to navigation by reference to aids to navigation, landmarks, seamarks, soundings, and radar data. Areas in which pilotage is customarily used are called *pilotage waters*, often shortened to *pilot waters*.

Unlike the somewhat leisurely process at sea, where navigation consists principally of dead reckoning, with occasional position fixing, and where mistakes can usually be detected and corrected with impunity, pilotage requires alertness, constant attention to detail, and the frequent exercise of good judgement. Mistakes can be costly, even fatal. In confined waters, as in a harbour, the navigator is concerned not only with almost continuous fixing of the position of his vessel, but also with projecting its movements ahead, to be confident that his vessel is not heading into danger, keeping always in mind its manoeuvering characteristics, and allowing an adequate margin of safety. Thorough knowledge of local conditions and the state of the tide, tidal stream, and weather is important, as is mastery of the principles of pilotage, and intimate acquaintance with large-scale charts and sailing directions of the area to be traversed.

2. Position Lines
Position determination by pilotage makes extensive use of *position lines* (*PL's*) (p. 17). Although measurements and

the usual means of representing them are subject to errors and approximations, carefully-established position lines are sufficiently accurate to serve well an important need of the navigator.

Customarily, position lines are utilized by plotting on the chart or plotting sheet. Usually, only a short segment of the line near the DR position is plotted, to avoid clutter and possible confusion. One should be particularly careful to avoid plotting the line through chart symbols, if this can be avoided, for charts are usually used many times, and repeated erasures might render the symbol indistinct. It is good practice to label a position line *at the time of plotting*, as a safeguard against error. In most cases an appropriate label consists of the time to the nearest minute, in four digits, above the line, and, if needed, identification of the line below it. An exception to the rule of always labelling a position line is sometimes made in congested waters where position fixing is almost continuous, when lines might be labelled at intervals, as when shifting from one observed object to another for position lines.

A position line might be part of a great circle, small circle, or some other curve, notably a hyperbola.

A great-circle position line is established by measuring the direction, or bearing (p. 21), of some identifiable object or point, the position of which is known with sufficient accuracy to make it useful for navigation, or occasionally by measurement of the direction of the craft from the object. Bearings can be measured in a variety of ways, but however measured, only *true bearings (TB)* are plotted, any other form being first converted to the equivalent true bearing. A true bearing is expressed as an angle in three digits, from 000° at true north clockwise through 360°.

Although a bearing is part of a great circle, its representation as a straight line on a Mercator chart is customary and of adequate accuracy unless the object is easterly or westerly and of greater than normal visual range or the vessel is in very high latitude. The error introduced by using a rhumb line to represent a bearing line is usually of significance only when the bearing is measured by a radio direction-finder (p. 481). The means of applying a suitable correction is explained on page 487. A typical bearing line is shown plotted in Fig. 501. Only the part in the vicinity of the craft, shown as a solid line, is plotted. If it serves a useful purpose, the bearing is shown as a three-digit number (080 in this case) below the line, under the time label. The unit (degree) is understood and need not be indicated. If the beacon bore 080° from the craft, the direction of the craft from the beacon is assumed to be the reciprocal of 080°, or 260°.

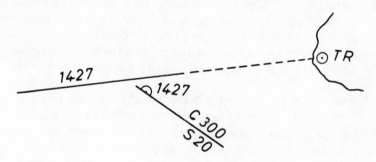

FIG. 501. Plot of a bearing line.

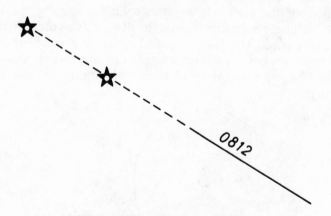

FIG. 502. Plot of a transit, or range.

A useful special case of a bearing occurs when two objects are seen in line, one directly behind the other. This is known as a *transit* or *range*. Any two identifiable objects can be used. If the positions of the two objects are located on the chart, a line through them, extended to the vicinity of the craft, constitutes the position line. No measurement of direction is necessary, but might be useful in identification of the objects. The label need consist only of the time, as shown in Fig. 502. Because of the usefulness of transits in providing immediate and sometimes continuous information, pairs of beacons are established in line with some channels, so that a vessel need only keep the beacons in line to stay in the channel. One must be careful, of course, to know when to turn to avoid running aground at the end of the channel. Sometimes a natural range can be found to mark a turning point, or perhaps this point might be marked by a buoy or other object which indicates the time to turn when it is abeam or at some preselected bearing.

If the distance to an object is known, the position line is a small circle with centre at the object and with radius equal to the known distance. At distances normally measured, the representation of the position line as the arc of a circle on the nautical chart, as shown in Fig. 503, does not introduce significant error. Only that part of the position line in the vicinity of the craft, shown as a solid line in Fig. 503, is plotted. The label indicates that the distance was measured at 1158. If desired, the distance (1.6M in this case) can be shown below the arc, under the time label. The unit (nautical mile) should be indicated if there is any possibility of mistaken identity.

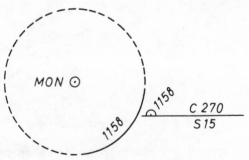

FIG. 503. Plot of a small-circle position line.

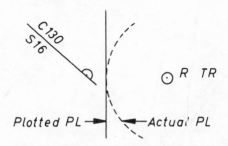

FIG. 504. Use of a tangent to represent
a small-circle position line.

If the distance is considerable and the craft is believed to be near the dead-reckoning position, a straight line perpendicular to a line from the object through the dead-reckoning position at the measured distance is adequate and may be more convenient to draw. If other information indicates error in the dead reckoning, a second approximation might be needed. If the bearing of the object is measured at approximately the same time as the distance, the tangent should be drawn perpendicular to the bearing line. Fig. 504 shows the nature of the principal error introduced by using a tangent to represent a small circle. The additional error introduced by using a rhumb line to represent the tangent is negligible. If a small-circle PL is always plotted as a circle, errors associated with the difference between a circle and its tangent are avoided.

Another means of establishing a small-circle PL is by determining the difference in bearing of two objects. The PL is a small circle through the two objects and the observer. With insignificant error, the centre of the circle can be considered to lie on the perpendicular bisector of the straight line joining the two objects, at a point where the angle subtended by the line joining the objects is twice the measured angle, as shown in Fig. 505.

If the difference in distance between two points is known, the position line is a *hyperbola*, and is referred to as a *hyperbolic position line*. Such a line, usually established by radio, is discussed in chapter X (p. 500).

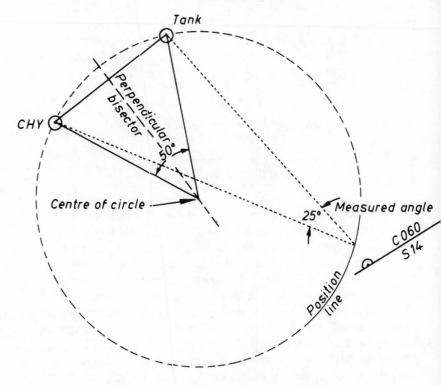

FIG. 505. A small-circle position line from
direction-difference measurement.

The time of making any reading for a position line, and the data observed, should be recorded in the navigator's notebook (p. 155).

3. The Fix

Two simultaneous intersecting position lines, however determined, cross at a point called a *fix*. Perhaps the most frequently-used combination of position lines in pilotage is two bearing lines. However, two distance circles, a transit (range) and a bearing line, a bearing line and distance circle, two direction-difference measurements, and two hyperbolic position lines are also used. If position lines intersect at more than one point, as might occur with a bearing line relating to one object and a distance circle relating to another, the correct intersection is usually apparent. If it is not, one might well use the less favourable one, run dead reckoning from both intersections until the correct one can be determined, or seek a third position line to resolve the ambiguity.

Fig. 506 shows a fix by two bearing lines. Note that the fix is indicated by a small circle enclosing the intersection of the position lines and by a label indicating the time. The plot and

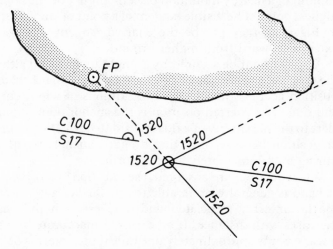

FIG. 506. A fix by two bearings.

symbol identifies the position as a fix, but the word 'Fix' might be added to the time label if desired. Note that the position-line labels are *along* the lines, and that the fix label is not, preferably being horizontal. A new DR plot is started from the fix.

When a choice of objects is available, the ones used should be selected carefully. An important consideration is the angle of cut (p. 32) of the position lines, the effect of which is illustrated in Figs. 108 and 109, indicating that the ideal is 90°. For this reason, simultaneous observations of both the bearing and distance of the same object is particularly desirable, the angle of cut always being 90°. An angle of cut of less than 30 should be avoided where possible. The general direction in which a pattern of objects observed provides the greatest fixing accuracy is called the *line of shoot*.

Correct identification both of the object and the part observed is essential to accurate position fixing. Where several similar objects are close together, care is needed to be certain of the identity of the one observed. A flagpole, cupola, or tower rarely presents a problem of the part of an object observed, but a prominent building might. The charted summit of a nearby mountain peak might not be the apparent highest point. The visible tangent of a point of land, as shown in Fig. 506, may not be the charted tangent if a low spit extends seaward from higher ground.

A buoy might be secured by a single anchor, and although the scope of the anchor cable might be small, *some* change of position occurs with changing conditions of wind, current, and tide. The charted position is the anchor. One should be alert to the possibility of a floating aid to navigation being out of position because of having dragged anchor, particularly during and immediately after a storm.

When bearings are observed, the selection of an object near at hand is generally preferable to one farther away, because the linear error associated with any error in the bearing increases with distance. If a bearing is inaccurate by 1, the linear error is approximately one mile if the object is 60 miles away, but only about 32 metres if the object is one mile distant.

Although two position lines intersecting at a good angle are adequate for establishing a fix, it is good practice to use a third line when one is available. The increase in accuracy is small, but the third position line provides a check on the other two. If the three position lines cross at a point, one can usually be confident of the reliability of the data used, but should not neglect the possibility of offsetting errors. Frequently, three position lines form a small triangle called a *cocked hat*, as shown in Fig. 507. If the navigator considers the error of reasonable size for the situation, and the position lines to be of equal accuracy, he uses as the fix that point within the triangle equidistant from the three sides.

However, if a series of fixes are cocked hats of about the

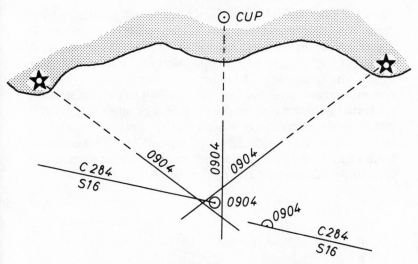

FIG. 507. A cocked hat from three bearings.

same size, the navigator might well suspect the presence of a constant error. Consider the situation of a fix determined by three bearings, as shown in Fig. 508. Each bearing is in error

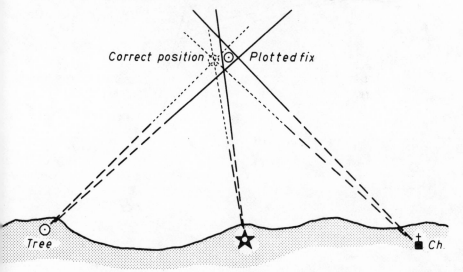

FIG. 508. Constant error in asymmetrical bearings.

by +3°. The pecked lines show the correct position of the craft. Note that the correct position lies *outside* the triangle. If the objects observed had been equally separated in bearing, as shown in Fig. 509, the correct position of the craft would be inside the triangle. Therefore, as a protection against constant error one should select three objects symmetrically separated in bearing when possible. But because this often is not possible, particularly when *coasting* (proceeding along a coast sufficiently close to fix position periodically by means of landmarks or aids to navigation), one should be alert to the possibility of constant error.

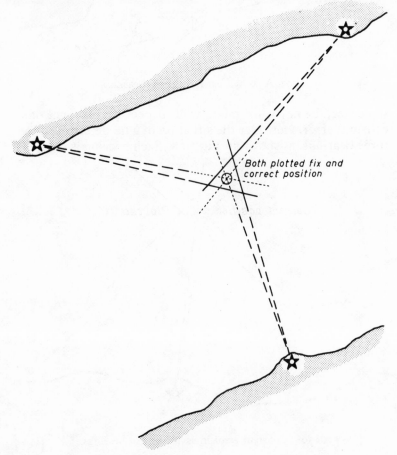

FIG. 509. Constant error in symmetrical bearings.

If one suspects a non-constant error, perhaps because of an unusually large cocked hat, the accuracy might be improved by making a new round of observations for a new fix. A different approach is to observe four objects, where possible. If only one of the position lines has a large error, its identity can be established by inspection of the plot, as shown in Fig. 510.

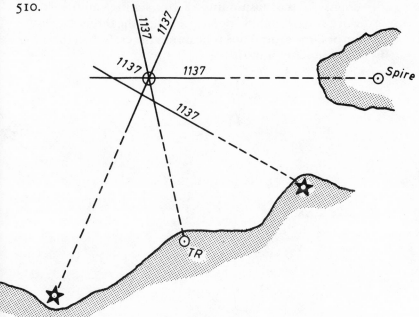

FIG. 510. Use of a fourth bearing to identify an erroneous bearing.

Direction-difference measurements are usually used in pairs. Three objects are selected and the angles between the central object and the other two are observed by sextant or the differences in bearings. Position is determined by setting the movable arms of a station pointer, or three-arm protractor, (p. 87) to the two measured angles and placing the device over the chart so that the three arms are directly over the three objects observed. The position of the observer is at the common intersection of the three arms. If a station pointer is not available, intersecting lines can be drawn on transparent material which is placed over the chart as before. The direction-difference method has the advantage of eliminating any constant error in measurement of direction. However, if the three objects and the observer are all on the same small circle, the two circular position lines coincide and no fix is obtained. Such a pair of angles, called a *swinger* or *revolver*, is analogous to bearings of two objects in the same or reciprocal directions. If the positioning of the station pointer is not critical, a swinger should be suspected. If the three objects are in line, or if the central one is nearer to the craft than the other two, a swinger is impossible.

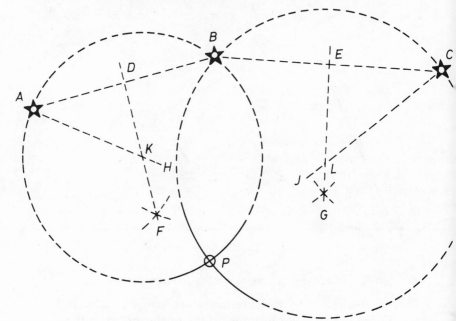

FIG. 511. Direction-difference position lines by plot.

A method of determining position of the craft from direction-difference measurements without use of a station pointer or transparent material is by plotting the small-circle position lines directly on the chart. Refer to Fig. 511. Observers aboard a ship simultaneously measure angles of 53° between lights A and B and 50° between lights B and C. On the chart, straight lines are drawn connecting A B and

BC. Lines D F and E G are drawn as perpendicular bisectors of AB and BC, respectively. Lines AH and C J are drawn with angle BAH being 37°, the complement of the measured angle between A and B, and angle BCJ being 40°, the complement of the measured angle between B and C. If either measured angle is more than 90°, the complement is the measured angle minus 90°, and is measured on the opposite side of AB, or CB, *away* from the craft. The centres of the small-circle position lines are at K and L, respectively, at the intersections of AH and C J with the perpendicular bisectors. Angles AKD and CLE are 53° and 50°, respectively, the measured angles. In Fig. 511 the entire small-circle position lines, ABP and BCP are shown, fixing the position of the craft at P, but only those parts in the vicinity of the craft, as shown by the solid arcs, need be drawn. This method has the advantage of being applicable when four objects are used for the two direction-difference measurements. Also, if the two angles are not measured simultaneously, the earlier position line can be advanced (section 4) by advancing the centre of the circle. The approach to a swinger is apparent by the acuteness of the angle of cut of the two small-circle position lines.

An alternative method of plotting when three objects are sighted, without drawing the small-circle position lines, is illustrated in Fig. 512, using the same data as in Fig. 511.

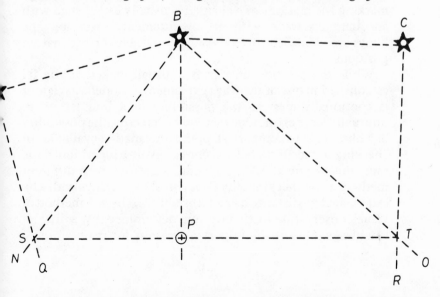

FIG. 512. Direction-difference position by plot.

Straight lines are drawn connecting AB and BC, as before. Lines BN and BO are drawn from B so that angle ABN is 37°, the complement of the measured angle between A and B, and angle CBO is 40°, the complement of the measured angle between B and C. If either measured angle is more than 90°, the complement (the measured angle minus 90°) is measured on the opposite side of AB and BC, or *away* from the craft. From A a line AQ is drawn perpendicular to AB, intersecting BN at S. Similarly, from C a line CR is drawn perpendicular to CB, intersecting BO at T. Points S and T are then connected by a straight line, and a line is drawn from B perpendicular to ST, intersecting that line at P, the position of the ship. The nearer S and T are together, the nearer the situation approaches a swinger. The assumption that the Earth is considered flat introduces negligible error at the distances usually involved.

Soundings can be helpful in establishing position of a vessel, as explained in section 9 (p. 256).

The simplest method of all of determining position of a craft has not been mentioned. This is by direct visual observation. If a vessel passes a buoy close aboard, its position is alongside the charted position of the buoy, allowing for any difference between the charted and actual positions. Similarly, the position of a ship midway between two buoys marking the margins of a channel is usually established with adequate accuracy without measurement, assuming the buoys are identified correctly and are in their correct charted positions.

While the position of a craft is usually taken as the fix established in one of the ways explained, a prudent navigator is continually alert to the possibility of a blunder or an unusually large error. One method of detecting the possibility of a blunder is to compare all of the information available. In checking the accuracy of a fix, one can avoid a repetition of the same mistake by checking the craft's position by a different method, as by checking a fix established by bearings with a fix established by distances, or a fix established by any method of visual observation with position determined by a line of soundings. One of the important reasons for maintaining a continuous dead reckoning is to provide a means of checking fix accuracy. Even an apparently reliable fix can be in error. If the discrepancy between a fix and the dead-reckoning position for the same time is larger than seems reasonable by considering the conditions involved, a wise navigator immediately seeks to either verify the difference or reconcile it. A practice helpful in avoiding mistakes is to ask oneself whether every item of information received, and every part of a calculation or plot, is reasonable. An understanding of the nature of navigational errors, discussed briefly in section 6 of chapter 1, a thorough acquaintance with local conditions, and experience are all helpful in evaluating a situation where reasonable doubt of the most probable position of the craft exists.

A new dead-reckoning plot is usually started from a fix. However, if the accuracy of a fix is in doubt, the navigator might elect to continue the previous dead-reckoning plot until the accuracy of the fix can be verified. If the craft is close to shoal water, good practice is to run the new plot from the most unfavourable position indicated by the data available. In congested waters where position fixing is almost continuous, a new dead reckoning plot might be started at intervals, or omitted entirely.

4. The Running Fix

When simultaneous or nearly simultaneous observations are not possible, one sometimes resorts to a *running fix*. This situation might occur when only one suitable object is available for observation, or during periods of restricted visibility.

A running fix is obtained by adjusting observations made at different times to a common time. The usual method of doing this is by *advancing* a position line for the distance and direction travelled between observations. Refer to Fig. 513. At 1523 the navigator of a ship steaming on course 300° at 20 knots observes a lighthouse bearing 000°. Six minutes later, at 1529, the ship has moved, by dead reckoning, two miles along its course line. The position line is advanced *parallel to itself* in the same direction and at the same speed as the ship, and given a double time-label to indicate both the time of observation and the time to which the line is advanced. The validity of this procedure is evident from the fact that if the ship is actually on the original position line at the time of observation, and makes good the distance and direction indicated, it will be on the advanced line at the time indicated, whatever its position on the original line at the time of observation.

The position of the advanced position line can be determined by measuring the course and distance from any point on the original line. A convenient point is often the intersection of the position line and the course line, point A, which is advanced to point A'. Another method, usually the most convenient for advancing a small-circle position line established by measurement of distance, is to advance the position of the object observed, as shown by the pecked line BB' in Fig. 513. This method has the advantage of not requiring the plotting of the original position line, before advancement, thus reducing the clutter on the chart. Another method is to drop a perpendicular from the DR position at 1523 to the position line, intersecting it at C. From the DR position at 1529 a new perpendicular is dropped parallel to the first and of the same length, locating C'.

If the position line had been moved *back* to an earlier time, rather than *ahead*, to a later time, it would be said to be *retired*.

In the example, the running fix is completed by observing the lighthouse at the time of the advanced position line, as shown in Fig. 514. In practice, these steps are reversed, the second observation being made and the resulting position line plotted, and the first position line then being advanced to the time of the second observation. The intersection of the adjusted position line with the other is the running fix and is labelled 'R Fix' (to distinguish it from a fix) and the time of the position line that was not adjusted. Note that the interval between observations was selected to allow sufficient change of direction between position lines to provide a good angle of cut, and at a convenient 6 minutes or 0.1 hour. A new DR plot is started from a running fix unless its accuracy is questioned.

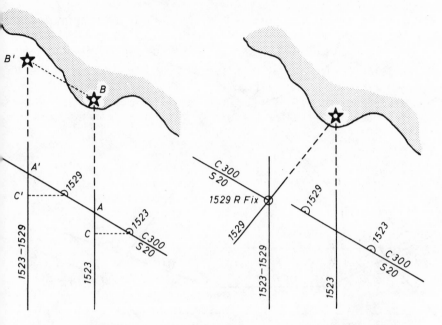

FIG. 513. Advancing a position line.   FIG. 514. A running fix.

If the craft changes course or speed between observations, the procedure is the same, but may be simplified if the equivalent single course and distance are substituted for the actual courses and distances, as shown in Fig. 515. In the illustration, a vessel rounds a point by steaming on the courses and at the speeds shown. At 1218 the light bears 040°, and at 1230 it bears 321°. The two bearing lines are plotted, as shown. The pecked line connecting the DR positions at 1218 and 1230 represents the equivalent course and distance between observations. From any convenient point A on the 1218 bearing line this equivalent course and distance is measured, locating point A', and the advanced position line is drawn through this point. The running fix is located at the intersection of the advanced 1218 position line and the 1230 position line, as shown. Note that the advanced 1218 position line has the same relationship to the 1230 DR position that the original position line does to the 1218 DR, and that the

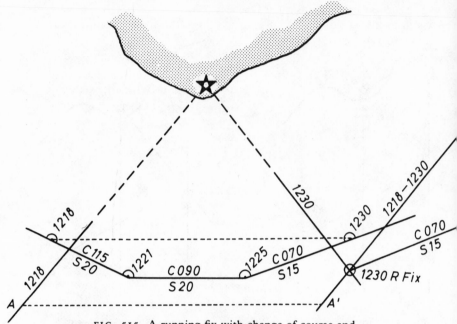

FIG. 515. A running fix with change of course and
speed between observations.

method of advancing the position of the object observed
would have resulted in the same position of the advanced
position line. Note, also, that the intersections of the position
lines with the course line have no significance, and that the
distance from the D R position at 1218 to the intersection with
the 1218 position line is not the same as the distance from the
1230 DR position to the intersection with the advanced
position line.

The observations for a running fix need not be of the same
object. Any position line intersecting the advanced line with a
good angle of cut is suitable.

Adjusted position lines, of course, are subject to all of the
errors inherent in lines that are not adjusted. In addition,
their accuracy is affected directly by any errors in course or
speed *over the ground*. Because these quantities are rarely
known accurately, a good fix from simultaneous or nearly
simultaneous observations is preferable to a running fix. Even

a marginal fix might be preferable to a running fix. As in all phases of navigation, judgment is an important factor in evaluating the relative merits of a fix of questionable reliability and a running fix. Angle of cut, reliability of the charted positions of objects observed, probable accuracy of observations, uncertainty of information on the effects of current and wind, time between observations, and perhaps other factors are all important considerations. As always, the prudent navigator uses all information available to him, evaluating it the best he can, keeps alert to indications of error or changing conditions, and gives dangers a wide enough berth to ensure safety, with ample margin for possible error. Proximity to danger and availability of water of adequate depth to ensure safety might limit the alternatives available. It is sometimes wiser to select a longer route around hazards than to risk grounding by passing between obstacles where the means of safe navigation are questionable.

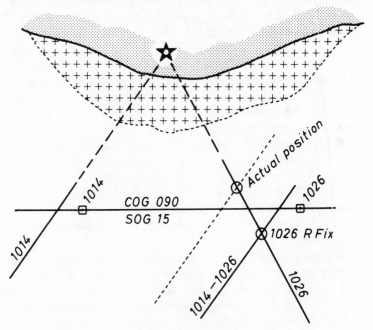

FIG. 516. A running fix and an unknown head current.

In advancing a position line in pilotage waters, one should consider current. In general, use of course and speed estimated to be made good over the ground can be expected to yield more accurate running fixes than use of course and speed through the water. However, one should be aware of the vagaries of current in pilotage waters, and the possibility of introducing error by use of incorrect current information. Consider the situation illustrated in Fig. 516. The navigator of a ship proceeding along a rocky coast at 13 knots estimates his course made good as 090°, and his speed over the ground as 15 knots, a following current of 2 knots being anticipated. A lighthouse bears 036° at 1014 and 332° at 1026. The navigator plots the two position lines and advances the earlier one 3.0 miles, resulting in the 1026 running fix shown. He might feel confident that he is farther offshore than shown by his EP track. But if the current is 1 knot from ahead, his earlier position line should have been advanced only 2.4 miles, as shown by the pecked line parallel to the original position line. His actual position, as shown, is nearer the rocky coast than indicated by either the plotted running fix or EP, a potentially dangerous situation. In this illustration, a better procedure would have been to use course and speed through the water and allow ample sea room, or use the most pessimistic estimate of current. If the danger were on the starboard side of the ship, the most optimistic estimate of speed would be in order.

The presence of a cross current, of course, has a direct effect in setting the vessel toward or away from the shore. The presence of an unknown cross current, like that of an unknown head or following current, is not apparent from the usual plot. An oblique current can be considered to be resolved into components along and perpendicular to the course line.

Three or more bearings on the same object can be used to determine the course being made good over the ground if the current remains the same between the first and last observations. Additional information is needed, however, for an accurate determination of position.

Fig. 517 is the plot of a ship steaming along a coast on

course 068°, speed 20 knots. The navigator obtains five bearings on a monument, at six-minute intervals, as shown. The time intervals need not be constant. The *first* bearing line is advanced to the time of each successive observation, as shown. The resultant running fixes are all in a straight line extending in direction 083°. This is the *direction* of the course being made good. The position of this pecked line, however, is not the track of the ship, except by coincidence. The fact that the course made good (083°) is to the right of the course steered (068°) indicates that the current has a component setting the ship toward the right.

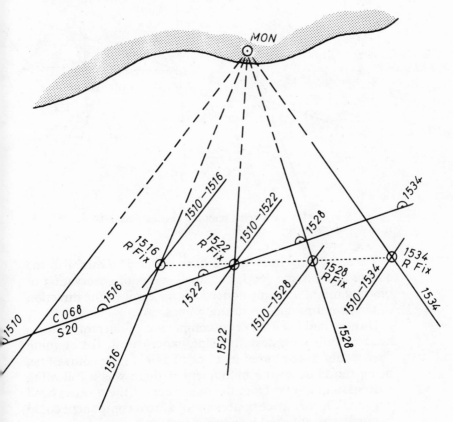

FIG. 517. Determining course made good by a series of bearings on the same object.

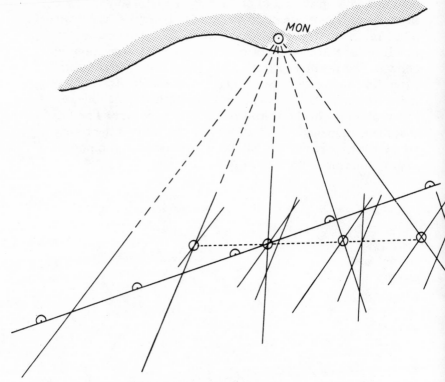

FIG. 518. Advancing multiple bearing lines relating
to the same object.

Three bearing lines would have sufficed to establish the course being made good, but small errors of observation or plotting might have introduced a large error in the direction of the line through the running fixes.

If there had been no cross component of current, *either* a head or following current being experienced, the running fixes would have plotted in a line parallel to the course line, being too close to the monument if there was a following current, and too far from the monument if there was a head current. The presence or absence of a cross component could be further established by advancing each bearing line except the last to the times of later observations. If the current is

242

constant, both in set and drift, and all work of the navigator is accurate, each multiple running fix would consist of several lines crossing at a common point of intersection if there is no cross component of current. If there is a cross component, the position lines would not all intersect at the same point, as shown in Fig. 518, in which the labels are omitted the better to indicate the principle illustrated. In this discussion, all references to 'current' refer to the total or resultant effect of all forces causing deviation from the course and speed used for plotting the dead reckoning.

In the discussion of Fig. 517 the statement was made that the line connecting the series of running fixes indicates the direction of motion but not the positions of the ship at the times indicated. It therefore does not provide means for determining the speed being made good over the ground or the set or drift of the current, unless the set is in line with the course steered. If any one of these quantities—speed over the ground, set, or drift—is known, the others can be determined. The position of the vessel at the time of each bearing can also be determined by drawing a line parallel to the course being made good and located so that the intercepts between bearing lines equal the distances made good during the intervals between observations. If the current has continued unchanged since the last fix (not running fix), a new course line can be laid off representing the course being made good. Its intersections with the various position lines then represent actual positions of the craft, and the speed can be determined by means of the time intervals and distances, along the new course line, between the bearing lines.

The assumption that current remains constant since the last fix, or even during the period between a series of observations, should not be made without justification. 'Current' as used here changes with the tidal cycle, a change in wind, geographical position, and even with a change of helmsman. Information from tidal stream (current) tables, nautical charts, pilot charts, and sailing directions should be combined with observations and the experience of the navigator. Familiarity with the vessel's characteristics with respect to wind is helpful. The practice of verifying or reconciling discrepancies between anticipated and encountered conditions can help develop the experience that will prove valuable at unfavourable times. The need for prior knowledge gained from perusal of available sources should also be evident, for there is often insufficient time to consult such sources when the information is needed.

Problems associated with running fixes can be avoided if simultaneous or nearly-simultaneous observations can be made for a fix. A strong case can be made for having means for determining both bearing and distance of an object when only one suitable object is available for observation.

5. Running Fix Without Plot

A running fix can be obtained mathematically, without plotting. This method might be desirable in rough weather, when plotting is difficult, or in small craft where plotting facilities are limited.

One approach is to solve the triangles by the course line (using the course made good over the ground, not the course steered or the heading) and bearing lines. Fig. 519 illustrates the plot of a ship steaming on COG 290° at SOG 15 knots. At 1105 lighthouse L bears 335°, and at 1113 it bears 000°. If the ship is making good a speed over the ground of 15 knots, it travels one mile each four minutes. Between 1105 and 1113 it travels 2.0 miles, so the length of side AB of the triangle ABL is known. If the course being made good is 290°, and the two bearings are accurate, one can mentally calculate the angle LAB to be $335° - 290° = 45°$. Angle ALB is the difference in the two bearings, or $360° - 335° = 25°$. The length of side BL can be calculated by means of the sine law, using the equation: BL = AB sin LAB csc ALB. Substituting numbers, BL = $2.0 \times 0.70711 \times 2.34620 = 3.3$M. A more rigorous solution would be obtained by solving the triangle ABL as a spherical triangle, but the error introduced by solving it as a plane triangle is negligible.

The solution indicates that the distance from the lighthouse to the ship at the time of the second bearing is 3.3 miles. Knowing both the distance and the direction, the navigator

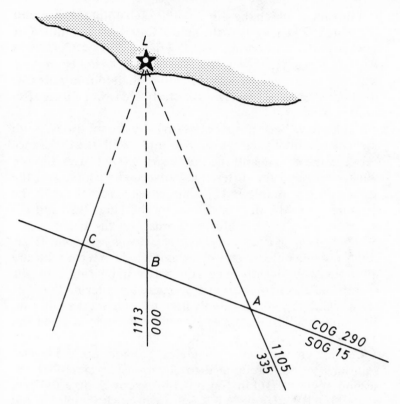

FIG. 519. The triangles of a running fix.

can determine his position at 1113, either by plotting or by the equations of plane and parallel sailings (pp. 171, 170). He can also calculate the distance off when the lighthouse will be broad on the starboard beam, assuming that the heading and the course over the ground are the same. He does this by solving triangle BCL. The angle LBC is $360° - 290° = 70°$. When the lighthouse is broad on the beam, angle LCB is $90°$, by definition. The angle BLC is therefore $180° - (90° + 70°) = 20°$. All three angles are known and side BL is known from the previous solution. Side CL can be computed from the equation: $CL = BL \cos BLC$. Substituting numbers: $CL = 3.3 \times 0.93969 = 3.1M$.

The time at which the ship should reach point C can also be calculated. The length of the side BC can be determined by solving the equation BC = BL sin BLC, or BC = 3.3 × 0.34202 = 1.1M. At a speed of 15 knots, the ship will cover this distance in a little more than four minutes, so the light should be broad on the starboard beam a little after 1117.

Tables have been prepared to simplify the solutions. With the usual form of such tables, one enters with the difference between the course and the first bearing (angle LAB in the illustration) and the difference between the course and the second bearing (angle LBC). One extracts from the table the distance off at the time of the second bearing (BL) and the distance off when the object is broad on the beam (CL), *assuming a run of exactly one mile between observations.* If the run is not one mile, the numbers extracted from the table are multiplied by the distance run between bearings. In the example of Fig. 519, the two differences for entering the table are 45° and 70°, and the two values taken from the table are 1.67 and 1.57. The distances sought are 2 × 1.67 = 3.3M and 2 × 1.57 = 3.1M, respectively, as before.

Certain combinations of angles provide simple mental solutions without reference to equations or tables. If the second angle (LBC in Fig. 519) is exactly double the first angle (LAB), triangle ABL is isosceles, with angles LAB and ALB equal. Sides AB and BL are also equal, so that the distance off at the time of the second observation is equal to the distance run between observations. This situation is called *doubling the angle on the bow.* If the first angle is 45° and the second one is 90°, the distance run is the distance off when the object is abeam. These angles are called *bow and beam bearings.*

While these are the two most commonly used combinations, others are useful. Several combinations of angles, in addition to the bow and beam bearing combination, result in the distance run between observations being equal to the distance off when the object is broad on the beam. A convenient one is 32° and 59°, but any two angles having natural cotangents differing by exactly 1 provide a solution. If the first angle is $63°.5$ and the second one is $90°$, the distance off at the time of the second observation (with the object broad on the beam) is twice the distance run between observations, and if the angles are $71°.5$ and $90°$, the distance off is three times the distance run. If the angles are $22°.5$ and $45°$, the distance off when abeam is $7/10$ of the distance run, if $22°.5$ and $26°.5$, the distance abeam is $7/3$ of the distance run, and if $30°$ and $60°$, the distance abeam is $7/8$ of the distance run between observations. In any combination of angles in which the second one is greater than $90°$, the object has already been passed and the distance abeam is the distance off when the object *was* broad on the beam.

In all of this discussion of combinations of angles, the two angles relate to the same object, which may be on either side of the craft. A change of course between observations complicates the solution discussed here, which is better avoided in favour of a new combination of angles or a graphical solution by plotting, as illustrated in Fig. 515. As in any form of running fix, the accuracy of this method is related to the accuracy of the observations and the accuracy of the estimate of course and speed made good between observations.

It is important to remember that the angles are the differences between the bearing lines and the COG line. Angles obtained by observing relative bearings, a method in common use, need to be corrected for any difference between the heading and the COG.

A variation of the method of using combinations of angles is to measure the time interval during which the bearing of an object changes from $8°$ forward of the beam to $8°$ abaft the beam. The distance off in nautical miles when the object is abeam is determined by multiplying the measured interval in seconds by the speed made good in knots, and dividing the product by 1,000 or

$$D = \frac{S \times t}{1,000},$$

where D is distance in nautical miles, S is speed in knots, and t is the time interval in seconds. This method is more accurate if a vessel is rounding a cape, keeping the object abeam and observing the change in true bearing. It is based upon the principle that if the bearing changes one radian (about $57°.3$), the distance óff is equal to the distance run (by definition of the radian), assuming the distance off remains constant during the change of bearing. Consequently, for a change of bearing of half (about $28°.5$), one-third (about $19°$), one-fourth (about $14°.5$), or one-fifth (about $11°.5$) of a radian the distance off is two, three, four, or five times the distance travelled, respectively, again assuming constant distance from the object during the change of bearing.

6. Estimated Position

An *estimated position* (*EP*) may be a D R position (based upon course and speed through the water) adjusted for (a) current, (b) a lone position line, or (c) both current and a lone position line, as shown in Fig. 520. It may also be a position determined by radio bearings.

The adjustment for current is no better, of course, than the estimate of the average current acting on the vessel since the last fix (not running fix). The cautions associated with the use of current in establishing a running fix, discussed in section 4, apply in the use of current for establishing an EP, but the

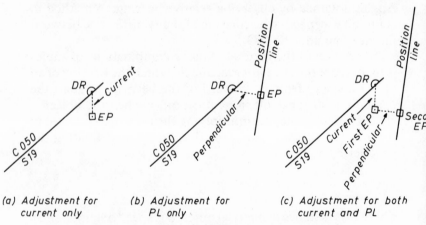

(a) Adjustment for current only

(b) Adjustment for PL only

(c) Adjustment for both current and PL

FIG. 520. Three methods of establishing an estimated position.

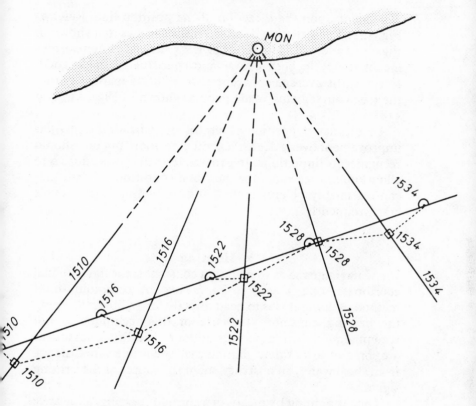

FIG. 521. Estimated positions from a series of bearing lines.

error of an incorrect estimate of current may be magnified when the time interval between the fix and the E P is greater than that between observations for a running fix.

If a lone position line is available, the E P is determined by dropping a perpendicular from the D R position at the time of observation to the position line, as shown in Fig. 520b, or, if an EP has already been established by adjustment for current, as shown in Fig. 520a, the perpendicular is dropped from that E P to the position line to establish a new E P, as shown in Fig. 520c. The method of dropping a perpendicular to a position line, like that of applying current only, is subject to considerable error. The position line itself is subject to possible error, and the location of the EP is directly dependent upon the direction of the position line. Refer to Fig. 521. The situation depicted is the same as that shown in Figs. 517 and 518. The series of EP's suggests a nonexistent inconsistency in both course and speed being made good. Further, the average apparent course differs markedly from the true course being made good as shown in Figs. 517 and 518.

An estimated position is useful in indicating a *possible* improvement over a dead-reckoning position, but one should recognize its limitations. In general, the safest procedure is to allow enough sea room for the worst conditions of drift that can reasonably be anticipated, and fix the position of one's craft frequently.

7. Homing

If one navigates so as to maintain constant some navigational coordinate, one is said to be *homing*. A commonly-used method of doing this is to head directly for an object, keeping the bearing constant. The use of this technique is not recommended during periods of poor visibility unless there are some means of determining that one is at a safe distance from shoal water, an obstruction, or the source of the homing signal.

If one is homing by means of a constant bearing, allowance for drift is needed when there is a cross current, if the true bearing is to remain constant. One method of detecting the presence of a cross component of current or tidal stream is to keep the object dead ahead and note any change in heading. If one finds such a current, one can make allowance for it by heading somewhat into the current. A variation is illustrated in Fig. 522. A yacht at point A by dead reckoning heads

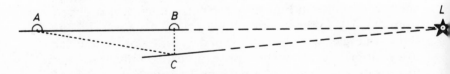

FIG. 522. Detecting and compensating for cross current in homing.

directly toward lighthouse L. The heading is kept constant and when the craft arrives at B by dead reckoning, the lighthouse is found to bear 5° red. This bearing line is plotted and C is located on the bearing line at the intersection of a line through B, perpendicular to the course line. Line A C then represents the track, and angle B A C, 10° by measurement, is the drift of the yacht to the right of the heading. By changing course 15° to port (5° to again head for the lighthouse and 10° to compensate for future drift), the yachtsman can keep the true bearing of the lighthouse constant. The solution is not exact and a small adjustment in the heading might be needed if additional cross drift is detected.

If one is homing by means of a transit, or range, the apparent opening of the transit as one object appears to move to the right or left of the other is immediate indication of cross set.

Homing is involved in the following of *any* position line. One might round a cape by keeping the distance-off constant, for example. In this case the existence of a cross current can be detected by keeping the object broad on the beam and periodically measuring the distance off.

Another use of the homing technique is explained on p. 324.

8. Safety Without a Fix

A fix is not always essential to safe piloting. Section 7 dealt with homing, which in many cases will ensure safety if used intelligently. It is important to know when to change course to avoid collision or grounding. Also, a vessel following a well-marked channel in clear weather should have no difficulty staying in the channel from fix to fix as it passes between pairs of buoys.

A method sometimes having utility is the use of a *clearing bearing*, also called a *danger bearing*, defined as the limiting bearing of an object, called a *clearing mark* or *danger mark*, to ensure safe passage of an off-lying obstruction. The principle is illustrated in Fig. 523. A vessel is proceeding along a rocky coast on course 292°. An off-lying shoal area with sunken

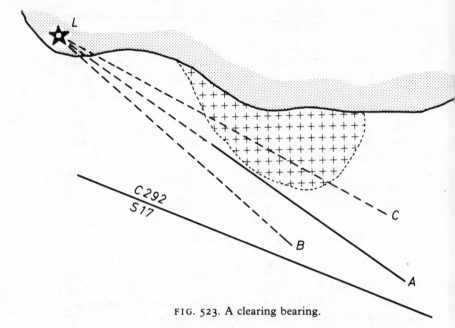

FIG. 523. A clearing bearing.

rocks, shown on the chart, is to be avoided. Objects for suitable fixes are not available. One lighthouse, L, well ahead on the starboard side, is expected to be visible. The navigator draws a line LA from the lighthouse, tangent to the shoal area, and measures the reciprocal direction, 305°. This is the clearing bearing. Any bearing *greater* than 305°, such as BL, indicates a safe position of the vessel, while any bearing *less* than 305°, such as CL, indicates a possibly dangerous situation, if the vessel is close enough to the shoal. An extra margin of safety can be achieved by drawing line LA some distance off the shoal to allow for errors in measurement or charting and to avoid the effect of a possible current setting the vessel toward the shoal.

It is important that all personnel concerned with safe navigation of the vessel understand whether the clearing bearing is the maximum or minimum safe bearing. Fig. 523 illustrates a minimum safe bearing. If the shoal had been on the port side, the clearing bearing would have been a maximum safe bearing.

For a clearing bearing to be effective, it should not differ greatly from the course. If the relative bearing, right or left, is large, it should be changing rapidly, and running fixes should be more useful than a clearing bearing.

A somewhat similar approach is to use a *clearing circle*, or *danger circle*, as illustrated in Fig. 524. The situation is similar to that shown in Fig. 523 except that now the lighthouse is located on the coast near the centre of the shoal area. A circle is drawn with its centre at the lighthouse and tangent to the shoal. Distances off are measured by one of the methods to be discussed in section 13. As long as the distance is greater than the *clearing distance*, or *danger distance*, the vessel is outside the clearing circle. As in other forms of navigation, one must use the clearing circle intelligently. The vessel might be outside the circle but heading for the shoal, as at point P in Fig. 524.

If the vessel is to pass between the obstruction and the shore, as in the case of a sunken rock well offshore, the clearing distance is maximum, not minimum, if distance is

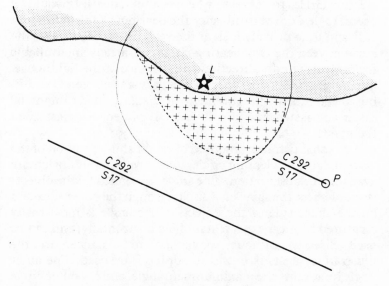

FIG. 524. A clearing circle.

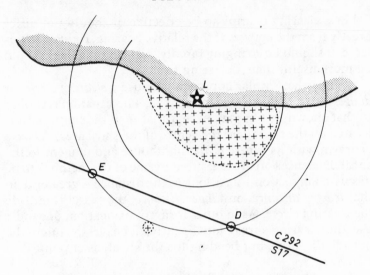

FIG. 525. Maximum and minimum clearing circles.

determined from an object on the shore. Fig. 525 illustrates the situation of a vessel using both maximum and minimum clearing circles to pass safely between two shoals. It would be useful to determine in advance the bearings of the lighthouse at D and E, to provide fixes as the vessel enters and leaves the area between the two clearing circles. If means are available for measuring both direction and distance of the lighthouse, fixes might be obtained during the passage between D and E, but the frequent measurement of distance alone might be easier and faster, and equally effective in ensuring safety of the vessel.

Fig. 526 illustrates a method of establishing position of the vessel relative to clearing circles when two suitable objects are available for observation. The angle subtended by the objects is everywhere the same on a circle through the objects (except on the shore side of the objects). The angle is most easily measured by means of a sextant held horizontally, and can be used directly without conversion to distance. In the illustration, gas tank O and standpipe S are used. The inner circle represents the maximum safe angle, and the outer circle represents the minimum safe angle, between points F and G.

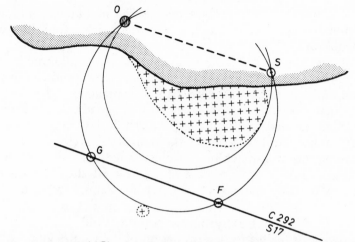

FIG. 526. Clearing circles defined by two objects.

These limiting values are called *horizontal clearing angles* or *horizontal danger angles*. Vertical angles between points, one above the other, differing in height by a known distance can be used in like manner as *vertical clearing angles*, or *vertical danger angles*.

In an area that has been well surveyed, with ample soundings shown on the chart, a *clearing sounding*, or *danger sounding*, can be highly useful. The technique is to determine the minimum safe sounding, considering the draught of the vessel, squat, range and state of the tide during passage of the area, the probability of shoaling since the survey was made, the depth gradient, possible error in measurements to be made, and any other pertinent factors, allowing ample margin for safety. A contour line is drawn on the chart through all points having the clearing sounding. A search is then made for any shoal areas outside the clearing sounding contour and contours are drawn around them. In an area where the bottom shoals abruptly, the clearing sounding should be selected at sufficient depth to permit action if the clearing sounding is measured while traversing the area. In an area of very steep bottom, no clearing sounding may be practical. In using a clearing sounding, one should note carefully the shape of its contour. An abrupt change of direction in the line identifies an area where there may not be adequate room for manoeuvre to avoid grounding after the clearing sounding is encountered.

It is good practice to use a pencil with bright-coloured lead to mark clearing bearing lines, clearing circles, and clearing sounding contours, to make them conspicuous and readily distinguishable from other lines. Red is a good colour unless red light is used to illuminate the chart desk at night. Some navigators like to accentuate the dangerous area by adding shading or crosshatching on the dangerous side of the coloured line, or in the case of an isolated shoal or other obstruction, to shade or cross hatch the dangerous area.

9. Bathymetric Navigation

Bathymetry relates to determination of depth of water, and *bathymetric navigation* relates to navigation by measurement of water depth.

The effectiveness of bathymetric navigation is related to the ruggedness of the bottom topography, the completeness and accuracy with which the bottom has been surveyed, the accuracy with which depth measurements are made aboard the vessel being navigated, and the skill of the navigator in interpreting the data available.

There are several methods of using depth data for determining the position or safety of the vessel. In general, they are all methods of locating the vessel relative to distinctive bottom features. If there are no such distinctive features, where the bottom is flat, or if there are so many similar features that identification is uncertain, depth information is of little or no value in determining position.

Section 8 discusses the use of clearing soundings, as a method of keeping the vessel in safe water without a fix. In an area where depth contours are charted or otherwise identifiable, the crossing of such a contour provides one with a position line that can be used as any other position line to help fix the position of the vessel. In the absence of other position lines, a depth contour might serve as an indication of the distance offshore, if the contour runs roughly parallel to the shore.

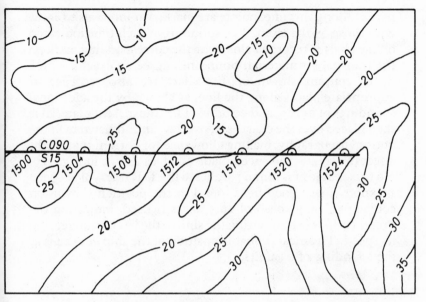

FIG. 527. Preparation of a chart for using a line of soundings.

If an echo sounder is available, a bottom profile can be matched to the bottom topography as shown on the chart. If *any* means of measuring depth at frequent intervals is available, a simple and effective way of using soundings is by means of a *line of soundings*, illustrated in Figs. 527, 528, and 529. A ship is steaming on course 090° at 15 knots. Dead-reckoning positions at intervals of one mile, or other convenient distance, are plotted on the chart, as shown in Fig. 527. A straight line is drawn on a piece of transparent material, as shown in Fig. 528, or along the edge of a piece of

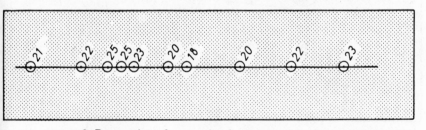

FIG. 528. Preparation of an overlay for using a line of soundings.

257

paper. Along this line, points are marked at intervals to agree with those on the chart. The sounding at each time indicated on the chart is recorded alongside the corresponding mark on the transparent material. Soundings agreeing exactly with a depth contour shown on the chart are also recorded at appropriate places along the line, as shown by the additional soundings of 25, 25, and 20 units. The transparent material is then placed over the chart as an overlay, and adjusted to fit the bottom topography, making allowance for current that might affect the course and speed made good, as shown in Fig. 529. No reasonable fit is found parallel to the D R track, or at speed 15 knots, but a good fit is found in the position shown, on course 085°, if a speed of 16.5 knots is used, indicating the presence of a current setting the ship to the left and increasing its speed. The most probable position of the ship at 1524 is at the sounding of 23 units.

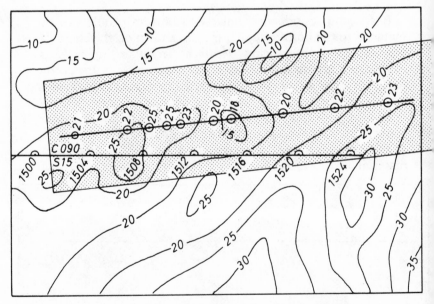

FIG. 529. A line of soundings placed over a chart.

In making the fit of a line of soundings one should try other possible solutions. If another reasonable fit is possible, the position of the vessel is in doubt. Additional soundings might resolve the ambiguity. The decision as to whether to consider the most probable position a fix and start a new D R plot from it is a matter of judgment. The neophyte should attempt to confirm the position by any means available, a procedure recommended to all navigators.

In using soundings to determine the position of one's vessel, one should study the chart for distinctive features. These can be helpful in identifying the correct fit of a line of soundings. Occasionally one passes directly over some feature that gives an immediate position line or a position, similar to passing a buoy close aboard. One should be careful of the identity of the feature, of course, if others in the area might be mistaken for it. If soundings are made by a hand lead with arming (p. 147), the bottom sample can be useful in fixing the position of the vessel if the nature of the bottom is shown on the chart, and has a distinctive pattern.

If sonar is available for making horizontal underwater measurements, both direction and distance of a prominent underwater feature such as a seamount might yield a fix similar to one taken visually on a lighthouse or other object above water.

In an area where the tidal range is appreciable, the state of the tide should be taken into account by correcting the depth readings an appropriate amount.

The accuracy of any method of bathymetric navigation, like that of other forms of pilotage, is directly dependent upon the accuracy with which the charted features have been located. When extreme care has been used to survey a limited area with unusual accuracy, bathymetric navigation has been used to establish positions of vessels to a very high degree of accuracy. In the ordinary practice of navigation, however, bathymetric navigation can prove helpful, but is generally somewhat less reliable than visual pilotage. It can, however, serve a useful function by providing an independent check on other methods, to help guard against gross errors, and sometimes it may be the best method available.

10. Visibility of Aids to Navigation

The distance at which an object can be seen is of interest to a navigator, for it helps him determine whether the object will be useful in establishing a visual position line. If he can determine the extreme distance at which an object is likely to be seen, he can draw an arc of its *circle of visibility* on the chart, with the object as the centre, and the distance as the radius, as shown in Fig. 530. The point at which his DR track crosses the arc of the circle is the point at which the object can be expected to be sighted. The direction of the object from this point is its anticipated bearing at the time of sighting. It is often convenient to convert a true bearing to a relative bearing, to assist the lookout in sighting the object. In Fig. 530, line AB represents the DR track of a vessel on course 080°, speed 17 knots. The anticipated time of crossing the circle of visibility is 0407, when the bearing of light L is expected to be 044° true, or 324° relative.

If the course line makes a small acute angle with the circle of visibility, a small error in course made good may result in a large error in anticipated position, time, and bearing of first sighting; or in missing the object altogether. In Fig. 530, CD represents the DR track of a vessel on course 265°, speed 20 knots. Light L is expected to be sighted at 2244, bearing 329°.

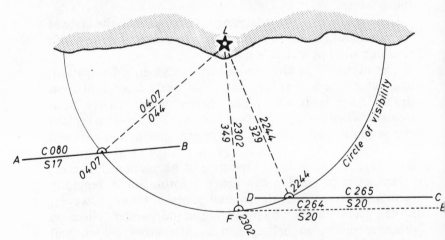

FIG. 530. Determining the time and bearing of sighting an object.

If the course made good is 264°, as shown by E F, the light will not be sighted for another 18 minutes, on bearing 349°. Any additional set to the left will keep the vessel outside the circle of visibility, and the light will not be sighted.

The distance at which an object can be seen through the Earth's atmosphere is a function of several factors:

Characteristic of the object. The shape and size of the object affect its visibility. The colour of a light affects the distance at which it can be seen, some colours being visible at greater distances than others. This fact should be considered when identifying a light by its characteristics, if the light displays more than one colour. The apparent brightness of a light of any colour is *not* a reliable indication of its distance.

Contrast with surroundings. A building or tower that may be prominent if standing alone might be difficult to see if it is surrounded by other structures, unless it is given some conspicuous marking. Lighthouses are often painted with stripes or given other distinctive markings to make them conspicuous relative to the background against which they will be viewed. A navigational light is given a distinctive sequence of light and dark periods to aid in its observation, as well as to assist in its identification.

Observer's perception threshold. Individual observers differ in their ability to see an object, or, stated differently, in the minimum illumination needed on the pupil of the eye to produce a sensation of perception. By international agreement, a threshold perception of 0.2 microlux is used in computing the distances at which navigational lights can be seen. This value is approximately four times greater than the threshold perception to which a 50 per cent probability would be given.

Atmospheric transparency. The transparency of the atmosphere is an elusive factor having a major influence on the distance at which an object can be seen. In an attempt to quantify visibility, the World Meteorological Organization has defined 'meteorological visibility' as 'the greatest distance at which a black object of suitable size can be seen and identified against the horizon sky under standard conditions of threshold contrast'. For convenience in telegraphic coding, various conditions of visibility are stated in a graduated scale, as follows:

Code	Description	Maximum Distance Nautical miles (M)	Kilometres (km)
0	Dense fog	0.027	0.05
1	Thick fog	0.11	0.2
2	Moderate fog	0.27	0.5
3	Light fog	0.54	1
4	Thin fog	1.1	2
5	Haze	2.2	4
6	Light haze	5.4	10
7	Clear	11	20
8	Very clear	27	50
9	Exceptionally clear	infinity	infinity

By definition, meteorological visibility relates to daytime conditions. It has been extended to observations of lights during darkness by international agreement that night visibility is that obtained by supposing that the general illumination is increased until it reaches the normal daylight intensity.

Following a 1966 recommendation of the International Association of Lighthouse Authorities (IALA), light lists tabulate a quantity called *nominal range*, which is defined as 'the luminous range in a homogeneous atmosphere with a meteorological visibility of ten nautical miles'. In effect, nominal range is a measure of the intensity of the light.

To determine the *luminous range* of a light, the extreme distance at which it can be expected to be seen if there is no intervening obstruction, one finds the nominal range in the appropriate light list, determines the meteorological visibility from marine weather forecasts and observation, and refers to a diagram given in the light list, similar to Fig. 531. From the intersection of the vertical line representing the nominal range with the curve representing the meteorological visibility (interpolating as necessary) one proceeds horizontally to the scale at the right or left of the diagram. The distance read from this scale is the luminous range, in nautical miles. Thus, if the nominal range of a light is 20 miles and meteorological visibility is three kilometres, the luminous range is 4.5 miles.

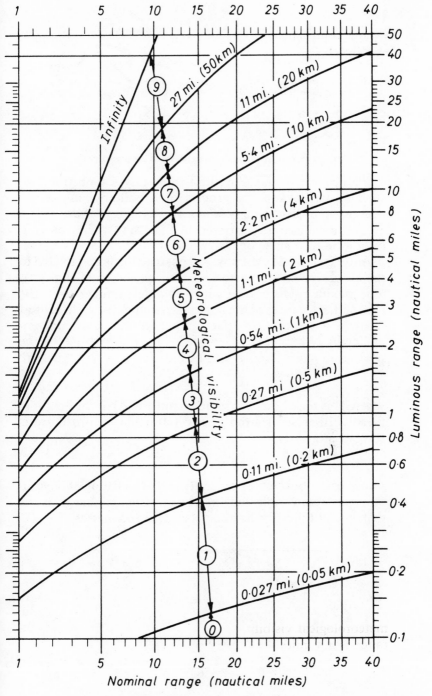

FIG. 531. Nominal and luminous ranges.

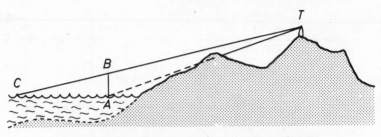

FIG. 532. Effect of position relative to an obstruction.

Physical obstruction. An intervening physical obstruction, such as an elevation of ground or a building, might not prevent an object being seen at a greater height of eye or at a greater distance, as illustrated in Fig. 532, where tower T cannot be seen at A, but is visible at B or C.

A somewhat different physical obstruction is that related to the curvature of the Earth's surface, as shown in Fig. 533. The maximum distance at which an object can be seen is the sum of the distances of the horizon from the object (MH) and from the observer (OH). Each of these distances is a function of height (MA, OB). Geometrically, the distance of the horizon in nautical miles can be calculated by the equation:

$$D = 1.92 \sqrt{h},$$

where D is the distance in nautical miles and h is the height in metres. Because of atmospheric refraction, the distance is somewhat greater:

$$D = 2.07 \sqrt{h}.$$

Books of nautical tables generally include a listing of horizon distance from various heights. The following table gives the distance in miles for heights from 1 to 100 metres.

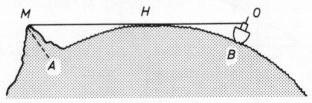

FIG. 533. Geographical range.

Height	Dist.	Height	Dist.	Height	Dist.	Height	Dist.
1	2.1	11	6.9	21	9.5	55	15.4
2	2.9	12	7.2	22	9.7	60	16.0
3	3.6	13	7.5	23	9.9	65	16.7
4	4.1	14	7.7	24	10.1	70	17.3
5	4.6	15	8.0	25	10.4	75	17.9
6	5.1	16	8.3	30	11.3	80	18.5
7	5.5	17	8.5	35	12.2	85	19.1
8	5.9	18	8.8	40	13.1	90	19.6
9	6.2	19	9.0	45	13.9	95	20.2
10	6.5	20	9.3	50	14.6	100	20.7

As an example of the use of the table, suppose the eye of the observer on the bridge of a ship is 15 metres above the water. His horizon is 8.0 miles away. If a light is on a promontory at a height of 30 metres, its horizon is 11.3 miles away. Thus, the maximum distance at which the observer can see the light is 8.0 + 11.3 = 19.3 miles. This is called the *geographical range*. This range for a height of eye of 15 feet is shown on older charts for lights of adequate power to be seen that far under standard conditions.

The information in the table is shown graphically in Fig. 534, and as a nomogram in Fig. 535. To use the nomogram, place a straight-edge so that it is over the height of eye of the observer on the right-hand scale and the height of the object on the left-hand scale. The point at which it crosses the middle scale is the geographical range of the object for the height of eye used. To determine the distance of the horizon, place the straight-edge over the height on one side scale and zero on the other side scale, and read the horizon distance on the middle scale.

If a light is sighted, one can sometimes determine whether it is at the geographical range by immediately lowering the height of eye, as by crouching near the deck or going to a lower deck. If the light disappears and then reappears when the observer returns to his original height, it is probably at the geographical range. This process is called *bobbing a light*. If there is excessive vertical motion of a vessel because of the condition of the sea, a light at the geographical range might alternately appear and disappear, a situation that could result

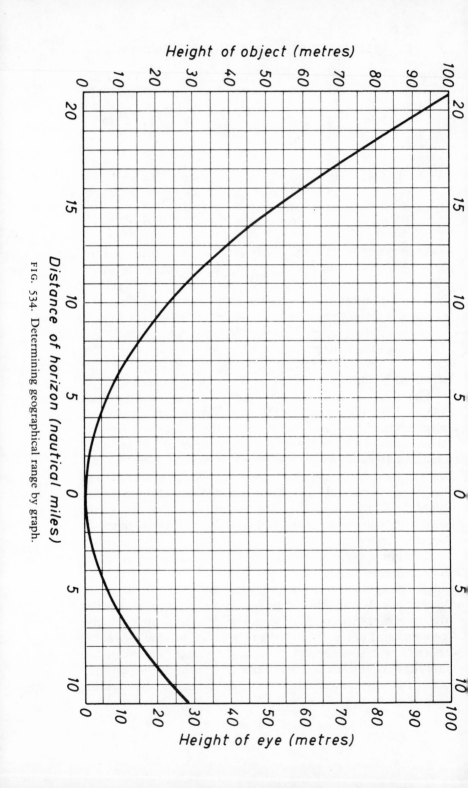

FIG. 534. Determining geographical range by graph.

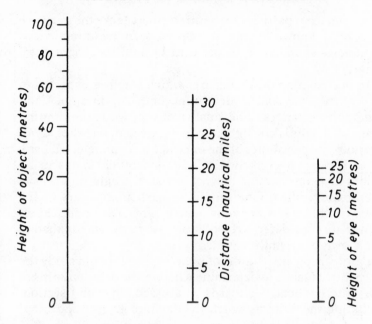

FIG. 535. Determining geographical range by nomogram.

in error in the identification of the light by means of its characteristics.

Although bobbing a light provides some indication of the distance of a light, one should be cautious in using this information for fixing the position of one's vessel. The equation, table, graph, and nomogram are all based upon standard atmospheric conditions and average radius of the Earth. At any given moment the distance can differ from the values given. Occasionally, objects can be seen at distances as much as 40 per cent or more greater than the calculated geographical range because of abnormal refraction, a phenomenon called *looming*. At other times the opposite condition, called *sinking*, occurs. Although the presence of a very warm air mass over cold water is particularly conducive to looming, and the opposite condition to sinking, either phenomenon is difficult to predict. There is always the possibility, too, that the light may be temporarily obscured by another vessel. Sometimes the *loom*, or glow, of a light by reflection from particles in the atmosphere make the presence of a light known before it can be seen by direct view, sometimes as much as 50 per cent beyond its geographical range.

In determining the distance at which a light is expected to be sighted, one should determine both the luminous and geographical ranges. The smaller of the two is the limiting range. If a light is not sighted when expected, one should not overlook the possibility of the presence of an undetected bank of fog between oneself and the light, or a low cloud obscuring a light at a considerable height; or that the light might have been extinguished. One should be particularly wary of the latter condition in a war zone, where lights may be turned off if they are considered to be of more use to the enemy than to one's own or friendly vessels.

Before using any volume of light lists, one should study the descriptive matter to determine whether the data conforms to the international standards discussed in this section, including the units in which the data are given.

11. Sound Signals

Sound signals are useful in navigation, both as a warning of the presence of other vessels when fog signals are sounded, and as aids in positioning one's vessel. For the latter application, sound is used as an indication of direction, depth, or distance, and the difference in distance from two established positions has been used. Sound can also create navigational problems, as when marine life is the source of sound that interferes with the reception of desired signals, or produces misleading echoes.

Unlike electromagnetic energy, sound is transmitted by a longitudinal wave motion causing alternate compression and rarefaction of the medium in which it travels. The amplitude or difference in pressure determines the intensity or loudness of a sound, and the frequency determines its pitch. The amplitude of the faintest sound that can be heard by the average person is about 0.0000000002 times normal atmospheric pressure, and the loudest that can be heard without experiencing pain is about 0.0002 times normal atmospheric pressure. The frequency of the audible range of the average person is about 20 Hertz (Hz) to 20,000 Hertz. This is the *sonic* range. Higher frequencies produce *ultrasonic* signals.

As sound travels outward from a source, its amplitude decreases by spreading. In the case of spherical spreading, where the sound travels outward in the form of an expanding sphere, the amplitude decrease attributable to spreading is inversely proportional to the square of the distance. If the propagation is other than spherical, the rate of decrease in amplitude is less, being proportional to the distance if the sound is confined to a narrow channel.

Amplitude is also reduced by absorption by the medium through which the sound travels. Absorption is less in water than in air. For this reason, in part, water is a better medium than air for propagating sound. Absorption increases with higher frequency. A 10 kHz signal typically carries only about 1 per cent as far as a 1 kHz signal.

Sound is also dissipated by scattering, which occurs when a sound wave encounters any significant change in sonic characteristics of the medium in which it is travelling. Particularly effective in water is the presence of gas bubbles.

The speed of sound increases with increased temperature and pressure and, in sea water, with increased salinity. Other factors, such as frequency or the presence of moisture in the atmosphere, have minor effects upon the speed of sound and can be neglected for all but precise scientific work. Temperature change is the principal parameter of speed change. In sea water, speed of sound increases about one metre per second with an increase of one-third degree Celsius in temperature, one part per thousand in salinity, or 55 metres in depth. At temperature 15°C the speed of sound in air is typically 340 metres per second, and in sea water 1,500 metres per second, or about 4.4 times the speed in air. The greater speed of sound in water, resulting primarily from its lesser compressibility, is a second reason that water is a better medium than air for the propagation of sound.

Sound waves, like those of light, radio, and water, are refracted toward regions of slower speed. As air temperature and pressure normally decrease with higher altitude, so does the speed of sound. Consequently, sound waves in the atmosphere tend to be refracted upward, precluding the propagation of sound over great distances across the surface of the Earth. When a temperature inversion is present, the increase of temperature with height reverses this situation, and *ducting* may take place as the sound waves are refracted back toward the surface of the Earth, where they are reflected upward, and again refracted downward, as illustrated in Fig. 536. When ducting occurs, sounds may be heard at much greater distances than normal. Because of vagaries in the atmosphere, sound signals are sometimes deceptive, seeming to come from the wrong direction or missing dead zones altogeher, so that a fog signal may not be audible within its normal range.

The propagation of sound in sea water is also quite complex. Except in polar regions, the ocean is composed of a surface *mixed layer* of relatively warm water having little temperature variation with depth, a bottom *deep layer* of relatively cold isothermal water, and an intermediate transition zone called the main *thermocline*, the lower limit of which is characteristically 300 to 1,000 metres deep in temperate latitudes. Its bottom is nearer the surface both in lower and in higher latitudes, reaching the surface in polar regions. Additionally, diurnal (daily) and seasonal thermoclines extending downward to a maximum depth of 7–10 metres and 50–100 metres, respectively, may further complicate the situation. Because of the nearly uniform increase of pressure with depth, the speed of sound increases with depth in the isothermal mixed and deep layers, while in

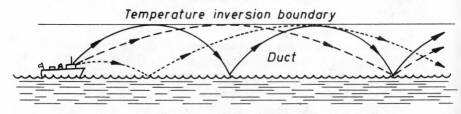

FIG. 536. Ducting in the atmosphere during a temperature inversion.

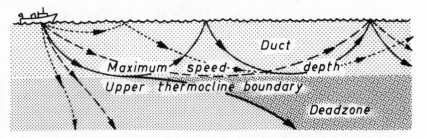

FIG. 537. Ducting in the surface mixed layer of the ocean.

the thermocline the speed decreases with depth because of the decreasing temperature. Therefore, the speed of sound reaches a maximum at the upper boundary of the thermocline, and a minimum speed at its lower boundary. Consequently, sound waves are refracted *away* from the upper boundary, and *toward* the lower boundary.

Sound propagated in the mixed layer is refracted upward. It is reflected at the air-water interface, as at any sharp discontinuity, and starts downward again, and is again refracted upward, as shown in Fig. 537. At some critical angle, sound reaching the maximum speed depth penetrates the thermocline and is refracted downward, creating a dead zone devoid of sound except for a small amount that enters because of scattering.

As sound crosses the minimum speed depth at the bottom of the thermocline, its direction of refraction reverses. If a sound originates at the minimum speed depth, it is refracted back toward this depth as it moves either upward or downward into regions of higher speed, as shown in Fig. 538. Low-frequency sound signals originating at the minimum

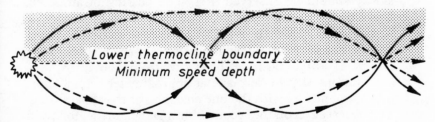

FIG. 538. Ducting at the lower thermocline boundary.

sound depth have been picked up by microphones thousands of kilometres away.

12. Direction Measurement

In pilotage, measurement of the direction of an object, or its bearing, for establishing a great-circle position line or determining the error of a compass, is accomplished by magnetic compass (p. 96), gyro compass (p. 127), compass repeater (p. 134), pelorus (p. 135), radio direction-finder (p. 481), or radar (p. 494).

In the visual measurement of bearings, a systematic *tilt error* is introduced if the device is not horizontal. Bearings are horizontal directions. A tilted circular compass card, when projected onto the horizontal, becomes an ellipse. The degree graduations near the ends of the long axis become compressed, and those near the ends of the short axis become expanded. As the angle of tilt increases, the error becomes larger.

An error may also be introduced if a reading is made while the sensitive element of an instrument is oscillating, the greatest error occurring at the ends of the oscillations, when the sensitive element is steadiest. If oscillation is continuous, the average of readings taken at opposite ends of the cycle may provide a reasonably accurate value, particularly if several readings are taken at each end.

Observations for position lines to be used for establishing a fix should be made simultaneously. When this is not possible, a series of observations in quick succession can often be made without introducing significant error. Certain precautions should be observed. The quantity that is changing most slowly should be observed first. The bearing of an object ahead or astern, for example, changes more slowly than the bearing of an object abeam. The distance to an object abeam changes at a slower rate than the distance to an object ahead or astern. If three position lines are to be obtained, five observations should be made at approximately equal short intervals, starting with the one changing at the slowest rate. The observation on the second object is then made, followed by the third, then the second again, and finally the first again.

The two readings on the first object are averaged, the two readings on the second object are averaged, and the single reading on the third object is used as read. The time of the fix is the time of the reading on the third object.

13. Distance-Off Measurement

Since radar has come into common use at sea, the measurement of distance between a vessel and an identifiable geographic point, for the purpose of establishing a small-circle position line, has become used more widely than previously. Sonar (p. 145) is also used for determining distance off, especially by naval vessels and fishermen. A primitive but sometimes effective method is to sound the ship's whistle and time the return of an echo from a mountain near the shore. Every eleven seconds of time indicate a distance of approximately one mile. Range finders (p. 144) and stadimeters (p. 145) provide other non-electronic means of measuring distance. Several high-accuracy electronic systems have been developed for distance-off measurements by surveyors.

The difference in speed of sonic and radio signals provides a means of measuring the distance between two points. A number of *distance finding stations* have been established throughout the world for this purpose. At these stations sound and radio signals are transmitted simultaneously. The user measures the time interval in seconds between reception of the two signals. To obtain distance in nautical miles, he multiplies this interval by 0.18 or divides it by 5.5 if the sound signal travels through air, or multiplies it by 0.8 or divides it by 1.25 if the sound signal travels through water. At some stations the radio transmits a number of short dashes following the synchronizing signal. The number of dashes received by the time the sound signal arrives is the distance in nautical miles. Accuracy of measurement by distance-finding station is about 10 per cent. Distance determined in this manner is between the observer and the source of the sound signal, which may differ from the source of the radio signal.

A useful approximation of distance off can be determined

by means of differences in bearing as a vessel steams past an object or rounds a cape, as discussed in section 5.

A sextant can be used for determining distance off. One method is to use the principle of the stadimeter. Both the top and bottom of the object observed must be visible if a vertical angle is measured, neither part being obscured by the horizon or other obstruction. The sextant is used to measure the angle, at the observer, between lines of sight to the top and bottom of the object. Distance off can then be calculated, using the equation:

$$D = \frac{H \cot \beta}{1852},$$

where D is distance off in nautical miles, H is the height of the object in metres, and β is the measured angle. Errors are introduced by the height of eye (unless the object is on the horizon), the curvature of the Earth, difference of refraction of the two lines of sight, and a bottom point not vertically below the top point. Generally, these errors are quite small, but may not be if the object is situated so that neither line of sight is approximately perpendicular to the object or if the bottom point is offset considerably from the vertical through the top of the object, as may be the case with a mountain peak. In the latter case, it may be possible to estimate the bottom point vertically below the top of the object.

The stadimeter principle can be used with any two points, not necessarily the top and bottom of the same object. For example, the horizontal angle between two lighthouses is suitable. The only requirements are that the distance between the two points, in the plane of the sextant, be known and the line of sight to one of the points be a right angle to the line connecting the two points. The calculated distance is that between the observer and the object at which the right angle occurs.

A second method of using a sextant to determine distance off is by measurement of the angle between lines of sight to the horizon and the water line of an object. The height of the object need not be known, but the object must be closer to the observer than the horizon if its water line is to be observed.

Distance off can be calculated by means of the equation:

$$D = 1.18\ [(\phi+d) - \sqrt{\{(\phi+d)^2 - d^2\}}],$$

where D is the distance off in nautical miles, ϕ is the measured angle in minutes of arc, and d is the dip of the horizon (p. 380), in minutes of arc. The dip of the horizon is the angle between the horizontal and the line of sight to the horizon, assuming standard atmospheric refraction. It increases with height of eye, and is tabulated in the *Nautical Almanac* (p. 386) and in various books of nautical tables. It can be calculated by the equation:

$$d = 1.76\ \sqrt{h},$$

where h is the height of eye above the water, in metres.

Some books of nautical tables include a table of distance when entered with the height of eye and the measured angle. For a constant height of eye, the only variable is the measured angle. If a table is not available, one can be calculated for the average height of eye used, if there is little variation in this height. For example, for a height of eye of 15 metres, the dip by computation is 6.8165. With this value, the table might take the following form:

Obs. Angle	Distance	Obs. Angle	Distance	Obs. Angle	Distance
′	M	′	M	′	M
0	8.04	7	2.12	30	0.75
1	4.71	8	1.96	35	0.66
2	3.81	9	1.82	40	0.59
3	3.25	10	1.70	45	0.53
4	2.85	15	1.29	50	0.48
5	2.55	20	1.04	55	0.44
6	2.32	25	0.87	60	0.41

If the observed angle is 0′, the object is on the horizon, and the value 8.04 miles is essentially the same as would be obtained by the distance of the horizon equation on p. 264. Note the big difference between the values for observed angles of 0′ and 1′, indicating that an error of only 1′ in the measured angle would introduce an error of 3.33 miles in distance off. Between 1′ and 2′ the error would be 0.9 mile.

These differences, and the maximum distance off that can be determined by this method, indicate its limitation. Because of the large differences in the first several entries, and the fact that the values are not linear, these entries might well be omitted from the table. The principal value of this method is that the height of the object need not be known. The distance determined in this manner is to the water line of the object observed.

If the measured angle is greater than 7′, a simpler equation can be used with an error only about 0.1 mile or less:

$$D = \frac{1.85h}{\phi + d}$$

where D, ϕ, and d are as before, and h is the height of eye in metres.

A similar but more widely-used method is to measure the angle between the lines of sight to the *top* of an object and the horizon. The height of the object must be known, but the horizon limitation does not apply. Distance off can be found by the equation:

$$D = \sqrt{\{[4100 \tan(\theta - d)]^2 + 4.429\,(H - h)\}} - 4100 \tan(\theta - d),$$

where D is distance off in nautical miles, θ is the measured angle in minutes of arc, d is the dip of the horizon in minutes of arc, H is the height of the object above sea level in metres, and h is the height of eye of the observer above sea level, in metres.

Books of nautical tables generally include a table for distance off by this method. In using such a table, one should be careful to note whether entry values are metres or feet, and whether the angle is the measured angle corrected only for index and instrumental errors or whether it should also be corrected for dip of the horizon. The values given in various tables may differ slightly because of differences in the refractive index lapse rate and the size of the Earth used in the computation of the tables. The constants used in the equation given here are the same as those used in computing the dip table in the *Nautical Almanac*. Maximum distance errors of the order of 0.1 mile may occur because of nonstandard refraction along the sight paths, resulting from variations from standard atmospheric conditions of temperature, pressure, and humidity.

If the horizon is not between the observer and the object observed, one may have difficulty making the observation. If the object is of little horizontal extent, a reasonably accurate estimate of the horizon level may be adequate. An alternate solution might be to make the observation from a lower position, with its nearer horizon. If neither of these solutions is practical, one might use the visible water line in place of the horizon, and substitute dip short of the horizon for dip of the horizon. Dip short is tabulated in some books of nautical tables, or it can be calculated by the equation:

$$ds = 0.4156D + \frac{1.856\,h}{D},$$

where ds is dip short of the horizon, D is distance off in nautical miles, and h is height of eye of the observer in metres. The equation for determing distance by means of the angle between the horizon and water line of an object was derived from this equation, substituting the equivalent $(\phi + d)$ for ds. The distance to the water line, which may not be the same as distance to the base of the object, particularly in the case of a mountain peak, is estimated, and the distance off is calculated. The horizontal distance from the part of the object observed to the water line is determined from the chart, and subtracted from the calculated distance off. The value thus obtained is used as a second estimate for determination of dip short, and the process is repeated as many times as necessary to obtain the same distance off on successive computations.

In using this method one should make certain that one correctly identifies the point used as the top of the object observed. An intervening high point of ground may obscure a higher point behind it, as illustrated in Fig. 532.

14. Direction-Difference Measurement

The difference in direction of objects, observed for use with a station pointer, or three-arm protractor, or other means of determining the position of a vessel, as discussed in section 3, is usually measured by a sextant turned on its side so as to be horizontal. Three objects are needed for the two angles required. They should preferably be in the same horizontal plane, or near enough to the horizontal so that a horizontal angle can be measured. Any deviation from the horizontal introduces an error that increases with increased tilt. Ideally, both angles are measured simultaneously, two observers being required. If this is not practicable, the lone observer should measure one angle, then the second, and then the first one again, the three measurements being made with as little elapsed time as practicable, consistent with accuracy. The average of the two readings of the first angle is used with the second angle, and the time of fix taken as the time of the second measurement. Ideally, the two time intervals should be equal. The measured sextant angles should be corrected for index error (p. 351) and any instrument error, if these are significant.

If horizontal sextant angles cannot be obtained, bearings of the three objects can be measured and the angles determined by subtraction. If simultaneous bearings cannot be obtained, one should measure bearings of the objects in the order 1, 2, 3, 2, 1 at equal short intervals of time, and average the two bearings each on objects 1 and 2, with time of fix at the measurement of the bearing of object 3. Any constant error in bearing measurement does not affect the results because it applies equally to all measurements, and the *differences* are the quantities used.

15. Depth Measurement

Depth of water has aroused man's curiosity throughout the centuries, and has been a practical concern since he first ventured away from land. Posidonius reported measurement of a depth of 1,000 fathoms in the Sea of Sardinia in the second century BC. The 27th chapter of the book of *The Acts of the Apostles* records that as the vessel bearing the Apostle Paul toward Rome approached Malta about midnight on a stormy night the 'shipmen', believing they approached land, 'sounded, and found it twenty fathoms: and when they had gone a little further, they sounded again, and found it fifteen fathoms,' and fearing shipwreck 'they cast four anchors out of the stern, and wished for the day,' a wish that can be appreciated by any mariner whose position in the vicinity of shoal water has ever been in doubt, especially during thick weather at night.

Modern 'shipmen' nearly always obtain soundings by means of an echo sounder, but this has not always been so. The hand lead had been used for many centuries, and is still one of the best safeguards against grounding. No vessel should be without at least one. It may have practical depth limitations, but even 'no bottom' soundings, if sufficiently deep, indicate adequate depth of water under the keel. In using a hand lead, the mariner should be familiar with the marks of the lead line and note particularly whether they mark metres, fathoms, or feet, and he should not forget to allow for the distance from his hand to the water surface. Some degree of skill is needed in effective sounding by lead, it being necessary to cast the lead some distance ahead so the line will be vertical when the lead touches the bottom.

In making and using soundings by any method one should not overlook the height of the tide. The adjustment of a sounding to the corresponding value from the chart datum is called *reduction of a sounding*. Also, one should not forget that shifting sand waves and silting can alter the depth as shown on the chart. There is always the possibility, too, that a shoal or isolated rock may have been undetected during the survey of the area.

16. Electronics and Pilotage

A number of the instruments used in pilotage and dead reckoning, as discussed in this and previous chapters, use electronics in some form. Examples are compass repeaters, electromagnetic logs, and echo sounders.

In addition to such indirect uses, electronics has a more direct application in the form of positioning systems that make possible the fixing of a suitably equipped vessel relative to geographic points at any time within effective range of the transmitting stations, virtually independent of weather. These systems are discussed in chapter X.

VI

Astronavigation

---

1. General

Astronavigation, or *astro*, (short for *astronomical navigation*), also called *celestial navigation*, involves the use of astronomical (celestial) bodies in the process of conducting a craft as it moves about its ways. The primary function of astronavigation is to fix the position of a craft at sea, out of sight of land. A secondary but important function is to verify the accuracy of the compass.

The primary function, position fixing, involves two distinct processes: observation and calculation. In its commonly-practised form, observation consists of measurement of the vertical angle between the horizon and an astronomical body, noting the time of observation. The process of observation is often called 'shooting' the body observed, and the resulting data are collectively called an 'observation' or 'sight'. The calculation involved in converting the sight to data for obtaining a position line is called *sight reduction*.

Astronavigation has been practised in some form since man first ventured out of sight of land, but it did not attain its modern form until astronomy had progressed to the extent that positions of astronomical bodies could be predicted for a considerable time in the future with adequate accuracy, and reliable means of measuring vertical angles and time became available in the eighteenth century. The 'discovery' of the astronomical position line by Thomas H. Sumner, captain of an American merchant ship, in 1837, and the introduction of the circle of equal altitude concept by Marcq St. Hilaire, then a commander in the French navy, in 1875, completed the development of the basic elements of the method of astronomical navigation now in common use. More recent developments have been refinements in the instruments for observation and the methods of sight reduction.

Since the emergence of electronic navigation, in the present century, emphasis on astronavigation has decreased somewhat. This decrease has been encouraged by the fact that astronavigation requires skies clear enough for observation of astronomical bodies, a relatively sharp horizon below the bodies observed, the development of some degree of skill in making observations, and the somewhat time-consuming process of observation and sight reduction. These disadvantages are somewhat offset by the fact that the equipment needed is relatively cheap and reliable and is easily understood by its user, there is no requirement for a source of power (except for receiving radio time-signals, not an absolute requirement), the method is free from the vagaries of electronic propagation and down time of transmitters, the method is not subject to jamming or termination in time of war, and there are no geographical limitations. Astronavigation is in wide use, and even those who place primary reliance on electronic methods would do well to develop the proficiency needed for reliable astronavigation, and practise this form of navigation from time to time to ensure the availability of the equipment and skill needed to use the method dependably.

2. The Celestial Sphere

Astronomy relates to astronomical bodies and their relationships to one another. The astronavigator's interest in this science is limited primarily to apparent positions of a relatively small number of the brighter astronomical bodies, their motions relative to him as an observer, celestial coordinates, and time. This limited part of astronomy related to navigation is called *navigational astronomy* or *nautical astronomy*.

Viewing the heavens on a clear, dark night, one sees what seems to be an almost countless number of stars of unequal brightness, unevenly distributed across the visible hemisphere above the horizon. Actually, under ideal conditions a person with good vision can see only about 2,500 stars at any time with the unaided eye. A total of about 6,000 stars in the entire heavens are thus visible, those below the horizon being obscured by the Earth, and the dimmer ones low in the sky not being visible because of absorption of their light by the greater amount of the Earth's atmosphere through which it must pass to reach the eye of the observer.

Thus observing the heavens, one is not aware of the vast distances involved or the great differences in distances of the various stars one can see, nor are these distances of direct concern, except for bodies of the solar system. It is easy to visualize all of the astronomical bodies one can see as being on the inner surface of a large sphere concentric with the Earth. In astronavigation the navigator uses these astronomical bodies as if this were so. This imaginary sphere he calls the *celestial sphere*.

As the observer continues to watch the sky, he notes that his imaginary celestial sphere seems to be in rotation, the various astronomical bodies appearing to move in a generally westerly direction, those toward the west setting below the horizon, and new ones rising above the eastern horizon. This *apparent motion* is the result of the rotation of the Earth on its polar axis. If the observer were to time this apparent rotation, he would find that the stars make one complete revolution around the Earth, arriving back at the same position they occupied at the start of the cycle, in a little more than 23 hours, 56 minutes, 4 seconds, called the *sidereal day*. 'Sidereal' means 'relating to the stars'. After 24 hours each star is about 1° beyond its position of the previous night. The sidereal day is shorter than the *solar day* because the Earth revolves around the Sun, nearly 150,000,000 kilometres (one *astronomical unit*, *AU*) away, completing one revolution in a year. Refer to Fig. 601. The relationships shown and the scale

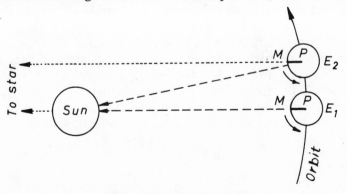

FIG. 601. Solar and sidereal days.

are distorted to better illustrate the principle shown. The Earth is rotating on its polar axis and revolving around the Sun, as shown by the arrows, being at positions E_1 and E_2 on consecutive days. The view is from above the North Pole, P. When the Earth is at position E_1, meridian PM is toward the Sun and a distant star, as shown by the broken and pecked lines, respectively. The local Sun time at this meridian is noon. A day later, when the Earth has moved along its orbit to position E_2, the meridian PM, after completing one revolution of 360°, is again toward the distant star, so far away that rays from it are essentially parallel at positions E_1 and E_2. But because of the changed position of the Earth with respect to the Sun, the Earth must turn an additional amount, approximately 1°, before the meridian is again lined up with the Sun. In a year there are one more of the shorter sidereal days than solar (calendar) days.

Note the difference in terminology between 'rotation' and 'revolution'. In astronomy, *rotation* is turning about an axis within the body, while *revolution* is motion of an astronomical body in its orbit. The Earth rotates about its polar axis daily and revolves about the Sun annually.

For an observer on the equator, the polar axis is horizontal, and the apparent rotation of the celestial sphere is perpendicular to the horizon, as shown in Fig. 602. All

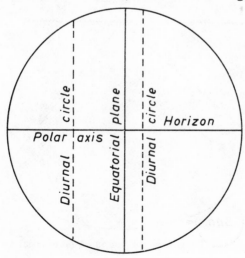

FIG. 602. Diurnal circles for an observer on the equator.

astronomical bodies rise somewhere along the eastern half of the horizon and set somewhere along the western half of the horizon.

As one travels away from the equator, either northward or southward, the apparent path traced by an astronomical body during one revolution, called its *diurnal circle* (diurnal meaning 'daily') tilts, as shown in Fig. 603. Some bodies rise and set, others remain above the horizon, and still others remain below the horizon. Observing the bodies that do not set, which are said to be *circumpolar*, one notes that they trace circles in the sky, each centred at the intersection of the celestial sphere with the extension of the Earth's polar axis.

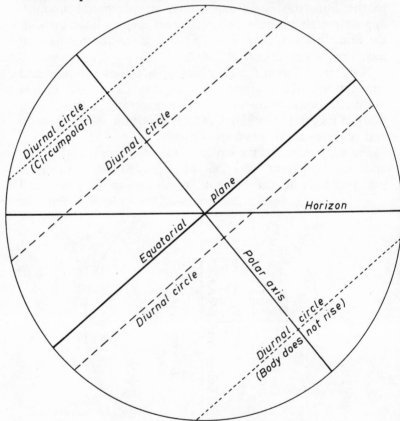

FIG. 603. Diurnal circles for an observer at lat 50° N.

The motion is anticlockwise in the northern hemisphere, and clockwise in the southern hemisphere. The radius of the diurnal circle of a circumpolar body is smaller for a body nearer the extended pole. Polaris, being less than 1° from the pole, appears almost stationary in the sky as the celestial sphere appears to rotate.

The tilting of the celestial sphere increases with higher latitude, more bodies becoming circumpolar. At the geographical poles of the Earth the polar axis is vertical and all diurnal circles are parallel to the horizon, as shown in Fig. 604, half the bodies being circumpolar and half remaining below the horizon. A body does not rise or set unless it changes its position northward or southward across the equator, which coincides with the horizon.

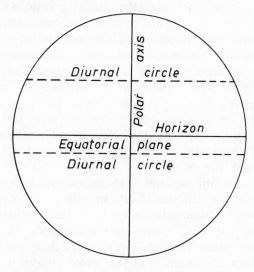

FIG. 604. Diurnal circles for an observer at the geographical North Pole.

As an observer watches the heavens, he notices that the position of the Moon on consecutive days, relative to the stars, changes from day to day, being farther east among the stars each succeeding day. In the course of approximately one month it makes a complete revolution relative to the stars, as if it were moving across the inner surface of the celestial sphere while that sphere is rotating. This apparent lunar motion relative to the stars is the result of the actual revolution of the Moon around the Earth. The period of one revolution of the moon is called a *lunar month*. Several different lunar months are defined, depending upon the reference used. For the *nodical month* of $27^d05^h05^m35\!\!\:.\!\!\:8$ the reference is the ascending node (p.289), for the *tropical month* of $27^d07^h43^m04\!\!\:.\!\!\:7$ it is the vernal equinox (p. 287), for the *sidereal month* of $27^d07^h43^m11\!\!\:.\!\!\:5$ it is the stars, for the *anomalistic month* of $27^d13^h18^m33\!\!\:.\!\!\:2$ it is the perigee (p. 289), and for the *synodical month* of $29^d12^h44^m02\!\!\:.\!\!\:8$ it is the Sun. These are average times that vary slightly from month to month.

During a synodical month the relative positions of the Sun and Moon, as seen by an observer on the Earth, change progressively, the Moon going through its various *phases*. When the Moon is at *conjunction*, approximately in line with the Sun, *new Moon* occurs. The Moon appears dark, the side toward the Sun and away from the Earth being illuminated. On succeeding days the Moon appears to move eastward, away from the Sun. A thin *crescent* appears, the *cusps*, or 'horns' pointing way from the Sun. On each succeeding day the crescent grows fatter as the *waxing* Moon appears to move farther from the Sun. After approximately a week, the *terminator*, the line separating the lighted and dark portions of the Moon, cuts the lunar disc in half, the Moon being at *first quarter*. On succeeding days more than half the surface toward the Earth is lighted by the Sun, the Moon being *gibbous* rather than crescent. After about a fortnight from new Moon, when the moon is at *full Moon* phase, it is on the opposite side of the Earth from the Sun, at *opposition*. The visible illuminated portion of the Moon then decreases from day to day as the *waning* Moon continues on to *third quarter*, sometimes called *last quarter*, when it changes from a gibbous to a crescent Moon, and on to conjunction, when it is again in about the same direction from the observer as the Sun. The elapsed time, usually expressed in days, from the last previous new Moon is called the *age of the Moon*.

If the Moon passes directly between the Earth and Sun at new Moon, it cuts off the light from the Sun, for a small area on the surface of the Earth, and a *solar eclipse* occurs. If the entire surface of the sun is obscured, the eclipse is said to be *total*, and if only part of the solar disc is obscured, the eclipse is said to be *partial*. Because of varying distances between the Earth, Moon, and Sun, the relative apparent diameters of the Sun and Moon vary. When the lunar disc is too small to cover the sun entirely, but leaves a thin ring of the solar surface visible around the Moon, the eclipse is said to be *annular*. When the Sun, Moon, and Earth are directly in line at full Moon, the Earth cuts off the light from the Sun, and the Moon is in the Earth's shadow, resulting in a *lunar eclipse*. The Moon is faintly visible by sunlight diffracted (scattered) by the Earth's atmosphere. An eclipse does not occur at each new or full Moon because the Moon usually passes a little above or below the line connecting the Earth and Sun.

The pattern of solar and lunar eclipses repeats with minor variation after a period of a little more than 18 years, or about 223 synodical months. This period is called the *saros*. The Sun, Moon, and line of nodes (p. 290) are in approximately the same relative positions at the start of each saros.

The Moon is not the only astronomical body that appears to change position on the celestial sphere. Planets, too, appear to move relative to the stars. It is this apparent wandering that gave the planets their name, 'planet' being derived from the Greek word meaning 'wanderer'.

The apparent wandering of the planets relative to the stars is the combined result of the motion of the Earth in its orbit around the Sun, and similar orbital motions of the other planets. Because of the Earth's orbital motion, the Sun appears to move nearly $1°$ eastward among the stars each day. The apparent path traced by the Sun in one year is called the *ecliptic*. Because the Earth's equatorial plane is inclined about 23.5 to its orbital plane, the Sun appears to move northward during half of the orbit, and southward during the other half, giving the Earth its seasons. As the Sun appears to cross the equator on its northward journey, about March 21, it is at *vernal equinox*, or *first point of Aries*. Days and nights are of about equal duration throughout the world. Six months later, about September 23, the Sun again crosses the equator, this time on its annual journey southward. It is then at *autumnal equinox*. Between the equinoxes the Sun reaches its maximum points north and south of the equator on about June 21 and December 22, the *summer solstice* and *winter solstice*, respectively. Maximum disparity between day and night occurs at the solstices. The words 'equinox' and 'solstice' are derived from the Latin. 'Equinox' means 'equal nights'; 'solstice' means 'sun stands still', as it reverses its direction of north-south motion, like the stand of the tide (p. 190). The attractive force of other bodies of the solar system on the equatorial bulge of the Earth (p. 18) causes a conical motion of the Earth's rotational axis about the vertical to the plane of the ecliptic, called *precession of the equinoxes*. The result is a slow westward motion of the equinoxes and solstices among the stars. Because of this motion, a *sidereal year*, one revolution of the Earth relative to the stars, is about 20 minutes longer than a *tropical year*, one revolution relative to the vernal equinox. The *anomalistic year*, the period of revolution from perihelion to perihelion (p. 289), is about five minutes longer than the sidereal year. A complete rotation of the equinoxes around the celestial sphere is made in about 25,800 years. Because of varying positions of bodies of the solar system, and especially the Moon, with respect to the ecliptic, the motion is somewhat erratic, the irregularities being called *nutation*.

The orbital motion of an astronomical body about another, called its *primary*, is governed by three laws defined by Johannes Kepler, and so known as *Kepler's laws*. As they relate to planets, these laws are:

1. *The orbits of the planets are ellipses, with the Sun at a common focus.*
2. *The straight line joining a planet and the Sun sweeps over equal areas in equal intervals of time.* The speed of a planet in its orbit is therefore variable.
3. *The squares of the sidereal periods of any two planets are proportional to the cubes of their mean distances from the Sun.*

The simple motion described by these laws is varied

slightly by the mutual attraction among planets. This is in keeping with the three *Newton's laws of motion* postulated by Sir Isaac Newton in 1687, as follows:

1. Every body continues in a state of rest or of uniform motion in a straight line unless acted upon by an external force.
2. When a body is acted upon by an external force, its acceleration is directly proportional to that force, and inversely proportional to the mass of the body, and acceleration takes place in the direction in which the force acts.
3. To every action there is an equal and opposite reaction.

From Kepler's laws and his own, Newton devised a single *universal law of gravitation* governing the relationship of bodies of the solar system, and perhaps of all bodies in space: *Every particle of matter attracts every other particle with a force varying directly with the product of their masses and inversely as the square of the distance between them.*

Although later studies, particularly those of Albert Einstein, have resulted in modification of the laws of Kepler and Newton, the difference in future positions of astronomical bodies, as predicted with and without the later information, is very small. As a planet thus revolves about the Sun (actually the centre of mass of the planet and the Sun) the point of closest approach is called the *perihelion*, and the point farthest from the Sun is called the *aphelion*. The Earth is at perihelion in January and at aphelion in July. The difference in maximum and minimum distance of planetary orbit is not great, the orbits being nearly circular, and all in nearly the same plane, that of the ecliptic.

The Moon's orbital motion about the Earth is similar to that of planets about the Sun. The points of minimum and maximum distance of the Moon's orbit are called the *perigee* and *apogee*, respectively. The straight line connecting the perihelion and aphelion of a planet, or the perigee and apogee of a satellite, is called the *line of apsides*.

The orbit of a planet or satellite intersects the ecliptic or the plane of the orbit of its primary, respectively, at two points called *nodes*. The node at which the planet or satellite has a northerly component of motion is called the *ascending node*.

The other is the *descending node*. The straight line connecting the two nodes is called the *line of nodes*.

The orbits of all planets being in nearly the plane of the ecliptic, apparent planetary motion relative to the stars is along nearly the same path as that taken by the Sun, but the apparent angular speed of the planets is much more erratic. It is usually eastward relative to the stars, the same as that of the Sun. But sometimes this *direct motion* reverses, resulting in westerly *retrograde motion* relative to the stars. Motion of bodies of the solar system relative to the stars is relatively slow compared with the apparent diurnal motion resulting from rotation of the Earth on its axis.

The planets Mercury and Venus, called *inferior planets*, are nearer to the Sun than is the Earth. They never appear far from the Sun. The angular distance east or west of the Sun, called *elongation*, is a maximum of about 28° for Mercury and 46° for Venus. When an inferior planet is nearest the line from the Earth through the Sun, it is said to be at *inferior conjunction* if it is between the Earth and Sun, and at *superior conjunction* if it is on the opposite side of the Sun. If one were to observe an inferior planet by telescope, one would find that the planet goes through all the phases of the Moon. Because of this changing phase, and the changing distance from the Earth, the apparent brightness of an inferior planet varies considerably.

Planets farther from the Sun than is the Earth are called *superior planets*. A superior planet may appear at any angle from the Sun. It is at *conjunction* when it is nearest the line from the Earth through the Sun, at *quadrature* when it is 90° from this line, and at *opposition* when it is on the opposite side of the Earth from the Sun. A superior planet never passes between the Earth and Sun, and is always in the gibbous or full phase.

Unlike bodies of the solar system, stars remain in almost the same apparent positions relative to one another over such long periods of time that they are sometimes referred to as *fixed stars* to further distinguish them from planets. It is this stability of position that makes possible the *constellations*, or groups of stars seeming to form imaginary figures. Although stars seem to be always in the same positions relative to one another, they, too, are in motion. This motion is hardly apparent to an observer without instruments capable of making minute measurements, because of the great distances of the stars from the Earth. While light from the Moon, travelling at the rate of approximately 300,000 kilometres per second, reaches the Earth in about a second and a quarter, and light from the Sun reaches the Earth in a little more than eight minutes, light from the nearest star travels more than four years to reach the Earth. With such distances, stars appear as mere points of light even in the most powerful telescopes, rather than as observable discs.

Stars visible to the unaided eye are all part of an island universe or *galaxy* of billions of stars all revolving around a point some 650,000,000,000,000,000 kilometres away. The Milky Way traces the edgewise direction of our galaxy, the milky appearance being the effect of this edgewise view of great numbers of faint stars. Millions of other galaxies similar to our own are at such great distances that they can be seen as groups of stars only by powerful telescopes.

The motion of a star in the line of sight does not change its apparent position relative to others. Slight change of apparent position is the result of the component of motion perpendicular to the line of sight, called *proper motion*.

Thus, all bodies are in motion, and all observable motion is relative to the observer. Actual motion relative to a fixed point in space, or *absolute motion*, could be determined only if one were able to identify such a fixed point. This has not been possible.

The apparent position of an astronomical body as observed from the surface of the Earth and as it would appear from the centre of the Earth is not measurably different for a star. Because of the great distances involved, rays of light from the stars are considered parallel over the entire surface of the Earth. Even from opposite sides of the orbit of the Earth the measured difference in position of the nearest star is less than two seconds of arc. For bodies of the solar system, however, the situation is different. The difference in apparent direction of a body as observed from different positions is called *parallax*, further designated *geocentric parallax* if the positions are the centre of the Earth and a point on its surface. The geocentric parallax of the Moon is greatest of all astronomical bodies because it is nearest to the Earth (about 385,000 kilometres away). Astronavigators make allowance for geocentric parallax of some bodies of the solar system.

As one observes the various astronomical bodies, one is aware of a great difference in apparent brightness. An arbitrary numerical scale of relative brightness, or *magnitude* (*mag*), has been established. About 20 of the brightest stars are considered to be of the first magnitude. The dimmest stars visible to the unaided eye are considered to be of the sixth magnitude. A first-magnitude body is considered to be 100 times brighter than a sixth-magnitude body. The fifth root of 100 being 2.512, the *magnitude ratio* of a body 2.512 times brighter than another is one magnitude. Stars brighter than magnitude 1.5 are generally referred to as 'first magnitude' stars. Those 1.51 to 2.50 magnitude are called 'second magnitude' stars, those 2.51 to 3.50 magnitude as 'third magnitude' stars, and so on. Negative magnitudes are used for bodies brighter than magnitude 0. The Sun has a magnitude of $(-)$ 26.7, and the Moon at full phase a magnitude of about $(-)$ 12.6. Venus, Mars, Jupiter, and Saturn sometimes have negative magnitudes. Two stars have negative magnitudes, Sirius being $(-)$ 1.6 and Canopus $(-)$ 0.9. The smallest magnitude difference observable by the unaided eye is about 0.1.

As commonly practised, astronavigation uses a very small number of astronomical bodies, considering the very large number available. The reason for this is that more bodies are not needed, and the tabulating of *ephemeridal information* (positional information with time) for a larger number would add to the bulk of almanacs without serving a useful purpose.

In the usual practice of astronavigation, each sight of an astronomical body yields one position line located relative to that point on the Earth where the body is vertically overhead. This point is called the *sub point* (*S*) or *geographical position* (*GP*) of the body. The intersection of two or more such position lines for the same time, or adjusted to the same time, identifies the fix.

3. Celestial Coordinates

Generally speaking, coordinates of the celestial sphere, called *celestial coordinates*, are similar to those of the Earth, shown in Fig. 101. The equator as the *primary great circle* of the terrestrial system, geographical poles, meridians, prime meridian, parallels, latitude, and longitude all have counterparts on the celestial sphere. In fact, there are several similar celestial coordinate systems based upon different primary great circles. The celestial equator, horizon, ecliptic, and galactic equator is each the primary great circle of a set of celestial coordinates.

Consider the *celestial equator system*. Refer to Fig. 605. If the plane of the Earth's equator is extended indefinitely, it intersects the celestial sphere at a great circle called the

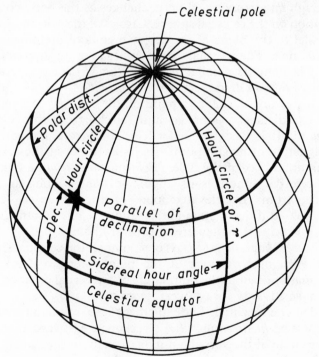

FIG. 605. The celestial equator system of coordinates relative to the celestial sphere.

celestial equator or *equinoctial*, the primary great circle of the celestial equator system of celestial coordinates. The two points 90° from the celestial equator, marking the intersections of the celestial sphere and the extension of the polar axis of the Earth, are the *celestial poles*, designated north and south to agree with the designations of their sub points. Except at the equator, the celestial pole having the same *name* (north or south) as the latitude of the observer is above his horizon, and the celestial pole having contrary name is below his horizon. These are designated the *elevated pole* and *depressed pole*, respectively.

Semi-great circles joining the north and south celestial poles are *hour circles, if they are fixed with respect to points on the celestial sphere and rotate with them.* Thus, the hour circle through an astronomical body changes as the body changes position on the celestial sphere. Circles of the celestial sphere parallel to the plane of the celestial equator are *parallels of declination.* The diurnal circle (p. 284) of an astronomical body is along its parallel of declination *if the body's position relative to the celestial equator is constant.*

Declination (d, dec) of a point on the celestial sphere is its angular distance, along an hour circle, from the celestial equator. It is designated north or south to agree with the designation of its sub point. Its limits are 0° at the celestial equator and 90° at the poles. *Polar distance (p)* of a point on the celestial sphere is its angular distance, along an hour circle, from the elevated pole of the observer. Thus, p = 90° − d if declination and latitude are of the same name, but p = 90° + d if they are of contrary name.

Sidereal hour angle (SHA) of a point on the celestial sphere is the angular distance of the point, along a parallel of declination, *west* of the hour circle of the vernal equinox (Υ). Because SHA is always west, from 0° to 360°, its direction need not be specified. The explement (360° minus an angle) of SHA is *right ascension (RA)*, reckoned eastward from the hour circle of the vernal equinox, usually in time units. It is seldom used by navigators.

Declination, sidereal hour angle, and right ascension of a fixed point on the celestial sphere change slightly from year to

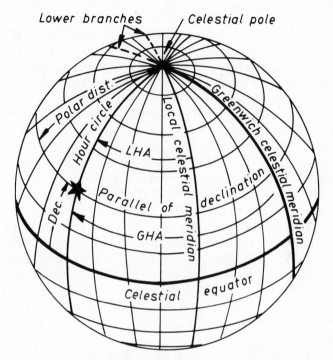

FIG. 606. The celestial equator system of coordinates
relative to the Earth.

year because of precession of the equinoxes and nutation
(p. 288). These coordinates of an astronomical body also
change as the body changes its position on the celestial
sphere. These coordinates constitute a celestial equator
system relative to the celestial sphere.

A second, similar set of coordinates constitutes a celestial
equator system relative to the Earth. Refer to Fig. 606. The
celestial equator, celestial poles, hour circles, parallels of
declination, declination, and polar distance are the same in
both systems. But the hour circle of the vernal equinox is
replaced as a reference by either of two great circles through
the poles. These *celestial meridians* are similar to hour circles,
with an important difference. Hour circles rotate with the
celestial sphere and so sweep over all the meridians of the

295

Earth each sidereal day. In contrast, celestial meridians remain fixed with respect to points on Earth, and so all hour circles of the celestial sphere sweep past them each sidereal day. The semi-great circle of a celestial meridian through the point vertically overhead at a place, and terminating at the celestial poles, is called the *upper branch* of the celestial meridian. The other half is called the *lower branch*, shown by broken lines in Fig. 606. The expression 'celestial meridian', used alone, usually refers to the upper branch.

Hour angle (HA) of a point on the celestial sphere is the angular distance, along a parallel of declination, of the point *west* of the reference celestial meridian. Hour angle always being west, from $0°$ to $360°$ (occasionally 0^h to 24^h), its direction need not be specified. The two reference celestial meridians are those over the prime meridian at Greenwich, England, and the observer. Hour angles with respect to these two references are distinguished by being designated *Greenwich hour angle (GHA)* and *local hour angle (LHA)*, respectively. The two are related by the expressions LHA = GHA − Lo(W.), and LHA = GHA + Lo(E.). Hour angle and sidereal hour angle are related by the expression HA (body) = HA Υ + SHA. Therefore SHA = HA (body) − HA Υ.

It is sometimes convenient to reckon a local hour angle either eastward or westward, from $0°$ to $180°$, like longitude on the Earth. It is then usually designated *meridian angle (t)*, and its direction (E. or W.) from the local meridian is specified. Meridian angle is not identified in Fig. 606. Occasionally, the designation hour angle (HA) is used for meridian angle (t).

Unlike SHA, hour angle of a fixed point on the celestial sphere changes rapidly, through $360°$ each sidereal day. The average rate for the Sun is $15°$ per hour.

As an astronomical body crosses the celestial meridian of a place, it is said to be at *meridian transit* or *meridian passage (mer pass)*, *upper transit* as it crosses the upper branch and *lower transit* as it crosses the lower branch.

A useful means of showing the relationship of the various types of hour angle is a diagram on the plane of the celestial

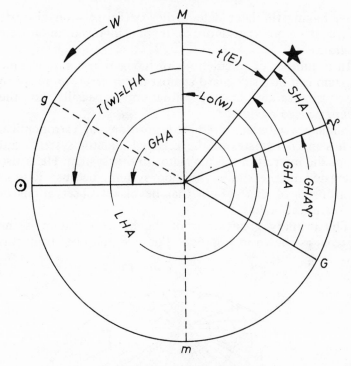

FIG. 607. Time diagram.

equator, called a *time diagram*. Refer to Fig. 607. The view is from above the *south* celestial pole, at the centre of the circle, which represents the celestial equator.

By convention, the local celestial meridian, Mm, is shown vertical with the upper branch at the top, the solid part being the upper branch and the broken part the lower branch. Similarly, Gg is the Greenwich celestial meridian. Hour circles of the vernal equinox (Υ), a star ($\bigstar$), and the Sun ($\odot$) are shown. Rotation of the celestial sphere is anticlockwise, as shown by the arrow outside the circle. The diagram shows that the observer is at longitude 120°W. The Sun is 90°W. of the observer, so his local time is 1800. Greenwich time is eight hours later, or 0200 the following day. When the Sun is between the lower branches of the two meridians, the dates at the two places differ by one day, the place to the east of the other having the later date. Other useful relationships are indicated. Note that latitude is not involved in a time diagram.

In a number of calculations of navigation a simple time diagram can be a safeguard against major error, or an aid to the visualization of the situation, especially to the inexperienced navigator.

Almanacs tabulate predicted positions of astronomical bodies in coordinates of the celestial equator system, and hence the interest of the navigator in this system. He is also interested in the similar horizon system, because it is in coordinates of this system that he makes observations of astronomical bodies.

The primary great circle of the horizon system is the *horizon*, as shown in Fig. 608. The two poles 90° from this

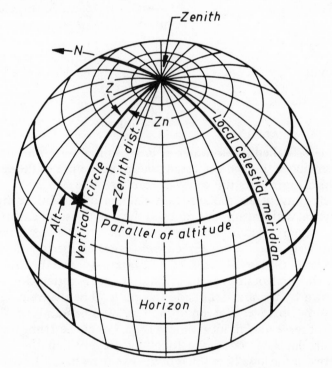

FIG. 608. The horizon system of coordinates.

great circle are the *zenith* (*Z*), the point vertically overhead, and the *nadir* (*Na*) not shown in Fig. 608, 180° from the zenith, and 90° below the horizon. Semi-great circles joining the zenith and nadir are *vertical circles*. The *principal vertical circle* passes through the north point on the horizon, and also through the celestial poles, and is therefore part of the celestial meridian of the place. The *prime vertical circle*, usually referred to as the *prime vertical* (*PV*), not shown in Fig. 608, passes through the east or west point of the horizon. Circles of the celestial sphere parallel to the plane of the horizon are *parallels of altitude*.

Altitude (*h*, *alt*) of a point on the celestial sphere is its angular distance, along a vertical circle, from the horizon. The altitude of a point below the horizon is negative. *Zenith distance* (*z*, *ZD*) of a point on the celestial sphere is its angular distance, along a vertical circle, from the zenith. Hence, $z = 90° - h$, and because h can be either positive or negative, z can have any value from 0° to 180°.

Azimuth (*Zn*, *Az*) of a point on the celestial sphere is the angular distance, along a parallel of altitude, of the point clockwise from the principal vertical circle, from 000° to 360°, or the *bearing* of the point. *Azimuth angle* (*Z*, *Az*) is the same as azimuth except that it is reckoned from the direction of the elevated pole, N. or S., toward the east or west, through 180°. It is given a prefix N. or S. to agree with the latitude, and a suffix E. or W. to indicate the direction from the reference direction, agreeing with the label of meridian angle. Occasionally, azimuth angle is reckoned from either north or south, through 90°, the prefix indicating whether the reference direction is north or south. *Amplitude* (*A*, *Amp*) is similar to azimuth angle but is reckoned from the *nearer* prime vertical circle, E. or W., toward the north or south. It is given a prefix E. or W. to indicate the reference direction, and a suffix N. or S. to indicate whether the point is north or south of the reference direction. Amplitude is usually used only for points on the horizon, for astronomical bodies at rising and setting. Azimuth angle or amplitude can be converted to azimuth by following the instructions of its labels, remembering that Zn starts with 000° at north, and increases eastward or clockwise through 090° at east, 180° at south, 270° at west, and to 360° or 000° back at north. Thus, if Z is S. 25° W., Zn = 180° + 25° = 205°. If A is E. 20° N., Zn = 090° − 20° = 070°. The integral degrees of azimuth, but not of azimuth angle or amplitude, are always stated in three figures. Thus, if Z is N. 6° E., Zn = 000° + 6° = 006°. In this case, A is E. 84° N. (Zn = 090° − 84° = 006°).

The horizon constituting the primary great circle of the horizon system of coordinates is more precisely identified as the *celestial horizon*. It is the intersection of the celestial sphere and a plane through the centre of the Earth and perpendicular to the zenith–nadir line, as shown in Fig. 609. A parallel plane through the eye of the observer intersects the celestial sphere at the *sensible horizon*, a small circle some

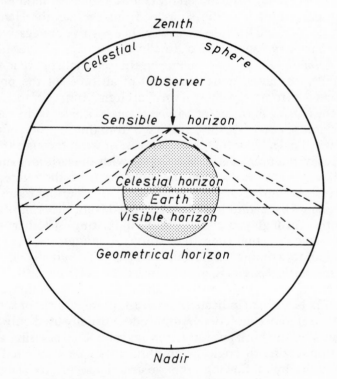

FIG. 609. Horizons.

distance above the celestial horizon, but at the great distance of the celestial sphere the difference is not measurable, and hence these two horizons are generally considered identical in navigation. However, some bodies of the solar system are so close to the Earth that their angular distances above the two planes may differ a small amount (parallax), requiring a correction to measured altitudes.

Because the eye of an observer is generally some distance above the surface of the Earth, the horizon he sees as the line of demarcation between Earth and sky differs appreciably from both the celestial and sensible horizons, the difference increasing with greater height of eye. A straight line from his eye, tangent to the surface of the Earth, intersects the celestial sphere on a small circle some distance below the celestial horizon, as shown in Fig. 609. This small circle is called the *geometrical horizon*, an expression occasionally used to refer to the celestial horizon. Because of refraction of light as it passes through the Earth's atmosphere, the *visible horizon* appears to be elevated somewhat above the geometrical horizon. The visible horizon is the one used by mariners in making observations of altitudes of astronomical bodies for position lines. Corrections are applied to convert measured readings to altitudes from the celestial horizon.

Because predicted positions of astronomical bodies are tabulated in coordinates of the celestial equator system, while the navigator observes bodies in coordinates of the horizon system, conversion of coordinates of one system to those of the other is a necessary part of astronavigation. This conversion is accomplished in the process known as sight reduction, discussed in chapter IX.

The interconversion of coordinates of the celestial equator and horizon systems is made possible by the fact that one great circle of the celestial sphere, the celestial meridian of the observer, is common to both systems. A diagram on the plane of the celestial meridian is instructive in demonstrating a number of relationships which can help a navigator visualize a situation and avoid major errors.

Refer to Fig. 610. The circle represents the celestial meridian of an observer, and so is common to both systems of

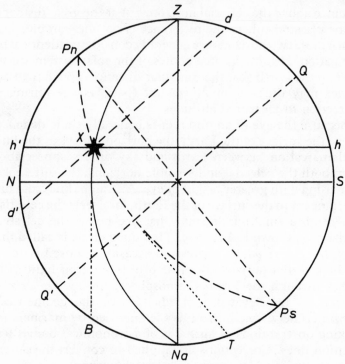

FIG. 610. Diagram on the plane of the celestial meridian.

coordinates. By convention, the zenith, Z, is placed at the top
of the diagram, and the nadir, Na, is placed 180° away, at the
bottom. The horizon is then midway between the zenith and
nadir, at NS, and parallels of altitude, such as hh′, are parallel
to it. These circles appear as straight lines because they are
viewed edge-on. By convention, the north point of the
horizon is placed to the left, at N, and the south point to the
right, at S. The prime vertical is represented by the vertical
circle ZNa, perpendicular to the horizon and midway
between the north and south points, and therefore, like the
horizon, seen edge-on. Any vertical circle except the prime
vertical and the principal vertical circle (the celestial
meridian) appears as an ellipse. The vertical circle through
the body X is shown by arc ZXNa. It is drawn as an arc of a
circle, rather than as an ellipse, through the three points for

ease in plotting. The results are satisfactory for illustrating the relationships involved.

The elements of the celestial equator system, except for the celestial meridian, are shown by broken lines for easy identification, though with a little experience one can abandon this refinement. The elevated pole is located on the celestial meridian at a point above the north or south point of the horizon equal to the observer's latitude. In Fig. 610 the north celestial pole, Pn, is 50° above the north point of the horizon (arc Nh'Pn = 50°), indicating that the observer is at latitude 50°N. A line from Pn through the centre of the diagram to the opposite side of the celestial sphere locates the south celestial pole, Ps, the depressed pole. Line PnPs represents an hour circle 90° from the celestial meridian, seen edge-on, and therefore a body on this line would have a meridian angle of 90°, either east or west. Line QQ′ represents the celestial equator, seen edge-on, midway between the celestial poles; and parallels of declination, such as dd′, are parallel to it. Any hour circle except the one coinciding with the celestial meridian (t = 0° or 180°) and that 90° from it appears as an ellipse, such as that shown by the arc PnXPs, again drawn as an arc of a circle for simplicity of construction.

Points on the celestial sphere can be located by either the celestial equator or horizon system of coordinates. If a point is located by one set, those of the other can be determined approximately by measurement. In Fig. 610, dd′ is the parallel of declination, seen edge-on, of point X. The declination, 30° N., is indicated by arc Qd or Q′d′. The meridian angle, 110° E. or W., is measured around the celestial meridian from Q to T, and then a perpendicular is dropped from T to the celestial equator. This is the equivalent of rotating the celestial equator through 90° so it will appear as a circle, measuring the meridian angle along the celestial equator, and then rotating it back into place. Measurement in similar manner along any parallel of declination would yield the same result. The hour circle is drawn as the arc of a circle through the celestial poles and the foot of the perpendicular from T to the celestial equator. The point X is located at the intersection of the parallel of declination and the hour circle.

The parallel of altitude, hh′ can then be drawn as a straight line (edge-on view) through point X, parallel to the horizon. The altitude of point X is arc Sh or Nh′, 11°. An arc of a circle through X and the zenith and nadir represents the vertical circle. By erecting a perpendicular at the intersection of the vertical circle and the horizon, one can locate point B. The azimuth angle of point X is represented by the arc Nd′Q′B, N. 56° E. or W. (north because the observer is in north latitude, and east or west to agree with meridian angle). This process is one of rotation through 90°, measurement, and return, as with meridian angle.

The process, of course, could be reversed, horizon system coordinates being used to locate point X, and celestial equator system coordinates then being determined by measurement. With a little practice, one can learn to draw a diagram on the plane of the celestial meridian easily and quickly, and by so doing gain a thorough understanding of the various definitions and relationships involved.

Refer again to Fig. 610. As the celestial sphere appears to rotate on its polar axis through Pn and Ps, a point on the sphere appears to move along its diurnal circle which is the parallel of declination, dd′, if declination does not change. If N is at the left and S is at the right, as shown, the east point of the horizon is at the centre of the diagram, directly behind the west point. As the body moves *upward*, from left to right, on the back side of the diagram (remembering that the circle represents a sphere), it rises at the point where its diurnal circle intersects the horizon. Its altitude is zero and its meridian angle is maximum while it is visible. As it continues along its diurnal circle, its altitude and azimuth angle increase, and its hour angle decreases. At the apparent intersection of the diurnal circle and PnPs its meridian angle is 90° and its LHA is 270°. As the body crosses the prime vertical, ZNa, its azimuth angle is N. 90° E., and its Zn is 090°. At d the body is at upper transit, at maximum altitude (arc ShQd). Its meridian angle is 0° and its azimuth is 180°. If the declination had been of the same name as the latitude and numerically greater, it would have crossed the celestial meridian north of the zenith at azimuth angle 0° and azimuth 000°, the arc ZQ, as arc PnN, being equal to the latitude of the observer. Azimuth angle would never be as great as 90°, the maximum value occurring at the point of tangency of its vertical and diurnal circles. At this point

$$\cos Z = \cot h \tan L = \sin d \sin t,$$

in which Z is the azimuth angle, h is the altitude, L is the latitude, d is the declination, and t is the meridian angle. The values of h and t at nearest approach can be determined as explained in section 12 of chapter IX. Only if latitude and declination were equal and of the same name would the body cross the celestial meridian at the zenith.

As the body continues downward along its diurnal circle, from right to left along the *front* side of the diagram, it crosses the prime vertical at Zn 270°, the 90° meridian angle point at LHA 90°, and finally sets as it again crosses the horizon in the north-western part of the sky. At each value of meridian angle, east or west, the altitude and azimuth angle are the same numerically but with opposite suffix. At point d′ the body is at lower transit, at maximum negative altitude. If the declination were greater than the co-latitude (90° − L)of the observer, the body would not set, being circumpolar. Only if a body were circumpolar and upper transit occurred on the opposite side of the zenith from the elevated pole would the body circle the sky with azimuths through 360° while visible.

A body having declination 0° rises and sets on the prime vertical, at meridian angle 90°, and is above the horizon half the time and below it half the time, regardless of latitude. This is the situation with the Sun at the time of the equinoxes, when day and night are of equal length throughout the world.

A body having declination of the same name as the latitude rise and sets on the side of the prime vertical toward the elevated pole, and is above the horizon more than half the time. This is the situation with the Sun during the summer, and why the northern summer is occurring at the same time that the southern hemisphere is having winter, for if the body and latitude have contrary names, the body rises and sets on the opposite side of the prime vertical from the elevated pole, is above the horizon less than half the time, and never crosses the prime vertical above the horizon. If a body's declination is contrary and greater than the co-latitude, it does not rise. Accordingly, bodies of high declination are never seen by many observers in the opposite hemisphere. If an observer is in higher latitude than the polar circle, the Sun remains above the horizon throughout the day and 'night' when it is at maximum same-name declination, and remains below the horizon all day during maximum contrary-name declination. Thus, the diagram can show various relationships related to the Sun during the year, neglecting such factors as atmospheric refraction, semi-diameter, parallax, changes in declination, position of the Earth in its orbit, and height of eye of the observer. It can also be used to show twilight relationships, such as why twilight lasts longer in higher latitudes. Note that longitude is not involved in these relationships.

Two additional sets of celestial coordinates are used by astronomers but are of little interest to the navigator. These are the *ecliptic system* and the *galactic system*, based upon the ecliptic and the galactic equator as primary great circles, respectively. One point of interest to navigators, however, is the fact that in the ecliptic system points on the celestial sphere are located by means of coordinates called *celestial latitude* and *celestial longitude*. It is incorrect, therefore, to use these expressions with respect to other systems of celestial coordinates.

Systems of spherical coordinates used by navigators are summarized in the following table:

Earth	Celestial Equator Relative to Cel. Sphere	Celestial Equator Relative to Earth	Horizon
equator	celestial equator	celestial equator	celestial horizon
poles	celestial poles	celestial poles	zenith, nadir
meridians	hour circles	celestial meridians	vertical circles
prime meridian	hour circle Υ	Greenwich or local celestial meridian	principal vertical circle, PV
parallels	parallels of dec	parallels of dec	parallels of alt
latitude	declination	declination	altitude
co-latitude	polar distance	polar distance	zenith distance
longitude	SHA, RA	GHA, LHA, t	Zn, Z, A

4. The Navigational Triangle

The principal calculation of astronavigation, like that of great-circle sailing, involves the solution of a spherical triangle called the *navigational triangle* sometimes called the *astronomical triangle*. Refer to Fig. 611, a diagram on the plane of the celestial meridian with the same coordinates and notation as those of Fig. 610. Point Z is the zenith of the observer; Pn his elevated pole; and X a point on the celestial sphere, usually an astronomical body. The navigational triangle of astronavigation consists of arcs PnZ, part of the celestial meridian; PnX, part of the hour circle; and ZX, part of the vertical circle. These arcs are all parts of great circles.

Arc QZ is the declination of the zenith, and arc PnZ is its polar distance. Then are QZ is numerically the same as the latitude of the observer, and arc PnZ is numerically equal to

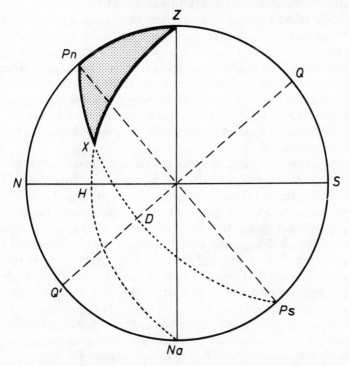

FIG. 611. The navigational triangle of astronavigation.

90° minus his latitude, (the co-latitude, co-L). Arc D X is the declination of the body, and arc PnX is its polar distance, or 90° ∓ its declination, minus if latitude and declinations are of the same name, and plus if of contrary name. Arc H X is the altitude of the body, and arc Z X is the zenith distance, or 90° minus the altitude (90° + negative altitude).

The angles of the triangle are Z PnX, the meridian angle (t); PnZX, the azimuth angle (Z); and PnXZ, the *parallactic angle* (X), or *position angle.*

If any three of the six elements of the navigational triangle (three sides and three angles) are known, the other three can be calculated, though two solutions are possible in some instances. In the usual practice of navigation the parallactic angle is not used. By using suitable trigonometric functions, the navigator can avoid complements of angles, using latitude, declination, and altitude directly.

The most common calculation involving solution of the navigational triangle is that used in sight reduction. An assumed latitude of the observer is used with the declination and meridian angle (for an assumed longitude) of an astronomical body, and the altitude and azimuth of the body are calculated. The methods of doing this are explained in chapter IX. Other solutions are sometimes needed, as in identification of an unknown body observed through a break in the overcast.

A terrestrial counterpart of the navigational triangle of the celestial sphere involves the sub points of the three vertices of the triangle, and the arcs of great circles joining them. Thus, the vertices are the position of the observer, his nearer geographical pole, and the sub point of the astronomical body. The sides are the co-latitudes of the observer and the sub point of the body and the arc of the great circle between these two points. The angles are the difference in longitude of the observer and the body's sub point and the initial great-circle direction of each from the other. If the position of the observer is the point of departure and the destination is substituted for the sub point of the body, the navigational triangle becomes that of great-circle sailing (p. 177). Thus, the methods of solution used for sight reduction can be used for great-circle sailing, and vice versa, if one substitutes the appropriate notation, and remembers that zenith distance, not altitude, is the equivalent of great-circle distance between points on the Earth.

5. Astro Position Lines

If the navigator observes an astronomical body in his zenith, vertically overhead, he is at the sub point of the body. Accordingly, if he knows the declination and GHA of the body at the instant of observation, he knows his position on the Earth. His latitude is the same as declination of the body, and his longitude is west, equal to the G H A if less than 180°, or east, equal to 360° − GHA if greater than 180°.

But since an astronomical body appears to revolve around the Earth, its sub point is in continual motion across the surface of the Earth, being at any particular point for only an instant and then moving on toward the west at a rate of approximately a quarter of a minute of arc of longitude per second. Further, it would be a coincidence if the sub point of a body of known declination passed through the position of the observer, rather than north or south of him. Finally, it is not easy to determine the instant at which a body is in the zenith.

The usual method of using an astronomical body for position determination is by establishing an astro *position line* to be crossed with others at the same time, or adjusted to the same time, as in pilotage.

Any specific altitude of an astronomical body defines a circle with the sub point at the centre and with a radius equal to the zenith distance. This is so because the rays of light from distant astronomical bodies are essentially parallel. This is not quite true of some bodies of the solar system, for which a small correction is needed to adjust for parallax. Refer to Fig. 612. The circle represents the Earth, with an observer at point O and his zenith at Z. The parallel lines represent parallel rays of light from an astronomical body having a sub point at S. The tangent line HH′ represents the horizon of the observer, h the altitude of the body at the observer, and z its zenith distance. Angle SCO and arc SO are equal,

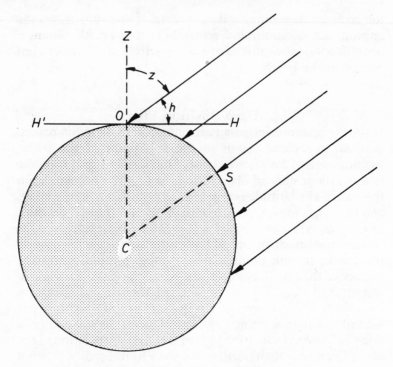

FIG. 612. The altitude of an astronomical body.

numerically, to the zenith distance. Arc SO is the radius of a *circle of equal altitude* surrounding point S, the altitude of the body being the same at every point on the circle. With a greater altitude the zenith distance and radius of the circle are smaller, decreasing to zero at the sub point.

The circle of equal altitude is the astro position line. Its radius can be very large, for each minute of arc is equivalent to one mile on the surface of the Earth. Thus, for a body at altitude $40°$ the zenith distance is $90° - 40° = 50°$, and with 60 miles in each degree, the radius is $50 \times 60 = 3{,}000$ miles. For a body on the horizon, the distance is $90 \times 60 = 5{,}400$ miles. For this reason, it is not practicable to plot the position line as a circle in the manner of plotting circular position lines in pilotage (p. 225), unless the body is near the zenith.

The usual procedure is to calculate the altitude (*calculated*

310

altitude or *computed altitude, Hc*) and azimuth for an *assumed position* (*AP*) in the vicinity of the actual position, and compare this altitude with the *observed altitude* (*Ho*), *corrected sextant altitude*, or *true altitude* (*T alt*), the measured altitude with certain corrections applied, to determine the *intercept* (*a, Int*), sometimes called the *altitude difference*. The intercept, in minutes of arc, is the difference in miles of the radii of the two circles of equal altitude, one through the assumed position, and the other through the position of the observer. This information is sufficient for plotting the astro position line. Refer to Fig. 613. Point S is the sub point of an astronomical body. The large arcs are parts of circles of equal altitude for two different zenith distances, A S and B S. The intercept is A B, and from either point the azimuth of the body is the direction, or bearing, of point S.

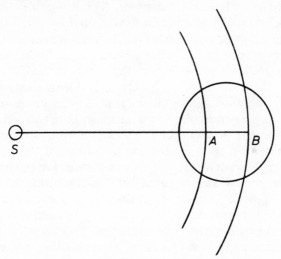

FIG. 613. Arcs of circles of equal altitude.

Now refer to Fig. 614, a larger-scale diagram of the part of Fig. 613 within the small circle. If point A is the assumed position, the arc through it represents the circle of equal altitude through A at the time of observation. If the calculated altitude (Hc) for this point and the observed altitude (Ho) are

311

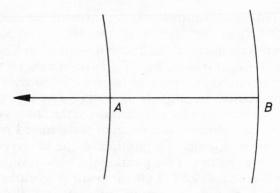

FIG. 614. Large-scale view of arcs of circles of equal altitude.

both known, the intercept can be calculated. If Hc is greater than Ho, the observer must be somewhere on a circle of equal altitude farther from the sub point. A point on this observer's circle of equal altitude can be established by drawing a line from the assumed position *away* (*A*) from the sub point, or in the reciprocal of the azimuth a distance equal to the intercept. This establishes point B, on the circle of equal altitude through the position of the observer. It does not establish his position. Because of the large radius of the circle of equal altitude, a perpendicular to the azimuth line, through B, can be used as the position line. For high altitudes a correction may be needed to allow for the curvature of the line. The observer is somewhere on this position line, within the accuracy of observation, calculation, and plotting. If B is the assumed position, Ho is greater than Hc, a is measured *toward* (*T*) the sub point, in the direction of the azimuth, and the perpendicular position line is erected at point A.

The actual plot of an astro position line is somewhat simpler than shown in Fig. 614. Refer to Fig. 615. The AP is plotted and labelled. The azimuth line is drawn toward or away from the sub point, as appropriate, for a distance in miles equal to the intercept in minutes of arc, and at the point thus determined, called the *intercept terminal point* (*ITP*) or J position, the perpendicular position line is plotted and labelled with the time of observation above the line and the name of the observed body below the line. The plot as shown

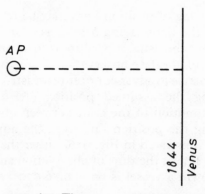

FIG. 615. The astro position line.

in Fig. 615 is in accordance with a widely accepted standard. Note the use of a broken line for the azimuth line. The plot should include all essential information but nothing extraneous.

As a safeguard against plotting the azimuth line in the wrong direction, one should invariably label the intercept as T (toward) or A (away) at the time it is calculated. It is easy to visualize the situation and determine the correct label, but some navigators prefer a memory aid. One frequently used among American navigators is 'Coast Guard Academy' using the initial letters of 'calculated greater away'. Any unambiguous memory aid one finds easy to remember is suitable.

Plotting of astro position lines is generally done directly on the plotting sheet or chart used for plotting the dead reckoning.

6. The Astro Fix

An astro fix, as one in pilotage, is established at the intersection of two or more position lines. However, astronomical observations are seldom made simultaneously, usually being spread over a period of perhaps 10 to 15 minutes. In astronavigation, position lines from a *round of sights* taken during a normal sight-taking period, adjusted to a common time, are considered simultaneous in the sense that the resulting position is called a *fix*, rather than a *running fix*.

The adjusting of position lines may be to any convenient time during the sight-taking period, as to an integral hour or half-hour, but the usual procedure is to *advance* earlier lines to the time of the last observation. To avoid clutter, it is common practice to advance or retire an astro position line by first plotting the assumed position (AP), moving it as required by motion of the craft between observations, and then plotting the position line from the adjusted assumed position, as illustrated in Fig. 616, rather than plotting both the position line at the time of observation and the advanced line. As shown, a vessel is on course 070°, speed 20 knots.

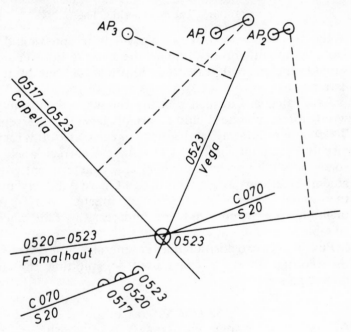

FIG. 616. The astro fix.

Observation and computation result in the following data:

Time	Body	a	Zn
0517	Capella	12.1A	045.1
0520	Fomalhaut	10.3T	171.8
0523	Vega	6.5A	293.2

The three assumed positions are plotted at AP_1, AP_2, and AP_3. The first is advanced 2 miles (the run for 6 minutes at speed 20 knots) in direction 070°, and from this advanced position the Capella position line is plotted and labelled as shown. Both the time of observation and the time to which the position line is advanced are given above the line, and the name of the body below the line. Similarly, the second AP is advanced 1 mile in direction 070°, and the Fomalhaut position line is plotted from this advanced position, and labelled. The Vega position line is plotted from the third AP, not advanced, and labelled. This line not being adjusted, the time of observation only is used in the label. The centre of the small cocked hat formed by the three position lines is taken as the 0523 fix, and labelled as shown. If desired, the word 'Fix' may be added after the fix-time label. A new DR plot is started from the fix. If the DR positions are used as AP's, all position lines are plotted from the DR position at the time of the fix.

Current is usually not used in advancing astro position lines over the short distances involved in plotting fixes, unless the time between observations is unusually long or the current is unusually strong. It *is* necessary to make allowance for any changes of course or speed between observations.

Much of what is said in section 3 of chapter V regarding two- and multiple-position-line fixes applies also to astro fixes. Two position lines provide a fix, but additional lines provide a small increase in accuracy; a possible means of eliminating systematic errors; and, most important, an indication of a possible blunder.

A great deal has been written on the subject of determining the most probable position from multiple position lines. Much of the discussion centres around the cocked hat involved when three position lines are plotted. Fig. 617 shows such a plot, with position-line labels omitted for clarity. If all positions are considered equally accurate, and their errors are considered random (p. 27), the position of the fix is considered to be the centre of the triangle, defined as that point, within the triangle, equidistant from the three position lines. Determination of this point by eye is generally of

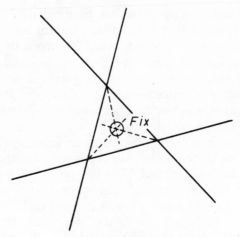

FIG. 617. The cocked hat.

sufficient accuracy for practical navigation, but it can be determined precisely by bisecting the three angles of the triangle, the centre being at the common intersection of the three bisectors, as shown.

If the total error of each position line is the same and of the same sign (all *toward* or all *away* from the bodies observed), and if the azimuths of the three bodies are not within a semi-circle, the fix is at the centre of the cocked hat. But if the azimuths are all within a semi-circle, the situation is different, as shown in Fig. 618. The azimuths of the two position lines

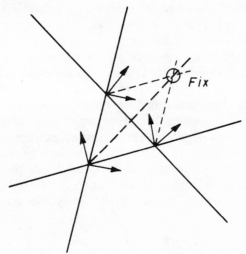

FIG. 618. A fix outside the cocked hat.

at each intersection are shown by the arrows. If the smaller angles between the *azimuth* lines at each intersection are bisected, the common intersection lies *outside* the cocked hat, at a point equidistant from the three position lines. For the three position lines shown, there are four possible combinations of azimuth: all may be either toward or away from the centre of the figure, or any two may be the same (toward or away) and the third contrary. Thus, there are four possible positions of the fix equidistant from the three position lines, as shown in Fig. 619.

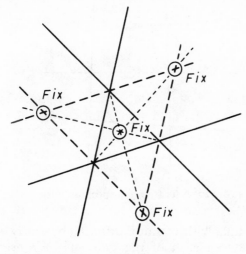

FIG. 619. Four positions equidistant from three position lines.

This situation might seem to indicate that the probability of the fix being within the cocked hat is only one in four. This is not the case, however. An analysis of a number of observations made at known positions, with all azimuths within a semi-circle, indicated clearly the superiority of the internal position, both in number of times it was nearer to the known position and in the magnitude of the error. This means that random error of astro sights generally exceeds systematic error.

However, the possibility remains that the actual position of the observer may be outside the cocked hat. Any constant error that does exist can be eliminated by observing bodies evenly distributed around the horizon, with azimuths 120° apart if three bodies are observed. This, of course, is not always possible. If four bodies are observed, the ideal is for them to be separated in azimuth by 90°. Fig. 620 shows the

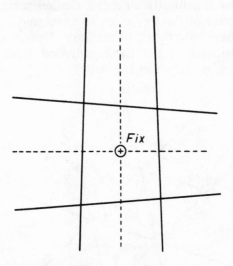

FIG. 620. A fix from four position lines.

plot of four lines with azimuths differing by nearly 90°. Lines midway between each of the two sets of nearly parallel position lines identify the fix. If four position lines are randomly spaced in azimuth, four cocked hats are likely to be obtained, as shown in Fig. 621, and unless one is very much in error, reasonable doubt exists as to the true position of the vessel. If a large number of position lines is available, the centre of the greatest concentration of intersections is a likely candidate for the most probable position, assuming one has no reason to favour some lines over the others. Unless one uses sights in pairs, as in Fig. 620, or a considerable number of sights, azimuth differences of less than 30° or more than 150° are best avoided, because azimuth differences exceeding these limits result in position lines with poor angles of cut (p. 32).

318

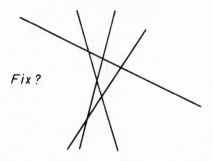

Fix?

FIG. 621. Four position lines with random azimuth.

The usual procedure is to make a number of observations, perhaps of seven bodies, if that number is available, and solve for the three or four considered most favourable, considering probable accuracy of observation and azimuth difference. If the resulting plot is reasonable, the other sights are not used, but in case of doubt, additional sights are reduced and plotted, giving them equal weight with those previously plotted, unless one has reason for weighting the lines.

One might be tempted to judge the accuracy of an astro fix by the size of the cocked hat. This is a dangerous procedure. A very small cocked hat or a common intersection of three position lines might seem close to perfection, but, because of offsetting errors or a common error in time, 'perfect' fixes may be as far from the true position as the centres of cocked hats of considerable size. The size of the cocked hat can serve one useful function, however. If it results in apparent errors, as indicated by the distance from the fix to each position line, larger than seems reasonable, one might well search for a blunder or reduce and plot additional sights, for two or three offsetting blunders are unlikely. The limiting magnitude of a 'reasonable' error varies with the conditions and the ability of the observer, dictated by experience. While no general rule suffices for all situations, one might reasonably question the accuracy of a sight with an apparent error of more than three miles, under normal conditions. An experienced navigator can usually measure altitude above a reasonably good horizon with an error of not more than two minutes of arc (two miles), and all errors of sight reduction and plotting should not add more than another mile, if tables and calculations to the nearest o.́1 are used. He might also question the accuracy of a fix father from his DR position than seems reasonable under existing conditions.

Position lines obtained by astronavigation can be crossed with position lines obtained in any other way, as by electronic positioning systems, or astro fixes can be compared with other fixes when the means for doing so are available. Astro sights are not usually taken when more accurate means of fixing the position of the vessel are available, as when one is in pilotage waters. However, an occasional observation at a position established accurately by other means, or even at anchor, can be helpful in assessing one's ability with the sextant, or in checking or establishing any personal error one may have.

When establishing a fix in which one has confidence, one can determine average current since the last previous fix (not running fix) by comparing the DR position and the fix. The direction from DR to fix is the set of the current. The distance between these positions is the total drift, which, divided by the interval, in hours, between fixes yields drift. A new DR plot is started from a reliable astro fix.

7. The Astro Running Fix

A *running fix* is obtained in astronavigation when the interval between observations is considerable. This occurs when only one body at a time is available in a favourable position, and a wait is needed for a suitable angle of cut on a second observation of the same or a different body.

A common use of the running fix in astronavigation is to provide a position of the vessel at or near noon. The Sun is observed during the morning and again about noon. The two position lines are plotted and the earlier one advanced to the time of the later sight, as shown in Fig. 622. The navigator of a ship on course 105°, speed 18 knots, obtains a morning Sun line at 0830. He plots the position line, which indicates that he is making better speed over the ground than through the

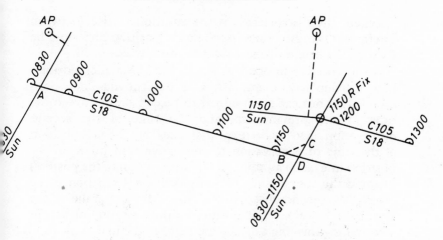

FIG. 622. A running fix from two observations of the Sun.

water, confirming a current set of 065°, drift 1.5 knots, established at a star fix at 0600, during morning twilight. Because one position line can yield useful information, the line itself, not just the AP, is plotted. At 1150 the navigator again *shoots* (observes) the Sun, and plots the position line. The earlier Sun line is advanced to 1150, allowing for current. The intersection of the two position lines constitutes the running fix, which serves as the origin of a new DR plot. It is necessary to make allowance for any changes of course or speed between observations.

Note that the earlier position line, not the AP, is advanced. A convenient method of doing so is to measure the distance run between 0830 and 1150, AB, along the course line, from point A, the intersection of the 0830 position line and the 0830 course line, and from point B measure BC a distance of 5.0 miles (the total drift during the interval between observations) in the direction of the drift, 065°, establishing point C. At this point the advanced position line is drawn parallel to the 0830 Sun line, and labelled appropriately. Note that the total drift is computed for the interval between observations, not between fixes. The current between the previous fix and the time of the first observation has already set the vessel from its 0830 DR position to the 0830 position line, and the distance BC is the additional offset between 0830 and 1150. Any point on the 0830 position line could be used as the origin of measurement for advancement.

An alternative method of advancing the earlier position line, particularly useful when a current has not been established but can be assumed to be constant between the time of the previous fix and the time of the second observation, is to measure the distance from the DR position at the time of observation to any convenient point on the position line, such as point A, the intersection of the position line and the course line. Then from the DR position at the time of the second observation a line is drawn parallel to the line from the earlier DR position to the position line at that time. Along this line a distance is measured equal to the ratio of time intervals from the previous fix to the times of the second and first observations. In the illustration:

$$\frac{1150-0600}{0830-0600} = \frac{5^h50^m}{2^h30^m} = \frac{5.83}{2.50} = 2.33$$

This makes possible the location of point D. By measurement, the distance from the 0830 DR position to point A is 2.4 miles, and 2.4 × 2.33 = 5.6 miles, the distance from the 1150 DR position to point D. The advanced position line is plotted through point D, parallel to the original position line.

Caution should be exercised in the use of this alternative method, for any error is magnified by the ratio of time intervals, in this case 2.33. If the interval between the previous fix and the first position line is short in comparison with the interval between observations, the ratio can be very large.

Some thought should be given to selection of the interval between observations. The ideal angle of cut of 90° would occur if the first observation were made at the time that the Sun crossed the prime vertical, and the second when it transmitted the celestial meridian. However, this would not be possible during the winter, when the Sun crosses the prime vertical below the horizon. Also, it might result in a very long interval between observations, with an attendant large error resulting from error in the current assumed to be acting to offset the vessel. Occasionally, the interval can be shortened without sacrificing desirability of angle of cut, by using two astronomical bodies, as the Sun and Moon. Their azimuths might be too nearly identical for a good angle of cut if sights are taken simultaneously, but might provide a good angle of cut if proper selection is made of the order of observation and a relatively short interval elapses between observations.

8. Utility of One Position Line

Although it is desirable to obtain a fix periodically, a lone position line can often provide useful information. If the body observed is directly ahead or astern, the position line is perpendicular to the course line, and so provides an indication of progress being made along the course line. If there has been no change of course or speed since the last fix, the distance from the last fix to the position line, divided by the elapsed time in hours, is the average speed of the craft over the ground. Consequently, a position line perpendicular to the course line, or nearly so, is called a *speed line*. A position line from a body on or near the beam is called a *course line* because it indicates how well the desired course is being maintained, and some indication of the cross component of combined current and leeway.

A body on or near the prime vertical indicates the longitude of the craft, while a body on or near the celestial meridian indicates the latitude. A body toward or away from the nearest coast indicates distance of the vessel offshore, useful information in maintaining a safe distance from shoal water or in predicting the time of landfall. A line perpendicular to the shore can be helpful in predicting the *place* of landfall.

If a passage is to be made between shoals or other dangers, with limited extent of safe water, frequent observation of a body abeam can be helpful in making a safe passage. The body's altitude at intervals during the passage might be calculated in advance with all corrections to measured altitudes applied with opposite sign, and the results plotted on cross-section paper, so that sextant readings can be compared with values from the curve for immediate indication of any deviation from the desired track.

A lone position line can be used for homing (p. 250). If a vessel is approaching a destination of limited horizontal extent, as a small island, and the position of the vessel is in doubt, there is a possibility that the destination will be passed unsighted. If only one astronomical body is available, a mariner can head well to one side of the destination, observe the body at intervals and calculate the altitude at the destination, and when the observed altitude is the same as the calculated value, he knows that he is on the position line through the destination, and its direction from him. He can then 'run down the position line' to the destination. Before the availability of electronic aids on various islands, this method was used frequently, especially by aviators. Before longitude could be determined accurately at sea, mariners sailed to the latitude of their destination, and then 'ran down the latitude (parallel)' to the destination.

It is sometimes helpful, when a lone position line is available, to use it for establishing an estimated position, as discussed in section 6 of chapter V, and illustrated in Fig. 520.

A lone astro position line might be used with a position line determined in some other manner to obtain a fix or running fix.

9. Time

The navigator's concern with time relates to the time of day and the measurement of time intervals. Thus, when a navigator speaks of 'time', he is referring to the measurement of time.

Time is involved in navigation in several respects. By its very nature, navigation involves motion from one place to another. Accordingly, a position, whether by dead reckoning or otherwise, is of little significance without identification of the related time. Further, navigators are concerned with estimated time of arrival; anticipated time of sighting a navigational light or making landfall; time of Sunrise, Sunset, and twilight; etc. In all of these applications, time is usually needed to the nearest integral minute.

In astronavigation, time has an additional significance. Because of rotation of the Earth, resulting in apparent rotation of the celestial sphere, sub points, to which astro position lines are related, are continuously moving westward at the rate of about one minute of longitude every four seconds. For the timing of observations of astronomical bodies, the navigator desires an accuracy of one second or better.

A third use of time in navigation relates to radar and electronic positioning systems, in which time intervals are measured in *microseconds* (*μs*, *μsec*, *Ms*) (millionths of a second), or, occasionally in *nanoseconds* (*ns*) (thousandths of a microsecond) or *picoseconds* (*ps*) (millionths of a micro-second).

The specific uses of time in navigation are, of course, distinct from the general use of time by all peoples for the regulation of the affairs of mankind—the times of starting and stopping some activity, keeping appointments, arising and retiring, etc.

Time measurement is based upon periodic repetition of some observable phenomenon. Of the many possibilities, three are in use generally today:

1. Rotation of the Earth on its polar axis.

2. Revolution of the Earth in its orbit around the Sun.

3. Transitions of the atom.

Time based upon rotation of the Earth can take several forms, depending upon (*1*) the reference meridian on Earth, and (*2*) the reference point on the celestial sphere. Three reference meridians are in common use: Greenwich, the local meridian of the observer, and a zone meridian used for all places within a band of longitudes. The times corresponding with these three meridians are designated Greenwich, local, and zone, respectively.

The time at any meridian differs from the *same kind of time* at any other meridian by the difference of longitude of the two reference meridians. The *day*, by any form of time based upon the rotation of the Earth, is the period of one rotation. The length of the day depends upon the celestial reference-point used. For the *sidereal day* the reference point is the vernal equinox (p. 287), for the *mean solar day* it is the mean Sun (p. 327), and for the *apparent solar day* it is the apparent Sun (p. 327). Whatever the reference, the day, of any length, is divided into 24 hours, each of 60 minutes, and each minute of 60 seconds. Because of differences in the length of the day, the smaller units also differ in length. In any kind of time based upon rotation of the Earth, a rotation of 360° is accomplished in 24 hours. Therefore:

$$360° = 24 \text{ hours,}$$
$$15° = 1 \text{ hour,}$$
$$1° = 4 \text{ minutes,}$$
$$15' = 1 \text{ minute,}$$
$$1' = 4 \text{ seconds.}$$

This relationship provides the basis for converting time at one place to the same kind of time at another. The process is simple and direct. Longitude difference is converted from arc units to time units, using the relationship given above or a table such as the 'conversion of arc to time' table in the *Nautical Almanac*, and this quantity is *added* to the time at the first meridian if the second meridian is toward the east, or *subtracted* if toward the west. The sign can be remembered if one keeps in mind the fact that the Earth rotates from west to east, giving the celestial sphere the appearance of moving from east to west, so that any event, such as the meridian transit of a body, occurs at a meridian east of another before it does at the more westerly meridian, so that time becomes progressively *later* as one travels eastward, and *earlier* as one travels westward. In making the conversion of time from one meridian to another, one should keep in mind that the meridians involved are those used for measurement of time. Thus, if the navigator is keeping the time of a reference meridian other than his own, he uses the reference meridian.

If one of the places is on the meridian of Greenwich, the longitude difference is the longitude itself. The time at Greenwich is earlier than at places in east longitude and later than at places in west longitude.

As an example of conversion of time at one meridian to the same kind of time at another, suppose the local time at Lo 127° 16ʹ8 W. is $7^h26^m14^s$, and it is desired to determine the corresponding time at the same instant at Greenwich. The time equivalent of $127°16'.8$ is $8^h29^m07^s$. Therefore, the time at Greenwich is:

$$\begin{array}{lr} \text{local} & 7^h26^m14^s \\ \text{Lo} & 8^h29^m07^s \text{ W.} \\ \hline \text{Greenwich} & 15^h55^m21^s. \end{array}$$

Conversely, if one knows the local time at two places, the longitude difference can be determined. Thus, if the time at Greenwich is $9^h44^m52^s$, and the local time at a second meridian is $13^h21^m18^s$, the longitude at the second place is:

$$\begin{array}{lr} \text{local} & 13^h21^m18^s \\ \text{Greenwich} & 9^h44^m52^s \\ \hline \text{Lo} & 3^h36^m26^s \text{ E.} \end{array}$$

The arc equivalent of $3^h36^m26^s$ is $54°\ 06'.5$, which is the longitude of the second place. It is east of Greenwich because the local time is later than that at Greenwich.

The celestial reference points used for time measurement are the apparent Sun, the mean Sun, and the vernal equinox (Υ). The corresponding times are designated apparent, mean, and sidereal, respectively.

Apparent time is designated *local apparent time* (*LAT*) or *Greenwich apparent time* (*GAT*), depending upon the reference meridian. Specifically, apparent time is the hour angle of the *apparent* (real) *Sun*, relative to the reference meridian, in time units, plus 12 hours. Apparent time based upon a reference meridian other than the local meridian is not ordinarily used. A Sun dial indicates local apparent time.

Because of the variable rate of motion of the Earth along its orbital path, in accordance with Kepler's second law (p. 288), and also because of the obliquity of the ecliptic, apparent time has a variable rate, and is therefore of limited utility. It is little used in navigation, but it does provide one means of determining the time of *local apparent noon* (*LAN*), when the Sun is at upper transit.

Time of a more uniform rate than that based upon the apparent Sun is provided by use of a fictitious *mean Sun* imagined to move eastward *along the celestial equator* at the average rate of the apparent Sun *along the ecliptic*. This *mean time* (*MT*) is further designated *local mean time* (*LMT*),

Greenwich mean time (GMT), or *zone time (ZT)*, depending upon the reference meridian. Specifically, mean time is the hour angle of the mean Sun, relative to the reference meridian, in time units, plus 12 hours.

The difference in length of a day by mean and apparent times does not exceed one minute, but the accumulated difference between these two forms of solar time, called the *equation of time (EqT)*, reaches a maximum of nearly 16½ minutes in early November. It is zero at four times during the year. Its value at 12-hour intervals is tabulated in the *Nautical Almanac*. If the tabulated Greenwich hour angle (GHA) of the Sun is a little more than 0° at GMT 1200, or a little more than 180° at GMT 0000, EqT is *added* to GMT to determine GAT; otherwise it is subtracted.

At any instant, LMT, like LAT, is different for every meridian, and is therefore not convenient for regulating the daily affairs of mankind. This shortcoming is overcome by the use of zone time. The Earth is divided into 24 *time zones*, each centred on a reference *zone meridian* exactly divisible by 15° (including the 0° meridian). These time zones are numbered from 0 at the Greenwich meridian to 12 at the 180° meridian. The numbers are given a plus (+) sign in west longitude, and a minus (−) sign in east longitude. This number, with its sign, is called the *zone description (ZD)* of the zone. Thus, the ZD of a place in Lo 75° W. is (+) 5, while that of a place in Lo 90° E. is (−) 6.

Zone time is the kind of time ordinarily kept throughout the world, with variations. Zone boundaries are quite regular at sea, the time change needed when one crosses a time-zone boundary usually taking place by adding or subtracting one full hour at some convenient time near the time of entering a new time zone. If the Captain should decide to change ship time once a day (probably during the night) to allow for the change of longitude during the day, a fractional ZD results.

On land, zone boundaries are modified somewhat for convenience, as to avoid large centres of population. During the summer months many areas of the world *advance* their standard time one hour, using the zone description of the zone one hour to the *east* of them. This 'fast' time is called *summer time* in many areas, but *daylight saving time* in others. The expression *standard time* is used to refer to the legal time at a place, usually the legal time when summer time is not in effect. In a few areas of the world a zone meridian other than a multiple of 15° is used. This may be the meridian of the capital or principal city of a country of limited longitudinal extent, or perhaps the nearest meridian differing in time from GMT by 30 minutes plus an integral number of hours. In some areas, such as the Austral Islands, LMT is generally kept, rather than the legal zone time. Other local variations are in use. Standard time of various places throughout the world are tabulated in the *Nautical Almanac*, and time-zone charts are provided by various publishers.

Time increasing eastward from Greenwich and decreasing westward from the same prime meridian meet at the 180° meridian, at which the ZD is both (+) 12 and (−) 12. This meridian, with some variations to accommodate local preferences, constitutes the international *date line*. A ship travelling eastward across the Pacific moves its clocks *ahead* at the passage of each time zone boundary, and compensates for these advances by changing the date *back* one day at the date line, without changing the time, the half of the zone in west longitude having a ZD of (+) 12, and the half in east longitude having a ZD of (−) 12. Thus, except at noon Greenwich time, two dates exist simultaneously somewhere in the world. The two meridians at which the date changes are that of the date line and that at which the Sun is at lower transit. At noon Greenwich time, these two meridians coincide, and the date momentarily is the same everywhere (ignoring local variations).

The principal navigational use of GMT is for tabulation, in almanacs, of Greenwich hour angle and declination. Zone time in some form is used for setting ship's clocks. Thus, the navigator, unless he elects to use GMT for his navigation, has frequent occasion to convert ZT to GMT. He does this simply by adding, algebraically, ZD to ZT. If the sum exceeds 24 hours, he drops 24 hours and increases the date by one day. If it is necessary to add 24 hours to ZT before subtracting a ZD, he subtracts one day to find the Greenwich date. These relationships are shown conveniently on a time diagram (p. 297). If GMT is to be converted to ZT, the ZD is applied with reversed sign, and the local date determined as before, adding one day if the sum exceeds 24 hours (in east longitude), and subtracting one day if GMT is less than ZD (in west longitude).

The principal navigational use of LMT is for tabulation, in almanacs, of times of Sunrise, Sunset, twilight, Moonrise, and Moonset. The LMT determined from the almanac is converted to ZT by means of the longitude difference between the local meridian and the zone meridian, remembering that times increase toward the east, and that ZT is the same as LMT at the zone meridian. The LMT is tabulated to the nearest integral minute. Thus, for each $15'$ of longitude between the local and the zone meridian, the time of the phenomenon differs by one minute of time, occurring earlier by ZT than the tabulated LMT if east of one's zone meridian, and later if west of it. For example, suppose one is at longitude $117°18.'4$ W., one is keeping ZT of the meridian $120°$ W., and the tabulated LMT of Sunset is 1858. One is $120° - 117°18.'4 = 2°41.'6$ or 11 minutes (to the nearest integral minute) *east* of the zone meridian. Therefore, the ZT of Sunset is $1858 - 11 = 1847$. If keeping summer time, one's zone meridian is $105°$ W., and one is $12°18.'4$ or 49 minutes *west* of it. The ZT of Sunset is $1858 + 49 = 1947$, the same result obtained by adding one hour to the standard time.

Marine chronometers are customarily set to GMT and not reset at sea, so that interconversion of *chronometer time* (*C*) and GMT is by means of *chronometer error* (*CE*). Similarly, *watch time* (*W*) and ZT are interconverted by means of *watch error* (*WE*). Even though a watch or chronometer may be graduated only to 12 hours, it is good practice in navigation always to express time on a 24-hour basis, principally to avoid error in date as times are interchanged.

The rotation rate of the Earth is not quite uniform. Two principal sources of error have been identified. One is a slight wobbling of the Earth's polar axis, called *polar motion*. The other is a seasonal variation thought to be caused principally by meteorological factors, resulting in a slight increase in rotational speed during the northern-hemisphere spring and summer, followed by a decrease during the remainder of the year, in a pattern that does not repeat exactly from year to year. Astronomers use the designation *universal time* (UT) as the equivalent of GMT. Three separate universal times are identified: UT_0 is universal time as determined directly by observation of astronomical bodies near the zenith by means of a photographic zenith tube, UT_1 (GMT) is UT_0 corrected for polar motion, and UT_2 is UT_1 corrected for the seasonal variation in the Earth's rotational rate. The corrections are of the order of tens of *milliseconds* (*ms*) (thousandths of a second).

Additional small variations in the Earth's rotational rate have been detected, but they are irregular and unpredictable. Because of this unpredictability, a *coordinated universal time* (*UTC*) approximating UT_2 was adopted by most time services so that radio time-signals will agree within several milliseconds. The UTC is coordinated by the Bureau International de l'Heure, in Paris. In practice, UTC is derived from time kept by atomic clocks. Starting in 1972, a step correction of exactly 1 second is applied to UTC, as needed, to bring it into agreement with UT_1. The maximum difference permitted is 0.9 second. The step increase is usually made at midnight on December 31 or June 30. The time signals of most nations are coded to indicate the difference to the nearest 0.1 second.

The third celestial reference for time measurement based upon rotation of the Earth is the vernal equinox (Υ). The resulting *sidereal time* is further designated *local sidereal time* (*LST*) or *Greenwich sidereal time* (*GST*), depending upon the reference meridian. Like apparent time, sidereal time based upon a reference meridian other than the local meridian is not ordinarily used. Sidereal time is the hour angle of the vernal equinox, converted to time units, and thus is reckoned from the *upper* branch of the meridian. As commonly used, sidereal time has no date. Because of the revolution of the Earth in its orbit around the Sun, a sidereal year has one more day than a solar year, and an hour of sidereal time is almost 10 seconds shorter than an hour of solar time. Sidereal time is the

331

basis of means used for star identification (p. 333), and has been used in some methods of sight reduction.

A second basic approach to time measurement is to base the time system on the revolution of the Earth in its orbit around the Sun. The result, called *ephemeris time* (*ET*), defines the second as some part of a year, rather than as part of the day, thus averaging out variations in the rotational rate of the Earth. Ephemeris time was defined in 1956 by the International Committee of Weights and Measures in terms of the Earth's orbital period in 1900. Being tied to a specific year, ET is, by definition, a uniform system. Because of variations in the orbital period of the Earth, ET, while being a close approximation of UT, has become out of step with it, the accumulated difference between the two currently being of the order of 40 seconds, ET being *fast* on UT. Although ET has the advantage of providing a uniform time-scale, it has the disadvantage of requiring several months of observation for determination to an accuracy of a tenth of a second.

A third approach to time measurement is based upon transitions of the atom. In 1967 the Thirteenth General Conference of Weights and Measures adopted a resolution defining the second of time in the International System (SI) of Units as 'the duration of 9,192,631,770 periods of the radiation corresponding to the transition between the two hyperfine levels of the ground state of the caesium atom 133'. Since January 1, 1972, SI time units have been used for UTC. The *atomic clock time* (*AT*) based upon this time scale provides a very uniform method of keeping time, but, unlike time based upon rotation of the Earth, depends upon the running of individual clocks, resulting in differences in AT indicated by different atomic clocks, and discrepancies between AT and time based upon rotation or revolution of the Earth. The *rate* adopted for AT is the same as that of the uniform ET, but the two are offset by a constant amount because of the accumulated difference between ET and UT at the time of adopting AT. The AT is particularly useful for very accurate measurements of short time *intervals*.

10. Identification of Astronomical Bodies

Although some 6,000 astronomical bodies on the whole celestial sphere are visible to the unaided eye, only a relatively small number are used in astronavigation. The *Nautical Almanac* provides positional information on its three-day pages for the Sun, Moon, four planets, and 57 'navigational' stars, with a monthly tabulation of information on 116 additional stars, making a total of 179 bodies. Of the 57 stars given favoured treatment, 20 are of first magnitude, 31 are of second magnitude, and 6 of third magnitude. No star of either tabulation is dimmer than third magnitude. A navigator may use perhaps 20 to 25 stars under normal circumstances, but when a limited number are available, as through holes in overcast, he may resort to unfamiliar stars.

If an astronomical body is to be used to establish a position line, its identity must be known, of course. Traditionally, navigators have prided themselves on their knowledge of the heavens. Under favourable conditions, on a dark night with clear skies, the identification of astronomical bodies is relatively easy. Even during early evening twilight, when stars and planets begin to appear, the challenge is not great, for there is little change from evening to evening, and one who is observing astronomical bodies regularly soon learns to know where to look for the brighter bodies. But when a body of the second or third magnitude appears suddenly through a break in an overcast, its identity may not be apparent.

General familiarity with the principal astronomical bodies used in navigation is relatively easy to attain. The Sun and Moon, of course, pose no problem. The four navigational planets—Venus, Mars, Jupiter, and Saturn—are not difficult to distinguish from stars, especially if one follows their positions among the stars from night to night. They all stay relatively close to the ecliptic, are relatively bright most of the time, and shine with steadier lights than the point-source, twinkling stars. A page of 'Planet Notes', followed by a planet diagram, in the *Nautical Almanac*, can be helpful. One should particularly be careful to avoid confusing Mercury with other planets, especially when it is near maximum elongation (p. 290).

The great number of stars visible in the clear night-time sky may seem bewildering to the neophyte, but with practice and some assistance, he soon learns to identify the navigational stars. Magnitude (p. 292), possibly colour, and particularly position relative to other stars provide ample means of identification.

The ancients grouped the stars in a number of configurations called *constellations*. A few of them are quite striking, while many are difficult to identify. Some of the imagined figures might not be apparent to a modern observer, and other groupings might seem more logical. The word 'constellation' is now used to designate a specific portion of the celestial sphere having well-defined limits. Every point on the celestial sphere is assigned to a constellation. Stars are given designations relating to their constellations, or to a particular catalogue. The 57 principal navigational stars, and some others, have names in addition to their constellation or catalogue designation. Relationships of stars of different constellations are sometimes more helpful in the identification process than relative position within constellations.

In the following discussion of the 57 principal navigational stars, reference to star charts in the *Nautical Almanac* or elsewhere might prove helpful. *Star charts* are generally constructed to present the celestial sphere as it appears from *inside* the sphere; that is, to an observer on Earth. Except for charts of celestial polar regions, north is at the top of the star chart, south at the bottom, east at the left, and west at the right (opposite to the usual map convention). When an observer is looking upward at the sky, toward his zenith, he should hold the chart over his head, with north on the chart toward north on the Earth. Other directions on the chart are then correctly oriented. In the following, stated directions refer to the celestial sphere. Some indicated relationships are not apparent on star charts because of distortion related to the map projection used for the charts.

Identification of stars by position relative to other stars might well begin with Ursa Major, the 'large' or 'great bear', sometimes known as the 'plough'. During northern-hemisphere spring evenings this group of stars, perhaps the best known of the constellations, is high in the northern sky of most northern-hemisphere observers, above the north celestial pole. Seven relatively bright stars of the constellation form an easily-recognized 'big dipper'. The last star in the handle of the dipper, farthest from the bowl, is Alkaid. The second star from Alkaid, or third from the end of the handle, is Alioth. The star at the outer lip of the bowl, away from the handle, is Dubhe. All three are second-magnitude stars.

Dubhe and Merak (not one of the 57 principal navigational stars), the other star forming the outer part of the bowl, are sometimes called the 'pointers' because a line from Merak through Dubhe (*downward* in spring evenings) leads to second-magnitude Polaris, not one of the 57 principal navigational stars but a useful one less than 1° from the north celestial pole. Polaris is part of Ursa Minor, the 'small' or 'lesser bear'. Seven relatively dim stars of this constellation form a 'little dipper' that is smaller and less conspicuous than the 'big dipper', and has a handle with a curvature toward the bowl, unlike that of the 'big dipper'. Polaris is at the far end of the handle, away from the bowl. Second-magnitude Kochab is at the lip of the bowl.

A line southward (*upward* in spring evenings) through the two stars of the bowl of the 'big dipper' nearest the handle leads first to first-magnitude Regulus, in a sickle-like group of stars forming the head of the constellation Leo, the lion, and then close to second-magnitude Alphard, in the constellation Hydra, the water monster. Regulus is the brightest star in this part of the sky. Denebola, tail of the lion, and second brightest star of the constellation Leo, is about the same distance east of Regulus that Alphard is to the south of it.

A curved extension of the arc of the handle of the 'big dipper' leads first to first-magnitude Arcturus, a little north of an extension of a line from Regulus through Denebola, then to first-magnitude, blue Spica, and finally to a group of four third-magnitude stars shaped much like the quadrilateral mainsail of a gaff-rigged schooner. The most north-westerly star of this group is Gienah. East of Arcturus is second-magnitude Alphecca, brightest star of a bowl-shaped group known as Corona Borealis, the northern crown. With Arcturus and Alphard, Alphecca forms a nearly isosceles triangle. A line from Regulus through Spica leads close to third-magnitude Zubenelgenubi, westernmost and second brightest star of box-like Libra, the balance (scales). A line through Gienah and the opposite star of the sail, the two brightest stars of the constellation, leads close to second-magnitude Menkent.

South of this area is a region with a number of relatively bright stars below the horizon of most northern-hemisphere observers. About 40° directly south of Gienah is Crux, the small, poorly-formed, unimpressive, but well known 'southern cross'. Second-magnitude Gacrux is at the northern end of the cross, and first-magnitude Acrux is at the southern end. A line through the other two stars of the cross, toward the east, leads close to two very bright first-magnitude stars nearby, Hadar and Rigil Kentaurus in that order. The easterly of the two pointer stars of the 'southern cross', Mimosa, is of the first magnitude but is not included among the 57 principal navigational stars because of its proximity to other bright stars providing better coverage of the area. A small triangle of one second- and two third-magnitude stars south-east of Hadar and Rigil Kentaurus includes Atria, the brightest and most southerly of the trio. No bright star is near the south celestial pole.

Turning next to the evening sky of the northern-hemisphere summer, Ursa Major is toward the west, to the left of Polaris, the pointers being nearly horizontal. The most conspicuous feature in the northern hemisphere at this season is a large right triangle dominating the eastern sky. The triangle is formed by three first-magnitude stars: Vega, the brightest star in the northern hemisphere of the celestial sphere; Denebola, at the eastern end of a large cross known as the 'northern cross' or Cygnus, the swan; and Altair, midway between two nearby fainter stars known as the 'guardians', in line with Vega. The right angle is at Vega. This star, with a declination of nearly 39° N., transits the meridian high in the sky for observers in middle northern latitudes. The triangle is east of Arcturus and Alphecca. Vega and Altair form a nearly equilateral triangle with second-magnitude Rasalhague, toward the west. A line from Altair through Vega leads to second-magnitude Eltanin, which is also nearly in line with the shorter arm of the 'northern cross'.

Low in the southern sky for northern-hemisphere observers, south and a little west of Rasalhague, is a conspicuous group of stars known as Scorpius, the scorpion. The brightest star in this area is first-magnitude Antares, a red star at the head of the well-formed scorpion. Shaula, a second-magnitude star, second brightest of the constellation, is at the tail. Antares, second-magnitude Kaus Australis and Nunki, and the third-magnitude Sabik form a large approximate parallelogram that is not conspicuous because of the proximity of a number of other second- and third-magnitude stars. Nunki is at the north-east corner and Kaus Australis at the south-east corner of the parallelogram.

During autumn evenings of the northern hemisphere, Ursa Major is low in the northern sky, below Polaris. Directly across the pole from Ursa Major, and at about the same distance from the pole, is a group of two second-magnitude and three third-magnitude stars forming a prominent M-shaped figure called Cassiopeia. The most southerly star of the group is Schedar. Mirfak is a second-magnitude star south of Cassiopeia, nearly on a line from Kochab through Polaris.

A line from Polaris southward (upward) through Caph, the westernmost and brightest star of Cassiopeia, but not one of the 57 principal navigational stars, leads to the eastern edge of a large, conspicuous square of one second-magnitude and three third-magnitude stars known as Pegasus, the winged horse. The second-magnitude star (actually part of the nearby constellation Andromeda, the chained woman) is Alpheratz, almost on the hour circle of the vernal equinox. Markab is at the opposite corner of the square. West of Markab, some distance, is second-magnitude Enif, nearly in line with the southern side of the square. The constellation Aries is about the same distance east of the centre of the square. Its brightest star is second-magnitude Hamal, midway between Pegasus and the well-known Pleiades, the legendary seven sisters. The vernal equinox, also known as the first point of Aries, is no longer in the constellation, because of precession of the equinoxes (p. 288).

A continuation of the line southward through the eastern side of the square of Pegasus leads close to second-magnitude Diphda. A line southward through the western side of the square leads to first-magnitude Fomalhaut. Diphda and Fomalhaut form a nearly equilateral triangle with second-magnitude Ankaa, farther south. Fomalhaut and Ankaa form another nearly equilateral triangle with Al Na'ir toward the south-west. Al Na'ir, Ankaa, and Diphda form a series of triangles of about equal size with second-magnitude Peacock to the south-west, first-magnitude Achernar a little east of south, and third-magnitude Acamar toward the east.

The northern-hemisphere winter-evening sky has the greatest concentration of bright stars of any season. Ursa Major is to the right of Polaris, and Cassiopeia to the left. The best known constellation of this season is Orion, the mighty hunter, astride the celestial equator, south of northern-hemisphere observers. Three closely-spaced second-magnitude stars form the belt of the hunter. The middle star of the belt is Alnilam. Two first- and two second-magnitude stars form the box-like body of the hunter. The first- but variable-magnitude star of the portion of the box north of the belt is red Betelgeuse. The second-magnitude star at the other northerly corner of the box, toward the west, is Bellatrix. The first-magnitude star at the south-western corner of the box is the blue Rigel.

A line eastward through the belt passes close to Sirius, the brightest star in the sky, with a magnitude of (−) 1.6. From Sirius, a northerly curving line forming a big inverted (for northern-hemisphere observers) teardrop passes through four first-magnitude stars and back through the belt of Orion to Sirius. The four first-magnitude stars, in order, are Procyon, Pollux, Capella, and Aldebaran. The Pleiades are west and a little north of Aldebaran. Second-magnitude Elnath is within the teardrop, between Capella and Aldebaran. A V-shaped group of stars including Aldebaran and Elnath points to third-magnitude Menkar, toward the south-west, brightest star in its area.

If the returning curve of the teardrop is continued on southward from Sirius, with reverse curvature, it passes a small triangle of three second-magnitude stars a short distance south of Sirius, and then leads to Canopus, the second brightest star in the heavens, with a magnitude of (−) 0.9. The brightest and westernmost of the three stars forming a small triangle is Adhara. Canopus forms a nearly equilateral triangle with Adhara and second-magnitude Suhail, toward the east, and another with Suhail and second-magnitude Miaplacidus, to the south. The side of the second triangle connecting Suhail and Miaplacidus passes through the false southern cross (a better, but less conspicuous cross than the southern cross). The brightest and most westerly star of this group is second-magnitude Avior.

An observation for establishing an astro position line consists of measurement of the altitude, and sometimes the azimuth, of an astronomical body. At sea the altitude is measured by determining the arc of a vertical circle between the visible horizon and the body. It is essential, then, that both the horizon and the body be visible, and that the horizon appear as a reasonably sharp line. This visibility requirement is the principal limitation of astronavigation. The horizon is not visible with sufficient sharpness during the night or during daylight periods of poor visibility. Except for the Sun, Moon, and perhaps Venus at or near maximum brilliance, astronomical bodies are not visible to the unaided eye during full daylight or periods of overcast. This leaves the two brief periods of twilight, when skies are clear and visibility is good, as the only times when both the horizon and most astronomical bodies are visible, and therefore the times when most observations are made.

Twilight is defined as the period of incomplete darkness following Sunset or preceding Sunrise. Thus, Sunset or Sunrise marks the brighter limit of twilight. Three different darker limits are specified. The darker limit of *civil twilight* occurs when the centre of the Sun is 6° below the celestial horizon, of *nautical twilight* when it is 12° below the celestial horizon, and of *astronomical twilight* when it is 18° below the celestial horizon. Because of height of eye above the surface of the Earth, semi-diameter of the Sun (Sunrise or Sunset occurring when the highest part of the *upper limb* (*UL*), that half of the visible disc having the greater altitude—the other half is the *lower limb* (*LL*)—is on the visible horizon) and atmospheric refraction, the period of civil twilight is considerably shorter than the periods between the other limits. Relatively few observations can be made during civil twilight, and when the Sun is 12° below the horizon, the horizon is indistinct. These limitations narrow the most effective sight-taking period to the interval between the darker limits of civil and nautical twilights, a period of some 24 minutes on the equator, and longer as the latitude increases. The most favourable period is the interval when the Sun is between about 8° and 10° below the horizon.

When only a few of the brighter stars are visible, the method of identification by position relative to other bodies is not available. This is particularly true during evening twilight, when stars are just beginning to appear. For this reason, and for general convenience, it is common practice to prepare, in advance, a list of navigational bodies that will be available for observation during twilight, with the approximate azimuth, altitude, and magnitude of each body. They are best listed in order of increasing azimuth. One may prefer to subtract the heading of the vessel from the true azimuths to determine the relative azimuths, as this may facilitate location of the bodies. Some navigators like to make diagrams of radial lines indicating the azimuths of the bodies, to help visualize the position of each body relative to their craft.

Several convenient aids are available to assist in the preparation of such a list. One is the *star globe*, a sphere representing the celestial sphere, mounted in such manner that the celestial poles can be titled, and the sphere can be rotated about its polar axis. In the usual form of the device, the globe is mounted inside a frame having a horizontal circle representing the horizon (or offset 6° below the celestial horizon), graduated to indicate azimuth. It also has a circle perpendicular to the horizon circle, through its north and south points, representing the celestial meridian and bearing a latitude scale to indicate the tilt of the elevated pole. An arc representing a vertical circle is pivoted at the zenith, the point at the top of the meridian circle, 90° from the horizon. This arc is graduated to indicate altitude. A scale representing LHA Υ, or its equivalent, is printed on the globe.

To use the star globe, one first tilts the polar axis to agree with the latitude, as indicated by the latitude scale on the meridian circle. The globe is then rotated about its polar axis until L H A Υ, as indicated by the scale on the globe, is under the meridian circle. The globe, representing the celestial sphere, is then oriented to the Earth at the position of the observer, at the time for which it is set. Any convenient time can be used, but the time of the darker limit of civil twilight, when the centre of the Sun is 6° below the celestial horizon, is a good time, representing about the brighter limit of the sight-taking period. This time, and LHA Υ, can be determined by means of the *Nautical Almanac*.

An alternative method of orienting the globe, eliminating the need for an almanac, is provided by some star globes. The position of the Sun each day is indicated on the globe. The horizon circle is offset 6° below the celestial horizon. The globe is then rotated until the indicated position of the Sun for the date is on the 'false horizon', the latitude having been set as before.

When the globe is set properly, the rotatable arc can be placed over any point on the visible portion of the celestial sphere, and the altitude and azimuth of that point can be read from the appropriate scales. If the altitude and azimuth of such a point are known from observation, these data provide an alternative means of setting the star globe without reference to an almanac.

The positions of the navigational stars are shown on the globe as they would appear from *outside* the celestial sphere, opposite the presentation of most star charts. Constellations thus appear reversed from their appearance in the sky or on most star charts. The position of a planet or the Moon at any time can be plotted on the globe by means of its declination and SHA, or equivalent, from the *Nautical Almanac* or other source.

Many navigators prefer some form of *star finder* to a star

globe. A number of different forms of star finder have been devised. A typical one consists of a thin, white, opaque, plastic disc called a *star base*, with the north celestial pole at the centre on one side, and the south celestial pole at the centre on the other side. The positions of navigational stars are printed on both sides. A graduated scale around the periphery indicates LHAϒ. A template is available for plotting the positions of planets and the Moon. A series of clear plastic templates, each with families of curves representing altitude and azimuth for a specific latitude, are included.

To use a star finder of this type one selects the template for latitude nearest one's own latitude, centres it with the correct north or south side up over the north or south side of the star base, according to one's elevated pole, and rotates the template until LHAϒ appears under the meridian line on the template. The altitude and azimuth of any point on that part of the celestial sphere above the horizon can then be read directly by means of the families of curves, using eye interpolation between curves if necessary. A slight increase in accuracy can be obtained by offsetting the template along the meridian line so the latitude of the observer is directly over the pole at the centre of the star base. Like the star globe, a star finder can be set without reference to an almanac if the position of the Sun on the star base is known (positioning the template so that the Sun is 6° below the horizon, by eye interpolation), or if altitude and azimuth of a known point on the celestial sphere are known.

A star finder is constructed on the same principle as a star globe, but utilizes a map projection to provide a two-dimensional presentation. It is cheaper and less bulky than a star globe, but can be set accurately for only those latitudes of the templates, and lacks the advantage of a three-dimensional presentation.

Either a star globe or a star finder provides a convenient means of making a list of bodies available for observation at specific times, in preparation for making a round of sights. These devices can also be used to identify a body that has not been identified at the time of observation. The procedure is to observe both the altitude and azimuth of the body, and then later to set the star globe or star finder for the latitude and time of observation, and note the body nearest the measured coordinates. If reasonable doubt exists as to the body observed, the celestial-equator coordinates of the point can be determined and converted to the corresponding coordinates at Greenwich. The coordinates can then be compared with those of planets and additional stars in the monthly tabulation, and if the body still cannot be identified, it may be an unlisted star or the planet Mercury.

Neither a star globe nor a star finder is essential for identification of a body unknown at the time of observation. A diagram on the plane of the celestial meridian (p. 302) is a relatively simple means of determining the celestial equator coordinates. Any method of sight reduction (chapter IX) can also be used for determining the local coordinates of the celestial-equator system, by solving the navigational triangle in reverse of the usual solution. That is, declination and altitude are interchanged, and so are meridian angle and azimuth angle. The calculated values can then be converted to their Greenwich equivalents and compared with tabulated values for identification of the body.

VII

Astronavigation Equipment

1. Marine Sextant

Mariners generally measure the elevation angle or *altitude* (*h, alt*) of an astronomical body above the visible horizon, as well as horizontal angles, by means of a *marine sextant*. The importance of this instrument to the traditionally dominant astronomical navigation has resulted in the marine sextant having become accepted widely as the symbol of navigation itself.

The principal parts of a marine sextant are shown in simplified form in Fig. 701. The telescope and horizon glass are fixed with respect to the frame, except that provision is usually made for slight adjustments to remove or reduce errors. The index mirror is similarly fixed relative to the index arm. The index arm is rotatable about a pivot at the centre of curvature of the arc, and bears a mark or *index* for reading the angle indicated by the arc. Means are provided for clamping the index arm at any position along the arc, and for making fine adjustments of this position. If the instrument is in correct adjustment, the index mirror and horizon glass are parallel when the index is set at zero on the arc. When the index arm is rotated, the index mirror rotates with it. As shown in Fig. 701, the index arm is set at 54°. Because of the double reflection of the ray of light, shown by the broken line, from a point on the celestial sphere, the index mirror has been rotated through only 27°, half the altitude shown on the arc. The arc is graduated accordingly, the 120° shown covering a span of 60°. It is this 60° arc that gives the instrument its name, the term 'sextant' being derived from a Latin word meaning a 'sixth part' (of a circle). Octants, quintants, and quadrants, of an eighth, fifth, and fourth of a circle, respectively, have also been made, but now the term *sextant* is generally applied regardless of the length of the arc. Modern

344

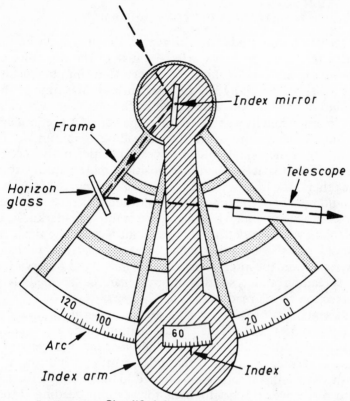

FIG. 701. Simplified diagram of a marine sextant.

instruments vary in respect to the length of the arc, but are generally graduated to more than 120°.

The index mirror is silvered over its entire surface, but only half of the horizon glass, that nearest the frame, is silvered. This arrangement permits a direct view of the horizon at the same time that one can see the double-reflected image of an astronomical body.

To measure the altitude of a body, the observer sets the index arm to zero, approximately, faces in the direction of the body, holds the sextant vertical, looks through the telescope, and rotates the sextant upward or downward until the horizon comes into view. He then moves the index arm along the arc until the body appears in the silvered half of the horizon glass, and then makes a fine adjustment to bring the image in line with the horizon. He, or an assistant, notes the time of the observation and reads the altitude on the arc, opposite the index mark on the index arm. Because of the difficulty of noting the time and making the observation simultaneously, the observer generally has an assistant note the time at the instant of observation, announced by the observer, who calls out 'mark' when he wants the time to be noted. A preliminary 'stand by' alerts the timer that a reading is imminent. In noting the time, one should observe the position of the second hand first, for it is changing position more rapidly than the others. If a light is needed to make a reading, the assistant should read both the time and the altitude while the observer looks away to maintain his adaptation to the semi-darkness. If the observer does not have an assistant to note the time, he should practise counting short intervals of time, or have someone time the interval between his making an observation and reading time, so this interval can be applied as a correction to his readings.

A sextant is provided with a device to permit reading of fractional parts of the smallest graduation of the arc. Details vary with different sextants. Older instruments generally have a vernier directly on the index arm, opposite the arc, with a small magnifying glass pivoted so that it can be rotated into place over the graduations for accurate reading. Most modern instruments are provided with micrometer drums that amplify the graduations and thus facilitate accurate reading. Readings are made in two or three steps, analogous to noting the time indicated by the hands of a clock or watch. One should acquire sufficient familiarity with the sextant to minimize the possibility of error in reading it.

Several alternative methods of making the altitude measurement are in use, particularly during the brighter part of twilight when stars and planets may be difficult to see, but the horizon is sharp. The index may be set to the predetermined approximate altitude, thus facilitating the finding of the double-reflected image of the body. Alternatively, one may set the index at zero, point the telescope directly at the body, and then rotate the index arm slowly, at the same time lowering the line of sight, keeping the image in view until the horizon appears, thus 'bringing the body down to the horizon'. Some navigators prefer the opposite procedure of 'bringing the horizon up to the body'. This is done by setting the index at zero, inverting the sextant, and sighting at the body. The index arm is then moved until the reflected image of the horizon comes into view. The sextant is then inverted and the fine adjustment is made.

If the horizon below the body is obstructed, as by another vessel, or is not as sharp as in the opposite direction, a *back sight*, may be made by facing away from the body and observing the supplement of the altitude, if the arc is sufficiently long. The altitude so measured is called a *back angle*. Appropriate adjustments are made in sextant altitude corrections (p. 397).

Whatever method is used to bring the image of the body into approximate line with the horizon, and this is a matter of personal preference, the final adjustment is made to bring the image of a star or planet exactly on the visible horizon. When the Sun is observed, the lower limb is usually brought to the horizon, the 'bottom' of the Sun then appearing to rest on the horizon. The upper limb may be brought to the horizon if one prefers, an appropriate adjustment then being made in the sextant altitude corrections. If a back sight is made, the lower limb appears at the top of the reflected Sun, and the upper limb at the bottom. When the Moon is observed, the choice of limb is usually dictated by the orientation of the terminator (p. 286).

In making an observation of the altitude of an astronomical body, one should be careful to make the measurement along its vertical circle. If the sextant is tilted, the observed angle is greater than the altitude. To ensure measurement along the vertical circle, one first makes the measurement as described, and then rotates the sextant several degrees clockwise and anticlockwise around the line of sight. This process is called *swinging the arc*, as the image of the body or the appropriate limb appears to move along an arc of a circle. The position of the index arm is then adjusted, if necessary, to bring the observed arc tangent to the horizon. The point of tangency is the intersection of the vertical circle and the horizon.

Shade glasses, not shown in Fig. 701, of different intensity are attached to the frame in such a manner that they can be rotated individually into the line of sight between the index mirror and the horizon glass, to shade the eye of the observer from the direct rays of the Sun when it is the body observed. A similar set of shade glasses can be rotated into place behind the horizon glass to reduce glare of the water or sky in the direction of the horizon. One shade glass of polaroid material that can be rotated to vary the intensity may be used in place of each set of shade glasses of different intensity.

The telescope is generally mounted so that it can be moved closer to the frame of the sextant during the brighter part of twilight, and farther from the frame during the darker portion. Thus, the major portion of light entering the telescope is from the area of the astromonical body when it is difficult to see, and from the horizon when it is indistinct to the unaided eye. The telescope can be removed from its collar, so that observations can be made without magnification if one prefers.

If angular measurements are to be made accurately to a fraction of a minute of arc, a good-quality sextant should be selected, kept in proper adjustment, and given suitable care.

In selecting a sextant one should consider weight, size, workmanship, and intended use. The frame should be rigid and strong, but of light weight. A heavy instrument induces fatigue, resulting in reduction in observational accuracy. A sextant having a radius of the arc of about 20 centimetres is a good size. A smaller radius reduces the interval between graduations of the arc, and a larger radius increases the weight and storage space needed. All moving parts should move freely without binding or excessive play. The arc should be easy to read clearly in dim light. Means should be provided for suitable adjustment, as described below. The length of the arc dictates the maximum altitude observable. If one desires an instrument capable of making back sights of bodies at moderate altitudes, or if one anticipates use of an artificial horizon (p. 356), or if the sextant is to be used for measuring horizontal angles of widely-spaced objects, a sextant with longer than normal arc should be selected. For measurement of horizontal angles, less accuracy is needed, for such angles are rarely needed to an accuracy better than $0°.1$.

A marine sextant is subject to seven principal sources of error. Three of these cannot be adjusted by the navigator, but the combined *instrument error* can be determined and a correction called *instrument correction* (*I*), applied. The instrument error is usually determined by the manufacturer and provided with the instrument. The three sources of error constituting instrument error are imperfections in (*1*) the location of the pivot for rotation of the index arm (*centring error*), (*2*) the graduations of the arc or vernier (*graduation error*), and (*3*) the parallelism of the two sides of the mirrors or shade glasses (*prismatic error*). If the navigator cares to check the accuracy of the instrument error, he can do so by making a number of measurements of angles determined accurately by other means. Horizontal angles between objects can be determined accurately by a surveying theodolite. Angles between stars can be calculated, but when they are measured, the stars should be at approximately the same altitude, and altitudes below $15°$ should be avoided. The instrument error of a well-made sextant is usually small enough to be ignored in the normal practice of navigation.

The four adjustable errors are of direct concern to the navigator, and the need for such adjustment should be checked periodically. Set screws are provided for making each adjustment. When making an adjustment of an instrument having set screws in pairs, one should invariably loosen one screw before tightening the other that bears on the same surface. Because of the inter-relationships of the errors, the adjustments should always be made in the order described.

Perpendicularity of the index mirror to the frame is checked by holding the sextant in a horizontal position with the index mirror upward, above the frame, and toward the observer, and moving the index arm to a position where the reflected view of the arc can be seen in the mirror. The index mirror is perpendicular to the frame when the reflected and direct views of the arc appear as a continuous, unbroken line. Any adjustment needed is made by means of a set screw or screws at the back of the mirror.

Perpendicularity of the horizon glass to the frame is checked by setting the index to zero, holding the sextant vertical, and observing the horizon. The setting of the index is adjusted, if necessary, to make the direct and double-reflected views appear as a continuous, unbroken line. The sextant is then rotated around the line of sight. The horizon glass is perpendicular to the frame when the direct and reflected views continue to appear as a continuous line. Adjustment, by means of a set screw or screws near the base of the horizon glass, is needed if *side error* exists, indicated by one portion of the horizon appearing to move upward or downward, with respect to the other portion, as the sextant is rotated.

For accurate readings, the index mirror and horizon glass should be parallel when the sextant reads zero. This parallelism is checked by holding the sextant vertical and observing the horizon, as in the second adjustment. The direct and double-reflected views of the horizon are brought together so that the horizon appears as a continuous, unbroken line. Several readings are desirable for accurate determination of the magnitude of the error. Between readings the index should be offset in alternate directions. The two glasses are parallel when the sextant reads zero while the two portions of the horizon are in line. An astronomical body, instead of the horizon, can be used to check for parallelism of the index mirror and the horizon glass. If a star or planet is used, the body as seen direct in the horizon glass is identical with the double reflected image when the index is set at zero, if the glasses are parallel. If they are not, the reflected image appears above or below the direct view. If the Sun or full Moon is used, the reflected image is brought into tangency with the direct view, both above and below. The glasses are parallel if the two readings, one positive and the other negative, are numerically equal. Low altitudes should be avoided because of rapid change of atmospheric refraction with altitude near the horizon. If an error exists, a second set screw or pair of screws near the base of the horizon glass can be used to produce the desired parallelism.

This error need not be removed. Instead, the reading of the sextant can be noted and applied as a correction to all observations. The error is called *index error (IE)*, and the resulting correction, of the same magnitude but opposite sign, is called *index correction (IC)*. Because of its direct effect upon the accuracy of any angle measured by the sextant, index error should be determined each time the sextant is used, and preferably when the horizon is clear and sharp. There is some merit in not making the adjustment each time an error is found, because the frequent change in the setting of the set screws may cause wear that renders the sextant incapable of maintaining an adjustment. One can determine the sign of index correction by remembering that a positive reading at alignment of the two views of the horizon results in measured angles greater than the correct values, and a negative reading results in measured angles less than the correct values. Thus the saying, 'If it's on it's off and if it's off it's on', meaning that a reading on the arc when it should read zero should be taken off measured angles (given a negative sign), and vice versa. Any adjustment for either perpendicularity of the horizon glass or index error may affect the other. Accordingly, after one is made, the other should be checked.

The last check to be made is for parallelism of the telescope to the frame of the sextant. If this condition does not exist, the sextant has *collimation error*. The existence of this error is determined by placing the sextant horizontally on a flat surface such as a table or desk. One then sights along the upper surface of the frame and has an assistant place a mark on the opposite bulkhead, in line with the frame. One then places a second mark above the first, at a distance equal to the distance between the frame and the telescope. The telescope is parallel to the frame when the second mark is in the centre of the field of view through the telescope. Any needed adjustment is made by means of a pair of set screws on the collar holding the telescope. If the telescope and frame are not parallel, measured angles are greater than the correct angles.

Once adjustments are made, they should remain essentially

unchanged and need not be checked more often than at intervals of several months, except for index error, unless one has reason to doubt the accuracy of the sextant. If frequent adjustments are needed for no apparent reason, the presence of excessive wear of some parts should be suspected, and the sextant should be ckecked by a competent instrument technician. If worn parts are not replaced, undetected errors may be present in the readings. Again except for index error, small errors can be ignored, for they have negligible effect upon the accuracy of measured angles, and frequent changes in the adjustment can cause undesirable wear.

With proper care, a good sextant can give satisfactory service almost indefinitely. Even a simple and rugged instrument is designed to measure angles to an accuracy that warrants gentle handling. A sextant should never for an instant be left unattended at any place where it might fall or be knocked off onto the deck, and when handled, it should be grasped firmly by the handle or frame, never by the arc, index arm, or any of its appurtances. The slightest bending of any part may introduce unacceptable inaccuracies. A sextant that has been dropped or subjected to other violent treatment should be checked by a competent instrument technician to determine its suitability for further service.

When a sextant is not in use, it should be secured properly in its box, and the box should be stored in such a place and in such a manner that it will not receive shocks or be subjected to vibration or excessive heat.

Moisture is an enemy to sextants, causing corrosion of some of the vital parts and deterioration of the mirrors. In use, a sextant should be protected from salt spray. If any part of the instrument becomes damp, it should be wiped dry with lens paper or linen before the instrument is returned to its box. Linen used for this purpose should be stowed in a manner that will protect it from collecting abrasive dust. Alcohol applied with clean lens paper is a suitable liquid for cleaning the mirrors. Excessive pressure on any part should be avoided. A small amount of a drying agent such as silica gel kept in the sextant box helps keep the instrument dry when not in use. The agent should be replaced from time to time or heated to remove the moisture it might have collected.

Recommendations of the manufacturer regarding lubrication and other matters of care should be followed. Even the best instrument can be rendered ineffective by neglect or abuse.

Because of the desirability of having simultaneous observations, to avoid the necessity of advancing or retiring position lines, multi-body sextants have been proposed from time to time, but these have never proved popular, primarily because of the difficulty of viewing two or more bodies simultaneously.

Horizontal references other than the visible horizon are discussed in the next section.

Accurate measurements by means of a marine sextant require some skill in the use of the instrument. Familiarity with a sextant and practice are helpful, but even an experienced observer can often benefit from an analysis of his technique. Help by another observer may prove beneficial. The other person, watching as one makes an observation, may be able to detect errors in one's use of the instrument. The other person may make an observation of a body at a relatively low altitude near the meridian, when the altitude is nearly constant, and quickly transfer the sextant to the person whose technique is being investigated so he can see how the body and horizon should appear. This procedure is particularly useful for observations of the Sun or Moon, for the novice frequently has a tendency to misjudge the condition of tangency. Some observers who have a problem with accurate detection are able to improve their technique by setting the instrument so that the horizon and the image of the body are not quite in contact, the upper limb being below the horizon for a rising body, and the lower limb above the horizon for a setting body, and then continuing to observe, noting the instant at which contact is made as the altitude of the body changes. An alternative procedure is to observe the opposite limb and note the moment that contact between the limb and the horizon is broken.

Simultaneous observations by two observers can be instructive. If the difference is erratic and more than perhaps

1′, practice is indicated. If the altitudes of one observer are consistently greater than those of the other, the two observers having alternated in calling the times of observation, and allowance having been made for any differences in heights of eye and index and instrument errors, an attempt should be made to account for the difference in measured altitudes.

The navigator can do several things to help evaluate his technique without the assistance of a second observer. One of the most productive is to compare his observations with correct values, which may be a more reliable guide than observations of another observer. This comparison is best made when one's vessel is at anchor, or at a pier with an open stretch of horizon visible, or when one's vessel is proceeding at constant course and speed with an accurate means of independently determining position. The procedure is to select a body that will be over an open horizon during the sight-taking period, and calculate the altitude at intervals of perhaps eight minutes. If the body will be near the celestial meridian, a shorter interval should be used because of the variable rate of change of altitude at such time. If the vessel is underway, one may need to determine its position at the times for which calculations are to be made, and do the calculating after the observations are completed. Whatever the procedure, all sextant altitude-corrections (p. 378) should be applied, with reverse sign, to the calculated altitudes to determine the corresponding sextant altitudes. Watch error is applied with reverse sign to determine watch times. A plot is then made of sextant altitude *vs.* watch time.

With such a plot, one can compare a large number of observations quickly, with relatively few calculations. The results are then analyzed, and an attempt made to account for differences. For best results the procedure should be repeated a number of times with different bodies and under different conditions of lighting, visibility, and fatigue. It is usually best to make several observations with short intervals between them, and then to rest eyes and arms a minute or two before making another series of observations. One might experiment somewhat with different techniques, such as use *vs.* non-use of the telescope, closing one eye *vs.* keeping both eyes open, placing the limb of the Sun or Moon on the horizon *vs.* letting it seek the horizon, etc. It is good practice for the observer to practise 'calling his shots', by attempting to recognize those observations that are more accurate than others.

If, after a number of attempts to improve his skill, an observer finds that he has a nearly constant error of uniform sign, he may have a *personal error*. He may be able to recognize different but consistent values of personal error for different astronomical bodies or under different conditions. If one is confident of the existence, magnitude, and sign of such an error, one may achieve better results by applying a *personal correction* (*PC*) of like magnitude but opposite sign than by attempting to eliminate it. Personal error should be verified from time to time, for it may change.

Even if accurate positions of a vessel are not available, one might find it instructive to make a series of observations, preferably at equal intervals of time, and plot the results. A body near the celestial meridian should be avoided. The slope of the line averaging the results can be determined by calculating the altitude for two times during the sight-taking period, plotting these points, and drawing a straight line through them. Four minutes is a convenient interval, for during this interval the hour angle changes $1°$. The difference between each plotted altitude and the altitude indicated for the same time on the plotted line is determined and a second line is drawn parallel to the first and offset by the average of these differences. By noting the positions of plotted observations relative to the second line one can determine the consistency of one's observations but not the magnitude of any constant error (p. 27). Some indication of consistency can be made without a graph by making several observations of a low-altitude body within seconds as it crosses the celestial meridian, when the altitude is nearly constant. The method is not accurate unless the vessel is stopped or on an easterly or westerly course.

If one has a tendency to be erratic, a plot of altitude *vs.* time, with a line of the correct slope through the average position of the individual plots, can be used for improving one's accuracy when observing for a position line. Any point on the line

355

averaging the observations can be used for the observation, the time and altitude of the point being taken from the graph. Preferably, a convenient point near the centre of the line should be used.

Traditionally, a navigator takes great pride in his ability to use his sextant skilfully.

2. Artificial Horizons

When the natural horizon is not visible with adequate clarity, because of darkness or poor visibility, astronomical observations can be made if some form of *artificial horizon* is available. The flat surface of a liquid has been used for this purpose. Mercury is the liquid commonly used in commercial artificial horizons, but a pan of some viscous fluid such as heavy oil will do. A glass or clear plastic cover is desirable to protect the surface from disturbance by wind.

An artificial horizon is used by bringing the double-reflected sextant image of an astronomical body into coincidence with the single-reflected image seen in the liquid. For a lower-limb observation of the Sun or Moon, the lower limb of the body is made tangent to the apparent upper limb as seen in the liquid, and vice versa. If the two images are brought into coincidence, the centre of the body is observed. The correction of an altitude observed by means of an artificial horizon of this type is explained on page 397.

An artificial horizon of the type indicated is useful ashore, but has little or no practical value afloat except on a flat calm sea with no rolling or pitching of the vessel, or aboard a ship in heavy pack ice, or on the ice itself.

Another type of artificial horizon, of use primarily in aircraft but of limited use afloat, is one provided by a bubble, pendulum, or gyroscope attached to or an integral part of the sextant itself. Such a device provides a visual horizontal reference. The centres of all bodies are customarily observed.

Because of the unsteadiness of a bubble or pendulum reference, an altitude measured by means of a sextant employing such a reference has a greater probable error than one determined by use of a sharp natural horizon as a reference. Because of this unsteadiness, it is common practice to observe continuously over some period of time, usually two minutes, and use the indicated average altitude and the mid time as the observation.

An additional problem associated with the use of an artificial-horizon sextant afloat is the presence of *acceleration error*, a deflection of the visual reference caused by motions of the platform on which the observer is situated. In a moderate sea an error of 30′ or more from this source is not unusual. Even a gentle roll may introduce an error of 10′ or more. Additionally, yawing of the vessel may introduce a *Coriolis error* of 10′ or more. Because of these limitations, an artificial-horizon sextant having a bubble or pendulum is seldom used afloat except under the conditions mentioned for using an external artificial horizon.

Details of construction, use, and care of artificial-horizon sextants differ considerably. Instructions are provided with each instrument or should be sought from the manufacturer.

3. Timepieces

The various timepieces used aboard ship are discussed in section 21 of chapter III. For astronavigation, time at a reference meridian, usually Greenwich, is needed because this is the time used in almanacs for the tabulation of coordinates of astronomical bodies. If accurate time at a reference meridian were not available, astronomical determination of longitude at sea would not be possible.

The timepieces customarily used for astronavigation are (*1*) one or more marine chronometers set to GMT approximately, with known error, determined by means of periodic comparison with radio time-signals, and between such comparisons by applying chronometer rate to the last such comparison; and (*2*) a hack watch, usually set to ZT, but possibly to GMT, with a known error determined by comparison with a chronometer or by direct comparison with radio time-signals, allowing for the difference between GMT and ZT if the latter is used for the watch. A stop watch may be used in place of a hack watch.

4. Publications

The various publications of interest to navigators are discussed in section 2 of chapter III. Those relating particularly to astronavigation are almanacs and sight-reduction tables.

An almanac intended for use by navigators tabulates celestial-equator-system coordinates of the astronomical bodies commonly used in navigation, plus times of Sunrise, Sunset, twilight, Moonrise, and Moonset; sextant-altitude corrections; and other astronomical information of interest to navigators. The almanac most commonly used by British and American mariners is the *Nautical Almanac*, published jointly by the Royal Greenwich Observatory and the United States Naval Observatory. This almanac is published annually, each edition having ephemeridal information for one calendar year. A somewhat similar joint publication designed primarily for use by aviators is called *Air Almanac*. Additional information of interest principally to astronomers is published in ephemerides. Almanacs are discussed in greater detail in chapter VIII.

Sight-reduction tables are used primarily to convert celestial-equator-system coordinates to horizon-system coordinates. A great variety of such tables have been produced, most recent ones providing means for determining both altitude and azimuth. While many of the older tables were small publications of certain trigonometric functions arranged conveniently for calculation, a number of excellent tables of altitude and azimuth are now available. Of these, a joint British-United States publication called *Sight-Reduction Tables for Marine Navigation* is of particular interest. Sight-reduction tables are discussed in greater detail in chapter IX.

5. Miscellaneous

The plotting equipment needed for dead reckoning and pilotage, discussed in section 3 of chapter III, is adequate for astronavigation.

In addition, a *sight book* should be available for recording times of Sunrise, Sunset, twilight, Moonrise, Moonset; predicted positions of astronomical bodies during twilight; the names of bodies observed, with the sextant altitude and time of each observation; and other pertinent data such as height of eye and index correction. A *work book* of sight-reduction calculations should also be kept. This might well take the form of a looseleaf notebook in which pages bearing printed sight-reduction work forms (p. 399) are inserted as calculations are made. The sight book and work book provide a permanent record to which the navigator, Master, or others may wish to refer later, particularly if the voyage should be marred by a mishap such as a grounding or collision.

A good torch (flashlight) and spare batteries should be kept in a convenient place for use in reading the sextant and watch when observations are made during semi-darkness. A torch might have other uses, also, as for illuminating the sight book, a watch used for timing navigation lights, and an unlighted pelorus. It is well to provide means to prevent the torch from disturbing the dark adaptation of the eyes of the bridge personnel. A red bulb or filter should be adequate.

It is desirable to have equipment available for observing azimuth of astronomical bodies, for use in locating such bodies during the brighter part of twilight, and for measuring azimuths of unidentified bodies.

VIII

Almanacs

---

1. The Nautical Almanac

The practice of astronavigation is dependent upon the availability, in convenient form, of accurate predictions of positions of the astronomical bodies of use to the navigator. Positions in coordinates of the celestial-equator system (p. 293) are tabulated in some form of *almanac*. The almanac of primary interest to British and American mariners is the *Nautical Almanac* (*NA*), an annual joint publication of the Royal Greenwich Observatory and the United States Naval Observatory. With minor modifications and changes of language this almanac has been adopted by a number of other countries.

The major portion of this publication (Figs. 801, 802) consists of hourly tabulations of the Greenwich hour angle (GHA) of 'Aries' (the first point of Aries, or vernal equinox), four planets, Sun, and Moon, with tabulations of sidereal hour angle (SHA) and declination of 57 selected stars, and times of twilight and rising and setting of the Moon at various latitudes. Some additional information is included on these 'daily' pages, the data for three consecutive days being given on the two facing pages of any almanac opening. The data for stars and planets are given on the left-hand pages, and those for the Sun and Moon on the right-hand pages. Monthly tabulations of SHA and declination of 173 stars, including the 57 given on the daily pages, are given near the back of the book, before a special Polaris table (Fig. 910) and a series of 'increments and corrections' tables (Fig. 803), printed on buff-coloured paper, providing data for interpolation of GHA and declination.

The *Nautical Almanac* also has tables for interpolation of times of rising, setting, and twilight (Fig. 805), sextant-altitude correction tables (Figs. 806, 807, 808, 809), a table for conversion of arc to time, and other useful data, as well as explanatory information. A loose bookmark has the most frequently-used altitude correction tables printed on one side and two indices of the 57 selected stars on the other side.

In general, data tabulated in the *Nautical Almanac* are correct to the nearest 0ʹ.1. The lone exception is the GHA of the Sun, which is adjusted slightly to minimize the error in interpolation resulting from assuming a constant rate of change of 15° per hour. The maximum adjustment is 0ʹ.15. Interpolated values of GHA and declination are somewhat less accurate than tabulated data because of (*1*) the accumulation of errors when two or more quantities are added and (*2*) the assumption that the rate of change of these quantities between tabulations is linear. The largest total error that can occur from these causes is 0ʹ.3 in the GHA of the Moon, 0ʹ.25 in the GHA of the Sun, and less than 0ʹ.2 in the GHA or declination of a star or planet. These are extreme values. Two thirds of the values of GHA and declination taken from the almanac can be expected to have errors of 0ʹ.05 or less, and only about one tenth of the values to have errors in excess of 0ʹ.1.

Tabulation error of sextant altitude-corrections is not greater than 0ʹ.05, but the total error, found by adding several quantities each tabulated to the nearest 0ʹ.1, can be greater. Also, atmospheric conditions differing from the standard conditions assumed in computation of the corrections can introduce additional error. Minor corrections not taken into account can add slightly to the total error.

2. Time and the Almanac

As shown in Figs. 801 and 802, positional information given on the daily pages of the *Nautical Almanac* is tabulated for each integral hour of Greenwich mean time, GMT. As used in the almanac and throughout this book, GMT is GHA of the mean Sun plus 12 hours, often designated universal time, UT, specifically UT_1 (p. 331). This differs slightly from the atomic time scale, coordinated universal time, UTC (p. 331), commonly used for radio time-signals, the difference arising from the fact that the rotational rate of the Earth is slightly variable. Step adjustments of exactly one second, as needed, are made to UTC to bring it into conformity with UT_1. Normally, an adjustment is made at midnight on December 31 or June 30, if needed. For the ordinary purposes of astronavigation, this slight discrepancy, which is not permitted to exceed 0.9 second, can be ignored, but if greater accuracy is needed, the correction should be applied. The correction is given by coding of the time signed, as explained in the British *Admiralty List of Radio Signals*, volume V, 'Navigation Aids', NP 275(5), and in the United States Defense Mapping Agency Hydrographic Topographic Center Publication 117, *Radio Navigational Aids*.

Greenwich apparent time (GAT) (p. 327), can be determined by converting GHA of the Sun to time units, by means of the table provided in the almanac, and adding 12 hours. Local apparent time (LAT) can be determined by adding east longitude to or subtracting west longitude from GHA of the Sun, converting the result to time units, and adding 12 hours.

Greenwich sidereal time (GST) (p. 331) can be determined by converting GHA Aries (GHAΥ) to time units. Similarly, LST is LHAΥ.

Times of twilight, Sunrise, Sunset, Moonrise, and Moonset are tabulated in local mean time (LMT) (p. 327). This can be changed to zone time (ZT) (p. 328), by converting from arc to time units the difference in longitude between the local meridian and the reference meridian used for zone time, and subtracting this difference if the local meridian is east of the reference meridian, and adding if west of the reference meridian.

3. Coordinates of Astronomical Bodies

Stars. The SHA and declination of each of the 57 selected stars tabulated on the left-hand daily page of the *Nautical Almanac* can be used throughout the three days of each tabulation without interpolation, with negligible error. To find the GHA of a star, add its SHA, the GHA Υ for the integral hour of GMT, and the increase in GHA ♈ for minutes and seconds of GMT, taken from the increments and corrections section of the almanac.

Suppose it is desired to determine GHA and declination of the star Vega at GMT 5^h 14^m 22^s on June 22. Refer to Fig. 801. From the star tabulation, Vega's SHA is found to be $80°56'.0$, and its dec $38°45'.9$ N. Next, from the Aries column, on the line for GMT 5^h on June 22 the tabulated GHA ♈ is found to be $344°47'.3$. Refer now to Fig. 803, the increments and corrections tables for 14^m and 15^m. Note that separate columns are provided for Sun and planets, Aries, and the Moon, respectively. Enter the table for 14^m, and on the line for 22^s, in the column for Aries, find the value $3°36'.1$. Add the three hour-angle values to obtain GHA of the star:

Vega

GMT	5^h 14^m 22^s June 22
SHA	$80°56'.0$
5^h	$344°47'.3$
14^m 22^s	$3°36'.1$
GHA	$69°19'.4$
dec	$38°45'.9$ N.

If the sum of the three hour-angle values exceeds $360°$, as in this example, subtract $360°$ from the answer, as shown.

The tabulation of 173 stars near the back of the almanac includes all stars of magnitude 3.0 and brighter, including the 57 selected stars tabulated on the daily pages, and a few fainter ones to fill some of the larger gaps. Stars are listed in order of increasing SHA, unlike the daily-page alphabetical tabulations. In the 173-star tabulation, constellation names are given, as well as the star names where well-known ones exist. The average value of each star's SHA and declination for each month is tabulated. In the ordinary course of navigation, these values can be used throughout the month without interpolation.

Planets. The GHA and declination of the planets Venus,

Mars, Jupiter, and Saturn are tabulated on the left-hand daily pages, at hourly intervals of GMT, as shown in Fig. 801. The average magnitude of each planet during the three-day period is shown at the top of the column, to the right of the planet name.

At the bottom of each planet column average values of v and d for the three days are shown. The quantity v is the excess of the actual change of GHA in one hour over the standard value of $15°$ per hour used in the increments table, and d is the change of declination during one hour. When the change of GHA in one hour is less than the standard value, a condition that occurs occasionally for Venus, v is given a negative sign. The sign of d can be either positive or negative, as determined by comparison of consecutive values of declination. The d value is used for interpolation of declination between hourly entries. A slight increase in accuracy can sometimes be obtained by using the actual differences between consecutive entries (minus $15°$ for v), rather than the tabulated values of v and d, but in the ordinary course of navigation this refinement is not justified.

To determine the GHA of a planet, find the value tabulated for the integral hour of GMT, as shown on the left-hand daily page; add the increase in GHA for the minutes and seconds of GMT, as taken from the increments table; and add (or subtract) any needed correction for v. To find a planet's declination, interpolate between the hourly entries on the daily pages, using the d value and corrections table if desired. A corrections table is given for each minute of GMT. The same integral minute is used for entering the GHA increments table and the v and d corrections table. The v and d corrections are given the same signs as v and d. The average three-day value of SHA of each of the four navigational planets is tabulated at the lower right-hand corner of each left-hand page. To find the value at any specific time, subtract GHA Υ from GHA of the planet.

Suppose it is desired to determine GHA and declination of the planet Venus at GMT $18^h 15^m 39^s$ on June 23. Refer to Fig. 801. The values tabulated for GMT 18^h are: GHA $107°56'.7$, v $(-)$ $0'.8$, dec $21°53'.2$ N., d $(+)$ 0.5. From the increments and corrections tables, Fig. 803, the planet GHA increment for 15^m 39^s is found to be $3°54.8$, the v correction $(-)$0.2, and the d correction $(+)$0.1. The calculations for the desired values are:

	Venus
GMT	$18^h15^m39^s$ June 23
18^h	$107°56.7$
15^m 39^s	$3°54.8$
v corr	$(-)$ 0.2 $\quad v$ $(-)$ 0.8
GHA	$111°51.3$
18^h	$21°53.2$ N.
d corr	$(+)$ 0.1 $\quad d(+)0.5$
dec	$21°53.3$ N.

Sun. The GHA and declination of the Sun are tabulated on the right-hand daily pages, at hourly intervals of GMT, as shown in Fig. 802. The GHA values are adjusted slightly, as explained in section 1 of this chapter, to avoid the necessity for a v correction. The average value of d for the three days is shown at the bottom of the declination column. To the left of d is shown the average value of semi-diameter of the Sun for the three days.

To determine the GHA of the Sun, find the tabulated value for the integral hour of GMT and add the increase for the minutes and seconds of GMT, as taken from the increments table. To find the Sun's declination, interpolate between the hourly entries on the daily pages, using the d value and the corrections table if desired. To find SHA of the Sun, subtract GHA Υ from GHA of the Sun.

Suppose it is desired to determine GHA and declination of the Sun at GMT 10^h 14^m 03^s on June 21. Refer to Fig. 802. The tabulated values for GMT 10^h are: GHA $329°36.6$, dec $23°26.3$ N., d 0.0. From the increments and corrections tables, Fig. 803, the Sun GHA increment for 14^m 03^s is found

JUNE 21, 22, 23 (THURS., FRI., SAT.)

G.M.T.	ARIES G.H.A.	VENUS −3.3 G.H.A.	Dec.	MARS +1.5 G.H.A.	Dec.	JUPITER −1.4 G.H.A.	Dec.	SATURN +1.1 G.H.A.	Dec.	STARS Name	S.H.A.	D
21 00	268 35.8	198 47.7 N21 21.6		214 28.0 N19 01.5		137 10.6 N18 42.1		107 40.7 N10 05.1		Acamar	315 38.2	S40
01	283 38.3	213 46.9 22.1		229 28.6 01.9		152 12.6 42.0		122 43.0 05.0		Achernar	335 46.3	S57
02	298 40.7	228 46.2 22.6		244 29.3 02.4		167 14.6 41.9		137 45.3 05.0		Acrux	173 38.0	S62
03	313 43.2	243 45.4 ·· 23.1		259 29.9 ·· 02.8		182 16.6 ·· 41.8		152 47.6 ·· 04.9		Adhara	255 33.1	S28
04	328 45.7	258 44.7 23.6		274 30.5 03.2		197 18.5 41.6		167 49.9 04.8		Aldebaran	291 19.3	N16
05	343 48.1	273 43.9 24.1		289 31.1 03.7		212 20.5 41.5		182 52.2 04.7				
06	358 50.6	288 43.1 N21 24.6		304 31.7 N19 04.1		227 22.5 N18 41.4		197 54.5 N10 04.7		Alioth	166 43.2	N56
07	13 53.0	303 42.4 25.1		319 32.4 04.6		242 24.5 41.3		212 56.8 04.6		Alkaid	153 19.0	N49
T 08	28 55.5	318 41.6 25.6		334 33.0 05.0		257 26.4 41.1		227 59.1 04.5		Al Na'ir	28 15.8	S47
H 09	43 58.0	333 40.8 ·· 26.1		349 33.6 ·· 05.5		272 28.4 ·· 41.0		243 01.4 ·· 04.5		Alnilam	276 12.9	S 1
U 10	59 00.4	348 40.1 26.6		4 34.2 05.9		287 30.4 40.9		258 03.7 04.4		Alphard	218 21.6	S 8
R 11	74 02.9	3 39.3 27.1		19 34.9 06.4		302 32.4 40.7		273 06.0 04.3				
S 12	89 05.4	18 38.6 N21 27.6		34 35.5 N19 06.8		317 34.3 N18 40.6		288 08.3 N10 04.3		Alphecca	126 32.6	N26
D 13	104 07.8	33 37.8 28.1		49 36.1 07.2		332 36.3 40.5		303 10.6 04.2		Alpheratz	358 10.2	N28
A 14	119 10.3	48 37.0 28.6		64 36.7 07.7		347 38.3 40.4		318 12.9 04.1		Altair	62 33.0	N 8
Y 15	134 12.8	63 36.3 ·· 29.1		79 37.3 ·· 08.1		2 40.3 ·· 40.2		333 15.2 ·· 04.0		Ankaa	353 41.2	S42
16	149 15.2	78 35.5 29.6		94 38.0 08.6		17 42.2 40.1		348 17.5 04.0		Antares	112 57.5	S26
17	164 17.7	93 34.7 30.1		109 38.6 09.0		32 44.2 40.0		3 19.9 03.9				
18	179 20.1	108 34.0 N21 30.6		124 39.2 N19 09.4		47 46.2 N18 39.9		18 22.2 N10 03.8		Arcturus	146 19.1	N19
19	194 22.6	123 33.2 31.1		139 39.8 09.9		62 48.2 39.7		33 24.5 03.8		Atria	108 22.0	S68
20	209 25.1	138 32.4 31.6		154 40.4 10.3		77 50.1 39.6		48 26.8 03.7		Avior	234 29.0	S59
21	224 27.5	153 31.7 ·· 32.1		169 41.1 ·· 10.8		92 52.1 ·· 39.5		63 29.1 ·· 03.6		Bellatrix	279 00.0	N 6
22	239 30.0	168 30.9 32.6		184 41.7 11.2		107 54.1 39.4		78 31.4 03.6		Betelgeuse	271 29.5	N 7
23	254 32.5	183 30.1 33.1		199 42.3 11.6		122 56.0 39.2		93 33.7 03.5				
22 00	269 34.9	198 29.3 N21 33.6		214 42.9 N19 12.1		137 58.0 N18 39.1		108 36.0 N10 03.4		Canopus	264 08.1	S52
01	284 37.4	213 28.6 34.1		229 43.6 12.5		153 00.0 39.0		123 38.3 03.3		Capella	281 13.0	N45
02	299 39.9	228 27.8 34.5		244 44.2 13.0		168 02.0 38.8		138 40.6 03.3		Deneb	49 48.6	N45
03	314 42.3	243 27.0 ·· 35.0		259 44.8 ·· 13.4		183 03.9 ·· 38.7		153 42.9 ·· 03.2		Denebola	183 00.0	N14
04	329 44.8	258 26.3 35.5		274 45.4 13.8		198 05.9 38.6		168 45.2 03.1		Diphda	349 21.8	S18
05	344 47.3	273 25.5 36.0		289 46.0 14.3		213 07.9 38.5		183 47.5 03.1				
06	359 49.7	288 24.7 N21 36.5		304 46.7 N19 14.7		228 09.9 N18 38.3		198 49.8 N10 03.0		Dubhe	194 23.5	N61
07	14 52.2	303 24.0 37.0		319 47.3 15.1		243 11.8 38.2		213 52.1 02.9		Elnath	278 45.6	N28
08	29 54.6	318 23.2 37.4		334 47.9 15.6		258 13.8 38.1		228 54.4 02.9		Eltanin	90 57.6	N51
F 09	44 57.1	333 22.4 ·· 37.9		349 48.5 ·· 16.0		273 15.8 ·· 38.0		243 56.7 ·· 02.8		Enif	34 12.2	N 9
R 10	59 59.6	348 21.6 38.4		4 49.1 16.5		288 17.7 37.8		258 59.0 02.7		Fomalhaut	15 52.3	S29
I 11	75 02.0	3 20.9 38.9		19 49.8 16.9		303 19.7 37.7		274 01.3 02.6				
D 12	90 04.5	18 20.1 N21 39.4		34 50.4 N19 17.3		318 21.7 N18 37.6		289 03.6 N10 02.6		Gacrux	172 29.5	S57
A 13	105 07.0	33 19.3 39.8		49 51.0 17.8		333 23.7 37.4		304 05.9 02.5		Gienah	176 18.8	S17
Y 14	120 09.4	48 18.5 40.3		64 51.6 18.2		348 25.6 37.3		319 08.2 02.4		Hadar	149 24.1	S60
15	135 11.9	63 17.8 ·· 40.8		79 52.2 ·· 18.6		3 27.6 ·· 37.2		334 10.5 ·· 02.4		Hamal	328 30.0	N23
16	150 14.4	78 17.0 41.2		94 52.9 19.1		18 29.6 37.1		349 12.8 02.3		Kaus Aust.	84 17.6	S34
17	165 16.8	93 16.2 41.7		109 53.5 19.5		33 31.5 36.9		4 15.1 02.2				
18	180 19.3	108 15.4 N21 42.2		124 54.1 N19 19.9		48 33.5 N18 36.8		19 17.4 N10 02.1		Kochab	137 18.3	N74
19	195 21.8	123 14.7 42.7		139 54.7 20.4		63 35.5 36.7		34 19.7 02.1		Markab	14 03.9	N15
20	210 24.2	138 13.9 43.1		154 55.3 20.8		78 37.5 36.6		49 22.0 02.0		Menkar	314 42.3	N 4
21	225 26.7	153 13.1 ·· 43.6		169 56.0 ·· 21.2		93 39.4 ·· 36.4		64 24.3 ·· 01.9		Menkent	148 37.8	S36
22	240 29.1	168 12.3 44.1		184 56.6 21.6		108 41.4 36.3		79 26.6 01.9		Miaplacidus	221 45.6	S69
23	255 31.6	183 11.5 44.5		199 57.2 22.1		123 43.4 36.2		94 28.9 01.8				
23 00	270 34.1	198 10.8 N21 45.0		214 57.8 N19 22.5		138 45.3 N18 36.0		109 31.2 N10 01.7		Mirfak	309 17.7	N49
01	285 36.5	213 10.0 45.5		229 58.4 22.9		153 47.3 35.9		124 33.5 01.6		Nunki	76 29.9	S26
02	300 39.0	228 09.2 45.9		244 59.1 23.4		168 49.3 35.8		139 35.8 01.6		Peacock	53 59.3	S56
03	315 41.5	243 08.4 ·· 46.4		259 59.7 ·· 23.8		183 51.3 ·· 35.7		154 38.1 ·· 01.5		Pollux	243 59.6	N28
04	330 43.9	258 07.6 46.8		275 00.3 24.2		198 53.2 35.5		169 40.4 01.4		Procyon	245 27.0	N 5
05	345 46.4	273 06.9 47.3		290 00.9 24.7		213 55.2 35.4		184 42.7 01.4				
06	0 48.9	288 06.1 N21 47.7		305 01.5 N19 25.1		228 57.2 N18 35.3		199 45.0 N10 01.3		Rasalhague	96 30.0	N12
07	15 51.3	303 05.3 48.2		320 02.2 25.5		243 59.1 35.1		214 47.3 01.2		Regulus	208 11.1	N12
S 08	30 53.8	318 04.5 48.7		335 02.8 25.9		259 01.1 35.0		229 49.6 01.1		Rigel	281 37.2	S 8
A 09	45 56.2	333 03.7 ·· 49.1		350 03.4 ·· 26.4		274 03.1 ·· 34.9		244 51.9 ·· 01.1		Rigil Kent.	140 26.4	S60
T 10	60 58.7	348 03.0 49.6		5 04.0 26.8		289 05.0 34.8		259 54.2 01.0		Sabik	102 41.8	S15
U 11	76 01.2	3 02.2 50.0		20 04.6 27.2		304 07.0 34.6		274 56.5 00.9				
R 12	91 03.6	18 01.4 N21 50.5		35 05.3 N19 27.6		319 09.0 N18 34.5		289 58.8 N10 00.9		Schedar	350 10.0	N56
D 13	106 06.1	33 00.6 50.9		50 05.9 28.1		334 11.0 34.4		305 01.1 00.8		Shaula	96 56.5	S37
A 14	121 08.6	47 59.8 51.4		65 06.5 28.5		349 12.9 34.2		320 03.4 00.7		Sirius	258 56.8	S16
Y 15	136 11.0	62 59.0 ·· 51.8		80 07.1 ·· 28.9		4 14.9 ·· 34.1		335 05.7 ·· 00.6		Spica	158 58.3	S11
16	151 13.5	77 58.3 52.3		95 07.7 29.4		19 16.9 34.0		350 07.9 00.6		Suhail	223 11.7	S43
17	166 16.0	92 57.5 52.7		110 08.3 29.8		34 18.8 33.9		5 10.2 00.5				
18	181 18.4	107 56.7 N21 53.2		125 09.0 N19 30.2		49 20.8 N18 33.7		20 12.5 N10 00.4		Vega	80 56.0	N38
19	196 20.9	122 55.9 53.6		140 09.6 30.6		64 22.8 33.6		35 14.8 00.4		Zuben'ubi	137 33.7	S15
20	211 23.4	137 55.1 54.0		155 10.2 31.1		79 24.7 33.5		50 17.1 00.3			S.H.A.	Mer.
21	226 25.8	152 54.3 ·· 54.5		170 10.8 ·· 31.5		94 26.7 ·· 33.3		65 19.4 ·· 00.2				
22	241 28.3	167 53.5 54.9		185 11.4 31.9		109 28.7 33.2		80 21.7 00.1		Venus	288 54.4	10
23	256 30.7	182 52.8 55.4		200 12.1 32.3		124 30.6 33.1		95 24.0 00.1		Mars	305 08.0	9
										Jupiter	228 23.1	14
Mer. Pass.	6 00.7	v −0.8 d 0.5		v 0.6 d 0.4		v 2.0 d 0.1		v 2.3 d 0.1		Saturn	199 01.0	16

FIG. 801. A left-hand daily page of the *Nautical Almanac*.

JUNE 21, 22, 23 (THURS., FRI., SAT.)

M.T.	SUN G.H.A.	Dec.	MOON G.H.A.	v	Dec.	d	H.P.
21							
00	179 38.0	N23 26.2	222 34.9	10.5	N12 32.7	8.0	57.2
01	194 37.9	26.2	237 04.4	10.5	12 40.7	7.9	57.2
02	209 37.7	26.2	251 33.9	10.5	12 48.6	7.8	57.2
03	224 37.6	·· 26.2	266 03.4	10.5	12 56.4	7.8	57.2
04	239 37.4	26.2	280 32.9	10.5	13 04.2	7.7	57.1
05	254 37.3	26.2	295 02.4	10.4	13 11.9	7.6	57.1
06	269 37.2	N23 26.2	309 31.8	10.5	N13 19.5	7.5	57.1
07	284 37.0	26.3	324 01.3	10.4	13 27.0	7.5	57.1
08	299 36.9	26.3	338 30.7	10.4	13 34.5	7.4	57.0
09	314 36.8	·· 26.3	353 00.1	10.4	13 41.9	7.3	57.0
10	329 36.6	26.3	7 29.5	10.4	13 49.2	7.2	57.0
11	344 36.5	26.3	21 58.9	10.4	13 56.4	7.2	57.0
12	359 36.3	N23 26.3	36 28.3	10.4	N14 03.6	7.1	57.0
13	14 36.2	26.3	50 57.7	10.4	14 10.7	7.0	56.9
14	29 36.1	26.3	65 27.1	10.3	14 17.7	6.9	56.9
15	44 35.9	·· 26.3	79 56.4	10.4	14 24.6	6.8	56.9
16	59 35.8	26.3	94 25.8	10.3	14 31.4	6.8	56.9
17	74 35.7	26.3	108 55.1	10.3	14 38.2	6.6	56.9
18	89 35.5	N23 26.3	123 24.4	10.3	N14 44.8	6.6	56.8
19	104 35.4	26.3	137 53.7	10.3	14 51.4	6.5	56.8
20	119 35.3	26.4	152 23.0	10.3	14 57.9	6.4	56.8
21	134 35.1	·· 26.4	166 52.3	10.2	15 04.3	6.4	56.8
22	149 35.0	26.4	181 21.5	10.3	15 10.7	6.2	56.8
23	164 34.8	26.4	195 50.8	10.3	15 16.9	6.2	56.7
22							
00	179 34.7	N23 26.4	210 20.1	10.2	N15 23.1	6.0	56.7
01	194 34.6	26.4	224 49.3	10.2	15 29.1	6.0	56.7
02	209 34.4	26.4	239 18.5	10.2	15 35.1	5.9	56.7
03	224 34.3	·· 26.4	253 47.7	10.3	15 41.0	5.9	56.6
04	239 34.2	26.3	268 17.0	10.2	15 46.9	5.7	56.6
05	254 34.0	26.3	282 46.2	10.1	15 52.6	5.6	56.6
06	269 33.9	N23 26.3	297 15.3	10.2	N15 58.2	5.6	56.6
07	284 33.7	26.3	311 44.5	10.2	16 03.8	5.4	56.6
08	299 33.6	26.3	326 13.7	10.2	16 09.2	5.4	56.5
09	314 33.5	·· 26.3	340 42.9	10.1	16 14.6	5.3	56.5
10	329 33.3	26.3	355 12.0	10.2	16 19.9	5.2	56.5
11	344 33.2	26.3	9 41.2	10.1	16 25.1	5.1	56.5
12	359 33.1	N23 26.3	24 10.3	10.2	N16 30.2	5.0	56.5
13	14 32.9	26.3	38 39.5	10.1	16 35.2	4.9	56.4
14	29 32.8	26.3	53 08.6	10.1	16 40.1	4.9	56.4
15	44 32.7	·· 26.3	67 37.7	10.1	16 45.0	4.7	56.4
16	59 32.5	26.3	82 06.9	10.1	16 49.7	4.6	56.4
17	74 32.4	26.2	96 36.0	10.1	16 54.3	4.6	56.4
18	89 32.2	N23 26.2	111 05.1	10.1	N16 58.9	4.4	56.3
19	104 32.1	26.2	125 34.2	10.1	17 03.3	4.4	56.3
20	119 32.0	26.2	140 03.3	10.1	17 07.7	4.3	56.3
21	134 31.8	·· 26.2	154 32.4	10.1	17 12.0	4.2	56.3
22	149 31.7	26.2	169 01.5	10.1	17 16.2	4.0	56.3
23	164 31.6	26.1	183 30.6	10.1	17 20.2	4.0	56.2
23							
00	179 31.4	N23 26.1	197 59.7	10.1	N17 24.2	3.9	56.2
01	194 31.3	26.1	212 28.8	10.1	17 28.1	3.8	56.2
02	209 31.1	26.1	226 57.9	10.1	17 31.9	3.7	56.2
03	224 31.0	·· 26.1	241 27.0	10.1	17 35.6	3.6	56.1
04	239 30.9	26.1	255 56.1	10.1	17 39.2	3.5	56.1
05	254 30.7	26.0	270 25.2	10.1	17 42.7	3.5	56.1
06	269 30.6	N23 26.0	284 54.3	10.1	N17 46.2	3.3	56.1
07	284 30.5	26.0	299 23.4	10.1	17 49.5	3.2	56.1
08	299 30.3	26.0	313 52.5	10.1	17 52.7	3.1	56.0
09	314 30.2	·· 26.0	328 21.6	10.1	17 55.8	3.1	56.0
10	329 30.1	25.9	342 50.7	10.2	17 58.9	2.9	56.0
11	344 29.9	25.9	357 19.9	10.1	18 01.8	2.8	56.0
12	359 29.8	N23 25.9	11 49.0	10.1	N18 04.6	2.8	56.0
13	14 29.6	25.9	26 18.1	10.1	18 07.4	2.6	55.9
14	29 29.5	25.8	40 47.2	10.2	18 10.0	2.6	55.9
15	44 29.4	·· 25.8	55 16.4	10.1	18 12.6	2.4	55.9
16	59 29.2	25.8	69 45.5	10.2	18 15.0	2.4	55.9
17	74 29.1	25.7	84 14.7	10.1	18 17.4	2.2	55.9
18	89 29.0	N23 25.7	98 43.8	10.2	N18 19.6	2.2	55.8
19	104 28.8	25.7	113 13.0	10.2	18 21.8	2.1	55.8
20	119 28.7	25.7	127 42.2	10.2	18 23.9	1.9	55.8
21	134 28.6	·· 25.6	142 11.4	10.2	18 25.8	1.9	55.8
22	149 28.4	25.6	156 40.6	10.2	18 27.7	1.7	55.8
23	164 28.3	25.6	171 09.8	10.2	18 29.4	1.7	55.7
	S.D. 15.8	d 0.0	S.D. 15.5		15.4		15.2

Lat.	Twilight Naut.	Civil	Sunrise	Moonrise 21	22	23	24
N 72	□	□	□	00 19	{00 10 / 23 55}	(□)	□
N 70	□	□	□	00 41	00 45	00 53	01 14
68	□	□	□	00 58	01 09	01 28	01 59
66	□	□	□	01 12	01 29	01 53	02 28
64	////	////	01 31	01 23	01 44	02 12	02 50
62	////	////	02 09	01 33	01 57	02 28	03 08
60	////	00 49	02 36	01 42	02 09	02 42	03 23
N 58	////	01 40	02 56	01 49	02 18	02 53	03 35
56	////	02 10	03 13	01 56	02 27	03 03	03 46
54	00 45	02 33	03 27	02 02	02 34	03 12	03 56
52	01 32	02 51	03 40	02 07	02 41	03 20	04 04
50	02 00	03 06	03 51	02 12	02 47	03 27	04 12
45	02 46	03 36	04 13	02 22	03 00	03 42	04 28
N 40	03 17	03 58	04 31	02 31	03 11	03 55	04 42
35	03 40	04 17	04 46	02 39	03 21	04 06	04 53
30	03 59	04 32	04 59	02 45	03 29	04 15	05 03
20	04 28	04 57	05 21	02 57	03 43	04 31	05 21
N 10	04 50	05 17	05 40	03 07	03 56	04 45	05 36
0	05 09	05 36	05 58	03 17	04 08	04 59	05 50
S 10	05 26	05 53	06 16	03 27	04 19	05 12	06 04
20	05 43	06 10	06 34	03 37	04 32	05 26	06 19
30	05 59	06 29	06 55	03 49	04 47	05 43	06 36
35	06 08	06 40	07 08	03 56	04 55	05 53	06 47
40	06 17	06 51	07 22	04 04	05 05	06 04	06 58
45	06 28	07 05	07 39	04 13	05 16	06 16	07 12
S 50	06 40	07 21	08 00	04 24	05 30	06 32	07 28
52	06 45	07 29	08 10	04 29	05 37	06 40	07 36
54	06 51	07 37	08 21	04 35	05 44	06 48	07 45
56	06 57	07 46	08 33	04 41	05 52	06 57	07 55
58	07 03	07 56	08 48	04 48	06 01	07 08	08 06
S 60	07 11	08 08	09 06	04 57	06 12	07 20	08 19

Lat.	Sunset	Twilight Civil	Naut.	Moonset 21	22	23	24
N 72	□	□	□	19 27	21 28	□	□
N 70	□	□	□	18 53	20 30	21 56	22 55
68	□	□	□	18 29	19 56	21 12	22 08
66	□	□	□	18 10	19 32	20 43	21 38
64	22 33	////	////	17 55	19 13	20 21	21 16
62	21 54	////	////	17 43	18 57	20 03	20 57
60	21 28	23 14	////	17 32	18 44	19 48	20 42
N 58	21 07	22 23	////	17 23	18 33	19 36	20 30
56	20 50	21 53	////	17 15	18 23	19 25	20 19
54	20 36	21 31	23 19	17 08	18 15	19 16	20 09
52	20 24	21 13	22 31	17 02	18 07	19 07	20 00
50	20 13	20 58	22 03	16 56	18 00	19 00	19 53
45	19 50	20 28	21 18	16 43	17 45	18 43	19 36
N 40	19 32	20 05	20 47	16 33	17 33	18 30	19 22
35	19 17	19 47	20 24	16 24	17 23	18 19	19 11
30	19 04	19 32	20 05	16 17	17 14	18 09	19 01
20	18 42	19 07	19 36	16 04	16 58	17 52	18 44
N 10	18 23	18 46	19 13	15 52	16 45	17 37	18 28
0	18 05	18 28	18 54	15 41	16 32	17 23	18 14
S 10	17 48	18 11	18 37	15 30	16 19	17 10	18 00
20	17 29	17 53	18 21	15 19	16 06	16 55	17 45
30	17 08	17 35	18 04	15 06	15 50	16 38	17 27
35	16 56	17 24	17 56	14 58	15 41	16 28	17 17
40	16 42	17 12	17 46	14 49	15 31	16 17	17 06
45	16 25	16 59	17 36	14 39	15 19	16 03	16 52
S 50	16 04	16 42	17 24	14 27	15 05	15 47	16 35
52	15 54	16 35	17 19	14 22	14 58	15 40	16 27
54	15 43	16 27	17 13	14 15	14 50	15 31	16 18
56	15 30	16 18	17 07	14 09	14 42	15 22	16 09
58	15 15	16 07	17 00	14 01	14 33	15 11	15 57
S 60	14 58	15 56	16 53	13 52	14 22	14 59	15 44

Day	SUN Eqn. of Time 00h	12h	Mer. Pass.	MOON Mer. Pass. Upper	Lower	Age	Phase
21	01 28	01 34	12 02	09 29	21 54	26	
22	01 41	01 47	12 02	10 20	22 45	27	
23	01 54	02 01	12 02	11 11	23 37	28	●

FIG. 802. A right-hand daily page of the *Nautical Almanac*.

to be 3°30′.8, and the *d* correction 0′.0. The calculations for the desired values are:

	Sun	
GMT	10^{h}14^m 03^s June 21	
10^h	329°36′.6	
14^m 03^s	3°30′.8	
GHA	333°07′.4	
10^h	23°26′.3 N.	
d corr	0′.0	*d* 0′.0
dec	23°26′.3 N.	

Moon. The GHA, *v*, declination, *d*, and horizontal parallax of the Moon are tabulated on the right-hand daily pages, at hourly intervals of GMT, as shown in Fig. 802. In the case of the Moon, the *v* values are the excess of the actual hourly change in GHA over 14°19′.0, resulting in all positive values. Each *d* value is the actual difference between the entry value and that for the next later hour. The horizontal parallax is used in determining a sextant altitude-correction (p. 390). The average semi-diameter for each of the three days is shown at the bottom of the Moon data columns.

To find the GHA and declination of the Moon, proceed as for a planet. To find SHA, proceed as for the Sun.

Suppose it is desired to determine GHA and declination of the Moon at GMT 2^h 15^m 53^s on June 21. Refer to Fig. 802. The values tabulated for GMT 2^h are: GHA 251°33′.9, *v* (+) 10′.5, dec 12°48′.6 N., *d* (+) 7′.8. From the increments and corrections tables, Fig. 803, the Moon GHA increment for 15^m 53^s is found to be 3°47′.4, the *v* correction (+) 2′.7, and the *d* correction (+) 2′.0. The computations for the desired values are:

INCREMENTS AND CORRECTIONS 15ᵐ

s	SUN PLANETS	ARIES	MOON	v/d or Corrⁿ	v/d or Corrⁿ	v/d or Corrⁿ	SUN PLANETS	ARIES	MOON	v/d or Corrⁿ	v/d or Corrⁿ	v/d or Corrⁿ
00	3 30·0	3 30·6	3 20·4	0·0 0·0	6·0 1·5	12·0 2·9	3 45·0	3 45·6	3 34·8	0·0 0·0	6·0 1·6	12·0 3·1
01	3 30·3	3 30·8	3 20·7	0·1 0·0	6·1 1·5	12·1 2·9	3 45·3	3 45·9	3 35·0	0·1 0·0	6·1 1·6	12·1 3·1
02	3 30·5	3 31·1	3 20·9	0·2 0·0	6·2 1·5	12·2 2·9	3 45·5	3 46·1	3 35·2	0·2 0·1	6·2 1·6	12·2 3·2
03	3 30·8	3 31·3	3 21·1	0·3 0·1	6·3 1·5	12·3 3·0	3 45·8	3 46·4	3 35·5	0·3 0·1	6·3 1·6	12·3 3·2
04	3 31·0	3 31·6	3 21·4	0·4 0·1	6·4 1·5	12·4 3·0	3 46·0	3 46·6	3 35·7	0·4 0·1	6·4 1·7	12·4 3·2
05	3 31·3	3 31·8	3 21·6	0·5 0·1	6·5 1·6	12·5 3·0	3 46·3	3 46·9	3 35·9	0·5 0·1	6·5 1·7	12·5 3·2
06	3 31·5	3 32·1	3 21·9	0·6 0·1	6·6 1·6	12·6 3·0	3 46·5	3 47·1	3 36·2	0·6 0·2	6·6 1·7	12·6 3·3
07	3 31·8	3 32·3	3 22·1	0·7 0·2	6·7 1·6	12·7 3·1	3 46·8	3 47·4	3 36·4	0·7 0·2	6·7 1·7	12·7 3·3
08	3 32·0	3 32·6	3 22·3	0·8 0·2	6·8 1·6	12·8 3·1	3 47·0	3 47·6	3 36·7	0·8 0·2	6·8 1·8	12·8 3·3
09	3 32·3	3 32·8	3 22·6	0·9 0·2	6·9 1·7	12·9 3·1	3 47·3	3 47·9	3 36·9	0·9 0·2	6·9 1·8	12·9 3·3
10	3 32·5	3 33·1	3 22·8	1·0 0·2	7·0 1·7	13·0 3·1	3 47·5	3 48·1	3 37·1	1·0 0·3	7·0 1·8	13·0 3·4
11	3 32·8	3 33·3	3 23·1	1·1 0·3	7·1 1·7	13·1 3·2	3 47·8	3 48·4	3 37·4	1·1 0·3	7·1 1·8	13·1 3·4
12	3 33·0	3 33·6	3 23·3	1·2 0·3	7·2 1·7	13·2 3·2	3 48·0	3 48·6	3 37·6	1·2 0·3	7·2 1·9	13·2 3·4
13	3 33·3	3 33·8	3 23·5	1·3 0·3	7·3 1·8	13·3 3·2	3 48·3	3 48·9	3 37·9	1·3 0·3	7·3 1·9	13·3 3·4
14	3 33·5	3 34·1	3 23·8	1·4 0·3	7·4 1·8	13·4 3·2	3 48·5	3 49·1	3 38·1	1·4 0·4	7·4 1·9	13·4 3·5
15	3 33·8	3 34·3	3 24·0	1·5 0·4	7·5 1·8	13·5 3·3	3 48·8	3 49·4	3 38·3	1·5 0·4	7·5 1·9	13·5 3·5
16	3 34·0	3 34·6	3 24·3	1·6 0·4	7·6 1·8	13·6 3·3	3 49·0	3 49·6	3 38·6	1·6 0·4	7·6 2·0	13·6 3·5
17	3 34·3	3 34·8	3 24·5	1·7 0·4	7·7 1·9	13·7 3·3	3 49·3	3 49·9	3 38·8	1·7 0·4	7·7 2·0	13·7 3·5
18	3 34·5	3 35·1	3 24·7	1·8 0·4	7·8 1·9	13·8 3·3	3 49·5	3 50·1	3 39·0	1·8 0·5	7·8 2·0	13·8 3·6
19	3 34·8	3 35·3	3 25·0	1·9 0·5	7·9 1·9	13·9 3·4	3 49·8	3 50·4	3 39·3	1·9 0·5	7·9 2·0	13·9 3·6
20	3 35·0	3 35·6	3 25·2	2·0 0·5	8·0 1·9	14·0 3·4	3 50·0	3 50·6	3 39·5	2·0 0·5	8·0 2·1	14·0 3·6
21	3 35·3	3 35·8	3 25·4	2·1 0·5	8·1 2·0	14·1 3·4	3 50·3	3 50·9	3 39·8	2·1 0·5	8·1 2·1	14·1 3·6
22	3 35·5	3 36·1	3 25·7	2·2 0·5	8·2 2·0	14·2 3·4	3 50·5	3 51·1	3 40·0	2·2 0·6	8·2 2·1	14·2 3·7
23	3 35·8	3 36·3	3 25·9	2·3 0·6	8·3 2·0	14·3 3·5	3 50·8	3 51·4	3 40·2	2·3 0·6	8·3 2·1	14·3 3·7
24	3 36·0	3 36·6	3 26·2	2·4 0·6	8·4 2·0	14·4 3·5	3 51·0	3 51·6	3 40·5	2·4 0·6	8·4 2·2	14·4 3·7
25	3 36·3	3 36·8	3 26·4	2·5 0·6	8·5 2·1	14·5 3·5	3 51·3	3 51·9	3 40·7	2·5 0·6	8·5 2·2	14·5 3·7
26	3 36·5	3 37·1	3 26·6	2·6 0·6	8·6 2·1	14·6 3·5	3 51·5	3 52·1	3 41·0	2·6 0·7	8·6 2·2	14·6 3·8
27	3 36·8	3 37·3	3 26·9	2·7 0·7	8·7 2·1	14·7 3·6	3 51·8	3 52·4	3 41·2	2·7 0·7	8·7 2·2	14·7 3·8
28	3 37·0	3 37·6	3 27·1	2·8 0·7	8·8 2·1	14·8 3·6	3 52·0	3 52·6	3 41·4	2·8 0·7	8·8 2·3	14·8 3·8
29	3 37·3	3 37·8	3 27·4	2·9 0·7	8·9 2·2	14·9 3·6	3 52·3	3 52·9	3 41·7	2·9 0·7	8·9 2·3	14·9 3·8
30	3 37·5	3 38·1	3 27·6	3·0 0·7	9·0 2·2	15·0 3·6	3 52·5	3 53·1	3 41·9	3·0 0·8	9·0 2·3	15·0 3·9
31	3 37·8	3 38·3	3 27·8	3·1 0·7	9·1 2·2	15·1 3·6	3 52·8	3 53·4	3 42·1	3·1 0·8	9·1 2·4	15·1 3·9
32	3 38·0	3 38·6	3 28·1	3·2 0·8	9·2 2·2	15·2 3·7	3 53·0	3 53·6	3 42·4	3·2 0·8	9·2 2·4	15·2 3·9
33	3 38·3	3 38·8	3 28·3	3·3 0·8	9·3 2·2	15·3 3·7	3 53·3	3 53·9	3 42·6	3·3 0·9	9·3 2·4	15·3 4·0
34	3 38·5	3 39·1	3 28·5	3·4 0·8	9·4 2·3	15·4 3·7	3 53·5	3 54·1	3 42·9	3·4 0·9	9·4 2·4	15·4 4·0
35	3 38·8	3 39·3	3 28·8	3·5 0·8	9·5 2·3	15·5 3·7	3 53·8	3 54·4	3 43·1	3·5 0·9	9·5 2·5	15·5 4·0
36	3 39·0	3 39·6	3 29·0	3·6 0·9	9·6 2·3	15·6 3·8	3 54·0	3 54·6	3 43·3	3·6 0·9	9·6 2·5	15·6 4·0
37	3 39·3	3 39·9	3 29·3	3·7 0·9	9·7 2·3	15·7 3·8	3 54·3	3 54·9	3 43·6	3·7 1·0	9·7 2·5	15·7 4·1
38	3 39·5	3 40·1	3 29·5	3·8 0·9	9·8 2·4	15·8 3·8	3 54·5	3 55·1	3 43·8	3·8 1·0	9·8 2·5	15·8 4·1
39	3 39·8	3 40·4	3 29·7	3·9 0·9	9·9 2·4	15·9 3·8	3 54·8	3 55·4	3 44·1	3·9 1·0	9·9 2·6	15·9 4·1
40	3 40·0	3 40·6	3 30·0	4·0 1·0	10·0 2·4	16·0 3·9	3 55·0	3 55·6	3 44·3	4·0 1·0	10·0 2·6	16·0 4·1
41	3 40·3	3 40·9	3 30·2	4·1 1·0	10·1 2·4	16·1 3·9	3 55·3	3 55·9	3 44·5	4·1 1·1	10·1 2·6	16·1 4·2
42	3 40·5	3 41·1	3 30·5	4·2 1·0	10·2 2·5	16·2 3·9	3 55·5	3 56·1	3 44·8	4·2 1·1	10·2 2·6	16·2 4·2
43	3 40·8	3 41·4	3 30·7	4·3 1·0	10·3 2·5	16·3 3·9	3 55·8	3 56·4	3 45·0	4·3 1·1	10·3 2·7	16·3 4·2
44	3 41·0	3 41·6	3 30·9	4·4 1·1	10·4 2·5	16·4 4·0	3 56·0	3 56·6	3 45·2	4·4 1·1	10·4 2·7	16·4 4·2
45	3 41·3	3 41·9	3 31·2	4·5 1·1	10·5 2·5	16·5 4·0	3 56·3	3 56·9	3 45·5	4·5 1·2	10·5 2·7	16·5 4·3
46	3 41·5	3 42·1	3 31·4	4·6 1·1	10·6 2·6	16·6 4·0	3 56·5	3 57·1	3 45·7	4·6 1·2	10·6 2·7	16·6 4·3
47	3 41·8	3 42·4	3 31·6	4·7 1·1	10·7 2·6	16·7 4·0	3 56·8	3 57·4	3 46·0	4·7 1·2	10·7 2·8	16·7 4·3
48	3 42·0	3 42·6	3 31·9	4·8 1·2	10·8 2·6	16·8 4·1	3 57·0	3 57·6	3 46·2	4·8 1·2	10·8 2·8	16·8 4·3
49	3 42·3	3 42·9	3 32·1	4·9 1·2	10·9 2·6	16·9 4·1	3 57·3	3 57·9	3 46·4	4·9 1·3	10·9 2·8	16·9 4·4
50	3 42·5	3 43·1	3 32·4	5·0 1·2	11·0 2·7	17·0 4·1	3 57·5	3 58·2	3 46·7	5·0 1·3	11·0 2·8	17·0 4·4
51	3 42·8	3 43·4	3 32·6	5·1 1·2	11·1 2·7	17·1 4·1	3 57·8	3 58·4	3 46·9	5·1 1·3	11·1 2·9	17·1 4·4
52	3 43·0	3 43·6	3 32·8	5·2 1·3	11·2 2·7	17·2 4·2	3 58·0	3 58·7	3 47·2	5·2 1·3	11·2 2·9	17·2 4·4
53	3 43·3	3 43·9	3 33·1	5·3 1·3	11·3 2·7	17·3 4·2	3 58·3	3 58·9	3 47·4	5·3 1·4	11·3 2·9	17·3 4·5
54	3 43·5	3 44·1	3 33·3	5·4 1·3	11·4 2·8	17·4 4·2	3 58·5	3 59·2	3 47·6	5·4 1·4	11·4 2·9	17·4 4·5
55	3 43·8	3 44·4	3 33·6	5·5 1·3	11·5 2·8	17·5 4·2	3 58·8	3 59·4	3 47·9	5·5 1·4	11·5 3·0	17·5 4·5
56	3 44·0	3 44·6	3 33·8	5·6 1·4	11·6 2·8	17·6 4·3	3 59·0	3 59·7	3 48·1	5·6 1·4	11·6 3·0	17·6 4·5
57	3 44·3	3 44·9	3 34·0	5·7 1·4	11·7 2·8	17·7 4·3	3 59·3	3 59·9	3 48·4	5·7 1·5	11·7 3·0	17·7 4·6
58	3 44·5	3 45·1	3 34·3	5·8 1·4	11·8 2·9	17·8 4·3	3 59·5	4 00·2	3 48·6	5·8 1·5	11·8 3·0	17·8 4·6
59	3 44·8	3 45·4	3 34·5	5·9 1·4	11·9 2·9	17·9 4·3	3 59·8	4 00·4	3 48·8	5·9 1·5	11·9 3·1	17·9 4·6
60	3 45·0	3 45·6	3 34·8	6·0 1·5	12·0 2·9	18·0 4·4	4 00·0	4 00·7	3 49·1	6·0 1·6	12·0 3·1	18·0 4·7

FIG. 803. An increments and corrections page of the
Nautical Almanac.

Moon

$$\text{GMT} \quad 2^h\ 15^m\ 53^s \quad \text{June 21}$$

2^h	$251°33'.9$
$15^m\ 53^s$	$3°47'.4$
v corr	$(+)\ 2'.7 \qquad v\ (+)\ 10'.5$
GHA	$255°24'.0$

2^h	$12°48'.6$ N.
d corr	$(+)\ 2'.0 \qquad d\ (+)\ 7'.8$
dec	$12°50'.6$ N.

4. Rising, Setting, Twilight

Sunrise, Sunset, Moonrise, and Moonset occur when the upper limb of the body is on the visible horizon; that is, when the body first appears above the horizon at rising, or when it drops out of sight below the horizon at setting. Because of semi-diameter of the body and atmospheric refraction, the average period from rising to setting is longer than the average period below the horizon. For the Sun the zenith distance at rising and setting is about $90°50'$. For the Moon the zenith distance is about $90°$ plus $0°34'.5$ for atmospheric refraction plus semi-diameter of the Moon minus horizontal parallax (because of the Moon's close proximity to the Earth). Zenith distances of the darker limits of civil, nautical, and astronomical twilight are $96°$, $102°$, and $108°$, respectively. That is, these limits occur when the *centre* of the Sun is at $6°$, $12°$, and $18°$, respectively, below the *celestial* horizon. Tabulated times of rising and setting are computed for zero height of eye above the sea surface. For greater heights, bodies rise earlier and set later because of dip of the horizon (p. 380).

Times of rising, setting, and twilight can be calculated by means of the equation:

$$\cos t = \sec L \sec d\ (\sin h - \sin L \sin d),$$

in which t is meridian angle, L is latitude, d is declination, and h is altitude. The altitude used is $90° - z$, where z is zenith distance, as given above. For the Sun, h is always negative. The time of the phenomenon is determined by converting the calculated meridian angle to time units and subtracting it from the time of meridian transit for rising, and adding it for setting. The times of meridian transit of the Sun and Moon are tabulated at the lower right-hand corner of each right-hand daily page of the *Nautical Almanac*, under the heading 'Mer. Pass.' Because of variations in atmospheric refraction, primarily, calculation of times of rising, setting, and twilight

Lat.	Sunset	Twilight		Moonset			
		Civil	Naut.	6	7	8	9
°	h m	h m	h m	h m	h m	h m	h m
N 72	□	□	□	23 02	■	■	■
N 70	□	□	□	23 46	23 59	24 36	00 36
68	□	□	□	00 02	00 16	00 41	01 27
66	23 11	////	////	00 18	00 38	01 09	01 59
64	22 15	////	////	00 32	00 56	01 31	02 22
62	21 43	////	////	00 43	01 10	01 48	02 41
60	21 20	22 49	////	00 52	01 22	02 03	02 56
N 58	21 01	22 11	////	01 01	01 33	02 15	03 09
56	20 45	21 45	////	01 08	01 42	02 26	03 21
54	20 32	21 24	22 56	01 15	01 51	02 35	03 31
52	20 20	21 08	22 20	01 21	01 58	02 44	03 40
50	20 10	20 54	21 56	01 26	02 05	02 51	03 47
45	19 49	20 25	21 14	01 38	02 19	03 08	04 04
N 40	19 32	20 04	20 45	01 48	02 31	03 21	04 18
35	19 17	19 47	20 23	01 56	02 41	03 32	04 30
30	19 05	19 32	20 05	02 03	02 50	03 42	04 40
20	18 44	19 08	19 37	02 16	03 05	03 59	04 58
N 10	18 25	18 48	19 15	02 27	03 19	04 14	05 13
0	18 08	18 31	18 57	02 38	03 31	04 28	05 27
S 10	17 52	18 14	18 41	02 48	03 44	04 42	05 41
20	17 34	17 58	18 25	03 00	03 57	04 57	05 57
30	17 13	17 40	18 09	03 12	04 13	05 14	06 14
35	17 02	17 30	18 01	03 20	04 21	05 24	06 24
40	16 48	17 18	17 52	03 28	04 32	05 35	06 36
45	16 32	17 05	17 42	03 38	04 44	05 48	06 49
S 50	16 12	16 50	17 31	03 50	04 58	06 04	07 06
52	16 03	16 43	17 26	03 56	05 05	06 12	07 13
54	15 52	16 35	17 21	04 02	05 13	06 20	07 22
56	15 40	16 27	17 15	04 09	05 21	06 30	07 32
58	15 27	16 17	17 09	04 17	05 31	06 41	07 43
S 60	15 10	16 06	17 02	04 25	05 42	06 53	07 55

FIG. 804. Table of the *Nautical Almanac* showing times of Moonset near midnight.

to greater precision than one minute is not justified. An approximation of the meridian angle at the time of rising, setting, or twilight can be determined graphically by means of a diagram on the plane of the celestial meridian (p. 302).

For most purposes, the simplest method of determining the times of rising, setting, and twilight is by means of the *Nautical Almanac*. Refer to Fig. 802, a right-hand page of the almanac. At various invervals of latitude between 72° N. and 60° S. the local mean times of Sunrise, Sunset, and the darker limits of civil and nautical twilight are tabulated for the middle of the three days of the page opening. Times for other days can be determined by interpolation. The times of Moonrise and Moonset are tabulated for each of the three days and the next succeeding day.

Note the following with reference to certain high-latitude entries: The symbol □ indicates that the Sun (or Moon) does not rise or set on the date indicated, remaining above the horizon during the entire day. The symbol ■ (shown in Fig. 804) indicates that the Moon (or Sun) does not rise, remaining below the horizon throughout the day. The symbol //// indicates that the Sun is below the horizon, but that twilight continues throughout the night. All three of these conditions can be verified by means of a diagram on the plane of the celestial meridian.

Because of the revolution of the Moon eastward around the Earth, Moonrise and Moonset generally occur later each day, as evident from the tabulations. The average interval between successive Moonrises or Moonsets is about 24^h 50^m. Accordingly, a little oftener than once a month the Moon rises, or sets, shortly before midnight, and the following Moonrise, or Moonset, occurs shortly after the next midnight, leaving the intervening day without a Moonrise, or Moonset. This is indicated in the tables by listing the same phenomenon twice, as 2436 on one day and 0036 on the following day. This occurs for Moonset at latitude 70° N., on July 8 and 9, as shown in Fig. 804. Successive Moonsets occur at 2359 on July 7 and at 0036 on July 9 (or 2436 on July 8). The opposite condition of two Moonrises or two Moonsets sometimes occurs in high latitudes when the change in declination of the Moon during the day more than offsets the retardation caused by revolution of the Moon around the Earth. Thus, two times of Moonrise are shown for latitude 72° N. on June 22 (Fig. 802). The Moon rises ten minutes after midnight, and again five minutes before the next midnight, or $23^h 45^m$ later.

Times for latitudes other than those tabulated are determined by interpolation. Where the difference in consecutive entries is small, in low and intermediate latitudes, eye interpolation usually suffices for practical purposes. However, the interpolation is not linear, as indicated by progressive increases in the differences between consecutive entries for the same latitude interval as latitude changes. Accordingly, an interpolation table is provided near the back of the almanac. Refer to Table I of Fig. 805. The tabular interval referred to at the upper left-hand corner of Table I refers to the difference between consecutive latitude entries on the daily pages. The correct column is selected and entered with the difference between the latitude of the observer and the tabular latitude next smaller to it. One then moves to the right along the line thus defined until one reaches the column headed by the difference between the times for the two latitudes between which the interpolation is being made, using eye interpolation as needed. The value taken from Table I is then added to or subtracted from the time for the tabular latitude used as the base for the interpolation, the sign being determined by noting whether the tabulated time for the next larger latitude entry is later or earlier than the base value.

Suppose it is desired to determine the LMT of Sunrise at latitude 47°21′.6 N. on June 22. From the daily page Sunrise table (Fig. 802) it is seen that Sunrise occurs at 0413 at latitude 45° N., the base entry, and at 0351 at latitude 50° N. This is a difference of 22^m for a tabular interval of 5°. The difference between the base latitude and the latitude of the observer is 47°21′.6 − 45° = 2°21′.6. In Table I (Fig. 805) this difference, in the tabular interval 5° column, lies between entries for 2°15′ and 2°30′. Following across, and interpolating by eye, one finds the correction to be 9^m for a

TABLES FOR INTERPOLATING SUNRISE, MOONRISE, ETC.

TABLE I—FOR LATITUDE

Tabular Interval 10°	5°	2°	Difference between the times for consecutive latitudes 5ᵐ	10ᵐ	15ᵐ	20ᵐ	25ᵐ	30ᵐ	35ᵐ	40ᵐ	45ᵐ	50ᵐ	55ᵐ	60ᵐ	1ʰ05ᵐ	1ʰ10ᵐ	1ʰ15ᵐ	1ʰ20ᵐ
0 30	0 15	0 06	0	0	1	1	1	1	1	2	2	2	2	2	0 02	0 02	0 02	0 02
1 00	0 30	0 12	0	1	1	2	2	3	3	3	4	4	4	5	05	05	05	05
1 30	0 45	0 18	1	1	2	3	3	4	4	5	5	6	7	7	07	07	07	07
2 00	1 00	0 24	1	2	3	4	5	5	6	7	7	8	9	10	10	10	10	10
2 30	1 15	0 30	1	2	4	5	6	7	8	9	9	10	11	12	12	13	13	13
3 00	1 30	0 36	1	3	4	6	7	8	9	10	11	12	13	14	0 15	0 15	0 16	0 16
3 30	1 45	0 42	2	3	5	7	8	10	11	12	13	14	16	17	18	18	19	19
4 00	2 00	0 48	2	4	6	8	9	11	13	14	15	16	18	19	20	21	22	22
4 30	2 15	0 54	2	4	7	9	11	13	15	16	18	19	21	22	23	24	25	26
5 00	2 30	1 00	2	5	7	10	12	14	16	18	20	22	23	25	26	27	28	29
5 30	2 45	1 06	3	5	8	11	13	16	18	20	22	24	26	28	0 29	0 30	0 31	0 32
6 00	3 00	1 12	3	6	9	12	14	17	20	22	24	26	29	31	32	33	34	36
6 30	3 15	1 18	3	6	10	13	16	19	22	24	26	29	31	34	36	37	38	40
7 00	3 30	1 24	3	7	10	14	17	20	23	26	29	31	34	37	39	41	42	44
7 30	3 45	1 30	4	7	11	15	18	22	25	28	31	34	37	40	43	44	46	48
8 00	4 00	1 36	4	8	12	16	20	23	27	30	34	37	41	44	0 47	0 48	0 51	0 53
8 30	4 15	1 42	4	8	13	17	21	25	29	33	36	40	44	48	0 51	0 53	0 56	0 58
9 00	4 30	1 48	4	9	13	18	22	27	31	35	39	43	47	52	0 55	0 58	1 01	1 04
9 30	4 45	1 54	5	9	14	19	24	28	33	38	42	47	51	56	1 00	1 04	1 08	1 12
10 00	5 00	2 00	5	10	15	20	25	30	35	40	45	50	55	60	1 05	1 10	1 15	1 20

Table I is for interpolating the L.M.T. of sunrise, twilight, moonrise, etc., for latitude. It is to be entered, in the appropriate column on the left, with the difference between true latitude and the nearest tabular latitude which is *less* than the true latitude; and with the argument at the top which is the nearest value of the difference between the times for the tabular latitude and the next higher one; the correction so obtained is applied to the time for the tabular latitude; the sign of the correction can be seen by inspection. It is to be noted that the interpolation is not linear, so that when using this table it is essential to take out the tabular phenomenon for the latitude *less* than the true latitude.

TABLE II—FOR LONGITUDE

Long. East or West	Difference between the times for given date and preceding date (for east longitude) or for given date and following date (for west longitude) 10ᵐ	20ᵐ	30ᵐ	40ᵐ	50ᵐ	60ᵐ	1ʰ+ 10ᵐ	20ᵐ	30ᵐ	1ʰ+ 40ᵐ	50ᵐ	60ᵐ	2ʰ10ᵐ	2ʰ20ᵐ	2ʰ30ᵐ	2ʰ40ᵐ	2ʰ50ᵐ	3ʰ00ᵐ
0	0	0	0	0	0	0	0	0	0	0	0	0	0 00	0 00	0 00	0 00	0 00	0 00
10	0	1	1	1	1	2	2	2	2	3	3	3	04	04	04	04	05	05
20	1	1	2	2	3	3	4	4	5	6	6	7	07	08	08	09	09	10
30	1	2	2	3	4	5	6	7	7	8	9	10	11	12	12	13	14	15
40	1	2	3	4	6	7	8	9	10	11	12	13	14	16	17	18	19	20
50	1	3	4	6	7	8	10	11	12	14	15	17	0 18	0 19	0 21	0 22	0 24	0 25
60	2	3	5	7	8	10	12	13	15	17	18	20	22	23	25	27	28	30
70	2	4	6	8	10	12	14	16	17	19	21	23	25	27	29	31	33	35
80	2	4	7	9	11	13	16	18	20	22	24	27	29	31	33	36	38	40
90	2	5	7	10	12	15	17	20	22	25	27	30	32	35	37	40	42	45
100	3	6	8	11	14	17	19	22	25	28	31	33	0 36	0 39	0 42	0 44	0 47	0 50
110	3	6	9	12	15	18	21	24	27	31	34	37	40	43	46	49	0 52	0 55
120	3	7	10	13	17	20	23	27	30	33	37	40	43	47	50	53	0 57	1 00
130	4	7	11	14	18	22	25	29	32	36	40	43	47	51	54	0 58	1 01	1 05
140	4	8	12	16	19	23	27	31	35	39	43	47	51	54	0 58	1 02	1 06	1 10
150	4	8	13	17	21	25	29	33	38	42	46	50	0 54	0 58	1 03	1 07	1 11	1 15
160	4	9	13	18	22	27	31	36	40	44	49	53	0 58	1 02	1 07	1 11	1 16	1 20
170	5	9	14	19	24	28	33	38	42	47	52	57	1 01	1 06	1 11	1 16	1 20	1 25
180	5	10	15	20	25	30	35	40	45	50	55	60	1 05	1 10	1 15	1 20	1 25	1 30

Table II is for interpolating the L.M.T. of moonrise, moonset and the Moon's meridian passage for longitude. It is entered with longitude and with the difference between the times for the given date and for the preceding date (in east longitudes) or following date (in west longitudes). The correction is normally *added* for west longitudes and *subtracted* for east longitudes, but if, as occasionally happens, the times become earlier each day instead of later, the signs of the corrections must be reversed.

FIG. 805. Rising-setting-twilight interpolation tables of the *Nautical Almanac*.

tabular difference of 20^m, and 11^m for a tabular difference of 25^m. Interpolating between these values, one finds the correction to be 10^m. The LMT of Sunrise at latitude $47°21'.6$ N. is therefore $0413 - 10 = 0403$. The double interpolation in Table I might be made easier by tabulating the applicable entries:

	20^m	22^m	25^m
$2°15'$	9^m		11^m
$2°21'.6$	9^m	10^m	11^m
$2°30'$	10^m		12^m

When interpolating for the Moon, one should exercise caution if the time of Moonrise or Moonset is near midnight, for the date on which one of these phenomena is missing may not be the same at all latitudes. Refer to Fig. 804. The time of Moonset on July 7 is shown as 2359 for latitude 70° N., and as 0016 for latitude 68° N. These are not the same, but are successive Moonsets, as indicated by the interval of $23^h 43^m$ between them. Interpolation in this case should be between 0016 on July 7 and 2346 on July 6. If the interpolated time is before midnight, this Moonset occurs on July 6 at the interpolated latitude. The next following Moonset is found by interpolation between 0041 on July 8 and 2359 on July 7.

Strictly, the tabulated times are GMT at the Greenwich meridian. The times of Sunrise, Sunset, and twilight change so little from day to day that the times taken from the table can be considered to be LMT without serious error. When tabulated times on consecutive days differ considerably, a condition sometimes encountered in high latitudes when the Sun is near the horizon at lower transit, accurate time of Sunrise, Sunset, or twilight is of little consequence, and calculated times may be in error by several minutes because of vagaries in atmospheric refraction.

The situation with respect to the Moon, however, is different because of the relatively great difference in times of consecutive Moonrises and Moonsets resulting primarily from the revolution of the Moon around the Earth. For this reason, interpolation for longitude may be desirable. Table

II, Fig. 805, is provided for this purpose, although a simple linear interpolation may be easier. The GMT (LMT at the Greenwich meridian) is first determined both for the day in question and for the preceding (east longitude) or succeeding (west longitude) Moonrise or Moonset. Table II is then entered with the longitude and the difference between these two times, and the quantity taken from the table is then applied to the time for the day in question with the appropriate sign so that the local time lies between the two times between which interpolation is made.

Suppose it is desired to find the LMT of Moonrise at latitude $39°44'.2$ S., longitude $153°27'.3$ E. on June 22. From the daily tabulations and Table I, Fig. 805, the LMT is found to be 0504 on June 22 and 0403 on June 21. The difference is $0504 - 0403 = 1^h 01^m$. Interpolating in Table II:

	60^m	$1^h 01^m$	$1^h 10^m$
$150°$	25^m		29^m
$153°27'.3$	26^m	26^m	30^m
$160°$	27^m		31^m

Thus, LMT of Moonrise occurs 26^m earlier at the observer than at the same latitude on the Greenwich meridian, or at $0504 - 26 = 0438$.

One additional step in determining the time of rising, setting, or twilight is generally desirable. The time found from the almanac tabulations is LMT, but ZT is usually desired. For each $15'$ of longitude difference between the observer's longitude and the reference meridian used for whatever ZT he may be keeping, the times of rising, setting, and twilight differ by one minute, occurring earlier by ZT than LMT if he is east of his reference meridian, and later if he is west of it. Thus, in the example of Moonrise, if the observer is keeping ZT of longitude $150°$ E., $(-)$ 10 ZT, the difference in longitude is $3°27'.3$, or 14^m to the nearest integral minute. The observer being east of his reference meridian, his ZT of Moonrise is 14^m earlier than his LMT, or $0438 - 0424$.

The entire calculation is conveniently shown as follows:

$$L \quad 39°44\!.2 \text{ S.}$$
$$Lo\, 153°27\!.3 \text{ E.}$$
$$\text{June 22}$$

	Moonrise	
35° S.	0455	June 22
T I	(+) 9	
LMT$_G$	0504	June 22
35° S.	0356	June 21
T I	(+) 7	
LMT$_G$	0403	June 21
LMT$_G$	0504	June 22
diff	(−) $1^h\,01^m$	
T II	(−) 26	
LMT$_G$	0504	June 22
LMT	0438	June 22
DLo	(−) 14	
ZT	0424	June 22

For Sunrise, Sunset, or twilight, the calculation is considerably simpler because of elimination of the need for the Table II correction. Suppose it is desired to find the zone times of Sunset and the darker limits of both civil and nautical twilights at latitude 32°18$\!.7$ S., longitude 78°41$\!.6$ W. on June 22. The calculations can be shown conveniently as follows:

L   32°18.7 S.
Lo 78°41.6 W.
June 22

	Sunset	Civil Twilight	Nautical Twilight
30° S.	1708	1735	1804
TI	(−) 5	(−) 5	(−) 3
LMT	1703	1730	1801
DLo	(+) 15	(+) 15	(+) 15
ZT	1718	1745	1816

Aboard a moving ship the position of the observer at the time of rising, setting, or twilight is normally in doubt because the time of the phenomenon is not known. Using a rough approximation of the position, one can calculate the time of the desired phenomenon at this place, then determine the dead reckoning or estimated position at this time, and then make a second calculation of the time, if needed. A third estimate should seldom be necessary. On an easterly or westerly course the first estimate can usually be used with any needed adjustment of the correction for longitude difference.

5. Sextant Altitude-Corrections

At sea, the altitude of an astronomical body above the visible horizon is customarily measured by means of a marine sextant. The quantity so measured is called *sextant altitude* (*hs*, *sext alt*). Certain *sextant altitude-corrections* are needed to convert sextant altitude to actual altitude above the celestial horizon. This corrected value, called *observed altitude* (*Ho*, *obs alt*), *corrected sextant altitude*, or *true altitude* (*T alt*), is needed for comparison with *calculated altitude* (*Hc*) at an assumed position for determination of the *intercept* (*a*, *Int*) needed for establishing an astronomical position line. The expression 'observed altitude' is occasionally used to refer to sextant altitude corrected for index error only. In practice, certain of the corrections are combined in a small number of convenient tables, and a number of the minor corrections are ignored. However, an understanding of the various corrections may prove useful to the navigator who desires to improve his sight-taking technique and account for seemingly anomalous results. Accordingly, a discussion of the various individual corrections will precede an explanation of actual altitude correction as practiced at sea.

Altitude corrections can be conveniently grouped under five headings:

1. Corrections for reading errors. Corrections of this group are discussed in section 1 of chapter VII, and summarized here. Even after adjustment, a sextant may have a small remaining error reflecting imperfection in manufacture. The *instrument correction* (*I*) needed to allow for this error is usually recorded, by the manufacturer, inside the instrument box. It may be either positive or negative, applies to all astronomical bodies, and usually varies with altitude. The instrument correction of a modern high-grade sextant is generally small enough to be ignored. However, the magnitude of this correction should be determined before a sextant is used for the first time, and a decision made whether to ignore it on all or certain altitudes.

The *index correction* (*IC*) is the reading of a sextant, with reverse sign, when the instrument should read zero. It should be determined each time the sextant is used, and applied equally to all readings of the sextant, for all bodies. It may be either positive or negative.

Personal correction (*PC*) is the angle to be applied to readings to correct for a personal bias. It may be either positive or negative, and may vary with the body and conditions of observation. It is usually the same at all altitudes. A navigator should develop skill in the use of his sextant adequate to eliminate the need for personal correction.

In summary of the corrections of the first group, only index correction is applied universally, but one should be alert to the possible existence of instrument and personal corrections, and apply them if their use results in significant improvement in accuracy.

2. Corrections for reference-level errors. The principal

correction of this group is dip of the sea horizon, commonly called *dip* (*D*, *d*). Because the eye of the observer is some distance above the surface of the sea, his visible horizon is depressed below the sensible horizon, as discussed in section 3 of chapter VI. The angular amount of this depression, reduced somewhat by refraction of light from the horizon, is the dip. Because of dip, the altitude measured by sextant is too great, and the correction is therefore negative. It increases numerically with increased height of eye above the surface of the sea. The correction applies to all bodies when the visible sea horizon is used as the horizontal reference.

The values of dip tabulated in the *Nautical Almanac* were computed by means of the equations $D = 1'.76 \sqrt{h}$ where h is height of eye in metres, and $D = 0'.97 \sqrt{h}$ where h is height of eye in feet.

Unfortunately, the refraction of light from the horizon is not constant. Anomalous conditions introduce errors in the dip. The possible existence, but not the magnitude, of such conditions can be anticipated within half an hour after passage of a squall, and when a temperature inversion is known to exist. Error may also be encountered when there is a large difference between air and sea temperatures at the interface in calm weather, especially if mirage effects are present. Dip is greater when the water is warmer than the air, and less when the air is warmer than the water. Distortion of the rising or setting Sun may indicate anomalous conditions. A *sea–air temperature difference correction* (*S*) is occasionally applied to sextant altitudes.

The difference between actual dip at any time and the tabulated or calculated value may be great enough to introduce a significant error in a position line. If one can assume a constant error in all directions, an assumption not entirely justified, one can eliminate it by observing astronomical bodies equally spaced in azimuth, thus changing the size of the cocked hat or other figure formed by the position lines but not altering the centre of the figure. It may be possible to determine the average dip in opposite directions by measuring the altitude of an astronomical body both as a direct sight and a back sight (p. 347), applying IC (and any instrument and personal corrections), subtracting 180° from the sum of the two observations, and dividing the result by two. The same limb of the Sun or Moon must be observed, and allowance must be made for any change of altitude between observations. Allowance for change of altitude can be made by making a direct sight, a back sight, and a second direct sight at equal short intervals of time, and using an average of the two direct sights.

The height of eye above the sea surface, from any point on a vessel, varies with the observer and with the loading, trim, roll, pitch, and heave of the vessel. It may also change with wave height, for waves tend to increase the apparent elevation of the sea surface. The principal error introduced by changes in height of eye is usually from pitching of the vessel. An observational position near the centre of the ship minimizes this error. Error from changing height of eye can also be minimized somewhat by observing from a position high in the vessel. A change in height from 15 to 16 metres increases the dip by 0.2, but a change from 5 to 6 metres increases it by twice this amount.

Dip is affected slightly by tilt of the sea surface because of tides, differences in density of sea water, and *deflection of the vertical* (slight differences in the direction of gravity because of differences in the density and distribution of the material constituting the crust of the Earth). No allowance for such irregularities is made in the ordinary practice of navigation.

If the horizon is obstructed, as by another ship, the visible water line of the obstruction can be used as the horizontal reference, and an increased value of dip used. This 'dip short of the horizon', commonly called 'dip short' can be calculated by the equation:

$$Ds = 0.4156 \, d + 1.856 \, h/d,$$

where Ds is dip short, d is distance in nautical miles, and h is height of eye in metres. The constant 1.856 becomes 0.5658 if the height of eye is in feet. Dip short tables have been published.

Two other corrections of this group apply only to sextants using a bubble or pendulum as a horizontal reference. *Coriolis correction* (*Z*) arises from a deflection of the artificial horizon because of motion of an observer across the surface of the rotating Earth, and yawing of the vessel. *Acceleration correction* (*C*) results from deflection of the liquid of a bubble chamber or pendulum when the instrument is accelerated. Coriolis resulting from yawing of the vessel and acceleration resulting from rolling and pitching vary from moment to moment in a somewhat erratic, unpredictable manner, and the combined error is of such magnitude aboard ship that the use of sextants having liquid or pendulous horizontal references is impractical under normal conditions at sea.

In summary of the corrections of the second group, only dip or dip short is applied in the normal course of navigation afloat.

3. Corrections for curved path of light from body. When a ray of light, travelling in a straight line, enters a medium of different density, it changes its direction of travel. This change of direction, called *refraction* (*refr*) is easily demonstrated by immersing part of a stick or other linear object obliquely in water. The object appears to be bent at the surface of the liquid. The direction of bending of a ray entering a more dense medium is toward the normal (vertical) to the surface of the denser medium. A ray of light from an astronomical body, in traversing the atmosphere of the Earth, is bent progressively toward the vertical, with the result that the body appears higher in the sky than it would if there were no atmospheric refraction.

The *mean-refraction correction* (*R*) for this condition is always negative because atmospheric refraction results in the measured altitude being too great, and it applies equally to all astronomical bodies. Refraction is zero at the zenith and increases as the altitude decreases, reaching an average value of about 34.5 at the horizon.

Atmospheric refraction of a ray of light from an astronomical body can be expected to be anomalous under the same conditions that affect dip of the sea horizon. Fortunately, however, atmospheric refraction decreases rapidly with elevation, near the horizon. Because of relatively large uncertainties in atmospheric refraction in this region, altitudes of less than 2° should be avoided, and any altitude less than 10° should be considered of doubtful accuracy.

Humidity, latitude, azimuth, wind velocity, and uncertainty of the exact value of the constant of refraction have all been shown to affect refraction slightly, but the principal sources of error in the refraction used in correction tables are differences between actual air temperature and atmospheric pressure and the standard values used in the computation of the tables. The *Nautical Almanac* uses 10° C (50° F) and 1010 millibars (29.83 inches of mercury) as the standards for its main altitude-correction tables. The *air-temperature correction* (*T*) and *atmospheric-pressure correction* (*B*) are combined in an almanac *temperature–pressure correction* (*TB*) table for non-standard conditions. This correction applies to all bodies, may be either positive or negative, and increases with decreased altitude and with increased departure from standard temperature or pressure. Navigators generally apply the TB correction only for altitudes of less than 15°, or when the temperature or atmospheric pressure differs greatly from the standard value.

Thus, the only correction of the third group normally applied is that for refraction, an additional correction for non-standard temperature and atmospheric pressure being applied for low altitudes or extreme values of temperature or atmospheric pressure.

4. Correction for off-centre observation. Tabulated coordinates of astronomical bodies are for the centres of the bodies. If some other part of a body is observed, a correction is needed. No problem is encountered with stars, which appear as points of light in the most powerful telescopes.

The situation is different with respect to other bodies. Using the visible horizon as the horizontal reference, one would have difficulty making an accurate observation of the centre of the Sun or Moon, for the centres of these bodies are not critically apparent to the eye. It is customary, therefore, to observe the lower or upper limb and apply a correction for *semi-diameter* (*SD*). A positive correction is needed for a lower-limb observation, and a negative correction for an upper-limb observation. It is customary to observe the lower limb of the Sun, unless it is obscured by clouds. The choice of limb of the Moon depends primarily upon the position of the terminator, unless the Moon is in 'full' phase. The planets ordinarily used for navigation also have measurable semi-diameters, but these range from less than 0ʹ.1 for Saturn at its greatest distance from the Earth to a little more than 0ʹ.5 for Venus at its closest approach. No attempt is made to observe a limb of a planet. With an artificial horizon, the centres of all bodies may be observed, and with artificial-horizon sextants, the centres are invariably observed.

The semi-diameter of an astronomical body varies not only with its distance from the Earth, but also with its altitude. When a body is on the horizon, its distance from the observer is approximately the same as its distance from the centre of the Earth. But when a body is in the zenith, the distance from the observer is decreased by the radius of the Earth, resulting in an apparent increase in the size of the body. This increase, called *augmentation* (A, *aug*) is greatest for the Moon because of the relatively close proximity of that body to the Earth. The Moon's augmentation from horizon to zenith is about 0ʹ.3. At any altitude the value is equal to the value at the zenith times the sine of the altitude. Augmentation of the Sun and planets is a small fraction of a second of arc, and therefore not significant in the ordinary practice of navigation. The effect of augmentation is to increase the semi-diameter correction, whether positive or negative. In the altitude-correction tables of the *Nautical Almanac*, augmentation is included only for the Moon.

The difficulty of observing the centre of the Moon is greater at certain phases of the Moon. Venus, too, goes through all phases, and other navigational planets are often in the gibbous phase. No *phase correction* (F) for the Moon is included in sextant-altitude correction tables for use with a marine sextant, because one of the limbs of this body is customarily observed. Phase corrections for Venus and Mars are included, however, because the centres of the illuminated portions of these planets are sometimes offset a significant amount from the centres of the bodies. The corrections are intended for use during twilight. It is sometimes possible to observe Venus at greatest brilliance during daylight. The *Nautical Almanac* provides information in its 'Explanation' section for calculating the correction for a daylight observation of this planet. Phase corrections for Jupiter and Saturn are too small to be significant, and are therefore not included.

One other correction of this group is called *irradiation correction* ($\mathcal{J}$). When a relatively bright area is observed adjacent to a darker area, the brighter area may appear enlarged. This effect is called *irradiation*. Thus, when a bright sky is adjacent to darker water, the visible horizon may appear depressed. An astronomical body may appear enlarged in size. The greatest effect of irradiation is with respect to the Sun. An observation of the lower limb is little affected because the effect of irradiation of both this limb and the horizon is in the same direction, and hence tend to cancel one another. For the upper limb, the effect is doubled. Because of the variables involved, including the fact that the magnitude of the effect varies considerably with different observers, no correction for irradiation is included in the *Nautical Almanac*. If the observer finds it a factor in his observations, he might include it in his personal correction. For most observers, however, the best practice is probably to avoid observations of the upper limb of the Sun.

In summary of the corrections of the fourth group, a correction for semi-diameter is applied to observations of the Sun and Moon, augmentation to observations of the Moon, and phase correction to observations of Venus and Mars.

5. Correction for observation near Earth's surface. After application of all corrections mentioned thus far, the value obtained is the altitude of the astronomical body above the sensible horizon. A correction for *parallax* (P) may be needed to convert this altitude to the altitude above the celestial horizon. For the stars, there is no measurable difference between these values, and for the more distant planets Jupiter and Saturn the difference is too small to be of consequence. But for the Moon and, to a lesser degree, the Sun and planets Venus and Mars, parallax is of sufficient magnitude to be a factor. Parallax is the difference in apparent position of an object as viewed from different places. In the case of bodies of the solar system, parallax increases from maximum value, called *horizontal parallax* (*HP*) when the body is on the horizon, to zero at the zenith. Between these extremes the *parallax in altitude* (*P in A*) is equal to horizontal parallax times the cosine of the altitude. The correction for parallax varies both with altitude of the body and with its distance from the Earth. Because parallax causes an astronomical body to appear lower in the sky than it would otherwise, the correction is always positive. Altitude correction tables of the *Nautical Almanac* include parallax corrections for the Moon, Sun, Venus, and Mars.

Summary of sextant altitude-corrections. The corrections normally applied to sextant altitudes, and their usual sources, are as follows:

Index correction (*I C*), either positive or negative, applies to all bodies. It is determined by measurement and varies with the instrument or with a change in the adjustment of the sextant. It is otherwise constant for all bodies and all altitudes.

Dip (*D*) is always negative, applies to all bodies, and increases with greater height of eye (HE) above the sea surface. A dip table for entry with either metres or feet is located on the inside front cover of the *Nautical Almanac* and repeated on the bookmark. An abbreviated dip table is located on the page facing the inside back cover of the almanac. Dip short, if needed, is obtained by calculation or table.

Mean-refraction correction (*R*) is always negative, applies to all bodies, and increases with decreasing altitude. For altitudes from a little less than 10° to 90° the mean-refraction correction is tabulated in the 'Stars and Planets' table on the inside front cover of the *Nautical Almanac* and repeated on the bookmark. For altitudes form 0° to 10°, mean-refraction correction is tabulated in the 'Stars/Planets' column on the page facing the inside front cover of the almanac.

An additional table for a combined *temperature–pressure correction* (*TB*) for non-standard air temperature and atmospheric pressure is located on the page next following the mean refraction correction for altitudes to 50°. A graph at the top of the page is entered with temperature and pressure to identify the column to be used in a table below the graph. The correction, either positive or negative, is found in this column, on the line indicated by the apparent altitude (p. 389) Interpolation may be needed for low altitudes. The temperature–pressure correction increases with decreasing altitude and with increasing departure of temperature or pressure from standard values. Some books of nautical tables tabulate these corrections separately.

Semi-diameter (SD) is positive for a lower-limb observation and negative for an upper-limb observation. It varies with distance of the body and increases slightly with increasing altitude because of augmentation. A correction for semi-diameter is applied only to altitudes of the Sun and Moon, and augmentation only to altitudes of the Moon. Semi-diameter is tabulated on the right-hand daily pages of the almanac. Semi-diameter is included in the Sun altitude-correction tables on the inside front cover, facing pages, and the bookmark of the *Nautical Almanac*. Semi-diameter and augmentation of the Moon are included in the Moon altitude-correction tables on the inside back cover and facing page of the almanac.

Phase correction (F) may be either positive or negative, varies with the phase, body, and aspect of the body, and applies only to the planets Venus and Mars. It is included in the additional correction tables for Venus and Mars on the inside front cover of the *Nautical Almanac*, and on the bookmark.

Parallax (P) is always positive, increases with decreasing altitude, and applies to the Sun, Moon, Venus, and Mars. It is included in the altitude-correction tables for these bodies. For the Sun, the separate value of parallax is about 0.1 for altitudes of $70°$, and zero for higher altitudes. For the Moon, horizontal parallax is tabulated on the right-hand daily pages of the *Nautical Almanac*. The separate values of horizontal parallax of Venus are tabulated as '*p*' in the 'Explanation' section of the almanac. Parallax in altitude can be determined by calculation.

In the ordinary practice of navigation, altitude corrections

ALTITUDE CORRECTION TABLES 10°-90°—SUN, STARS, PLANETS

SUN

OCT.—MAR. App. Alt.	Lower Limb	Upper Limb	APR.—SEPT. App. Alt.	Lower Limb	Upper Limb
° ′	′	′	° ′	′	′
9 34			9 39		
	+10·8	−21·5		+10·6	−21·2
9 45			9 51		
	+10·9	−21·4		+10·7	−21·1
9 56			10 03		
	+11·0	−21·3		+10·8	−21·0
10 08			10 15		
	+11·1	−21·2		+10·9	−20·9
10 21			10 27		
	+11·2	−21·1		+11·0	−20·8
10 34			10 40		
	+11·3	−21·0		+11·1	−20·7
10 47			10 54		
	+11·4	−20·9		+11·2	−20·6
11 01			11 08		
	+11·5	−20·8		+11·3	−20·5
11 15			11 23		
	+11·6	−20·7		+11·4	−20·4
11 30			11 38		
	+11·7	−20·6		+11·5	−20·3
11 46			11 54		
	+11·8	−20·5		+11·6	−20·2
12 02			12 10		
	+11·9	−20·4		+11·7	−20·1
12 19			12 28		
	+12·0	−20·3		+11·8	−20·0
12 37			12 46		
	+12·1	−20·2		+11·9	−19·9
12 55			13 05		
	+12·2	−20·1		+12·0	−19·8
13 14			13 24		
	+12·3	−20·0		+12·1	−19·7
13 35			13 45		
	+12·4	−19·9		+12·2	−19·6
13 56			14 07		
	+12·5	−19·8		+12·3	−19·5
14 18			14 30		
	+12·6	−19·7		+12·4	−19·4
14 42			14 54		
	+12·7	−19·6		+12·5	−19·3
15 06			15 19		
	+12·8	−19·5		+12·6	−19·2
15 32			15 46		
	+12·9	−19·4		+12·7	−19·1
15 59			16 14		
	+13·0	−19·3		+12·8	−19·0
16 28			16 44		
	+13·1	−19·2		+12·9	−18·9
16 59			17 15		
	+13·2	−19·1		+13·0	−18·8
17 32			17 48		
	+13·3	−19·0		+13·1	−18·7
18 06			18 24		
	+13·4	−18·9		+13·2	−18·6
18 42			19 01		
	+13·5	−18·8		+13·3	−18·5
19 21			19 42		
	+13·6	−18·7		+13·4	−18·4
20 03			20 25		
	+13·7	−18·6		+13·5	−18·3
20 48			21 11		
	+13·8	−18·5		+13·6	−18·2
21 35			22 00		
	+13·9	−18·4		+13·7	−18·1
22 26			22 54		
	+14·0	−18·3		+13·8	−18·0
23 22			23 51		
	+14·1	−18·2		+13·9	−17·9
24 21			24 53		
	+14·2	−18·1		+14·0	−17·8
25 26			26 00		
	+14·3	−18·0		+14·1	−17·7
26 36			27 13		
	+14·4	−17·9		+14·2	−17·6
27 52			28 33		
	+14·5	−17·8		+14·3	−17·5
29 15			30 00		
	+14·6	−17·7		+14·4	−17·4
30 46			31 35		
	+14·7	−17·6		+14·5	−17·3
32 26			33 20		
	+14·8	−17·5		+14·6	−17·2
34 17			35 17		
	+14·9	−17·4		+14·7	−17·1
36 20			37 26		
	+15·0	−17·3		+14·8	−17·0
38 36			39 50		
	+15·1	−17·2		+14·9	−16·9
41 08			42 31		
	+15·2	−17·1		+15·0	−16·8
43 59			45 31		
	+15·3	−17·0		+15·1	−16·7
47 10			48 55		
	+15·4	−16·9		+15·2	−16·6
50 46			52 44		
	+15·5	−16·8		+15·3	−16·5
54 49			57 02		
	+15·6	−16·7		+15·4	−16·4
59 23			61 51		
	+15·7	−16·6		+15·5	−16·3
64 30			67 17		
	+15·8	−16·5		+15·6	−16·2
70 12			73 16		
	+15·9	−16·4		+15·7	−16·1
76 26			79 43		
	+16·0	−16·3		+15·8	−16·0
83 05			86 32		
	+16·1	−16·2		+15·9	−15·9
90 00			90 00		

STARS AND PLANETS

App. Alt.	Corrn
° ′	′
9 56	
	−5·3
10 08	
	−5·2
10 20	
	−5·1
10 33	
	−5·0
10 46	
	−4·9
11 00	
	−4·8
11 14	
	−4·7
11 29	
	−4·6
11 45	
	−4·5
12 01	
	−4·4
12 18	
	−4·3
12 35	
	−4·2
12 54	
	−4·1
13 13	
	−4·0
13 33	
	−3·9
13 54	
	−3·8
14 16	
	−3·7
14 40	
	−3·6
15 04	
	−3·5
15 30	
	−3·4
15 57	
	−3·3
16 26	
	−3·2
16 56	
	−3·1
17 28	
	−3·0
18 02	
	−2·9
18 38	
	−2·8
19 17	
	−2·7
19 58	
	−2·6
20 42	
	−2·5
21 28	
	−2·4
22 19	
	−2·3
23 13	
	−2·2
24 11	
	−2·1
25 14	
	−2·0
26 22	
	−1·9
27 36	
	−1·8
28 56	
	−1·7
30 24	
	−1·6
32 00	
	−1·5
33 45	
	−1·4
35 40	
	−1·3
37 48	
	−1·2
40 08	
	−1·1
42 44	
	−1·0
45 36	
	−0·9
48 47	
	−0·8
52 18	
	−0·7
56 11	
	−0·6
60 28	
	−0·5
65 08	
	−0·4
70 11	
	−0·3
75 34	
	−0·2
81 13	
	−0·1
87 03	
	0·0
90 00	

App. Alt.	Additional Corrn
VENUS	
Jan. 1-Jan. 15	
° 0	′
46	+ 0·3
Jan. 16-Mar. 3	
° 0	′
47	+ 0·2
Mar. 4-Dec. 31	
° 0	′
42	+ 0·1
MARS	
Jan. 1-Dec. 28	
° 0	′
60	+ 0·1
Dec. 29-Dec. 31	
° 0	′
41	+ 0·2
75	+ 0·1

DIP

Ht. of Eye	Corrn	Ht. of Eye
m	′	ft.
2·4		8·0
	−2·8	
2·6		8·6
	−2·9	
2·8		9·2
	−3·0	
3·0		9·8
	−3·1	
3·2		10·5
	−3·2	
3·4		11·2
	−3·3	
3·6		11·9
	−3·4	
3·8		12·6
	−3·5	
4·0		13·3
	−3·6	
4·3		14·1
	−3·7	
4·5		14·9
	−3·8	
4·7		15·7
	−3·9	
5·0		16·5
	−4·0	
5·2		17·4
	−4·1	
5·5		18·3
	−4·2	
5·8		19·1
	−4·3	
6·1		20·1
	−4·4	
6·3		21·0
	−4·5	
6·6		22·0
	−4·6	
6·9		22·9
	−4·7	
7·2		23·9
	−4·8	
7·5		24·9
	−4·9	
7·9		26·0
	−5·0	
8·2		27·1
	−5·1	
8·5		28·1
	−5·2	
8·8		29·2
	−5·3	
9·2		30·4
	−5·4	
9·5		31·5
	−5·5	
9·9		32·7
	−5·6	
10·3		33·9
	−5·7	
10·6		35·1
	−5·8	
11·0		36·3
	−5·9	
11·4		37·6
	−6·0	
11·8		38·9
	−6·1	
12·2		40·1
	−6·2	
12·6		41·5
	−6·3	
13·0		42·8
	−6·4	
13·4		44·2
	−6·5	
13·8		45·5
	−6·6	
14·2		46·9
	−6·7	
14·7		48·4
	−6·8	
15·1		49·8
	−6·9	
15·5		51·3
	−7·0	
16·0		52·8
	−7·1	
16·5		54·3
	−7·2	
16·9		55·8
	−7·3	
17·4		57·4
	−7·4	
17·9		58·9
	−7·5	
18·4		60·5
	−7·6	
18·8		62·1
	−7·7	
19·3		63·8
	−7·8	
19·8		65·4
	−7·9	
20·4		67·1
	−8·0	
20·9		68·8
	−8·1	
21·4		70·5

Ht. of Eye	Corrn
m	′
1·0	− 1·8
1·5	− 2·2
2·0	− 2·5
2·5	− 2·8
3·0	− 3·0
See table ←	
m	′
20	− 7·9
22	− 8·3
24	− 8·6
26	− 9·0
28	− 9·3
30	− 9·6
32	−10·0
34	−10·3
36	−10·6
38	−10·8
40	−11·1
42	−11·4
44	−11·7
46	−11·9
48	−12·2
ft.	′
2	− 1·4
4	− 1·9
6	− 2·4
8	− 2·7
10	− 3·1
See table ←	
ft.	′
70	− 8·1
75	− 8·4
80	− 8·7
85	− 8·9
90	− 9·2
95	− 9·5
100	− 9·7
105	− 9·9
110	−10·2
115	−10·4
120	−10·6
125	−10·8
130	−11·1
135	−11·3
140	−11·5
145	−11·7
150	−11·9
155	−12·1

App. Alt. = Apparent altitude = Sextant altitude corrected for index error and dip.

FIG. 806. Inside front cover of the *Nautical Almanac*.

may be applied in any order, using sextant altitude as the entering argument where altitude is needed. But for low altitudes, where refraction changes rapidly with differences in altitude, or if a very large index correction or dip short correction is involved, the use of hs may introduce a significant error in observed altitude. It is good practice, therefore, to apply corrections of the first two groups to obtain *apparent altitude (ha, App alt)* for use as the entry value for obtaining the other corrections.

Sextant altitude-correction by body. Index correction, dip, mean refraction correction, and temperature–pressure correction (when applicable) are required for all bodies. In addition, corrections for semi-diameter and parallax are needed for the Sun and Moon, and corrections for phase and parallax are needed for Venus and Mars. Some of the corrections are combined in the *Nautical Almanac*.

Some of the almanac tables are of the critical type. Consecutive values of the corrections are tabulated, with the limiting values of the entering argument for each correction offset half a line above and below the correction. Interpolation is not needed. If the entering value is a tabulated limiting value, the correction half a line *above* the entering value is taken. Thus, in the dip table, a correction of 5ʹ.3 applies to heights of eye of 8.9 to 9.2 metres, or 29.3 to 30.4 feet.

Sun. The Sun table on the inside front cover of the almanac, and repeated on the bookmark, is shown in Fig. 806. It is a critical table combining corrections for mean refraction, semi-diameter, and parallax. Separate tables are given for two periods of the year, to allow for differences in semi-diameter as the distance between the Earth and Sun varies during the Earth's annual revolution around the Sun. Separate tabulations are given for the lower and upper limbs. Corrections are for altitudes of a little less than 10° to 90°. A non-critical table of the corrections for altitudes for 0° to 10° is located on the page facing the inside front cover, as shown in Fig. 807. For the Sun, one first applies index correction and dip to hs to obtain ha, which is then used to find the combined Sun correction from the Sun table on the inside front cover or facing page, and the temperature-pressure correction (if applicable) from the table on the page following the low-altitude corrections, as shown in Fig. 808. These corrections are applied to ha to determine Ho.

Suppose it is desired to determine the observed altitude for a sextant altitude of the lower limb of the Sun of $41°09'.6$ taken on November 17 from a height of eye of 10.5 metres, with a sextant having an index correction of $(+)$ $1'.5$ (off the arc). From the critical dip table, the dip is found to be $(-)$ $5'.7$. Applying IC and D to hs, one finds ha to be $41°09'.6 + 1'.5 - 5'.7 = 41°05'.4$. Using ha as the entering argument, one finds the main Sun correction to be $(+)$ $15'.1$. Applying this to ha, one finds Ho to be $41°05'.4 + 15'.1 = 41°20'.5$. Note that the Sun correction would have been $(+)$ $15'.2$ if hs had been the entering argument. The entire solution can be arranged conveniently as follows:

	Sun LL
hs	$41°09'.6$
IC	$(+)$ $1'.5$
D	$(-)$ $5'.7$
ha	$41°05'.4$
LL	$(+)$ $15'.1$
Ho	$41°20'.5$

In this solution, LL stands for lower limb.

Moon. Non-critical Moon correction tables on the inside back cover, and facing page, Fig. 809, combine corrections for mean refraction, semi-diameter including augmentation, and parallax. The combined correction is separated into two parts. The main correction is taken from the upper table with apparent altitude as the entering argument. The second correction is found in the lower table, in the same column as the main correction, using horizontal parallax (HP) from the right-hand daily page of the almanac as the entering argument. In the lower table, separate corrections are given for lower and upper limbs. Both corrections are always positive, but $30'.0$ is subtracted from upper-limb

ALTITUDE CORRECTION TABLES 0°–10°—SUN, STARS, PLANETS

App. Alt.	OCT.–MAR. SUN Lower Limb	Upper Limb	APR.–SEPT. Lower Limb	Upper Limb	STARS PLANETS	App. Alt.	OCT.–MAR. SUN Lower Limb	Upper Limb	APR.–SEPT. Lower Limb	Upper Limb	STARS PLANETS
0 00	−18·2	−50·5	−18·4	−50·2	−34·5	3 30	+3·3	−29·0	+3·1	−28·7	−13·0
03	17·5	49·8	17·8	49·6	33·8	35	3·6	28·7	3·3	28·5	12·7
06	16·9	49·2	17·1	48·9	33·2	40	3·8	28·5	3·5	28·3	12·5
09	16·3	48·6	16·5	48·3	32·6	45	4·0	28·3	3·7	28·1	12·3
12	15·7	48·0	15·9	47·7	32·0	50	4·2	28·1	3·9	27·9	12·1
15	15·1	47·4	15·3	47·1	31·4	3 55	4·4	27·9	4·1	27·7	11·9
0 18	−14·5	−46·8	−14·8	−46·6	−30·8	4 00	+4·5	−27·8	+4·3	−27·5	−11·8
21	14·0	46·3	14·2	46·0	30·3	05	4·7	27·6	4·5	27·3	11·6
24	13·5	45·8	13·7	45·5	29·8	10	4·9	27·4	4·6	27·2	11·4
27	12·9	45·2	13·2	45·0	29·2	15	5·1	27·2	4·8	27·0	11·2
30	12·4	44·7	12·7	44·5	28·7	20	5·2	27·1	5·0	26·8	11·1
33	11·9	44·2	12·2	44·0	28·2	25	5·4	26·9	5·1	26·7	10·9
0 36	−11·5	−43·8	−11·7	−43·5	−27·8	4 30	+5·6	−26·7	+5·3	−26·5	−10·7
39	11·0	43·3	11·2	43·0	27·3	35	5·7	26·6	5·5	26·3	10·6
42	10·5	42·8	10·8	42·6	26·8	40	5·9	26·4	5·6	26·2	10·4
45	10·1	42·4	10·3	42·1	26·4	45	6·0	26·3	5·8	26·0	10·3
48	9·6	41·9	9·9	41·7	25·9	50	6·2	26·1	5·9	25·9	10·1
51	9·2	41·5	9·5	41·3	25·5	4 55	6·3	26·0	6·0	25·8	10·0
0 54	−8·8	−41·1	−9·1	−40·9	−25·1	5 00	+6·4	−25·9	+6·2	−25·6	−9·9
57	8·4	40·7	8·7	40·5	24·7	05	6·6	25·7	6·3	25·5	9·7
1 00	8·0	40·3	8·3	40·1	24·3	10	6·7	25·6	6·4	25·4	9·6
03	7·7	40·0	7·9	39·7	24·0	15	6·8	25·5	6·6	25·2	9·5
06	7·3	39·6	7·5	39·3	23·6	20	6·9	25·4	6·7	25·1	9·4
09	6·9	39·2	7·2	39·0	23·2	25	7·1	25·2	6·8	25·0	9·2
1 12	−6·6	−38·9	−6·8	−38·6	−22·9	5 30	+7·2	−25·1	+6·9	−24·9	−9·1
15	6·2	38·5	6·5	38·3	22·5	35	7·3	25·0	7·0	24·8	9·0
18	5·9	38·2	6·2	38·0	22·2	40	7·4	24·9	7·2	24·6	8·9
21	5·6	37·9	5·8	37·6	21·9	45	7·5	24·8	7·3	24·5	8·8
24	5·3	37·6	5·5	37·3	21·6	50	7·6	24·7	7·4	24·4	8·7
27	4·9	37·2	5·2	37·0	21·2	5 55	7·7	24·6	7·5	24·3	8·6
1 30	−4·6	−36·9	−4·9	−36·7	−20·9	6 00	+7·8	−24·5	+7·6	−24·2	−8·5
35	4·2	36·5	4·4	36·2	20·5	10	8·0	24·3	7·8	24·0	8·3
40	3·7	36·0	4·0	35·8	20·0	20	8·2	24·1	8·0	23·8	8·1
45	3·2	35·5	3·5	35·3	19·5	30	8·4	23·9	8·1	23·7	7·9
50	2·8	35·1	3·1	34·9	19·1	40	8·6	23·7	8·3	23·5	7·7
1 55	2·4	34·7	2·6	34·4	18·7	6 50	8·7	23·6	8·5	23·3	7·6
2 00	−2·0	−34·3	−2·2	−34·0	−18·3	7 00	+8·9	−23·4	+8·6	−23·2	−7·4
05	1·6	33·9	1·8	33·6	17·9	10	9·1	23·2	8·8	23·0	7·2
10	1·2	33·5	1·5	33·3	17·5	20	9·2	23·1	9·0	22·8	7·1
15	0·9	33·2	1·1	32·9	17·2	30	9·3	23·0	9·1	22·7	7·0
20	0·5	32·8	0·8	32·6	16·8	40	9·5	22·8	9·2	22·6	6·8
25	−0·2	32·5	0·4	32·2	16·5	7 50	9·6	22·7	9·4	22·4	6·7
2 30	+0·2	−32·1	−0·1	−31·9	−16·1	8 00	+9·7	−22·6	+9·5	−22·3	−6·6
35	0·5	31·8	+0·2	31·6	15·8	10	9·9	22·4	9·6	22·2	6·4
40	0·8	31·5	0·5	31·3	15·5	20	10·0	22·3	9·7	22·1	6·3
45	1·1	31·2	0·8	31·0	15·2	30	10·1	22·2	9·8	22·0	6·2
50	1·4	30·9	1·1	30·7	14·9	40	10·2	22·1	10·0	21·8	6·1
2 55	1·6	30·7	1·4	30·4	14·7	8 50	10·3	22·0	10·1	21·7	6·0
3 00	+1·9	−30·4	+1·7	−30·1	−14·4	9 00	+10·4	−21·9	+10·2	−21·6	−5·9
05	2·2	30·1	1·9	29·9	14·1	10	10·5	21·8	10·3	21·5	5·8
10	2·4	29·9	2·1	29·7	13·9	20	10·6	21·7	10·4	21·4	5·7
15	2·6	29·7	2·4	29·4	13·7	30	10·7	21·6	10·5	21·3	5·6
20	2·9	29·4	2·6	29·2	13·4	40	10·8	21·5	10·6	21·2	5·5
25	3·1	29·2	2·9	28·9	13·2	9 50	10·9	21·4	10·6	21·2	5·4
3 30	+3·3	−29·0	+3·1	−28·7	−13·0	10 00	+11·0	−21·3	+10·7	−21·1	−5·3

Additional corrections for temperature and pressure are given on the following page.
For bubble sextant observations ignore dip and use the star corrections for Sun, planets, and stars.

FIG. 807. Page facing the inside front cover of the *Nautical Almanac*.

ADDITIONAL REFRACTION CORRECTIONS FOR NON-STANDARD CONDITIONS

Temperature

App. Alt.	A	B	C	D	E	F	G	H	J	K	L	M	N	App. Alt.
0 00	−6·9	−5·7	−4·6	−3·4	−2·3	−1·1	0·0	+1·1	+2·3	+3·4	+4·6	+5·7	+6·9	0 00
0 30	5·2	4·4	3·5	2·6	1·7	0·9	0·0	0·9	1·7	2·6	3·5	4·4	5·2	0 30
1 00	4·3	3·5	2·8	2·1	1·4	0·7	0·0	0·7	1·4	2·1	2·8	3·5	4·3	1 00
1 30	3·5	2·9	2·4	1·8	1·2	0·6	0·0	0·6	1·2	1·8	2·4	2·9	3·5	1 30
2 00	3·0	2·5	2·0	1·5	1·0	0·5	0·0	0·5	1·0	1·5	2·0	2·5	3·0	2 00
2 30	−2·5	−2·1	−1·6	−1·2	−0·8	−0·4	0·0	+0·4	+0·8	+1·2	+1·6	+2·1	+2·5	2 30
3 00	2·2	1·8	1·5	1·1	0·7	0·4	0·0	0·4	0·7	1·1	1·5	1·8	2·2	3 00
3 30	2·0	1·6	1·3	1·0	0·7	0·3	0·0	0·3	0·7	1·0	1·3	1·6	2·0	3 30
4 00	1·8	1·5	1·2	0·9	0·6	0·3	0·0	0·3	0·6	0·9	1·2	1·5	1·8	4 00
4 30	1·6	1·4	1·1	0·8	0·5	0·3	0·0	0·3	0·5	0·8	1·1	1·4	1·6	4 30
5 00	−1·5	−1·3	−1·0	−0·8	−0·5	−0·2	0·0	+0·2	+0·5	+0·8	+1·0	+1·3	+1·5	5 00
6	1·3	1·1	0·9	0·6	0·4	0·2	0·0	0·2	0·4	0·6	0·9	1·1	1·3	6
7	1·1	0·9	0·7	0·6	0·4	0·2	0·0	0·2	0·4	0·6	0·7	0·9	1·1	7
8	1·0	0·8	0·7	0·5	0·3	0·2	0·0	0·2	0·3	0·5	0·7	0·8	1·0	8
9	0·9	0·7	0·6	0·4	0·3	0·1	0·0	0·1	0·3	0·4	0·6	0·7	0·9	9
10 00	−0·8	−0·7	−0·5	−0·4	−0·3	−0·1	0·0	+0·1	+0·3	+0·4	+0·5	+0·7	+0·8	10 00
12	0·7	0·6	0·5	0·3	0·2	0·1	0·0	0·1	0·2	0·3	0·5	0·6	0·7	12
14	0·6	0·5	0·4	0·3	0·2	0·1	0·0	0·1	0·2	0·3	0·4	0·5	0·6	14
16	0·5	0·4	0·3	0·3	0·2	0·1	0·0	0·1	0·2	0·3	0·3	0·4	0·5	16
18	0·4	0·4	0·3	0·2	0·2	0·1	0·0	0·1	0·2	0·2	0·3	0·4	0·4	18
20 00	−0·4	−0·3	−0·3	−0·2	−0·1	−0·1	0·0	+0·1	+0·1	+0·2	+0·3	+0·3	+0·4	20 00
25	0·3	0·3	0·2	0·2	0·1	−0·1	0·0	+0·1	0·1	0·2	0·2	0·3	0·3	25
30	0·3	0·2	0·2	0·1	0·1	0·0	0·0	0·0	0·1	0·1	0·2	0·2	0·3	30
35	0·2	0·2	0·1	0·1	0·1	0·0	0·0	0·0	0·1	0·1	0·1	0·2	0·2	35
40	0·2	0·1	0·1	0·1	−0·1	0·0	0·0	0·0	+0·1	0·1	0·1	0·1	0·2	40
50 00	−0·1	−0·1	−0·1	−0·1	0·0	0·0	0·0	0·0	0·0	+0·1	+0·1	+0·1	+0·1	50 00

The graph is entered with arguments temperature and pressure to find a zone letter; using as arguments this zone letter and apparent altitude (sextant altitude corrected for dip), a correction is taken from the table. This correction is to be applied to the sextant altitude in addition to the corrections for standard conditions

FIG. 808. Non-standard temperature-pressure correction table of the *Nautical Almanac*.

observations. The non-standard temperature–pressure correction (if applicable) is found from the table, Fig. 808.

Suppose it is desired to determine the observed altitude for a sextant altitude of the Moon of 29°14.′7 taken about GMT 1900 on June 22 from a height of eye of 11.0 metres, with a sextant having an IC of (−) 2.′2 (on the arc). Find Ho if the observation is of (*1*) the lower limb (LL), and (*2*) the upper limb (UL).

(*1*)	Moon LL		(*2*)	Moon UL
HP	56.′3		HP	56.′3
hs	29°14.′7		hs	29°14.′7
IC	(−) 2.′2		IC	(−) 2.′2
D	(−) 5.′8		D	(−) 5.′8
ha	29°06.′7		ha	29°06.′7
Main	(+) 59.′3		Main	(+) 59.′3
add'l LL	(+) 3.′4		add'l UL	(+) 2.′7
Ho	30°09.′4		UL ☾	(−) 30.′0
			Ho	29°38.′7

Note that the height of eye is a tabulated value, the dip correction used being the value half a line *above* the entering argument argument.

Planets. Altitudes of Jupiter and Saturn are corrected the same as altitudes of stars, discussed later. For Venus and Mars, apparent altitude is corrected for mean refraction taken from the critical 'Stars and Planets' table on the inside front cover of the almanac, and repeated on the bookmark, Fig. 806, or from the non-critical table on the page facing the inside front cover, Fig. 807, for non-standard temperature and atmospheric pressure (if applicable), Fig. 808, and also the additional combined correction (add'l) for parallax and phase, taken from the inside front cover or bookmark, Fig. 806. If Venus is observed when the Sun is above the horizon, the additional correction should be calculated as explained in the 'Explanation' section of the almanac. The main planet correction is always negative. The additional correction may be either positive or negative.

393

ALTITUDE CORRECTION TABLES 0°–35°—MOON

App. Alt.	0°–4° Corrⁿ	5°–9° Corrⁿ	10°–14° Corrⁿ	15°–19° Corrⁿ	20°–24° Corrⁿ	25°–29° Corrⁿ	30°–34° Corrⁿ	App. Alt.
00	$0°$ 33·8	$5°$ 58·2	$10°$ 62·1	$15°$ 62·8	$20°$ 62·2	$25°$ 60·8	$30°$ 58·9	00
10	35·9	58·5	62·2	62·8	62·1	60·8	58·8	10
20	37·8	58·7	62·2	62·8	62·1	60·7	58·8	20
30	39·6	58·9	62·3	62·8	62·1	60·7	58·7	30
40	41·2	59·1	62·3	62·7	62·0	60·6	58·6	40
50	42·6	59·3	62·4	62·7	62·0	60·6	58·5	50
00	$1°$ 44·0	$6°$ 59·5	$11°$ 62·4	$16°$ 62·7	$21°$ 62·0	$26°$ 60·5	$31°$ 58·5	00
10	45·2	59·7	62·4	62·7	61·9	60·4	58·4	10
20	46·3	59·9	62·5	62·7	61·9	60·4	58·3	20
30	47·3	60·0	62·5	62·7	61·9	60·3	58·2	30
40	48·3	60·2	62·5	62·7	61·8	60·3	58·2	40
50	49·2	60·3	62·6	62·7	61·8	60·2	58·1	50
00	$2°$ 50·0	$7°$ 60·5	$12°$ 62·6	$17°$ 62·7	$22°$ 61·7	$27°$ 60·1	$32°$ 58·0	00
10	50·8	60·6	62·6	62·6	61·7	60·1	57·9	10
20	51·4	60·7	62·6	62·6	61·6	60·0	57·8	20
30	52·1	60·9	62·7	62·6	61·6	59·9	57·8	30
40	52·7	61·0	62·7	62·6	61·5	59·9	57·7	40
50	53·3	61·1	62·7	62·6	61·5	59·8	57·6	50
00	$3°$ 53·8	$8°$ 61·2	$13°$ 62·7	$18°$ 62·5	$23°$ 61·5	$28°$ 59·7	$33°$ 57·5	00
10	54·3	61·3	62·7	62·5	61·4	59·7	57·4	10
20	54·8	61·4	62·7	62·5	61·4	59·6	57·4	20
30	55·2	61·5	62·8	62·4	61·3	59·6	57·3	30
40	55·6	61·6	62·8	62·4	61·3	59·5	57·2	40
50	56·0	61·6	62·8	62·4	61·2	59·4	57·1	50
00	$4°$ 56·4	$9°$ 61·7	$14°$ 62·8	$19°$ 62·4	$24°$ 61·2	$29°$ 59·3	$34°$ 57·0	00
10	56·7	61·8	62·8	62·3	61·1	59·3	56·9	10
20	57·1	61·9	62·8	62·3	61·1	59·2	56·9	20
30	57·4	61·9	62·8	62·3	61·0	59·1	56·8	30
40	57·7	62·0	62·8	62·2	60·9	59·1	56·7	40
50	57·9	62·1	62·8	62·2	60·9	59·0	56·6	50

H.P.	L U	L U	L U	L U	L U	L U	L U	H.P.
54·0	0·3 0·9	0·3 0·9	0·4 1·0	0·5 1·1	0·6 1·2	0·7 1·3	0·9 1·5	54·0
54·3	0·7 1·1	0·7 1·2	0·7 1·2	0·8 1·3	0·9 1·4	1·1 1·5	1·2 1·7	54·3
54·6	1·1 1·4	1·1 1·4	1·1 1·4	1·2 1·5	1·3 1·6	1·4 1·7	1·5 1·8	54·6
54·9	1·4 1·6	1·5 1·6	1·5 1·6	1·6 1·7	1·6 1·8	1·8 1·9	1·9 2·0	54·9
55·2	1·8 1·8	1·8 1·8	1·9 1·9	1·9 1·9	2·0 2·0	2·1 2·1	2·2 2·2	55·2
55·5	2·2 2·0	2·2 2·0	2·3 2·1	2·3 2·1	2·4 2·2	2·4 2·3	2·5 2·4	55·5
55·8	2·6 2·2	2·6 2·2	2·6 2·3	2·7 2·3	2·7 2·4	2·8 2·4	2·9 2·5	55·8
56·1	3·0 2·4	3·0 2·5	3·0 2·5	3·0 2·5	3·1 2·6	3·1 2·6	3·2 2·7	56·1
56·4	3·4 2·7	3·4 2·7	3·4 2·7	3·4 2·7	3·4 2·8	3·5 2·8	3·5 2·9	56·4
56·7	3·7 2·9	3·7 2·9	3·8 2·9	3·8 2·9	3·8 3·0	3·8 3·0	3·9 3·0	56·7
57·0	4·1 3·1	4·1 3·1	4·1 3·1	4·1 3·1	4·2 3·1	4·2 3·2	4·2 3·2	57·0
57·3	4·5 3·3	4·5 3·3	4·5 3·3	4·5 3·3	4·5 3·4	4·6 3·4	4·6 3·4	57·3
57·6	4·9 3·5	4·9 3·5	4·9 3·5	4·9 3·5	4·9 3·5	4·9 3·5	4·9 3·6	57·6
57·9	5·3 3·8	5·3 3·8	5·2 3·8	5·2 3·7	5·2 3·7	5·2 3·7	5·2 3·7	57·9
58·2	5·6 4·0	5·6 4·0	5·6 4·0	5·6 4·0	5·6 3·9	5·6 3·9	5·6 3·9	58·2
58·5	6·0 4·2	6·0 4·2	6·0 4·2	6·0 4·2	6·0 4·1	5·9 4·1	5·9 4·1	58·5
58·8	6·4 4·4	6·4 4·4	6·4 4·4	6·3 4·4	6·3 4·3	6·3 4·3	6·2 4·2	58·8
59·1	6·8 4·6	6·8 4·6	6·7 4·6	6·7 4·6	6·7 4·5	6·6 4·5	6·6 4·4	59·1
59·4	7·2 4·8	7·1 4·8	7·1 4·8	7·1 4·8	7·0 4·7	7·0 4·7	6·9 4·6	59·4
59·7	7·5 5·1	7·5 5·0	7·5 5·0	7·5 5·0	7·4 4·9	7·3 4·8	7·2 4·7	59·7
60·0	7·9 5·3	7·9 5·3	7·9 5·2	7·8 5·2	7·8 5·1	7·7 5·0	7·6 4·9	60·0
60·3	8·3 5·5	8·3 5·5	8·2 5·4	8·2 5·4	8·1 5·3	8·0 5·2	7·9 5·1	60·3
60·6	8·7 5·7	8·7 5·7	8·6 5·7	8·6 5·6	8·5 5·5	8·4 5·4	8·2 5·3	60·6
60·9	9·1 5·9	9·0 5·9	9·0 5·9	8·9 5·8	8·8 5·7	8·7 5·6	8·5 5·4	60·9
61·2	9·5 6·2	9·4 6·1	9·4 6·1	9·3 6·0	9·2 5·9	9·1 5·8	8·9 5·6	61·2
61·5	9·8 6·4	9·8 6·3	9·7 6·3	9·7 6·2	9·5 6·1	9·4 5·9	9·2 5·8	61·5

DIP

Ht. of Eye (m)	Ht. of Eye (ft)	Corrⁿ	Ht. of Eye (m)	Ht. of Eye (ft)	Corrⁿ
2·4	8·0	−2·8	9·5	31·5	−5·5
2·6	8·6	−2·9	9·9	32·7	−5·6
2·8	9·2	−3·0	10·3	33·9	−5·7
3·0	9·8	−3·1	10·6	35·1	−5·8
3·2	10·5	−3·2	11·0	36·3	−5·9
3·4	11·2	−3·3	11·4	37·6	−6·0
3·6	11·9	−3·4	11·8	38·9	−6·1
3·8	12·6	−3·5	12·2	40·1	−6·2
4·0	13·3	−3·6	12·6	41·5	−6·3
4·3	14·1	−3·7	13·0	42·8	−6·4
4·5	14·9	−3·8	13·4	44·2	−6·5
4·7	15·7	−3·9	13·8	45·5	−6·6
5·0	16·5	−4·0	14·2	46·9	−6·7
5·2	17·4	−4·1	14·7	48·4	−6·8
5·5	18·3	−4·2	15·1	49·8	−6·9
5·8	19·1	−4·3	15·5	51·3	−7·0
6·1	20·1	−4·4	16·0	52·8	−7·1
6·3	21·0	−4·5	16·5	54·3	−7·2
6·6	22·0	−4·6	16·9	55·8	−7·3
6·9	22·9	−4·7	17·4	57·4	−7·4
7·2	23·9	−4·8	17·9	58·9	−7·5
7·5	24·9	−4·9	18·4	60·5	−7·6
7·9	26·0	−5·0	18·8	61·9	−7·7
8·2	27·1	−5·1	19·3	63·8	−7·8
8·5	28·1	−5·2	19·8	65·4	−7·9
8·8	29·2	−5·3	20·4	67·1	−8·0
9·2	30·4	−5·4	20·9	68·8	−8·1
9·5	31·5		21·4	70·5	

MOON CORRECTION TABLE

The correction is in two parts; the first correction is taken from the upper part of the table with argument apparent altitude, and the second from the lower part, with argument H.P., in the same column as that from which the first correction was taken. Separate corrections are given in the lower part for lower (L) and upper (U) limbs. All corrections are to be **added** to apparent altitude, but 30′ is to be subtracted from the altitude of the upper limb.

For corrections for pressure and temperature see page A4.

For bubble sextant observations ignore dip, take the mean of upper and lower limb corrections and subtract 15′ from the altitude.

App. Alt. = Apparent altitude = Sextant altitude corrected for index error and dip.

FIG. 809. Part of Moon altitude correction table of the *Nautical Almanac*.

Suppose it is desired to determine the observed altitude for a sextant altitude of Venus of 24°01′.2 taken on December 2 from a height of eye of 5.6 metres, with a sextant having an IC of (+) 3′.0 (off the arc).

	Venus
hs	24°01′.2
IC	(+) 3′.0
D	(−) 4′.2
ha	24°00′.0
Main	(−) 2′.2
add'l	(+) 0′.1
Ho	23°57′.9

Stars. Apparent altitudes of stars and the planets Jupiter and Saturn are corrected only for mean refraction, the correction (always negative) being tabulated in the 'Stars and Planets' correction table on the inside front cover, repeated on the bookmark, Fig. 806, the page facing the inside front cover, Fig. 807, and the TB correction from the graph, Fig. 808 (if applicable).

Suppose it is desired to determine the observed altitude for a sextant altitude of Procyon of 68°47′.5 taken from a height of eye of 12.5 metres, with a sextant having an IC of (−) 1′.0 (on the arc).

	Procyon
hs	68°47′.5
IC	(−) 1′.0
D	(−) 6′.2
ha	68°40′.3
Main	(−) 0′.4
Ho	68°39′.9

Low altitudes. Although it is good practice to avoid altitudes of less than 2°, because of uncertainty in the magnitude of the refraction corrections, and to consider any altitude of less than 10° to be of doubtful accuracy, low-altitude observations may be the only ones available. The

395

navigator then uses them in the same manner as he uses any data of questionable accuracy.

Corrections for low-altitude observations are applied as for any altitude. However, the application of corrections for the first two groups to determine ha for use as an entering argument is particularly important with low altitudes, as is the application of the TB correction for non-standard temperature and pressure. Suppose hs is $2°10'.9$, IC $(-)$ $3'.5$ (on the arc), and height of eye 11.9 metres, and the observation is of the lower limb of the Sun during winter. The ha is $2°10'.9 - 3'.5 - 6'.1 = 2°01'.3$. If hs is used as the entering argument in the Sun table of Fig. 807, the main lower-limb correction is found to be $(-)$ $1'.1$, but if ha is used, the correction is $(-)$ $1'.9$. If the temperature is $(-)$ $16°$ C and the pressure 1022 millibars (mb), the TB correction is $(-)$ $3'.0$ if ha is used as the entering argument. In the usual convenient form, the solution appears as follows:

	Sun LL
hs	$2°10'.9$
IC	$(-)$ $3'.5$
D	$(-)$ $6'.1$
ha	$2°01'.3$
LL	$(-)$ $1'.9$
TB	$(-)$ $3'.0$
Ho	$1°56'.4$

If the observer notes the time that a body, either the lower or upper limb if the body is the Sun or Moon, is exactly on the horizon, he has an observation of hs $0°$ without need of a sextant, and consequently without need for a correction of the first group, with the possible exception of personal correction. This procedure can be useful in an emergency, as in a lifeboat without a sextant, or if the only available sextants have been damaged. If ha is negative, corrections using ha as an entering argument can be determined by extrapolation. Corrections are applied algebraically, so that a negative correction is added numerically, and a positive correction is subtracted numerically.

Back sight. If a back sight (p. 347) is made, the corrections of the first two groups are applied in the usual way to obtain ha, which is then subtracted from 180° before other corrections are applied.

Suppose it is desired to determine the observed altitude for a back sight of the Sun's upper (apparent lower) limb taken on January 25, with the following data: hs 112°36ʹ.1, IC (+) 1.0 (off the arc), height of eye 8.7 metres.

	Sun UL
	Backsight
hs	112°36ʹ.1
IC	(+) 1ʹ.0
D	(−) 5ʹ.2
180° − ha	112°31ʹ.9
ha	67°28ʹ.1
UL	(−) 16ʹ.5
Ho	67°11ʹ.6

Artificial-horizon observations. When an observation is made on land by artificial horizon, as explained on page 356, corrections of the first group are first applied, the result is divided by 2, and corrections of groups three through five are then applied. Corrections of the second group are not applied, although, to be exact, a correction for deflection of the vertical is applicable. Aboard a moving vessel, Coriolis and acceleration errors are so large and unpredictable that artificial-horizon observations at sea are usually impracticable. If the centre of the Sun or Moon is observed, corrections for both limbs are averaged. For the Moon, this is easiest done by correcting ha for the main moon correction from the upper table of Fig. 809, half the sum of the lower and upper limb corrections from the lower table of Fig. 809, and using (−) 15.0 as the additional correction.

Suppose it is desired to determine the observed altitude for an observation of the Moon made by means of an artificial horizon at approximately GMT 0700 on June 21, considering the sight (*1*) a lower-limb observation, and (*2*) an

397

observation of the centre of the body, with the following data:
hs 69°14.3, IC (−) 2.0 (on the arc).

(1)	Moon LL		(2)	Moon centre
HP	57.1		HP	57.1
hs	69°14.3		hs	69°14.3
IC	(−) 2.0		IC	(−) 2.0
2 ha	69°12.3		2 ha	69°12.3
ha	34°36.2		ha	34°36.2
Main	(+) 56.7		Main	(+) 56.7
LL	(+) 4.3		½(LL+UL)	(+) 3.8
Ho	35°37.2		☾	(−) 15.0
			Ho	35°21.7

Artificial-horizon sextant observations. Sights taken on land
by an artificial-horizon sextant are subject to the same
corrections as those taken by marine sextant with an artificial
horizon, except that measurement is of the altitude, not twice
the altitude. However, artificial-horizon sextants normally do
not have significant instrument or index errors. The latter is
avoided by permanent setting of the index at the time of
manufacture of the instrument. Also, no tilt error is present
because the instrument is vertical when the artificial horizon
is in correct position for observation. Thus, unless one has a
personal error, no correction of the first group is needed. It is
customary with an artificial-horizon sextant to observe the
centre of the Sun and Moon, thus eliminating correction for
semi-diameter and augmentation. Because of the difficulty of
making observations by artificial-horizon sextant, readings
are customarily recorded to a precision of one minute of arc,
which is well within the probable error of observations.
Accordingly, no phase correction is applied, and parallax is
ignored except for the Moon.

In practice, then, artificial-horizon sextant observations
made on land are corrected only for refraction, with an
additional correction for parallax in the case of a Moon
observation. The temperature-pressure correction is usually
ignored. Refraction is tabulated in the 'Stars and Planets'

correction table, and parallax in altitude of the Moon is found by multiplying the horizontal parallax, tabulated on the right-hand daily pages of the *Nautical Almanac*, by cosine of the apparent altitude corrected for refraction. The *Air Almanac* has a table for parallax in altitude of the Moon, but if this almanac is not available, such a table can be constructed for each minute of horizontal parallax between 54′ and 62′.

Aboard a moving vessel, altitudes obtained by a gyro-horizon sextant are corrected as just explained. However, bubble sextants and pendulum sextants are generally subject to such large unpredictable Coriolis and acceleration errors that use of these instruments is seldom practicable afloat.

Horizontal angles. If a marine sextant is used to measure horizontal angles between objects, only corrections of the first group are applicable, and usually this means only index correction. If such angles are to be used for fixing the position of the craft (p. 228), the sextant reading is normally of sufficient accuracy without the application of any corrections unless the index error is unusually large.

Other sources of corrections. Sextant altitude-correction tables are not limited to those in the *Nautical Almanac*. The *Air Almanac* has been mentioned. Various books of nautical tables have sextant altitude-correction tables. The observer should use the tables most suitable to his personal taste.

Work forms. It is good practice to have a work form applicable to the usual procedure with all astronomical bodies, perhaps a composite of the various forms used here. In practice, the form adopted should be part of the overall form used for sight reduction, as discussed in section 13 of the next chapter.

6. Additional Almanac Data

Between the sextant altitude-correction tables at the front of the *Nautical Almanac* and the daily pages are given religious calendars, lists of the principal anniversaries and holidays of the British Commonwealth and the United States of America, a list of the days and GMT's of the phases of the Moon, a calendar giving days of the week and days of the year, data on lunar and solar eclipses, notes relating to planets, and a planet diagram.

The daily pages tabulate, in addition to hour angle, declination, and rising–setting–twilight data, the magnitudes, SHA at GMT 0000, and GMT's of Greenwich meridian transits of the four navigational planets on the mid day of each page opening; GMT of Greenwich meridian transit of the vernal equinox (Aries) for the middle day of the three on the page; the semi-diameters and GMT's of Greenwich meridian transits of the Sun and Moon; the equation of time (p. 328) at twelve-hour intervals; and the age, phase, and horizontal parallax of the Moon. Transit times at meridians other than Greenwich can be determined by interpolation or by finding the time at which LHA is zero. A heavy line between entries of equation of time indicate a change of sign.

Between the daily pages and the 'Increments and Corrections' section near the back of the Nautical Almanac are given an explanation section including instructions for setting a star globe and instructions for use of the almanac for the Sun and stars for the following year, a list of zone descriptions of places throughout the world, star charts, the list of SHA and declination of 173 stars at monthly intervals, Polaris tables (p. 452), and a conversion of arc-to-time table.

An 'Index to Selected Stars' table, between the rising–setting–twilight interpolation tables and altitude-correction tables for the Moon, has separate tabulations, in alphabetical order and order of decreasing SHA, of the 57 navigational stars listed on the daily pages.

A 'List of Contents' is given on the outside back cover of the Nautical Almanac.

7. Other Almanacs

Although the Nautical Almanac is the principal source of ephemeridal information for mariners, other almanacs are available. Some of these are intended primarily for mariners, some for aviators, some for surveyors, and some for astronomers. Some are published by government organizations and some by non-government publishers.

The *Air Almanac* (*A A*), published jointly by the Royal Greenwich Observatory and the United States Naval Observatory, is similar in many respects to the *Nautical Almanac*, but with some differences in arrangment to provide a faster, in some cases less precise, solution. The daily-page data are tabulated at 10-minute intervals, data for the Sun, Aries, three planets, and the Moon for 12 hours being on each page. Each volume has data for a six-month period.

Ephemerides with detailed data to a high precision, for use primarily by astronomers, are published jointly by the Royal Greenwich Observatory and the United States Naval Observatory, and by others.

Abbreviated, long-term almanacs have been published, and can be used for navigation, but generally with less convenience and reduced accuracy. Such an almanac for the Sun is published in volumes II and III of *Sight Reduction Tables for Air Navigation*, publication AP 3270 of the Royal Greenwich Observatory and Pub. No. 249 of the United States Defense Mapping Agency Hydrographic Topographic Center. A long-term almanac for the Sun and stars is published by the United States Defense Mapping Agency Hydrographic Topographic Center in its Pub. No. 9, *American Practical Navigator* (originally by Nathaniel Bowditch). The *Nautical Almanac* is available several months in advance, but if one has not acquired a copy by the first of the year, one can use the volume for the previous year, for Sun and star observations, by following the instructions given in the 'Explanations' section of that publication. The error thus introduced should not exceed 0.4. The previous year's almanac cannot be used for the Moon or planets.

Starting with the edition for 1977 an *Almanac for Computers* has been published by the United States Naval Observatory, in Washington. The publication contains ephemeridal information and constants for astronomical and navigational applications in a form suitable for use with digital computers of programmable desk- or hand-calculators. A similar publication is contemplated by the Royal Greenwich Observatory.

IX
Sight Reduction

1. General

In its broadest sense, the expression 'sight reduction' refers to the entire process of converting an astronomical observation or group of observations to position of the observer. A number of ways of making this conversion have been devised. The most common approach is to convert each observation to a position line, and derive the position of the observer from a plot of two or more position lines, adjusted to a common time if necessary. Each observation consists of a timed sextant altitude of an astronomical body. In the usual process of converting these data to a position line one applies needed sextant altitude-corrections, determines from an almanac the body's celestial-equator-system coordinates at the Greenwich meridian at the time of observation, converts these coordinates to similar ones at an assumed local meridian, calculates the body's horizon-system coordinates at an assumed latitude on the assumed local meridian, compares the calculated and observed altitudes, and, with the difference and the calculated azimuth, plots the position line relative to the assumed position. The assumed position might be the dead-reckoning position, an estimated position, or a convenient position selected to simplify the solution.

In a more restricted sense, the expression 'sight reduction' applies to the solution of the navigational triangle for data needed to establish the observer's position. Tables intended primarily for this purpose are called *sight-reduction tables*. To make the calculation by means of conventional tables, one needs to know the latitude of the assumed position for which the horizon-system coordinates are to be determined, the body's hour angle or meridian angle at the meridian of the assumed position, and the body's declination. Sight-reduction tables can be used for solution of any spherical triangle, as in great-circle sailing.

Any astro position line is sometimes called a *Sumner line,* after Thomas H. Sumner, who 'discovered' it in 1837, although, strictly, the expression refers to an astro position line established by identifying two points on the circle of equal altitude and drawing a line through these points, thus establishing a chord of the circular position line. The establishment of an astro position line by comparison of calculated and observed altitudes is often referred to as the *Marcq St. Hilaire method,* after the French naval officer who introduced the concept of circles of equal altitude centred at the sub points of the bodies observed. Because of its universal application, this method has largely replaced all others. It can be used whenever an accurately-timed observation of the altitude of an astronomical body can be made. However, some methods of limited application have utility under favourable conditions.

The large number of methods of sight reduction can be grouped in five classifications: (*1*) 'inspection tables', (*2*) trigonometric methods, (*3*) graphical methods, (*4*) mechanical methods, and (*5*) unconventional methods.

2. Inspection Tables

Modern inspection tables, produced by large computers, generally consist of tabulations, in parallel columns, of altitude and azimuth angle for various entry values of local hour angle or meridian angle, declination, and assumed latitude, with appropriate auxiliary tables to facilitate interpolation. It is customary for each volume to include an explanation of the use of the tables. As convenient inspection tables have become available, other methods of sight reduction have decreased in popularity. The principal disadvantage of inspection tables is their bulk, several large volumes being needed to provide solutions of the large number of spherical triangles involved with three variables.

The inspection tables in common use by British and American mariners are entitled *Sight Reduction Tables for Marine Navigation,* further designated NP 401 in the United

Kingdom, and Pub. No. 229 in the United States. The tables represent collaborative efforts of the Royal Greenwich Observatory, the United States Naval Observatory, and the United States Defense Mapping Agency Hydrographic Topographic Center. The tables are published in identical format by both the British Ministry of Defence as a Hydrographic Department publication and by the United States Defense Mapping Agency Hydrographic Topographic Center.

The tables consist of six volumes, each covering 16° of latitude north and south, with a 1° overlap between volumes. Although designed primarily for use with the Marcq St. Hilaire (intercept) method of sight reduction, the tables can be used for solution of any spherical triangle of which two sides and the included angle are known, including great-circle sailing. For sight reduction, the tables are entered with local hour angle, declination, and latitude. All combinations of these three variables, at intervals of 1°, are included. For each combination, altitude is given to the nearest 0.'1, and azimuth angle to the nearest 0.°1. Also tabulated is the altitude difference (d) between each tabulated value of altitude and the value of tabulated altitude for a declination 1° greater. This difference is used with interpolation tables at the inside front and back covers and facing pages to interpolate for declination. The tables are designed for use with integral degrees of latitude and local hour angle, without interpolation. This is accomplished by selecting an appropriate *assumed position* (*AP*) consisting of the integral degree of latitude (*assumed latitude*, *aL*) nearest the dead-reckoning or estimated position, and the nearest longitude (*assumed longitude*, *aLo*) having a local hour angle of an integral degree. Such an assumed position is sometimes called a *chosen position* (*CP*). In west longitude this assumed meridian has the same number of minutes of arc as GHA, and in east longitude the sum of minutes of longitude and GHA is 60'. If interpolation is desired, as in great-circle sailing, it can be accomplished in the same manner as for declination, the difference being determined by subtraction of consecutive entry values.

Each double-page opening of the main tabulation has entries for $1°$ of LHA in each quadrant, the values being prominently displayed at the top and bottom of each page. Each page has eight groups of columns of figures, one for each degree of latitude. Each volume has two sections, the first for the first eight degrees of latitude of the range of the volume, and the second for the other eight degrees. A separate line is provided for each integral degree of declination from $0°$ to $90°$. Each left-hand page, Fig. 901, has local hour angles of the first and fourth quadrants ($0°–90°$ and $270°–360°$), for declination and latitude of the same name, both north or both south. For LHA $90°$, the right-hand and left-hand pages are identical. For other values of LHA, each right-hand page, Fig. 908, is divided into two parts. The upper part has altitude and azimuth angle tabulations down to altitude $0°$ for values of declination and latitute of contrary name, and LHA of the first and fourth quadrants. The lower part of each right-hand page has tabulations down to altitude $0°$ for values of LHA in the second and third quadrants ($90°–270°$). The two portions of each right-hand page are separated by a horizontal line, called the C–S (contrary-same) line, between entries. Altitude entries beyond the C–S line, either up or down, can be considered negative values (zenith distance more than $90°$).

The interpolation tables, Fig. 902, in the front and back of each volume are entered with the declination increment (Dec Inc), which is the difference between the entering integral value of declination and the actual declination, in the left-hand column, and the altitude difference, d, across the top. Normally, the correction, d corr, is extracted in two parts. The first part, d_1 corr, is found in the column for the tens of altitude difference. The second part, d_2 corr, is for the excess of d over the value used for determining d_1. A separate d_2 corr tabulation is given for each 10 entries ($1'$) of Dec Inc. Units are given across the top and tenths along the left side. When the value of d in the principal table is shown in *italic* type and dotted, Fig. 901, a 'double second difference' (DSD) is determined by taking the difference between the values of d immediately above and below the value for the entry value of

16°, 344° L.H.A. — LATITUDE SAME NAME AS DECLINATION

Dec.	38° Hc	38° d	38° Z	39° Hc	39° d	39° Z	40° Hc	40° d	40° Z	41° Hc	41° d	41° Z	42° Hc	42° d	42° Z	43° Hc	43° d	43° Z
0	49 14.6	+56.5	155.0	48 20.1	+56.7	155.5	47 25.4	+56.9	156.0	46 30.5	+57.1	156.4	45 35.4	+57.4	156.8	44 40.2	+57.5	15
1	50 11.1	56.4	154.5	49 16.8	56.6	155.0	48 22.3	56.9	155.5	47 27.6	57.1	155.9	46 32.8	57.2	156.4	45 37.7	57.4	15
2	51 07.5	56.2	154.0	50 13.4	56.5	154.5	49 19.2	56.7	155.0	48 24.7	56.9	155.5	47 30.0	57.1	155.9	46 35.1	57.3	15
3	52 03.7	56.0	153.4	51 09.9	56.3	154.0	50 15.9	56.5	154.5	49 21.6	56.8	155.0	48 27.1	57.0	155.5	47 32.4	57.2	15
4	52 59.7	55.9	152.8	52 06.2	56.2	153.4	51 12.4	56.4	154.0	50 18.4	56.5	154.5	49 24.1	56.9	155.0	48 29.6	57.1	15
5	53 55.6	+55.6	152.2	53 02.4	+55.9	152.8	52 08.8	+56.3	153.4	51 15.0	+56.6	154.0	50 21.0	+56.8	154.5	49 26.7	+57.0	15
6	54 51.2	55.5	151.6	53 58.3	55.8	152.2	53 05.1	56.1	152.8	52 11.6	56.3	153.4	51 17.8	56.6	154.0	50 23.7	56.9	15
7	55 46.7	55.2	150.9	54 54.1	55.6	151.6	54 01.2	55.9	152.2	53 07.9	56.2	152.9	52 14.4	56.4	153.5	51 20.6	56.7	15
8	56 41.9	55.0	150.2	55 49.7	55.3	150.9	54 57.1	55.7	151.6	54 04.1	56.0	152.3	53 10.8	56.3	152.9	52 17.3	56.6	15
9	57 36.9	54.7	149.4	56 45.0	55.1	150.2	55 52.8	55.4	151.0	55 00.1	55.8	151.7	54 07.1	56.2	152.3	53 13.9	56.4	15
10	58 31.6	+54.4	148.7	57 40.1	+54.9	149.5	56 48.2	+55.3	150.3	55 55.9	+55.6	151.0	55 03.3	+55.9	151.7	54 10.3	+56.2	15
11	59 26.0	54.1	147.9	58 35.0	54.5	148.7	57 43.5	54.9	149.6	56 51.5	55.4	150.3	55 59.2	55.7	151.1	55 06.5	56.1	15
12	60 20.1	53.7	147.0	59 29.5	54.3	147.9	58 38.4	54.7	148.8	57 46.9	55.1	149.6	56 54.9	55.5	150.4	56 02.6	55.8	15
13	61 13.8	53.4	146.1	60 23.8	53.8	147.1	59 33.1	54.4	148.0	58 42.0	54.9	148.9	57 50.4	55.3	149.7	56 58.4	55.7	15
14	62 07.2	52.9	145.1	61 17.6	53.6	146.2	60 27.5	54.1	147.2	59 37.1	54.4	148.1	58 45.7	55.0	149.0	57 54.1	55.3	14
15	63 00.1	+52.4	144.1	62 11.2	+53.0	145.2	61 21.6	+53.6	146.3	60 31.4	+54.2	147.2	59 40.7	+54.7	148.2	58 49.4	+55.2	14
16	63 52.5	52.0	143.0	63 04.2	52.7	144.2	62 15.2	53.3	145.3	61 25.6	53.8	146.4	60 35.4	54.3	147.3	59 44.6	54.8	14
17	64 44.5	51.3	141.8	63 56.9	52.1	143.1	63 08.5	52.8	144.3	62 19.4	53.5	145.4	61 29.7	54.0	146.5	60 39.4	54.5	14
18	65 35.8	50.7	140.6	64 49.0	51.5	142.0	64 01.3	52.3	143.2	63 12.9	53.0	144.4	62 23.7	53.6	145.5	61 33.9	54.2	14
19	66 26.5	50.0	139.3	65 40.5	51.0	140.7	64 53.6	51.8	142.1	64 05.9	52.5	143.3	63 17.3	53.2	144.6	62 28.1	53.8	14
20	67 16.5	+49.2	137.9	66 31.5	+50.2	139.4	65 45.4	+51.1	140.9	64 58.4	+51.9	142.2	64 10.5	+52.7	143.5	63 21.9	+53.4	14
21	68 05.7	48.3	136.4	67 21.7	49.4	138.0	66 36.5	50.5	139.6	65 50.3	51.4	141.0	65 03.2	52.2	142.4	64 15.3	52.9	14
22	68 54.0	47.4	134.8	68 11.1	48.6	136.5	67 27.0	49.7	138.2	66 41.7	50.7	139.8	65 55.4	51.6	141.2	65 08.2	52.4	14
23	69 41.4	46.2	133.0	68 59.7	47.6	134.9	68 16.7	48.8	136.7	67 32.4	49.9	138.4	66 47.0	50.9	139.9	66 00.6	51.8	14
24	70 27.6	45.0	131.2	69 47.3	46.5	133.2	69 05.5	47.9	135.1	68 22.3	49.1	136.9	67 37.9	50.2	138.6	66 52.4	51.1	14
25	71 12.6	+43.6	129.1	70 33.8	+45.3	131.3	69 53.4	+46.8	133.4	69 11.4	+48.2	135.3	68 28.1	+49.3	137.1	67 43.5	+50.5	13
26	71 56.2	42.0	127.0	71 19.1	43.9	129.3	70 40.2	45.5	131.5	69 59.6	47.0	133.6	69 17.4	48.5	135.5	68 34.0	49.6	13
27	72 38.2	40.2	124.6	72 03.0	42.3	127.2	71 25.7	44.2	129.5	70 46.6	45.9	131.8	70 05.9	47.3	133.8	69 23.6	48.7	13
28	73 18.4	38.2	122.1	72 45.3	40.6	124.8	72 09.9	42.7	127.4	71 32.5	44.5	129.8	70 53.2	46.2	132.0	70 12.3	47.7	13
29	73 56.6	36.0	119.4	73 25.9	38.5	122.3	72 52.6	40.9	125.0	72 17.0	43.0	127.6	71 39.4	44.9	130.0	71 00.0	46.5	13
30	74 32.6	+33.5	116.4	74 04.4	+36.4	119.5	73 33.5	+38.9	122.5	73 00.0	+41.3	125.3	72 24.3	+43.3	127.8	71 46.5	+45.2	13
31	75 06.1	30.6	113.2	74 40.8	33.8	116.6	74 12.4	36.7	119.8	73 41.3	39.3	122.7	73 07.6	41.6	125.5	72 31.7	43.7	12
32	75 36.7	27.5	109.8	75 14.6	31.0	113.4	74 49.1	34.2	116.8	74 20.6	37.0	120.0	73 49.2	39.7	123.0	73 15.4	41.9	12
33	76 04.2	24.1	106.2	75 45.6	27.9	110.0	75 23.3	31.4	113.6	74 57.6	34.6	117.0	74 28.9	37.4	120.2	73 57.3	40.1	12
34	76 28.3	20.4	102.3	76 13.5	24.4	106.3	75 54.7	28.2	110.2	75 32.2	31.7	113.8	75 06.3	35.0	117.2	74 37.4	37.8	12
35	76 48.7	+16.3	98.3	76 37.9	+20.6	102.4	76 22.9	+24.8	106.5	76 03.9	+28.6	110.3	75 41.3	+32.1	114.0	75 15.2	+35.3	11
36	77 05.0	12.0	94.0	76 58.5	16.6	98.3	76 47.7	20.9	102.5	76 32.5	25.1	106.6	76 13.4	29.0	110.5	75 50.5	32.5	11
37	77 17.0	7.4	89.6	77 15.1	12.2	94.0	77 08.6	16.8	98.4	76 57.6	21.3	102.7	76 42.4	25.4	106.8	76 23.0	29.4	11
38	77 24.4	+2.9	85.1	77 27.3	7.6	89.5	77 25.4	12.4	94.0	77 18.9	17.1	98.5	77 07.8	21.6	102.8	76 52.4	25.8	10
39	77 27.3	-1.9	80.5	77 34.9	2.9	84.9	77 37.8	7.8	89.5	77 36.0	12.6	94.0	77 29.4	17.3	98.5	77 18.2	21.9	10
40	77 25.4	-6.5	75.9	77 37.8	-1.8	80.3	77 45.6	+3.0	84.8	77 48.6	+7.9	89.5	77 46.7	+12.9	94.1	77 40.1	+17.6	98
41	77 18.9	11.1	71.3	77 36.0	6.6	75.6	77 48.6	1.9	80.1	77 56.5	3.1	84.7	77 59.6	8.0	89.4	77 57.7	13.1	94
42	77 07.8	15.4	66.9	77 29.4	11.2	71.0	77 46.7	6.6	75.4	77 59.6	1.9	79.9	78 07.6	3.2	84.6	78 10.8	8.2	89
43	76 52.4	19.5	62.6	77 18.2	15.6	66.5	77 40.1	11.3	70.7	77 57.7	6.7	75.1	78 10.8	1.9	79.8	78 19.0	3.2	84
44	76 32.9	23.4	58.5	77 02.6	19.8	62.2	77 28.8	15.8	66.1	77 51.0	11.5	70.4	78 08.9	6.8	74.9	78 22.2	1.9	79
45	76 09.5	-26.8	54.6	76 42.8	-23.6	58.0	77 13.0	-20.0	61.7	77 39.5	-16.0	65.8	78 02.1	-11.7	70.1	78 20.3	-6.9	74
46	75 42.7	30.1	50.9	76 19.2	27.1	54.1	76 53.0	23.9	57.5	77 23.5	20.2	61.3	77 50.4	16.2	65.4	78 13.4	11.8	69
47	75 12.6	32.9	47.4	75 52.1	30.4	50.3	76 29.1	27.5	53.5	77 03.3	24.2	57.0	77 34.2	20.5	60.9	78 01.6	16.5	65
48	74 39.7	35.5	44.2	75 21.7	33.2	46.9	76 01.6	30.4	49.8	76 39.1	27.8	53.0	77 13.7	24.5	56.7	77 45.1	20.8	60
49	74 04.2	37.8	41.2	74 48.5	35.8	43.6	75 31.0	33.6	46.3	76 11.3	31.0	49.2	76 49.2	28.1	52.5	77 24.3	24.8	56
50	73 26.4	-39.8	38.4	74 12.7	-38.1	40.6	74 57.4	-36.1	43.1	75 40.3	-33.9	45.7	76 21.1	-31.3	48.7	76 59.5	-28.5	51
51	72 46.6	41.6	35.9	73 34.6	40.1	37.8	74 21.3	38.4	40.0	75 06.4	36.4	42.4	75 49.8	34.3	45.1	76 31.0	31.7	48
52	72 05.0	43.3	33.5	72 54.5	42.0	35.3	73 42.9	40.5	37.2	74 30.0	38.8	39.4	75 15.5	36.8	41.8	75 59.3	34.6	44
53	71 21.7	44.7	31.3	72 12.5	43.5	32.9	73 02.4	42.2	34.7	73 51.2	40.8	36.6	74 38.7	39.1	38.8	75 24.7	37.3	41
54	70 37.0	46.0	29.2	71 29.0	45.0	30.7	72 20.2	43.9	32.3	73 10.4	42.6	34.0	73 59.6	41.2	36.0	74 47.4	39.4	38
55	69 51.0	-47.1	27.3	70 44.0	-46.2	28.6	71 36.3	-45.3	30.1	72 27.8	-44.1	31.6	73 18.4	-42.9	33.4	74 08.0	-41.5	35
56	69 03.9	48.1	25.6	69 57.8	47.4	26.7	70 51.0	46.5	28.0	71 43.7	45.6	29.4	72 35.5	44.5	31.0	73 26.5	43.3	32
57	68 15.8	49.1	23.9	69 10.4	48.4	25.0	70 04.5	47.6	26.1	70 58.1	46.8	27.4	71 51.0	45.8	28.8	72 43.2	44.8	30
58	67 26.7	49.8	22.4	68 22.0	49.2	23.3	69 16.9	48.4	24.4	70 11.3	47.9	25.5	71 05.2	47.1	26.8	71 58.4	46.2	28
59	66 36.9	50.6	21.0	67 32.8	50.1	21.8	68 28.3	49.5	22.8	69 23.4	48.9	23.8	70 18.1	48.2	24.9	71 12.2	47.4	26
60	65 46.3	-51.2	19.6	66 42.7	-50.8	20.4	67 38.8	-50.3	21.2	68 34.5	-49.7	22.2	69 29.9	-49.1	23.2	70 24.8	-48.4	24
61	64 55.1	51.8	18.4	65 51.9	51.4	19.1	66 48.5	51.0	19.8	67 44.8	50.5	20.7	68 40.8	50.0	21.6	69 36.4	49.4	22
62	64 03.3	52.3	17.2	65 00.5	52.0	17.8	65 57.5	51.6	18.5	66 54.3	51.2	19.3	67 50.8	50.7	20.1	68 47.0	50.2	21
63	63 11.0	52.9	16.1	64 08.5	52.5	16.7	65 05.9	52.2	17.3	66 03.1	51.8	18.0	67 00.1	51.5	18.7	67 56.8	51.0	19
64	62 18.1	53.2	15.1	63 16.0	53.0	15.6	64 13.7	52.7	16.1	65 11.3	52.4	16.7	66 08.6	52.0	17.4	67 05.8	51.7	18
65	61 24.9	-53.7	14.1	62 23.0	-53.4	14.6	63 21.0	-53.1	15.1	64 18.9	-52.9	15.6	65 16.6	-52.6	16.2	66 14.1	-52.2	16
66	60 31.2	54.0	13.2	61 29.6	53.8	13.6	62 27.9	53.6	14.0	63 26.0	53.3	14.5	64 24.0	53.0	15.0	65 21.9	52.8	15
67	59 37.2	54.3	12.3	60 35.8	54.2	12.7	61 34.3	54.0	13.1	62 32.7	53.8	13.5	63 31.0	53.5	14.0	64 29.1	53.2	14
68	58 42.9	54.7	11.5	59 41.6	54.4	11.8	60 40.3	54.3	12.2	61 38.9	54.1	12.6	62 37.5	54.0	13.0	63 35.9	53.7	13
69	57 48.2	54.9	10.7	58 47.2	54.8	11.0	59 46.0	54.6	11.3	60 44.8	54.4	11.7	61 43.5	54.2	12.0	62 42.2	54.1	12
70	56 53.3	-55.2	9.9	57 52.4	-55.1	10.2	58 51.4	-54.9	10.5	59 50.4	-54.8	10.8	60 49.3	-54.6	11.1	61 48.1	-54.4	11
71	55 58.1	55.4	9.2	56 57.3	55.3	9.5	57 56.5	55.2	9.7	58 55.6	55.1	10.0	59 54.7	55.0	10.3	60 53.7	54.8	10
72	55 02.7	55.6	8.5	56 02.0	55.5	8.8	57 01.3	55.4	9.0	58 00.5	55.3	9.3	58 59.7	55.1	9.5	59 58.9	55.1	9
73	54 07.1	55.8	7.9	55 06.5	55.2	8.1	56 05.9	55.7	8.3	57 05.2	55.6	8.5	58 04.6	55.5	8.8	59 03.8	55.3	9
74	53 11.3	56.0	7.3	54 10.8	56.0	7.5	55 10.2	55.8	7.6	56 09.7	55.8	7.8	57 09.1	55.6	8.1	58 08.5	55.6	9

FIG. 901. Part of left-hand page of NP 401/Pub. No. 229.

Dec. Inc.	Tens 10'	20'	30'	40'	50'	Decimals ↓	Units 0'	1'	2'	3'	4'	5'	6'	7'	8'	9'	Double Second Diff. and Corr.
44.0	7.3	14.6	22.0	29.3	36.6	.0	0.0	0.7	1.5	2.2	3.0	3.7	4.4	5.2	5.9	6.7	1.1
44.1	7.3	14.7	22.0	29.4	36.7	.1	0.1	0.8	1.6	2.3	3.0	3.8	4.5	5.3	6.0	6.7	3.2 0.1
44.2	7.3	14.7	22.1	29.4	36.8	.2	0.1	0.9	1.6	2.4	3.1	3.9	4.6	5.3	6.1	6.8	5.3 0.2
44.3	7.4	14.8	22.1	29.5	36.9	.3	0.2	1.0	1.7	2.4	3.2	3.9	4.7	5.4	6.2	6.9	7.5 0.3
44.4	7.4	14.8	22.2	29.6	37.0	.4	0.3	1.0	1.8	2.5	3.3	4.0	4.7	5.5	6.2	7.0	9.6 0.4
44.5	7.4	14.8	22.3	29.7	37.1	.5	0.4	1.1	1.9	2.6	3.3	4.1	4.8	5.6	6.3	7.0	11.7 0.5
44.6	7.4	14.9	22.3	29.7	37.2	.6	0.4	1.2	1.9	2.7	3.4	4.2	4.9	5.6	6.4	7.1	13.9 0.6
44.7	7.5	14.9	22.4	29.8	37.3	.7	0.5	1.3	2.0	2.7	3.5	4.2	5.0	5.7	6.5	7.2	16.0 0.7
44.8	7.5	15.0	22.4	29.9	37.4	.8	0.6	1.3	2.1	2.8	3.6	4.3	5.0	5.8	6.5	7.3	18.1 0.8
44.9	7.5	15.0	22.5	30.0	37.5	.9	0.7	1.4	2.2	2.9	3.6	4.4	5.1	5.9	6.6	7.3	20.3 0.9
45.0	7.5	15.0	22.5	30.0	37.5	.0	0.0	0.8	1.5	2.3	3.0	3.8	4.5	5.3	6.1	6.8	22.4 1.0
45.1	7.5	15.0	22.5	30.0	37.6	.1	0.1	0.8	1.6	2.4	3.1	3.9	4.6	5.4	6.1	6.9	24.5 1.1
45.2	7.5	15.0	22.6	30.1	37.6	.2	0.2	0.9	1.7	2.4	3.2	3.9	4.7	5.5	6.2	7.0	26.7 1.2
45.3	7.5	15.1	22.6	30.2	37.7	.3	0.2	1.0	1.7	2.5	3.3	4.0	4.8	5.5	6.3	7.1	28.8 1.3
45.4	7.6	15.1	22.7	30.3	37.8	.4	0.3	1.1	1.8	2.6	3.3	4.1	4.9	5.6	6.4	7.1	30.9 1.4
45.5	7.6	15.2	22.8	30.3	37.9	.5	0.4	1.1	1.9	2.7	3.4	4.2	4.9	5.7	6.4	7.2	33.1 1.5
45.6	7.6	15.2	22.8	30.4	38.0	.6	0.5	1.2	2.0	2.7	3.5	4.2	5.0	5.8	6.5	7.3	35.2 1.6
45.7	7.6	15.3	22.9	30.5	38.1	.7	0.5	1.3	2.0	2.8	3.6	4.3	5.1	5.8	6.6	7.4	
45.8	7.7	15.3	22.9	30.6	38.2	.8	0.6	1.4	2.1	2.9	3.6	4.4	5.2	5.9	6.7	7.4	
45.9	7.7	15.3	23.0	30.6	38.3	.9	0.7	1.4	2.2	3.0	3.7	4.5	5.2	6.0	6.7	7.5	
46.0	7.6	15.3	23.0	30.6	38.3	.0	0.0	0.8	1.5	2.3	3.1	3.9	4.6	5.4	6.2	7.0	1.2
46.1	7.7	15.3	23.0	30.7	38.4	.1	0.1	0.9	1.6	2.4	3.2	4.0	4.7	5.5	6.3	7.1	3.5 0.1
46.2	7.7	15.4	23.1	30.8	38.5	.2	0.2	0.9	1.7	2.5	3.3	4.0	4.8	5.6	6.4	7.1	5.8 0.2
46.3	7.7	15.4	23.1	30.9	38.6	.3	0.2	1.0	1.8	2.6	3.3	4.1	4.9	5.7	6.4	7.2	8.1 0.3
46.4	7.7	15.5	23.2	30.9	38.7	.4	0.3	1.1	1.9	2.6	3.4	4.2	5.0	5.7	6.5	7.3	10.5 0.4
46.5	7.8	15.5	23.3	31.0	38.8	.5	0.4	1.2	1.9	2.7	3.5	4.3	5.0	5.8	6.6	7.4	12.8 0.5
46.6	7.8	15.5	23.3	31.1	38.8	.6	0.5	1.2	2.0	2.8	3.6	4.3	5.1	5.9	6.7	7.4	15.1 0.6
46.7	7.8	15.6	23.4	31.2	38.9	.7	0.5	1.3	2.1	2.9	3.6	4.4	5.2	6.0	6.7	7.5	17.4 0.7
46.8	7.8	15.6	23.4	31.2	39.0	.8	0.6	1.4	2.2	2.9	3.7	4.5	5.3	6.0	6.8	7.6	19.8 0.8
46.9	7.9	15.7	23.5	31.3	39.1	.9	0.7	1.5	2.2	3.0	3.8	4.6	5.3	6.1	6.9	7.7	22.1 0.9
47.0	7.8	15.6	23.5	31.3	39.1	.0	0.0	0.8	1.6	2.4	3.2	4.0	4.7	5.5	6.3	7.1	24.4 1.0
47.1	7.8	15.7	23.5	31.4	39.2	.1	0.1	0.9	1.7	2.5	3.2	4.0	4.8	5.6	6.4	7.2	26.7 1.1
47.2	7.8	15.7	23.6	31.4	39.3	.2	0.2	0.9	1.7	2.5	3.3	4.1	4.9	5.7	6.5	7.3	29.1 1.2
47.3	7.9	15.8	23.6	31.5	39.4	.3	0.2	1.0	1.8	2.6	3.4	4.2	5.0	5.8	6.6	7.4	31.4 1.3
47.4	7.9	15.8	23.7	31.6	39.5	.4	0.3	1.1	1.9	2.7	3.5	4.3	5.1	5.9	6.6	7.4	33.7 1.4
																	36.0 1.5

FIG. 902. Part of the interpolation table of NP 401/Pub. No. 229.

declination. This D S D is used in the interpolation table for finding a third part of the correction, d_3, which is tabulated in a critical table to the right of the tabulations for d_1 and d_2 corrections. For strictest accuracy, the d_3 correction should always be applied, but if it is neglected when d is not printed in *italics* and dotted, the error thus introduced is generally negligible, and is rarely as large as 0'.2. The d_3 correction is always positive.

Having determined the declination of the body, and its LHA for an assumed position, one proceeds as follows:

1. Select the volume and section having tabulations for the assumed latitude.

2. Open to the pages for the LHA.
3. Select the left-hand or right-hand page according to LHA and whether the declination and latitude are of same or contrary name.
4. Select the column group headed by the assumed latitude.
5. Select the line for the integral value of declination, a dec. If declination of the body is not an integral degree, use the next smaller value, regardless of the number of minutes. Thus, if declination is $12°56'.8$, use $12°$. The minutes of declination, in this example $56'.8$, constitute the declination increment (Dec Inc) used for entering the interpolation table.
6. Record (a) the tabulated calculated altitude (Tab Hc); (b) altitude difference (d) with its tabulated sign; (c) double second difference (DSD) if the tabulated d is printed in *italics* and dotted; (d) tabulated azimuth angle (Tab Z); and (e) the azimuth angle difference (Z diff), the difference between the tabulated azimuth angle and the value on the next line below it in the column ($1°$ greater declination), with its sign determined by inspection.
7. Select the appropriate interpolation table on the inside front cover or facing page if Dec Inc has a value of $0'.0$ to $31'.9$, or on the inside back cover or facing page if Dec Inc has a value of $28'.0$ to $59'.9$. If d has a value of $60'.0$, no interpolation table is needed because d corr is then identical with Dec Inc.
8. Find Dec Inc in the left-hand column, and on the same line find d_1 corr in the column for the tens of d. Give d_1 corr the sign of d.
9. In the next tabulation to the right, find d_2 corr in the column for units of d, on the line for tenths of a minute of arc. Give d_2 corr the sign of d.
10. If DSD has been recorded, enter the critical double second difference correction table for the entry value of Dec Inc, and extract d_3 corr, which is always positive.
11. Determine azimuth angle correction (Z corr) in the same manner as the d_2 corr (d_1 corr plus d_2 corr if Z diff is sufficiently large), and give it the sign of Z diff. If the interpolation tables are entered with minutes of arc, the

408

corrections are in minutes of arc, as shown, but if the tables are entered with degrees, the corrections are in degrees.

12. Apply d_1, d_2, and d_3 corrections in accordance with their signs (add algebraically) to Tab Hc to determine calculated altitude (Hc).

13. Apply Z corr in accordance with its sign (add algebraically) to Tab Z to determine Z.

14. Convert azimuth angle (Z) to azimuth (Zn) in accordance with instructions (not shown in illustration) given on each double page. That is, in north latitude, Zn = Z if LHA is greater than 180°, and Zn = 360° − Z if LHA is less than 180°; and in south latitude, Zn = 180° − Z if LHA is greater than 180°, and Zn = 180° + Z if LHA is less than 180°.

Suppose it is desired to determine Hc and Zn by NP 401/Pub. No. 229 for the following data: DR lat 41°53′4 N., DR long 51°18′3 W., GHA 67°33′2, dec 46°45′7 N. (a fictitious body). First, one determines the entering arguments. The assumed latitude is the *nearest* integral degree of latitude to the DR position, or 42° N. The declination is 46°45′7 N., as given. The LHA = GHA − aLo (W.) = 67°33′2 − 51°33′2 W. = 16°. With these values, one is ready to follow the steps of solution by NP 401/Pub. No. 229. Refer to Figs. 901 and 902.

1. Volume 3 covers the latitude range 30° to 45°, and latitude 42° is included in the second section of the volume (for latitude 38° to 45°).

2. The tabulations for LHA 16° are given on pages 216 and 217 (page number not shown in Fig. 901).

3. Latitude and declination both being north, of same name, and LHA 16° being in the first quadrant, the left-hand page (p. 216) is selected.

4. The column group headed by 42°, the assumed latitude, is selected.

5. The *a* dec is 46°, the integral value next smaller than the declination. The Dec Inc is 45′7.

6. The tabulated values extracted are: Tab Hc 77°50′4, d (−) 16′2, DSD 20′5 − 11′7 = 8′8, Tab Z 65°4, Z diff 65°4 − 60°9 = 4°5, recorded (−) 4°5 because tabulated Z

decreases with increasing dec. Note that for Tab dec 43°
the DSD is the difference between $(+)$ 3$'$.2 and $(-)$ 6$'$.8, or
10$'$.0.

7. The left portion of the interpolation table on the inside
back cover has tabulations for Dec Inc 45$'$.7.

8. On the line for Dec Inc 45$'$.7, in the column headed 10$'$ (the
tens of d), the value of d_1 corr is found to be 7$'$.6. It is
recorded $(-)$ 7$'$.6 to agree with the sign of d.

9. In the next tabulation to the right, in the column headed 6$'$
(the units of d), on the line for 0$'$.2 (the tenths of a minute of
d), the value of d_2 corr is found to be 4$'$.7. It is recorded $(-)$
4$'$.7 to agree with the sign of d.

10. In the critical table for the double second difference
correction, for DSD 8$'$.8, the d_3 corr is found to be 0$'$.4,
recorded $(+)$ 0$'$.4 because DSD correction is always
positive.

11. In the tabulation used for determining the d_2 corr, in the
column headed 4$'$, on the line for 0$'$.5, the value of Z corr is
found to be 3°.4. It is recorded $(-)$ 3°.4 because Z diff is
negative. The correction is in degrees, not minutes of arc as
shown in the table, because degrees are used for entering
the table.

12. Applying the three parts of the d correction algebraically
to Tab Hc, one finds Hc to be 77°50$'$.4 $-$ 7$'$.6 $-$ 4$'$.7 $+$
0$'$.4 $=$ 77°38$'$.5.

13. Applying Z corr to Tab Z, one finds Z to be
65°.4 $-$ 3°.4 $=$ 62°.0.

14. The observer is in north latitude, and LHA is less than
180°. Therefore, Zn $=$ 360° $-$ Z $=$ 360° $-$ 62°.0 $=$ 298°.0.
The solution can be arranged as follows:

GHA 67 33$'$.2		DR L 41 53$'$.4 N.
a Lo 51 33$'$.2 W.	dec 46°45$'$.7 N.	DR Lo 51 18$'$.3 W.
LHA 16°	*a* dec 46° N. Dec Inc 45$'$.7	*a* L 42 00$'$.0 N.

Tab Hc 77°50$'$.4	d $(-)$ 16$'$.2 DSD 8$'$.8 Z diff $(-)$ 4$'$.5	Tab Z 65°.4
d_1 corr $(-)$ 7$'$.6		Z corr $(-)$ 3°.4
d_2 corr $(-)$ 4$'$.7		Z N. 62.0 W.
d_3 corr $(+)$ 0$'$.4		Zn 298°.0
Hc 77°38$'$.5		

The Hc determined in this manner is compared with Ho to

determine the intercept (a) for use with Zn for plotting the position line. The intercept is measured from the assumed position (AP) toward or away from the azimuth, depending upon whether Hc is smaller or larger than Ho.

If it is desired to use the dead reckoning, estimated, or some other position as the AP such that the assumed latitude and LHA are not integral values, the Hc determined as above is further interpolated for the increments of latitude and LHA. Thus, in the example given above, suppose the Hc and Z are desired for the dead-reckoning position. The latitude increment is the difference between the assumed latitude shown above and the actual latitude, or $42° - 41°53.4 = 6.6$. From the main table of NP 401/Pub. No. 229, Fig. 901, the tabulated Hc and Z for latitude 41°, declination 46°, are $77°23.5$ and 61.3, respectively, and the differences between the values for latitude 42°, declination 46°, and these values are $(-)26.9$ and $(-)4.1$, respectively. Using these values for entering the interpolation tables in the same manner as for declination (this part of the interpolation table is not shown in Fig. 902), one finds the corrections to be $(-)2.9$ for Hc, and $(-)0.4$ for Z. Using similar procedure for LHA, which in this case is $16°$ 14.9, and the values of Hc and Z for latitude 42°, declination 46°, same name, and LHA 17° (not shown in Fig. 901), one finds the differences to be $(-)40.6$ for Tab Hc, and $(+)0.7$ for Tab Z. The corrections are $(-)10.1$ for altitude, and $(+)0.2$ for azimuth angle. Applying these corrections to the Hc and Z found in the example above one finds Hc at the DR position to be $77°38.5 - 2.9 - 10.1 = 77°25.5$, and Z to be $62.0 - 0.4 + 0.2 = 61.8$. The azimuth, then, is $360° - 61.8 = 298.2$.

A somewhat simpler, graphical solution for the correction to Hc for latitude and LHA increments is possible. The azimuth line is drawn from the chosen position, and a perpendicular is dropped from the position for which Hc is desired to this azimuth line. The correction in minutes of arc is the distance in nautical miles from the chosen position to the foot of the perpendicular, positive if an extension of the azimuth line in the reciprocal direction is needed, and negative if it is not.

When the altitude is high, as in this example, the curvature of the small-circle position line might be a consideration. This situation is discussed in section 7.

A set of inspection tables somewhat similar to the NP 401/Pub. No. 229 tables, previously published in both the United Kingdom and the United States, is entitled *Tables of Computed Altitude and Azimuth*, and further designated HD 486 in the United Kingdom, and Pub. No. 214 in the United States. A Spanish edition with identical tables has been published in Spain. These tables have been largely replaced by the *Sight Reduction Tables for Marine Navigation*, but because of the large number of the older tables distributed, a brief description of them is included here.

The British edition of HD 486 is arranged in six volumes, each covering 15° of latitude, while the United States edition of Pub. No. 214 is arranged in nine volumes, each covering 10° of latitude. The main tables are identical in the two editions.

The entry arguments in HD 486/Pub. No. 214 are assumed latitude consisting of the integral degree nearest the dead reckoning or estimated position; meridian angle (not LHA), labelled 'H.A.', in integral degrees; and declination. Latitude and meridian angle entries are in increments of 1°. Declination entries are in increments of 0°.5 from 0° to 29°, to accommodate bodies of the solar system; for greater values of declination, 37 entries, each an integral or half degree, are given to accommodate the stars listed on the daily pages of the *Nautical Almanac* and most of the additional stars listed near the back of the almanac.

A group of 12 double-page tables are provided for each 1° of latitude. Each page has eight vertical sections, each one having tabulations for one declination entry. Each line is for 1° of meridian angle. Each left-hand page has meridian-angle entries for declination and latitude of the same name, with a maximum of 91 entries (0° to 90°). The right-hand pages have the same declination entries as the left-hand pages. Most right-hand pages are for declination and latitude of contrary name, with the overflow of same-name entries for meridian angles of more than 90°, if any, below the contrary-name entries. At higher values of declination and latitude there may be no contrary-name entries.

In the main tables, four quantities are tabulated for each entry of the three variables. The first is tabulated altitude, labelled 'Alt'. The second is the change of altitude for a change of 1′ of declination, labelled 'Δd'. The third is the change of altitude for a change of 1′ of meridian angle, labelled 'Δt'. The fourth is the azimuth angle, labelled 'Az'. These four quantities are given for all entries of the three variables in which the altitude is 5° or greater. Altitude is given to the nearest 0′.1, Δd and Δt to the nearest 0′.01, and azimuth angle to the nearest 0°.1.

The main table is entered with the *nearest* tabulated value of each entering argument, and the sign of the interpolation corrections derived from Δd and Δt are determined by inspection of adjacent values of altitude in the main tables. The usual method of using the tables is to select an assumed position such that latitude and meridian angle are integral degrees, as with the NP 401/Pub. No. 229 tables, and interpolate for declination increment only, using a 'multiplication table' on the inside back cover and facing page of each volume. If interpolation for the other two entering values is desired, Δt and the same multiplication table are used for the meridian-angle increment, and an additional table on the two pages preceding the multiplication table is used for the latitude increment. Instructions regarding the sign of latitude increment correction are given at the bottom of the table. Azimuth angle is interpolated, if desired, by inspection of consecutive entries. Azimuth angle is converted to azimuth by giving azimuth angle a prefix N. or S. to agree with the latitude of the observer (or declination of the body if latitude 0° is used for entering the tables), and E. or W. to agree with the meridian angle. One then follows the instructions of the labels, N. representing 000° or 360°, and S. representing 180°; while the label E. indicates the azimuth angle is to be added to 000° or subtracted from 180° and W. indicates that azimuth angle is to be subtracted from 360° or added to 180°.

A two-page star-identification table follows each main-table latitude section. A speed–time–distance table is given on the inside front cover and facing page, followed on the next page by a table for conversion of arc to time. Detailed instructions for use of the tables are given in each volume.

A third set of inspection tables, designed particularly for aviators, is entitled *Sight Reduction Tables for Air Navigation*, and further designated AP 3270 in the United Kingdom, and Pub. No. 249 in the United States. The main tables of the two editions are identical.

The tables consist of three volumes, Volume I being for selected stars, and Volumes II and III for bodies of the solar system. In Volume I, the entering arguments are latitude to the nearest integral degree, LHA Υ to the nearest integral degree (nearest *even* degree for latitudes greater than 69°), and the name of the star. A separate list of seven stars is given for each 15 entries of LHA Υ. Because of precession of the equinoxes and nutation (p. 288), the tabulated data becomes inaccurate with the passage of time. Accordingly, a new edition of Volume I is published at five-year intervals, and each edition has a table of corrections *to be applied to the fix* in years other than that for which the data are computed. The data extracted are tabulated Hc to the nearest 1', and azimuth (not azimuth angle) to the nearest 1°. No interpolation is needed. A two-page opening is adquate for all entries for each 1° of latitude from 69° N. to 69° S. For latitudes 70° to 89°, one page is adequate for each 1° of latitude. Various tables of auxiliary data are included. The method is somewhat shorter than the others described above, but is of less precision, and is limited to the seven stars for which data are tabulated. One may sometimes be under the necessity of determining the approximate LHA Υ in advance, to be sure of observing stars that are tabulated. Any star having a declination of not more than 29° can be used with Volumes II or III.

Volumes II and III are in many respects similar to NP 401/Pub. No. 229. Entering arguments are the nearest integral degree of latitude, integral degree (*even* degree for latitudes 70° to 89°) of LHA of the body, and integral degree of declination equal to or next smaller than the actual declination. Data extracted from the tables are tabulated Hc to the nearest 1′; d, the difference (including sign) between the tabulated altitude and the altitude for declination 1° greater; and azimuth angle to the nearest 1°. An auxiliary table for interpolation of altitude for declination increment is provided on the page facing the inside back cover. Volume and page selection are by latitude. Volume II is for latitudes 0° to 39°, and Volume III is for latitudes 40° to 89°. Column selection is by declination, separate sections being provided, in order, for declination 0° to 14° same name as latitude, 0° to 14° contrary name, 15° to 29° same name, and 15° to 29° contrary name. Line selection is by LHA. Data are tabulated for entry arguments having any altitude from the zenith to several degrees below the celestial horizon, zenith distances greater than 90° being shown as negative altitudes. Rules for converting Z to Zn are given on each page. Auxiliary tables of useful data are included.

Each volume has detailed instructions for its use. All volumes are designed primarily for use with the *Air Almanac*, but they can be used with the *Nautical Almanac*.

Inspection tables are by no means a recent innovation. The desirability of such tables has long been recognized, but the enormous task involved in trigonometric calculation, checking, typesetting and proof reading, before the development of large computers and modern reproduction techniques, served as a deterrent. Some indication of the size of the task can be gained by realizing that the NP 401/Pub. No. 229 tables represent the solution of approximately one and one half million spherical triangles for two quantities, in addition to the computation of the d value for each triangle. The first volume of HD 486/Pub. No. 214 printed was produced by calculation using tables of trigonometric functions, each triangle being solved independently by two persons as a check on accuracy. Although all reasonable care was exercised in the production, some errors were found in the printed book. With modern methods, errors are rare.

Because of the magnitude of the task of producing inspection tables before the availability of modern aids, early attempts were usually limited in scope. They generally

415

suffered, also, from the absence of a simple means of interpolation, especially those requiring triple interpolation before the introduction of the assumed-position concept early in the twentieth century. Before the intercept approach introduced by Marcq St. Hilaire became fully established in relatively recent times, it was not uncommon for navigators to regard the establishment of position as separate problems of determining latitude and longitude, and azimuth was not a part of the calculation. Accordingly, the need for calculated azimuth was related to other uses, notably the determination of compass error. Because of this situation, and the fact that calculation of azimuth is a relatively simple operation, inspection tables of azimuth only, often related specifically to the Sun, as by the use of local apparent time as an entering argument, came into common use well before the emergence of the modern universal-application inspection tables providing tabulations, in parallel columns, of calculated altitude and azimuth. Because of the notorious conservatism of mariners and their reputed reluctance to abandon an older, well-established method in which they have confidence, in favour of a newer method until its reliability and superiority have been established, and the fact that the modern tables described above are a relatively recent innovation, some of the older tables may be encountered. Explanation of their use generally accompany the tables, and may also be found in older texts.

3. Trigonometric Methods

Trigonometric methods involve calculations for solution of the navigational triangle by means of spherical trigonometry. The basic equations are:

$$\sin Hc = \sin L \sin d + \cos L \cos d \cos t,$$

$$\sin Z = \cos d \sin t \sec Hc,$$

in which Hc is calculated altitude, L is latitude, d is declination, t is meridian angle, and Z is azimuth angle.

When azimuth angle is calculated by the second equation, it is reckoned from *either* north or south, depending upon

416

which is nearer. In many cases one can tell the quadrant by noting the position of the body when the observation is made. However, if the body is near the prime vertical, reasonable doubt may exist. One method of resolving this ambiguity is to determine the meridian angle or altitude when the body is on the prime vertical, and comparing this value with the actual value. The prime vertical values can be calculated by the equations:

$$\cos t = \tan d \cot L,$$

$$\sin Hc = \sin d \csc L.$$

The azimuth angle should be labelled N. or S. to agree with latitude if t is greater or Hc is less than the values when the body is on the prime vertical. Azimuth angle should be given contrary name to the latitude if t is less or Hc is greater than the prime vertical value. Tables and graphs showing the prime vertical values have been published.

The basic equations for Hc and Z require strict attention to the signs of the values in various quadrants. To avoid possible error because of ambiguity or an incorrect sign, navigators using trigonometric solutions have generally preferred the use of haversines, which increase from $0°$ to $180°$ without change of sign. The applicable equations are:

$$hav \; z = hav \; (L \sim d) + \cos L \cos d \; hav \; t,$$

$$hav \; Z = \sec L \sec Hc \; [hav \; p - hav \; (L \sim Hc)],$$

in which z is zenith distance $(90° - Hc)$, p is polar distance $(90° - d$ for L and d same name, $90° + d$ for L and d contrary name), and the symbol $\sim$ means the algebraic difference. The other notation is the same as before. By this solution, Z is given a prefix to agree with the latitude and a suffix to agree with the meridian angle.

Another method of finding azimuth is by means of amplitude (p. 299), which is similar to azimuth angle but is reckoned from the prime vertical (p. 299) rather than from the meridian. Its use is normally confined to checking compass error by means of an astronomical body, usually the Sun, when it is on the horizon. Amplitudes of bodies when their *centres* are on the *celestial* horizon are tabulated in some books of nautical tables, or they can be calculated by the equation:

$$\sin A = \sec L \sin d,$$

in which A is the amplitude, L is the latitude, and d is the declination.

The centre of the Sun is on the celestial horizon when its lower limb is approximately two thirds of a Sun diameter above the visible horizon. Its position varies slightly with height of eye of the observer above the sea surface. The centre of the Moon is on the celestial horizon when its upper limb is about on the visible horizon. Stars and planets are on the celestial horizon when they are little more than one Sun or Moon diameter above the visible horizon.

Amplitude is converted to azimuth by giving it a prefix of E. if it is rising, and W. if it is setting, and a suffix N. or S. to agree with its delination, and following the instructions of the labels.

Books of nautical tables having amplitudes generally include an additional table of corrections to be applied if the body is observed when its centre is on the visible horizon. Alternatively, its azimuth angle at this time can be calculated by the equation:

$$\cos Z = \sec Hc \sec L \, (\sin d + \sin Hc \sin L),$$

in which Hc is the altitude, L is the latitude, and d is the declination. The altitude is the algebraic sum of dip (negative), refraction at the negative altitude of the dip (negative), and horizontal parallax (positive).

A large number of 'short methods' have been devised to facilitate sight reduction. These methods consist of convenient arrangements of tabulated data and applicable 'rules' for the calculation. While some of the methods use the undivided triangle, perhaps with some transformation of the equations, the more common approach has been to divide the triangle into two right spherical triangle by dropping a perpendicular from one vertex to the opposite side, extended if necessary.

If the perpendicular is dropped from the zenith to the hour circle, the azimuth angle becomes divided and is determined in two parts, which are added together. This approach, which has been most popular, is used in the British *Rapid Navigation Tables* by W. Myerscough and W. Hamilton, the *Hughes Tables for Sea and Air Navigation* largely devised by P. V. H. Weems and compiled and designed by L. J. Comrie; the American *Line of Position Book* by P. V. H. Weems, *Navigation Tables for Mariners and Aviators* by J. Y. Dreisonstok, and the *Manual of Celestial Navigation* by Arthur A. Ageton; the French *Tables du Point Auxiliaire* by F. Souillagout (the first to drop a perpendicular from the zenith); and the Japanese *New Altitude and Azimuth Tables* by Sinkiti Ogura; among others. The Weems tables provide a diagram for finding azimuth angle, and an auxiliary diagram for resolving the prime vertical ambiguity.

If the perpendicular is dropped from the body to the meridian, the parallactic angle (p. 308), which is not computed, is divided. The American *Dead Reckoning Altitude and Azimuth Table* by Arthur A. Ageton, and the Brazilian *Altitude and Azimuth Tables* by Radler de Aquino are among those using this approach. The Ageton tables became particularly popular because of the claim that interpolation was unnecessary.

If the perpendicular is dropped from the elevated pole to the vertical circle, both the meridian angle and zenith distance or altitude are divided into two parts. This has not been an attractive alternative, except in great-circle sailing. The only known published tables using this approach are the Yugoslavian *Tables for the Abbreviated Computation of Zenith Distance and Azimuth of Celestial Bodies* by Frane Flego.

The attraction of 'short methods' has been the convenience of their arrangement, and their small bulk, one small volume containing the tables, explanation, and instructions for their use, including the necessary 'rules'. Some methods, however, have limitations. For example, the *Rapid Navigation Tables* of Myerscough and Hamilton are limited to 70° of both altitude and latitude, and large errors can be encountered if Ageton's *Dead Reckoning Altitude and Azimuth Table* is used for meridian angles near 90°.

The equations of short methods can be solved by ordinary tables of the applicable natural or logarithmic trigonometric functions if one is careful to observe the sign of each function in each quadrant.

Some 'short methods', as well as some inspection tables, provide solutions for azimuth only, for use primarily in determining compass error by comparison of the observed bearing of the Sun or other astronomical body with its true azimuth. Perhaps the best known 'short' azimuth tables are the celebrated *A B C Tables* found in some books of nautical tables and for many years popular with British merchant seamen.

With the availability of modern, convenient inspection tables with altitude and azimuth or azimuth angle tabulated in parallel columns, trigonometric solutions have lost much of their popularity.

4. Graphical Methods

Much of the calculation involved in sight reduction is generally avoided by means of inspection tables, which are tabulations of precomputed solutions of the navigational triangle for various combinations of entering arguments. An alternative approach is to use a diagram rather than tables. While the diagrams needed for graphical solutions can be drawn by the user, a number of printed ones have been produced.

As appealing as a graphical solution might be, very few have proved popular. The reasons for this lack of acceptance have varied somewhat with the individual methods. In general, however, graphical solutions have suffered from the need for portraying the entire navigational triangle, or its equivalent, on a single diagram, requiring one of unpractical size or of a scale too small for useful results, except to serve as a check to avoid a major error, or to obtain approximate results that might be useful for instructional or other purposes. Some suggested solutions have been capable of division of the graph into small segments, similar to the pagination of a set of inspection tables, but the method of locating the needed part of any such diagram is not always simple. Azimuth diagrams have had better acceptance than other graphical solutions, primarily because azimuth has not been needed to the same precision.

Several different types of graphical solution have been proposed. One is a diagram that solves an equation, or part of one. One enters the diagram with certain quantities or combinations of quantities and, by following the instructions accompanying the diagram, one is able to determine other needed qualities. Lines may need to be drawn as with a nomogram. This type of solution, generally reducing but not eliminating calculation, has been particularly popular among the French, but has found little favour elsewhere.

A more popular approach among British and American navigators has been the use of a map projection. The celestial equator and horizon systems of coordinates are similar and related by the celestial meridian, which is common to both. Accordingly, the coordinates of one system can be superimposed on those of the other if the two are correctly oriented with respect to the assumed latitude. The position of the body is located by means of its celestial-equator system of coordinates, declination and meridian angle. The altitude and azimuth angle are then read from the horizon-system graduations. This process, of course, can be reversed. A common example of this approach is the diagram on the plane of the celestial meridian (p. 302). The stereographic (p. 47), orthographic (p. 47), and gnomonic (p. 47) projections have been used extensively. The transverse Mercator (p. 44) and zenithal equidistant (p. 51) projections have also been used. An alternative approach is to construct the navigational triangle on the map projection by drawing arcs of the three great circles involved (celestial meridian, hour circle, and vertical circle), and measuring the parts needed.

A variation of the map-projection approach that has been used with probably more success than any other graphical solution has been to print, on a suitable map projection, curves, at intervals, representing arcs of the circles of equal altitude of specific stars, two or three bodies being used. One has then only to draw, by eye interpolation, a short segment of each observed body's circle, identified by its observed altitude, and locate the position of the observer at the common intersection of the position lines drawn. From this intersection one can read directly the latitude of the observer and the local sidereal time. Longitude is found by comparing this time with Greenwich sidereal time (p. 331), found by means of the almanac. If observations are not made simultaneously, they must be adjusted to a common time. In this case the position lines are adjusted both for the motion of the observer and the interval of time between observations. Azimuth, if needed, can be determined by measuring the direction perpendicular to the position line. The 3-body *Star Altitude Curves*, published by the American P. V. H. Weems are undoubtedly the most successful of any graphical method of sight reduction, having had wide usage among aviators, particularly those of allied nations during World War II. Position line curves are printed at 10′ intervals on the Mercator projection, except for the Arctic, where the polar stereographic projection is used. A separate volume was published for each 10° of latitude from 50° south to 70° north, with one volume for latitude 70° to 90° north. In a sense, the curves might be considered a graphical version of the *Sight Reduction Tables for Air Navigation* (p. 414). Like the tables, the curves need to be updated periodically for precession of the equinoxes and nutation (p. 288). The *Star Altitude Curves* have had limited use among mariners, and with the introduction of convenient inspection tables their use by aviators has declined.

Other variations have been suggested from time to time, but none has had wide acceptance. One approach worthy of mention is a group of diagrams for suitable intervals (perhaps 1°) of latitude and LHA ϒ. Each diagram consists of a series of radial lines with a common origin, each line extending in the direction of the azimuth of a specific star. The common origin represents calculated altitude. Graduations on the azimuth line indicate various values of observed or sextant altitude. By means of a transparency properly oriented over the diagram, one can plot each position line perpendicular to the azimuth line. The fix derived from two or more such plots, adjusted to a common time, can be transferred to the chart or plotting sheet.

The use of a sphere in navigation is of ancient origin, as attested by its presence in pictures of early navigators at work. Two principal ways of using a sphere for sight reduction have been suggested. One is to construct the navigational triangle for the assumed position of the observer and the meridian angle and declination of the body, and measure the calculated altitude and azimuth angle. The second approach is to locate the sub point (p. 292) of each body observed and use it as the centre for drawing a segment of the circle of equal altitude constituting the position line. If observations are not simultaneous, the adjustment to a common time must include both the motion of the observer and the elapsed time between observations. The position of the observer is at the common intersection of the position lines. The method provides an excellent means of visualizing the real-world situation, and so is useful for instructional purposes. However, it suffers from scale problems. One suggested solution of the second type proposed a sphere of a little more than 35 centimetres, on which one centimetre represented some 190 nautical miles!

An interesting variation of the sphere approach is to use the celestial sphere itself. This would be done by locating the zenith among the stars and referring to a graduated star chart. One way of locating the zenith would be to photograph the sky with a vertically stabilized camera having a reticle to mark the zenith. An alternative approach would be to compare a previously-made photograph or star chart of the proper scale directly with the sky. In either approach, one would determine latitude and LHA Υ, which would be compared with GHA Υ to determine longitude. Vertical stabilization would be critical, and scale and identification of the observed zenithal point might be problems.

5. Mechanical Methods
An alternative to both tabular and graphical methods is offered by mechanical methods. The step from diagram to

mechanical device is often a small one. In some instances the dividing line between them is indistinct, as when a plastic overlay or a globe is involved. Like graphical solutions, mechanical devices have been prolific but generally not well received. The advantages and disadvantages of each relative to tabular methods is essentially the same. Relative to graphical solutions, mechanical solutions eliminate the need for plotting, but generally are more expensive and are more susceptible to mechanical damage. An imperceptible bending of one part of a mechanical device may introduce intolerable error.

The common slide rule is a familiar example of a mechanical device that solves an equation or part of one. Slide rules designed specifically for solving problems of astronavigation have appeared in many forms, linear, circular, and cylindrical.

The use of a map projection in which one set of coordinates is superimposed over another is particularly attractive to mechanization. The diagram on the plane of the celestial meridian (p. 302), for example, is readily mechanized by placing one set of coordinates on an opaque plastic disc and the second set of coordinates on a transparent overlay pivoted at the centre. The two discs are oriented by rotating the overlay until the elevated pole is in correct position, established by latitude, on the celestial meridian. Such devices on the stereographic (p. 47) and orthographic (p. 47) projections have been used by American navigators, but generally as a check on major errors or for instructional purposes. During World War II a precision instrument of this kind was made in Germany and used for sight reduction by aviators. Similar instruments were made in France and Russia. A device using the same principle but increasing the scale by limiting the device to one fourth of a hemisphere, and pivoting the two parts at one corner, uses the zenithal equidistant projection (p. 51).

The principle of the *Star Altitude Curves* (p. 422) has been mechanized in various forms. Earlier versions generally consist of a device with the altitude curves and a plotting sheet on separate surfaces. One or the other is on transparent material wound on rollers arranged so that the transparent material can be moved relative to the opaque material. This arrangement provides mechanical orientation of the two parts for the time of each observation. If the plotting sheet is on the transparent overlay, the position line can be marked on it directly. If the altitude curves are on the transparent overlay, the position line can be traced on the plotting sheet by means of carbon paper. Some of the devices of this type include provision for bodies of the solar system, particularly the Sun, by having curves for different values of declination, permitting interpolation for the declination of the body, or by providing means of offsetting curves for a limited range of declination.

A more sophisticated device for use of precomputed altitude curves was devised by H. C. Pritchard and F. E. Lamplough, of the British Royal Aircraft Establishment, during the early part of World War II. Altitude curves of selected stars were placed on film used in a projector placed over a plotting sheet on the Mercator projection (p. 41) so as to project the curves onto the plotting sheet. The curves can be moved to allow for rotation of the Earth, thus reducing the work involved in adjusting non-simultaneous sights to a common time. The orientation of the device, called an *astrograph*, for 'astrograph mean time' must be done carefully if accurate results are to be obtained. The device was used by some allied aircraft during World War II. A plastic computer based upon the principle of the astrograph was intended primarily for determination of longitude.

A somewhat different method of using precomputed altitude curves has been suggested in various forms from time to time. Arcs of concentric circles, representing a family of circles of equal altitude, are drawn, with a bisecting azimuth line. These curves are mounted on rollers with the azimuth line extending in the direction of roll. A transparent plotting sheet mounted over the curves can be rotated. A table of calculated altitude and azimuth for various values of declination and meridian angle at the centre of each plotting sheet is needed. The curves are adjusted so the calculated altitude is through the centre of the plotting sheet, which is rotated so the azimuth line extends in the correct direction. The curve, interpolated as necessary, representing the observed altitude is then correctly placed and can be traced on the plotting sheet. Some adjustment may be needed to allow for distortion of the map projection. With some variations, this technique has been suggested with several different map projections, including the stereographic (p. 47) zenithal equidistant (p. 51) and polyconic (p. 46).

The use of a sphere has been especially attractive to those who would mechanize the sight-reduction problem. A typical device of this kind has a fixed arc representing the celestial meridian, and movable arcs representing the hour circle and the vertical circle. The movable arcs are mounted in such manner that the navigational triangle can be formed. Suitable scales and verniers are provided for reading the various quantities involved. In normal usage the arcs are set for latitude, meridian angle, and declination. The altitude and azimuth angle can then be read from appropriate scales. A particularly successful device of this kind was used by Japanese navigators during World War II. Its disadvantage is its bulk and susceptibility to mechanical damage.

Attempts have been made to combine observation and sight reduction. The usual approach is to orient a spherical device to the celestial sphere by aligning it to the celestial meridian, the vertical, and the line of sight to a body of known celestial coordinates. Information needed for establishing a position line or fix is then determined by means of the appropriate graduations on the device. If two bodies are observed simultaneously, the need for an accurate directional reference is eliminated. Observation with such a device, particularly if two bodies are to be observed simultaneously, is difficult. It has not been possible, with simple shipboard equipment, to meet the directional and vertical reference accuracy requirements. The principle has been used successfully by means of an inertial stable platform (p. 535) to establish the directional and vertical references, and mounting a small equatorial telescope over the sensors. The telescope is then set to the declination of the body, and the body is brought into view in the telescope. The latitude and meridian angle are read from the device, and the longitude is determined by comparison of the meridian angle with GHA, determined from the almanac. A more sophisticated approach has been to combine an inertial stable platform, an electronic astro-tracker, and a computer.

A device designed for sight reduction can generally be used in reverse to determine declination and meridian angle of a body whose altitude and azimuth are known, for use in identification of observed bodies. Similarly, a star globe (p. 340) or star finder (p. 341) can be used to determine approximate altitude and azimuth as a rough check on sight-reduction accuracy.

6. Unconventional Methods

Different approaches to the problem of sight reduction have been proposed from time to time, and some have enjoyed a degree of acceptance by mariners. Some of the suggested methods have practical application under favourable conditions, while others are primarily of academic interest. The broad scope of the suggested methods is indicated by the following brief review of a number of them.

Plot of arc of circle of equal altitude. The zenith distance $(90° - Ho)$ is the radius of the circle of equal altitude through the observer's position, to the accuracy of observation and sextant altitude-correction. The sub point of the body at the time of observation is the centre of the circle. Thus, if one has a chart or plotting sheet of sufficient extent, one can plot part of the circle of equal altitude in the vicinity of one's dead-reckoning or estimated position, without need for calculated altitude. This method is practical for high altitudes, discussed in section 7, but at altitudes usually observed, the long radius—3,000 miles for altitude 40°—would require a very small scale for a chart or plotting sheet of practical size, and distortion of the circle or displacement of its centre by the chart projections usually used by mariners would introduce difficulty or error.

Plot of position line through two points on circle of equal altitude. The position line as usually plotted by means of intercept and azimuth is tangent to the circle of equal altitude. A chord of the circle can be drawn if two points on the circle are known. It was this approach that led to the 'discovery' of the astro position line by Captain Thomas H. Sumner in 1837. In his day the common practice was to determine latitude the best one could, usually by observation of a body on or near the celestial meridian, and use this latitude in the calculation of the meridian angle of a second body observed as near the prime vertical as practical. Meridian angle was compared with GHA to find longitude. If only one body was available, it was observed twice with a suitable time interval between observations, and the calculated latitude was adjusted for the run between observations. An error in latitude introduced an error in longitude, the longitude error increasing with larger latitude error and also with increasing difference between the azimuth and the direction of the prime vertical.

Captain Sumner was approaching the Irish coast from the west. His position was in considerable doubt because overcast skies had prevented astronomical observations for several days. An observation of the Sun was obtained about 1000. The longitude was calculated for his dead-reckoning latitude and also for latitudes 10′ and 20′ farther north. The three points thus established were on the circle of equal altitude, and in approximately a straight line—the position line. This method of locating an astro position line became generally accepted and was widely used until replaced by the intercept method of Marcq St. Hilaire. The Sumner method is rarely used by modern navigators supplied with inspection tables or 'short-method' tables.

Another method of establishing two points on the position line is by calculating the intercept for two assumed positions several miles apart and plotting a circle around each assumed position as a centre, using the intercept at each AP as the radius. A common tangent to the two circles is the position line, the two points of tangency being the two points on the circle of equal altitude. One needs to know the general direction of the body to distinguish among the four common tangents. If the correct tangent is in doubt, a third circle, from an additional AP, should resolve the ambiguity. A 'short-method' table providing for calculation of altitude, but not azimuth, was produced for use with this approach, which has little to recommend it.

Azimuth and one point on circle of equal altitude. A method resembling both the method of Captain Sumner and the intercept method involves the calculation of one point on the circle of equal altitude and the azimuth at that point. The position line is drawn through the calculated point, perpendicular to the azimuth line. This method differs from that of Captain Sumner in that only one position is calculated, and from the intercept method in that no intercept is involved. The method has little to recommend it.

Assumed altitude. Rear Admiral Thomas D. Davies, USN (Ret.), has suggested the publication of tables listing, for each integral degree of latitude and altitude, the LHA ϓ and azimuth of selected stars. The position line would be plotted in the usual manner from an assumed position consisting of the integral degree of latitude nearest the dead-reckoning latitude, and the longitude differing from the dead-reckoning longitude by the difference between the tabulated LHA ϓ and LHA ϓ at the dead-reckoning position at the time of observation, as determined from the almanac, the assumed position being east of the dead-reckoning position if the tabulated LHA ϓ were greater than the calculated LHA ϓ, and west if smaller. The Hc used with Ho for determining the intercept would be the assumed altitude used for entering the table. The identity of the star need not be known. A somewhat modified procedure would be needed for a star near the celestial meridian.

Combined almanac and sight-reduction tables. Starting with the edition for 1944, the Japanese Hydrographic Office published tables of altitude and azimuth of selected astronomical bodies at intervals, for specific locations. Several versions were published, usually for a time interval of 10 minutes. The first edition used important positions in the western Pacific. Later editions used positions differing in latitude by exactly 5°. The use of specific places, such as an important air field, led to the appellation 'destination tables' sometimes applied to these *Altitude and Azimuth Almanacs*, which were discontinued after several years' publication. The method provided a rapid, easy means of sight reduction, but error was sometimes introduced by the curvature of long intercept lines and long position lines. A separate table, or auxiliary correction tables, would be needed for each assumed position and each body, making the method impracticable for long voyages. However, a table of altitudes at a destination would provide a simple means of determining the great-circle distance of the observer from his destination, for the intercept would be this distance.

Parallactic angle. The parallactic angle (p. 308) can be calculated by the equations of spherical trigonometry or by using any azimuth table, interchanging latitude and declination. The latitude and meridian angle at that point of the circle of equal altitude nearest the assumed position can then be calculated by Napier's rules of circular parts, dividing the navigational triangle into two right spherical triangles. The longitude of the nearest point can be determined by means of the meridian angle and GHA of the body. The azimuth at the nearest point can be determined by calculation or table, and the position line drawn perpendicular to it. Alternatively, coordinates of a second point on the circle of equal altitude can be calculated by using a slightly different value of parallactic angle, and the two points connected by a straight line, a chord of the circle of equal altitude. This method was suggested by Eli Gradsztajn of the Department of Physics and Astronomy at Tel Aviv University, Israel.

Triangles other than PZX. Spherical triangles other than the navigational triangle composed of arcs of the celestial meridian, hour circle, and vertical circle can be used to calculate altitude and azimuth. One such method, proposed by Dr. Stjepo Kotlarić, Assistant Director of the Hydrographic Institute of the Yugoslav Navy, and published as *Tables K_1, Short Method of Computation of Altitude and Azimuth in Astronomical Navigation*, is based upon solution of the three right spherical triangles defined by arcs of the celestial horizon, hour circle, and (*1*) celestial equator, (*2*) vertical circle, (*3*) lower branch of celestial meridian. The rules are few and simple, and only four table entries are needed. The method might have enjoyed wider acceptance if it had not appeared after convenient inspection tables came into general use.

Some of the methods of calculation of position without plot, discussed later, involve a spherical triangle other than the navigational triangle.

Azimuth position line. The usual astro position line is an approximation of an arc of the circle of equal altitude. If azimuth or rate of change of altitude could be measured to adequate accuracy, the azimuth line could be used as a position line. The obvious way of doing this would be to plot a radial line from the sub point, in the direction of the reciprocal of the azimuth, as is done when the bearing of a terrestrial object is observed and plotted. For strict accuracy, the great-circle direction of the observer from the sub point should be plotted. The method is practical only for high altitudes, when the distance is short and the difference between the azimuth at the observer and its reciprocal at the sub point is negligible. Alternatively, one point on the azimuth position line might be calculated and the line drawn through that point, in the direction of the azimuth, or two points on the line might be computed and the position line drawn through them. The intercept approach might also be used. The azimuth 'intercept' would be the difference between the measured azimuth and the calculated azimuth for an assumed position, multiplied by the cosine of the altitude. The 'intercept' would be measured from the assumed position, in a direction perpendicular to the azimuth, and the position line drawn in the direction of the azimuth. The weakness of any azimuth position line method is the difficulty of measuring azimuth to the required accuracy. An error of $1'$ in azimuth would offset the position line a distance in miles equal to the cosine of the altitude.

Position from observation of one body. When only one body is available for observation, as the Sun might be during the day, it is common practice to establish a running fix by two observations of the body with sufficient interval of time between observations to produce two position lines having a suitable angle of cut. When a body transits the celestial meridian near the zenith, the required time interval near transit can be quite short.

Other methods of establishing position of the observer by observation of one body have been suggested. If both altitude and azimuth are observed to adequate accuracy, a simple means of establishing position of the observer would be to plot both altitude and azimuth position lines. These lines are always mutually perpendicular. The weakness of the azimuth position line limits the value of this method.

If one could measure altitude and rate of change of altitude to adequate accuracy, it would be possible not only to establish mutually perpendicular position lines, but also to calculate latitude and meridian angle, which could be compared with GHA to determine longitude. Measurement of azimuth and rate of change of azimuth could serve the same purpose. The weakness of either approach is the difficulty of observing rate of change of altitude to the required accuracy. Even more difficult would be the accurate measurement of azimuth and its rate of change.

A suggestion has been made that position on the surface of the Earth can be established by observing the position of the Moon relative to the background of stars, and comparing this data with the Moon's position as might be observed at the centre of the Earth. Accuracy would be greatest near the sub point of the Moon, diminishing with increased distance from that point. Even in the vicinity of greatest accuracy the method would require an accuracy of observation exceeding practical capability.

A total eclipse of the Sun offers a rare opportunity to obtain a fix by observation of one body. The shadow of the Moon moves across the surface of the Earth with such speed that, under the most favourable situation, the timing of the beginning or ending of totality to an accuracy of one second would provide a position line accurate to approximately one third of a mile. A second position line would be obtained by observation of the altitude, with sight reduction in the usual manner.

Calculation of position from observation of two or more bodies. An approach that has been popular with mathematicians, but

432

which the modern navigator considers primarily of academic interest, is the determination of position by calculation, rather than by plot.

A large number of suggestions have been made for calculation of the latitude and some form of hour angle by means of simultaneous observation of two bodies, or non-simultaneous observations adjusted to a common time. Special tables have been suggested or published to facilitate the calculations. Before position-line navigation came into general use, the common practice was to calculate latitude from an observation of a body near the celestial meridian, and use this latitude, adjusted for any difference in time of observation, to calculate longitude from an observation of a body near the prime vertical, as discussed above. Some of the methods of calculating position from observation of two bodies require unique relationship of the bodies, as those having the same altitude, the same azimuth, or nearly the same hour angle. Another approach has been the solution of three simultaneous equations from observation of three bodies or three observations of the same body.

A basic method of calculating the direction and distance of a two-position-line fix from a common assumed position is illustrated in Fig. 903. Point AP is the assumed position for both observations, a_1 is the intercept for the first observation, a_2 the intercept for the second observation, and a' the line from the AP to the fix. The directions of a_1 and a_2 from AP are the azimuths of the two bodies observed if the intercepts are 'toward', and the reciprocal if 'away'. If A_1 is the difference between the directions of a_1 and a_2, and A_2 is the difference between the directions of a_1 and a', the values of A_2 and a' can be calculated by the equations:

$$\tan A_2 = \frac{a_2 - a_1 \cos A_1}{a_1 \sin A_1},$$

$$a' = a_1 \sec A_2.$$

The position of the fix can be determined by plotting the vector a' from the AP or by calculation, using one of the sailings (chapter IV), with the direction of a' being substituted for course, and the length of a' being substituted

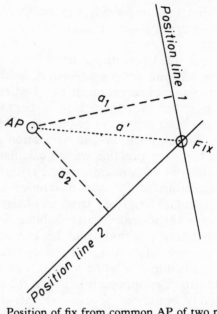

FIG. 903. Position of fix from common AP of two position lines.

for distance. If observations are not made simultaneously, the adjusted AP should be the same as the other AP. Thus, if the first AP or position line is to be advanced to the time of the second observation, the AP for reduction of the first observation is in the direction of the reciprocal of the course from the second AP, at a distance equal to the run between observations. If the dead-reckoning position at the time of each observation is used as the AP for reduction of that observation, the DR position at the time for which the fix is desired is the AP for the calculation of the fix.

A unique set of tables using two astronomical bodies for direct determination of position without plotting was proposed by Dr. Stjepo Kotlarić, Assistant Director of the Hydrographic Institute of the Yugoslav Navy, and published as *Tables* K_{11}, *Two-star Fix Without Use of Altitude Difference Method*. The unique feature of these tables is the tabulation of corrections to be applied to the common assumed position to obtain the position of the observer, without computation of the intercept.

7. High Altitudes

Observation of bodies near the zenith is generally avoided because of the difficulty of making such an observation, especially when the azimuth is changing rapidly, near meridian transit. Also, as the altitude increases, the radius of the circle of equal altitude decreases, resulting in increased discrepancy between the circle and the position line, whether a tangent or chord.

If a body is in the observer's zenith, the circle of equal altitude shrinks to a point. If the navigator could determine that a body was exactly in his zenith, he would know that he was at the sub point of the body. His latitude would be the declination of the body, and his longitude would be its GHA, or 360° − GHA. However, it is a rare occasion that one might observe a navigational body exactly in the zenith, and determination of the condition might be difficult.

If a body is within two or three degrees of the zenith, as the Sun might be near noon for an observer in the tropics, an arc of the circle of equal altitude might conveniently be drawn by locating the sub point of the body and using the zenith distance (90° − Ho) as the radius. Alternatively, one might plot the azimuth line from the sub point, but azimuths of bodies near the zenith are difficult to observe accurately. However, if both altitude and azimuth are observed, a fix can be obtained from one body.

The more commonly-used procedure for obtaining a fix from one body near the zenith is to observe it twice a few minutes apart, once shortly before meridian transit, and again shortly after transit. The interval between observations is dictated by the rapidity of the change of azimuth. A change of 90° results in the ideal orthogonal position lines. If in doubt, one might make several observations and use all of them or those producing the best fix. Observations made at different times need to be adjusted to a common time, of course. This is done most conveniently by adjusting the sub points.

The usual procedure for obtaining a fix in this manner is illustrated in Fig. 904.

1. Several observations of the altitude of the body are made near meridian transit, the time of which can be determined

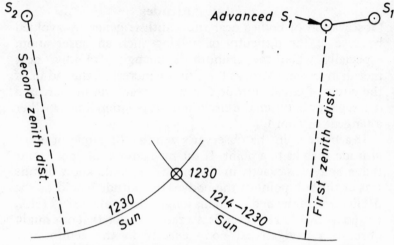

FIG. 904. A fix by two circular position lines of a body near the zenith.

by observation or by noting the time at which the GHA or $360° - $ GHA is the same as the longitude.

2. The sub point (S) of the body at the time of each observation is determined. Generally, any change in declination between observations can be ignored.

3. Each S is plotted and earlier ones are advanced for the run between the time of observation and the time of the fix.

4. Zenith distance ($90° - $ Ho) at the time of each observation is determined.

5. An arc of the circle of equal altitude for each observation is plotted, using the S (advanced for earlier observations) as the centre of the circle, and zenith distance (z) as the radius. The fix is at the intersection of the arcs of the circles of equal altitude.

Two circles intersect at two points. Any doubt regarding which intersection constitutes the fix might be resolved by noting whether the body transits to the north or south, by noting the azimuth at the time of either observation, or by other information.

As the zenith distance increases, the method of drawing the circles of equal altitude becomes less desirable, because of the long radii involved and the departure of the great-circle

436

azimuth lines from straight lines on the chart or plotting sheet. The *Sight Reduction Tables for Marine Navigation* (p. 403) can be used with modified procedure, as follows:

1. Select the assumed latitude (aL) within 30′ of the dead reckoning or estimated position, such that the minutes of latitude are the same as the minutes of declination (60′ minus minutes of latitude if of contrary name, near the equator). Select the assumed longitude (a Lo) in the usual way, to determine LHA to the nearest integral degree.

2. Record the tabulated calculated altitude (Tab Hc) and the tabulated azimuth angle (Tab Z) from adjacent columns, using entering values of declination and latitude differing by 1° bracketing the actual values.

3. Determine altitude difference (d) and azimuth angle difference (Z diff) by subtraction of the recorded values.

4. Using the declination increment and the value of d found in step 3 (*not* the tabulated d), find d_1 corr (usually zero) and d_2 corr in the usual way, and apply them to Tab Hc at the smaller value of declination used for entering the table, to determine Hc for comparison with Ho to determine the intercept (a).

5. Using the declination increment and the value of Z diff found in step 3, find Z corr and apply it to the Tab Z for the smaller value of declination used for entering the table.

6. Plot the position line in the usual manner, from the assumed position in step 1.

Suppose it is desired to determine Hc and Zn by NP 401/Pub. No. 229 for the following data: DR lat 16°27′.7 S., DR long 155°44′.3 E., GHA 207°23′.8, dec 17°45′.1 S. Refer to Figs 905 and 902.

1. The nearest latitude meeting the requirements is 16°45′.1 S., the 45′.1 agreeing with the minutes of declination, and 16°45′.1 being within 30′ of the DR latitude. The LHA = GHA + aLo(E) = 207°23′.8 + 155°36′.2 = 363°, or 3°.

2. Enter the table with L 16°, dec 17° same name and extract Tab Hc 86°57′.3, Tab Z 70°4. Enter the table again, with L 17° dec 18° same name and extract Tab Hc 86°58′.2, Tab Z 70°3.

3°, 357° L.H.A. LATITUDE SAME NAME AS DECLINATION

Dec.	15° Hc	d	Z	16° Hc	d	Z	17° Hc	d	Z	18° Hc	d	Z	19° Hc	d	Z	20° Hc	d
°	° ′	′	°	° ′	′	°	° ′	′	°	° ′	′	°	° ′	′	°	° ′	′
0	74 42.6	+58.8	168.6	73 43.7	+59.0	169.2	72 44.7	+59.1	169.8	71 45.6	+59.2	170.4	70 46.4	+59.3	170.9	69 47.1	+59.4 17
1	75 41.4	58.6	167.8	74 42.7	58.8	168.6	73 43.8	59.0	169.2	72 44.8	59.1	169.8	71 45.7	59.2	170.4	70 46.5	59.3 17
2	76 40.0	58.5	166.9	75 41.5	58.6	167.8	74 42.8	58.8	168.6	73 43.9	59.0	169.2	72 44.9	59.1	169.8	71 45.8	59.2 17
3	77 38.5	58.1	165.9	76 40.1	58.5	166.9	75 41.6	58.7	167.8	74 42.9	58.8	168.6	73 44.0	59.0	169.2	72 45.0	59.1 16
4	78 36.6	57.8	164.7	77 38.6	58.2	165.9	76 40.3	58.4	166.9	75 41.7	58.7	167.8	74 43.0	58.8	168.6	73 44.1	59.0 16
5	79 34.4	+57.4	163.3	78 36.5	+57.8	164.7	77 38.7	+58.2	165.9	76 40.4	+58.5	166.9	75 41.8	+58.7	167.8	74 43.1	+58.9 16
6	80 31.8	56.8	161.6	79 34.6	57.4	163.3	78 36.9	57.9	164.7	77 38.9	58.2	165.9	76 40.5	58.5	166.9	75 42.0	58.7 16
7	81 28.6	55.9	159.5	80 32.0	56.8	161.6	79 34.8	57.4	163.3	78 37.1	57.9	164.7	77 39.0	58.3	165.9	76 40.7	58.6 16
8	82 24.5	54.8	156.9	81 28.8	56.0	159.5	80 32.2	56.8	161.6	79 35.0	57.4	163.3	78 37.3	57.9	164.8	77 39.2	58.3 16
9	83 19.3	53.1·153.6		82 24.8	54.8	157.0	81 29.0	56.0	159.6	80 32.4	56.9	161.7	79 35.2	57.4	163.4	78 37.5	57.9 16
10	84 12.4	+50.4·149.3		83 19.6	+53.1·153.7		82 25.0	+54.9	157.0	81 29.3	+56.0	159.6	80 32.6	+56.9	161.7	79 35.4	+57.5 16
11	85 02.8	46.2·143.5		84 12.7	50.5·149.4		83 19.9	53.2·153.7		82 25.3	55.0	157.1	81 29.5	56.1	159.7	80 32.9	56.9 16
12	85 49.0	39.1·135.4		85 03.2	46.3·143.6		84 13.1	50.6·149.5		83 20.3	53.2·153.8		82 25.6	55.0	157.1	81 29.8	56.2 15
13	86 28.1	27.6·124.1		85 49.5	39.3·135.5		85 03.7	46.3·143.7		84 13.5	50.7·149.5		83 20.6	53.3·153.9		82 26.0	55.0 15
14	86 55.7	+10.4·108.6		86 28.8	27.7·124.2		85 50.0	39.4·135.7		85 04.2	46.4·143.8		84 13.9	50.8·149.6		83 21.0	53.4·15
15	87 06.1	– 9.6·	89.6	86 56.5	+10.5·108.7		86 29.4	+27.9·124.3		85 50.6	+39.6·135.8		85 04.7	+46.6·143.9		84 14.4	+50.8·14
16	86 56.5	27.1·	70.5	87 07.0	– 9.7·	89.6	86 57.3	+10.6·108.7		86 30.2	28.0·124.4		85 51.3	39.7·135.9		85 05.2	46.8·14
17	86 29.4	38.8·	54.9	86 57.3	27.1·	70.4	87 07.9	– 9.7·	89.6	86 58.2	+10.6·108.8		86 31.0	28.1·124.6		85 52.0	39.8·13
18	85 50.6	45.9·	43.4	86 30.2	38.9·	54.7	86 58.2	27.2·	70.3	87 08.8	– 9.7·	89.5	86 59.1	+10.7·108.9		86 31.8	28.2·12
19	85 04.7	50.3·	35.2	85 51.3	46.1·	43.2	86 31.0	39.0·	54.5	86 59.1	27.3·	70.2	87 09.8	– 9.8·	89.5	87 00.0	+10.9·10

FIG. 905. Part of left-hand page of NP 401/Pub. No. 229 showing high altitudes.

3. Altitude difference (d) is $86°58'.2 - 86°57'.3 = (+)0'.9$. Azimuth angle difference (Z diff) is $70°3 - 70°4 = (-)0°1$.

4. The declination increment (Dec Inc) is $45'.1$. Enter the interpolation table with this value and $0'.9$ and extract the d_2 corr of $(+)$ $0'.7$. Applying this correction, find Hc $= 86°57'.3 + 0'.7 = 86°58'.0$.

5. Enter the interpolation table with Dec Inc and Z diff $0°.1$ and extract the Z corr of $(-)$ $0°.1$. Applying this correction, find $Z = 70°.4 - 0°.1 = 70°.3$. Azimuth $(Zn) = 180° + 70°.3 = 250°.3$.

6. Plot the position line from the assumed position, aL $16°45'.1$ S., a Lo $155°36'.2$ E.

The solution can be arranged conveniently as follows:

```
GHA   207°23'.8                              DRL   16°27'.7 S.
 a Lo 155°36'.2 E.        dec 17°45'.1 S.      Lo  155°44'.3 E.
LHA     3                                     a L   16°45'.1 S.

L 16° S. dec 17° S.              Tab Hc 86°57'.3      Tab Z    70'.4
L 17° S. dec 18° S.              Tab Hc 86°58'.2      Tab Z    70.3
                                  d (+) 0'.9           Z diff  (−) 0.1

Tab Hc  86°57'.3                                      Tab Z    70'.4
 d corr  (+) 0'.7                                     Z corr (−) 0'.1
   Hc   86°58'.0                                         Z   S. 70.3 W.
                                                        Zn    250.3
```

This modified procedure is needed because interpolation by the usual method is inaccurate near the zenith. The modified procedure utilizes the principle that interpolation is adequate when the difference between entering arguments, in this case latitude and declination, is constant. It is good practice to use the modified procedure when the altitude exceeds 86° or the double second difference is greater than the values shown in the interpolation table.

The use of a straight line on the chart, a rhumb line for a Mercator chart, to represent a small segment of the circle of equal altitude generally does not introduce a significant error. However, for any given distance from the point of tangency the discrepancy increases with increased altitude of the body.

A one-page auxiliary 'Table of Offsets' is provided in each volume of NP 401/Pub. No. 229 to adjust the position line for the curvature of the circle of equal altitude. Part of this table is shown in Fig. 906. The table is entered with the observed altitude (Ho) and the distance along the position line from the intercept terminal point (p.312). The offsets, in miles, taken from the table with interpolation, if necessary, are measured perpendicular to the position line, in the direction of the body observed. Customarily, two offsets are used, at a five-mile interval, to bracket the DR position. A line connecting the ends of the offsets is the offset position line, a chord of the circle of equal altitude.

TABLE OF OFFSETS (ALTITUDES 0° TO 89°)

DISTANCE ALONG POSITION LINE FROM INTERCEPT					
00'	05'	10'	15'	20'	25'
ALT.				OFFSETS	
85. 0	0. 0	0. 0	0. 2	0. 4	0. 7	1. 0
85. 5	0. 0	0. 0	0. 2	0. 4	0. 7	1. 2
86. 0	0. 0	0. 1	0. 2	0. 5	0. 8	1. 3
86. 5	0. 0	0. 1	0. 2	0. 5	1. 0	1. 5
87. 0	0. 0	0. 1	0. 3	0. 6	1. 1	1. 7
87. 5	0. 0	0. 1	0. 3	0. 8	1. 3	2. 1
88. 0	0. 0	0. 1	0. 4	0. 9	1. 7	2. 7
88. 5	0. 0	0. 2	0. 6	1. 3	2. 3	3. 5
89. 0	0. 0	0. 3	0. 8	1. 9	3. 4	5. 5

FIG. 906. Part of Table of Offsets of NP 401/Pub. No. 229.

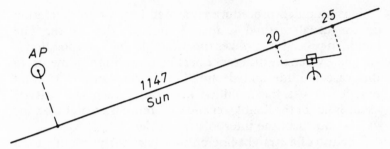

FIG. 907. Plot of offset position line.

A plot illustrating the use of offsets is shown in Fig. 907. The Sun is observed at 1147 with the following results: Ho 87°39'.5, Hc 87°34'.5, Zn 163°.0. From these data, the intercept (a) is 87°39'.5 − 87°34'.5 = 5'.0 T. The position line is plotted, as shown. From the Table of Offsets the offsets for Ho 87°39'.5 at distances of 20 and 25 miles, bracketing the DR position, are found to be 1.4 and 2.3 miles, respectively. These offsets are measured in direction 163°.0, from points on the position line 20 and 25 miles from the intercept terminal point, as shown. The estimated position (EP) at the time of observation, assuming no current has been established, is at the foot of the perpendicular from the DR position at 1147 to the line connecting the offsets, as shown.

The question of when to use offsets is a matter of personal judgment. For strict accuracy, they should always be used, but for many observations this would be an unrealistic nicety. A rule sometimes followed is that any offset of 0.5 mile or greater is used. This may require reference to the offset table for every observation. If the use of offsets is limited to values of Ho greater than 60°, the minimum offset will be 0.5 mile. A realistic modification of this rule would be to use offsets if Ho is 80° or more or if Ho is greater than 60° and the distance is 25 miles or more.

8. Low Altitudes

An observation of a body near the horizon requires no special treatment, as far as sight reduction is concerned, if one is careful with signs. Thus, if *either* Ho or Hc is negative, *and* the other is positive, the intercept is the numerical sum of the two values, the positive value being the greater. If *both* Ho and Hc are negative, the smaller numerical value is the greater value in determining whether the intercept is toward or away from the body.

Interpolation in NP 401/Pub. No. 229 when negative altitudes are involved requires some care. Refer to Fig. 908, part of the tables for L H A 78°, 282° contrary name (above the C–S line), and LHA 102°, 258° same name (below the C–S line). For latitude and declination same name the altitudes above the C–S line are negative for the values of LHA at the bottom of the page (102°, 258°). For latitude and declination contrary name the altitudes below the C–S line are negative for the values of LHA at the top of the page (78°, 282°). Also, for contrary name, altitudes on the left-hand pages of the tables (not shown) are negative for values of LHA at the bottom of the right-hand pages (102°, 258°). When a tabulated altitude is negative, the azimuth angle is the supplement of the value shown in the tables, and the sign of d is opposite to that shown.

Dec.	45° Hc	d	Z	46° Hc	d	Z	47° Hc	d	Z
°	° ′	′	°	° ′	′	°	° ′	′	°
0	8 27.2	-42.9	98.5	8 18.2	-43.6	98.7	8 09.1	-44.4	98.8
1	7 44.3	43.0	99.3	7 34.6	43.7	99.4	7 24.7	44.4	99.5
2	7 01.3	43.0	100.0	6 50.9	43.8	100.1	6 40.3	44.5	100.2
3	6 18.3	43.2	100.7	6 07.1	43.8	100.8	5 55.8	44.5	100.9
4	5 35.1	43.1	101.4	5 23.3	43.9	101.5	5 11.3	44.6	101.5
5	4 52.0	-43.2	102.1	4 39.4	-43.9	102.1	4 26.7	-44.6	102.2
6	4 08.8	43.3	102.8	3 55.5	44.0	102.8	3 42.1	44.6	102.9
7	3 25.5	43.3	103.4	3 11.5	43.9	103.5	2 57.5	44.7	103.6
8	2 42.2	43.3	104.1	2 27.6	44.0	104.2	2 12.8	44.6	104.2
9	1 58.9	43.3	104.8	1 43.6	44.1	104.9	1 28.2	44.7	104.9
10	1 15.6	-43.3	105.5	0 59.5	-44.0	105.5	0 43.5	-44.7	105.6
11	0 32.3	-43.3	106.2	0 15.5	-44.0	106.2	0 01.2	+44.7	73.8
12	0 11.0	+43.4	73.1	0 28.5	+44.0	73.1	0 45.9	44.7	73.1
13	0 54.4	43.3	72.4	1 12.5	44.0	72.4	1 30.6	44.7	72.4
14	1 37.7	43.3	71.7	1 56.5	44.0	71.7	2 15.3	44.7	71.8
15	2 21.0	+43.3	71.0	2 40.5	+44.0	71.1	3 00.0	+44.6	71.1
16	3 04.3	43.3	70.3	3 24.5	43.9	70.4	3 44.6	44.6	70.4
17	3 47.6	43.2	69.6	4 08.4	43.9	69.7	4 29.2	44.6	69.8
18	4 30.8	43.2	68.9	4 52.3	43.9	69.0	5 13.8	44.5	69.1
19	5 14.0	43.1	68.2	5 36.2	43.8	68.3	5 58.3	44.5	68.4

FIG. 908. Part of right-hand page of NP 401/Pub. No. 229 showing low altitudes.

If interpolation is between two negative altitudes, it is done in the usual manner. The resulting Hc is given a negative sign, and the supplement of the tabulated Z is used. If interpolation is between positive and negative altitudes (across the C–S line), the same modification of the tabulated data is needed. The interpolated altitude might be either positive or negative, depending upon the magnitude of the d corr with respect to Tab Hc and whether the Tab Hc is positive or negative.

Suppose it is desired to find Hc and Zn for the following data: DR lat 46°21′.4 N., DR long 31°47′.6 W., GHA 313°33′.7, dec 11°45′.4 S. Refer to Figs. 908 and 902.

GHA 313°33′.7		DR L 46 21′.4 N.
a Lo 31°33′.7 W.	dec 11 45′.4 S.	DR Lo 31 47′.6 W.
LHA 282°	a dec 11° S. Dec Inc 45′.4	a L 46 00′.0 N.
Tab Hc 0°15′.5	d (−) 44′.0 Z diff (+)0°.7	Tab Z 106.2
d$_1$ corr (−)30′.3		Z corr (+) 0′.5
d$_2$ corr (−) 3′.0		Z N. 106.7 E.
Hc(−)0°17′.8		Zn 106.7

If the combined d$_1$ and d$_2$ corrections had been less than Tab Hc, Hc would have been positive. Note that interpolations for Z is between 106°.2 and 106°.9, the supplement of the next entry down the page.

Suppose it is desired to find Hc and Zn for the following data: DR lat 46°21′.4 N., DR long 31°47′.6 W., GHA 289°33′.7, dec 11° 45′.4 N. Refer to Figs. 908 and 902.

GHA 289°33′.7		DR L 46 21′.4 N.
a Lo 31°33′.7 W.	dec 11°45′.4 N.	DR Lo 31 47′.6 W.
LHA 258°	a dec 11° N. Dec Inc 45′.4	a L 46 00′.0 N.
Tab Hc (−)0°15′.5	d (+)44′.0 Z diff (−)0°.7	Tab Z 73°.8
d$_1$ corr (+) 30′.3		Z corr (−) 0′.5
d$_2$ corr (+) 3′.0		Z N. 73°.3 E.
Hc 0°17′.8		Zn 073°.3

Note that this is the same as the previous example except that GHA is different and latitude and declination are same name. Also note that when entering with LHA at the bottom of the page, one reverses the sign of Tab Hc and d above the line, and uses the supplement of the Z, as shown. If the combined d$_1$ and d$_2$ corrections had been numerically less than Tab Hc, Hc would have been negative.

9. High Latitudes

An azimuth line is a great circle. A circle of equal altitude is a small circle with radius equal to zenith distance. It is customary to plot both of these circles as straight lines (rhumb lines) on a Mercator chart or plotting sheet. The error thus introduced is generally negligible. Near the geographical poles, however, the departure of a rhumb line from either a great circle or a small circle is considerable. In high latitudes, poleward of perhaps 60°, it is good practice to use a chart or plotting sheet on a projection other than Mercator, such as the polar stereographic (p. 47), Lambert conformal (p. 46), or transverse Mercator (p. 44), particularly if one plots the position circle of a high-altitude observation, using the sub point as the AP. Alternatively, one might use the dead-reckoning or estimated position as the assumed position, interpolating for latitude and LHA as well as for declination, thus limiting the lengths of azimuth and position lines. If the position of the vessel is in considerable doubt, and the fix is more than several miles from the dead-reckoning or estimated position, the fix might be used as an assumed position for a second calculation.

Offsets, which are as applicable in high latitudes as elsewhere, do not solve the problem of map-projection distortion, for offsets are differences between a great circle and a small circle.

A simple method of sight reduction unique to polar regions is to use the nearer geographical pole as the assumed position. The declination of the body is then the calculated altitude (Hc), negative if the latitude and declination are of contrary name, and GHA replaces azimuth. That is, all meridians meet at the poles, and the body is over the meridian of a place having the same longitude, measured westward through 360°, as the GHA of the body. A chart on the polar stereographic, Lambert conformal, or transverse Mercator projection is used with little error within several degrees of the pole. Offsets should be used with long position lines.

Special, short tables for use near the poles have been devised, but these are not needed if tables with neither latitude or altitude limitations are used.

10. Low Latitudes

Very long azimuth or position lines may occur near the equator because meridians have maximum separation there. Accordingly, offsets are needed more often than elsewhere, and directions should be measured carefully. An error of $0°.5$ in azimuth may introduce an error of more than 0.3 mile in position. If high accuracy is needed, one might consider using the dead-reckoning or estimated position for the assumed position.

If the assumed position is exactly on the equator, with assumed latitude $0°$, there is no elevated pole, and either may be used as such in the calculation. The one used dictates the conversion of azimuth angle to azimuth. It is customary in inspection tables to use the pole nearer the body (agreeing with declination) as the elevated pole. That is, declination, rather than latitude, is used to determine the N. or S. prefix of Z. In all cases, the instructions accompanying the tables should be followed. Unless the body is near the prime vertical, a check can be provided by noting the approximate azimuth at the time of observation.

11. Latitude

When a body is on the celestial meridian, either the upper or lower branch, its azimuth is either $000°$ or $180°$. A position line resulting from observation of a body in this position, being perpendicular to the azimuth line, extends in an east–west direction, thus defining latitude. Modern navigators equipped with inspection tables generally reduce such an observation in the usual manner, rather than giving it special consideration. This has not always been so, for two principal reasons. First, and most important before the development of the chronometer, accurate calculation of latitude, from a meridian altitude, is possible without accurate time. Second, when a body is on the celestial meridian, the navigational triangle is a straight line, and its solution is a simple problem of arithmetic. Accordingly, numerous solutions, including a number of variations of the celebrated 'double-altitude problem', were devised. Two

444

methods of finding latitude, other than by sight reduction in the usual manner, have survived and are still in limited use. These are the *meridian altitude* and *Polaris altitude* methods.

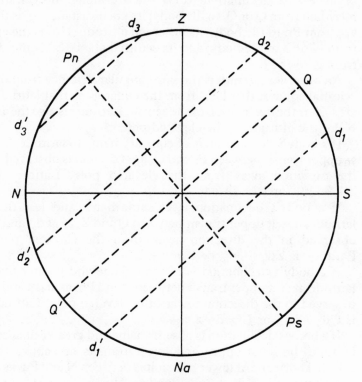

FIG. 909. Meridian altitudes.

Meridian altitude. Refer to Fig. 909, a diagram on the plane of the celestial meridian (p. 302) for latitudes 50° N. In the diagram, the semi-circle PnQPs is the upper branch of the celestial meridian, and arc PnQ′Ps is the lower branch of the celestial meridian. Point N is the north point on the celestial horizon, Pn the elevated pole, Z the zenith, Q the intersection of the celestial equator and the upper branch of the celestial meridian, S the south point on the celestial horizon, Ps the depressed pole, Na the nadir, and Q′ the intersection of the celestial equator and the lower branch of the celestial

445

meridian. Three parallels of declination are shown, with upper transits at d_1, d_2, and d_3, and lower transits at d_1', d_2', and d_3', respectively. When a body is at transit, either upper or lower, its declination (d) is the arc along the celestial meridian from Q or Q' to the body; its polar distance (p) is the arc from Pn to the body; its observed altitude (Ho) is the arc from N or S to the body; and its zenith distance (z) is the arc from Z to the body.

An observer's zenith is the same angular distance from the celestial equator that he is from the equator, so that latitude, arc QZ, is the declination of the zenith. Latitude is also the arc NPn, the altitude of the elevated pole.

If a body's declination is of contrary name to latitude, it is at upper transit between Ps and Q, as at d_1, and is observed in the direction away from the elevated pole. Latitude is $Zd_1 - Qd_1$, or $L = z - d$.

If a body's declination is of same name and less than latitude, it is at upper transit between Q and Z, as at d_2, and is observed in the direction away from the elevated pole. Latitude is $Zd_2 + Qd_2$, or $L = z + d$.

If a body's declination is of same name and greater than latitude, it is at upper transit between Z and Pn, as at d_3, and is observed in the direction toward the elevated pole. Latitude is $Qd_3 - Zd_3$, or $L = d - z$.

If a body's declination is of same name and greater than co-latitude, both its upper and lower transits are above the celestial horizon. At lower transit it is between N and Pn, as at d_3'. Latitude is $Nd_3' + Pnd_3'$, or $L = Ho + p$.

A problem associated with a meridian altitude observation is the need to make an observation at a prescribed time. Observations are usually more accurate if made when the observer believes he has made the proper setting of his sextant. That is, the observer, rather than the timer, should determine the time of observation.

Another problem is determination of the time of transit. Traditionally, the approximate time of transit is calculated in advance, using an estimated longitude, and a series of observations is started several minutes before the calculated time. At upper transit the altitude gradually increases until it reaches a maximum at transit, and then *dips*, or starts to decrease. At lower transit, the altitude decreases to a minimum and then starts to increase. The maximum, or minimum, altitude is taken as the meridian altitude. Some navigators prefer to plot the sextant altitude *vs.* time on cross-section paper, and fair a curve through the plotted points to determine the maximum or minimum altitude and time of transit, because the greatest or least sextant altitude might be in error.

A problem with using the maximum altitude is that the altitude is changing very slowly at the time of meridian transit, and if the vessel has a considerable north or south component of speed, or if the body is changing declination rapidly, the maximum or minimum altitude does not occur at transit. If the longitude is known accurately, the observation can be made at the precalculated time of transit of the body, explained below. If the azimuth can be measured accurately, the observation can be made when the body bears exactly 180° or 000°.

Another alternative is to apply a correction to the time of transit or to the maximum or minimum altitude measured. The difference between the time of transit and maximum or minimum altitude can be calculated by the equation:

$$t = 0.25465\ (\Delta L \pm \Delta d)\ \sin\ (L - d)\ \sec L \sec d,$$

in which t is the time interval in minutes, ΔL is the rate of change of latitude in minutes of arc per hour, Δd is the rate of change of declination in minutes of arc per hour, L is the latitude, and d is the declination. If ΔL and Δd are in opposite directions, they are added, but subtracted if in the same direction. The question of whether the maximum or minimum altitude occurs before or after transit should be apparent from the geometry involved. For example, if the upper transit of the Sun is south of the observer and the vessel's motion has a northerly component, with the declination changing toward the north at a slower rate, or toward the south, the altitude is decreasing, and the maximum altitude occurs *before* meridian transit. The correction to maximum or minimum altitude can be calculated by the equation:

$$C = 1.9635 \ t^2 \cos L \cos d \csc (L \sim d),$$

where C is the difference in altitude in minutes of arc, $L \sim d$ is the algebraic difference between latitude and declination (the numerical sum if of opposite sign and the numerical difference if of the same sign). The correction for one minute of time, called *altitude factor* (*a*) is tabulated in some books of nautical tables.

The time of meridian transit, or passage, at a known longitude can be calculated by letting the GHA equal the longitude in west longitude, or 360° minus longitude in east longitude, and working, in reverse, the usual problem of finding GHA. Suppose it is desired to find the watch time of transit of the Sun at longitude 131°51′.8 E. on June 22, if the watch is 6ˢ slow on ZT of ZD (−) 9. Refer to Figs. 802 and 803. The GHA at transit is 360° − Lo = 228°08′.2. From the daily page of the almanac, Fig. 802, it is seen that at GMT 3ʰ the GHA of the Sun is 224°34′.3, leaving 3°33′.9 to go to reach the celestial meridian. From the Increments and Corrections table, Fig. 803, it is seen that the Sun travels 3°33′.9 in 14ᵐ 16ˢ. Therefore, the GMT of transit at Lo 131°51′.8 E. is 3ʰ 14ᵐ 16ˢ. The ZT is 9ʰ later, or 12ʰ 14ᵐ 16ˢ. The watch is 6ˢ slow on ZT, and reads 12ʰ 14ᵐ 10ˢ at transit. The solution can be arranged conveniently as follows:

	June 22
Lo	131°51′.8 E.
GHA	228°08′.2
3ʰ	224°34′.3
14ᵐ 16ˢ	3°33′.9
GMT	3ʰ 14ᵐ 16ˢ
ZD (−) 9	(rev)
ZT	12ʰ 14ᵐ 16ˢ
WE	(S) 6ˢ
W	12ʰ 14ᵐ 10ˢ

For a body requiring a *v* correction, the correction is subtracted from the GHA difference (3°33′.9 in the example) before the time interval is determined from the Increments and Corrections table. Aboard a moving vessel, it is customary to use the best longitude at 1200 and then make a second calculation for the longitude at the time of transit determined in the first calculation, or adjust the time by 4ˢ for each minute of longitude between 1200 and the calculated time, adding if the ship is west, and subtracting if east, of the 1200 position.

Another problem associated with meridian altitudes is that observation at transit is sometimes missed, perhaps because the observer cannot get a good observation at the right time, the time of observation is miscalculated, or perhaps because overcast obscures the body at transit, but not several minutes before or after transit. In former days it was customary, under such circumstances, to calculate the difference between the altitude at the time of observation, called an *ex-meridian altitude,* and at the time of transit, and add the calculated difference to the observed altitude to determine the equivalent meridian altitude *at the time of observation* (not at transit). For lower transit the difference would be subtracted. An observation near the celestial meridian, to be thus adjusted, was called an *ex-meridian observation,* and the process of adjusting it to the equivalent meridian altitude was called *reduction to the meridian.* Some books of nautical tables include a tabulation of the correction, or it can be calculated by means of the correction equation given above, using for t the interval between the time of meridian transit and the time of observation. The equation should not be used for intervals of more than half an hour, or if the body is within 4° of the zenith, without reduced accuracy.

Knowledge of the longitude is needed for accurate results by reduction to the meridian. Where it is later determined that the longitude used was in error, a correction can be applied to the results by means of the *latitude factor* (f), the change in latitude along the position line for a 1′ change in longitude. The latitude factor is tabulated in some books of nautical tables, or can be calculated by the equation:

$$f = \cos L \tan Z,$$

where L is the latitude and Z is the azimuth angle.

Add to these various problems the fact that a ZT 1200 noon

position is usually desired, and that meridian transit, or passage, of the Sun is as likely to occur after 1200 as before, and one finds it easy to understand why the use of inspection tables for an observation at or shortly before noon has largely replaced the traditional meridian-altitude observation.

Polaris altitude. Refer to Fig. 909. If a body had a declination of exactly 90°, it would be located at one of the celestial poles, Pn or Ps. The altitude of the body would be the latitude of the observer. No bright star is at either pole, and none is near the south celestial pole. However, Polaris is less than 1° from the north celestial pole. A correction can be applied to its altitude to determine the altitude of the north celestial pole, thus providing a simple method of determining latitude in the northern hemisphere.

As Polaris revolves along its diurnal circle, making one revolution each sidereal day (p. 282), it passes directly above the pole, when its altitude is greater than that of the pole by the polar distance of the body. Half a sidereal day later it passes directly below the pole, with altitude less than that of the pole by the same amount. Twice each sidereal day its altitude is the same as that of the pole, once to the left of the pole and once to the right. At other points along the diurnal circle the difference in altitude of the pole and Polaris is between these extreme values, the amount being approximately equal to the extreme value multiplied by the cosine of the body's local hour angle.

For an observer on the equator, the plane of the parallel of declination of any body is perpendicular to the plane of the horizon. The points at which the pole and Polaris have the same altitude are at LHA 90° and 270°. But at any other latitude, the plane of the parallel of declination, being parallel to the plane of the equator, is tilted with respect to the plane of the horizon, as shown in Fig. 909. Consequently, the points at which the pole and the star have the same altitude are offset. This situation is shown exaggerated in Fig. 909, where it is seen that the altitude of Pn is greater than the point of intersection of the 90°–270° hour circle with the parallel of declination $d_3 d_3{}'$. The amount of this offset increases with higher latitude, requiring an adjustment to the Polaris correction.

If one correction table is to suffice for an entire year, a second adjustment to the Polaris correction is needed because of precession of the equinoxes and nutation (p. 288) and aberration, which affect the apparent position of Polaris. *Aberration* is the apparent displacement of an astronomical body in the direction of motion of the Earth in its orbit. It is greatest for bodies perpendicular to the direction of motion of the Earth in its orbit, and therefore quite large for Polaris.

The total correction at any time can be calculated by means of the equation:

$$C = -p \cos t + \tfrac{1}{2} p \sin p \sin^2 t \tan L,$$

in which C is the correction, p is the polar distance in the same units as C, t is the meridian angle, and L is the latitude.

The total correction is tabulated in three parts in the *Nautical Almanac*. The first part, a_0, is the total correction at latitude 50° for the mean position of Polaris during the year. The second part, a_1, is the adjustment to a_0 for latitude. The third part, a_2, is the adjustment to a_0 for the actual position of Polaris. The computed values of the three parts are increased 58.8 for a_0 and 0.6 each for a_1 and a_2, resulting in all tabulated values being positive. To compensate for the additions to computed values, the user subtracts 1° from the sum of the three parts to obtain the total correction, which is applied in accordance with its sign to Ho to determine the latitude.

Refer to Fig. 910, one of the three pages of the table. The LHA of Aries, not the LHA of Polaris, is used to identify the column to be used for extracting all three parts of the correction. The value of a_0 is taken from the upper part of the table by mental interpolation. The value of a_1 is taken from the second part of the table on the line identified by the latitude, without interpolation. The value of a_2 is taken from the third part of the table, on the line identified by the month at Greenwich, again without interpolation. Latitude is equal to Ho $+ a_0 + a_1 + a_2 - 1°$. Azimuth is tabulated at the bottom of the page, where it can be obtained by mental interpolation. The position line should be plotted perpendicular to the azimuth line through the latitude on the meridian used for determining LHA ϒ.

451

POLARIS (POLE STAR) TABLES
FOR DETERMINING LATITUDE FROM SEXTANT ALTITUDE AND FOR AZIMUTH

L.H.A. ARIES	240°–249°	250°–259°	260°–269°	270°–279°	280°–289°	290°–299°	300°–309°	310°–319°	320°–329°	330°–339°	340°–349°	350°–359°
	a_0	a_0	a_0	a_0	a_0	a_0	a_0	a_0	a_0	a_0	a_0	a_0
	° ′	° ′	° ′	° ′	° ′	° ′	° ′	° ′	° ′	° ′	° ′	° ′
0	1 43·2	1 38·7	1 33·0	1 26·2	1 18·6	1 10·4	1 01·8	0 53·1	0 44·6	0 36·5	0 29·1	0 22·6
1	42·9	38·2	32·3	25·5	17·8	09·5	00·9	52·3	43·8	35·7	28·4	22·0
2	42·4	37·7	31·7	24·7	17·0	08·7	1 00·1	51·4	42·9	35·0	27·7	21·4
3	42·0	37·1	31·0	24·0	16·2	07·8	0 59·2	50·5	42·1	34·2	27·0	20·8
4	41·6	36·6	30·4	23·2	15·4	07·0	58·3	49·7	41·3	33·4	26·4	20·2
5	1 41·1	1 36·0	1 29·7	1 22·5	1 14·6	1 06·1	0 57·5	0 48·8	0 40·5	0 32·7	0 25·7	0 19·7
6	40·7	35·4	29·0	21·7	13·7	05·3	56·6	48·0	39·7	32·0	25·0	19·2
7	40·2	34·8	28·3	21·0	12·9	04·4	55·7	47·1	38·9	31·2	24·4	18·6
8	39·7	34·2	27·6	20·2	12·1	03·5	54·9	46·3	38·1	30·5	23·8	18·1
9	39·2	33·6	26·9	19·4	11·2	02·7	54·0	45·4	37·3	29·8	23·2	17·6
10	1 38·7	1 33·0	1 26·2	1 18·6	1 10·4	1 01·8	0 53·1	0 44·6	0 36·5	0 29·1	0 22·6	0 17·1
Lat.	a_1	a_1	a_1	a_1	a_1	a_1	a_1	a_1	a_1	a_1	a_1	a_1
	′	′	′	′	′	′	′	′	′	′	′	′
0	0·5	0·4	0·3	0·3	0·2	0·2	0·2	0·2	0·2	0·3	0·4	0·4
10	·5	·4	·4	·3	·3	·2	·2	·2	·3	·3	·4	·5
20	·5	·5	·4	·4	·3	·3	·3	·3	·3	·4	·4	·5
30	·5	·5	·5	·4	·4	·4	·4	·4	·4	·4	·5	·5
40	0·6	0·5	0·5	0·5	0·5	0·5	0·5	0·5	0·5	0·5	0·5	0·6
45	·6	·6	·6	·5	·5	·5	·5	·5	·5	·6	·6	·6
50	·6	·6	·6	·6	·6	·6	·6	·6	·6	·6	·6	·6
55	·6	·6	·7	·7	·7	·7	·7	·7	·7	·7	·6	·6
60	·7	·7	·7	·8	·8	·8	·8	·8	·8	·7	·7	·7
62	0·7	0·7	0·8	0·8	0·8	0·8	0·8	0·8	0·8	0·8	0·7	0·7
64	·7	·7	·8	·8	·9	0·9	0·9	0·9	·9	·8	·8	·7
66	·7	·8	·8	0·9	0·9	1·0	1·0	1·0	0·9	·9	·8	·7
68	0·7	0·8	0·9	1·0	1·0	1·1	1·1	1·0	1·0	0·9	0·9	0·8
Month	a_2	a_2	a_2	a_2	a_2	a_2	a_2	a_2	a_2	a_2	a_2	a_2
	′	′	′	′	′	′	′	′	′	′	′	′
Jan.	0·5	0·5	0·5	0·5	0·5	0·6	0·6	0·6	0·6	0·7	0·7	0·7
Feb.	·4	·4	·4	·4	·4	·4	·4	·5	·5	·5	·6	·6
Mar.	·4	·3	·3	·3	·3	·3	·3	·3	·3	·4	·4	·5
Apr.	0·5	0·4	0·4	0·3	0·3	0·3	0·2	0·2	0·2	0·3	0·3	0·3
May	·6	·5	·5	·4	·4	·3	·3	·2	·2	·2	·2	·2
June	·8	·7	·6	·6	·5	·4	·4	·3	·3	·2	·2	·2
July	0·9	0·8	0·8	0·7	0·7	0·6	0·5	0·5	0·4	0·4	0·3	0·3
Aug.	·9	·9	·9	·8	·8	·7	·7	·6	·6	·5	·5	·4
Sept.	·9	·9	·9	·9	·9	·9	·8	·8	·8	·7	·7	·6
Oct.	0·8	0·8	0·9	0·9	0·9	0·9	0·9	0·9	0·9	0·9	0·8	0·8
Nov.	·6	·7	·8	·8	·9	·9	·9	1·0	1·0	1·0	1·0	0·9
Dec.	0·5	0·5	0·6	0·7	0·8	0·8	0·9	0·9	1·0	1·0	1·0	1·0
Lat.	AZIMUTH											
	°	°	°	°	°	°	°	°	°	°	°	°
0	0·4	0·6	0·7	0·7	0·8	0·8	0·8	0·8	0·8	0·7	0·6	0·5
20	0·5	0·6	0·7	0·8	0·8	0·9	0·9	0·9	0·8	0·8	0·7	0·5
40	0·6	0·7	0·8	1·0	1·0	1·1	1·1	1·1	1·0	0·9	0·8	0·7
50	0·7	0·9	1·0	1·1	1·2	1·3	1·3	1·3	1·2	1·1	1·0	0·8
55	0·8	1·0	1·1	1·3	1·4	1·4	1·4	1·4	1·4	1·2	1·1	0·9
60	0·9	1·1	1·3	1·4	1·6	1·6	1·7	1·6	1·6	1·4	1·3	1·0
65	1·0	1·3	1·5	1·7	1·9	1·9	2·0	1·9	1·8	1·7	1·5	1·2

Latitude = Apparent altitude (corrected for refraction) − 1° + a_0 + a_1 + a_2

The table is entered with L.H.A. Aries to determine the column to be used; each column refers to a range of 10°. a_0 is taken, with mental interpolation, from the upper table with the units of L.H.A. Aries in degrees as argument; a_1, a_2 are taken, without interpolation, from the second and third tables with arguments latitude and month respectively. a_0, a_1, a_2 are always positive. The final table gives the azimuth of *Polaris*.

FIG. 910. Part of Polaris tables of the *Nautical Almanac*.

Suppose it is desired to determine the latitude by Polaris altitude, and the azimuth, for the following data: DR lat 31°14.7 N., DR long 171°33.6 E., at 4ʰ 15ᵐ 16ˢ on June 23, WE 9ˢ fast, hs 31°26.4, ht of eye 9.3 metres, IC (−) 2.0 (on the arc). Refer to Fig. 910.

	June 23		Polaris		DR L	31°14.7 N.
W	4ʰ15ᵐ16ˢ	a_0	0 28.7		DR Lo	171°33.6 E.
WE	(F) 9ˢ	a_1	0.5			
ZT	4ʰ15ᵐ07ˢ	a_2	0.2		hs	31°26.4
ZD	(−)11	sum	0 29.4		IC	(−) 2.0
GMT	17ʰ15ᵐ07ˢ June 22	(−) 1			D	(−) 5.4
17ʰ	165°16.8	corr (−)	0 30.6		ha	31°19.0
15ᵐ07ˢ	3 47.4				Main	(−) 1.6
GHA♈	169 04.2				Ho	31 17.4
Lo	171 33.6 E.					
LHA♈	340 37.8					
Ho	31 17.4					
corr	(−) 30.6					
L	30°46.8 N.					
Zn	000.8					

Reduction of Polaris observations need not be by special method. Any method of sight reduction can be used if suitable entry values are provided. Since the appearance of the NP 401/Pub. No. 229 inspection tables, the almanac method explained above has lost much of its popularity.

Latitude by calculation is discussed further in section 6 of this chapter.

12. Longitude

When a body is on the prime vertical, either east or west of the observer, its azimuth is 090° or 270°. A position line resulting from observation of a body in this position, being perpendicular to the azimuth line, extends in a north-south direction, thus defining longitude. Modern navigators equipped with inspection tables generally reduce such an observation in the usual manner, rather than giving it special consideration.

Before the introduction of the intercept method by Marcq St. Hilaire in 1875 the common practice was to observe a body on or near the prime vertical and, with the declination and observed altitude of the body and the best determination of latitude, calculate the meridian angle. The following equation might be used:

$$\cos t = \sec Ho \sec d \ (\sin Ho - \sin L \sin d),$$

in which t is the meridian angle, Ho the observed (corrected sextant) altitude, d the declination, and L the latitude. Comparison of t with GHA of the body at the time of observation yielded longitude. Various 'horary tables' appeared from time to time to facilitate the solution. An observation made to determine longitude in this manner is called a *time sight*.

Not all bodies cross the prime vertical above the horizon. Refer to Fig. 909. If a body has declination of contrary name to latitude, it crosses the prime vertical below the horizon, as shown by d_1d_1', the parallel of declination of such a body. In the figure, ZNa is the prime vertical. The nearest approach of the body when visible is at rising and setting. A body having declination the same name as, but greater than, latitude does not cross the prime vertical, as shown at d_3d_3'. Its nearest approach occurs at maximum azimuth angle.

There are several methods of determining when a body is on the prime vertical or at its nearest approach. A diagram on the plane of the celestial meridian, such as Fig. 909, can be used for approximate results. Inspection tables such as NP 401/Pub. No. 229 can be used, noting the LHA when the azimuth angle is 90° or maximum, and converting LHA to GHA, using the approximate longitude, and finding the time at which the calculated GHA occurs. Tables of meridian angle and altitude when a body is on the prime vertical, or at nearest approach, for various entering values of latitude and declination, are included in some books of nautical tables. The meridian angle and altitude can be calculated. When a body is on the prime vertical,

$$\cos t = \tan d \cot L,$$

$$\sin h = \sin d \csc L,$$

in which t is meridian angle, d is declination, L is latitude, and h is the altitude. At nearest approach of a body that does not cross the prime vertical,

$$\sec t = \tan d \cot L,$$

$$\csc h = \sin d \csc L,$$

with notation as above.

The longitude determined by a time sight is that at the intersection of the position line and the assumed parallel. The error of the position so determined increases with increasing error of latitude and increasing departure of the body from the prime vertical. Some books of nautical tables include a table of *longitude factor* (F), the change of longitude along a position line for unit change of latitude, to simplify correction of the calculated longitude if a correction to latitude is established subsequent to the time-sight calculation. Longitude factor can be calculated by the equation:

$$F = \sec L \cot Z = 1/f,$$

in which L is the latitude, Z is the azimuth angle, and f is the latitude factor (p. 449).

A variation of the time-sight method is to determine the instant of meridian transit of a body. At that instant the meridian angle is zero, and the GHA of the body ($360° - $GHA in east longitude) is the longitude of the observer. Knowledge of the latitude is unnecessary, and the calculation is simple. The principal problem with this approach is the difficulty of determining the instant of meridian transit. Azimuth observation is not sufficiently accurate for practical results, and the altitude changes very slowly near transit. If the declination is changing rapidly, or if the observer's motion has a north or south component, the maximum (or minimum) altitude does not occur at transit (p. 446). For a stationary observer and a body of nearly constant declination the time midway between two observations of the body at the same altitude on each side of transit might produce practical results. Better procedure might be observation of the altitude over a period of several minutes each side of transit. A plot of altitude *vs.* time provides an indication of the time of transit.

Any method of determining longitude dependent upon

GHA at the time of observation requires accurate knowledge of time at the Greenwich meridian. It was this need that led to the development of the marine chronometer. Before the availability of this instrument, various ingenious methods of determining Greenwich time were conceived. The most popular was the method of *lunar distances*, which involved observation of the position of the Moon relative to other astronomical bodies. Other methods included observation of an eclipse of the Moon, the eclipse of Jupiter's four principal satellites by their primary, occultations of stars by the Moon, and the time of transit of the Moon. All of these approaches but one depend upon the changing position of the Moon on the celestial sphere. Variations of this principle are still suggested from time to time, for use in emergency situations when other means of establishing Greenwich time are not available.

Longitude by calculation is discussed further in section 6 of this chapter.

13. Complete Solution

The complete reduction of an astronomical observation involves the following separate calculations: (*1*) sextant altitude-correction; (*2*) conversion of watch time to GMT; (*3*) determination of GHA and declination from an almanac; (*4*) selection of an assumed position and determination of LHA or t for the assumed longitude; (*5*) calculation of Hc and Zn; and (*6*) comparison of Hc and Ho to determine *a*. With AP, *a*, and Zn, one plots the position line. With minor variations, the sight-reduction process is the same for all bodies. It is good practice to adopt a standard method of solution. The use of a duplicated work form saves time and reduces the probability of error. Such forms, either separately or in a bound volume, may be available commercially, but a navigator may prefer to devise his own and have it duplicated or a rubber stamp made. If loose sheets are used, the completed sheets should be inserted in a looseleaf work book for possible reference later.

A suitable work form for use with NP 401/Pub. No. 229

and the *Nautical Almanac* is shown in Fig. 911, filled in with a complete solution of an observation of the star Enif, for the following data: DR lat 41°26'.2 N., DR long 20°54'.6 W., June 21, W 5^h 14^m 18^s, WE 13^s (F), hs 55°41'.6, ht of eye 10.6 metres, IC (+) 1'.5 (off the arc). It is good practice to make the solution in several steps, completing each step for all bodies observed before proceeding to the next step:

1. Fill in all given data, record the assumed latitude (two places), and solve for GMT and date and for Ho. For an observation of the Moon, the solution for Ho cannot be completed at this point. Record Ho below Hc in the left-hand column.

2. Record all applicable data from the appropriate daily page of the almanac (SHA, GHA and declination for the integral hour of GMT, v and d values, and horizontal parallax if a Moon sight). Be careful to record signs of v and d and whether declination is N. or S.

3. Record and apply the applicable data from the Increments and Corrections part of the almanac. When this step is completed, one should have LHA; assumed longitude (two places), assumed declination, declination increment, assumed latitude (two places), and Ho (two places).

4. Record the applicable data, including signs, from the main table of NP 401/Pub. No. 229. One should now have Tab Hc, d, DSD (if applicable), Tab Z, and Z diff. It is good practice at this point to record in their places the signs of d_1, d_2, and Z corrections.

5. Complete the calculation, using the data from the interpolation table of NP 401/Pub. No. 229.

If this work form is used, the four quantities needed for plotting the position line (*a*, Zn, *a* L, and *a* Lo) are clustered together at the bottom of the form. The time diagram is not essential, but provides a useful check to help one visualize the situation and avoid a major error. If used, it is completed as one proceeds, the Greenwich meridian and the hour circle of the Sun being drawn as part of step *1*, and the remainder as part of step *3*.

Because of the time-saving value of parallel solution of all observations of a round of sights, some navigators prefer to

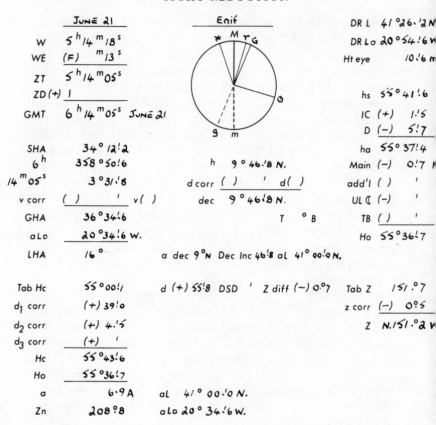

	JUNE 21		Enif	
W	$5^h 14^m 18^s$			DR L 41°26.'2 N
WE	(F) $^m 13^s$			DR Lo 20°54.'6 W
ZT	$5^h 14^m 05^s$			Ht eye 10.'6 m
ZD (+)	1			
GMT	$6^h 14^m 05^s$ JUNE 21			hs 55°41.'6
				IC (+) 1.'5
				D (−) 5.'7
SHA	34° 12.'2			ha 55°37.'4
6^h	358°50.'6		h 9°46.'8 N.	Main (−) 0.'7 M
$14^m 05^s$	3°31.'8	d corr ( ) ' d( )		add'l ( ) '
v corr	( ) ' v( )	dec 9°46.'8 N.		UL ☾ (−) '
GHA	36°34.'6		T °B	TB ( ) '
aLo	20°34.'6 W.			Ho 55°36.'7
LHA	16°	a dec 9°N Dec Inc 46.'8 aL 41°00.'0 N.		
Tab Hc	55°00.'1	d (+) 55.'8 DSD ' Z diff (−) 0.°7	Tab Z 151.°7	
d_1 corr	(+) 39.'0		z corr (−) 0.°5	
d_2 corr	(+) 4.'5			
d_3 corr	(+) '		Z N.151.°2 W	
Hc	55°43.'6			
Ho	55°36.'7			
a	6.9 A	aL 41° 00.'0 N.		
Zn	208°8	aLo 20° 34.'6 W.		

FIG. 911. Complete solution of a star sight.

use a work form in one column, with several columns, for several bodies, on one page. This avoids page-turning during calculation, but does not always place related data together on one line or in close proximity. Personal preference should be one's guide in adoption of a work form.

Although parallel solution of several observations reduces the total time of sight reduction, one might prefer complete individual solutions until one becomes thoroughly familiar with the process.

14. Precalculation

The normal sequence of tasks involved in fixing position by astronavigation is (*1*) advance planning, including determination of time of Sunrise or Sunset for twilight observations; (*2*) observation; (*3*) sight reduction; and (*4*) plotting. The time needed for sight reduction and plotting introduces a delay between observation and the establishment of a fix. This delay can be shortened by reversing steps (*2*) and (*3*). This process is called *precalculation*. A number of variations have been suggested. The following is a simple procedure:

1. Select in advance the bodies to be observed and the watch times of observation.

2. Calculate Hc for each proposed observation.

3. Using Hc, determine altitude corrections, reverse the sign of the total correction, and apply to Hc to obtain *precalculated altitude* (*Hp*). For best accuracy, particularly for altitudes of less than 15°, use Hp to make a second determination of the altitude corrections, and apply this to Hc to obtain an improved value of Hp.

4. Make each observation at the appointed time and compare Hp (in place of Hc) and hs (in place of Ho) to determine the intercept (*a*).

5. Plot each position line and the fix.

Experience in astronavigation is useful in establishing a realistic schedule of observations. Observation at exactly the prescribed times is not essential. For each second of time that the observation is late the assumed position is moved 0.́25 westward along the parallel. If the observation is early, the AP is moved eastward. This movement of the AP assumes constant declination and a constant rate of apparent motion of 15° per hour, reasonable assumptions over a period of a few minutes, except for the Moon, for which the adjustment should not be for more than a minute and a half if errors of longitude greater than 1′ are to be avoided.

An alternative procedure is to make a number of observations over a period of several minutes, starting a minute or two before the preselected time, make a graph of sextant altitude *vs.* watch time, and take the sextant altitude at the preselected time from the graph.

Precalculation can be used for any body. It is particularly attractive for a noon sight of the Sun, to permit determination of a noon position of maximum accuracy with minimum delay following observation. Precalculation is not suitable when overcast obscures much of the sky, thus dictating the selection of bodies and the times of observation.

X

Electronic Aids

1. Electromagnetic Radiation

If an alternating current is flowing through a conductor half a wave length long, nearly all of the energy that is not dissipated in the form of heat is radiated into the space surrounding the conductor at about the speed of light (300,000 kilometres per second). This emission of energy into the space surrounding an oscillating circuit is called *electromagnetic radiation*, the energy thus transmitted having both electrical and magnetic properties. The radiated energy is conceived as travelling in the form of waves called *radio waves*, if of a suitable rate for radio communication.

The conception of radiated electromagnetic energy as waves is strengthened by the fact that the electromagnetic energy increases and decreases in proportion to the sine of the *phase*, the portion of completion of the cycle, a complete cycle being considered as 360°. Refer to Fig. 1001. Starting with zero at the left, the energy increases with time until it reaches a maximum at a quarter of the cycle, then decreases to zero at half cycle, reaches a maximum negative value at three-quarters of the cycle, and returns to zero at the completion of the cycle. The maximum value is the *amplitude* (*A, Amp*) of the signal, occurring at either the positive or negative *peak*.

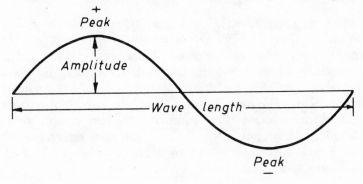

FIG. 1001. A radio wave.

The distance travelled by a signal during one complete cycle is the *wave length* (λ). The *frequency* (f) is the number of cycles in unit time. A unit of one cycle per second is called a *Hertz* (*Hz*) after the German scientist Heinrich Hertz. Frequency may be expressed in Hertz, but more often in some large multiple of Hertz, such as 1,000 (kiloHertz, kHz), 1,000,000 (megaHertz, MHz), or 1,000,000,000 (gigaHertz, GHz).

Wave length varies with the speed of travel, which does not vary greatly from 300,000 kilometres per second, or 300,000,000 metres per second. If wave length is expressed in metres and frequency in Hertz, the approximate value of either can be found by dividing 300,000,000 by the other. Thus, if the frequency is 150 MHz (150,000,000 cycles per second), the approximate wave length is 300,000,000/150,000,000 = 2 metres.

Radio spectrum. The range of electromagnetic radiation suitable for radio communication, called the *radio spectrum*, extends from about 10kHz to about 300 GHz. It is divided into a number of bands, as follows:

Designation	Frequency	Wave Length
Very low frequency (VLF)	10–30 kHz	30–10 km
Low frequency (LF)	30–300 kHz	10–1 km
Medium frequency (MF)	300–3,000 kHz	1–0.1 km
High frequency (HF)	3–30 MHz	100–10 m
Very high frequency (VHF)	30–300 MHz	10–1 m
Ultra high frequency (UHF)	300–3,000 MHz	100–10 cm
Super high frequency (SHF)	3–30 GHz	10–1 cm
Extremely high frequency (EHF)	30–300 GHz	10–1 mm

The upper limit in each band is included, while the lower limit is not. The VLF band is occasionally given as 3–30 kHz (100–10 km), and an extremely low frequency (ELF) band of 1–3,000 Hz (300,000–100 km) is included. Frequencies of less than about 20 kHz are in the audible range. Frequencies greater than EHF exist in the form of heat, infra-red, visible light, ultra-violet, x-rays, gamma rays, and cosmic rays. Radiations shorter than VHF are sometimes referred to as *microwaves*, further broken down into *decimetric* (UHF), *centimetric* (SHF), and *millimetric* (EHF) waves.

Letter designations are sometimes used to define certain small ranges of the higher frequencies, but these have no official sanction. Some of these bands are:

Band	f(GHz)	λ(cm)	Band	f(GHz)	λ(cm)
L	1.00–1.88	30.00–15.96	X	8.20–12.40	3.66–2.42
S	2.35–4.175	12.77–7.816	K	16.00–28.00	1.88–1.07
C	3.60–7.45	8.33–4.03	Q	33.00–50.00	0.91–0.60

Attenuation. As radio waves travel outward from their source, the amplitude decreases, the signals becoming weaker. The decrease in amplitude, called *attenuation*, is the result of (*1*) the expansion of the wave in a three-dimensional manner similar to the two-dimensional increase in the circumference of a circular ripple caused by dropping a pebble in water; (*2*) *absorption* by the medium through which it travels (principally water in gas, liquid, or solid form in the atmosphere) and any surface (e.g. of the Earth) with which it has contact; and (*3*) *scattering* by water droplets, ice, and solid particles in the atmosphere. The amount of attenuation varies greatly with conditions, aerial characteristics, and frequency of the signal.

Reflection. Radio waves are reflected in a manner similar to reflection of light waves. Any solid or liquid surface can cause reflection. In addition, rain, clouds, the ionosphere (p. 465), and even sharp discontinuities in the atmosphere, as along the frontal surface between air masses of different characteristics, cause reflection of radio waves. The nature of the surface influences the amount and nature of the reflection. The surface of a good conductor reflects better than the surface of a poor conductor. If the surface is rough relative to the length of the wave, or composed of small particles, the reflection is diffuse. Thus, frequency is a factor. So is the angle of encounter of the signal with the reflecting surface.

At reflection, a wave may undergo a phase change. The phase of a reflected wave received some distance away may differ from another portion of the same wave received without reflection because of this phase change at reflection, and also because of a difference in the lengths of the paths followed by the two parts. The effect of this *multipath* is the receipt of two or more signals from one transmitted signal. The different components of the received wave strengthen one another if they arrive in phase, but may weaken one another if they arrive out of phase, the total signal received being the vector sum of the individual components. Complete cancellation occurs if two components have the same amplitude and are 180° out of phase. If the difference in time of reception is sufficiently long, the same signal arriving by two or more routes may arrive as separate signals, as shadows sometimes seen on a television screen.

Refraction of radio waves when a signal enters a medium of different density is similar to refraction of visible light (p. 382), but somewhat greater. As a radio wave travels across the surface of the Earth, the upper portion of the wave, travelling in thinner air, moves faster than the lower portion, and the wave front is bent toward the Earth. This bending being greater than that of visible light, the *radio horizon* is more remote than the visible horizon. The distance in miles to the geometrical horizon (p. 301) is about $1.92\sqrt{h}$, to the visible horizon about $2.09\sqrt{h}$, and to the radio horizon typically about $2.21\sqrt{h}$, where h is the height of eye or aerial above the surface of the Earth, in metres. If the height of eye is in feet, the constants are 1.06, 1.15, and 1.22, respectively. However, the distance to the radio horizon varies somewhat with frequency, being greater for lower frequencies. In a warm air mass, particularly one over water, with a sharp decrease of humidity with height, the lapse rate with height above the surface tends to decrease, resulting in greater than normal atmospheric refraction, called *super-refraction*. As a result, the radio horizon is extended and radar ranges are greater than normal. Under extreme conditions, when a strong temperature inversion exists, the refraction may be equal to the curvature of the Earth, resulting in *ducting*. The anomalous propagation occurring when this condition exists results in reception of signals at far greater distances than normal, the expansion being essentially two-dimensional rather than three-dimensional and the decrease in signal strength being proportional to the distance rather than the square of the distance. Ducting occurs principally at VHF and UHF frequencies.

Ground effects. Refraction of radio waves also takes place in the horizontal as a wave travelling across the surface of the Earth enters an area having a surface with different conducting and reflecting properties, as when it crosses a coast line. This phenomenon is sometimes called *coastal refraction* or *land effect.* A similar but generally weaker effect may occur when a radio wave crosses a mountain range or a magnetic anomaly (p. 104).

Radio waves penetrate the ocean and solid Earth somewhat, the depth decreasing with increasing frequency. This permits reception of signals at the lower end of the frequency spectrum several metres below the surface of the ocean. The speed of radio waves penetrating the more dense liquid or solid upper portion of the Earth's crust decreases. If a radio wave of sufficiently low frequency travels across the surface of the Earth, the lower portion penetrates the Earth and slows, causing bending downward of the wave front additional to that caused by atmospheric refraction. This results in the waves at lower frequencies following the curvature of the Earth. These *ground waves* may be received at great distances from the transmitter.

Ionosphere. Radiation from outside the Earth's atmosphere, principally ultra-violet radiation from the Sun, produces several layers of ionized gas in the rarefied upper atmosphere, principally in the region of about 50 to 1,000 km above the surface of the Earth. Collectively, these layers are called the *ionosphere.* The layers affecting radio-wave propagation are designated the D, E, and F layers, in order of increasing height. The height, orientation, and intensity of the various layers vary with the amount and type of radiation received, and with atmospheric conditions, time of day, season, and the phase of the 11-year sunspot cycle. The F layer, in the thinnest part of the upper atmosphere, is most erratic. During daylight hours, it separates into two layers designated F_1 and F_2. During the night, the layers are generally weaker and at higher altitudes than during the day.

The D layer may disappear entirely. For short periods at about the times of Sunrise and Sunset, changes are rapid, resulting in unstable conditions. The related disturbance of some radio signals at these times is called *night effect* or *polarization error*.

The principal effects of the ionosphere upon radio propagation are absorption and refraction. Absorption is greatest in the D layer, and in the HF range of about 500 to 1,500 kHz. Refraction of lower-frequency signals occurs principally in the D layer, but as frequency increases, the waves increasingly penetrate the D layer and are refracted by higher layers. Refer to Fig. 1002. As a radio wave encounters

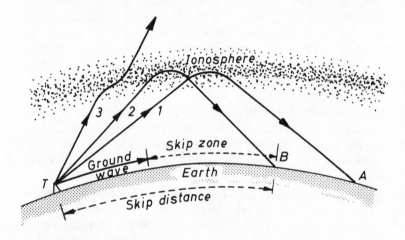

FIG. 1002. Ionospheric refraction of radio signals.

a refractive layer of the ionosphere at an oblique angle, the upper portion of the wave reaches the ionized layer first and its speed increases, resulting in bending, or refracting of the wave front. Ray 1, leaving the transmitter T at a low angle to the horizontal, is refracted by the ionosphere and returns to the Earth at some point A. Ray 2, leaving at a steeper angle, returns at a point closer to the transmitter, at B. Ray 3, at a still steeper angle, is bent but not sufficiently for it to return to the Earth. As it passes through the ionosphere, it is refracted in the opposite direction, and passes out into space. The minimum distance at which a signal can be received by refraction in the ionosphere, shown here as ray 2, is called the *skip distance*. At shorter distances, signals can be received only by ducting or as ground waves or *direct waves*—those that travel in an essentially straight line from the transmitter to the receiver. The area between the maximum limit of reception of ground waves and the minimum limit of reception of waves arriving after refraction in the ionosphere, called *sky waves*, in which no signal is received, is called the *skip zone*. A number of different sky waves may reach the Earth from one transmitted wave, being refracted by different layers of the ionosphere. *Multihop sky waves* may also be received when sky waves are reflected by the Earth and refracted one or more additional times by the ionosphere.

Sky waves are attenuated less than ground waves, and thus make possible the reception of some signals at greater distances than would be possible otherwise. This increased distance of reception is particularly noticeable during the night, when the ionosphere is weaker. The bending of radio waves is then more gradual, increasing the distance between the transmitter and the return of the waves to the surface of the Earth. The disappearance of the D layer, which has a relatively high absorption of radio energy at some frequencies, also contributes to the greater reception distance at night.

The effects of the ionosphere upon radio-wave propagation are not all good. The amount of bending depends upon the intensity of the ionization and the frequency of the radio signal, as well as upon the angle of incidence. The amount of bending is greatest at the lowest frequencies, decreasing with increased frequency until a *maximum usable frequency* (*MUF*) is reached, beyond which the waves pass through the ionosphere and travel outward into space. The maximum usable frequency depends not only upon the condition of the ionosphere, but also upon the distance between the transmitter and the receiver, for the skip distance is a consideration. The strongest signals are received at a frequency near the maximum usuable frequency, but this frequency is somewhat variable because of fluctuations in the intensity of ionization of the ionosphere. Because of this variability, it is customary to use 85 per cent of the maximum usable frequency as the optimum. During a sudden ionosphere disturbance (p. 96) ionization decreases, resulting in decreased maximum usable frequency. Absorption by the D layer increases, thus increasing the lower limit of usable frequency. If the change is great enough, the maximum and minimum frequencies overtake one another, resulting in a radio *blackout*, when arriving signals are too weak for use if communication is dependent upon sky waves. Sky waves can usually not be received at any distance at a frequency of more than 30 MHz.

Radio waves undergo some change of phase during refraction by the ionosphere. They may also change direction of travel because of tilting of the ionosphere. Because of continual changes in intensity, position, and orientation of the somewhat patchy ionosphere, the signal arriving at a receiver may be composed of several components, arriving by paths of different lengths, with various strengths and phase. Such components sometimes strengthen one another, and sometimes interfere, resulting in variable strength of the total signal, a condition called *fading* when the signal strength decreases. Signals reflected by the F layer are particularly erratic.

Diffraction. Obstacles in the paths of radiant energy produce shadows. For visible light and the higher radio frequencies the demarcation between illuminated and shadow areas is quite sharp, but as frequency decreases, the line of separation becomes more diffused, and increasing amounts of radiant energy enter the shadow area. This effect is called *diffraction*.

Noise. Radio receiving equipment is responsive to all signals of adequate magnitude at the frequency to which the receiver is tuned, whatever the source. Unwanted stray signals are called *noise*. A number of sources of noise have been identified. It may originate within the receiver itself, or at other electrical equipment in the vicinity of the receiver or aerial. Sparks are particularly productive of noise.

Unwanted signals may also be received from transmission at the same or nearly the same frequency as that of the desired signals. Reception of signals transmitted at a frequency different from that to which the receiver is tuned is called *spillover*. Deliberate, intentional interference with reception of desired signals by transmission or re-radiation of signals on the same frequency is called *jamming*. While unwanted signals from transmissions on the same or nearly the same frequency as that of the desired signals is not noise in the strict sense, the effect is similar.

Natural sources also contribute to noise. Stray signals originating in the discharge of static electricity in the atmosphere are called *atmospherics* or *static*. They are particularly strong in the vicinity of thunderstorms. *Precipitation static* is sometimes produced when precipitation strikes a conducting surface, giving it a negative charge of static electricity that produces noise as it discharges into the atmosphere surrounding the surface. Friction of solid or liquid particles as they strike an exposed conducting projection may also produce a charge of static electricity on the projection. As the charge builds up, the energy tends to leak off in a luminous and sometimes audible *corona discharge* often called *St. Elmo's fire*. Noise is particularly troublesome at lower frequencies, those higher than 30 MHz being relatively noise-free, except for some *cosmic noise* originating outside the atmosphere.

The effect of noise is to interfere with the reception of wanted signals. The ratio of the strength of wanted signals and noise is called *signal-to-noise ratio* (S/N). The ratio can be improved by either increasing the signal strength or reducing the noise, or by changing the frequency to a more favourable one. Increasing the range of frequency received seldom helps, because it lets in more noise. Reduction of noise has limitations, because much of it is beyond control. Noise is usually of mixed frequency. That having a wide range of frequency is called *white noise*, after white light, composed of all frequencies of the visible spectrum.

A relatively simple signal of limited frequency range can sometimes be identified with quite a low signal-to-noise ratio, but as the complexity of the signal increases, so does the difficulty of identifying it in the presence of noise. If the signal-to-noise ratio cannot be improved, signal identification might be enhanced by redundancy, either by repetition of the signal or by inclusion of sufficient information to permit identification if some of the message is missed. An example would be the missing of one letter of a word or message which could be constructed from the letters or words received.

Doppler effect. The *Doppler effect* is the change of frequency of arriving radiant energy when the distance between the source and the receiver or observer is changing. The received frequency is higher than the transmitted frequency if the distance is decreasing, and lower if the distance is increasing. The Doppler effect is present in all forms of radiation, including sound and radio waves.

Range. The maximum distance at which a usable signal can be received depends upon a number of factors, such as frequency and power of transmission, the path of travel of the radio waves, noise level, condition of the ionosphere, presence of precipitation, aerial (both transmitting and receiving) design and efficiency, and characteristics of the receiver.

Propagation characteristics. Selection of appropriate frequency is an important consideration in the development of an electronic navigation or communication system because of the differences in propagation characteristics at various frequencies. A summary of the principal characteristics follows:

Very low frequency (VLF) waves travel great distances, essentially as ground waves, but the lower portion of the ionosphere also contributes to the great distance at which these signals are received. Reception of VLF signals travelling in opposite directions around the Earth is not unknown. There is relatively little reflection from obstacles, and diffraction is maximum. Penetration of the Earth and especially sea water is maximum, making possible reception of VLF signals at depths of several metres below the surface. Sudden ionospheric disturbances have relatively little effect, but atmospherics are a problem. Because of the long wave length, very large aerials are needed, but even these do not approach half a wave length, resulting in low aerial efficiency and great power requirements. The propagation speed is slightly variable, depending upon direction of travel of the waves, a condition that can affect the use of these frequencies for navigation.

Low frequencies (*L F*). The effects of higher frequency are apparent. The distance of reception is less, reflection is greater, diffraction is less, penetration of the surface of the Earth is greatly reduced, as compared with V L F propagation. But aerial efficiency is much greater. Atmospherics are still a problem. The L F band is useful for communication at distances to several thousand miles, and for radio direction-finding (p. 480).

Medium frequency (*M F*). The ground wave is the stronger signal during daylight hours, but at distances of several hundred miles the sky wave predominates during the night. Interference between ground waves and sky waves may occur when both are received. This problem is particularly critical when night effect occurs near the times of Sunrise and Sunset. Ionospheric absorption is greatest in the M F band, peaking at about 1,400 kHz. Distance at which M F signals can be received reliably varies considerably, depending upon atmospheric conditions and critically upon the frequency selected.

High frequency (*H F*). Ground waves are usable only within a few miles of the transmitter, leaving a dead space between the outer limits of reception of these waves and the inner limit of reception of sky waves. Thus, the skip distance is of considerable importance in selecting frequency. The height of the aerial determines the distance at which direct waves can be received. Because H F propagation at considerable distance is dependent upon sky waves, the condition of the ionosphere is critical, and sudden ionospheric disturbances are disruptive of H F communication.

Very high frequency (*V H F*). Sky waves are unreliable and ground waves extend only for very short distances. Accordingly, communication at VHF frequencies is limited essentially to direct waves, waves reflected by the surface of the Earth (and by ducting), inefficient *scatter* transmission utilizing the energy scattered by reflecting patches in the ionosphere, and signals retransmitted by relay stations on artificial Earth satellites. The availability of satellites has made VHF available for reliable communication at great distances at sea, thus displacing the less dependable HF to some extent. Nearer the transmitting aerial, when satellites are not used, some interference between direct and reflected ground waves may occur. Atmospheric noise is virtually nonexistent at VHF and higher frequencies. Directional aerials of reasonable efficiency are possible in the VHF band.

Ultra high frequency (UHF) signals are sharply directional, so that directional aerials are practicable, and the principal type in use. Although direct waves and waves reflected by the surface of the Earth (and by ducting) may be used, interference between waves is a problem. Sky waves are virtually nonexistent. Accordingly, direct waves are the principal ones used, although some weak signals may be received by atmospheric scatter by particles in the atmosphere. Propagation of UHF signals is thus essentially line-of-sight, the radio horizon at these frequencies being some 6 per cent more distant than the visible horizon, the difference being the result of greater atmospheric refraction of the radio waves than of light waves. There is very little diffraction at UHF frequencies, and reflection is strong. Atmospherics are not a problem, and there is almost no fading.

Super high frequency (SHF). Sky waves, diffraction, and atmospherics are virtually nonexistent, but slight interference by cosmic noise may be encountered. Also, reflections by clouds, precipitation, or solid particles in the atmosphere increases the scatter, causing some wave interference and fading. Atmospheric absorption is present to some extent, particularly at the higher end of the frequency band. Highly-effective directional aerials are practicable.

Extremely high frequency (EHF). The effects of short waves are most evident in this band. There is no diffraction, wave interference, fading, atmospheric noise, sky waves, or ground waves. Only direct, line-of-sight waves and reflected waves are available. Scattering by reflection from particles in the atmosphere is pronounced, and absorption is extensive. Propagation at EHF frequencies approaches that of heat, infra-red, and visible light.

Forms of transmission. Electromagnetic energy is transmitted in several different forms. In *continuous wave* (*CW*) transmission a continuous series of waves is transmitted at identical amplitude and frequency. This type of transmission is useful for some purposes, as in radio direction-finding.

Variation of some characteristic of the basic wave pattern in accordance with instantaneous values of another wave is called *modulation*. When this occurs, the basic wave system is called the *carrier wave*, and a wave system producing the variation is called the *modulating wave*. A common example of a modulating wave is the wave system at audio frequency resulting from human speech. Continuous wave transmission produces an unvarying tone of a pitch too high to be audible except at the lower end of the VLF band. But if the carrier wave is varied by the modulating wave, the intelligence thus imposed can be recovered by *demodulation* at the receiver.

The variation of the carrier wave in the form of changing its amplitude is called *amplitude modulation* (*AM*), a form commonly used in commercial broadcasting. The variation of the frequency of the carrier wave is called *frequency modulation* (*FM*), also used in commercial broadcasting and in the audio portion of television transmissions. In *phase modulation* the phase of the carrier wave is varied. Another form of modulation, not suitable for transmission of voice signals but used in some navigation systems, is called *pulse modulation* (*PM*). This form of transmission consists of a series of very short bursts of carrier wave, separated by relatively long periods without transmission. By this means large peak-power transmission can be achieved with very small average power. The pulses may be varied in time, amplitude, or arranged in groups.

Audible transmissions, unless of a continuous, unvarying tone, involve a range of frequency called *bandwidth*.

473

Modulation of radio waves also requires bandwidth, as does the Doppler effect if there is relative motion between the transmitter and the receiver. Narrowing the bandwith conserves the radio spectrum but limits the rate at which information can be transmitted, and this adversely affects the accuracy of some types of navigation systems. At some point of narrowing the bandwidth the system becomes useless. An analogy is the transmission of music. As the bandwidth is narrowed, the highest and lowest notes are eliminated. As the narrowing continues, the range of notes decreases until finally a single tone is transmitted. An important consideration in the selection of an electronic navigation system is its bandwidth requirements, especially if it operates in a crowded part of the radio spectrum. One method of reducing the bandwidth requirement without sacrifice of accuracy when AM is used is by *single-sideband transmission* (*SSB*). In AM transmission, two *sidebands* are involved, with frequencies consisting of the sum and difference, respectively, of the carrier and modulating frequencies. The intelligence is carried by the sidebands. By suppressing one of the sidebands and perhaps the carrier wave also, one reduces the bandwidth required.

Aerials. An *aerial*, also called an *antenna*, is a conductor or system of conductors for radiating or receiving radio waves. A lone radiating element connected at its centre to the transmitter or receiver is called a *dipole aerial*. The efficiency of a dipole increases as its length increases until a maximum is reached when the length of the dipole is half a wave length, beyond which the efficiency decreases. For the higher frequencies, the dipole is very short, as indicated by the table of the radio spectrum, given on p. 462. At lower frequencies, the length becomes so long that efficient transmitting aerials aboard ship are impractical. At MF frequencies, transmitting aerials can be used on very large vessels. For most commercial vessels, HF aerials are the practical limit, and for small craft, VHF aerials.

Receiving aerials are another matter. As the efficiency increases, the strength of desired signals also increases, but so does the strength of noise and any other unwanted signals.

Therefore, an inefficient receiving aerial is satisfactory.

The waves transmitted by an aerial vibrate in the direction of the aerial; e.g., waves from a vertical aerial vibrate vertically. The direction of vibration is said to be the *polarization* of the waves. Thus, a vertical aerial transmits vertically polarized waves, and a horizontal aerial transmits horizontally polarized waves. Circular polarization can be achieved by means of a helical coil aerial or by appropriate circuitry within the transmitter. Received signal strength is greatest when the receiving aerial is correctly oriented to the polarization of the arriving signal; e.g. a vertical aerial for a vertically polarized signal. However, polarization of signals may change during transmission, particularly those under-going refraction or reflection, resulting in somewhat uncertain polarization of signals arriving at the receiving aerial.

If the same aerial is used both for transmitting and receiving, a device is fitted to disconnect the receiver during transmission, to protect the receiver from the strong signals of the transmitter.

The large horizontal transmitting aerials used for lower frequencies are elevated from the ground because of inter-action between the ground and the aerial. The maximum beneficial effect of this interaction would occur when the distance between the aerial and the ground was one quarter of the wave length if the Earth were a perfect conductor. Because it is impractical to elevate aerials to optimum height for transmission of the lowest frequencies, or to make vertical aerials half a wave length long, the efficiency of these aerials is relatively low, requiring greater transmitter power than for higher-frequency transmissions. This inefficiency at lower frequencies is offset somewhat by the greater distance at which usable signals at these frequencies can be received for the same radiated power.

The relative signal strength of radiated signals is not uniform in an expanding sphere. For a lone wire aerial the greatest signal strength is in the plane perpendicular to the wire, and minimum signal strength is in the directions along the wire. The signal strength from a vertical aerial is the same in all horizontal directions. In many installations one desires to concentrate transmitted energy within a limited arc, and suppress it in others. The increase in signal strength in the desired arc over the average in all directions if there were no directivity is called the *gain* of the aerial.

Concentration of transmitted energy within a limited arc can be accomplished in several ways. If a second dipole of appropriate design is placed from one-eighth to one-quarter of a wave length from the transmitting aerial, and not connected to the transmitter, it acts as either a reflector or a director, according to its characteristics. The result in either case is a stronger signal transmitted in one direction than in the opposite direction. If several such dipoles are placed in a line, the transmitted signal becomes strongly directive. This type aerial is also used for reception of transmitted signals, a familiar example being the common household Yagi television aerial. If the dipoles are all connected to the transmitter, the transmission is strong in the two directions perpendicular to the line of dipoles. Transmission in one of these directions might be suppressed by a properly placed reflecting screen of appropriate design. Weaker transmissions, called *side lobes*, may be present in other directions. A *polar diagram* showing relative signal strength transmitted in various directions by such an array might appear as shown in Fig. 1003. At the higher frequencies, highly directive transmission is accomplished by a parabolic reflector that concentrates the radiated energy into a narrow beam. Directivity in a receiving aerial improves the signal-to-noise ratio.

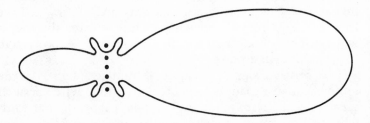

FIG. 1003. Polar diagram of a directional aerial array.

At HF and lower frequencies, the power is led from the transmitter to the aerial by wire, but as the frequency increases, power loss in the transmission lines increases also. At higher frequencies, particularly in the VHF and UHF bands, *coaxial cable* is used. This cable consists of two concentric conductors insulated from each other. At still higher frequencies the resistance encountered in a coaxial cable would be too great, and a *waveguide* is used. This consists of a hollow tube through which the signals travel. A horn at the outer end directs them to the surface of the parabolic reflector that beams them out into the surrounding space.

Transmitter. A radio-wave transmitter consists essentially of an *oscillator* to generate the alternating-current carrier wave pattern. Unless the transmission is to be of a continuous tone, a *modulator* is needed to modulate the carrier wave. A power supply is needed to provide direct current. An *amplifier* increases the strength of the output of the oscillator. An aerial radiates the signal into surrounding space. Additional components are added as needed in a particular installation.

Receiver. The function of a radio receiver is to detect the presence of radio signals intercepted by an aerial, amplify them and extract the intelligence conveyed through modulation, which intelligence is then delivered in audible form or in some form of display or control. A receiver is designed for a preselected frequency range, and provided with means of selecting a desired frequency from among the many at which different signals are received by the aerial. Standards for certain types of receiving equipment are established by governmental or quasi-governmental organizations to provide guidance for manufacturers and establish some degree of uniformity for the benefit of users.

Display. The output of a receiver may be presented audibly in head-phones or by a loudspeaker, or it may be displayed in the form of a dial, meter, or on a *cathode ray tube (CRT)*. The output may also be used to control equipment automatically.

A cathode ray tube, Fig. 1004, the familiar 'picture tube' of television, consists essentially of (*1*) a cathode which together

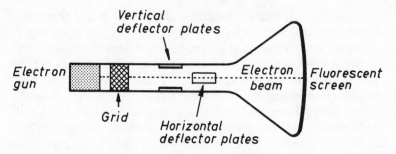

FIG. 1004. A cathode ray tube.

with a focusing anode and accelerator constitutes an *electron gun* that emits a stream of electrons, and (2) a screen coated with fluorescent material that glows when the electrons impinge on it. The fluorescence may be given some degree of persistence if it is desirable that the spot of light produced by the electrons does not fade too quickly. Between the electron gun and the screen the electron stream passes a cylindrical grid on which a negative charge can be imposed to reduce the strength of the beam and thus control the brightness of the spot of light on the screen. The stream of electrons also passes two sets of deflector plates or coils arranged so that positive and negative charges can be applied on opposite sides of the stream to deflect it horizontally and vertically. By this means the spot of light can be moved to any point on the screen, and thus provide a means of displaying information.

2. Techniques

The use of electronics in navigation began early in the twentieth century with the broadcast of radio time signals (p. 152), thus improving the accuracy of timekeeping at sea. This was followed several years later by the use of radio to provide navigational warnings, marine weather forecasts, and other information of interest to mariners.

The direct use of radio for position fixing began with the development of the M F radio direction-finder (p. 481) in the early 1920's. This device provided a means of determining direction of a known point out of sight of land and in periods

478

of restricted visibility. More recently, other techniques have been used to determine direction, as by directional receiving aerials as used in radar (p. 494), directional transmitting aerial arrays as in the L F four-course airway ranges formerly in extensive use, rotating patterns of electronic signals as in consol, and signals emitted by leader cables (p. 492) used to guide vessels along a channel.

Another method of using electronics for navigational purposes is to measure distance, for establishing a circular position line. In radar this is done by measuring the elapsed time between emission of a short burst of energy, or pulse, and the return of an echo from an identifiable point. Distance can also be determined by noting the time of arrival of a signal transmitted at a known time, if the timekeeping equipment at the receiver is synchronized accurately with that controlling the transmission. If sound signals, transmitted through air or water, are synchronized with radio signals, the difference in reception time can be used to determine distance (p. 273).

The *difference* in distance between the receiver and two transmitters can be used to establish hyperbolic position lines. The difference in distance is commonly determined either by measuring the difference in arrival times of synchronized pulse signals from the two stations or by measuring the difference in the phase of synchronized CW signals.

If the *sum* of the distances between the receiver and two transmitters is determined, an elliptical position line is obtained with the two transmitters at the foci. No system of this type is operational.

The Doppler effect (p. 470) is used in the first operational navigation satellite system (p. 542). Additional uses of electronics for navigation include the measurement of the speed of the vessel and the use of radio astronomy (p. 518). Additionally, electronic équipment is used in such navigation equipment as echo sounders (p. 148), sonar (p. 145), underwater logs (p. 138), compass repeaters (p. 134), inertial navigators (p. 532), and electronic computers (p. 527).

The International Telecommunications Union has defined

the following terms relating to the use of electronics:

Radiodetermination. Determination of position, or obtaining information relating to position, by means of the propagation properties of radio waves.

Radionavigation. Radiodetermination used for navigation, including obstruction warning.

Radiolocation. Radiodetermination used for purposes other than navigation.

3. Direction Measurement

The direction from which incoming radio signals are arriving can be measured by means of a loop aerial. Refer to Fig. 1005.

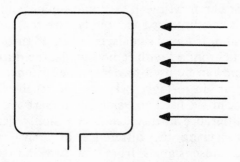

FIG. 1005. A loop aerial.

Vertically polarized signals (p. 475) arriving at the aerial induce voltages in the two vertical sections of the aerial. The output of the aerial is the *difference* in these induced voltages. If the direction of travel of the radio waves is perpendicular to the plane of the aerial, the currents resulting from the induced voltages in the two vertical sections are equal in amplitude and phase. There is no aerial output, a condition called a *null*. If the aerial is rotated about a vertical axis, the incoming signal arrives at the two vertical sections at slightly different times, resulting in a phase difference of the two currents, and an output from the aerial. If the distance between the two vertical sections is half a wave length or less, nulls occur only in the directions perpendicular to the plane of the loop, and maximum output only when the direction of the incoming

480

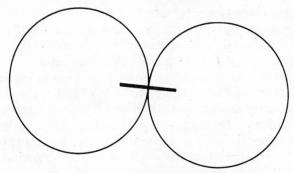

FIG. 1006. Polar diagram of a loop aerial.

signals is in the plane of the loop. The polar diagram (p. 476) of a loop aerial is shown in Fig. 1006. The null direction is more sharply defined than the direction of maximum strength, and thus is used to orient the aerial relative to the incoming signal.

A device consisting essentially of a loop aerial and the accompanying receiver and indicator is called a *radio direction-finder (RDF)*. The simple device described above suffers from a 180° ambiguity, signals arriving from opposite directions producing the same output. This ambiguity can be resolved by the addition of a *sense aerial* consisting of a vertical wire with amplitude and phase relationship to the loops as shown in Fig. 1007. The two small circles shown as

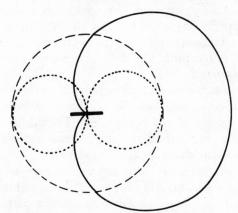

FIG. 1007. Polar diagram of a loop aerial with a sense aerial.

pecked lines represent the output of the loop alone, the two parts being 180° out of phase with respect to each other. The larger circle shown as a broken line represents the output of the sense aerial alone, in phase with the right-hand loop output circle. The cardiod shown as a solid line is the vector sum of the individual outputs of the loop and sense aerials. The lone null of this pattern makes possible the unambiguous determination of direction of the incoming signal. However, the null of the cardiod is less sharply defined than those of the loop alone. It is therefore customary to use the sense and loop aerials together to resolve the ambiguity, and the loop aerial alone to make the direction measurement. If a radio direction-finder does not have a sense aerial, the ambiguity can be resolved, unless the transmitter is nearly dead ahead or dead astern, by taking several bearings and noting the direction of change. If the sense interpretation is correct, the relative bearing, right or left, increases.

A variation of the radio direction-finder described above has a rapidly rotating loop aerial connected to a cathode ray tube (p. 477) that provides a continuous visual display of relative-output signal strength in various directions, thus providing an indication of direction of arrival of an incoming signal.

Another variation has two fixed loops perpendicular to each other. The output of each loop is sent to a field coil, the two being mutually perpendicular so the signals from the two loops are reproduced on a reduced scale. Within the two coils a rotatable coil aligns itself with the vector output to indicate the direction of the null. The direction-indicating element is called a *goniometer*.

A radio direction-finder is subject to several errors in addition to the personal, installation, and calibration errors involved in the use of any equipment. The additional errors can generally be grouped into those relating to (1) propagation vagaries, and (2) environment.

However perfectly an outgoing signal may be vertically polarized, the signal arriving at a receiving aerial is a mixture of signals that may have travelled by a direct path and those that have undergone refraction, reflection from various surfaces, and possible influence from having travelled over the surface of the nonhomogeneous Earth. The result is some induction in the horizontal sections of the loop aerial, and this *polarization error*, or *night effect*, which is particularly troublesome when the ionosphere is undergoing maximum change near the times of Sunrise and Sunset, may offset and broaden the null positions. Coastal refraction (p. 464) may introduce error, especially when a signal travels obliquely across a coast line some distance from the transmitting aerial.

The vessel itself and its equipment, such as other aerials, metal booms and masts, etc., may disturb incoming radio signals, suggesting care in the selection of the site for the RDF aerial to avoid, so far as possible, close proximity to disturbing forces. The principal effect is called *quadrantal error*, so named because its maxima are usually near relative bearings of $045°$, $135°$, $225°$, and $315°$. A table of corrections for various relative bearings, similar to a deviation table (p. 125), can be made by taking a series of simultaneous radio and visual bearings on a transmitting aerial. Metal booms, cranes, davits, etc. should be in their normal positions during the operation, and also when the equipment is being used for navigation. Quadrantal error may change somewhat with changes in trim or loading of the vessel and the nature of its cargo. Additional error may be introduced by the tilt of the loop aerial when the vessel rolls or pitches.

Radio direction-finders are required to be installed aboard all merchant vessels of more than 1,600 tons. They are also in extensive use on smaller ships of various types, and aboard pleasure craft. The type of equipment varies from relatively simple, portable, battery-powered, manually-operated equipment to highly sophisticated, permanently-installed, automatic equipment with various features designed to improve performance and simplify operation. Some of the features available are internal calibration for quadrantal error, automatic sense determination, cathode-ray-tube display, automatic signal-level control to minimize the effect of signal fading, and solid-state construction for greater reliability. Some are mounted over compass repeaters (p. 134) for a direct reading of gyro or compass bearings.

Before taking a reading with such a device one should check the accuracy of the repeater. Some installations are provided with means for manually or automatically positioning a reference mark to permit direct reading of true bearings. The setting of the reference mark should be checked when a reading is taken, particularly if the vessel is yawing.

With the best modern equipment one has little difficulty in obtaining radio bearings to an accuracy of $2°$ under favourable conditions. With the simplest equipment some skill and near-ideal conditions are needed to obtain such accuracy, $5°$ being a more realistic figure for average conditions. If the signals travel a considerable distance over land, or if they are at a frequency differing considerably from that at which the radio direction-finder is calibrated, the error may be larger.

A radio direction-finder can be used to obtain a bearing on any appropriate signal within its frequency range. If the bearing is to be useful for navigation, one must know the position of the transmitting aerial. Marine *radiobeacons (R Bn)* operating in the MF or upper portion of LF band have been installed throughout the world to assist mariners in position determination. Many of these operate intermittently, some groups on coordinated time-sharing schemes. Rotating-loop radiobeacons are installed at some places to permit determination of direction aboard ship without a radio direction-finder. The shore-based loop of such a radiobeacon rotates at the rate of one rotation per minute. The number of seconds from the receipt of the north signal to the arrival of the null, multiplied by six, is the bearing from the transmitter. Instructions for the use of radiobeacons of various types and data on their locations, frequencies, powers, ranges, and operating schedules are given in various publications (section 18), and their locations are indicated on nautical charts.

Direction-finding equipment may be located ashore to assist in position determination. The locations of these *radio-direction-finder stations* are indicated on nautical charts by an appropriate symbol accompanied by the designation RDF. The bearings so determined are communicated by radio to the vessel requesting them. These bearings are corrected by the station for all errors except conversion angle (p. 181), and are normally accurate within 2° for distances to 150 miles. Words such as 'doubtful', 'approximate', or 'second-class' are used in reporting bearings suspected of having larger errors. Two or more stations may operate in a group to provide information to assist in vessel position determination.

A different principle that can be used for direction finding is by means of the Doppler effect (p. 470). A rapidly revolving vertical aerial receives signals at the same frequency as the incoming signals when it is travelling perpendicular to the direction of motion of the signals, but at a higher frequency when travelling toward the incoming signal, and at a lower frequency when travelling in the same direction as the incoming signal, thus providing an indication of the direction of arrival of the signal.

Another approach, used ashore, is to install a number of aerials in a circle of appropriate diameter relative to the frequency. Direction of the incoming signal is determined by comparison of the phase of the signal as received in the various individual aerials. Directional signals can be transmitted from a circular array by suitable control of the phase of the transmitted signal from individual aerials.

Another method of measuring the direction of arrival of an incoming signal or transmitting a directional signal is by means of an *Adcock array*, consisting of two vertical aerials fed by signals so related in phase as to produce maximum signal strength in the plane of the two aerials. A sense aerial might be added to restrict the direction to one. Two Adcock arrays operating together were formerly used extensively for L F ranges marking airways. The two arrays, sometimes with an additional aerial, were arranged so that equal-signal strength of the two arrays were in the directions of the airways. A rotatable Adcock array, or two fixed Adcock arrays with a rotatable goniometer, or a cathode ray tube, can be used for direction finding.

A marine counterpart of the radio range is an aerial array providing a strong equisignal or beam in only one direction to guide vessels along a channel. Electronic beams have been used to guide aircraft in landing and as marker beacons to indicate progress of aircraft along a desired track.

Another approach used ashore for transmitting signals directionally is to use three vertical aerials in a straight line spaced appropriately for the frequency of the signals to be transmitted. If the phase of the signals in the two outer aerials is shifted systematically, the pattern of transmitted signals can be caused to rotate. If dots and dashes are transmitted in alternate lobes, a person can determine his direction from the station by counting the signals from alternate lobes during a specified interval, and referring to a special chart or table. This method of transmission is used in the *consol system*, discussed in section 5. A rotating pattern is also used in the *omniranges* operating at VHF to guide aircraft.

Both transmission and reception of signals at higher frequencies, as those used in radar, is by means of parabolic reflectors (p. 476).

The use of radio bearings is discussed in the next section.

4. Radio Bearings

Any bearing, whether visual or by radio, is a great circle (neglecting any bending of the ray of radiant energy). If the bearing line is to be plotted as a position line, it requires no adjustment if plotted on a chart portraying a great circle as a straight line or nearly so. However, on the Mercator projection commonly used for nautical charts a great circle appears as a curve convex to the nearer pole. Accordingly, if the equivalent straight rhumb line is desired for plotting, the conversion angle (p. 181) is needed. It can be determined by computation or graphically, as explained in section 9 of chapter IV, or by table. Books of nautical tables generally contain values of conversion angle. Its value in degrees can also be determined by multiplying the longitude difference between transmitter and receiver by the factor shown in the following critical table:

Mid lat	Conv. angle factor
$0°$	
$6°$	$0°0$
$17°$	$0°1$
$30°$	$0°2$
$44°$	$0°3$
$64°$	$0°4$
$90°$	$0°5$

Because of simplifying assumptions used in the computation of this table, a longitude difference of $7°5$ is a practical limit to its use.

Except for long visual bearing lines in very high latitudes, the adjustments to visual bearings are too small to have practical significance. Radio bearings, however, may need adjustment. The question of whether to adjust is a matter of judgment based upon experience. A good rule to follow until one acquires adequate experience is to determine the conversion angle and apply it if one can plot the difference between the rhumb line and the great circle.

To plot a radio bearing, one first corrects it for quadrantal and any other known errors, and, if necessary, converts it to a true direction. One then determines the conversion angle and applies it as a further correction to the observed bearing. One should be careful to use the correct sign. The rhumb line is always farther from the direction of the nearer pole than the great circle. If one has trouble with the sign, one might refer to the following table:

Receiver Lat	Transmitter	Sign
North	Eastward	+
North	Westward	−
South	Eastward	−
South	Westward	+

The sign refers to the adjustment *at the receiver*, whether it is aboard one's vessel or at a radio direction-finder station ashore.

For strict accuracy, one should plot the position line as a tangent to the great circle at the meridian of the dead-reckoning or estimated position used to determine the conversion angle. Refer to Fig. 1008. The conversion angle is applied to the radio bearing, and the equivalent rhumb line is plotted. At the point of intersection of the rhumb line and the meridian of the observer the position line is drawn in the direction of the observed radio bearing before adjustment for conversion angle. If the bearing is measured ashore, the conversion angle is applied with the same sign to the rhumb-line direction from the vessel to the transmitter to determine the direction of the position line.

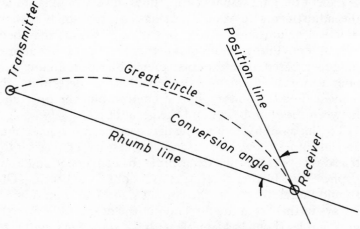

FIG. 1008. Plotting a radio bearing.

Because of the small magnitude of the conversion angle and the short length of the position line, as well as the low accuracy of radio bearings, this plotting refinement is generally not justified. It is common practice to plot the equivalent rhumb line and consider it the position line, labelled as any bearing line (p. 223). Because radio bearings are generally less accurate than visual bearings, one may wish to indicate the nature of the line by adding '(Radio)' or '(RDF)', as appropriate, after the direction label below the line. Because of the lesser reliability of radio bearings, compared with visual bearings, a position determined entirely by radio bearings is generally considered an estimated position (p. 17) rather than a fix, and a new dead-reckoning plot is not started from the position. However, if an EP, or series of EP's, indicates that one might be standing into dangerous waters, one might with prudence take appropriate action and seek confirmation of one's position by whatever means might be available, not forgetting the possible value of soundings.

In plotting radio bearings, one should be careful to use the position of the transmitting aerial. This caution is particularly applicable when bearings are taken on commercial radio stations, which generally have aerials at considerable distances from their studios. Their programs, too, are sometimes retransmitted by other stations.

For bearings taken at a longitude difference of more than $7°\!.5$, or if the transmitter and receiver are on opposite sides of the equator, one should use other means of adjustment, as by special chart or correction table designed for such conditions, for the simplifying assumptions used in the usual conversion angle table, including the one given above, are not valid over great east-west distances or across the equator. Bearings obtained by radio direction finders or radio direction-finder-stations ashore are generally well within the limits of the usual conversion-angle table, but consol (p. 489) bearings may not be.

Radio bearings, as visual bearings, can be used for homing (p. 250), but in periods of low visibility one should be careful of distance from the transmitter, to avoid running aground or ramming a vessel on which the transmitter is located.

5. Consol

A consol station transmits signals in the 250 to 370 kHz range from three vertical aerials in line at intervals of approximately three wave lengths (3 kilometres or 1.6 nautical miles at 300 kHz). The result is a pattern of hyperbolic position lines (section 9), but because of the relatively short base line, the position lines are essentially great circles beyond a distance of about 25 miles from the central aerial, and are used as bearing lines.

With this configuration, there are a number of sectors averaging about 15° in width, but becoming wider with increasing angular distance from the line of shoot, the perpendicular bisector of the line of aerials, to a maximum in the direction of the line of aerials. It is recommended not to use the station at a greater angle than 60° from the line of shoot. Thus, a station has a usable sector of 120° on each side, or a total of 240°, with unusable sectors of 60° in each of the two directions in line with the aerials, or a total unusable area of 120°.

In alternate 15° sectors signals consisting of 1/8 second dots and 3/8 second dashes are transmitted and coordinated so that both are received with equal amplitude. The result is a steady tone. Thus, 60 dots and 60 dashes are transmitted each 30 seconds, the 'keying cycle'. Between keying cycles a continuous tone and a station identifying signal are transmitted. The sectors are made to rotate slowly, as explained in section 3.

To obtain a bearing, one counts the dots and dashes received during a keying cycle, noting which were received first. As the dots give way to dashes, or vice versa, a brief monotone 'equisignal' is heard. It may extend over several characters. To complete the count, one adds the number of dots and dashes, subtracts the sum from 60, and applies half the difference to each count. Thus, if one counts 37 dashes followed by 19 dots, the sum of the two is 56, and $60 - 56 = 4$. Thus, the count is $37 + 2 = 39$ dashes followed by $19 + 2 = 21$ dots. This is known as a 39-dash count. If the difference between 60 and the initial count is an odd number, as 55, the smaller number (2 in this example) is added to the first count because one finds it easier to follow a merging a signal than to pick up an emerging one. With the count, one refers to a special chart or table to determine the equivalent bearing. Because the count is repeated in alternate sectors, one must know one's approximate bearing to an accuracy of perhaps 10° and 12° to resolve the ambiguity. The dead-reckoning position is usually adequate for this purpose, but if one is in doubt, an RDF bearing might be used. If the table is used to interpret the reading, the resulting bearing line needs adjustment to convert the great circle to the equivalent rhumb line, as explained in section 4. The time of the bearing is the time of the equisignal.

A narrow-band receiver is best, to reduce the noise. Automatic gain control, if available, should not be used. A vertical or open aerial is recommended. If a loop aerial is used, it should be turned so as to receive maximum or near maximum signal strength.

The range at which usable signals can be received varies greatly, being a function of the power of the transmitter, conductivity of the surface over which the signals travel, the bandwidth of the receiver, noise level, condition of the ionosphere, and the skill of the operator. A station might not be usable at a distance of 100 miles, or its signals might be identified at 2,000 miles or more. As a general rule, the usable range is from 25 miles to a maximum of 1,000 to 1,200 miles by day, and to a maximum of 1,200 to 1,500 miles by night. The range is somewhat less if the signals travel over land.

Accuracy of bearings is a function of transmission equipment and siting of the transmitting aerials, propagation conditions, and the receiving equipment and skill of the operator. Accuracy is greatest along the line of shoot. The error increases with angular distance from the line of shoot to about double at 60°, the edge of the usable sector. Greatest angular error occurs when both ground waves and sky waves are received, generally at distances of about 250 to 400 miles from the station. As a very general guide, an accuracy along the line of shoot of about 0°.3 by day and 0°.7 by night can be expected under favourable conditions. An error of 0°.5 translates into an error of one mile for each 120 miles, approximately, from the station, or 10 miles at 1,200 miles. A reasonable estimate of error in miles at 1,000 miles from a station is 6 to 24 miles by day and 10 to 40 miles by night. The error can be much larger under unfavourable conditions. Accuracy might be improved by averaging several readings. A wide equisignal and big variations in consecutive counts are an indication of low accuracy. Because a reading is to an integral number of dots and dashes, the system has an inherent error of as much as half a character, which translates to an average of about one mile for each 360 miles from a station.

Consol coverage is provided along the coasts of northern Europe and the Arctic coast of the U.S.S.R. Details of the stations are given in appropriate publications (p. 525).

Because of the possibility of large errors in consol bearings, they should be used with caution, particularly in the vicinity of dangers and in making landfall. In spite of the short-comings of the system, it is popular along the coasts where it is available, particularly by small craft, fishing vessels, and coasters. The primary reason for the popularity is the fact that an ordinary LF/MF receiver can be used.

6. Leader Cables

Experimentally, cables have been laid along the bottom to provide guidance to vessels along narrow channels. A simple method is to energize such a cable with alternating current. The resulting magnetic field is horizontal directly above the cable, and has a vertical component on each side. A properly oriented coil on each side of a vessel detects the vertical component. A sharp null indicates that the vessel is directly over the cable. Shifting of the positions of cables and other problems have limited the use of leader cables.

7. Distance Measurement

Electronic measurement of distance is based upon the nearly-constant speed of radio waves of 6.18 *microseconds* (μs, μsec, *Ms*) (millionths of a second) per nautical mile, or nearly 300 metres per microsecond. For highly accurate work, units of *nanoseconds* (*ns*) (thousandths of a microsecond) or even *picoseconds* (*ps*) (millionths of a microsecond) are used. In such precise work, allowance must be made for travel time of the signals through the circuitry of the transmitting and receiving equipment, for a signal travels 0.3 millimetres in one picosecond. A crystal oscillator is commonly used for timing.

A widely-used technique for electronic distance measurement is by direct measurement of the elapsed time between transmission and reception of a signal. If this involves one-way travel, the timing equipment or clocks at both ends of the transmission path must be coordinated, for any difference would appear as an error in distance measurement. A more commonly used technique is to measure the two-way travel time, the transmitter and receiver being at the same place. The extremely short interval of time involved is thus essentially error-free. This is the technique used in radar (p. 494). The signal may be returned by reflection or by retransmission from a *transponder*, which is a combined receiver-transmitter that transmits a signal when an incoming signal is received from an *interrogator*. Pulse modulation (p. 473) is used, and the leading edge of the pulse is used for the measurement. A shorter wave length produces a sharper leading edge, and therefore greater accuracy. Because the leading edge is used, multipath (p. 464) is no problem, the direct signal being the first to arrive. It is necessary to have the interval between pulses longer than the travel time if erroneous readings are to be avoided. Because of the very short time of transmission relative to the long time between pulses, high peak power can be achieved with low average power.

Sonar (p. 145) and the echo sounder (p. 148) use the same principle, but with sonic signals in water.

Another technique for measuring distance is by measurement of the phase of a continuous wave transmission. One complete cycle occurs over one wave length. If one can measure the phase to one-hundredth of a cycle, one can thus determine distance to 1/100 of a wave length for a one-way transmission, or 1/200 of a wave length for a two-way transmission. Thus, by decreasing the wave length, one can increase the accuracy. But as the wave length decreases, so does the ambiguity, for the same phase occurs at intervals of one wave length (half a wave length for two-way travel). This ambiguity can be resolved by (*1*) using a wave length longer than the distance of travel of the signal, (*2*) starting at a known distance and counting the full cycle changes, or (*3*) by

493

switching periodically to a lower frequency. Continuous-wave phase measurement also has the disadvantage that direct signals cannot be distinguished from those travelling by a longer path. This technique has the advantages of using very little spectrum and being capable of measurement of very short distances with great accuracy.

Another technique for using phase measurement is to generate signals at two different frequencies at each of the two points between which the distance is to be measured. The two signals produce beat frequency signals at the sum and difference of the two frequencies. If one of these beat frequency signals is transmitted at one station and received at the other, the phase of the received signal can be compared with that generated at the second station for determination of distance. It is necessary that the signal generators at the two stations be synchronized.

A different approach to distance finding is by means of synchronized radio and sound signals, utilizing the *differences* in travel time of the two signals. This technique is used in distance-finding stations (p. 273).

8. Radar

The name *radar* is an acronym derived from *r*adio *d*etection *a*nd *r*anging. By transmitting a series of brief bursts of electromagnetic energy (pulse modulation, p. 473) and timing the intervals between transmission and return of *echoes*, radar measures the distance to the object, called the *target*, that returns the echo. Transmission and reception of the signals are by the same directional aerial, a T R (transmit-receive) switch changing from one to another to protect the receiver from the strong signals of the transmitter. Direction of the target is indicated by the orientation of the rotating directional aerial, called a *scanner*. Microwaves are used, the most commonly-used wave lengths being of the order of 3 and 10 centimetres. The shorter wave length provides a sharper image, but is more susceptible to returns from precipitation and clouds, and requires more power for the same range. Many vessels are equipped with both 3-cm and 10-cm radars, while radar-equipped fishing vessels, tugs, and small craft generally have only 3-cm equipment, their operators preferring a sharp display to longer range with available power.

The information is displayed on a cathode ray tube. Several different types of display have been devised. That commonly used afloat is known as a *plan position indicator* (*PPI*). A faint radial line rotates in synchronization with the aerial to indicate direction of 'look'. When an echo is received, the line glows, the distance from the centre of rotation to the illuminated portion providing an indication of distance of the target. Several range scales are generally provided. The display somewhat resembles that of television, but differs in that no picture of the surroundings is displayed, thus requiring some interpretation, discussed below.

In a 'heading-up' display, the forward or 'up' direction of the display coincides with the heading of the craft. Bearings indicated by the radar are therefore relative (p. 21). Because of persistence of the fluorescent material coating the tube, some smearing of echoes occurs when the vessel yaws or changes course. In a 'stabilized' display, the 'up' direction is slaved to a repeating compass, generally a gyro compass. Thus, compass or gyro (essentially true) directions are indicated. A stabilized display is generally superior, but provision may be made for display selection by the operator. Some equipment has provision for offsetting the origin of the polar presentation from the centre of the display tube face to provide greater range in one direction than in the reciprocal direction. *True-motion radar* has a display on which the origin moves with the vessel, until reset. The actual, rather than relative, motion of other vessels is shown, permitting ready determination of their courses, speeds, and aspects if there is no current. Stationary objects appear without motion, making them readily distinguishable from moving objects. However, if an object known to be stationary appears to move, it is an indication of error in the course or speed, or both, of the vessel in which the radar is installed. Some mariners consider this feature the principal value of true-motion radar.

Radar repeaters may be installed so that the display is available at locations remote from the radar.

Because the radar receiver is disconnected from the aerial during transmission, the theoretical minimum distance that can be measured by radar is governed by the pulse length. For a 0.05-microsecond pulse, about the shortest used, the minimum distance is approximately 7.5 metres. However, the practical minimum is perhaps 50 metres under favourable conditions because of such factors as receiver recovery time, side-lobe echoes, and sea return.

The maximum range is limited by the peak power, pulse length, *pulse repetition rate* (*PRR*), frequency, beam width, receiver sensitivity, aerial rotation rate, aerial height (the radio horizon, p. 464, being in this case called the *radar horizon*), atmospheric condition (weather, presence of ducting, etc.), and target characteristics (size, shape, aspect, height, composition, texture). When ducting (p. 464) occurs, the maximum range may be extended to several times its normal value. Super-refraction and subrefraction also affect the maximum range. If the aerial height is increased to extend the radar horizon, increased sea return is encountered.

Because of interference between direct waves and those reflected by the surface of the sea, the transmission in the vertical is not uniform, but consists of a number of lobes, the number dependent upon the aerial height and the frequency. As a result, some objects of small vertical extent might be missed while smaller objects at greater range are observed.

Some skill, developed by experience, is needed for the accurate interpretation of the scope display. Radar is usually considered a low-visibility aid, but it can be useful in clear weather, and practice in scope interpretation when visual confirmation is possible can be helpful in developing ability to interpret the display accurately.

Resolution is the ability to separate targets that are close together. *Resolution in range* is a function of pulse length. If a target consists of a flat surface perpendicular to the direction of travel of the radio waves but of negligible extent in range, the echo continues to be received throughout the period of one pulse, and appears to have a measurable extent in range. If a second target in the same direction is within half a wave length (because of the two-way travel of the signal) of the first target, the two images merge and the objects cannot be separated. Because of this condition, in part, detailed features of a land mass might not be distinguishable, and echoes from surf or from vessels or offlying islands or rocks close to the shore might merge with the echoes from the shore, giving a false indication of the shore line.

Similarly, *resolution in bearing* is a function of *beam width*, defined as the angular extent of the beam between some percentage, usually 71 per cent, but sometimes 50 per cent, of maximum signal strength. Because of beam width, an object appears wider than it is. As the beam sweeps past an object, an echo is received when sufficient energy reaches the object to return a detectable echo. The centre of the beam is still to one side. Similarly, as the beam sweeps past the object, the echo continues until signal strength is too low to return a detectable echo. Targets within one beam width, at the same range, appear as a single object. Beam width depends upon frequency and the size and design of the aerial. Typical beam widths are two-thirds of a degree to two degrees in the horizontal, and $15°$ to $30°$ in the vertical. The greater vertical extent allows for pitching and rolling of the vessel, and permits observation of objects at a range of heights.

Thus, sharpness of image is a function of pulse length and beam width. The echo is also affected by the reflecting quality of the target and clutter from atmospherics (p. 469), precipitation echoes, sea return, etc. Return from precipitation might appear as a land mass. Because of sea return, small craft and partly-submerged ice might not be detected. Clutter can be reduced somewhat by shortening the pulse length. Rain clutter can be reduced by using circular polarization (p. 475). Wanted echoes can sometimes be distinguished from clutter by the fact that they appear relatively stable, while clutter echoes are erratic.

Ghosts are echoes returned by discontinuities in the atmosphere or other sources not identifiable. Ghosts sometimes appear to move at incredible speed and to perform amazing manoeuvres. Interference from other radars operating on the same frequency is usually identifiable by appearing as sporadic spirals of dots, because the pulse repetition rates of two radars are rarely identical.

Shadows might hide objects, although there is some penetration of shadow areas because of diffraction (p. 468). If a land mass is beyond the radar horizon, the lower portion of the land might not be visible. Relatively flat or gently sloping land might not return a detectable echo.

The aspect of the target affects the size and strength of the echo. A small ship broadside to the radar beam might appear larger than a large vessel end-on to the beam.

Echoes from parts of the vessel on which the radar is mounted, such as masts or stacks, might appear on the scope. Outgoing signals and returning echoes might be reflected from a stack or bulkhead, giving a false direction of the target. Because of the various distortions, it is not always easy to pinpoint specific targets that might be used for navigation. Advance study of the chart to determine targets that can be expected to return strong echoes, experience in an area, and the identification of each prominent target as it appears are all helpful. Some objects, such as buoys and small craft, are provided with *corner reflectors*, also called *radar reflectors*, to return a stronger echo then might be expected from the object itself. The fact that a buoy has a corner reflector might be indicated on the chart.

If the limitations of radar are understood, this device can be a valuable navigational aid. A fix can be obtained by means of distance and direction of one object, distances from two objects, or bearings of two objects. Radar bearings are generally less accurate than visual bearings, and one should be particularly wary of tangents, particularly when there is a possibility of a low sandy spit or mud flat off a prominent headland. A visual bearing and a radar distance measurement sometimes provide the most accurate fix available. In using distances, one should be careful to identify the part of the land or object returning the echo. It may not be the shore line, particularly if there is a possibility that the shore line is beyond the radar horizon. Another way of using radar is by direct comparison of the radar image and a chart, keeping in mind the differences.

Radar beacons have been installed in various parts of the world to assist in navigation. Some of these installations are experimental and may not be shown on charts. Two types of radar beacon are in use. The more common, called a *racon* (from *ra*dar bea*con*), is a form of *secondary radar*, using a transponder (p. 493) to return a characteristic signal when triggered by a vessel's radar, in contrast with *primary radar*, which uses reflections. Each racon sweeps over the frequency range of the radar sets in use in its part of the spectrum, to accommodate all potential users. The sweep may be relatively slow (perhaps a minute in length) or very fast (a number of sweeps per second). Nearly all of the racons currently in use are in the 3-cm band. The usual presentation is a coded radial line or narrow sector extending outward from the position of the racon, with a gap of perhaps a hundred metres, because of reaction time of the beacon.

A second type of radar beacon is called a *ramark*, which transmits continuously without being triggered by an incoming signal. Its signals appear on the scope as a radial line indicating the direction of the beacon, but giving no indication of distance.

Radar beacons might cause interference at short ranges. This can be reduced by means of the 'rain clutter' control on the radar.

Radar stations have been installed in some locations along the coast to provide assistance, not control, to vessels. A radar station established primarily to provide distance and direction information to vessels by means of radar, rather than radio direction-finding equipment, is indicated on the chart by the abbreviation Ra alongside the symbol indicating the position of the station. A radar station might suspend operations at intervals, without notice, for maintenance or because of failure of some part of the system.

Surveillance radar has been installed in some harbours to supervise the flow of traffic and to give navigation assistance to craft in the harbour, as explained in section 24 of chapter XII.

Radar can also be useful in avoiding collision with other vessels and fixed obstructions. The primary value of radar for this purpose is in providing early information on the locations and movements of other vessels and dangers. The subject of collision avoidance is discussed in greater length in section 27 of chapter XII.

9. Distance-Difference Measurement

If a person measures the *difference* in his distance from two identifiable points, he establishes a position line in the shape of a *hyperbola*. If the curve is on the surface of a sphere, it is a *spherical hyperbola*, and if on the surface of a spheroid, a *spheroidal hyperbola*. A position line representing a distance difference is thus called a *hyperbolic position line*.

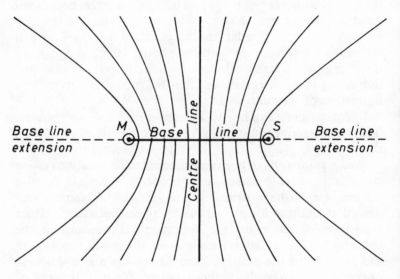

FIG. 1009. Hyperbolic position lines.

Refer to Fig. 1009. If radio stations M and S transmit signals at the same instant, the two signals arrive at the same time at every point equidistant from the two transmitters, assuming equal speed of travel of the two signals. The locus of all equidistant points is a great circle, called the *centre line*, forming the perpendicular bisector of the *base line*, the great circle joining the two stations. If one is not on the centre line, the signal of the nearer station arrives first, and the locus of all points of constant distance difference is a hyperbola. Thus, a family of hyperbolas is associated with the two transmitters. The interval between consecutive curves is least along the base line, increasing outward from it. The interval also increases from the centre line to a maximum along the *base line extensions*. The decrease in accuracy of position determination because of this fanning out of position lines and more acute crossing angles of position lines, assuming equal accuracy of measurement, is called *geometric dilution of precision* (*GDOP*).

Note that each curve has a counterpart on the opposite side of the centre line. If signals from the two stations are transmitted simultaneously, it is necessary to provide means of identifying the origin of each signal, so one will know which signal arrives first. One way of providing identification is by delaying one of the signals sufficiently so that the other always arrives first, resulting in a time difference increasing progressively from the base line extension past the station sending the later signal to the base line extension of the other station. This is accomplished by designating one station as the *master station* (*M*), and the other as the *slave station* (*S*). Signals from the master control those of the slave, thus accomplishing both the delay and synchronization.

If two or more pairs of stations have intersecting families of position lines, the resulting pattern, called a *lattice*, provides information needed for a fix. The user measures the distance difference of each pair of stations and locates his position by referring to a chart on which the position lines are printed at intervals, a separate colour generally being used for each family of curves to augment identification by designation. If necessary, hyperbolas can be constructed by drawing circles at equal distance intervals around the two stations, and connecting successive intersections of the two families of circles. Coordinates of curves representing difference readings are also tabulated at frequent intervals in special tables. By means of the charts or tables one plots a short segment of each position line and determines one's position at their intersection. Hyperbolic position lines are used as any others, being advanced, retired, and crossed as needed. The angle of cut is an important consideration, as with any position lines.

Beyond distances of about five times the base line, or a little more, hyperbolas become essentially great circles. This principle is used with short base lines to provide an essentially radial system such as consol (p. 489).

The disadvantage of needing two stations to establish one position line is partly overcome by using two or more slaves with each master. A group of related stations producing a lattice is called a *chain*.

Distance difference is usually determined directly by measurement of the interval between reception of synchronized pulse-modulated signals, or indirectly by measurement of the phase difference of the signals. The latter method lends itself to very high accuracy by the use of relatively high frequency, but is has the disadvantage of having any reading duplicated in a number of different *lanes*. As the frequency increases, the accuracy also increases, but width of the lane decreases. Along the base line one lane width is equal to half a wave length. Lane identification can be accomplished by keeping a count of lane changes from a known position, but this is subject to error if one loses count, as by temporary loss of signal or power, and it is useless if one enters the pattern from the outside, as one approaching land from seaward. A more certain method is to use a series of frequencies to provide wide lanes for approximating position and narrower lanes for greater accuracy. A phase-comparison system is also subject to large, indeterminate errors when both ground waves and sky waves are received. The accuracy of any distance-difference system is related to the constancy of propagation conditions over the coverage area.

10. Decca

The Decca Navigator system is a privately owned and operated, medium-range, unmodulated continuous-wave, phase-comparison, hyperbolic system operating in the 70 to 130 kHz frequency range. Each chain consists of a master station surrounded by three (two in a few chains) slave stations at distances of 60 to 120 miles from the master, as shown in Fig. 1010.

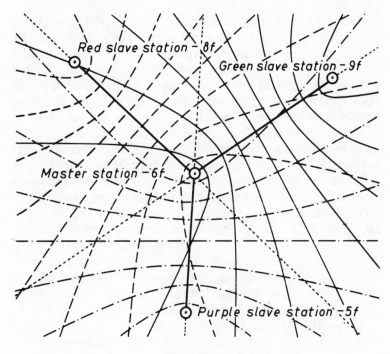

FIG. 1010. A Decca chain.

For identification purposes, the slaves are designated red, green, and purple. All stations of a chain transmit harmonically-related frequencies consisting of multiples of a basic frequency of about 14 kHz, the actual basic frequency varying slightly from chain to chain. If the basic frequency, not transmitted, is designated f, the transmitted frequencies are 6f for the master, 8f for the red slave, 9f for the green slave, and 5f for the purple slave. It is not the transmitted frequency that is compared, but a *comparison frequency* consisting of 24f for the red frequency, 18f for the green frequency, and 30f for the purple frequency. Lane width along the base line is approximately 440, 590, and 350 metres for the red, green, and purple stations, respectively. The lanes are grouped in *zones* about 6 miles wide along the base lines, a red zone encompassing 24 lanes, a green zone 18 lanes, and a purple zone 30 lanes.

Receiving equipment consists of five separate receivers, one tuned to each of the four transmitters of a chain, and the fifth to a lane-identification frequency. A phase meter called a *decometer* is provided for each slave. Each decometer indicates fractional parts of a lane, being graduated in hundredths of a lane. As one crosses a lane from one in-phase position to the next, the decometer pointer makes one complete revolution. At intervals of 20 seconds the transmissions automatically shift to the lane-identification frequency, and the lane within a zone is indicated by a separate lane meter. Zones are designated by letter, and lanes by number. The zone letter and lane number are set manually on the decometer, and indicate changes as they occur as long as there is no *lane slippage* because of interruption or disturbance of transmission or power or operation difficulty at the receiver. In the case of interruption or disturbance of the transmissions, warnings are broadcast by some coastal radio stations. Two types of lane identification systems are in use. Some receivers do not have lane identification capability.

To use the Decca system, one obtains a reading, consisting of the colour, zone letter, lane number, and fractional part of a lane for each pair of stations, and refers to a chart overprinted with the hyperbolic position lines, generally one line for each lane, printed in the colour of the slave. Only the two colours providing the best cut may be printed on the chart. In some areas it is possible to obtain readings from two chains, with a better angle of cut than provided by position lines generated by one chain. One must know one's position by independent means accurately enough to identify the zone in which one is located. A *track plotter* is available on which a pen traces the track of the vessel on a plotting sheet distorted to show two families of hyperbolic position lines as straight, mutually perpendicular lines. If a digital computer is available, it might be programmed to indicate latitude and longitude directly.

Although Decca signals have been received in excess of 1,000 miles from the transmitters, the system is not considered usable at such a distance because intermixture of sky waves and ground waves introduces error, and at such distances the position lines are essentially great circles with very small angle of cut. The useful range is somewhat variable, but 175 miles by night and 350 miles by day might be considered about average. Interchain fixing is particularly useful at longer ranges.

Accuracy of Decca is associated with distance from the transmitters, angle of cut, characteristics of the terrain over which the signals travel, and propagation conditions. Skill in taking readings is not involved because readings are indicated automatically, a favourable feature of the system. In general, the repeatable error varies from several tens of metres to several miles. The geographical error is somewhat greater.

Two types of error are involved. *Fixed error* is caused by differences in conductivity of the terrain over which the signals travel, resulting in distortion of the hyperbolic position lines. Because the fixed error is related to the path of travel of the signals, it is a constant for any geographical location. The 'pattern correction' for fixed error at various locations, determined by monitoring the readings at positions whose coordinates are determined by other means, is furnished to users by The Decca Navigator Company, Ltd. Fixed error is minimum for a signal travel path entirely over sea water. It is maximum where rugged land is traversed by the signals, where it can exceed half a lane width. Where no pattern correction data are available, the accuracy of Decca fixes should be considered doubtful.

In contrast with fixed error, *variable error* is largely unpredictable. It is associated primarily with changing propagation conditions, particularly with the ionosphere. It varies with the time of day, season of the year, and geographical locations of the transmitters and the receiver. It is greatest at long ranges, and is greater at night than during the day, and in winter than in summer. At distances greater than about 150 miles, particularly during twilight or darkness, the lane identification signals may be too weak to provide accurate lane identification, so that lane slippage might not be detected.

Full information on the system, coverage, accuracy, and use of the equipment is contained in *Decca Navigator Operating Instructions and Marine Data Sheets* issued by The Decca Navigator Company, Ltd. to users of the systems.

11. Loran

A navigation system establishing position lines by transmitting synchronized pulse-modulated signals from two transmitters is free from the lane ambiguity associated with phase comparison systems. With properly spaced pulses one can measure the difference in arrival time directly. Loran, an acronym from *lo*ng *ra*nge *n*avigation, is such a system. Several versions of loran have been devised, each identified by letter.

Loran A, called *standard loran*, is a medium-frequency, pulse-modulated, hyperbolic navigation system operating in the 1850–1950 kHz range. Both ground waves and sky waves are used. A transmitted pulse may arrive as a *train* of several signals, having travelled by different routes. If a ground wave (p. 465) signal is received, it is the first to arrive.

Usable signals can be received at ranges of about 500 to 700 miles by day, and about two thirds this distance during the night. Usable sky waves extend to about 1,400 miles.

Transmitters are generally arranged in groups or *chains* along a coast, at intervals typically of 200 to 400 miles.

The amount of radio spectrum used is minimized by transmitting several signals on the same frequency, each at a slightly different pulse repetition rate (p. 496).

A basic loran A receiver accepts loran signals from the receiving aerial and displays them on a cathode ray tube. User equipment with automatic tracking and digital read-out has also been produced. The reading is referred to a chart overprinted with loran A position lines, or a position line is drawn on a plotting sheet by reference to a table of coordinates corresponding with loran A readings. By either method, a line can be advanced or retired to the time of any other position line. Sky-wave corrections to convert the readings to equivalent ground-wave readings are shown at intervals on the loran A charts, and tabulated in the volumes of loran A coordinates.

Accuracy of loran A fixes varies with the accuracy of the individual position lines and the angle of cut. An experienced observer under average conditions can usually make a reading, when ground waves are matched, with an error of not more than one microsecond. This translates to about 0.08 mile along the base line, becoming greater at other positions in the coverage error because of geometric dilution of precision (p. 501). Near the base line extensions the error can become very large. When sky waves are used, the error is typically five to seven miles.

Loran A is being phased out in favour of the more accurate loran C.

Loran B was an experimental system involving the addition of cycle matching to loran A pulse matching. Efforts were unsuccessful because of the large ratio of pulse build-up time to cycle time.

Loran C represents a successful attempt to combine pulse matching, as in loran A, for coarse readings with phase comparison for increased accuracy. All stations operate at 100 kHz, and are required to keep 99 per cent of the radiated energy within 90 to 110 kHz.

Each chain consists of a *master station*, designated M, and two or more *secondary stations* designated, W, X, Y, or Z. The master station transmits groups of nine pulses with individual pulses being at intervals of 1,000 microseconds except for the last pulse, which is delayed an additional 1,000 microseconds to provide means of identification of the master signals. Each secondary station transmits groups of eight pulses with individual pulses being at intervals of 1,000 microseconds. The interval between the beginning of consecutive groups of pulses is called the *group repetition interval* (*GRI*). Each station transmits one group of pulses during each GRI, and the transmission of all pulses of a chain is timed so there is no overlap of pulses. Thus, there is a minimum GRI which is a function of the number and spacing of stations in the chain. The actual GRI used is selected to prevent interference by adjacent chains, which operate on the same frequency.

The loran C system is designed for use of ground waves primarily. Two separate means are used to prevent error by sky-wave contamination of signals. A sky-wave signal may arrive as early as 35 or as late as 1,000 or more microseconds after arrival of the ground wave from the same transmitted signal. Each pulse is of about 200 microseconds duration, increasing to peak strength about 60 microseconds after start of the pulse and then gradually tailing off to the end of the pulse. Only the first three cycles, arriving within the first 30 microseconds, are used. Thus, the matching of the first pulse is completed before a sky wave is received. The first parts of later pulses of a group might be contaminated by sky waves, causing fading and change of shape of pulses. These later pulses are given coded phase reversals which, in addition to providing means of identification of individual pulses, provide some protection against interference, and aid in identification of the stations transmitting the signals.

Vertical transmitting aerials that may be more than 400 metres high are used to provide omnidirectional radiation of signals. The range of usable signals is dependent upon transmitter power, losses over the signal path, noise level, and sensitivity of the receiver. Base lines of 600 to 800 miles are used to provide good angles of cut out to the limit of ground-wave reception, which is 800 to 1,200 miles. This greater range than that of loran A signals is possible because of lower propagation losses in LF ground waves, and the use of groups of pulses to increase the average power without increasing peak power. One-hop-E signals have been received at 2,300 miles, and multihop sky waves have been received at more than 3,400 miles from the transmitter.

The earliest receivers used cathode ray tubes to assist in making the reading, but in later models the signals are acquired and matched automatically. Equipment that can be used with both loran A and loran C has been produced, but such equipment generally has provision for matching pulses only, and thus does not take advantage of the cycle-matching feature that provides the greater accuracy of loran C over loran A. Development of low-cost combined loran C/omega receivers is anticipated.

Because all stations transmit on the same frequency of 100 kHz, no frequency control is needed. To acquire signals from a specific chain, one enters the group repetition interval in the receiver, turns on the power, and the equipment automatically searches for the signals, and after acquisition it continues to track the signals until the power is turned off or another GRI is inserted. Most receivers acquire and commence tracking of the desired signals within five minutes of being turned on or adjusted to the GRI, but a longer time may be needed, particularly near the outer limit of the coverage area, where ten minutes may be a more representative time. A warning light remains lighted until satisfactory tracking has started. However, near the outer limit of coverage the light may be extinguished because of temporary loss of signal.

When the receiver is tracking satisfactorily, time-difference readings of two pairs of stations appear continuously on dials.

If the synchronization tolerance of between 0.15 and 0.2 microsecond is exceeded, the signals are caused to blink until the transmission tolerance is restored. *Blinking* consists of turning off and on, by a specified code, of the ninth pulse of the master station and the first two pulses of the offending secondary station.

Two ground waves are matched whenever possible, but if both ground waves and sky waves are available from one station, and only a sky wave is available from the other station of the pair, the ground wave of the first is matched with the sky wave of the other.

If a digital computer is available, it might be programmed to provide a direct indication of latitude and longitude. Alternatively, the time-difference readings provided by the receiver might be referred to charts overprinted with curves of the hyperbolic position lines, or to tables providing geographical coordinates of various points along each position line, so a segment of the line can be plotted. Sky-wave corrections are provided so the equivalent ground-wave readings can be used for plotting.

Station pairs are identified by the first four digits of GRI, and the letter designation of the secondary station; and the time difference readings are identified as T_G for ground waves, T_S for sky waves, T_{GS} for a ground wave from the master matched to a sky wave from the secondary station, and T_{SG} for a sky wave from the master matched to a sky wave from the secondary station.

Individual position lines can be advanced, retired, and crossed with other loran C position lines, or with lines determined in some other manner. A position line is suitably labelled with the time (or times for an adjusted line) above the line, and the station pair and time difference reading below the line. In the case of a sky-wave reading, it is good practice to indicate the equivalent ground-wave reading in parantheses following the reading obtained.

Each volume of loran C tables contains general information on the loran C system. Details of operation and maintenance of user equipment are given in the equipment manual provided by the manufacturer.

Phase measurement is accurate to about 0.03 microsecond in the best equipment. Cesium frequency standards used to maintain the timing accuracy of the transmitted signals prevent meaningful error from faulty timing. The principal sources of error in loran C fixes are GDOP (p. 501) and propagation instability.

The speed of ground waves travelling across the surface of the Earth is slightly less than that in free space. Compensation for this slowing of ground waves is made by introduction in the tables and the positions of overprinted curves of a *secondary phase factor* (SF) if the path is entirely over sea water, and an *additional secondary phase factor* (ASF) if the signals travel over land. These are average values. Because of slight variations in travel path and speed, some error can be expected. As a general rule, the 95 per cent accuracy of ground-wave loran C positions is of the order of 0.25 mile, and the error of individual lines is 0.1 microsecond. The repeatable error is 15 to 100 metres. The error of sky-wave position lines is of the order of one microsecond.

Accuracy of loran C positions can be improved by using the system in a *differential mode*. That is, if one is near land, the reading of a monitor receiver at a position of known coordinates can be compared with the predicted reading at the position of the monitor, and any difference transmitted to the vessel and applied as a correction to the readings obtained there. This procedure reduces propagation errors, the validity of the correction decreasing with increasing distance between the vessel and the monitor.

It is also possible to use loran C in a range-range mode. The actual one-way travel time of signals is measured and the resulting position line is plotted as a circle with the transmitter at its centre. Thus, only one station is needed for a position line, extending the useful range of the system, and reducing somewhat the GDOP error. To use the method, one needs a stable, accurate time source synchronized with or having known differences from the time standards of the transmitters, and accurate information on propagation conditions.

Loran D is a transportable, lower-power, shorter-range version of loran C intended primarily for military use.

12. Omega

The omega navigation system is a VLF, continuous-wave, phase-comparison, hyperbolic system operating in the 10–14 kHz frequency band. A pulse system in this band is precluded because of large bandwidth (p. 473) requirements. Because of the efficiency of propagation of ground waves of VLF, signals from the 10 kilowatt omega transmitters can be received throughout the world, sometimes by two routes in opposite directions. Only eight transmitting stations (the eighth, in Australia, expected to be in operation some time in 1981) provide worldwide coverage with multiple position lines. The stations, typically with 5,000-mile base lines, operate singly, rather than in master-slave configurations, so that any two stations can be used for establishing a position line.

All omega stations transmit on the same frequency of 10.2 kHz, on a time-sharing basis. A lane width being half a wave length, the lane width along the base line is approximately eight miles, and with a base line of 5,000 miles there are approximately 600 lanes between stations. Because of the long base lines, the lane widths do not increase greatly with GDOP (p. 501) except in the vicinity of base-line extensions.

←——————————————— 10 seconds ———————————————→

Station	0.9	1.0	1.1	1.2	1.1	0.9	1.2	1.0
A	10.2	13.6	$11\frac{1}{3}$			11.05		
B		10.2	13.6	$11\frac{1}{3}$			11.05	
C			10.2	13.6	$11\frac{1}{3}$			11.05
D	11.05			10.2	13.6	$11\frac{1}{3}$		
E		11.05			10.2	13.6	$11\frac{1}{3}$	
F			11.05			10.2	13.6	$11\frac{1}{3}$
G	$11\frac{1}{3}$			11.05			10.2	13.6
H	13.6	$11\frac{1}{3}$			11.05			10.2
0.2 sec between segments								

FIG. 1011. Omega signal format.

If lane count is maintained accurately without interruption, lane identification is not a problem. However, lane identification is aided by the transmission of a second frequency of 13.6 kHz. The difference between this frequency and 10.2 kHz is 3.4 kHz, giving a lane width of about 24 miles. A third frequency of 11.333 kHz provides a beat frequency with 10.2 kHz of 1.133 kHz, giving lane widths of approximately 72 miles, which should provide lane resolution adequate for any reasonable situation. A fourth frequency of 11.05 kHz is being added to provide lane widths of 288 miles for use primarily in search and rescue operations. Another method of lane identification, particularly applicable when a single-frequency receiver is used, is to obtain several position lines from different pairs of stations. They should all intersect at only one common point.

The full omega signal format is shown in Fig. 1011. Stations are identified by letter, A through H. The entire cycle is ten seconds long, divided into eight 'segments' of different duration as shown, with 0.2 second between segments to avoid overlapping of signals. The pattern of segment length aids in station identification, as does the relative strength of signals. The relatively long integration times (approximately one second) are used because of low signal-to-noise ratio sometimes encountered, especially in the tropics. Each station may transmit an additional unique frequency in the VLF range during the unused time segments for purposes other than navigation afloat. Synchronized cesium time standards set to coordinated universal time (p. 331) are used to keep the various transmissions on schedule.

Because only one station transmits a specific frequency during any one time segment, direct comparison of the phase of signals from two stations is not possible. Instead, the phase of the signal of one station is compared with the frequency of a signal generated within the user equipment. This information is stored until a like comparison is made between the locally generated signal and the signal of the second station. The two comparisons are then compared to determine the phase difference of signals from the two stations. Because of the relatively long period of time between reception of the signals from the two stations, an error might be introduced in a very fast-moving craft such as a high-speed aircraft, but at ship speeds the error is negligible.

Cheaper user equipment may have provision for receiving only the basic 10.2 kHz frequency. This is the frequency used for navigation, the additional frequencies being provided only for lane identification.

The omega readout is generally by digital display indicating hundredths of a cycle, called *centicycles* (*cec*). Each centicycle identifies one hundredth of a lane, or one *centilane* (*cel*). Lines representing zero phase difference are printed on omega plotting charts, and coordinates of the curves are tabulated in volumes of omega lattice tables. The reading in centicycles is used for interpolating between zero isophase lines. Development of low-cost combined omega/loran C receivers is anticipated.

Signals at VLF have relatively good phase stability over long ranges. The accuracy of omega readings depends primarily upon the ability to predict phase variations along the propagation path. Several sources of error have been identified. Sudden ionospheric disturbances (p. 96) may cause position errors of the order of two to three miles over a period of half an hour to an hour. Signals traversing the *auroral zones* surrounding the geomagnetic poles (p. 92) may be subject to an advance in phase. When there is a concentration of high-energy particles in the vicinities of the geomagnetic poles, a disruption of VLF signals known as *polar cap disturbance* (*PCD*) takes place. Signals crossing large ice fields with their low conductivity, such as that covering Greenland, are attenuated more than signals travelling over other areas. The height of the ionosphere also affects VLF propagation. The height varies with the zenith distance of the Sun, so that time of day, season, and geographic position all affect propagation.

The corrections, in centicycles, to be applied to omega readings are determined by the application of known theory, verified by extensive monitoring expected to be completed in 1982, when the system will be considered fully operational. The corrections are tabulated for time of day and date, new tables being provided at intervals of about two years to allow for changes in solar activity and other anomalies. The corrections are applied to the readings obtained for the 10.2 kHz signals, to obtain the values needed for use on plotting charts or for entering the omega lattice tables. During the day the correction is relatively small but variable. During the night it is larger but less variable. A navigator may wish to construct a graph of the correction for his area, to better visualize the times of rapid change, when it is best not to use the affected station pair. Such a graph, constructed from the correction tables, might show the correction *vs.* time of day. A new graph should be constructed at intervals of about a fortnight or when the vessel enters a new area for which different corrections are tabulated. The use of a digital computer to provide automatic application of the correction or direct indication of latitude and longitude is possible.

A relatively simple vertical whip aerial about 3 metres long is adequate for reception of omega signals.

The overall accuracy of omega position lines when readings are corrected is of the order of one mile during the day and two miles during the night. When omega signals are known to be unreliable or disrupted, appropriate warnings are broadcast and published in *Notices to Mariners* and *Daily Memorandum*.

Omega signals are considered generally unreliable within 450 miles of the transmitters, and any readings in these areas should be avoided if signals from other stations are available. Position-line curves in these areas are shown as broken lines on omega plotting charts.

Because propagation anomalies are the major source of error in omega readings, differential (p. 511) omega is a possibility for achieving considerable improvement in accuracy, which might be especially desirable in the approaches to a harbour entrance, or when avoiding an isolated danger at sea, or when making rendezvous with another vessel. Differential omega is effective to a range of perhaps 300 miles. The propagation correction is not applied when differential omega is used.

Omega can be used in a range-range mode if synchronized time to sufficient accuracy is available to the user. In this mode the circular lanes are approximately 16 miles wide and do not vary over the coverage area. Phase changes along the transmission path do not affect accuracy because distance is determined by measurement of time of transit of the signals, not by phase measurement. However, disruption of signals, as by a polar cap disturbance, introduces a larger error in range position lines than in hyperbolic lines.

The attenuation in sea water of VLF signals at omega frequencies is less than half that at 100 kHz, the loran C frequency. Omega signals can be received for depths of several metres, making possible their use by submerged vessels near the surface.

A handbook intended primarily for the non-technical user of omega has been published by the United States Coast Guard.

13. Special-Purpose Systems

A number of applications require special considerations, such as great accuracy. So important is this requirement that some relaxation of other features, such as cost, may be acceptable. Examples of special-purpose applications are for hydrographic and oceanographic surveying; geophysical exploration; cable laying and recovering; research; and positioning of oil-drilling rigs, missile and spacecraft-tracking stations, aids to navigation, and transmitting aerials for electronic navigation systems.

Before the availability of electronic capability, high-accuracy positioning near a coast was accomplished visually, frequently by means of horizontal sextant angles (p. 228). On land, astronomical observations were used. Visual systems are limited by visibility, range, accuracy of the positions of objects used, and accuracy of observation and use of data. Astronomical observation is limited by visibility, deflection of the vertical (p. 381), and accuracy of observation and use of data, as well as requiring a large number of observations extending over a considerable period of time, as several days.

A large number of electronic systems have been devised to meet the requirements of special applications without some of the limitations of visual and astronomical methods. Electronic systems generally provide means for measurement of distance or distance difference. Distance measurement has the advantage of not requiring special charts or tables for location of position lines, and needing only one station for each position line, but hyperbolic systems are available and provide satisfactory service.

Following the development of radar, pulse techniques were used for measurement of distance. Accuracy over primary radar was achieved by the use of transponders in some form of secondary radar. Different versions of this approach took such names as *oboe*, *shoran* (*sho*rt *ran*ge *n*avigation), *hiran* (*hi*gh precision sho*ran*), *electronic position indicator* (*EPI*), and *Trident III*.

Higher accuracy can generally be achieved by use of phase-comparison techniques, as there is virtually no limitation to the theoretical accuracy that can be achieved by this technique if lane ambiguity and range limitation are acceptable. As frequency increases, the width of a lane decreases. In the vicinity of 2 MHz, the frequency used by several special-purpose systems, a lane width along the base line of a hyperbolic system is about 75 metres. If phase can be measured to one hundredth of a cycle, the minimum error at this frequency is less than one metre. Practical accuracies of the order of one to ten metres are claimed for some of the phase-comparison systems. The problem of lane ambiguity is generally overcome by starting operations at a known position, or with the interrogator and transponder at the same position, and then counting the lanes as position changes. If the frequency is increased sufficiently, the system becomes essentially line-of-sight, direct waves (p. 467) only being available.

The high-accuracy systems are generally of relatively short range, either line-of-sight or extending only to several hundred miles, within the region where ground waves are uncontaminated by sky waves. *Raydist*, *lorac* (*lo*ng *r*ange *ac*curacy), and *toran* are high-accuracy systems of this type. A special version of Decca, called *Hi-Fix*, uses light-weight, compact equipment to provide mobility for use to a maximum distance of about 100 miles. It operates in the 2 MHz region and can be used in either the usual hyperbolic configuration or in a ranging configuration to provide circular position lines.

For high accuracy beyond the range of the systems mentioned above, artificial Earth satellites (p. 542) might be used, or an integrated system using several different components (p. 551).

Special-purpose systems are generally available commercially or are limited to government-operated applications.

14. Radio Astronomy

With the discovery of discrete sources of emission of energy at radio frequencies in space came consideration of the possible use of such sources for all-weather astronavigation. Several requirements would have to be met before the new science of radio astronomy would be useful to navigation, including the following:

The equivalent point sources of radiation would have to be identified and their positions made available to navigators.

The sources would have to be stable in terms of position, frequency, and radiated power.

User equipment of reasonable size and cost would be needed.

The results in terms of useful information and acceptable accuracy would have to justify the addition of another method.

Several thousand sources of radio emission have been identified. Each source is generally referred to as a 'radio star', although this name is not entirely appropriate because of the wide variety of sources, including the Sun, Moon, planets, stars, nebulae, galaxies, and a number of objects that are not visible optically. A number of these sources are very large, being thousands of light years in diameter. The Sun is a relatively weak source compared to nebulae and galaxies, but because of its close proximity to the Earth, its emission is the strongest received. Emission from the Moon is much weaker than that from the Sun, but relatively strong signals are received at the short distance of the Earth. The planets Venus and Jupiter emit strong signals but of such variabilty that they are not reliable sources. The strongest signals received from outside the solar system are from the vicinity of α Cassiopeia.

The strength of radio signals received at the Earth peaks in the vicinity of 15 and 35 GHz, with wave lengths of approximately 2 cm and 9 mm, respectively. The lower frequency is the more desirable because signals at this frequency are less disturbed by clouds and rainfall, although the parabolic aerial needed for the higher frequency is only a third to a half the diameter of that needed for the lower frequency. At frequencies above 35 GHz molecular absorption and attenuation when water drops are present in the atmosphere result in unreliable signals. As the frequency decreases, the strength of the signals from the Sun and Moon increases, while those of sources outside the solar system decreases. Below 15 GHz variable radiation from point sources on the solar disc result in an unacceptable shifting of the centre of solar radiation.

Refraction of radio signals is similar to that of light, and can be predicted with reasonable accuracy by reference to wet- and dry-bulb temperatures and barometric pressure. However, a sort of pseudo-refraction, which has been called 'atmospheric pulling' is caused by radiation of sources within the Earth's atmosphere. The result is an offset of the apparent centre of radiation, thus introducing an error in tracking the source. The effect is proportional to the relative strengths of the wanted signals and the disturbing atmospheric signals. For the Sun the 'pulling' effect is quite small, permitting accurate tracking through moderately heavy rainfall and all but the most intensive thunderheads. Tracking of the Moon is practicable, but with larger error in the vicinity of large cumulus clouds, thunderheads, and precipitation. Because of this 'pulling' effect, primarily, impracticably large aerials would be needed for accurate tracking of other sources. For the most powerful such source, that of α Cassiopeia, an aerial of about 5 metres in diameter would be needed.

As a result of the various limitations, the Sun and, to a lesser extent, the Moon are the only sources of radio emission that have been considered practical for navigation. Several versions of a *radio sextant* operating at about 15 GHz, with a parabolic aerial generally less than one metre in diameter, have been constructed for this purpose. With inertial quality stabilization, the equipment is capable of providing continuous information on altitude and relative azimuth of the Sun or Moon to an accuracy approaching that of visual navigation with a marine sextant.

If both the Sun and Moon are available in favourable positions relative to one another, a fix can be obtained. If only one body is available, a fix is theoretically possible by measurement of both altitude and azimuth, but a reference direction is rarely available with sufficient accuracy for this purpose. A fix might also be obtained by means of altitude and rate of change of altitude (p. 432), but rate of change is generally not sufficiently accurate. The common use of the data is to provide a series of running fixes. It has been suggested that the most effective use of the radio sextant is in conjunction with an inertial stable platform (p. 535), which is needed for stabilization. With this combination the radio sextant can be used to update the inertial equipment, and the inertial equipment can be used to provide stability for the vertical reference and to carry an accurate dead reckoning during periods of non-availability of radio astronomy.

The principal advantage of the radio sextant is that it provides limited astronavigation capability during periods of overcast. It also provides highly accurate relative-direction capability. However, because of its limited applicability, the emergence of electronic systems providing continuous coverage, and the relatively high cost and bulk of the equipment, use of the radio sextant has been confined to naval vessels, where its passive nature and freedom from possible jamming and destruction of ground transmitters by enemy action are important considerations.

15. Speed Measurement

Various methods of measuring the speed of a vessel are discussed in section 18 of chapter III. With the lone exception of Doppler radar logs (p. 141), which are seldom used afloat, electronics are of secondary utility, when used at all: they are involved in the equipment but not used directly for the measurement of speed.

An electronic method of direct measurement of the speed of ships, using the Doppler effect, has been applied successfully to very accurate calibration of ships' speed determination by engine revolution counters. A Doppler radar is installed on the vessel. An efficient corner reflector (p. 498) is placed at a prominent reference point such as a lighthouse. The vessel steams directly toward or away from the reflector. Because of the motion of the vessel relative to the reflector, the returned echo has a frequency differing slightly from that of the transmitted signal. The difference is directly proportional to the instantaneous speed of the vessel relative to the ground.

Average speed over some periods of time can be determined by averaging the readings or by counting the difference between the number of cycles transmitted and the number received, the difference being directly proportional to the distance travelled, and noting the time interval involved. Distance divided by time is average speed. For accurate calibration, measurement should be made while the engine revolutions and speed are essentially constant.

Speed relative to the water can be determined either by averaging readings taken when going toward and away from the reference point, or by using a drifting reference point, as another ship or an unanchored buoy. In the first method the runs should be made with minimum intervening time, to avoid changes in speed of the water relative to the ground. In the second method the area selected should be one in which the difference in water velocity over the ground at the reference point and the vessel being calibrated is minimal.

For accurate results, several runs should be made and the results averaged. Under these conditions an error of less than 0.1 per cent can be achieved. The principal source of error is inaccurate steering of a steady course toward or away from the reference point. Electronic errors arising from inaccurate assumption of the speed of propagation, variation in the frequency of the transmitted signals, and measurement errors are negligible in a well-designed and carefully-used system.

16. Air-Navigation Aids Use Afloat

Electronic aids designed especially for use by air navigators consist principally of directional beacons, non-directional or marker beacons, equipment for determining distance, and landing aids. Of these, the directional beacons are most likely to be of possible use to mariners.

The principal directional beacon is known as a *VOR* beacon, from 'VHF omnirange'. This beacon operates in the

108–118 MHz band. Each beacon transmits two synchronized signals. One signal has a cardiod pattern that rotates 30 times per second, generating a sine wave at the receiver, with a frequency of 30 Hz. The other signal, which is omnidirectional (all-directional), is frequency modulated at 30 Hz. The phase difference of the two signals received at the craft is measured, providing an indication of direction. Zero phase difference occurs in direction *magnetic* north from the transmitter. Position lines radiating outward from the transmitter are known as *radials*, and are identified by the *magnetic* direction from the transmitter.

Special user equipment is needed, consisting of a receiver, phase comparator, and a dial indicator, with the necessary aerial, filters, switches, etc. A switch may be provided for selecting the indication of bearing FROM or TO the station. Equipment designed expressly for use afloat has been developed, but because of its limited application is not used widely.

Bearings obtained by VOR are used in the same manner as any other bearings to establish radial position lines.

Because of the very high frequencies used, signals are free from contamination by sky waves, atmospherics, and other undesirable effects associated with lower frequencies, but the ranges at which signals can be received are limited essentially by the curvature of the Earth. Sites are not selected with the marine user in mind. High ground or other obstructions between the transmitting aerial array and the receiver may interfere with reception in some directions.

The principal sources of error are instrumental and site of the transmitter. The instrumental error is small, being of the order of 1°. Site error is more troublesome, arising principally from reflection of signals by objects near the transmitting aerial array. The most desirable location is on flat ground with no trees, buildings, or other obstructions within a quarter of a nautical mile. With unfavourable sites, errors of as much as 15° have been noted. This problem has been largely overcome by the development of a different version called *Doppler VOR*, with a somewhat different aerial array design and a reversal of the role of the two parts of the array.

By this means the site error has been reduced nearly 90 per cent. The same user equipment can be used with either version.

Distance measuring equipment (*DME*) is a form of secondary radar operating in the 1025–1150 MHz band to provide suitably-equipped craft with means of determining distance of the craft from the transponder. When the transponder is located at a VOR station, both distance and direction information is available for obtaining a fix relative to one reference point. A system with this capability is called a *rho-theta system*. *Tacan* (acronym from *ta*ctical *a*ir *n*avigation) is a military rho-theta system operating at UHF. *Vortac* is a combined VOR-tacan system providing rho-theta information for both civil and military craft with suitable equipment.

The locations and other information relating to some air navigation aids that might be useful to mariners are shown on nautical charts. Full information on all such aids is given in appropriate publications designed for use by aviators, and principal information is given on aeronautical charts.

17. Information by Radio

Radio time signals (p. 152) and weather reports are broadcast regularly from stations throughout the world. In addition, medical advice can be obtained, upon request, from a number of locations.

Radio navigational warnings are also broadcast. These messages include information of an urgent or temporary nature that affect safe navigation. Several different types of warnings are broadcast.

Local warnings, broadcast by most maritime nations, are directed primarily. to local traffic and small craft. The warnings, often in English as well as in the local language, may be quite detailed, covering information relating to harbours and coastal areas in the vicinity of the broadcast. Frequently the broadcasts are both by voice and radio-telegraph. Usually, broadcasts are from only one station in each area.

Long-range warnings are directed primarily to mariners on the high seas, and include major ocean areas, coast lines, and major ports and harbours and their approaches. Messages are usually sent by radiotelegraph, and sometimes by radio-teleprinter. Dissemination of long-range warnings is coordinated by the Inter-Governmental Maritime Consult-ative Organization (IMCO). Sixteen areas, each called a *NAVAREA* and designated by a Roman numeral, have been established to provide world-wide coverage, except for polar regions, in English, using a standard format and procedure. Local and coastal warnings may be broadcast separately by each nation as desired.

World-wide coverage is provided by the United States, in addition to its responsibility for NAVEREAS IV and XII. HYDROLANTS are warnings covering the eastern North Atlantic, South Atlantic, North Sea, Baltic Sea, English Channel, Mediterranean Sea, and contiguous areas. HYDROPACS are warnings for the western North Pacific, South Pacific, South China Sea, Indian Ocean, Red Sea, Persian Gulf, and contiguous areas. The remainder of the world's ocean areas are included in NAVAREAS IV and XII.

The long-range and world-wide warnings usually include such information as casualties suffered by major or approach aids to navigation, establishment of new offshore aids or alteration of existing ones, floating dangers such as large derelicts that might endanger the safety of ships at sea, dangerous wrecks and other obstructions, new information on important changes in shoal depths, marine and air disasters or overdue arrivals and searches for survivors, selected military operations that might affect the safety of shipping, live ordnance that might be hazardous to vessels, mobile drilling rig and seismic geophysical exploration operations, malfunction and scheduled off-time of electronic aids including navigation satellites, the presence of large unwieldy tows in congested waters, and any special events or changes that might have a bearing upon safe navigation.

Navigational warnings are numbered serially and accounted for. When one is no longer applicable, it is cancelled, not merely dropped. Warnings are published in *Daily Memorandum* and *Notices to Mariners* unless cancelled before publication. Permanent messages are not cancelled sooner than six weeks after publication in *Notices to Mariners*.

In addition to the usual navigational warnings, the International Ice Patrol Service broadcasts iceberg warnings at GMT 0000 and 1200 during the iceberg season, usually from February or March through August or September, using information furnished by ships passing through the area and aircraft of the Ice Patrol. The area covered is the vicinity of the Grand Banks of Newfoundland, generally at latitudes south of 48°N. If many bergs are present in the area, only isolated ones or those near the southern limit of sea ice are reported. Positions derived from drift rates from the latest reported sightings become increasingly unreliable with the passage of time, and after five days should be discounted. It is in the interest of mariners to report all iceberg contacts, as well as sea-water temperature and weather information. One should be aware of the possible existence of undetected bergs, and also that radar is not an infallible means of detecting them. When the presence is indicated by radar the average distance of first detection is only four miles.

Detailed information on the presence of ice, and forecasts for the future are available for specific areas such as the Gulf of St. Lawrence, Hudson Bay, and the Great Lakes of North America.

Significant solar and geophysical data are broadcast hourly by stations WWV and WWVA of the United States National Bureau of Standards, the message being changed daily at 0400 UTC (essentially GMT). Provision is also made for real-time data alerts of outstanding occurring events.

18. Radio Information Sources

Detailed information on the locations and use of the various electronic aids to navigation is given in British Admiralty Publication NP 275. *Admiralty List of Radio Signals*, volume V, 'Navigation Aids', and in the United States Defence Mapping Agency Hydrographic Topographic Center

Publication 117, *Radio Navigational Aids*. These publications also have detailed information on radio time signals; radio navigational warnings; distress, emergency, and safety traffic; medical advice by radio; the United States Flag Merchant Vessel Locator Filing System (USMER); procedures in time of war, emergency, or nuclear fallout warnings; and miscellaneous information.

Light lists, sailing directions, and nautical charts include limited information on specific installations. *Notices to Mariners* and *Daily Memorandum* publish information on navigational warnings and changes to aids to navigation. The United States Defence Mapping Agency Hydrographic Topographic Center Publication 118 *Radio Weather Aids* gives detailed information on marine weather broadcasts. Chart indexes of mapping agencies give information on lattice charts of the various electronic systems. Agents of these organizations generally have information on the various publications and charts available from both government and non-government sources.

Among publications of the International Telecommunications Union (ITU), Geneva, of possible interest to mariners are *Radio Regulations*, containing regulations concerning distress, emergency, and safety traffic; and *List of Radiodetermination and Special Service Stations*, giving full information on stations transmitting medical advice.

Electronic user equipment is generally accompanied by a manual provided by the manufacturer, giving detailed information on the use and care of the equipment. The *Decca Navigator Operating Instructions and Marine Data Sheets* furnished by The Decca Navigator Company, Ltd., to users of their equipment contains useful information concerning the Decca system.

A number of good texts on electronics and electronic navigational aids are available for the person who wishes to delve deeper into the subject. Some of these are listed in Appendix A.

XI

Advanced Systems

---

1. Computers

A computer, as generally conceived, is an electronic device for performing almost instantaneous mathematical calculations. Computers vary in size, shape, complexity, and cost from a small, simple, cheap device that adds, subtracts, multiplies, and divides to a large, complex, costly piece of equipment with incredible capability. A *general-purpose computer* may have many uses, while other computers may be designed to perform specific tasks.

Navigation might be considered to consist of the six steps of (*1*) planning, (*2*) sensing, (*3*) logging, (*4*) calculation, (*5*) interpretation, and (*6*) application. The function of a computer is to perform steps (*3*) and (*4*) more rapidly and with greater reliability than can be accomplished by a person. Any step involving judgment, as number (*5*), is best done by a human.

Because of rapidly changing computer technology, the discussion here is limited primarily to generalizations related particularly to the use of computers in navigation.

Computers have been used in the design and construction of navigation equipment, and have virtually eliminated errors in almanacs and sight-reduction tables. More direct navigational applications include the logging of data, solution of equations involved in navigation, collision avoidance, traffic regulation, and ship routing. The advantages of using computers for navigation include the following:

1. Reduction in time needed to perform navigational calculations.
2. Increase in accuracy by reduction or elimination of human error.
3. Reduction or virtual elimination of lag between acquisition of data and determination of the position of a vessel.

4. Remote display of data.
5. Practical use of systems involving complex and lengthy calculations.
6. Practical assimilation of large masses of data.

While it is true that the output of a computer is no more accurate than the input data, the redundance provided by data from a number of sources, rendered more practicable by the use of a computer, reduces the probability of a major error.

The use of computers in navigation can result in reduction in distance run between ports because of smaller deviations from desired tracks, greater safety because of reduction in uncertainty of the position of a vessel, and improved accuracy in estimated times of arrival. The reduction in time needed to perform routine operations provides additional time to the navigator for other tasks such as interpretation of data, assessment of the current situation, and decision-making.

There is almost no limit to the capability that might be provided by a computer, if one is willing to pay the price in terms of cost and maintenance. If the requirements are stated accurately, a computer can probably be designed to accomplish virtually any desired task. The question is whether the intended application is cost effective. It would be difficult, for instance, to justify a large expenditure for complex equipment to perform a simple task easily accomplished by a human at relatively long intervals of time. However, the calculations associated with some advanced navigation systems are so complex and extensive that the systems would be impracticable without computers.

A *digital computer* solves mathematical equations, providing numerical answers on a counter, to any desired degree of precision. While there is a great variety of digital computers, a typical one consists essentially of separate units: input–output, arithmetic, memory, and control.

The *input–output unit*, while not strictly a part of the computer itself, is the means for communication with the computer. There is considerable variation in this unit, depending upon the type of computer and its intended function. Instructions to the computer are inserted as a series of sequential or parallel operations, called the *computer program*. The *Almanac for Computers*, published by the United States Naval Observatory, contains information to help the navigator programme a digital computer for astronavigational applications. The output of a digital computer may be in the form of a display of numbers or a signal to control other equipment.

The *arithmetic unit* makes the calculation by a series of steps consisting of additions, subtractions, multiplications, divisions, and comparisons. The arithmetical steps are generally some form of addition, using a *binary code* consisting of just two digits, 1 and 0. Numbers are indicated by a series of pulses and spaces, each pulse or space being called a *bit* (*binary unit*). A pulse represents 1 and a space 0. Bits are assembled in *words*, each successive bit in the word *in reverse order* (right to left) representing a power of 2: $2^0 = 1$, $2^1 = 2$, $2^2 = 4$, $2^3 = 8$, and so on. Thus, the word length depends upon the size of the number. A 10-bit word accommodates numbers to 1,023, a 20-bit word to 1,048,575, and a 30-bit word to 1,073,741,823. As an example, the number 723 requires 10 bits, consisting of $1 \times 2^9 + 0 \times 2^8 + 1 \times 2^7 + 1 \times 2^6 + 0 \times 2^5 + 1 \times 2^4 + 0 \times 2^3 + 0 \times 2^2 + 1 \times 2^1 + 1 \times 2^0 = 723$, or $512 + 0 + 128 + 64 + 0 + 16 + 0 + 0 + 2 + 1 = 723$. This number would be indicated by pulse, space, pulse, pulse, space, pulse, space, space, pulse, pulse. A pulse being represented by 1 and a space by 0, the number 723 is represented in binary code as 1011010011. Similarly, the number 164 in binary code is 10100100. The two numbers 723 and 164 are added as follows:

$$
\begin{array}{rl}
723 = & 1011010011 \\
164 = & \underline{10100100} \\
887 = & 1021110111
\end{array}
$$

Each 2 is replaced by a 1 in the next bit to the left, so the binary code representation appears as 1101110111.

The *memory unit* stores instructions and data. The memory capacity required depends upon the type and amount of data to be processed.

The *control unit* is essentially a clock that times the transfer of data to and from the memory and the various computer processes. A program counter maintains a record of which instruction is being processed. An index register stores information that may be used to modify instructions received from the memory. Modifications are accomplished by adding a number in the index register to one in the original instructions.

A number of steps are involved in even a relatively simple calculation, yet a digital computer accomplishes even very complex operations with astonishing speed, each step being completed in a tiny fraction of a second, perhaps only a small number of nanoseconds.

One of the advantages of a digital computer is its great flexibility. A special-purpose computer may have the programme permanently wired in. Other computers can be adapted to different problems by merely changing the *software*, a term indicating the instructions, or programs, collectively, to distinguish it from the physical computer, called the *hardware*. Simple, hand-held calculators are generally not programmable, each step of a calculation being performed separately by pushing appropriate buttons, but there are exceptions.

With the application of miniaturization to computers to produce relatively small, cheap *microcomputers* with all the capability of larger devices, the use of digital computers in navigation has increased. There has also been a tendency to use one computer for a number of applications, replacing various special-purpose hardwired computers.

An *analog computer* establishes a physical or electrical analogy to the physical problem to be solved. A mechanical solution of the navigational triangle (p. 423) is a common example. An analog computer is suitable for use in such applications as performing coordinate transformations, integration, multiplication, computing trigonometric functions, and in solving certain relatively simple equations. The accuracy is limited by hardware and electrical tolerances, and tends to change in time, as mechanical parts wear, thus requiring recalibration from time to time. Analog computers have been used in navigation since antiquity. They can provide continuous, essentially instantaneous solutions, and are applicable where a small number of algebraic or differential equations are to be solved with an accuracy of 0.1 per cent or a little better. They are not suitable for involved solutions or voluminous processing, or where great accuracy is required.

Pulse-analog computers use pulse duration or pulse repetition rate as an analogy of physical quantities, thus eliminating the need for mechanical parts. In comparison with a straight analog computer, a pulse-analog computer is lighter in weight, cheaper, more accurate, more reliable, and has greater versatility.

When considering the purchase of a computer one should take into account a number of factors, including the following:

1. Intended function of the computer.
2. Type and format of input–output data.
3. Memory capacity requirement.
4. Data and computation rates.
5. Accuracy and precision requirements.
6. Flexibility and growth potential.
7. Reliability and maintenance requirements.
8. Cost effectiveness.

The relative importance of these items is a consideration, too, for some compromise may be needed.

If computers are to be used effectively afloat, it is essential that those who will use them be given adequate education and training. It is not important that the seagoing officer have complete knowledge regarding their construction, but he should understand their capabilities and limitations and be thoroughly conversant with their use. The extent of knowledge of programming needed depends upon the type of computer involved. The user should be able to detect a malfunction, and someone aboard ship should be able to replace defective modules or otherwise maintain the computer. The need for redundancy depends upon how vital a computer is to the operation of the vessel, and the maintenance capability of the crew. The extent of computer knowledge needed afloat may be quite modest in the case of a simple hand-held calculator, but extensive if a complex general-purpose computer of many applications is installed.

2. Inertial Navigation

The expression *inertial navigation* refers to the determination of (*1*) position relative to an established starting point, (*2*) velocity, and (*3*) heading, by measurement of accelerations in known space-oriented directions, and processing the data by a computer. The name 'inertial' is derived from Sir Isaac Newton's laws of motion (p. 289) which are based upon inertia relative to 'fixed stars'. Modern inertial navigation relies on the work done by Newton in 1687, Foucault in 1851 (p. 128), and Schuler in 1908 (p. 130). The marine gyro compass was the first limited inertial navigation device, but the development of a full *inertial navigator*, or *inertial navigation system* (*INS*), as a mechanization of spacial inertia had to await major advances in technology.

Relative to other methods, inertial navigation has the following advantages:

1. It has world-wide application without weather limitations.
2. It is self-contained and passive, not requiring ground-based transmitters or transmission from the craft, and therefore free from interference, jamming, propagation anomalies, power failures ashore, physical damage to aerials, and political vagaries.
3. Readouts are instantaneous and continuous.

There are disadvantages:

1. Initial alignment with position and the coordinate frame is needed.
2. Readout information degrades with time, whether the craft is moving or stationary, and thus needs updating at intervals.
3. Equipment is expensive and requires expert service and maintenance.

In effect, inertial navigation is a form of dead reckoning relative to the Earth, not the water through which the vessel moves. Its use is particularly attractive in military vessels, especially submarines; in aircraft and missiles, where flight time is relatively short; and in spacecraft, which have long periods of 'coasting' between short powered manoeuvres. Because of its disadvantages, inertial navigation in civilian vessels has been limited primarily to special-purpose craft such as those used for geophysical exploration or hydrographic or oceanographic surveys. As advancing technology lessens the impact of these shortcomings, increased use of inertial navigation in the merchant service can be anticipated. In addition to its direct use in positioning a vessel, its velocity information is useful in determining position by means of the United States Navy Navigation Satellite System (p. 542), and its stable platform can be useful in stabilizing other equipment aboard the vessel. Conversely, because of its need for periodical updating, its use afloat is most likely to be in conjunction with other systems (p. 551).

Principles of operation. According to Newton's second law, the acceleration of a body acted upon by an external force is directly proportional to the force, and inversely proportional to the mass of the body, with the acceleration taking place in the direction of application of the force. Thus, if a is acceleration, F the force, and m the mass, $a = F/m$, or, as generally stated, $F = ma$.

Imagine a body at rest on a non-rotating Earth that is either stationary in space or travelling in a straight line at constant speed, with no gravity. There would be no acceleration. If, now, a force acts on the body, causing it to change position, and the acceleration in the direction of motion is measured, its speed can be determined by integration of the acceleration, and the distance travelled by a second integration of acceleration. Thus, if the initial position and direction of motion are known, the position at any future time can be determined.

Effects of accelarations other than that caused by motion of the body over the surface of the Earth need to be removed. Examples of such other accelerations are those resulting from change in the direction of gravity because of change of position of the body on the curved surface of the Earth; rotation of the Earth on its axis and its revolution around the

Sun; gravity; Coriolis (p. 193); and such craft rotations as roll, pitch, and yaw. Some accelerations are so small that they are beyond the capability of present technology. An example is the variation of the Earth's speed of revolution about the Sun in accordance with Kepler's second law (p. 288).

Thus, requirements of a practical inertial navigator are means for:

1. Establishment of initial conditions of position, the horizontal, and direction.
2. Maintenance of a platform aligned perpendicular to the direction of gravity.
3. Measurement of horizontal direction of motion of the craft over the surface of the Earth.
4. Measurement of space (inertia)-referenced acceleration, including gravity.
5. Removal of effects of unwanted accelerations.
6. Maintenance of a suitable coordinate reference frame.
7. Integration of acceleration to obtain speed, and a second integration to obtain distance travelled.
8. Power supply, a suitable display, console, etc.

Alignment consists of establishing initial conditions. This involves the following:

1. *Position* in latitude and longitude or other suitable coordinates. This requires an independent means of establishing position.
2. *Velocity,* set at zero if the craft is stationary on the surface of the Earth, or at an established value by independent means if underway.
3. *Horizontal,* determined by rotating the platform on two mutually perpendicular horizontal axes until the horizontal acceleration is zero. Two gimbals permit such rotation. Any tilt results in an indication of acceleration because of gravity.
4. *Direction,* by alignment with a reference direction. A third, vertical gimbal is provided for this purpose.
5. *Gyro drifts* noted at the time of switching from 'alignment' to 'navigate' mode.

Before an inertial navigator is aligned, it should be permitted to warm up. As long as 30 minutes may be required. If the device is aligned prematurely, large errors might result. The availability of another platform, accurately aligned, or recorded settings of a previous alignment can be helpful in reducing alignment time. Advancing technology is reducing the time and simplifying the process of placing an inertial navigator in service.

Stable platform. A critical function of an inertial navigator is its ability to maintain its alignment with respect to the horizontal and a reference direction as a craft rolls, pitches, and yaws, and the local vertical changes direction as the craft moves across the surface of an Earth that is rotating on its axis and revolving around the Sun. This is accomplished by means of gyroscopes (p. 128) that sense any deviation from alignment in any of the three mutually perpendicular axis (two horizontal and one vertical) and provide inputs to stabilization servos. A tremendous amount of research has been and is still being devoted to the development of more accurate gyroscopes. Floated gyroscopes with one or two degrees of freedom are generally used in inertial navigators, but electrostatically-suspended gyroscopes are coming into use. Research is continuing to provide even greater accuracy by the possible use of other kinds of gyroscopes such as laser, cryogenic, nuclear, and fluid (rotor).

In addition to its primary function of stabilizing the acceleration sensors, the stable platform of an inertial navigator provides a convenient indication of roll, pitch, and yaw. Its method of mounting also protects the sensitive elements from large angular motions and from vibration, temperature, and magnetic influences.

A considerable amount of research has been devoted to possible elimination of the stable platform. An inertial navigator of this type is called a *strapdown* system. The gyroscopes and acceleration sensors are mounted in fixed positions and their outputs are converted by the computer to the equivalent of outputs from a stable platform. This configuration eliminates the need for a stable platform, but is fraught with problems of considerable magnitude.

Accelerometers measure the acceleration of the craft. The principle of the accelerometer is illustrated in Fig. 1101. A

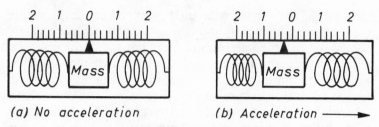

(a) No acceleration   (b) Acceleration ⟶

FIG. 1101. A simple accelerometer.

mass is mounted between two springs. If there is no acceleration, as in *a*, the pointer at the top of the mass indicates 0 on the scale at the top of the case. If the case is accelerated to the right, as in *b*, the mass moves toward the left, compressing the spring on that side and extending the spring on the other side. The pointer indicates the movement by being offset from 0. A greater acceleration would produce a larger offset. If the craft steadies on some speed, acceleration ceases and the mass returns to the centre position. As the craft slows, the acceleration and direction of movement of the mass are reversed. As the craft comes to a stop, the mass is again centred. Typically, one accelerometer is aligned with each of the three mutually perpendicular axes of the stable platform.

Unwanted accelerations. If an inertial navigator is to indicate accurately the progress of a vessel across the surface of the Earth, all unwanted accelerations must be eliminated.

If a stable platform is truly level, the horizontal accelerometers do not indicate an acceleration because of gravity, but if there is any tilt, a vertical component is registered. The effect of gravity on the vertical accelerometer is eliminated in the computer.

The effect of rotation and revolution of the Earth, resulting in a continuous change in the direction of gravity in space, is eliminated by precessing the gyroscopes at the rate of rotation of their axes because of Earth motion. The gyroscopes must also be precessed to compensate for change in the direction of the vertical as the craft moves across the surface of the Earth. A *Schuler-tuned* system, having an 84.4-minute period, accomplishes this function. Additionally, the gyroscopes require compensation, called *gyro bias*, for gyro drift caused by such factors as mass imbalance and friction.

Any accelerometer- or gyro-bias error, or any disturbance of the stable platform from the horizontal, tends to cause an oscillation of the stable platform about the horizontal with a period of 84.4 minutes, the period of a pendulum having a length equal to the radius of the Earth. This effect is minimized by a system of damping, using a velocity source independent of gravity and other accelerations.

The effect of Coriolis in causing false readings of the accelerometers may be removed by computation.

Coordinate reference frames. A number of different coordinate systems may be used in inertial navigators. Each system is rectangular in nature, having three mutually perpendicular axes. Those most commonly used are space-oriented with respect to the centre of the Earth, Earth-oriented with respect to the axis of rotation of the Earth, and horizontal-referenced with respect to a point on the surface of the Earth. The stable platform is oriented with respect to the horizontal system, using true north, east, and the vertical as the axes.

Computer. Generally, an inertial navigator is provided with its own digital computer, but a central navigation computer or even a general-purpose computer of many functions may be used. The calculation involved in converting the outputs of the sensors to velocity, position, and altitude of the craft are too extensive and lengthy to be solved manually in a practical system. The actual nature of the computer needed depends upon the type of inertial navigator and the outputs desired.

Auxiliary features. Not only are suitable housing, adequate power, and appropriate displays essential, but the actual inertial navigator is considerably more complex than the simple device described above. If one is interested in delving deeper into the subject, there is extensive literature, both in texts and in technical journals.

Errors. Inertial navigator errors arise from (*1*) imperfections in the components and the assembled system, (*2*) inaccurate alignment, and (*3*) limitations in knowledge of the physical environment in which the system operates. The problem of producing an accurate system is compounded by (*1*) the interrelation of errors; (*2*) the cumulative nature of the total error; and (*3*) the fact that some imperfection effects, such as gyro drift, tend to change in a random manner.

Two principal cyclic errors have been identified. Any tilt of the stable platform, as one caused by inaccurate initial alignment or later disturbance, causes an 84.4-minute oscillation of the platform, resulting in a rhythmic error superimposed on other errors. Another cyclic error has a period of 24 hours. Its source is imperfections in position or heading alignment or incorrect gyro bias. Its 24-hour period arises from the fact that the effect of gravity acting on any misalignment or gyro imbalance reverses its direction in opposite halves of the 24-hour rotation of the Earth.

Small but significant errors arise from natural causes. The principal one is imperfect knowledge of the Earth's gravity field, particularly with respect to gravity anomalies and deflections of the vertical (p. 381) by the non-homogeneity of the Earth. The problem arises from the fact that the accelerometers cannot distinguish accelerations caused by gravity from those caused by motions. Minute effects such as precession of the equinoxes (p. 288) and polar motion (p. 330) also affect the accuracy of an inertial navigator.

Because of the cumulative nature of the total error of an inertial navigator, its accuracy is generally stated in terms of miles (or fractions of a mile) per hour. An error that might be quite small over a short interval may in time become intolerably large, requiring updating of the navigator by means of position information from another source.

Improvement of accuracy involves (*1*) greater perfection in manufacture, particularly the development of gyroscopes with lower drift rates; (*2*) better alignment techniques; (*3*) increased knowledge of the physical environment; and (*4*) more accurate independent sources of velocity and position to provide better inputs for damping and for periodic updating.

3. Acoustic Navigation

Acoustic energy in some form has been used in navigation for a very long time. An early technique, still useful under suitable conditions, is to determine distance from precipitous terrain by blowing the ship's whistle and timing the interval until return of an echo. Distance off in miles is approximately one eleventh the interval in seconds. Somewhat the same principle is used for distance-finding stations (p. 273) except that synchronized radio and sound signals are used and the difference in reception time is used as one-way travel time. The travel time of sound signals is also the principle used in echo sounding (p. 148) for depth measurement and sonar (p. 145) for distance measurement.

A somewhat similar approach has been the use of submerged acoustic beacons, particularly by deep submergence craft and their surface-ship escorts. The usual technique is to place one or more acoustic transponders (p. 493) at previously-established positions and then to determine range by means of sonic or ultrasonic signals transmitted by a *transducer*, a device that converts electrical to acoustic energy, aboard the vessel. If one transponder is used, an array of two or more hydrophones aboard the vessel receives the return signal. The two-way travel time provides a measurement of distance, and the difference in reception times at different hydrophones provides means for determining direction. If more than one transponder is used, the distance from each is determined, and positon is established by means of the resulting circular position lines.

A method proposed for guiding a vessel along a straight channel would place a submerged beacon on each side of the channel with the line connecting the beacons being perpendicular to the centre line of the channel. As long as signals from the two beacons arrived simultaneously, the vessel would be on the centre line of the channel. A series of beacon pairs, suitably coded, might be used for long channels or those with legs on different courses. The beacons could be either transponders or synchronized transmitters. The same principle could be used to provide bearing position lines in fixed positions.

Another method of providing channel guidance or fixed bearing position lines would be to have a submerged beacon transmit alternately in two narrow, intersecting lobes. When signals from the two lobes would be received with equal amplitude, the vessel would be on the centre line of the two lobes. A probably more satisfactory arrangement would be to transmit coded signals in each lobe. The Morse code letters A ($\cdot$—) and N (—$\cdot$) have been suggested. If these signals were synchronized properly, a continuous tone would be received when the vessel was on course. This is the principle used in low-frequency radio ranges formerly used to mark the Federal Airways of the United States. Other, more sophisticated systems patterned after more advanced aircraft electronic systems could undoubtedly be devised.

Doppler sonar navigators have been used successfully by deep submergence vessels, geophysical exploration vessels, and others. Ultrasonic signals beamed downward at an angle from the vessel are reflected back by the ocean floor. The frequency of the returning, reflected signals differs from that of the transmitted signals because of the Doppler effect (p. 470) if the vessel has components of motion, either positive or negative, in the directions of the beams. The difference of frequency between the transmitted and return signals is directly proportional to the component of speed in the direction of that beam. With two beams, ideally 90° apart in horizontal direction, and a reference direction indication, one can determine the course and speed of the vessel. Integration of speed determines distance travelled.

Doppler sonar is subject to several sources of error. Misalignment of the transducers, or an undetected compass error, results in an error in indicated direction of travel of the vessel. The orientation of the transducers changes with change in the trim of the vessel. Vessel motions—roll, pitch, yaw, and heave—also introduce errors. The error resulting from rolling and pitching can be reduced, but not completely eliminated, by using four beams, ideally spaced 90° apart in horizontal direction, instead of two beams. This arrangement is called a *Janus configuration* after the Roman mythical god who was supposed to have two faces, one looking forward and the other looking back. The accuracy of the indicated velocity is affected by changes in the speed of the ultrasonic signal in the immediate vicinity of the transducers. This speed in water varies with temperature, pressure, and salinity. The pressure change is generally quite small, but the temperature between high latitudes and the tropics is considerable, and the change in salinity as a vessel enters or leaves an estuary receiving fresh water from the land can be quite large. A device called a *velocimeter* is used in some installations to measure the speed of the ultrasonic signal in the vicinity of the transducers. If some echos are missed because of loss by absorption, scatter, spreading, a smooth bottom, or other reason, the vessel speed indication is too low. A too-low indication of speed also results if returns from side lobes are greater than those from the main beam.

The overall accuracy of a good Doppler sonar navigator is of the order of 0.5 per cent or better in calm water not more than about 400 metres deeper than the transducers. Like indications of an inertial navigator, the speed determined by a Doppler sonar navigator in shallow water is relative to the ground. In water deeper than about 400 metres, the return signals are by water reverberation rather than by ground reflection, and the measured speed is therefore relative to the water. Unlike inertial equipment, Doppler sonar error increases with distance travelled, rather than time.

The principle of the Doppler sonar navigator is also used as a *docking aid* for very large vessels, which require accurate data on speed. With these vessels a speed of a very small fraction of a metre per second can result in damage to a pier or loss of anchor and chain.

Frequency and the type of sound transmission are important considerations in the selection of a Doppler sonar navigator or docking aid. Higher frequency reduces the size of the transducers and maximizes the Doppler shift, but the absorption loss in sea water is greater, resulting in higher power requirements. Also, with higher frequency the size of a bottom irregularity constituting a rough bottom is smaller, resulting in better reflecting properties. Frequencies of 150 to 600 kHz are most popular. Doppler sonar navigators generally use pulse modulation to provide greater peak power, and therefore greater maximum depth capability, with relatively low average power. Continuous-wave transmission is more popular for docking aids because this type of signal is capable of greater accuracy resolution, and it has virtually no minimum depth limitation, an important consideration for a deep-draught vessel in the vicinity of berthing areas.

4. Navigation Satellites

One of the first practical uses suggested for artificial Earth satellites was for navigation. A number of techniques were suggested, including measurement of elevation angle (as in astronavigation), distance, distance-difference, Doppler shift, and various combinations of ground and satellite transmissions. The first practical navigation satellite system, known as the *United States Navy Navigation Satellite System* (*NNSS*) became operational for restricted military use in January 1964, and was released to world-wide civilian use on July 29, 1967.

The Navy system, also known as the 'Transit System', uses five satellites (sometimes four temporarily) in nominally circular polar orbits at heights of about 1,100 kilometres above the surface of the Earth. At this height the orbital period is about 107 minutes. A fix is obtained during a pass of any one satellite. During a pass, a satellite remains above the horizon for a period of any duration from a momentary appearance to approximately 18 minutes. With five satellites there are about 15 to 20 useful passes per day, the number increasing with higher latitude until mutual interference reduces the number in polar regions. Because of random distribution of the satellites in their orbits, and a slightly different precession rate of the different orbits, the interval between consecutive passes varies from a few minutes to several hours.

Each satellite is observed continuously, while it is above the horizon, by four widely-separated *tracking stations*. The observed data are sent to a computing centre in California where the best orbital fit is computed and extrapolated for the next 16 hours. At approximately 12-hour intervals these orbital data are transmitted to the satellite by one of three *injection stations*, replacing the orbital data stored there previously. The 16-hour period of data provides a reserve in case of delayed injection.

During each two-minute period each satellite transmits its orbital data in two parts. One part is the fixed data that remains constant over the 16-hour period. The other part consists of variable parameters that are considered constant for only the two-minute transmission period.

User equipment receives the signals and computes the position of the receiving aerial. The computed position is determined relative to the satellite orbit. The computer converts this to latitude and longitude.

The principle used is the Doppler effect (p. 470) of the transmitted signals as the satellite approaches ('up Doppler'), passes ('no Doppler'), and recedes ('down Doppler') from the user, as shown in Fig. 1102. The Doppler pattern during a pass is unique for each user, being a composite of (*1*) motion of the satellite in its orbit, (*2*) motion of the user over the surface of the Earth, and (*3*) rotation of the Earth on its polar

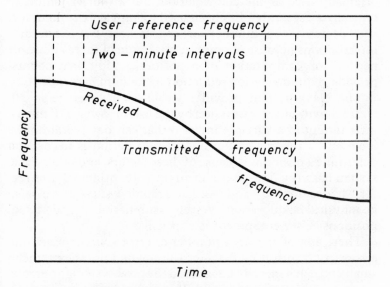

FIG. 1102. Doppler effect during a pass of a United States Navy Navigation Satellite.

axis. The receiving equipment includes a stable oscillator that provides frequencies that differ from the transmitted frequencies by a little more than the variation because of the Doppler effect. The measurement consists of a count of the difference, during each measurement period, between the number of cycles received and the number of cycles generated by the user equipment. This number is called the *integrated Doppler count* because it can be represented by an integral of the difference frequency during the time period of the count. The number representing the constant difference between the transmitted and user-generated reference cycles during the same period is subtracted to obtain the *Doppler cycle count*, which represents an accurate measure of the difference in slant range between the user and the satellite, for each cycle is one wave length, which at 400 MHz is about 0.75 metre.

The actual computation determines the slant range from an assumed position of the user and compares this with the measured values, using successive iterations until the results converge. The two-minute transmission period was originally used as the count period, but a shorter period— typically 23 seconds—has been used to improve the accuracy and decrease the number of counts lost by temporary interruptions because of noise. A minimum of three counts is needed for computation of a position. Additional counts provide redundancy for reduction of random error.

The Navy system provides world-wide coverage in all weather, without transmission by the user. However, fixing is intermittent at a variable interval that can be several hours long, and a relatively long observation period is needed to determine a position. Because of these factors, and others, the system has very limited use in aircraft. Its principal uses are for hydrographic and oceanographic survey vessels, geophysical exploration vessels, submarines, and fixed positions. User equipment is expensive.

There are, of course, a number of error sources. Random errors (p. 27) resulting from measurement noise is extremely small and can generally be ignored. Several systematic errors (p. 27) are more troublesome. The Doppler effect relates to the *difference* in velocity vectors, in space, of the satellite and

544

user. The component of vessel motion parallel to the satellite motion is rather critical for accurate results, an error of one knot in vessel speed in this direction introducing an error of about 0.2 nautical mile in the fix. Where maximum accuracy is required, the vessel is provided with an independent means of establishing its velocity vector relative to the surface of the Earth. Doppler sonar (p. 540) and inertial navigators (p. 532) have been used for this purpose.

Another major source of error is variable ionospheric refraction. This error is minimized by transmitting on two frequencies: approximately 400 MHz and 150 MHz. Both frequencies are derived from the same oscillator, and so the relationship is very stable. The ionospheric refraction is very nearly inversely proportional to frequency, and so the use of two frequencies can be used to compute the error from this source. However, during periods of anomalous ionospheric refraction the error increases. Some relatively inexpensive user equipment, designed for use where maximum accuracy is not needed, uses only the 400 MHz signals. The error introduced by using only the higher frequency might be as large as 0.5 mile, or as small as 0.1 mile. The error would be larger if the lower frequency were used alone.

Additional error sources are errors in the orbital positions of the satellites, error in the velocity component of the user perpendicular to the satellite motion, error in the height of the aerial above the surface of the geoid (p. 18), error in the reference frequency standard in the user equipment, and tropospheric refraction. The frequency standards in the satellites are sufficiently accurate to introduce negligible error.

Satellite passes having maximum elevation between about 15° and 75° are usuable. Below 15° the pass is too short to provide enough counts, the reception tends to be noisy with possible loss of counts, and the error in the direction of satellite motion (essentially latitude except in polar regions) is large relative to the error in a transverse direction. For high satellite passes the error in the transverse direction is least accurate, and counts near the zenith may be lost because of aerial design.

545

All satellites transmit on the same frequencies, which provide essentially line-of-sight transmission. If two or more satellites are above the horizon at the same time, mutual interference might occur, preventing a fix from any satellite. This sutuation is quite common in high latitudes, but can occur anywhere.

The overall accuracy of a satellite fix by the Navy system, if two frequencies are used, the user equipment has a good frequency standard, the pass is favourable, and the velocity vector of the vessel over the ground is known to a fraction of a knot speed, is of the order of 0.1 nautical mile or better. Under ideal conditions with the best equipment and careful analysis of all data, accuracy of the order of 50 metres has been achieved at sea. At a fixed location, as in positioning an oil-drilling rig offshore or establishing the position of a survey marker on land, where there is no vessel motion and the user equipment can remain in the same position for several days, accuracies of the order of 5 metres have been achieved with 25 to 30 good passes. When the system is used in a differential mode (p. 511), even higher accuracies are possible.

In addition to their use in position fixing, the Navy navigation satellites can be used for time signals. At the start of each two-minute period, a 400 Hz audible 'beep' signal is transmitted, and these signals are synchronozied with UTC (p. 331) to an accuracy of about 0.02 second.

A more sophisticated satellite system providing world-wide, continuous, highly-accurate, all-weather, three-dimensional fixing capability and time and user velocity information is under development. If development continues as predicted, limited two-dimensional capability of moderate accuracy will be available possibly as early as 1981, and full three-dimensional capability of high accuracy by 1984. The system, under development by elements of the United States Department of Defense, based upon studies made independently by the United States Navy and United States Air Force, is known as the *NAVSTAR Global Positioning System (GPS)*. It consists of three segments: space, control, and user.

Space segment. The fully operational system will have 24

satellites, eight each in three circular 12-hour orbits at a height of a little more than 20,000 kilometres, the orbits having an inclination of 63° to the equatorial plane. The satellites will have a design life of five years and will have means of maintaining assigned positions for eight years. An average of nine and minimum of six satellites will be above the horizon at any time at any point on the Earth. Each satellite will have a mass of approximately 430 kilograms and at the end of five years will have a power of 400 watts provided by solar panels that track the Sun, with three nickel-cadmium batteries to store energy for use when the satellite is in the Earth's shadow.

Each satellite will transmit at 1,575.42 MHz and 1,227.6 MHz to provide for reduction of error because of ionospheric refraction. Pseudo-random noise, spread-spectrum signals will be used. The pseudo-random noise sequence will be unique to each satellite so that all satellites can transmit on the same carrier frequency. A rubidium or caesium atomic clock with a stability of the order of one part in 10^{13} will be used to time the signals.

Control segment. The control system will consist of a number of monitor stations, a master control station, and an upload station. The operational system is expected to have additional stations of all three parts to provide redundancy in case of need. The monitor stations will track the satellites and send the data to the master control station, where known corrections will be made and satellite orbit and clock drift will be computed. The control station will ensure satellite clock synchronization to within a few nanoseconds. The upload station will transmit necessary data to the satellites daily or more often.

User segment. The user equipment will consist of an aerial, receiver, computer, and display unit. The signals received from the satellites will be used to measure pseudo range and pseudo-range rate from each of four suitably located satellites. These data will be converted to three-dimensional Earth-centred position, velocity (if required), and time. The positional information will be converted to latitude and longitude, or other desired coordinates, and altitude (in aircraft). The need for high precision clocks in the user equipment will be avoided by using three independent range-difference equations based upon the data received from four satellites to calculate the unique intersection of three hyperboloids of revolution. If user velocity data are required, Doppler measurements can be made. Satellite-transmitted data will include satellite velocity. An inertial navigator may be integrated with satellite user-equipment to enhance the ability to acquire and track the satellite signals when jamming occurs.

Even though the system is being designed to minimize user equipment complexity, the equipment for utilization of the full accuracy potential of the system will not be simple, resulting in high cost. Simplified, single-frequency, moderate-accuracy user equipment will perhaps alleviate this situation somewhat.

Accuracy. The principal consideration in determining user positioning accuracy is the ranging error. Several sources of error can be allowed for with negligible error. These include polar motion (p. 330), precession of the equinoxes (p. 288), solar wind pressure, and the effect of relativity on the relative indications of the satellite-based and ground-based clocks. More troublesome are errors in the positions of the satellites, satellite clock-drift between updates, ionospheric and tropospheric propagation delays, user receiver noise, and multipath. Considerable research and careful analysis predict that the overall ranging error of highest-accuracy user equipment can be limited to three to five metres 50 per cent of the time, resulting in horizontal positioning accuracy of the order of ten metres on the average. Higher accuracy might be achieved by averaging repeated measurements over a period of time at one place. Typical accuracy at sea by equipment likely to be available to the merchant service is probably of the order of 100 metres.

The Summer 1978 issue (Vol. 25, No. 2) of *Navigation*, Journal of The Institute of Navigation (U.S.A.), devoted to the NAVSTAR Global Positioning System, contains a wealth of detailed information on the system.

5. Astro-Trackers

Automation of astronavigation involves the use of an *astro-tracker*, a device that detects and remains pointed toward an astronomical body as the craft in which it is mounted moves as a result of its own motion and the motion of the Earth. Such a device, suitably mounted on a stable platform (p. 535) and provided with adequate computing capability, can provide position-line or fix information day and night during clear weather, directional information, and attitude control of aircraft and spacecraft. Afloat, its principal users are special-purpose craft and submarines. The high cost and complexity of the equipment precludes its wide use for ordinary navigation. Because a high-grade stable platform of inertial quality is needed, the use of an astro-tracker is particularly attractive in conjunction with an inertial navigator.

While a radio sextant (p. 519) can be considered one form of astro-tracker, the term more generally applies to an optical device that senses the light from various astronomical bodies, principally stars.

The heart of an astro-tracker is a *photoelectric sensor* that distinguishes the light of the astronomical body from the background light. Three types of photoelectric sensors have been used. A *photovoltaic sensor* establishes an electrical voltage when subjected to light. Despite its high internal noise and decreasing efficiency with higher temperature, silicon is the most widely used photovoltaic sensor. Selenium oxide and gallium arsenide are also used. A *photoconductive sensor* undergoes a change in electrical resistance when subjected to light. The photoconducting material is deposited on the surface of an imaging valve, or tube, such as the vidicon used in a television camera. The material generally used is lead sulfide, cadmium sulfide, or cadmium selenide. A *photoemissive sensor* is a valve on which light which strikes the surface emits electrons which are accelerated toward secondary emission stages for amplification. Several different types of valves have been used, the photomultiplier and photodiode having been the most popular. Some imaging valves have also been used.

The ability of an astro-tracker to detect the light from a star

549

depends upon the *photoelectric magnitude* of the body (the brightness as observed by a photoelectric sensor), which may differ from the optical magnitude (p. 292), and the effective area of the sensor. The principal problem in daylight tracking is distinguishing the light of the astronomical body from that of the background, as the latter may be many times brighter and more variable than the former. Internal noise within the sensor and amplifier may also interfere with detection of the wanted signal. Some form of modulation is used to change the characteristic of the wanted signal from the essentially direct-current nature of the noise. An efficient astro-tracker can detect perhaps 100 of the brightest stars during daylight. By night, stars of magnitude 3.5 or fainter can be detected. Means must be provided for protecting the sensor from the direct or indirect rays of the Sun, and also to prevent a false acquisition, as from the bright edge of a cloud or from a star image reflected from a surface outside or inside the device.

Because of the need for distinguishing between the image of an astronomical body and the background, the field of view of an astro-tracker is quite limited, being of the order of six to ten minutes of arc. Typically, the altitude and azimuth of the body to be tracked are computed for the best position of the craft, and the tracker is pointed toward the computed position. If the body is within the field of view, either (*1*) the pointing of the tracker is adjusted to centre the body, and the altitude and azimuth of the setting are noted; or (*2*) the difference between the centre of the field of view and the body is measured and applied as a correction to the setting of the tracker. If the body is not in the field of view, the tracker goes into a search mode until the body is located, and then the measurement is made as above. The body is identified by some pre-established characteristic, usually magnitude. Wide-angle astro-trackers that would identify the wanted body by pattern recognition have been proposed, but the technology needed for such a device has been inadequate. Simultaneous or consecutive observation of two or more bodies is needed for a fix.

The principal sources of error are in pointing of the sensor and in the stable platform. A good astro-tracker should be able to point toward an astronomical body with an accuracy of 0.́1 or better. The stable-platform error depends critically upon the quality of the platform. Overall accuracy of one minute of arc or better has been achieved.

6. Integrated Systems

With the proliferation of methods and systems of navigation, one has the capability of position determination in a variety of ways. Even though some systems have limitations relating to geography, weather, or electromagnetic propagation conditions, and any mechanical or electronic system is subject to failure, a navigator nearly always has more than one means of determining position other than by dead reckoning, which is always available in some form.

Traditionally, different means of determination of the vessel's position have been employed independently. A dead-reckoning position is checked by astronavigation or an electronic system, and a position obtained by cross bearings may be compared with soundings. With the increase in the use of electronics in navigation, and particularly with the development of relatively cheap digital computers, considerable attention has been given to the automatic combining of results from more than one source, to provide a single result. A simple application of the principle involves the weighting of results from different positioning systems to determine one most probable position.

A more sophisticated approach is to use the results of one method to improve results of another. An example is the use of an inertial navigator to provide a good velocity vector for determining position by means of the United States Navy Navigation Satellite System. In turn, the position so determined can be used to update positions determined by the inertial navigator, which are subject to increasing error because of gyro drift, primarily. Similarly, the stable platform of an inertial navigator may be used to provide a reference for measurements of altitudes of astronomical bodies by an astro-tracker (p. 535), and the resulting fix used to update the inertial navigator.

Complex systems in great variety, involving a number of different inputs, have been proposed or developed. Generally, an integrated navigation system involves the use of some form of electronic filtering to smooth, weight, and evaluate the noisy input data from a number of redundant, complementary sources to provide a single output of position, velocity, and possibly attitude for display to bridge personnel or to guide the craft along a predetermined path on an established schedule, as shown in Fig. 1103.

FIG. 1103. Function of integrated navigation system.

Thus, an obvious reason for combining the various inputs of navigation data in one integrated system is to improve accuracy. Another reason is to improve reliability by detecting anomalous conditions or malfunction of a component, rejecting such inputs, and providing outputs from reliable input data. A third reason is to shorten or virtually eliminate the lag between observation and the availability of results.

Integrated navigation systems have been particularly attractive to operators of special-purpose craft such as hydrographic survey and geophysical exploration vessels, who desire greater accuracy, reliability, and real-time outputs.

Other users may also benefit, if cost effectiveness can be established. An integrated system is expensive, but there are benefits. Certain components of electronic equipment may be duplicated in different systems if kept separate, but the duplication eliminated if the systems are combined. One computer might replace several that would be needed if equipments were used separately. This elimination of duplication might be carried a step further by including collision-avoidance or communication equipment in the integration. Even internal vessel functions such as centralized control of some machinery might use the same computer. Increased automation might lead to reduction of manpower needed to operate the vessel. Increased safety and reliability resulting from integration of navigation systems might lead to reduction of insurance premiums, more reliable schedules, and shorter passages from port to port, resulting in more efficient utilization of vessels, reduction of operating and stevedoring costs, and improved relations with passengers and shippers of goods.

For maximum effectiveness, an integrated system should be designed to fit the particular requirements of the vessel in which it is to be used. The ship as a whole should be considered, and each candidate function for automation should be considered carefully, as some functions might benefit more than others by automation. Further, cost considerations should not be limited to initial acquisition, but should include, also, such factors as operation, maintenance, and useful life (including obsolescence).

The proper role of an integrated navigation system is to enhance the decision-making role of the officer afloat by freeing him of the burdensome task of observation and calculation.

7. The Future

Over the centuries navigation has evolved from a very simple process to a highly complex scientific art. Although there has probably been greater advance in the science of navigation during the twentieth century than in all previous history of mankind, the mariner is basically conservative, and fundamental changes come slowly. This situation is attributable, in part, to the fact that each new generation of navigators learns from the preceding one, and afloat the young officer generally finds that his relations with the captain are most amicable if the junior uses methods favoured by, or at least understood by, the senior.

Nevertheless, change has come, and continues to do so.

One should not suppose, however, that every vessel is equipped with advanced navigation equipment, and that all seagoing personnel are profficient in the use of all modern devices. Quite the contrary. Very few ships, for instance, are equipped with inertial or Doppler sonar navigators, or with equipment for fixing position by satellite. There are still many smaller vessels without radar, Decca, or omega equipment. The ordinary practice of navigation as described throughout this book is still the norm in the vast majority of craft afloat. It has been argued, and with merit, that greater improvement in safety and efficient ship operation could be achieved by proper training and effective utilization of equipment and methods now available than by further development of more advanced aids. Mechanical or electronic marvels are not a substitute for skilful personnel.

One of the problems of orderly improvement in navigation has been the lack of effective communication between the mariner on the one hand and the engineer and scientist on the other. The mariner has been unwilling or unable to define his requirements clearly. Perhaps his lack of knowledge of the capabilities of engineering and science has contributed to this situation. The engineer and scientist, on their part, have not always sought to understand the needs and problems of the navigator, but have too often proceeded to find a solution and then seek a problem for its application. Happy, but rare, has been the situation where one understood both positions.

As in the past, change will come in the future. Although there will undoubtedly be some surprises, one can anticipate some changes in the near future by noting the present trends and problems being attacked. As one looks further into the future, predictions become more uncertain and less specific.

Some of the changes taking place in the navigation environment provide an indication of some things to be anticipated. The number, size, speed, and draught of ships are increasing, and small pleasure craft are taking to sea in ever increasing numbers. The mammoth, deep-draught tanker is less manoeuvrable than its smaller counterpart, and has more limited area in which it can operate. At the same time, the addition of man-made obstructions is increasing as man's search for and extraction of petroleum and minerals, and other exotic activities in the oceans, continue to advance.

As the cost of ship operation increases, the need for more efficient ship utilization becomes more acute. Scheduling of traffic for economic utilization of port facilities becomes more important, and delays because of poor scheduling, weather, or inaccurate navigation become les tolerable. While shipping is increasing, adequately trained personnel is becoming more expensive, and the supply is drying up as seagoing careers seem to have decreasing appeal to modern youth.

As a result of greater congestion with limited sea room and port facilities, one can expect more attention to be given to the establishment of one-way traffic lanes, particularly in the coastal confluence and harbour areas, with more regulation and requirements, perhaps eventually paralleling the situation in the air, where the volume and speed of traffic that must of necessity keep moving in all kinds of weather has required a highly advanced system of traffic control. The traditional privilege, cherished by mariners, of using any part of the water area of the Earth at will, as long as it is suitable to accommodate the craft, is likely to be increasingly restricted. As the number of vessels, of widely varying manoeuvrability, increases, greater navigational accuracy will be needed to ensure compliance with traffic regulations. With this requirement, faster ships, and a decreasing supply of seagoing personnel, automation, with less lag between observation and answers, can be expected to use available personnel more efficiently, reduce the stress on watch officers, and make a career afloat more attractive.

Traditionally, navigation has been a personal matter, each mariner pursuing it in his own way, using the methods and techniques that appealed most to him. A current trend is toward a systems approach both in the integration of components and in the concept that each vessel is but a subsystem in the overall navigation picture. This is partly a result of the trend toward greater regimentation. As the trend continues, one can expect more control, and perhaps, as communication capability increases, a greater share of the navigation function on the high seas being handled ashore. A logical outgrowth of this situation is a requirement for more detailed international standardization, again paralleling the situation with respect to aircraft.

Safety is an important consideration, but, unfortunately, the acceptable risk at sea has not been defined. Again, if every vessel operated as well as the best, with the means now available, a very high standard of safety would be achieved.

At some point, one can expect a demand that the legal aspects of shipping catch up with modern technology. Court decisions are based largely upon precedent, and, with a few notable exceptions, the previous cases cited were in an environment quite different from that encountered by the ships of the case under consideration. Not only are ships and their navigation and communication facilities vastly different, but most cases in the past have involved two-ship encounters, while many modern cases involve multi-vessel encounters. Further, national territorial interests are steadily encroaching upon the free access to the seas.

Although more effective utilization of presently-available facilities is more promising as a means of improving safety at sea, and the majority of mariners now going to sea will continue to navigate much as they do today, man's search for improved equipment and techniques to provide safer, easier voyages will undoubtedly continue. Improvement in communication between mariner and developer of navigational aids is being achieved by the Institutes of Navigation established in various countries, these organisations providing forums for discussions of navigational problems and proposed solutions. Better education of mariners is also contributing to improvement in communications and understanding among those involved in advancing navigation. As man's knowledge of his seagoing environment continues to increase, and as technology continues to advance, the various instruments used by the navigator can be expected to improve in accuracy and reliability, but cost effectiveness will be an increasing consideration. Some of the specific developments now in progress provide an indication of some changes to anticipate, although not all efforts can be expected to meet with equal success, or to enjoy equal acceptance by the navigator.

Limited metrication of navigation is rapidly becoming almost universal. But although the metre and its derivatives have largely replaced the foot, yard, and fathom, unity is lacking on the advisability of discarding the nautical mile and traditional angular and time units because of their logical convenience in navigation, whether astronavigation or dead reckoning. Because of this relationship and the widespread use of traditional methods, these units are likely to remain in use for quite a long time.

As meteorology advances and accurate forecasts are extended further into the future, with better dissemination of such information, weather routing of ships to take advantage of favourable conditions for faster and more comfortable voyages can be expected to increase. Although shore-based facilities to provide such service have been available, they have not enjoyed wide acceptance. Rather, the upgrading of facilities and the education of shipmasters to permit this function to be performed at sea has increased in popularity, and this trend is likely to continue, aided by an ever-increasing availability of suitable computers.

In addition to reflecting increasing metrication of navigation, the nautical chart will undoubtedly continue to evolve to meet the changing need of the navigator. Improvement in accuracy and methods of acquiring data should result in greater accuracy and reliability of charts. But perhaps the most welcome change will be in the introduction of simpler, less time-consuming methods of chart and publication updating, perhaps accompanied by more convenient methods of chart stowage and display, as by projection of film images on a suitable surface.

For dead reckoning, the present trend is toward greater automation and greater accuracy. One important area needing more attention is the development of a cheap, universally-applicable, accurate, reliable log to provide a continuous velocity vector relative to the solid Earth, rather than with respect to the continuously-moving water. Satisfactory solution of this problem is not yet in sight.

Pilotage is perhaps the area in which least change can be anticipated, for it is used in areas of close proximity to danger, where alertness, constant evaluation, and application of judgment based upon experience are the important ingredients of successful navigation. This situation does not preclude the improvement of the instruments, and limited automation, nor does it rule out the introduction of electronic systems of greater accuracy to guide the vessel through confined areas of high traffic density in periods of limited visibility.

The principal change in traditional astronavigation is likely to be in the manner of converting observations to craft positions. Although astro-trackers and computers have largely automated the process for the few adequately-equipped vessels, the vast majority of navigators still make observations with hand-held sextants that differ little from those in use two centuries ago, and perform sight reduction by means of an almanac and sight-reduction tables. With the increasing acceptance of relatively cheap computers, one can expect greater use of this device for computation of ephemeridal information, refraction corrections, and for sight reduction. An *Almanac for Computers* (p. 401) has been introduced for this purpose.

The use of a night-vision image-intensification telescope or low-light-level television camera with a sextant promises to extend the use of this instrument throughout the night in clear weather. Digital readout capability simplifies reading of the instrument and thus reduces the probability of error. It also makes possible remote readout and automatic introduction to a computer. The extent of acceptance of an instrument of this kind is yet to be determined. It certainly should be cheaper than an astro-tracker or radio sextant (p. 519) both of which require expensive stable platforms of inertial quality. The night-vision telescope and low-light-level television camera may have additional application in piloting, permitting observation of land and objects not normally visible during darkness.

Timepieces are presently quite adequate for astro-navigation, but they might become relatively less expensive and more convenient, with provision for automatic insertion in automatic calculation processes.

Astro-tracker development relates primarily to technological improvements in photoelectric sensors. Increasing use of solid-state sensors can be anticipated to reduce size, weight, and power requirements. Larger arrays of cells are likely to increase the field of view. Increased light sensitivity and reduced sensor noise will increase the capacity of the device to sense dimmer bodies or to make observations during reduced visibility.

The past has witnessed a proliferation of electronic navigational aids, and while additional ones will undoubtedly be proposed, the present trend is to consolidate the available systems, emphasizing those with wide, preferably world-wide, application. Present thinking seems to justify two types of systems, because no one system has yet met all requirements for universal application, although such a system remains as the ideal.

Omega promises to meet the requirements of a world-wide system of moderate accuracy, while Decca and loran C seem adequate for the high-accuracy coastal confluence areas. If either of these two systems proves adequate to do the entire job, it may ultimately replace the other. Ultra-accurate systems for harbour navigation have been proposed, but the most promising aid is perhaps improved radar using pulses measured in nanoseconds. Loran A is being phased out. Consol is not likely to be expanded, and may in time be considered redundant. An area for consolidation sometimes considered is greater coordination of air and marine aids. Increased international cooperation would be helpful in standardizing and perhaps reducing the proliferation of electronic aids.

Several references have been made to increased use of computers. The development of the microcomputer—a full-scale computer in miniature—is likely to decrease the cost and increase the reliability of computers, thus encouraging their more widespread use. Another trend that should contribute to the same result is the development of simplified computer-user interface to make programming capability available directly to the user. Another software trend is to give computers the ability to detect errors where redundant sensors are available and to ignore faulty inputs. The rapid increase in digital computer application does not rule out continued use of analog computers (p. 530), which are quite suitable for some applications. The versatility and reliability of these devices are likely to be enhanced in the future.

Inertial navigator development trends are along two lines. One is to increase accuracy for application in special-purpose craft such as survey vessels and by the military. The devices being developed are very expensive and have little justification for ordinary merchant-service application. For these high-accuracy systems research is being conducted on unconventional gyroscopes such as laser, cryogenic (very low temperature), nuclear, and fluid (rotor). While the laser gyroscope is perhaps the most promising, especially for a strapdown system (p. 535), none of these is likely to be used in the near future. The second line of development is for a relatively cheap, moderate-accuracy system for use with some form of independent fixing-system to provide continuous position indication for the general user. The prediction has been made, perhaps over-optimistically, that nearly every moving craft will ultimately be equipped with some kind of inertial device because of its versatility in providing a continuous, instantaneous indication of important information independent of external inputs.

Acoustic systems, both Doppler sonar and submerged beacon systems (p. 539), are likely to continue in use by special-purpose vessels, but their use for general navigation is likely to be very restricted because of their limitations.

An accurate, continuous, world-wide navigation system using satellites is currently under development (p. 546) with every prospect of successful culmination of the project, but its use is likely to be limited because of high cost of user equipment. If this cost can be reduced, use of the system should expand. Increased use of satellites for communication is probable.

Use of integrated systems is likely to expand as automation increases, primarily for economic reasons, but also to increase reliability, accuracy, and safety, and to meet increasing demands of traffic regulation.

The possible use of laser gyroscopes in inertial navigators has been mentioned. Laser logs have been used experimentally (p. 142). Other possible navigational uses of lasers, particularly for distance measurement, have been investigated, with the general conclusion that other solutions are more promising, except for very specialized applications.

Similarly, the use of infra-red for navigation has been investigated, indicating possible limited military and space applications, but not promising for navigation afloat, with the possible exception of using an infra-red device for sensing the horizon during periods of darkness and somewhat reduced visibility.

Whatever changes may take place in the navigational equipment, methods, and techniques of the future, it is clear that in the foreseeable future, there will be no lessening of the need for vigilance on the part of the navigator and the application of sound judgment backed by all the experience available aboard the craft being navigated. It is also clear that the advances taking place today will have so little impact upon the practice of navigation as performed by the vast majority of mariners that the principles learned today are likely to be useful with relatively modest changes in their application for many years to come. Even those mariners who will depend in varying degree upon sophisticated, advanced equipment will, if prudent, be prepared to fall back upon more primitive, basic methods when their modern methods are denied them, whether because of malfunction, power failure, accident, international conflict, or the vagaries of nature.

XII

The Practice of Navigation

1. General

The safe navigation of a vessel from one place to another involves the application of certain principles and the use of available equipment, as described in previous chapters. Adequate education and training are highly important, but not enough for safe navigation under all conditions. The mechanics of navigation can be learned in the classroom, but navigation involves, additionally, the application of human judgment based upon both knowledge and experience. Finally, the most knowledgeable person with a wealth of experience may be an unreliable navigator if he is not constantly alert. Effective navigation, then, is a combination of knowledge, judgement, and alertness. To this might be added some skill in the use of available equipment.

The knowledge involved goes beyond that included in previous chapters of this book. The prudent navigator becomes acquainted with the manoeuvring characteristics of his vessel under various conditions of wind, sea, water depth, loading, and trim. Speed is a lesser consideration. In making a turn, a vessel follows a curve, as shown in Fig. 1201. The distance travelled in the initial direction is called the *advance*, and the distance travelled perpendicular to the initial direction of travel is called the *transfer*. Additionally, the navigator needs to know the response of his vessel to a given rudder angle, how far the stern moves in the opposite direction during a turn, and the response time to a change of speed. Such information may be of little importance when a vessel is alone on the high seas, but vitally important in a busy harbour or when traversing a tortuous channel. Although such matters may well be considered to be in the realm of seamanship, rather than navigation, there is an important relationship.

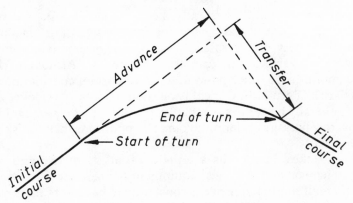

FIG. 1201. Advance and transfer during a turn.

Other areas of information might also be important to the navigator. Meteorological knowledge and the relationship of weather and sea state are important if one is to engage in effective weather routing (p. 634). One needs to be familiar with applicable Rules of the Road, government and international regulations, the sources of needed information, the capabilities and limitations of equipment, and how to detect anomalous performance or conditions.

If every condition and situation to be encountered could be determined in advance, navigation could be fully automated. But the unexpected does occur, and while automation can serve the useful function of relieving the navigator of the drudgery and much of the mechanics of navigation, it needs monitoring. Further, if the navigator relies too fully upon an automated operation, he may lose his ability to perform essential functions in the event of an emergency, when this ability is most needed. He should attempt to explain seemingly anomalous conditions and predict results when means are at hand for checking, so that the abilities and limitations of methods and devices can be understood better and accurate judgments can be made when conditions are unfavourable. A cardinal principle of good navigation is never to rely on one solution alone if it can be checked by a different method. Redundancy is the friend of the navigator.

Vigilance is essential to successful navigation. The

navigator should constantly keep 'ahead' of his vessel, anticipating results and watching for any sign of uncertainty in the safety of his vessel. Assumption of safe conditions, without verification, can be disastrous. Although the economics of a quick passage are an important consideration, the risk of grounding or collision should not be overlooked. It is generally better to slow, haul off to deeper water, or avoid a narrow passage under unfavourable conditions than to risk an accident.

Mistakes being characteristic of all humans, and all mechanical and electrical equipment being subject to errors and malfunction, one needs constantly to be alert to incorrect results. A good means of detecting large errors is to constantly ask oneself, 'Is this result reasonable?' An unusually large cocked hat (p. 17) or a fix indicating a current differing widely from that previously established, for instance, should be regarded with suspicion unless it can be explained satisfactorily in the light of existing conditions. If a series of consistent positions obtained by electronics is followed by a fix inconsistent with the others, one should be alerted to a possible error. With experience, one should develop the ability to predict accurately most results obtained in navigation. But when the unexpected is encountered, one should be prepared to accept anomalous conditions if the situation warrants. Because of the possibility of a mistake, one should not overlook the value of a check by another person, who may be able to detect an error more readily than the person making the mistake. All available sources of information should be used and the results checked and analysed.

Throughout the book the term 'navigator' has been used loosely to indicate anyone involved in the navigation of a craft. Whilst it is true that the Master has final responsibility for the navigation of his vessel, and may be involved in varying degree in the actual process of navigation, he of necessity relies to some extent upon others, generally delegating responsibility for determining the charts and publications needed, keeping them properly stowed and up-to-date, maintaining equipment in good condition, and the actual process of dead reckoning and fixing the position of the vessel. It is important that each person involved in navigation has a clear, definite understanding of exactly what is expected of him and his relationship to others involved in the process. Each should be adequately trained to perform the functions required of him, and the proper procedures and communication among members of the navigation team should be observed. Responsibility for maintaining and checking accurate records, such as entries in the navigator's notebook (p. 155) should be clearly established.

A prolific source of grounding and collision accidents is human error. There is no adequate substitute for well trained, alert, motivated personnel. With a continual increase in the number, size, speed, and variety of vessels, safety becomes more elusive. Professional pride among mariners is of ever-increasing importance. If the promise of a successful career afloat is not sufficient motivation, safety should be. This involves not only effective navigation, but compliance with laws and regulations designed to further safety at sea. Vessels differ considerably in the navigation equipment carried. It is the responsibility of the owners to provide adequate, but not excessive, equipment. The crew has responsibility for seeing that the equipment is kept in good operating condition and is used expertly, and for bringing any deficiency to the attention of the owners. The possible advantages of acquiring such additional equipment as might improve the safe navigation of the vessel might also be brought to the attention of the owners.

Navigation can be an interesting and pleasant part of life afloat, or it can be an onerous task, depending upon the attitude of the person involved. The well-informed, conscientous navigator is likely to enjoy his work, be effective at it, and have good reason to look foward to a successful career afloat.

2. Preparation for a Voyage

Advance preparation for a voyage is an important part of safe navigation. The preparation logically consists of three parts:

(*1*) checking the availability and condition of equipment, (*2*) voyage planning, and (*3*) preparation for getting underway.

The first part is best done as far in advance as practicable, to provide adequate time and allow for unforeseen delays. Navigational equipment is checked for availability, proper installation, and operating condition (perhaps during the last previous voyage), and deficiencies are corrected.

When information is available regarding destination, time schedule, and other pertinent items, the route is selected and the necessary charts and publications are seen to be on board or are acquired. They are checked to determine whether they are the latest edition, and that all available corrections since publication have been made. *Notices to Mariners* (p. 78), *Daily Memoranda* (p. 78), and navigational warnings (p. 523) are available for this purpose.

It is customary to plot, in advance, the entire route on a small-scale (large-area) chart, for planning purposes. The larger-scale charts, pilot charts (p. 79), lattice (p. 501) and any special charts needed are determined and acquired if not already available.

Required publications are determined and acquired if not on board. These include such items as the appropriate editions of tide and tidal stream (tidal current) tables (p. 209), light lists (p. 62), sailing directions (p. 84), the *Nautical Almanac* (p. 360), sight reduction tables (p. 402), and tables and other data for electronic navigation systems to be used. If any periodical such as the *Nautical Almanac* or tide or current table will expire during the voyage, the edition for the next period should be obtained, or provision made for acquiring it before expiration of the current volume.

The second part of preparation for a voyage consists of detailed planning. The large-scale charts, sailing directions, and light lists are studied carefully. Units of depths of water and heights above water are noted. The smallest unit of latitude and longitude scales is determined. Useful landmarks; aids to navigation with their designations and characteristics; transits, or ranges (p. 224); the locations of shoals and other obstructions; channels; and notes on charts are studied. Suitable radar targets are noted. Useful information is added to charts. Clearing bearings (p. 251) and clearing circles (p. 253) are drawn if appropriate. Circles of visibility (p. 260) for the height of eye of the observer are drawn around coastal lights likely to be seen. Useful turning bearings are indicated on charts. Soundings are studied, unique features noted, and clearing soundings (p. 255) are drawn if appropriate, avoiding use of red pencil marks if red light is to be used to illuminate the charts. Danger and restricted areas should be avoided and the locations of dredging operations should be noted.

Tides and tidal streams (tidal currents) expected to be encountered are determined. Tidal information is useful in converting soundings to depth of water, and if depth over a bar or other shoal or clearance under a bridge or other overhead obstruction is critical, the time of passage may need to be established relative to tidal conditions. Tidal-stream information is useful in converting speed through the water to speed over the surface of the Earth. Probable weather, particularly with respect to wind and visibility, and sea state should be noted. Variation of various points along the route, updated if necessary, should be observed. Time-zone boundaries, if zone time is kept, might be indicated on the chart. The point of changing from inland or local Rules of the Road to international rules should be noted.

Distances and elapsed time intervals (if speed is known in advance) between turning or check points may be indicated on the charts. The significance of the length of the vessel and its turning characteristics relative to the scale of the chart should be determined.

From the sailing directions one can determine regulations regarding pilot and tug assistance.

The information relating to the departure area should be studied thoroughly. That relating to later parts of the voyage should not be overlooked during advance planning, and should be studied with greater thoroughness as each area is approached.

If foreign charts are to be used, one should be sure that one understands the units, symbols, and terminology used, as these might differ somewhat from those with which one is familiar. One should also consult the applicable *Notices to Mariners* of the nation publishing the charts to ensure currency of the charted information.

The third part consists of the preparations for getting underway. This part usually starts several hours before departure, with turning on the gyro compass, if it was not kept running, so that it will have ample time to settle on the meridian. Shortly before getting underway the gyro error is determined, the vicinity of the magnetic compass is checked for magnetic items, synchronization of gyro compass and repeaters is checked, magnetic compass error on the heading of the vessel is noted and compared with the previously-recorded value, and the operation of equipment is checked. Equipment checked may include the steering engine, engine-room telegraph, internal communication-equipment, depth finder, electronic navigation-equipment, radio, navigational lights, whistle, and siren. The Master and all personnel to be engaged in navigation are briefed on pertinent information. A check is made to ensure that charts, plotting equipment, and publications needed for clearing the harbour and taking departure (p. 160) are in place and ready for use. The chart to be used first should be secured in place, preferably by masking tape, and all pencil marks from previous use should be erased. If it is necessary to fold the chart, at least one latitude and one longitude scale should be left exposed. A check should be made to be sure that personnel to be involved in the navigation of the craft are on station and ready to perform their assigned duties.

It is good practice to prepare a check-off list of things to be done, particularly in the third part of the preparation, to avoid overlooking an important item. The preparations that have been outlined are typical but not necessarily all-inclusive. The steps to be taken, and their order, should be determined for each vessel in accordance with its needs.

For a vessel following the same route repeatedly, the preparations as stated may seem unduly detailed. Some reduction is undoubtedly justified. Permanent items such as routes, distances between check points, danger soundings, and visibility circles might well be recorded in ink. However, there is always the danger of over complacency. It is easy to assume that one knows the way and need not be thorough in one's preparation. Changes do occur, and memory is not infallible. It is good practice to follow the entire procedure. If much of the planning phase involves familiar information, it might be covered rapidly, but it is better to be thorough and repetitious than superficial and overlook an item that might endanger the safety of the vessel and the lives of those aboard. Remember that constant vigilance is an essential ingredient of safe navigation.

3. Leaving Port

The period from leaving the dock or anchorage to taking departure at the sea buoy is one requiring constant attention, alertness, and the exercise of good judgment. Whether or not a pilot is on board, the ship's personnel should keep a constant check on position and progress of the vessel. The actual technique used varies from craft to craft and aboard the same vessel at different times and geographical locations. Judgment based upon experience dictates the procedure to use at any specific time.

Whatever the circumstances, it is important that the position of the vessel and its direction of motion be known at all times. Where there are stretches of open water with few aids to navigation and light or moderate traffic, as in a large bay, a dead-reckoning plot is kept, with a new dead-reckoning track being started at periodic fixes, as on the high seas away from land. Anticipated arrival times at check points are recorded on the chart as a guide to identification of aids to navigation and an indication of the strength of the tidal stream or other current.

When traversing a narrow channel marked by buoys, or in congested areas, the navigator may prefer to plot the intended track in advance and plot fixes frequently, labelling only the position lines associated with a change in landmark or aid to navigation used. As a departure from the desired track is noted, the course steered is changed slightly to bring the vessel back on track. Subsequent small changes are made as necessary to keep the departure from the desired track minimal.

Whatever technique is used, a continuous plot with accurate and meaningful labels, as appropriate, but devoid of unnecessary clutter, is a valuable part of safe navigation, and if fog should set in unobserved, the plot will have added value. It is wise, too, to record in the navigator's notebook the bearings (indicating whether true, magnetic, etc.), important soundings (indicating the units), course and speed changes, times of passing check points, and other pertinent information. The data thus recorded can be useful in writing the log, as a guide for future passages of the same area, and as a record in the event of accident.

All available data should be used, as a check on error or anomalous results. Soundings, corrected for tidal conditions, should be taken continuously and compared with values shown on the largest-scale chart (which should be used because it shows more detail than smaller-scale charts). The passage of distinctive features or certain depth contours provides a valuable check on position. Lights should be timed for identification, for a mistake in this respect can be disastrous. Transits, or ranges, both natural and man-made, are particularly useful for checking positions and compass error, and are easy to use. Fixed objects are preferable for fixing aids because they do not change position. An anchored buoy swings with the tidal stream, and may drag anchor and be out of position. A wise navigator is alert to any indication of a change in current or leeway. Ripples on the surface of the water, the direction and extent of leaning of buoys, eddies around obstructions, the limpness of flags, and the drift of smoke are all indicators of conditions affecting the progress of the vessel. If one practises the interpretation of such signs in periods of favourable conditions, confidence in their use at other times is likely to increase.

With the increased use of radar and other electronic aids there is a natural tendency to rely on such equipment to such an extent that other aids are neglected. Valuable as electronic aids are, they are not infallible, interpretation is essential, and failure can occur. The prudent rule is to check all results for consistency by comparison with other means of establishing position.

It is not wise to become so absorbed in the use of any one aid, or all available ones, that a person becomes oblivious to conditions about him. It is well to keep generally informed of the situation of one's own craft relative to its surroundings and other craft in the vicinity, and the need to reduce speed in the vicinity of dredging operations, construction work, small craft, etc., to avoid damage to them. Timely action to prevent dangerous situations from arising is the best protection from accidents. The practice of looking ahead starts with planning, and carries through until the voyage is completed. If a choice is available, courses are not laid close to obstructions that a small undetected change in current in the wrong direction, an unexpected failure of equipment, or the sudden onset of fog is likely to result in grounding of the vessel. *Spoil grounds* (areas designated for depositing dredged material), fish havens (obstructions created to attract fish), and *fish trap areas* are avoided. Sufficient clearance over shoals is allowed to take into account possible negative tides; uncharted shoaling; errors in depth measurement; errors in fixing; and rolling, pitching, heaving, and squat of the vessel. The planned distance at which other vessels are passed is not so short that a slight change in course or speed of the other vessel will jeopardize the safety of both.

Records indicate that most accidents are the result of human error. Prominent among these errors are the following:

Lack of alertness—failure to keep an adequate lookout.
Failure to identify aids to navigation positively.
Failure to use all available means of fixing position.
Lack of good judgment.
Failure to correct charts and publications.
Inadequate or faulty interpretation of data.
Failure to plot.
Faulty use of the magnetic or gyro compass.
Undue reliance upon others (following another vessel).
Failure to be informed of or use available information.
Lack of coordination among navigation personnel.

4. Coastal Navigation

Outside the congested waters of a busy harbour, but within sight of land or off-lying aids to navigation, navigation is similar to that discussed in section 3, but generally with less pressure. However, this is not always the case. An area such as the Dover Strait is often more congested than many harbours. Further, the traffic in the coastal confluence areas may be at higher speeds and more random in direction of travel than in a harbour area where traffic is largely confined to dredged channels. Because of the density of traffic in some areas, and other considerations, traffic lanes (p. 638) have been established as an aid to traffic separation. All the skill and judgment available to an alert navigator may be needed for safe navigation of a coastal area of heavy traffic at higher speeds than usual for harbour areas. In such an area there is likely to be an abundance of aids available—possibly more than can be effectively monitored while keeping a watch on other vessels. This situation requires nice judgment to determine the optimum division of one's attention.

While high-traffic-density areas pose special problems to the navigator, the more common situation in a coastal area is one of less congestion. Navigation consists essentially of running from one headland or major lighthouse to the next, with an occasional fixing aid or landmark between. Where only one object for viewing is available at one time, running fixes, clearing bearings (p. 251), and clearing angles (p. 255) are employed. Radar can be used for fixing by providing both direction and distance of one object. One should be particularly careful to identify the target correctly, especially when it consists of land. A low, sandy area shown on the chart as the shoreline may not return an echo, and the part of a gently sloping area providing an echo may not be apparent. Similarly, the use of a visual or radar tangent for a bearing line may be deceptive in the presence of a sandy spit.

In a coastal area the drawing of circles of visibility of navigational lights is particularly important. If a light is not sighted when expected, one should consider the angle at which the circle of visibility is approached, as shown in Fig. 530, the possibility of the light being extinguished, and the possibility of it being obscured by fog even though visibility at the vessel might be good. In any event, the absence of sighting the light is cause for intensified checking by other methods, as radar or other electronic means, soundings, or even astronavigation if conditions are suitable.

Soundings can be particularly helpful in coastal navigation. Where depth contours run roughly parallel to the shore, they can serve as reliable guides of distance offshore. This knowledge is particularly valuable if one is running close to the shore. In this situation one should be careful not to select desired tracks too close to dangers, for an undetected set toward the land can be disastrous. This warning is especially applicable to areas off the mouths of estuaries, where tidal streams and other currents may be particularly strong. If one is approaching land at an oblique angle, a line of soundings (p. 257) may be particularly useful.

The information and recommendations given in sailing directions can be of considerable value when coasting. One would do well to be thoroughly conversant with the volumes for the areas traversed.

Although there may appropriately be some slowing of pace while coasting well offshore, alertness is needed there as elsewhere, as attested by the numerous wrecks shown on charts of such areas.

5. Daily Routine at Sea

As the navigator clears the harbour, *takes departure* (p. 160) from the land, and heads out to the open sea, he shifts from the intensive routine of harbour navigation to a more leisurely pace. Navigation becomes a more intermittent process with fixes spaced more widely in time, and soundings becoming of less interest. Courses are likely to be followed over longer distances, and speed may be more uniform. A small-scale chart will probably be used to indicate daily progress, but routine plotting of dead-reckoning and position lines will probably be done on some form of plotting sheet (p. 53). Radar will be used primarily for collision avoidance. Use of distant electronic fixing aids will have increased emphasis.

The extent of use of astronavigation at sea and the details of the daily routine vary according to the inclinations of the individual Master and navigator. The use of advanced systems such as satellites and inertial navigators depends upon their availability and the mission of the vessel. Whether astronavigation is the primary or standby method, the maintenance of proficiency in its use is best achieved by its daily use, which, with modern methods, is not difficult. An unfamiliar method used in an emergency is an unreliable one.

A typical daily routine during periods of good visibility at sea, called the navigator's *day's work*, consists of the following:

Plot of dead reckoning throughout the day. The dead reckoning may be run from astro fix to fix for determination of average current, even though a new track for dead-reckoning position may be started at each running fix or other position. If positions are obtained frequently, as hourly, by an electronic or advanced system, the desired track may be plotted without gaps when shifting to a new fix, with course-steered adjustments as needed to keep the vessel close to the desired track, a procedure sometimes used in harbours. A number of variations of plotting are possible. The important point to observe is that the Master and all those doing the plotting are in agreement and understand the technique used, and that all use the same standards of plotting, symbols, and labelling.

Morning twilight observations of astronomical bodies, with sight reduction and plotting for a fix and determination of average set and drift of the current since the last fix. If conditions permit, five to seven bodies (more if conditions are marginal or an unusually long period has elapsed since the previous fix) should be observed. Three may be enough for a good fix, but it is well to have additional data in the event of uncertainty of position from the plot of three position lines. Several observations of each body should be made, and those observations considered most accurate should be indicated.

The bodies selected for observation should preferably be evenly distributed in azimuth throughout the entire 360°, as protection against an undetected constant error (p. 315) in the observations. The least brilliant bodies toward the east should be observed first because they are first to fade from view as twilight becomes brighter. Observations should be made quickly, with short rests between observations, to avoid error because of eye or arm fatigue. Each observation, adequately labelled, should be recorded as made. A separate notebook for this purpose might be used.

Identification of bodies during morning twilight should not be difficult if skies are clear, for one has opportunity to observe the constellations before starting observations. During overcast conditions, with a few breaks in the clouds, identification may not be certain. Under these conditions it is good practice to observe the bodies available, whether or not they are those planned for observation, and note and record the azimuth of each body observed, for use later in identification, if necessary. If the approximate altitude and azimuth of each body has been determined in advance, as an aid in finding and identifying the body, allowance should be made for changes between the time for which the coordinates were determined and the time of observation, remembering that bodies toward the east and west rise and set, respectively, faster than those toward the north or south, but that the latter may change azimuth more rapidly.

If the Moon is observed, one should be careful to select the correct limb, and during the darker part of twilight one should be alert to possible false indication of the horizon in the direction of the Moon, whether the Moon or another body is observed. The apparent horizon, illuminated by moonlight, may not be the actual horizon.

If a hack watch is used to time observations, its error should be determined both before and after a round of observations. The index correction of the sextant should be determined each time observations are made, preferably when the horizon is sharpest (usually *after* observations during morning twilight), if the horizon is used for this purpose.

Sight reduction should be accomplished by a familiar method. If an error is suspected but not found, a different method, and perhaps a different almanac, might be used. The use of standard sight-reduction forms is recommended. If available forms are not to the liking of the navigator, he might consider making his own and having them duplicated for filing in a looseleaf binder, or a rubber stamp made for use with a permanently bound book. In any event, a suitable record of the sight reductions should be kept for future reference.

Winding of chronometers and determination of chronometer error and rate. Comparison of chronometers, if more than one is carried, should also be noted. The data should be recorded in a permanent record as a guide to the functioning of the chronometers. The daily winding of the chronometers should be duly reported and recorded in the ship's log.

Azimuth of the Sun for a check on compass and gyro errors. This might be an amplitude (p. 299) observation at Sunrise or an observation of azimuth at the time of observation of altitude later in the morning.

Morning Sun line. The altitude of the Sun is measured, followed by sight reduction and plotting of the resulting position line. During the summer, this observation might be made when the Sun is on or near the prime vertical, for a check on the longitude, and to provide a good angle of cut with a meridian transit observation later. The position line, with the dead-reckoning position at the same time, and the current established at the time of the morning twilight fix, provides means for determining an estimated position. If the Moon or Venus is available at a favourable azimuth, relative to the Sun, a fix can be obtained. It is often possible to obtain a good observation of the Sun when it is partly obscured by thin clouds, its disc being visible with reasonable clarity.

Noon observation. The altitude of the Sun is observed at meridian transit or at 1200 or a few minutes earlier. The sight is reduced and plotted to obtain a latitude line. The morning Sun line is advanced to the time of the noon observation to obtain a running fix, or, if conditions are favourable, a fix is obtained by crossing the noon Sun line with a position line resulting from an observation of the Moon or Venus. When the declination of the Sun is nearly the same as the latitude, a good fix or running fix can sometimes be obtained over a relatively short time-interval near meridian transit, when the azimuth is changing rapidly. If the advanced morning Sun line is adjusted for the current established at the time of the morning twilight fix, one should remember that total drift (p. 163) is calculated for the interval of time between the two observations of the Sun, not from the time of the morning twilight fix until the noon observation. Traditionally, the noon position is considered the most important position of the day, and is established with great care, for it is the basis of the daily reckoning of progress of the vessel. A noon position determined a little before or after 1200 is adjusted to that time, and any other available means of determining position, as by an electronic fixing system, is used to obtain the best possible 1200 position of the vessel.

Computation of the day's run from 1200 of the last preceding day to 1200 of the present day.

Preparation of a 1200 position report for the Master. This position, in coordinates, or plotted on a small-scale chart, or both, with the distance travelled since the last previous report, may be posted for the benefit of the crew and any passengers.

Afternoon Sun line. The altitude of the Sun is observed, the sight reduced, and the resulting position line plotted. During the summer the observation might be made when the Sun is on or near the prime vertical to provide a check on the longitude. An estimated position might be obtained by dropping a perpendicular from the dead-reckoning position, adjusted for the best estimate of current, to the position line. Alternatively, if the Moon or Venus is available at a favourable azimuth, a fix might be obtained. If Venus is observed when the Sun is above the horizon, the instructions in the 'Explanation' section of the *Nautical Almanac* should be followed for determining the additional altitude correction for parallax and phase, rather than using the values on the inside front cover of the Almanac.

If current is established by an afternoon fix, a dead-reckoning position run forward from the last *fix*, not running fix, should be used. In the event that observations cannot be made during evening twilight, and a fix cannot be obtained during the afternoon, the noon Sun line can be advanced to the time of the afternoon Sun observation to obtain a running fix.

Morning and afternoon Sun lines provide means for a check on the sight-taking accuracy of the observer. If the morning Sun line indicates a consistent set toward the west, and the afternoon Sun line indicates a consistent set toward the east, the image of the Sun is being brought down too far, rather than to a correct position relative to the visible horizon. This error is reasonably common among inexperienced observers. If the navigator has trouble correcting such an error, he might find that he obtains more accurate results by observing the upper limb of the Sun, or both limbs and averaging the results, or applying a personal correction to his observations of the Sun.

Azimuth of the Sun for a check on compass and gyro errors. This might be an observation of azimuth at the time of observation of altitude for the afternoon Sun line, or an amplitude observation at Sunset.

Sunset, Sunrise, twilight calculations and preparation of lists of bodies available for observation. The zone times of Sunset, ending of evening civil and nautical twilight, beginning of morning nautical and civil twilight, and Sunrise at the vessel are calculated. Using any suitable method, such as a star globe (p. 340) or star finder (p. 341), one prepares a list of stars and planets above the horizon at the time of each civil twilight, with the approximate altitude, azimuth, and magnitude of each body. Some navigators prefer to include the Moon, if available, in the list. It is necessary, of course, to plot the positions of bodies of the solar system on the star globe or star finder. For bodies that change position, relative to the stars, slowly, notably Jupiter and Saturn, the plotted positions can be updated less frequently than daily.

When observations are made daily, one soon remembers from day to day the positions of the stars and planets most used, resulting in less reliance on the prepared list. However, the preparation of the list should not be neglected, for one may encounter partly cloudy skies obscuring one's favourite astronomical bodies, and making identification of others difficult. The bodies should be listed in some logical order, as by increasing azimuth of all bodies listed. Some navigators prefer to convert the true azimuth to directions relative to the heading, and some prefer to show the bodies, relative to one another, by a polar diagram. The best method is the one that is easiest to use and most meaningful to the individual, according to his personal preference. The list, in whatever form, is of particular value during evening twilight, when the various bodies first begin to appear and must be identified without benefit of position in constellation.

Calculation of the times of Moonrise and Moonset, if needed.

Evening twilight observations of celestial bodies with sight reduction and plotting for a fix and determination of average set and drift of the current since the last fix, using a dead-reckoning position run forward from that fix.

The same comments made relative to morning twilight observations apply generally to evening twilight observations, except that the *brightest* bodies toward the east should be observed first, because they are first to appear. By setting the sextant for the predicted altitude, adjusted as necessary for the difference in time between the time for which the predictions were made and the time of observation, and facing in the predicted direction, also adjusted as necessary, one can often see a body considerably sooner than by merely searching an entire region of the sky. The brightest bodies can often be seen a very few minutes after Sunset, or, under favourable conditions, even shortly *before* Sunset. The advantage of early observations is that the horizon is usually sharper at this time, becoming less distinct as daylight fades. If the horizon is used for determining the index correction, the observation should be made *before* making the round of observations, when the horizon is sharp.

Preparation of data for the Master's night order book, if required. If the Master prepares a set of instructions regarding courses and speeds to be used, lights expected to be sighted, and other data for guidance of the deck watch officers during the night, he probably expects the navigator to provide him with pertinent navigational information.

Electronic and advanced systems, as available, are used on a

579

regular basis. If positions are plotted at a uniform interval, as each hour, the consistency of plotted positions can be observed, and any deviation can serve as an immediate warning of possible error. This is particularly helpful near the outer edge of the coverage area of an aid, where errors may be greatest because of contamination by signals arriving by more than one path, or because of poor reception.

Miscellaneous. Some Masters prefer to have observations of the Sun, and any other bodies available, at hourly intervals as a precaution against the onset of overcast or deterioration of the visible horizon. Some observers claim the ability to obtain astro observations of acceptable accuracy during the night by dark-adapting their eyes and using red light or an assistant, with light shielded from the observer, to read the sextant and time of observation.

Regular frequent comparisons of a steering gyro repeater and magnetic compass, as every half hour, can help one catch an error before the vessel has strayed far from its intended track. Ships have grounded far from their supposed positions because of failure to observe this precaution and to be alert to other indications of error. It is also a wise precaution to compare gyro repeaters with the master gyro compass periodically, as once each watch.

The navigator should be alert to the change of local time as one travels eastward or westward. The policy for change of ship's time to keep pace with changing position is not uniform aboard all vessels. Some keep zone time differing from Greenwich mean time by an integral number of hours, as generally done on land, changing time one hour at the integral hour nearest the time of crossing a time zone boundary, or during the night nearest the time of crossing the boundary. Others schedule small changes over several watches for more equitable sharing of the gain or loss of time. Still others change the time the appropriate number of minutes at a uniform time each night. The method in use is not as important as understanding of the method by all concerned, and the navigator needs to know the relationship of the time being kept to Greenwich mean time. Some navigators find it desirable to keep a navigational watch set to Greenwich mean time, and do all navigating by this time, to minimize the probability of error and simplify astronavigation. When Greenwich time is used, one should be careful to be informed of the *date* at Greenwich, which, of course, may differ from the local date.

In some areas special precautions are needed. An example is the lookout for icebergs at certain times of the year in the vicinity of the Grand Banks in the western North Atlantic. Weather conditions, particularly the positions and movements of violent tropical storms, and the presence of other vessels with which one's craft might collide are important items demanding the attention of the mariner. While these are not matters of direct concern to the navigator, as such, any avoiding action can affect the navigation. Changes in wind velocity and sea state should be noted and evaluated relative to their effects upon the progress of the craft, often requiring changes in the estimate of speed made good, current, and leeway. The same is true of crossing the boundary of a well-established ocean current such as the Gulf Stream. Pilot charts can provide useful information regarding currents, and one should be alert to changes in colour and other aspects of appearance of sea water that might indicate a change of conditions affecting navigation.

Although navigation at sea may be somewhat more leisurely than in a busy harbour, one should guard against a natural tendency to become less alert and overly casual in one's navigation. Constant vigilance is required whenever one's vessel is underway.

6. Returning to Port

The return to port after an extended voyage at sea is a part of the trip of considerable interest, both navigationally and otherwise. Of particular interest is the first visual or radar contact with land, called *landfall*. Before the days of electronic navigational aids, visual landfall was generally the first contact with land, although there were often previous indications that the vessel was approaching land. Shoaling, the pattern of waves, and the presence of birds are some of these indicators. As the range of electronic aids has increased, so has the distance at which there has been some navigational contact with land. Since omega (p. 511) has become available, the mariner has had the capability of retaining such contact throughout a voyage.

Landfall remains an event of considerable importance to the navigator. It is the counterpart of his taking departure (p. 160) on the outbound part of the voyage. Essentially, it marks the end of the high-seas phase of the voyage and the beginning of the second pilotage phase, the terminal phase; a change from the geographical reference phase to a topographical phase.

Traditionally, navigators pride themselves on their ability to make accurate landfalls; that is, to predict accurately the point and time of first visual or radar contact with land. The preparation starts a considerable distance offshore. The largest-scale chart of the approach area, sailing directions, light lists, lists of radio aids to navigation, tide and tidal stream (tidal current) tables, radio navigational warnings, and any other available sources of pertinent data are studied systematically and thoroughly to determine the locations and characteristics of available aids to navigation, the locations and natures of dangers, the pattern of the depth contours, the appearance of land and similarities in appearance and configuration that might lead to mistaken identity, the availability of harbour surveillance radar, and regulations regarding lanes for separation of inbound and outbound traffic, the locations of suitable emergency anchoring areas, and any other pertinent information. With the availability of electronic fixing aids, such preparation may seem unnecessary, but the number of wrecks near the entrances to extensively-used ports indicates the value of careful navigation during the approach phase.

Having made his advance preparation, the navigator uses particular care in fixing the position of his vessel while still a considerable distance offshore, perhaps several hundred miles. Additional astronomical bodies are observed, the sights reduced, and the position lines plotted. Electronic fixes, if available, are made more frequently. Additional attention is given to current. Separate dead-reckoning and estimated-position tracks may be plotted, and an attempt is made to estimate reasonable error of position. The extent and thoroughness of the preparation is a matter of judgment, considering the length of time at sea since last sighting of land or an aid to navigation, the consistency of fixes and the time interval between them, the time since the last good fix, the state of the sea and weather, and the angle at which the coast line is approached. If the approach is perpendicular or nearly so, or if the land on both sides of the entrance to the estuary is of similar appearance, and the position of the vessel is in considerable doubt, one may wish to head far enough to one side of the entrance to be reasonably certain of which way to turn if the entrance is not sighted soon after making landfall.

Soundings may provide a reasonably reliable indication of distance offshore, but generally give little help in determining position along the coast. It is particularly important that the first point of visual or radar contact be identified accurately, particularly where similarities in appearance exist. Every available means of fixing the position of the vessel should be used, and, if possible, a position determined by one means should be checked by one or more additional methods. Soundings, navigational lights, landmarks, radar, short-range electronic aids, and even perhaps astronavigation should all be considered, as available. Lights should be identified carefully by timing their characteristics. Radar targets and any other aids should be identified with equal care.

One should keep constantly in mind the possibility of anomalous conditions, destruction or removal of a charted aid, malfunctioning of a mechanical device, extinguishing of a light, and the possibility of fog. In the event that the position of the vessel cannot be determined with sufficient accuracy, considering the proximity of dangers, one may have no safe alternative but to anchor or stand off and await more favourable conditions. It would be difficult to justify a decision to proceed rashly without tangible evidence of an almost total probability of a safe entrance into port.

The distance from the sea buoy to the dock or anchorage may be very short, in the case of an open harbour, or may be long and perhaps tortuous, involving a number of channels, shoals, and perhaps several different stages of the tide and tidal stream. Tidal conditions may be an important consideration in the light of the draught and manoeuvring characteristics of the vessel. One may find it desirable to time the entrance to take advantage of favourable conditions.

Navigation within the estuary is similar to that of leaving port, discussed in section 3. One should be certain that all suitable preparations are made, needed equipment is in place and ready for use, and all personnel that will participate in the navigation are at their stations and prepared to perform their assigned duties.

The approach to the vessel's berth alongside a wharf should be made carefully, considering the probable effects of wind and current, and the availability of tug assistance.

If the vessel is to anchor or moor, the anchorage should be selected carefully, considering depth of water, holding quality of the bottom, adequate room for swinging with the tide and wind, the availability of adequate approach and anchorage fixing aids, and local regulations. Submerged pipelines, which may stand as much as two metres above the sea bed, and submarine cables should be avoided.

If an assigned berth is to be used, or if space is limited, the anchoring manoeuvre should be planned carefully. It is desirable, when practicable, to make the final approach to the point of letting go in a direction heading directly into the current or wind, whichever will have greater effect upon the vessel, for better control of the craft. It is desirable, too, to have a transit, or range, dead ahead as a steering guide during the final approach. In the absence of such a transit, or range, the bearing of a prominent object might be used. The desired track of the vessel is plotted, and from the desired position of the anchor one measures *back*, along the desired track, a distance equal to the length of the vessel from the hawsepipe to the point at which bearings are taken. From this point the bearing of a prominent object is measured to determine the point of letting go the anchor. Points at which any turns are to be made during the approach to the anchorage, allowing for advance during a turn (p. 562) and for distance between hawsepipe and bearing measurement position, are marked on the plot, and the bearing of a prominent object at this point is determined and recorded. If practicable, objects for turning bearings should be selected so that the bearings approximate the new courses, to minimize the danger from possible error in the positions of the vessel. A transit, or range, at any point at which a bearing is needed, is superior to a measured bearing.

During the approach to the anchorage, fixes are obtained continuously, and any needed adjustments are made to the heading. As the vessel nears the point of letting go, the speed is reduced so that the vessel will be nearly dead in the water when the anchor is let go. As the vessel slows, and as long as steerageway is maintained, additional care, perhaps with larger rudder angles, is exercised to keep the vessel on the desired track. Immediately after the anchor is let go, the position of the vessel is determined by a quick round of bearings, horizontal sextant angles (p. 228), or whatever means are available. From these data the position of the anchor is determined, plotted, and recorded. When the vessel has settled into position at a distance from the anchor, another carefully-determined fix should be obtained. Using the position of the anchor as a centre, and the distance between it and the last position obtained, one draws a circle to indicate different positions of the vessel as it swings at anchor. Periodically after that, the position is checked by a round of bearings to determine whether the vessel has dragged anchor.

7. Unfavourable Conditions

Although adequate knowledge, suitable preparation, sound judgment, and constant vigilance are desirable ingredients of good navigation, the process of conducting a craft as it moves about its ways is not particularly difficult, and can be enjoyable, when conditions are favourable. The real test of a navigator comes when conditions are unfavourable.

Sometimes data are conflicting. Under some conditions of

the atmosphere, dip (p. 380) and atmospheric refraction (p. 382) are anomalous, resulting in unreasonable astro fixes. When the sky is overcast, astronavigation is not possible at all unless one is equipped with a radio sextant (p. 519).

The absence of reliable astro fixes is not generally a serious problem, for this form of navigation is used primarily at sea, far from shoal water. Its principal effect is an increase in uncertainty of the dead-reckoning position. This uncertainty may lead to a slightly longer path to the destination. This situation need not arise if one has capability of fixing position by satellite or a long-range electronic fixing system such as omega. In the absence of such capability, a navigator may find his position, after a period of several days without a fix, to be at considerable distance laterally from his desired track. A decision is then needed whether to set a course to return gradually to that track or to determine a new desired track to the destination. Conditions in individual cases govern the decision, but, in general, a new track is justified if it is expected to result in a significant saving of time or in avoiding other anticipated unfavourable conditions such as heavy seas.

As a vessel nears landfall, the absence of a good position is of greater concern. Unless one is able to fix position accurately, one may have no alternative but to anchor or haul off and await more favourable conditions. In a gradually shoaling area, soundings may provide an indication of distance offshore.

Astro fixes may also be unavailable in the absence of a good horizon, although astronomical bodies may be visible. The horizon may be obscured by fog, mist (thin fog or very light drizzle), haze (dust or salt particles suspended in the air), or smoke. Even when fog is dense, it has little direct effect upon navigation at sea other than precluding astro fixes. But if the vessel slows as a precaution against possible collision, the chief concern during periods of reduced visibility, the dead reckoning is affected. If the horizon is obscured but astronomical bodies are visible, an artificial-horizon sextant (p. 356) might be used to obtain astro fixes, but unless the sea is calm, such fixes may be less accurate than dead-reckoning positions.

As one approaches and enters pilotage water, visibility becomes a prime consideration to the navigator. Even when radar and other electronic aids are available, the presence of fog denies the navigator a direct view of the general situation. He is feeling his way, and needs all available assistance. Precise courses, with carefully-controlled changes of course and speed, are important. During passage through a channel, each buoy in succession should be observed and definitely identified, and any lateral drift should be noted. If a buoy is not seen within a short time of that anticipated, a serious situation has arisen, and every effort is needed to determine the position of the vessel relative to safe water. If risk of grounding is considerable, a decision is needed whether to continue on or to anchor and await better visibility.

When the position in pilotage water is in doubt for any reason, soundings are particularly important, and may be the means of keeping the craft afloat even when its position is not known with certainty.

In fog it is often wise to station a lookout aloft and another at the bow, as well as maintaining a sharp lookout at the bridge, for the visibility may be different at different heights. One should be alert, too, to the possibility of fog obscuring an aid to navigation or land when there is no fog in the vicinity of the vessel, particularly during darkness, when the presence of fog even a short distance away might not be apparent. The opposite effect might also be encountered. Fog-signal apparatus may not be in operation because of absence of fog at the aid. One should listen for fog signals, both of navigational aids and of other vessels, but one should be aware of the vagaries of sound transmission, both in air and in water. Its apparent intensity is not a reliable guide to its distance, and its apparent direction can be deceptive.

One should not overlook the fact that currents and tidal streams have relatively greater effect at slow vessel speeds because the vessel velocity vector (p. 165) is shorter, while that of the current is unchanged, resulting in an altered vector sum.

Reduced visibility might occur at any time, but its presence is more likely in a warm air mass than in a cold one. If the condition is anticipated, either on the basis of weather forecasts or one's own observations and experience, a position as accurate as possible should be determined at frequent intervals, and one should be prepared to navigate with caution when the reduced visibility is encountered. If additional personnel will be needed, as additional lookouts, they should be alerted that their services might be needed. A reliable forecast of an extensive, persistent fog area might be reason for changing the route to a more favourable one.

The effect of ice on navigation is discussed in section 8.

Wind is another factor affecting navigation. Its direct effect is to impede or assist the progress of the vessel, by increasing or decreasing its speed through the water or causing leeway. It may have a secondary effect by causing dust near land, and by affecting the movement of water. Wind-induced currents (p. 211) affect the velocity vector of a vessel relative to the ground, and therefore it is wise to be alert to wind changes when allowing for current or interpreting the position of a fix relative to the dead-reckoning position. Wind also affects the state of the sea. The relatively long, regular waves, called *swell*, that continue beyond the area of generation may produce rolling and pitching, resulting in reduced horizontal speed of the vessel. If resonance occurs, the effect can be quite large, resulting in excessive loss of speed, discomfort to crew and passengers, and possible shift of cargo or damage to the vessel. A relatively small change of course or speed may reduce the undesirable motion considerably. Within its area of generation the sea may be confused and the motions of the vessel complex. The subject of vessel routing to take advantage of favourable conditions is discussed in section 23.

Violent tropical cyclones, known variously as *hurricanes* and *typhoons*, and sometimes locally by other names, are best avoided. Information on their intensity and movements are usually broadcast in sufficient time to permit avoiding action. For maximum benefit of the information, one needs a basic understanding of the characteristics and habits of these storms. A person having travelled through a fully-developed tropical cyclone has little relish for another encounter.

Although there is considerable variation in the number and

location of violent tropical cyclones, the maximum number in any area is generally during late summer or early autumn. They form over water areas in the tropics and drift slowly westward. Those in the northern hemisphere curve gradually toward the north, and some of them continue curving until they have an easterly component of motion. Others continue on in a generally north-westerly direction. Those in the southern hemisphere curve southward, and some of them finally acquire an easterly component of motion. In either hemisphere, the storms increase in speed as they reach higher latitudes, and expand until they finally dissipate. If they encounter land, they dissipate more rapidly, but often cause extensive damage before doing so.

The track, or path, of a particular storm is established principally by the pattern of barometric pressure, any cyclonic storm tending to avoid high pressure areas. The only tropical area in which violent tropical cyclones are never encountered is the South Atlantic.

A tropical cyclone becomes known as a hurricane or typhoon when its winds reach a speed of 64 knots. The expressions *tropical disturbance*, *tropical depression*, and *tropical storm* apply to various cyclonic conditions of lesser intensity than a hurricane or typhoon. A violent tropical cyclone may have winds that attain a speed of more than 150 knots at the maximum stage of the storm.

At first, the circular area of the storm has a diameter of perhaps 100 miles, surrounded by a region of gale-force winds extending outward another 150 miles. Within the storm there are areas of heavy rain from bands of thick clouds. The direction of the wind is anticlockwise in the northern hemisphere, and clockwise in the southern hemisphere, in each case with a component toward the centre, where the barometric pressure is very low.

The *eye of the storm*, at its centre, is a relatively clear, nearly calm area perhaps 10 to 25 miles in diameter. Seas in this area are tempestuous and confused. The eye is surrounded by strong vertical currents of air. The passage of the eye of a violent tropical cyclone is spectacular. The strong winds, thick clouds, and heavy rainfall stop suddenly. Winds are light and variable, and the sky is clear or nearly so. As the opposite side of the eye passes, extreme conditions resume, but with the wind blowing in the opposite direction.

Marine weather forecasts and bulletins are the best guides to avoidance of violent tropical cyclones. As each bulletin is received, the position of the storm should be plotted and its predicted motion recorded.

There are other indications of the approach of such a storm. Several days before arrival of the storm, swell about twice as long as normal is encountered, coming from the location of the centre of the storm at the time of generation of the waves. When the storm approaches to within 500 to 1,000 miles, skies are relatively clear, with perhaps a few cumulus clouds of limited vertical development, and the barometer rises slightly with a vertical oscillation of a millibar or two. As the storm comes nearer, streaks of cirrus clouds appear to converge toward the direction of the storm centre. The barometer starts falling slowly. The cirrus gradually gives way to a continuous sheet of cirrostratus. The clouds increase in density and the weather becomes unsettled.

By the time the barometer has fallen perhaps three millibars, fine mist falls alternately with showers. The rate of decrease in barometric pressure increases and the wind increases in speed and gustiness. The appearance of a wall of cumulonimbus clouds in the distance announces the imminent arrival of the storm. The barometer falls rapidly, the winds increase in speed, seas become tempestuous, and squall lines in ever increasing intensity are encountered. As the heavy clouds reach the craft, the barometer plunges, winds mount, the day becomes very dark, and the rain falls in torrents. The violent tropical cyclone has arrived, although its centre may still be 100 miles or more away, and the wind, sea, and precipitation continue to increase until the eye of the storm is encountered.

Even the most sturdy vessel may become unmanageable and sustain damage. Smaller or weaker ones may founder. The safety of the vessel becomes the paramount consideration. The visualization of the furious conditions within a fully-developed hurricane or typhoon at sea is virtually impossible by anyone who has not experienced them.

As the storm passes, the sequence of events is essentially the same as during the storm's approach, but in the reverse order.

If one is to avoid a violent tropical cyclone, one needs to know where it is and its direction and speed of motion. The forecasts and bulletins are helpful but not infallible. They are adequate when the storm is still a considerable distance away, but if it approaches nearer, one should follow closely the indications stated above. Of these, the direction of the wind between squalls is perhaps the best indication. If one faces directly into the wind, the centre of the storm is to one's right in the nothern hemisphere and to one's left in the southern hemisphere. In either case it is a little more than 90° from the direction he faces. Radar might be helpful in locating the position of the storm centre.

If the navigator is not able to avoid a violent tropical cyclone entirely, but finds himself within its outer parts, his best course of action depends upon his position relative to the storm centre. In the northern hemisphere, the half of the storm area to the right of the storm track, as one faces in the direction of travel of the storm, is considered the *dangerous semi-circle*, and the other half the *navigable semi-circle*. In the southern hemisphere these are reversed. In the dangerous semi-circle the winds are generally strongest and the waves highest because the winds are the vector sum of those caused by the pressure gradient and those caused by motion of the storm. Also, the direction of the wind and sea is such that the vessel tends to be driven into the path of the storm (if it is ahead of the storm centre). In the navigable semi-circle the winds are diminished by the storm movement and the vessel is driven away from the storm centre.

If the storm is still a considerable distance away, one avoids it by simply running in a direction away from the storm track. If the vessel speed is greater than the speed of the storm, there is no problem in outdistancing it. But if one is unable to avoid the storm entirely, the best action in the northern hemisphere is generally to set a course such that the wind is on the starboard bow in the dangerous semi-circle and on the starboard quarter in the navigable semi-circle, and make as much way as possible. On the storm track ahead of the storm, the wind sould be brought to about 160° relative until the vessel is well within the navigable semi-circle, and then to the starboard quarter. In the southern hemisphere, the instructions are the same except that port is substituted for starboard.

If it becomes necessary to heave to, this should be done heading into the sea in the dangerous semi-circle, and away from the sea in the navigable semi-circle, unless individual ship characteristics dictate different action. In avoiding a violent tropical cyclone one should be alert to the possibility of a change in direction of travel of the storm.

These are very general rules. Each situation should be considered with respect to the characteristics of the storm and the vessel. One should particularly try to avoid being caught between the storm track and land in such a position that there is insufficient sea room to avoid the storm. One should also avoid being driven onto the storm track. If a ship is in port when a violent tropical cyclone approaches, the best procedure is generally to get underway and head out to sea, if there is sufficient time to clear the storm track.

If one approaches land when a violent tropical cyclone is in the vicinity, or has passed recently, one should be alert to abnormal tides and the possibility of aids to navigation having been carried away, moved, or damaged, and landmarks having been altered in appearance.

8. High Latitudes

As a vessel proceeds to higher latitudes, additional problems are encountered, arising either from the high latitude itself or from meteorological factors. For this reason, acquisition of information available from the literature and forecasts of weather and ice conditions, careful planning, and adequate preparation for a voyage to high latitudes are highly desirable. The latitude considered 'high' varies with the area and individual judgment. As a general rule, relatively few severe high-latitude problems are encountered below latitude 70°, a parallel rarely exceeded by most vessels. However, ships do go to higher latitudes. Shipping along the northern coast of Siberia is by no means scarce, and in 1977 the Soviet icebreaker *Arktika* navigated across the North Pole. Previously, in 1958 and 1960, the United States nuclear submarines *Nautilus* and *Skate*, respectively, crossed the North Pole under the ice, the latter surfacing at the pole. It is good practice for any navigator to be aware of high-latitude problems because such knowledge should help him gain a better understanding of navigation generally, and because some of these problems, such as those associated with ice, are sometimes encountered at considerably lower latitudes.

Some reorientation of one's thinking is necessary in polar regions. As one travels poleward, a degree of longitude becomes shorter at an increasing rate because the convergence of the meridians becomes greater. At the equator a degree of longitude is about equal in length to a degree of latitude. At latitude 60° it is only half as long, at latitude 70°.5 it is one-third as long, and at latitude 75°.5 it is one-fourth as long. As the latitude increases, the difference between a rhumb line and a great circle increases, except along a meridian, where they are identical. At some latitude this difference, and the increasingly rapid change of scale with latitude (distorting shapes and affecting accuracy of distance measurement) becomes excessive, and the familiar Mercator chart is discarded in favour of a chart on a polar projection. The transverse Mercator (p. 44), polar stereographic (p. 47), modified Lambert conformal (p. 46), gnomonic (p. 47), and zenithal equidistant (p. 51) projections are all used for polar charts. On any of these projections the meridians converge toward the nearer pole, and a great circle is a straight line, or nearly so. Compass roses (p. 43) are generally not shown, and directions are best plotted by some form of protractor or plotter (p. 87), the measurement being made at the nearest printed meridian.

The primary problems associated with charts of polar regions is the lack of accurate detail and the absence of large-scale charts. Surveys in these areas may not have been made with the same thoroughness as elsewhere, both because of lack of demand for such charts and because of the difficulty of making accurate surveys where position is difficult to determine accurately and snow and ice distort the appearance of the surroundings, sometimes obliterating an estuary and masking the true coast line. The lack of numerous soundings is partly offset by an absence of many shoals. However, it is good practice, when entering an estuary, to send a boat in ahead to make soundings.

Charts on a polar projection are generally overprinted with a *grid*, a series of lines parallel (on the chart) to the prime meridian, as shown in Fig. 1202. In the illustration, the radial

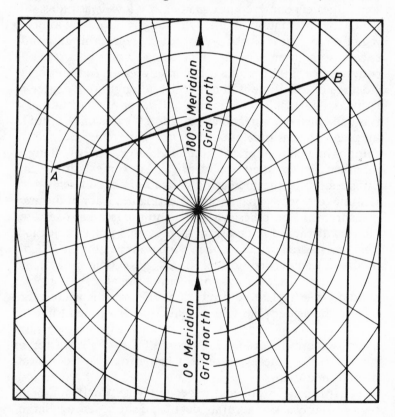

FIG. 1202. Polar grid.

lines are true meridians meeting at the North Pole. The circles are parallels. *Grid north* coincides with true north along the prime meridian, *in both polar regions*. The value of *grid direction* (*G*), relative to grid north, is apparent if one notes that the true direction of the straight line (great circle) from A to B changes true direction 120°, from 327° to 207°, while the grid direction is a constant 072° throughout. Interconversion of true and grid directions in the arctic is accomplished by the relationship: grid direction equals true direction plus west longitude, or minus east longitude. In the Antarctic, the signs are reversed. In subpolar regions, where the convergence is less than unity, the conversion is the same except that longitude is multiplied by the faction of a degree difference in direction (on the chart) between consecutive meridians 1° apart. The difference between grid north and magnetic north is called *grid variation* (*GV*), or *grivation*. It is the sum of variation and convergence of the meridians. Lines of equal grivation, called *isogrivs*, are customarily shown on the charts of polar regions.

A number of references to information relating to high latitudes are given in Appendix A. Appropriate volumes of sailing direction, particularly NP 100, *The Mariner's Handbook*, and tide and tidal stream (tidal current) tables are also helpful, but their coverage is incomplete and their information is less reliable than in areas where there have been a greater number of observations, over a longer period. Generally, tidal ranges are small and tidal streams (tidal currents) are weak, but there are some well-defined ocean currents, particularly around Antarctica and in narrow straits. Winds near land in polar regions are often very strong, and sometimes gusty and variable in direction.

The presence of ice, both that formed in the sea and land ice that has been discharged into the sea in the form of icebergs, is an ever-present problem in polar regions, although at times it can be an aid. Icebergs should be avoided, if possible. Because most of an iceberg is under water, projections below the surface might not be apparent. The drift of a berg is affected more by the local current than by the wind, and so the berg may move in a different direction, at a different speed, than floating sea ice, which moves primarily in response to wind action. It is generally not difficult to avoid bergs if they can be detected in time. A sharp lookout is important in iceberg areas. Radar and sonar (p. 145) can help, but they are not infallible, especially for smaller bergs. Observations from aircraft and satellites, as well as reports of sightings from ships, are important inputs to radio broadcast warnings.

Sea ice, too, should be avoided where possible, because of the possibility of damage to the vessel, especially its rudder and screws, and because of the possibility of becoming *beset* (immobilized) by the ice. If ice cannot be avoided, the route through it should be selected with care, using all available information, to find the path of least resistance. It is better to keep moving in a direction generally toward the destination than to risk complete immobility.

The presence of sea ice affects navigation in a number of ways. Dead reckoning is difficult because progress is variable both regarding speed and direction of travel. An underwater log may become inoperative because of clogging by ice. An engine revolution counter should not be considered an accurate indicator of speed when a vessel is forcing its way through ice. Speed and direction of motion are sometimes best determined by tracking some landmark. Ice can be used for this purpose if it is not moving. If it is in motion, it can be used to determine progress through the water, if the drift of the ice is the same as that of the vessel.

Ice and snow change the appearance of landmarks, alter the appearance of radar returns, hinder the establishment and maintenance of aids to navigation, affect propagation of radio signals, influence weather, complicate hydrographic surveying, alter atmospheric refraction, and obscure the visible horizon. Extensive fields of ice do, however, calm the sea and make practical the use of an artificial-horizon sextant (p. 356) afloat.

The accumulation of ice on exposed surfaces of the vessel can be hazardous to personnel and equipment. Excessive accumulation can affect the stability of the vessel. Accumulation on aerials can adversely affect radio transmission and reception.

Accurate measurement of direction is more difficult in high latitudes than elsewhere. The proximity of the magnetic poles, some distance from the geographical poles, results in greater magnetic dip (p. 92) and reduced intensity of the horizontal component of the Earth's magnetism, the directive force of the magnetic compass. Frictional errors are greater, the compass is more sluggish and has a longer period of oscillation, deviating forces have a greater effect, and interactions between compass magnets and correctors become greater. Further, the magnetic poles apparently move daily in an approximately elliptical orbit having a major axis of more than 100 miles, resulting in a diurnal change of variation of several degrees. Magnetic storms (p. 96) cause deviation to change as much as $45°$. Further, severe magnetic anomalies are located in polar regions. Because relatively few magnetic observations have been made in high latitudes, magnetic information there is of limited reliability. The magnetic compass works best in a calm sea. When the compass is subjected to very low temperatures, danger of freezing can generally be avoided by keeping the compass light burning.

The gyro compass, too, is of reduced utility in high latitudes because the directive force decreases with latitude, and some models do not have provision for applying certain corrections beyond some limiting latitude. Most gyro compasses give satisfactory service to latitude $70°$, but one should be alert to possible greater gyro errors as the latitude increases. Use of the gyro compass at latitudes exceeding $70°$ should be guided by recommendations of the manufacturer. In areas where neither the magnetic nor gyro compass provides satisfactory directional reference, one may need to have recourse to a *Sun compass*, using the direction of the shadow of the Sun; *astro compass*, using the direction of any celestial body having known coordinates; or a *sky compass*, using polarized solar light at the zenith. These devices require an unobstructed view of some part of the sky. An inertial navigator (p. 532) or a directional gyro (p. 131) may provide directional guidance over a limited period of time.

Visual bearings are great circles and should be plotted as

such. If they are plotted on a Mercator chart, they may need to be corrected as radio bearings (p. 486). There are relatively few aids to navigation in high latitudes, and those that have been established might be damaged or carried away by ice or weather. There are relatively few distinctive landmarks, and the appearance of these may change with the season, as the amount and distribution of snow and ice vary. Mirages are common in polar regions, distorting the appearance of the landscape. Fog, frost smoke (p. 218), and blowing snow are all impediments to visual observations. However, during clear weather the visibility is often excellent, and sound transmissions in both the cold polar air and cold sea water is generally very good. Positions obtained by reference to landmarks sometimes differ considerably from positions obtained by other means because of chart inaccuracies.

In high latitudes, the apparent diurnal motion of the heavens is quite different from that familiar to persons accustomed to conditions in lower latitudes. The extreme difference occurs at the poles, where bodies circle the sky, always at the same altitude except for change of declination. Day and night each lasts six months, and some 32 hours are needed between Sunrise and the appearance of the entire solar disc. The band of twilight, extending perpendicular to the direction of the Sun, rotates with apparent movement of the Sun. Twilight lasts for several weeks. Time zones all meet at the poles. During the brighter part of twilight no astronomical bodies may be available for observation, and during the long polar day only the Sun, and occasionally the Moon at a favourable azimuth relative to the Sun, are available for observation.

Astronavigation is further complicated by extreme abnormal refraction, fog, overcast skies, frost smoke, blowing snow, ice-obscured horizons, false horizons, and the frequent availability of bodies only at low altitudes. It is sometimes possible to obtain observations during the polar night because of illumination of the white horizon by stars, planets, aurora, and the Moon.

When only one body, usually the Sun, is available, good practice suggests hourly observations, with a series of running fixes using the last several observations. All available observations are used regardless of altitude, and the additional correction for refraction given on page A4 of the *Nautical Almanac* is applied to nearly all observations.

When the horizon is obscured or refraction is anomalous, acceptable results might be obtained by means of an artificial-horizon sextant (p. 356), an artificial horizon (p. 356), or a theodolite, if there is relatively little vessel motion other than along its course line. Better results are sometimes possible by observation from nearby ice.

Rising, setting, and twilight information beyond the range of the tables customarily used is given by graphs near the back of the *Air Almanac*.

Sight reduction in high latitudes is discussed in chapter IX, section 9.

Because of the convergence of the meridians towards the poles, an error in time has less effect upon accuracy of an astro position line in high latitudes than elsewhere.

An astro fix showing a position on land may not be in error geographically if chart errors are large.

Magnetic storms sometimes impair the use of electronic aids in high latitudes. This should not be reason for neglecting the use of such aids whenever they can contribute to safe navigation.

Radar is probably the most useful electronic aid in polar regions. It is valuable for detecting the presence and type of ice in the vicinity of the vessel. However, considerable experience is needed for valid scope interpretation. Also, even large icebergs are occasionally undetected by radar at ranges of only two or three miles. This occurs principally when the berg presents a smooth, sloping surface to the radar, a condition more likely to be encountered in the Arctic than in the Antarctic. The principal danger is the difficulty of detecting *growlers* (small icebergs or pieces broken from icebergs, large enough to be a hazard to ships), particularly in the presence of considerable sea clutter caused by floating sea ice or rough seas. Sonar (p. 145) can be helpful in detecting bergs of all sizes because of their large underwater portions. Radar can be helpful in detecting areas of open water in sea ice.

Radar can also be useful in fixing the position of the vessel, but it is handicapped in this use by similarity of aspect of ice-covered land, even more evident by radar than visually; by the difficulty in distinguishing a shore line masked by ice; and by the difficulty in distinguishing between icebergs and islands. Radar bearings, like others, may need correction for convergence of the meridians. Shorter-wave-length radar provides greater resolution than radar with longer waves, but is more susceptible to seriously reduced range capability in the presence of precipitation.

A radio direction-finder is useful primarily for rendezvous, particularly in an area where radar may not distinguish between ships and icebergs. It can, of course, be used with radiobeacons in the few areas where these are available.

Of long-range aids, omega (p. 511) is available world-wide, and loran C (p. 507) and consol (p. 489) have limited coverage. Navigation satellites (p. 542) are available, and inertial navigators (p. 532) can be useful.

An echo sounder (p. 148) can be a valuable aid in high latitudes, as elsewhere, but depth information on charts is minimal.

9. Inland Waterways

Navigation of inland waterways varies greatly with conditions. It is important that the navigator of these waterways be familiar with local regulations, especially in canals, and the aids to navigation available, their characteristics, and the identification system used, as there may be important differences from those familiar to an ocean navigator. The intracoastal waterway along the Atlantic and Gulf coasts of the United States, as an example, has a unique system of buoyage suiting the conditions of the waterway, differing from both the general buoyage system and the system on United States rivers. These buoys are important aids to navigation, while in some areas buoys and other aids are little used or are non-existant.

Navigation on large inland lakes such as the Great Lakes in North America is much the same as coastal navigation, except that greater use is made of ship-to-ship and ship-to-shore radio telephones, which are also widely used on navigable rivers.

Navigation on busy rivers is complicated by the mix of traffic, consisting of ships, small craft, and numerous tows, some quite long. Navigation consists essentially of a highly-developed form of pilotage at close quarters. Characteristically, channels are narrow, shoals shift position, currents are variable but sometimes very strong, and depth of water varies with height of the river. Where tides are encountered, they are generally of little range, and the effect of tidal streams is generally to alter the flow of river water, although in some areas the flood stream is of sufficient strength to reverse the flow of water in the river. The strongest river currents and deepest water are generally toward the outer part of bends, unless the flow of water is deflected by a system of breakwaters, as in the Rhine River in Europe.

Radar is a valuable aid in reduced visibility, to indicate the position of the vessel relative to the shore. On rivers it is little used for collision avoidance, except to indicate the presence of another vessel. A short-wave, high-resolution radar is desirable. A mosaic of photographs of the radar scope during the transit of a river is of value, but with repeated transit of the same waterway, one becomes familiar with the appearance of the radar scope in different areas, and relies less upon a mosaic, just as one uses a chart less as one's knowledge of the river increases. Multi-pier bridges can be a problem in periods of reduced visibility unless the piers are marked in some way to make them distinguishable, on the radar scope, from the bridge itself. The usual procedure is to use radar to determine the correct position from the river bank to pass between piers.

An echo sounder is valuable, particularly during periods of higher-than-normal water level, when it can be used effectively to guide the vessel on short-cuts across shoals, where the current is weaker. Compasses, both magnetic and gyro, may be of relatively little use aboard a vessel winding its way along a river with few straight courses. A rate-of-turn indicator is of greater value in controlling the movements of the vessel.

10. Very Large Ships

The development of very large ships, which may have a deadweight tonnage (DWT) of several hundred thousand, has been accompanied by unique problems of navigation and collision avoidance. The increase in size has been accomplished primarily by increasing the draught and beam, rather than the length, because the diameter of the turning circle is dictated primarily by length.

At sea, in deep water, the navigation of a very large ship is the same as that of any other similarly-equipped vessel. The difficulty in pilotage waters is associated with the size and mass of the vessel, the principal problem being the inability of the vessel to stop quickly, the backing power usually being a small fraction of the ahead power. A mammoth tanker at cruising speed may require as much as two hours to stop, during which time it may have travelled 15 to 20 miles. Because of this fact, turns are usually more effective than attempts to stop in avoiding other vessels, if there is sufficient sea room. Speed in the vicinity of a dock or anchorage is critical, because of the inertia of so large a mass. One study indicated that for a 312,000 DWT vessel the maximum safe docking speed is of the order of 0.06 metre per second, and the safe anchoring speed is about 0.15 metre per second. Because of the necessity of having accurate knowledge of speed over the ground in relatively shallow water, a Doppler sonar navigator (p. 540) is a valuable part of the navigation equipment of a very large ship.

The deep draught of very large vessels precludes their use of many harour areas. In pilotage areas where such vessels operate, the depth of water can be a problem, as the presence of obstructions near their depth limits may not have received attention during the surveys. Also, a large vessel proceeding with little clearance over the ground undergoes a reduction in speed, and the draught changes as the vessel rolls and pitches or as the trim changes because of *squat*, the difference in the way the vessel sits in the water when underway as compared with the condition when the vessel is dead in the water.

A deep-draught vessel is particularly vulnerable to sandwaves, which may form in an area where a strong current, tidal stream, or heavy seas move across a sandy bottom. The waves thus formed, similar to sand dunes on land, vary in size from ripples to waves as much as 20 metres in height. Some sandwaves are relatively permanent, and may be reflected in the soundings shown on the chart, although means of readily detecting them have only been available in relatively recent times. Other sandwaves are transitory and therefore cannot be shown in detail on charts. However, *areas* in which extensive sandwaves are known to exist, as in parts of the southern North Sea, in the Dover Strait, and in Japanese waters, are indicated by appropriate symbol on nautical charts, and known details are given in sailing directions.

Because of the size and manoeuvring characteristics of very large ships, their navigation requires detailed planning, careful routing, alertness, and constant anticipation of future needs.

11. Vessels with Limited Equipment

The navigation equipment of vessels varies from an elaborate assemblage of the latest sophisticated aids to the total lack of aids in the usual rowboat. It is important that a vessel be equipped with the navigational capability needed to carry out its intended mission, but even ships with similar capabilities and identical missions vary considerably in their navigation equipment.

Any lack of equipment needs to be made up by increased knowledge and skill on the part of the navigator. This requirement probably reaches its maximum in the navigation of a lifeboat, discussed in section 20. Although there is undoubtedly some feeling of security in knowing that one has extensive equipment, the navigator of a vessel with limited equipment might take comfort in the realization that navigators sailed the oceans of the world successfully for thousands of years before the development of modern navigation equipment. They did so by developing to a high degree the *art*, as contrasted with the *science*, of navigation. They developed a keen sense of interpreting what they saw, and heard, and felt. They were alert to all conditions affecting the progress of their vessels. With the availability of each new instrument or aid the navigator has become more dependent upon dials and other mechanical or electronic indicators, with a corresponding loss of some of his ability to read the messages of nature.

The successful navigator is one who becomes thoroughly acquainted with all available aids, both man-made and natural, and develops skill in their use; uses all available sources of information; exercises judgment in interpreting the data available; plans carefully; and remains always vigilant. The availability of advanced equipment is desirable but not essential to safe, if sometimes limited, navigation.

12. Sailing Vessels

A vessel propelled solely by wind is limited in its speed and direction of motion by its design, the type and amount of sail carried, the state of the sea, and the wind itself. If the wind is variable, so is the motion of the vessel. Dead reckoning is further complicated by variable amounts of leeway, which is greatest when the craft is close-hauled, and by the need, at times, to tack periodically to maintain progress in the desired direction. Currents, too, need careful attention at the relatively slow speeds of sailing vessels.

Except for these limitations, navigation of a sailing ship at sea does not differ greatly from the navigation of other craft, unless the lack of an adequate supply of electric power limits or precludes the use of electronic devices.

However, nearly all modern sailing is in relatively small pleasure craft that generally remain close to the shore, except in ocean racing. Near the shore, navigation is a matter of rather simple pilotage, but should not be neglected. Much of what is said in the next section applies to sailing boats operating near land.

While the principles involved in navigating a small sailing vessel at sea are identical with those applying to other vessels, there are some differences in application. Advance planning is important, selecting a route to take advantage of prevailing or forecast conditions of wind and sea, but recognizing that neither source of information is infallible. It is generally not practical to attempt to follow a pre-selected track, whether great-circle or rhumb-line, because of the need for frequent changes of heading to make maximum use of the wind. A more realistic approach is generally to plan each day's run from the current position of the craft, toward the destination. Selecting the course to steer relative to a headwind is a matter of judgment and personal preference, recognizing that faster speed might be possible a little farther off the wind, but that the distance covered would be greater. In crossing a tidal stream, it is usually preferable to drift with the current, depending upon a countercurrent to cancel out the set, than to experience a reduction in speed by fighting the current. Allowance is then made for the net drift.

Taffrail logs (p. 138) are little used because of their drag. Magnetic compasses are generally used for direction measurement, and these should be given care commensurate with their importance. Because of the absence of deviating forces in a wooden sailing vessel without auxiliary power, some ocean sailors prefer to remove the correcting magnets, to prevent their being accidently set incorrectly by someone unfamiliar with their function. Deviation should be determined periodically so that timely information is available. A miniature hand-held magnetic compass is useful for measuring bearings.

An automatic dead-reckoning computer has been developed, and is a boon to sailing-vessel sailors, but is generally not permitted by ocean racing rules.

Astronavigation is the usual means of fixing position aboard sailing craft at sea. The low height of eye can be a problem unless the sea is calm. Because of the relative unsteadiness of the observing platform, it is standard practice to average several observations of each body. Small electronic calculators and some graphical and mechanical methods are popular for sight reduction, but any method is suitable if it can be used effectively.

Electronic gear is limited by the circumstances, in some cases by power requirements, and sometimes by ocean racing rules. Of various electronic gear, the radio direction-finder is probably the most useful.

The prudent sailing-craft navigator, like his counterpart in other craft, adapts his practices to the equipment available and conditions under which it is used. He acquires skill and develops judgment by experience, and keeps always alert.

13. Small Craft

The great majority of small craft consists of small pleasure boats that stay near land, and are used only when weather conditions are favourable during daylight hours. Navigation consists largely of simple visual pilotage, and navigation equipment is minimal. But these vessels can encounter sudden, unexpected onset of fog, and weather changes can delay their return to land until after darkness has set in. Thus, any craft that ventures any considerable distance from land should be navigated, and operators of such craft should have adequate equipment and knowledge of its use.

Small craft are characterized by shallow draught, considerable manoeuvrability, and generally by limited equipment, much of it designed for such craft. Charts and publications relating to the area of operations should be kept current and be on hand ready for use. In some areas frequented by small craft, special charts have been designed for their use. If space is limited, or if plotting is difficult in seas sometimes encountered, some sort of portable plotting board, with provision for securing a chart, should be provided. Some form of plotter (p. 87) is generally preferable to parallel rulers, and the danger of flying dividers can be prevented by using a straight-edge on which a distance scale is or can be inscribed. A plastic circular slide rule or pocket calculator is useful.

Equipment should be compatible with the operations of the craft. The deviation of the magnetic compass on various headings should be checked frequently. A hand-held compass for taking bearings is useful. A corner reflector (p. 498) is desirable for use if the craft needs to be located in an emergency. If the craft is to make long voyages out of sight of land, astronavigation equipment should be carried. The electronic devices most useful are an echo sounder, radio direction-finder, marine radiotelephone, and a portable radio receiver capable of receiving marine weather forecasts. Radar and other electronic positioning aids might be considered if conditions warrant. Small-craft autopilots (p. 153) are available and can be useful, but should not be left unattended. A hand lead, fog signalling device, binoculars, and a torch (flashlight) should be kept in place for use when needed.

Advance planning is desirable, as in other forms of navigation. Nowhere is this more needed than in offshore powerboat racing, where the slamming of the craft makes chart work virtually impossible. Detailed planning and precalculation, with appropriate notes, makes possible the checking of progress and keeping track of one's position.

It is important that the small-craft mariner be adequately educated and appreciate the need to navigate his craft. However casual the process, one should be aware at all times of the position of one's craft, so that this position can be used as a point of departure in case of fog or darkness. Definite courses from buoy to buoy or headland to headland should be steered, with changes of course at specific places. A plot of the progress of the craft is generally desirable. Speed determined by means of a device generally called a *speedometer* in the case of small craft is usually not as reliable as that indicated by engine revolution counter. One should keep always alert to the possibility of fog or other unfavourable weather conditions, and return to land, if practicable, before the onset of such conditions. The usefulness of soundings should not be overlooked. They may be useful in determining distance offshore, and sometimes one can follow a depth contour for a considerable distance to locate aids to navigation or otherwise assist in the return to port.

Safety demands that all who venture any distance from shore navigate intelligently.

14. Fishing Vessels

The navigational requirements of fishing vessels vary with the fishing method employed. Tuna fishing often involves far-ranging activities. Navigation to and from fishing areas is essentially the same as that of any deep-water vessel. On station, location of fish is critically related to temperature, without any particular relationship to the bottom or depth of water. Positional accuracy afforded by omega is adequate.

Trawlers, on the other hand, require position to a much higher accuracy, which has been defined as 0.05 to 0.1 mile. Within range, systems such as Decca and loran C provide the needed accuracy. The use of these systems with automatic track plotters is particularly attractive. Differential omega (p. 511) has possibilities if it is implemented in areas where it is needed.

Satellites can provide the needed accuracy, but the United States Navy Navigation Satellite System, in addition to involving expensive user equipment, has serious limitations. One is the intermittent nature of the fixes it provides, requiring the availability of an accurate dead-reckoning capability between fixes. Another is the need for an accurate user velocity vector for accurate results. Both of these problems are acute in the case of a trawler with frequent course changes and slow speed, affecting its course made good in the presence of current. A Doppler sonar navigator can be helpful in meeting both objections in water not deeper than about 400 metres. The NAVSTAR Global Positioning System, if the user equipment is within the acceptable price range of fishermen, might find wider acceptance than the older Navy system.

The echo sounder is a particularly valuable aid to trawlers, not only to assist in locating fish, but also to help avoid obstructions. Fish are often found near obstructions, so the trawler captain may want to fish as close to such obstructions as he can without snagging his net.

Special charts of some areas have been produced for fishing vessels. These charts are of larger scale than ordinary offshore charts, have more closely spaced depth contours, and show additional detail of interest to fishermen. They may or may not be overprinted with lattice lines of useful electronic fixing aids. Devices that automatically trace, on the chart, the progress of the vessel have been devised to provide continuous indication of position.

15. Special-Purpose Craft

Marine craft engaged in such operations as hydrographic or oceanographic surveying, cable- or pipe-laying, geophysical exploration, or tracking spacecraft have unique navigational requirements. Perhaps the most obvious is the need for high accuracy, in some cases stated in metres. Soundings used by mariners to fix the positions of their vessels or determine whether they are in safe water are of little value if the soundings, however accurately determined, are not charted in correct positions. The location of a potential oil drilling site outside the area controlled by a customer is of little value to him.

In the ordinary practice of navigation, where the safety of a vessel is paramount, it is important to know where the vessel *is*, and where it is likely to be in the future if the present course and speed are continued. Where the vessel *was* at some previous time is of little interest beyond use of the information in establishing set and drift of the current. Various types of survey and cable-laying vessels are also interested in safety and, additionally, they desire a continuous real-time indication of present position relative to the ground, to ensure operations as planned. For this purpose, an integrated system providing automatic, continuous readout of present position is highly desirable. Such vessels may have an even greater need for information in where they were when data were obtained. For this purpose a detailed post-operational analysis is made, using all available data, to reconstruct as accurately as possible the actual track of the vessel over the surface of the Earth, without the gaps customary when a new dead-reckoning track is started from a fix. To aid in this analysis, it is customary for a survey vessel to run several survey lines perpendicular to its series of parallel tracks, to determine the degree of correlation at the points of intersection. The various means of obtaining the desired position accuracy are discussed in section 13 of chapter X.

Another aspect of accuracy seldom considered by the navigator of a vessel going from port to port, but of primary importance in some operations, is the reference ellipsoid (p. 18) used. A position has different coordinates on different ellipsoids, and while the difference is generally too small to be of practical significance in ordinary navigation, being at most of the order of a few hundred metres, it may be highly important in positioning a pipeline or locating an oil drilling rig. Similarly, a relatively small error in an astronavigation position because of deflection of the vertical (p. 381) is of importance where high geodetic accuracy is needed.

In summary, a typical special-purpose operation involves three phases: careful advance planning, the operation itself, and post-operational analysis. Each of these steps involves knowledge, judgment, and alertness.

16. Military Ships

Basically, the navigation of a military ship does not differ from that of other vessels. However, there may be some differences in the practice of navigation and in requirements.

Military ships may operate in areas or under conditions not normally encountered by non-military vessels, and it is not unusual for a military vessel to be required, perhaps on short notice, to leave its normal operating area and proceed to unfamiliar waters. Accordingly, military ships generally carry a larger number of charts and navigational publications than other vessels, requiring additional work to keep them current. If a pilot is not used, thorough knowledge of local conditions is essential.

If a ship is to launch aircraft or guided missiles, it may need more accurate position and reference-direction determination than would otherwise be needed at sea.

When ships operate in groups, station keeping is sometimes more important than geographical-position determination. When ships in company manoeuvre, changing position relative to one another, or rendezvous with other ships or aircraft, relative-movement problems not normally encountered by vessels operating alone become important.

Military ships often anchor, rather than tying up at wharves, and may be assigned specific berths. A thorough knowledge of approach and anchoring procedures, with practice in their application, is desirable.

A thorough knowledge of basic and alternative methods is desirable for any navigator, and the prudent navigator periodically uses alternative methods to retain proficiency in their use. For the military navigator this practice is particularly important because in time of combat familiar methods may be denied him because of damage to his vessel or equipment, or power loss. If the gyro compass ceases to operate, for example, and the deviation of the magnetic compass has changed because of the impact of shells or missiles, a thorough knowledge of magnetism and compass correction is essential. For this reason, partly, military navigators may be required to perform routine compass correction and other tasks not required of their merchant-service counterparts.

Although the military navigator might have more demands made upon him than upon others, he may have more advanced, modern equipment, greater redundancy, and more personnel to assist him. A larger navigation team may lessen the work load of individuals, but if the work is to be performed efficiently, thorough training and a clear understanding of one's duties and their relationship to those of other members of the team are essential. Standard terminology and practices are important.

17. Submerged Craft

A submarine operating on the surface is navigated much the same as any other vessel. However, the submarine may have limited equipment in exposed positions outside the hull. Because of the shielding effect of a steel hull, a magnetic compass is of reduced utility inside a submarine, and may not be installed. Because most of the vessel is below the water, a submarine is a relatively stable platform for astro or pilotage observations and for efficient operation of a gyro compass. However, the low height of eye limits the range of visibility and, in a rough sea, makes the position of the visible horizon uncertain, and may interfere with keeping observational instruments dry. With little exposed surface, a submarine experiences relatively little leeway. At night, astro observations by dark-adapted eyes, or by artificial-horizon sextant may be possible under favourable conditions.

At periscope depth a submarine has additional limitations. Bearings of natural landmarks and aids to navigation can be obtained through the periscope. With a properly equipped periscope, one can observe altitudes and azimuths of astronomical bodies, the altitude being corrected as those of artificial-horizon sextants. If azimuths of a body are observed near the zenith, when the azimuth is changing rapidly, a fix or running fix can be obtained from one body with a relatively short period of observation. If an aerial can be exposed, an electronic positioning or satellite system might be used. Usable VLF omega signals might be obtained by means of a submerged aerial within a few metres of the surface.

When totally submerged, a submarine's navigation capability is very limited, particularly if it is too far below the surface to receive radio signals. Careful dead reckoning is of even greater importance than on the surface. A gyro compass or inertial equipment is used for heading reference. An electromagnetic log (p. 139) is generally superior to a pitot-static log (p. 138) for determining speed through the water. At the slow speeds of non-nuclear submarines, current has relatively large effect, and because of the Ekman spiral (p. 211), the current at submarine depth may differ considerably from that on the surface. Inertial and Doppler sonar navigators are very useful in determining progress of the vessel over the ground. However, inertial equipment requires updating periodically, as by surfacing during the pass of a navigation satellite, but an inertial navigator may continue to provide the best available heading reference after it becomes unreliable as a position indicator. The use of Doppler sonar for determination of progress of the vessel relative to the bottom is limited to times when the submarine is within about 400 metres of the bottom. Further, in a miliary submarine operating on a war patrol, the use of any device transmitting acoustic signals may be prohibited for security reasons, and the vessel may not be equipped with Doppler sonar.

If its use is permitted, an echo sounder can be of considerable help in areas where sufficiently thorough hydrographic surveys have been made. Similarly, sonar can be helpful in avoiding obstacles and providing bearings of identifiable seamounts. Forward and upward pointing sonars are particularly useful in under-ice operations, where downward extensions of the ice may be encountered. They are also useful in avoiding surface ships and such man-made obstacles as drilling rigs, fishing trawls, and oceanographic research equipment. With adequate surveys of bottom features, side-scanning sonar might be used with a map-matching technique similar to analogous aircraft operations with side-scanning radar. In the use of any sonic device, whether active or passive, the vagaries of sound transmission in sea water is a problem, particularly in the vicinity of the thermocline (p. 270). The best method of avoiding most man-made obstacles is careful planning. This is particularly important in an area where geophysical exploration is being conducted by means of underwater explosions, which may be of a magnitude to constitute a danger to submerged craft.

Deep submergence craft operating near the bottom for research purposes generally require navigation techniques differing somewhat from those used by submarines. These research craft are much smaller than the usual submarine, and have limited operational range, being carried by a surface vessel to the area of operations. Larger deep submergence vessels having a range of tens or even hundreds of miles may be navigated in a manner similar to that of completely submerged submarines, except that a Doppler sonar navigator (p. 540) is very useful because of proximity of the bottom and the absence of need of security precautions. Heading reference is provided by gyro compass or perhaps by inertial equipment.

For research operations in a very limited area, high

accuracy relative to one or more reference points is usually needed. Geographic accuracy may be of secondary importance. A seamount or other identifiable underwater terrain feature may serve as a reference, but a more common approach is to station a network of acoustic beacons. A number of variations of this approach are used, but in a typical operation, position of the deep submergence craft is determined by means of ranges, bearings, or both, on the beacons. Geographic position accuracy, of course, depends upon the accuracy of positioning the beacons. A major problem in the use of acoustic beacons is refraction of the sonic signals. Visual reference is very limited in extent, a distance of 12 metres being considered excellent.

In some operations the position of a deep submergence craft is determined by the accompanying surface ship remaining directly over the submerged craft and determining the surface ship position by any means available. Maintenance of the position of the surface vessel over the submerged craft may be accomplished by means of narrow-beam sonar. The operation may be simplified by equipping the submerged craft with a transponder to provide a strong return. The surface vessel is directly over the submerged craft when the distance between the two is minimum.

A diver may navigate by means of a magnetic compass strapped to his wrist, and estimation of distance travelled. Visual reference is used within the stringent limitations of this method. Often a diver remains tethered to his craft, the tether providing a reference for distance travelled and facilitating return to the craft.

18. Hydrofoil Craft

At slow speeds a vessel equipped with hydrofoils handles and is navigated the same as any other displacement-type vessel. At speeds sufficiently high, the craft rises on its hydrofoils. If these foils are of a design to be only partly submerged, the craft still tends to align itself with the water surface, as it does during hull-borne operation. But if the design is for total submergence of the hydrofoils, the craft tends to align itself with inertial space, giving it greater stability and comfortable riding qualities at speeds to perhaps 100 knots.

Because of the high speeds involved in hydrofoil craft operations, continuous, real-time display of navigational information is desirable. A fully integrated system consisting of an inertial navigator, equipment for using an external-reference system, a digital computer, and an appropriate display, possibly with other inputs, is perhaps the ideal, but is not cost effective for many hydrofoil operations.

For many operations, particularly those involving relatively short runs in restricted waters, cheaper equipment is adequate. To a maximum of about 55 knots, speed can be measured to an accuracy of about 1 per cent (0.2 knot below 20 knots) by an electromagnetic log (p. 139). Two such logs may be installed, one in the hull for hull-borne operation, and the other in a fibreglass pod attached to a forward strut for hydrofoil operation. At speeds higher than 55 knots, an aircraft-type Doppler radar log (p. 141) or air Pitot-tube type speed-measuring device might be used, the former measuring speed relative to the water, and the latter measuring speed relative to the air. Speed over the bottom might be measured by a Doppler sonar navigator if water depth is not more than about 400 metres, or by a computer coupled to a receiver of a continuous position-indicating system such as Decca. A gyro compass provides a satisfactory directional reference, particularly when an autopilot is used.

Radar is desirable, both for navigation and collision avoidance. True-motion radar is generally preferable to other types, which, at hydrofoil speeds, tend to blur the image unless they have high rates of scanner rotation and low persistence of the cathode ray tube phosphor.

For purely local operations in good weather, minimal navigation equipment might be adequate, consisting of little more than a compass. For such operations navigation consists almost entirely of visual reference to one's surroundings.

Because of the high speeds involved in hydrofoil operations, drift angles are small. Another advantage of hydrofoil craft is their ability, even at maximum speed, to come to a complete stop in a very short distance, typically only three or four craft lengths. This stopping ability is a significant factor in collision avoidance.

19. Air-Cushion Craft

Craft that ride on an air cushion, a few centimetres to perhaps as much as two metres *above* the surface, are known variously as *air-cushion craft, hovercraft, surface-effect ships (SES)*, and *ground-effect machines (GEM)*. Unless the craft has sidewalls extending below the surface, it is entirely airborne and can travel over any surface—water, marsh, land, or ice—and may be capable of speed in excess of 100 knots. If designed for marine operation, it may also be capable of operating at slower speeds as a displacement-type vessel. At slow speeds there is considerable wake and spray, the craft generally being propelled by aircraft-type propellers, but above a critical *hump speed* of 12 to 20 knots, there is virtually no wake or spray.

The advantages of an air-cushion craft are its potential for high speed; ability to travel over shoal areas and other areas not accessible to other craft; and manoeuvrability, having very rapid acceleration, deceleration, and turning ability.

The craft has several disadvantages. It tends to follow the surface over which it travels, resulting in a rough ride over a rough surface. In fact, over rough water, strapping of crew and passengers to their seats is sometimes desirable. Although a hull-borne craft also tends to follow the surface of the water, its motion is quite different from that of an air-cushion craft. Over rough water, navigation of air-cushion craft is difficult and plotting is virtually impossible. Because the craft is airborne, leeway can be very large, and both leeway and speed can be quite variable, further adding to the problem of navigation. The handling characteristics are related principally to the state of the wind and sea relative to the longitudinal axis of the craft, and secondarily to its trim and loading.

Above the hump speed it is desirable to have continuous, automatic indication of present position, the relationship of this position to the intended position, direction of motion (which might be quite different from heading), required heading to allow for leeway, and speed. An integrated system, controlled by a digital computer, with a moving map display or equivalent, is ideal, but not cost effective for many air-cushion craft operations.

In pilotage waters, radar is highly effective, both for navigation and collision avoidance, a particular problem at air-cushion craft speeds. Because of the high speeds involved, true-motion radar is generally the preferred type. A popular way of using radar is by matching its image to a chart of the same scale. Because depth of water and tide and current information are irrelevant, simplified charts showing primarily topographical information are preferred. Radar can also be used for determining position by means of bearings and ranges on identifiable landmarks and seamarks. Electronic fixing aids are also useful. In Decca coverage areas, aircraft-type equipment with flight-log pictorial display has been used effectively.

If continuous position-indication is available, direction of motion and speed can be determined by comparison of successive positions. In the absence of this capability, an aircraft-type compass is usually considered most desirable for direction indication. Speed measurement is a problem because neither ship- nor aircraft-type equipment is entirely suitable. A method that has proved effective is by means of the Doppler effect upon radio signals. The signals are transmitted astern, at a depression angle of $45°$ to the horizontal. Two receivers are used, one on each side, pointing inward at an angle of $45°$. By comparing the Doppler at the two receivers, one can determine speed and leeway angle relative to the water, to an accuracy of about 2 per cent. A laser (p. 142) is an effective means of measuring height above the surface.

In purely local operations in favourable weather, visual reference to one's surroundings may be adequate for navigation. Also, below the hump speed and aboard air-cushion craft with sidewalls extending below the surface of the water, conventional navigation techniques can be used. But for operation of air-cushion craft without sidewalls, at speeds exceeding the hump speed, thorough training of personnel and careful advance planning are highly desirable.

Air cushion craft are required to comply with the international Rules of the Road.

20. Lifeboats

The methods and techniques used for navigation in a lifeboat are determined principally by the equipment available. If one is fortunate enough to have ample equipment, navigation is essentially the same as aboard ship, except for the low height of eye, limited electric power, and the need for added caution to protect the instruments from damage or loss overboard. If the available equipment is minimal, one is obliged to use it to best advantage, and often to apply ingenuity and some improvisation in order to find one's way to safety. Under these conditions a thorough knowledge of the fundamental principles involved can be of great assistance. The prudent navigator acquires such knowledge, which can be useful even though he may never have to use it in a lifeboat.

The time of abandoning ship, when there is much to think about and time may be short, is perhaps the poorest time to prepare for the emergency. Advance planning and preparation can pay big dividends if it ever becomes necessary to resort to lifeboats. Advance preparation properly consists of two parts: equipping each lifeboat and life raft with emergency navigation equipment, and preparation of a last-minute check-off list.

The equipment required to be carried in lifeboats and life rafts relates generally to survival, with minimal attention to navigation. With relatively little effort and expense one can prepare a kit of items that are highly useful in a lifeboat. The kit should be stowed in a watertight container securely lashed to the lifeboat. The following are useful items to be included:

Notebook in which useful data are recorded, such as the latitude and longitude of a number of ports in the operating area of the vessel, information on prevailing winds and ocean currents in the area, a simplified traverse table (p. 172), declination and sidereal hour angles of a number of widely-scattered stars and how to identify them, equations for sight reduction and other applications, and any other items of choice. Blank pages should be left for keeping a log and making calculations. A copy of a long-term almanac having data for stars, such as that included in Pub. No. 9, *American Practical Navigator* (originally by Nathaniel Bowditch), published by the United States Defense Mapping Agency Hydrographic Topographic Center, is even better than a list of star coordinates. Altitude correction tables, as those printed on the loose bookmark of the *Nautical Almanac*, are also useful.

Charts of small scale, preferably summer and winter pilot charts (p. 79) of the operating area or *ships' boats' charts*, prepared by the British Admiralty for lifeboats.

Plotting equipment consisting of pencils, knife or other means of sharpening them, eraser, straight-edge, and protractor or plotter (p. 87).

Graph paper, preferably in decimal graduations, and paper in polar coordinates (concentric circles and radial lines).

Sextant (inexpensive lifeboat type) or material for constructing one.

Sight-reduction tables or tables of trigonometric functions and sight-reduction equations.

Slide rule, preferably one with trigonometric functions. This item may eliminate the need for sight-reduction tables. An electronic calculator is of limited value because of its dependence upon batteries as a source of power.

Flashlight.

Each lifeboat might also be equipped with a deviation table for its magnetic compass (checked periodically for accuracy) and a folding corner reflector (p. 498) to enhance possibility of location by searching vessels and aircraft equipped with radar. If space permits, a book of nautical tables and detailed information on navigation in emergencies might be included.

The check-off list of data and equipment to be obtained at the time of abandoning ship, if time and circumstances permit, should be posted or kept in a place known to all bridge personnel, for immediate reference in the time of emergency. Appropriate items to be included are:

Radio receiver, battery operated, for receiving time signals and for possible use as radio direction-finder, and spare batteries.

Timepiece, preferably a quartz crystal watch, and its error and rate. If such a watch is not available, the ship's chronometer might be taken.

Position of ship.

Weather, current and forecast.

Distress message—whether transmitted, and whether an acknowledgement of its receipt was received.

It is good practice to assemble this equipment and information at each lifeboat drill. All data should be recorded, rather than trusted to memory. A responsible person should know what equipment is available in the lifeboat, and know how to use it.

After the lifeboat is clear of the ship, several important steps are needed preliminary to heading for safety. The first is to establish command. The person selected in each boat should be a natural leader whose authority to make decisions will be accepted by all aboard.

The next step is to collect all available information. The equipment and data should be checked. Each person aboard should be interrogated to determine his knowledge of navigation, mathematics, meteorology, astronomy, etc., and whether he has a watch and knowledge of its error and rate.

Probably the most important decision to be made is whether to head for safety or stay and await rescue. An important consideration is whether a distress message was sent prior to abandoning ship, and the probability of search and rescue (SAR) operations. The probability of rescue has been greatly enhanced since the establishment of various vessel-position reporting systems. Details of these systems are given in publications of the Inter-Governmental Maritime Consultative Organization (IMCO). Other considerations include the ability of the lifeboat to reach land, and the proximity of heavily-travelled shipping lanes. The only practical motive power for a long journey is sail, even if of a crude, improvised form.

If the decision is to leave the area, the decision of where to go should be made carefully, considering all factors. The nearest land, particularly if of limited extent, in a direction of unfavourable wind and current, or located so as to take the lifeboat away from shipping lanes or into an area of hazards or intense cold for which adequate protection is not available, may not be the best choice. In selecting the course, one should keep in mind the fact that latitude might be determined more accurately than longitude, so that it might be advisable to head well to one side of the objective, to leave no doubt of which way to sail when the latitude has been reached. Similarly, one might head well to one side of the objective if it is flanked by a long coast line, to avoid possible turning away from help after landfall.

Whatever the decision, it should be made deliberately, after careful consideration of all available information. If the decision is to head for land, the estimated time of arrival should be determined and rations of available food and water set accordingly.

Morale is important. Harmony and the will to succeed may be the difference between success and failure of the operation. Decisions and the reasons for them should be explained, and all aboard should be kept informed of the situation. Within existing constraints, consideration should be given to the health and comfort of those aboard. A definite routine should be established, with regular assigned duties. This is particularly important if the decision is to remain and await rescue. Activities such as singing, story-telling, reading (if books are available), and devotional services to invoke divine assistance and encourage those aboard might be scheduled on a regular basis. If more than one lifeboat is in the vicinity, there is merit in keeping together, sharing information and possibly exchanging personnel from time to time.

A deck log should be kept from the outset, starting with the position at the time of abandoning ship. Navigational information, major decisions, and important events should be recorded, rather than leaving these to memory and possible dispute later.

If the decision is to remain and await rescue, the position should be checked as opportunity affords, and an effort made, if practicable, to regain the original position to counteract drift and leeway.

Whenever an attempt is made to move from present position to a destination, whether the position of abandoning ship or a point on shore, dead reckoning is important. Because of the relatively large uncertainty in any fix obtained in a lifeboat out of sight of land, the dead-reckoning position during the first several days may be more accurate. If reasonably accurate means for determining direction and distance of travel are available, the dead-reckoning position should be given considerable weight throughout the time spent in the boat, and not abandoned until its error is demonstrated clearly.

As soon as convenient after abandoning ship, one should determine the compass error. The true azimuth of any astronomical body can be calculated or determined by a diagram on the plane of the celestial meridian (p. 302) if the declination of the body and Greenwich mean time are known. The difference between true azimuth and the direction of the body by compass is the compass error. The observation of compass error may be made easier by heading directly toward the body. The shadow of the Sun is particularly useful. Even during twilight or when the sun is obscured by fog or overcast, there may be a strong enough shadow to indicate the azimuth. Whenever a shadow is available, the use of a knife blade held vertical may help make an accurate measurement, the shadow being thinnest when the blade is parallel to the azimuth line.

If true azimuth cannot be determined, Polaris can be used to indicate true north in the northern hemisphere. The leading star in the belt of Orion (p. 338), δ Orionis, is almost exactly on the equator, and so rises and sets at nearly true east and true west. Because of atmospheric refraction, primarily, the star is on the celestial horizon when it is about half a degree above the visible horizon.

Deviation of the magnetic compass can be determined by heading directly away from an object in the water, then turning and heading back toward it, noting both compass headings. The magnetic direction is midway between one compass heading·and the reciprocal of the second heading. Variation can be determined from a pilot chart, if available.

If no compass is available, accurate steering is more difficult, but not impossible. Astronomical bodies can serve as guides if allowance is made for diurnal motion. The direction of the wind, clouds, or sea should be used with caution because of changes, but might be useful short-period guides. The direction of the wake of the boat or a trailing line secured amidships can also be a useful guide over a short period, but is no protection from slow drift of course over an extended period of time.

For determining speed, one might rig a chip log or Dutchman's log (p. 137). If a watch with second indications is not available, seconds might be estimated quite accurately by one accustomed to comparing a watch and a chronometer or timing the characteristics of a lighted aid to navigation. A crude pendulum might be devised. If it is one metre long, its swing from one side to the other is almost exactly one second in duration.

Before the development of devices for measurement of direction, speed, and time, people in various parts of the world, notably the Pacific, regularly made voyages of great length out of sight of land, with remarkable accuracy. The use of their senses was developed to a proficiency not likely to be attained by a navigator who depends upon instruments. When modern aids are no longer available, one's ability to estimate the needed elements of dead reckoning becomes sharpened through practice.

Progress in a lifeboat is likely to be slow. Therefore drift and leeway become a greater consideration than in a faster vessel. Maximum use should be made of favourable currents and winds. When they are unfavourable, it is sometimes advisable to rig a *sea anchor*, an object towed to keep the craft heading into the sea or to reduce leeway, to minimize motion away from the intended destination.

Periodically, as daily, the best available position of the boat should be logged. Progress by dead reckoning can be plotted directly on a pilot chart, or determined mathematically. For this purpose a traverse table is useful. The following is a simple one that might be copied in the lifeboat notebook if a more complete table is not available:

Angle   0° 18° 32° 41° 49° 57° 63° 70° 76° 81° 87° 90°
Factor 1.0 0.9 0.8 0.7 0.6 0.5 0.4 0.3 0.2 0.1 0.0

To determine change of latitude in minutes of arc, multiply the distance run by the factor from this table, the angle being the difference between north or south and the true course. To determine the change in longitude in miles, multiply the distance run by the factor, using the difference between east or west and the true course as the angle. To convert miles to minutes of longitude, divide by the factor from the table, using the mid latitude as the angle. The factors in this table are natural cosines, and therefore any source of this trigonometric function can be substituted for the table. One additional decimal place can be obtained by interpolation in the table given above by considering the tabulated value correct for the angle midway between the tabulated angles, except that the factor 1.0 is correct for an angle of 0°, and the factor 0.0 is correct for an angle of 90°.

Cosines and other trigonometric functions can be determined graphically as shown in Fig. 1203. The radius of the circle is considered 1.0, and the other values can be scaled from the diagram. A haversine is one-half of the versine, or 0.5 (1 − cos). If a table of trigonometric functions is not included in the lifeboat kit, a diagram similar to that of Fig. 1203 might be included in the notebook.

Astronavigation is likely to be the principal means of fixing position. If a sextant is not available, a crude device for measurement of altitude or zenith distances of astronomical bodies might be devised. A protractor, plotter, compass rose, or any graduated circle can serve as a sextant. The vertical can be established by gravity, or the horizontal by sighting along a diameter at the horizon. Another technique is to use a right angle. A vertical peg attached to a board floated in a bucket of water casts a shadow when the Sun is visible. The height of the peg divided by the length of the shadow is the tangent of the altitude, and the length of the shadow divided by the slant distance from the top of the peg to the end of the shadow is the

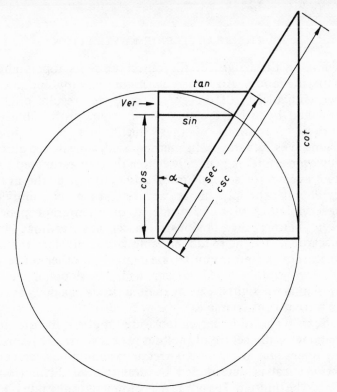

FIG. 1203. Graphical representation of trigonometric functions.

cosine. For bodies other than the Sun, two pieces of wood or other material can be held perpendicular to one another, as shown in Fig. 1204, and the device oriented to the horizon, as shown. The vertical piece is changed in height or moved along the horizontal piece until the body appears in the position shown. The same result is obtained by holding a stick or straight-edge vertical at arms length and aligning the position of the thumb, holding the object, with the horizon,

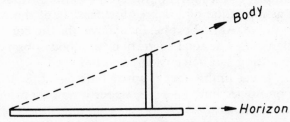

FIG. 1204. Measurement of altitude by right angle.

changing the length of the object until its top is aligned with the body. An assistant might help by judging the perpendicularity of the object, or better results might be obtained by using a string and a weight to establish the vertical. Variations of these techniques might suggest themselves. Whatever the method used, a measured altitude, however crude, is generally better than an estimated value. The average of several timed observations, at the average time, is generally more accurate than an individual observation. A plot of altitude *vs.* time, on graph paper, is even better, the obviously inaccurate readings being discarded. If sight-reduction tables are available, the change in altitude in four minutes (one degree), or other convenient interval, can be used to establish the slope of the line averaging the sights. The 'sextant' altitude of a body at rising or setting is, of course, $0°$.

Sextant altitude-corrections are applied in the usual manner. If the centre of the Sun is observed, as by shadow, the upper and lower limb corrections should be averaged. If the vertical is determined by gravity, the dip correction should be omitted. If a crude measurement of altitude is used, the only corrections needed are for refraction, semi-diameter of the Sun and Moon, and parallax of the Moon. Refraction, always negative, is as follows:

Alt.	$0°.0$	$0°.1$	$0°.7$	$1°.5$	$2°.8$	$5°.6$	$17°.7$	$90°.0$
Refr.	$0°.6$	$0°.5$	$0°.4$	$0°.3$	$0°.2$	$0°.1$	$0°.0$	

Semi-diameter of the Sun and Moon can be considered $0°.3$, positive if the lower limb is observed, negative if the upper limb, and zero if the centre is observed. The factor of the traverse table, given above, or the cosine of the altitude , can be used as a fraction of a degree for parallax of the Moon, always positive. At lifeboat heights of eye, the dip correction is less than $0°.1$. The total correction for a body observed at rising or setting can be considered to be:

Sun, lower limb $(-)0°.3$, upper limb $(-)$ $0°.8$
Moon, lower limb $(+)$ $0°.6$, upper limb $(+)$ $0°.1$
Star or planet, $(-)0°.6$

Some of these values do not check exactly with the values

given above because of rounding off to the nearest 0°.1.

If an almanac is not available for obtaining the coordinates of astronomical bodies, the approximate declination of the Sun can be determined graphically as shown in Fig. 1205. Alternatively, the declination can be found by multiplying 23°.45 by the factor from the traverse table given above, the number of days before or after the nearer solstice being used as degrees for entering the table. If the latitude is known accurately, as immediately after abandoning ship, declination can be determined by solving a meridian altitude (p. 445) or Polaris altitude method (p. 450) in reverse. The value of GHA Υ is equal to Greenwich mean time (in angular units) on September 23, and increases from this value at the rate of 90° between each equinox and solstice (nearly 1° per day). The GHA of the Sun is approximately equal to GMT ± 180°.

If no sight-reduction tables are available, approximate

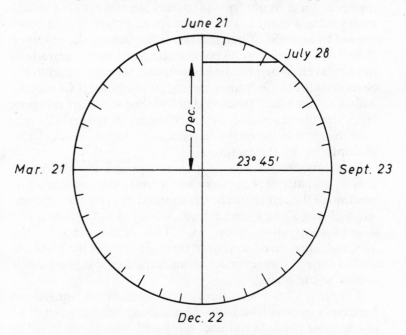

FIG. 1205. Graphical determination of Sun's declination.

627

sight reduction might be accomplished by means of a diagram on the plane of the celestial meridian. However, the best procedure might be to determine latitude and longitude separately.

If the accuracy of time or GHA is uncertain, the latitude can be determined more accurately than longitude. Latitude can be determined by meridian altitude, Polaris altitude, observing a body in the zenith, or by the length of daylight.

For a meridian altitude observation, it is desirable to make a number of observations of altitude and plot these on graph paper *vs.* time. Accurate time is not required, but the time interval between observations is needed. A curve in the form of an arc of a circle through the observations should indicate the meridian (maximum or minimum) altitude.

If Polaris correction-tables are not available, the correction can be determined approximately by estimation. A line through the trailing stars of Cassiopeia (p. 337) and the big dipper of Ursa Major (p. 334) passes approximately through both Polaris and the north celestial pole. Polaris is on the side toward Cassiopeia. When this line is horizontal, the observed altitude of Polaris can be considered equal to the latitude of the observer. When the line is vertical, the correction to the observed altitude is approximately 50′, negative if Cassiopeia is above Polaris, and positive if below. For any other position, enter the traverse table, or other source of natural cosines, with the angle between the reference line and the vertical, and multiply 50′ by the factor.

If an astronomical body passes through the observer's zenith, his latitude is the same as the body's declination. The position of the zenith can be determined by lying face upward and sighting along a plumb bob. A body is in the zenith of a desired destination when its GHA is the same as the longitude, measured westward through 360°, of the place. At such a time it can serve as an indication of the great-circle course to the place.

The interval between Sunrise and Sunset (or Sunset and Sunrise) varies with latitude. The elapsed time between these phenomena is measured and compared with the interval as indicated by a table of Sunrise and Sunset. If no such table is available, a diagram on the plane of the celestial meridian can be used. The measured interval should be increased one minute for each 15′ of longitude travelled eastward between observations, and decreased for each 15′ of longitude travelled westward. The method is not very accurate, particularly near the times of the equinoxes and in low latitudes.

Longitude can be determined by time sight, time of meridian transit of an astronomical body, time of rising and setting, lunar distance, or lunar position line.

Determination of longitude by means of a time sight and by the time of meridian transit is explained in section 12 of chapter IX.

The local mean times of Sunrise and Sunset are tabulated in the *Nautical Almanac* and elsewhere. If the GMT is noted, the longitude can be determined, being equal to the difference between LMT and GMT, in angular units. The LMT of Moonrise and Moonset needs to be corrected for longitude. The times of rising and setting of any body can be determined by means of a diagram on the plane of the celestial meridian.

If the longitude is known, any of the astronomical methods of finding longitude can be solved in reverse to determine time.

Time, and hence longitude, can be determined by taking advantage of the relatively rapid change of apparent position of the Moon relative to other astronomical bodies. The classical method is by lunar distance, the method used by mariners before an accurate timepiece was generally available during a long voyage. The sextant angle between the Moon and the Sun or a star near the ecliptic is observed and the measured angle corrected for semi-diameter and any instrument error. This angle is designated Do. The altitude of each body is observed simultaneously or adjusted to the same time. The equivalent geocentric distance, Do_G, is then calculated by means of the equation:

$$\cos Do_G = \sin Ho_M \sin Ho_S +$$

$$\frac{(\cos Do - \sin ha_M \sin ha_S) \cos Ho_M \cos Ho_S}{\cos ha_M \cos ha_S},$$

where ha is the apparent altitude (sextant altitude corrected for dip and index error), Ho is the observed altitude (apparent altitude corrected for refraction, semi-diameter, and parallax), and subscripts M and S indicate Moon and Sun or star, respectively. Next, the 'calculated' value of lunar distance, Dc, is determined by means of the equation:

$$\cos Dc = \sin d_M \sin d_S + \cos d_M \cos d_S \cos (SHA_M - SHA_S),$$

where d is declination, SHA is sidereal hour angle, and subscripts M and S are as before. The Dc should be calculated for a time believed to be earlier than the correct time, and again for a time believed to be later than the correct time. The Do_G and the two values of Dc are compared and the correct time determined by interpolation (or extrapolation).

An easier but less accurate variation of the lunar distance method is by lunar position line. Proceed as follows: Observe the altitude of several astronomical bodies, including the Moon. The most favourable position of the Moon is on the prime vertical. Reduce the sights for times believed to be earlier than the correct times, and plot the position lines, advanced or retired to the time of the Moon observation. Repeat the process for times believed to be later than the correct times. The Moon position line in the two plots should be on opposite sides of the fix established by the other position lines. Interpolate (or extrapolate) to find the position at which the Moon position line intersects the fix. The time corresponding to that position is the correct time.

Opportunities for using electronic navigation techniques are likely to be limited. A battery-operated radio receiver might be used to obtain radio time-signals, and may have directional properties permitting its use as a crude radio direction-finder. The receiver should be used sparingly to avoid early discharging of the batteries. If no corner reflector is available, the probability of being located by radar might be increased by elevating any metal object, such as a bucket.

One should be alert to signs of nearby land. The appearance of the sea and sky, and disturbances in the regularity of the swell are possible indicators. The presence of birds, which often fly away from land in the early morning and toward it at dusk, is a possible indicator.

When land has been sighted, one should overcome the impulse to beach the boat immediately. The landing place should be selected with care, to avoid disaster while attempting to negotiate the surf, which looks less dangerous when viewed from seaward than from land. A lagoon or other sheltered area might be found to offer some protection during the landing operation. If landfall is made at a remote area, there may be merit in paralleling the coast until a more favourable landing area can be reached.

Whatever the circumstances at the time of abandoning ship, the exercise of calm good judgment, the application of ingenuity and knowledge, and the display of determination and courage can result in survival which might not otherwise be possible.

21. Swimmers

For short distances in still water, navigation of a swimmer is a simple matter of reference, usually visual, to one's surroundings. When currents are involved, the situation is different.

Speed of the swimmer in the conditions to be encountered is an essential ingredient to accurate planning, and should be determined carefully by timing, for estimates tend to be high. The importance of knowing one's speed is apparent when one realizes that swimming speed is generally less than two knots, which may be less than the current speed. Swimmers in surf areas have been carried out to sea because they sought to swim against rip currents that moved too fast to be overcome, rather than swimming parallel to the coast until they were out of the currents and could then reach land with relatively little effort.

In crossing a current flowing continuously in one direction, as in a river, one either swims in a direction somewhat upstream to allow for the current, or starts at a point sufficiently far upstream of the intended arrival point on the far shore to allow for the drift during the crossing. The latter procedure involves less distance *through the water*, and therefore less effort on the part of the swimmer.

If a swimmer can select the time of departure for a long-distance swim, as across the English Channel, he can plan the swim to take advantage of favourable conditions. The general principle involved is to drift with the current rather than fight it, letting it take him first to one side of the mark and then return him as the direction of the current reverses. If the swimmer's speed and that of the current at different times of its cycle are known, one can plot progress on different courses for different starting times to find the optimum, determining the course and speed at each stage by vector diagram (p. 164), allowing for the possibility of encountering obstructions or unfavourable sea surface conditions.

During a long-distance swim the determination of direction and position is usually made in an accompanying boat, although it may be possible for the swimmer to have a compass strapped to his wrist, and the possibility of incorporating some sort of electronic or acoustic homing system in his headgear has been suggested. A swimmer determines the distance he has travelled by estimation, knowing his speed, that of the current, and the elapsed time.

22. Marine Animals

The remarkable ability of some members of the animal kingdom to navigate accurately over long distances, in some cases measured in thousands of miles, at speeds of hundreds of miles per day, is well known. The long migrations of some birds over water and the return of salmon to their breeding grounds long after their departure are cases in point.

The methods used for animal navigation have been studied extensively. While considerable success has been achieved, data have often been contradictory, leaving some doubt as to whether alleged abilities are not merely reasonable possibilities. The navigational capability of birds is better understood than that of marine animals, partly, at least, because of the fact that the motions of the former are more easily observed. Whatever the methods used, the navigation of animals, like that of man, requires the ability to sense some parameters and to process the data sensed. Before the development of artificial sensors, man possessed a relatively well-developed ability of this type, the remarkable feats of the Polynesian navigators bearing record of this fact, but lost much of his natural ability as he became increasingly dependent upon instruments.

It is well established that certain birds are able to sense direction, and perhaps altitude and even rate of change of altitude, of the Sun, Moon, and stars. The maximum altitude of the Sun, and the position of the elevated pole (p. 294) by the location of circumpolar constellations (p. 284) might also be detected. These data, with an accurate circadian-rhythm clock and excellent memory, may provide the means for establishing travel direction, which might be maintained by some means during periods of overcast. Secondary data might be provided by visual reference to landmarks, and by detection of sounds (perhaps at ultrasonic frequencies), odours, the direction and speed of the wind, and the magnetic field of the Earth. The head of a bird in flight is very steady, providing a stable platform for sensing navigational data. Less likely sources of navigational information are barometric pressure, electromagnetic radiation, polarized light, and inertial parameters. There might be other sensing ability that has not been considered. Whether birds have a bi-coordinate ability to determine position, in addition to homing ability, is a matter of conjecture.

That some marine animals may have abilities similar to those of birds, particularly the ability to use the Sun for orientation, is probable. But some marine animals are able to navigate at great depths and in turbid water where little or no sunlight penetrates. These animals have developed sensing ability not shared by birds to the same degree. Perhaps the most remarkable sensing ability of some marine animals is that of detecting minute concentrations of chemical substances, by odour. This ability is probably the means used by salmon for identifying the stream in which they were spawned. Eels have similar ability to detect odours. Some species also have the ability to establish an electric field by muscle activity, and to detect objects entering the field. In some cases they are able to detect the presence of their prey by minute electric fields established by the other animals. Some marine animals, notably porpoises and whales, have highly-developed ability to detect and determine the direction of sonic signals. Porpoises have been found to emit short bursts of ultrasonic signals and detect the presence of small objects by the return echoes, perhaps in three dimensions, with some ability of discrimination! This built-in sonar system has some characteristics similar to the system used by bats. Inertial sensing to provide a vertical reference has been observed, but additional use of this ability for navigation has not been demonstrated. Navigational use of pressure, electromagnetic radiation, and favourable currents have been postulated but not established.

23. Weather Routing

Although the great-circle track is considered the shortest path between two places, it is not always the least-time, or safest route. *Weather routing* is the determination of the most favourable route for a particular voyage, based upon predictions of weather, seas, ice, and ocean currents to be encountered and ship characteristics and loading. Favourability is construed to mean least time between ports, minimum fuel consumption, maximum safety, an acceptable level of crew and passenger comfort, or some combination of these conditions. Weather routing is generally done by a shore-based agency, either governmental or commercial, but might be carried out aboard ship by a knowledgeable person provided with the necessary information. Weather routing by a shore-based agency is purely advisory, the captain retaining full command and responsibility for his vessel.

Of prime consideration is the predicted height, period, and direction of travel of waves, the principal factor in slowing the progress of a vessel and causing damage to the ship or its cargo. Waves and wind coming from ahead have greater effect in decreasing a vessel's speed over the ground than following waves and wind aid its progress. In fact, only relatively small following waves help at all, larger ones impeding the vessel's progress. The probability of encountering fog or floating ice, the temperatures and ocean currents to be encountered, the density of shipping and fishing operations in fog-prevalent areas, the locations and probable movements of high- and low-pressure areas and violent storms, and local adverse conditions are additional considerations. Temperature is involved as it affects other factors, such as the formation of ice on the exposed portions of the vessel and its rigging, increasing the difficulty of deck operations, causing discomfort and hazard to the crew, and possibly influencing the stability of small vessels.

In general, unfavourable conditions increase with higher latitude. Unfavourable conditions generally have greater adverse effect upon low-powered vessels, small ships, vessels towing or being towed, and ships with deck cargoes than upon other craft. For any vessel, a prolonged period of moderately rough seas may be more unfavourable than a more severe storm of short duration.

Weather routing is based upon forecasts of conditions to be expected in the area of operations during the voyage, and to some extent upon climatic data. The latter may be of primary importance in an area where reliable extended forecasts are not available. Typically, a weather-routing agency may provide the following recommendation services, as applicable:

Long-range *planning route* based primarily upon climatic data.

Initial route, issued two or three days in advance of sailing, based upon forecasts, climatic data, and experience.

Alteration of departure time or date to change time of transitting certain areas, particularly if no very favourable route appears to be available at the scheduled departure time and date.

Final route before departure, constituting an update of the initial route.

Diversion, a change of route after departure, either to encounter more favourable conditions or to follow a shorter track with satisfactory conditions.

Adjustment of speed to alter the time of transitting a particular area, and perhaps to avoid a diversion.

Evasion, a recommendation to the Master to take whatever action is needed to cope with a dangerous situation, ship handling and safety being the prime considerations. With adequate warning, the Master should start evasive action soon enough for reasonable anticipation of success. Once the fury of a severe storm is encountered, the probability of delay and severe or even catastrophic damage is increased greatly.

The effectiveness of shore-based weather routing depends upon the validity of long-range weather and seas forecasts, the experience and ability of the persons doing the routing, the availability of two-way communications (so the ship can notify the routing agency of conditions encountered, and the routing agency can send its recommendations to the ship), and the use made of the recommendations.

24. Traffic Regulation

Traditionally, ship owners and Masters have jealously guarded and defended their independence, resisting every effort to erode their authority. However, some forms of traffic regulation have been accepted in the interest of safety and the orderly flow of traffic in all kinds of weather, but not to the same extent as on land or in the air.

As early as 1854 a proposal for traffic separation in the North Atlantic resulted in recommended separate routes for east-bound and west-bound traffic. Both traffic separation and weather (climate) were considerations. Routing to avoid ice was introduced in 1875, and in 1898 a number of shipping companies voluntarily signed the North Atlantic Track Agreement. In the meantime the international Rules of the Road were approved in 1889, based upon uniform regulations adopted by Great Britain and France in 1863, and subsequently accepted by other nations. Traffic separation on the Great Lakes of North America, introduced in 1911 by the Lake Carriers Association, was followed by a dramatic reduction in the number of collisions. During World Wars I and II traffic routing was instituted to avoid such dangers as mines.

Following World War II the volume of traffic increased

dramatically, resulting in greater congestion and increased risk of collision. Fortunately, means for alleviating this condition became available as radar was released for non-military use, electronic positioning systems were developed, and communication capability was improved. *Vessel traffic systems* were developed for a number of ports for the primary purpose of enhancing maritime safety by providing means for more orderly flow of traffic.

Each system was designed to meet the unique needs of the individual port. A system might consist simply of the designation of separate lanes for inbound and outbound traffic, with the aids necessary to permit compliance with the scheme. A vessel-movement reporting system might be added to permit a central unit to monitor the flow of traffic. A shore surveillance-system, possibly by visual observation but more often by radar installations at appropriate locations, with remote indication at a common point, provides more positive monitoring. If a communication system is included, the vessels in the area can inform the monitoring station of conditions encountered, and be informed of matters of concern to them. Maps of the area showing positions of shore lines, channels, aids to navigation, and other pertinent data might be superimposed on the radar scopes, and the scope displays might even be relayed to suitably equipped vessels.

In addition to providing guidance for ships in its coverage area, a traffic-surveillance system can monitor the positions of buoys and anchored ships, apprise port authorities of the arrival of ships at the harbour entrance, and help guide pilot vessels to incoming vessels. It is possible for ships to be provided with transponders to provide positive identification.

Desirable characteristics of a traffic-surveillance radar are high resolution, capability of detecting small targets anywhere in the coverage area, and minimum display of extraneous data such as sea return and precipitation. The radar equipment may be designed specifically for the area in which it is to be used.

The Inter-Governmental Maritime Consultative Organization (IMCO) came into being in 1958 as a result of a proposal made ten years earlier at a United Nations Maritime Conference in Geneva. The purpose of IMCO is to promote higher safety standards at sea. This is accomplished partly through discussions at international conferences held from time to time, recognizing the importance of international cooperation and standardization.

The establishment of IMCO provided a convenient vehicle for introducing traffic-separation schemes in international waters. The first such scheme, based upon a recommendation of a working group of the British, French, and German Institutes of Navigation convened in 1961, was established in the Dover Strait in 1967. Since that year nearly all traffic separation schemes, of which there are more than a hundred, have been established either by IMCO or national governments. The need for international coordination is evident from the fact that some national schemes have been at variance with IMCO recommendations and the 1972 Rules of the Road (officially titled *International Regulations for Preventing Collisions At Sea*), which became effective in July 1977.

The typical IMCO traffic-separation scheme consists of the establishment of separate, parallel *traffic lanes*, with an intervening buffer zone, analogous to a major divided highway for automobiles. The ability of a vessel to stay within its lane depends upon the width of the lane, vagaries of local currents, availability of appropriate navigational aids, the manoeuvrability of the vessel, and the skill and alertness of the crew. The marking of lanes by closely-spaced buoys is generally not practical because of expense and proliferation of aids. The usual means is by positioning systems, but in some areas surveillance by shore-based radar or patrol vessels or aircraft is available. If a surveillance centre has been established, it can provide information on the positions and movements of other vessels and navigational warnings of hazards, shifting of aids to navigation, etc.

Originally, the objective in establishing an IMCO traffic-separation scheme was only to reduce the risk of collision in meeting situations. Six additional objectives were adopted later: (*1*) reducing danger in crossing situations,

(*2*) simplification of traffic patterns in converging areas, (*3*) organization of traffic in areas of offshore exploitation, (*4*), routing vessels to keep out of areas to be avoided by certain vessels, (*5*) establishment of *deep water routes* for deep-draught vessels (to be avoided by others) to reduce risk of grounding, and (*6*) guidance of traffic through or around fishing areas. Areas to be avoided are identified as those where (*1*) adequate surveys have not been conducted, (*2*) adequate aids to navigation are not available, (*3*) local knowledge is essential for safe passage, (*4*) unacceptable damage to the environment could result from a casualty, and (*5*) ships might be a hazard to a vital aid to navigation.

The establishment of traffic-separation schemes has been accomplished by an impressive reduction in collisions between vessels in a close-quarter situation. Reduction of collisions in crossing encounters has been less impressive than in meeting situations, and the improvement in safety has been greater in some areas than in others. As the concept continues to evolve, and compliance becomes more universal, the safety record should continue to improve. As the advantages of traffic separation have become more apparent, and the means for complying have improved, the acceptance of the concept among mariners has increased.

The big step from voluntary to mandatory compliance with traffic regulation schemes has been taken by some countries. The trend toward regulation continues as traffic increases, and in some high-density areas, such as busy ports, the scheme borders on *traffic control* similar to that used to regulate traffic on land or in the air, but generally leaves a greater degree of freedom to the mariner in the selection of route, speed, and time of encounter.

Detailed information on traffic regulation schemes is given in *Ship's Routeing*, published by IMCO.

25. Accuracy

A discussion of navigational errors is given in section 6 of chapter I, and notes on accuracy of various methods and systems are included in the discussions relating to them.

What remains to be discussed is certain considerations relating to overall accuracy of navigation. It would be convenient if some general accuracy figure could be given that would apply to all situations. Unfortunately, there are too many variables involved, and any attempt to produce such a figure would be a misleading oversimplification that could lead to a dangerous complacency.

A number of studies of navigational errors have been conducted, with widely differing conclusions because of differences in assumptions, definitions, or conditions for collection of data. A basic problem of all such studies is the difficulty of determining the true values on which the errors depend, under operational conditions at sea.

The accuracy of position determination, of course, varies widely with the method used. Moreover, accuracy associated with a method involving skill of observation varies widely among different navigators. For example, a British five-year study of the accuracy of astronavigation found that the overall average error of the 'best' third of observers responding to the survey was only about one third that of the average of the poorest observers. In contrast, the accuracy of an automatic system depends primarily upon quality of equipment, proper installation, proper maintenance, and perhaps the environment, and is likely to be equally accurate for all users, unless there is a difference in reading or interpreting the output.

While the results of studies of navigational accuracy are interesting, they are of limited value. It is of greater importance that the individual navigator become thoroughly familiar with his navigation facilities, learning the capabilities and limitations of each item, developing what skill may be needed in its use, seeing that it is given adequate care and maintenance, and acquiring the ability to detect signs of malfunction or erratic operation. If the navigator checks the performance of an item under favourable conditions, he is in a better position to know how much to rely upon it when conditions are unfavourable.

The true test of a navigator is not how well he performs the mechanics of his work, but how accurately he interprets the available data, particularly when it seems to be conflicting. A good navigator not only knows his equipment and how to use it, but understands the principles of errors, recognizing that very large errors can sometimes occur by a method having a small average error. He also recognizes the value of using all available data, noting the degree of consistency of results and attempting to explain any seemingly anomalous results. He is alert to possible blunders, questioning the accuracy of results that appear to be unreasonable. But he accepts the possibility that unexpected results might be accurate, and plans future movements of his craft accordingly, verifying results by whatever means may be available. The development of sound judgment, based upon knowledge and experience, and applied with skill and alertness, is the basis of safe and reliable navigation.

26. Grounding Avoidance

The best protection against grounding is intelligent planning, effective navigation, and constant alertness. The court of inquiry investigating the Point Honda disaster in 1923, when seven destroyers in formation were lost and two others damaged by grounding off the California coast, included in its report a classic statement that might well serve as a guide to deck personnel of all ships:

> The sound navigator never trusts entirely to the obvious. The price of good navigation is constant vigilance. The unusual is always to be guarded against and when the expected has not eventualized, a doubtful situation always arises which must be guarded against by every precaution known to navigators. . . . It is always the captain who is sure in his own mind, without the tangible evidences of safety in his possesion, who loses his ship.

Some of the human errors leading to marine accidents, including grounding, are enumerated in section 3 of this chapter.

Even with careful planning, frequent position-fixing, and constant vigilance a vessel might ground on an uncharted rock or shoal. In a shoal area where the survey is very old, where relatively few soundings are shown on the chart, or where there are many small obstructions or shifting of the material making up the bottom, the sending of one or more boats ahead to make soundings or drag the area may be justified.

Sonar can be particularly useful as an antigrounding tool. A sonar device designed specifically for this purpose has been developed. It uses both a vertical beam and a forward-looking one. A series of vertical soundings is used to predict the distance to grounding, based upon the slope of the bottom and the speed and forward draught of the vessel. The forward-looking beam indicates the distance from obstructions of a depth to constitute hazards. Predictions are based upon several returns, rather than individual ones, to eliminate false alarms by returns from sea life.

The prudent navigator becomes familiar with the operation, capabilities, and limitations of the available equipment, and uses it intelligently to keep his vessel afloat, realizing that the essence of good navigation is keeping water between his keel and the ground beneath it.

27. Collision Avoidance

The hopes of those who expected modern science and technology to solve the age-old collision problem have not been realized because the most sophisticated, advanced equipment is not an infallible solution, but only an *aid*. The best equipment can provide information faster, perhaps more accurately, and in greater quantity than a human, but ultimate decisions rest with the human. The most promising approach, then, to collision avoidance is the adequate training of personnel regarding the nature, use, capabilities, and limitations of the various aids available to him, followed by the development of judgment through experience.

One can learn considerably by supplementing one's training with a study of previous collisions, which reveals that human failure, rather than lack of adequate data, is the underlying cause of most collisions. Lack of knowledge, disregard of rules and laws, non-use of available data, failure to appreciate the situation, and failure to take early action to avoid a close-quarter situation are common human failings. One needs to keep constantly in mind the time and distance requirements for manoeuvring.

The training and competence of ship's officers, and the aids available to them, vary widely among ships. Improved standards aboard ships with least capability is likely to be more effective in decreasing accidents at sea than providing the best ships with even better capability. If all ships performed as well as the best, there would be few accidents.

As might be expected, most collisions occur in congested areas, particularly where two or more vessels pose threats at the same time. The head-on encounter is the most frequent one resulting in collision, often because the conning officers interpret the situation differently or fail to recognize the margin of error of data. In a crossing situation a constant bearing with decreasing range indicates a collision course, but in a meeting situation the change of bearing, before a close-encounter occurs, is too slow to be conclusive, and small errors in data might lead one conning officer to expect a port-to-port passage, and the other a starboard-to-starboard passage, and a manoeuvre by either vessel to increase the passing distance may increase the danger of collision, a condition that might not be apparent until too late to avoid contact. In the few minutes left for evasive action a turn away from the other vessel may present one's broadside to the other vessel, when a turn toward the approaching vessel might have resulted in a close but safe encounter.

The Rules of the Road are intended primarily to reduce the risk of collision by assigning responsibility for taking evasive action, and prescribing certain lights and signals to be used to inform others of one's aspect or intentions. The relative positions of the forward (lower) and after (higher) mast lights are particularly helpful not only in estimating the aspect of another vessel but also in providing an immediate indication of a change of heading of the other vessel. A voluminous literature suggests various manoeuvres for applying the Rules effectively. The addition of bridge-to-bridge VHF telephone

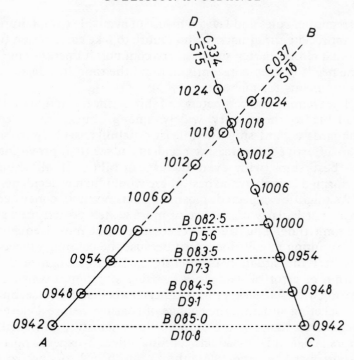

FIG. 1206. A true plot.

more positions for a vessel are plotted, future positions can be determined by extrapolation, as shown in Fig. 1206.

In the illustration, AB represents the track of own ship, on course 037°, speed 18 knots. At 0942 another ship is observed, bearing 085°, distant 10.8 miles. At 0948 it bears 084.°5, distant 9.1 miles; at 0954 it bears 083.°5, distant 7.3 miles, and at 1000 it bears 082.°5, distant 5.6 miles. The positions of the other vessels are plotted from successive positions of own ship. By scaling from the plot, one finds that the other ship travels 1.5 miles each six minutes, or at a speed of 15 knots. The direction of the line through the successive positions of the other vessel indicates that it is on course 334°. The bearing is decreasing very slowly, and the distance is also decreasing, indicating that the other vessel will pass ahead of own ship, at close range. By plotting future positions of both communication can be a positive factor in collision avoidance, by each vessel informing others of his course, speed, and intentions. Language differences and identification of which vessel is being heard are sometimes problems.

Traffic-separation schemes and other forms of traffic regulation are being used increasingly, with some effectiveness, to reduce collisions in high-density areas. However, traffic separation, like other aids, is no panacea. Its effectiveness depends upon the establishment of safe, easy-to-navigate traffic lanes and responsible, intelligent use of them.

The development of radar was accompanied by great expectations of its effectiveness in reducing collisions. Not only has this hope failed to materialize, but for a time the number of collisions between radar-equipped ships increased as ships took action, based upon faulty interpretation of radar information, that put them in the paths of other vessels that might otherwise have been avoided.

The principal value of radar as an anticollision device is its ability to give early warning, in virtually any weather, of the locations and movements of other vessels within its detection range. A major failure in effective use of radar information is the lack of appreciation of the fact that radar data are not the equivalent of visual information, in that they generally provide no direct information on the aspect or size of the other vessel. Also, some officers seem to have difficulty separating, in their minds, relative and true motion.

The use of relative- or true-motion radar is a matter of personal preference. If true-motion radar is used, it should be stabilized relative to the water, rather than to the ground, for anticollision purposes. When true-motion radar is used, any error in the log input introduces an additional error in the data displayed.

Whether information on the positions and movements of another vessel is obtained visually or by radar, a plot of the situation is an excellent aid to successful collision avoidance. In general, two types of plot are in use. In the *true*, or *geographical*, *plot*, the positions of one's vessel and any others in the vicinity are plotted at intervals of several minutes, using distance and bearing from own vessel. After two or vessels, one determines that the other vessel, following track CD, will pass ahead of own vessel at 1018, at a distance of 0.6 mile. The *closest point of approach* (*CPA*), not indicated, occurs a minute later, at *time at closest point of approach* (*TCPA*), when the other vessel bears 357°, distant 0.5 mile. This point is not evident from a true-motion plot. The effect of any change of course or speed by either vessel is evident if one continues to plot, which one should do until the other vessel is well clear. A true-motion plot does not directly indicate the evasive action to take to produce any desired result.

A different type of plot, a *relative plot*, provides additional information. In this plot, own ship is considered stationary, as it appears on the scope of a relative-motion radar, and positions of the other vessel are plotted relative to it. Refer to Fig. 1207, the relative plot of the same situation shown in the true plot of Fig. 1206. Successive positions of the other vessel being relative to own ship, the direction of the line connecting successive positions is the *direction of relative movement* (*DRM*), 267°, and the speed indicated by the spacing of the successive positions of other ship is the *speed of relative movement* (*SRM*), 17.4 knots. A perpendicular from own ship's position to the DRM line identifies the CPA, which occurs at 1019, when the other vessel bears 357°, distant 0.5 mile.

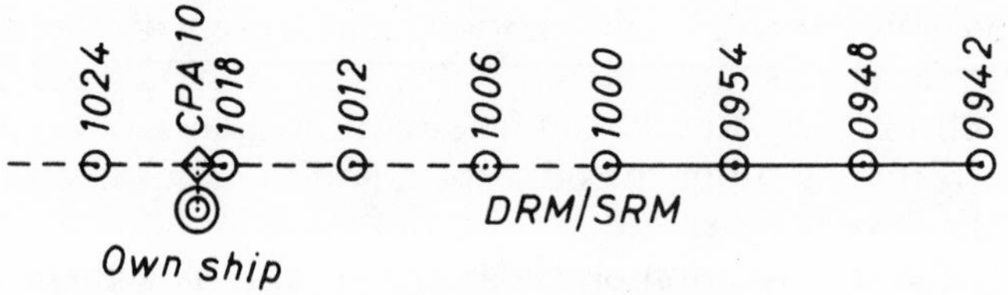

FIG. 1207. Determining DRM/SRM by relative plot.

The true course and speed of the other vessel is determined by a velocity vector diagram, usually superimposed over the DRM plot with the vector diagram origin, e, at the position of

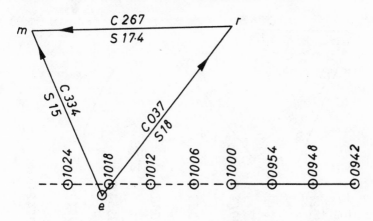

FIG. 1208. Determining course and speed of contact by relative plot.

own ship, as shown in Fig. 1208. From point e, the course and
speed vector of own ship, er, is plotted to any convenient
scale, which need not be the same scale as that used for the
DRM plot. All parts of the velocity vector plot, however,
must de drawn to the same scale. From r, vector rm (relative
movement), is plotted parallel to DRM, its length equal to
SRM. This locates point m. Vector em is the true course and
speed of the other vessel.

Any change of course or speed of either vessel changes the
relative movement line, and therefore the vector diagram. In
Fig. 1208 the CPA of 0.5 mile is considered too close for
safety. Own ship being the one required by the Rules of the
Road to give way, it is decided to take action at 1006 to
increase CPA to two miles. Refer to Fig. 1209. An arc of a
circle of radius 2.0 miles is drawn with e as the centre, and
from the 1006 position of the other vessel a line is drawn
tangent to this line, to identify the new DRM. If it is decided
to maintain speed but change course, an arc of radius 18 knots
is drawn with e as the centre. From m a line is drawn in the
reciprocal direction of the new DRM. The intersection of this
line with the 18-knot arc identifies point r′, and er′ is the new
course of own vessel, 075°. The relative speed, r′m, on this
course is 25.6 knots, giving time at CPA of 1014. If the
original course had been maintained and the speed reduced,

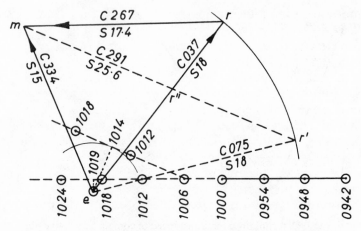

FIG. 1209. Determining manoeuvring to achieve desired CPA.

the vector r″m 14.0 knots, would have represented the new relative-speed vector, and the time of arrival at CPA would have been 1020 (not shown).

In collision-avoidance problems, one should be aware of all applicable provisions of the Rules of the Road, and should take into account the manoeuvring characteristics of own vessel, not shown in Fig. 1209. Plots of all vessels in the vicinity should be continued as long as danger of collision exists, and any contemplated manoeuvre should be considered in terms of its effect upon the relative situation with respect to all vessels in the vicinity. A manoeuvre to avoid one vessel might create a collision situation with respect to another.

The plot can be made on any suitable surface, but a printed polar-coordinate diagram is helpful. Diagrams of this kind, and plastic devices mechanizing such a diagram, have been produced. A *reflection plotter* has been devised to fit directly over the radar scope, to facilitate plotting without the need for transferring observed positions to a separate diagram or device.

A number of electronic devices have been devised for attachment to a radar to provide the equivalent of a hand plot. Such a device is generally referred to as a *collision avoidance system* (*CAS*), but might better be called an 'automatic (or semi-automatic) plotting and collision-risk assessment aid'. There is a variety of such devices varying in complexity, sophistication, capability, effectiveness, and cost. A typical CAS consists of digital processors to compute the tracks of radar contacts, and the CPA and time to reach the CPA of each contact. The results are displayed on a cathode ray tube. Some models provide means of displaying the results of selected changes of course or speed of own vessel. The addition of a digital computer to calculate potential solutions has been suggested.

The principal benefits of a CAS are (*1*) a reduction in the work load of personnel, giving them more time to evaluate the situation and decide on any action needed, and (*2*) the display of information on a number of different contacts. A display separate from the radar itself is most favoured. However, such a device is expensive, in most cases the cost being comparable to that of the radar. Also, a CAS is not infallible, as contacts can be lost. A CAS is not an antidote for incompetent or poorly-trained personnel. It is, after all, an *aid*, and intelligent use is essential. As in all navigation there is no substitute for a well-educated, well-trained, alert individual exercising good judgment based upon experience.

APPENDICES

APPENDIX A

Bibliography

Abbreviations

D.M.A.H.C. United States Defense Mapping Agency Hydrographic Topographic Center, Suitland, Maryland.

G.P.O. United States Government Printing Office, Washington.

H.M.S.O. Her Majesty's Stationery Office, London.

U.S.N.I. United States Naval Institute, Annapolis, Maryland.

J.N. *The Journal of Navigation, The Journal of the Institute of Navigation*, London.

Nav. *Navigation*, journal of The Institute of Navigation, Washington.

ABELL, G. O., *Exploration of the Universe*, 3rd ed., Holt, Rinehart and Winston, New York, 1975.

ADAMS, O. S., see Deetz, C., and O.S. Adams.

ALBERS, V. M., *Underwater Acoustics Handbook*, Pennsylvania State University Press, State College, Pennsylvania, 1960.

ALLEN, William H. (Editor), *Dictionary of Technical Terms for Aerospace Use*, NASA SP-7, National Aeronautics and Space Administration, Washington, 1965.

ALTER, D., and C. H. CLEMENSHAW, *Pictorial Astronomy*, Crowell, New York, 1952.

ANDERSON, E. W., 'A Philosophy of Navigation', *J.N.*, **XIV**, 1, 1961.

ANDERSON, E. W., *Man, The Navigator*, Priory Press, London, 1973. A philosophical, historical treatise on navigation.

ANDERSON, E. W., *The Principles of Navigation*, Hollis and Carter, London, 1966. An overview of navigation in which land, sea, air, and space navigation are treated as parallel developments.

ANDERSON, E. W., and D. M. ELLIS, 'Error Distributions in Navigation', *J.N.*, **24,** 429, 1971.

ANDERSON, E. W., and J. B. PARKER, *Observational Errors*, John Murray, London, 1956. An elementary discussion of the ideas behind the statistical theory of errors.

ANDERSON, R. E., see Fiore, A. E., R. E. Anderson, and L. J. Kapanka.

ANDERSON, R. K., *et al.*, *Applications of Meteorological Satellite Data in Analysis and Forecasting*, National Oceanic and Atmospheric Administration, Washington, 1974.

ANON., *Admiralty Manual of Hydrographic Surveying*, 2 vols., Hydrographer of the Navy, London, 1965.

ANON., *Admiralty Manual of Navigation*, H.M.S.O. The standard navigation text and reference book for the Royal Navy.

ANON, *A Fundamental Glossary of Ice Terminology*, D.M.A.H.C. Pub. No. 609, G.P.O.

ANON., *A Seaman's Guide to the Rule of the Road*, U.S.N.I., 1975.

ANON., *Compendium of Meteorology*, American Meteorological Society, Boston, 1951.

Anon., *Glossary of Meteorology*, American Meteorological Society, Boston, 1970.

ANON., *Glossary of Navigation Terms*, BS 4883, British Standards Institute, 1973.

ANON., *Guidance to Merchant Ships Navigating in Ice in Canadian Waters*, Operations Branch, Department of Transport, Ottawa, 1966.

ANON., 'Handling a Vessel in Ice', *J.N.*, **XII,** 141, 1959. Prepared by U.S. Navy Hydrographic Office.

ANON., *Hurricane the Greatest Storm on Earth*, U.S. Environmental Services Administration, G.P.O., 1967.

ANON., *Ice Atlas of the Northern Hemisphere*, D.M.A.H.C. Pub. No. 550, G.P.O.

ANON., *Manual of Current Observations*, Rev. ed., U.S. Coast and Geodetic Survey Special Pub. No. 215, G.P.O., 1950.

ANON., *Manual of Tide Observations*, U.S. Coast and Geodetic Survey Pub. 30-1, G.P.O., 1965.

ANON., *Marine Surface Observations*, U.S. Weather Service Handbook No. 1, G.P.O., 1974.

ANON., *Meterology for Mariners*, H.M.S.O., 1967.

ANON., *Navigation Dictionary*, D.M.A.H.C. Pub. No. 220, G.P.O., 1969.

ANON., *Physics of the Earth – Oceanography*, National Research Council Bulletin No. 85, ch. V, the National Academy of Sciences, Washington, 1932.

ANON., *Radar Navigation Manual*, D.M.A.H.C. Pub. No. 1310.

ANON., *Radar Plotting Manual*, D.M.A.H.C. Pub. No. 257, 1960.

ANON., *Ships' Routeing*, Inter-Governmental Maritime Consultative Organization.

ANON., *Smithsonian Meteorology Tables*, 6th ed., Smithsonian Institution, Washington, 1951.

ANON., *Tables of Distances Between Ports*, D.M.A.H.C. Pub. No. 117, G.P.O.

ANON., *Technical Nautical Dictionary*, Libreria Mario Bozzi, Genova, Italy, 1967. Italian–English and English–Italian texts.

ANON., *The Marine Observer's Handbook*, 7th ed., H.M.S.O., 1950.

ANON., *The Mariner's Handbook*, NP100, British Admiralty.

ANON., *The Navy Navigation Satellite System*, U.S. Navy Astronautics Group, Point Mugu, California, January 1967.

ANON., *The Planispheric Astrolabe*, The National Maritime Museum, Greenwich, 1976.

ANON., *The Preparation and Use of Weather Maps by Mariners*, World Meteorological Organization, Geneva, 1976.

ANON., *Weather Glossary*, U.S. Weather Bureau, G.P.O. 1946.

ANON., *Wind, Sea, and Swell: Theory of Relations for Forecasting*, D.M.A.H.C. Pub. No. 601, G.P.O.

ATKINSON, G. D., *Forecasting Guide to Tropical Meteorology*, U.S. Air Force, Air Weather Service, 1971.

BAKER, B. B., Jr., W. R. DEEBEL, and R. D. GEISENDERFER, *Glossary of Oceanographic Terms*, 2nd ed., D.M.A.H.C. Special Pub. SP 35, G.P.O., 1966.

BAKER, R. H., *Astronomy*, 8th ed., Van Nostrand, Princeton, New Jersey, 1964.

BAKER, R. H., *Introduction to Astronomy*, 6th ed., Van Nostrand, Princeton, New Jersey, 1961

BARRIAC, J., see Prabonneau., P., et J. Barriac.

BASSETT, Frank E., and Richard A. SMITH, *Farwell's Rules of the Nautical Road*, 5th ed., U.S.N.I., 1977.

BEATTIE, J. H., 'Routing at Sea 1857–1977', *J.N.*, **31**, 167, 1978.

BECK G. E. (Editor), *Navigation Systems – A Survey of Modern Electronic Aids*, Van Nostrand Reinhold, London, 1971. A compendium, the work of 12 contributing authors.

BEERS, N. R., see Berry, F. A., Jr., E. Bollay, and N. R. Beers.

BERESFORD, P. C., 'Map Projections Used in Polar Regions', *J. N.*, **VI**, 29, 1953.

BERGER, M., see Schnegelsberg, L., M. Berger, and J. Kraus.

BERRY, F. A., Jr., E. BOLLAY, and N. R. BEERS, *Handbook of Meteorology*, McGraw-Hill, New York, 1945.

BEST, K. N., 'Through the Proper Channels'. *J.N.*, **27**, 383, 1974. A discussion of the need for more stringent marine traffic regulation.

BIJLSMA, S. J., *On Minimal-time Routing*, Royal Netherlands Meteorological Institute No. 94, 1975.

BINI, Mario, *Navigazione Astronomica*, Accademia Navale, Livorno, 1954. Text in Italian.

BLAISE, Pierre, and Paul PÉTRY, 'The Luminous Intensity and Range of Lights', *J.N.*, **21**, 285, 1968.

BLEWITT, Mary, *Celestial Navigation for Yachtsmen*, 6th ed., Stanford Maritime Ltd., London, 1975.

BLEWITT, Mary, *Navigation for Yachtsmen*, Iliffe Books, London, 1964.

BOLLAY, E., see Berry, F. A., Jr., E. Bollay, and N. R. Beers.

BOURNE, William, edited by E. G. R. Taylor, *A Regiment for the Sea and Other Writings on Navigation*, Cambridge University Press (for the Hakluyt Society), 1963.

BOWDITCH, Nathaniel, *American Practical Navigator*, D.M.A.H.C. Pub. No. 9, G.P.O., vol. I, 1977, and vol. II, 1975.

BOWMAN, W. N., and R. J. RENARD, *Digest of Tropical Cyclones in the Eastern North Pacific*, Environmental Prediction Research Facility, Monterey, California, Technical Paper, December 1975.

BOYLE, R. J., *Ice Glossary*, U.S. Naval Electronics Laboratory, San Diego, California, 1965.

BRADFORD, J. D., 'Sea-ice Pressure Generation and its Effect on Navigation in the Gulf of St. Lawrence Area', *J.N.*, **24**, 512, 1971.

BRADLEY, Charles M., 'Small Craft Navigation', *Nav.*, **10**, 368, 1963.

BRANDENBURG, H. J., 'Port and Terminal Navigation and Control', *J.N.*, **25**, 67, 1972. A discussion of the problems of port and terminal navigation in the 1980's.

BREWINGTON, M. V., *Navigating Instruments, Peabody Museum Collection*, The Anthoensen Press, Portland, Maine, 1963. A catalogue of the navigation instruments in the extensive Peabody collection.

BRITTING, Kenneth R., *Inertial Navigation Systems Analysis*, John Wiley & Sons, New York. A reference book for the practising engineer.

BROUWER, D., and G. M. CLEMENCE, *Methods of Celestial Mechanics*, Academic Press, New York, 1961.

BROWN, Charles H., *Nicholl's Seamanship and Nautical Knowledge*, Brown, Son & Ferguson, Glasgow.

BROWN, R. G., 'Integrated Navigation Systems and Kalman Filtering: A Perspective', *Nav.*, **19**, 355, 1972–1973.

BUDLONG, John P., *Sky and Sextant, Practical Celestial Navigation*, Van Nostrand Reinhold, 1975. A small book covering only the essentials of astronavigation, including the use of calculators.

BURGER, William, *Radar Observer's Handbook for Merchant*

Navy Officers, 6th ed., Brown, Son & Ferguson, Glasgow, 1978.

BURGER, W., and A. G. CORBET, *Marine Gyro-Compasses and Automatic Pilots*, Macmillan, New York, 1964. A reference book for merchant service officers.

BURGESS, C. R., *Meteorology for Seamen*, 3rd ed., Brown, Son & Ferguson, Glasgow, 1973.

BURKARD, Richard K., *Geodesy for the Layman*, USAF Chart and Information Center, St. Louis, Missouri, 1959.

BURROUGHS, J., see Magini, P., and J. Burroughs.

BURTON, S. M., *Burton's Nautical Tables*, 5th ed., Burton's Navigational Publications (distributed by George Philip), London, 1951.

BURTON, S. M., *The Art of Astronomical Navigation*, Burton's Navigational Publications (distributed by Brown, Son & Ferguson, Glasgow), 1956.

BYERS, Horace R., *General Meteorology*, 4th ed., McGraw-Hill, New York, 1974.

CARPENTER, Max H., and Wayne M. WALDO, *Real Time Method of Radar Plotting*, Cornell Maritime Press, Cambridge, Maryland.

CESTONE, J. A., R. J. CYR, and E. ST. GEORGE, Jr., 'Latest Highlights in Acoustic Underwater Navigation', *J.N.*, **30**, 246, 1977 and *Nav.*, **24**, 7, 1977.

CESTONE, J. A., and E. ST. GEORGE, Jr., 'Hydrospheric Navigation', *Nav.*, **19**, 199, 1972. A review of underwater navigation techniques used by short-range deep submergence craft.

CESTONE, Joseph A., and Emery ST. GEORGE, 'Underwater Arctic Navigation', *J. N.*, **27**, 242, 1974.

CHAMBERLIN, Wellman, *The Round Earth on Flat Paper*, National Geographic Society, Washington, 1947.

CHAPMAN, Charles F., *Piloting, Seamanship, and Small Boat Handling*, Motor Boating, New York.

CHAUVENET, W., *A Manual of Spherical and Practical Astronomy*, 1906.

CHILTON, D., 'The Navigation Collection at the Science Museum', *J.N.*, **VIII**, 358, 1955.

CIMA, N. E., and W. F. DUPIN, *Predicting Individual*

Ship Performance from Real Time Environmental Observations, Society of Naval Architects and Marine Engineers, September 1974.

CLARK, Ralph F., 'The Use and Development of Modern Navigational Instruments on Western Rivers', *Nav.*, **2**, 363, 1951.

CLEMENCE, G. M., see Brouwer, D., and G. M. Clemence.

CLEMENSHAW, C. H., see Alter, D., and C. H. Clemenshaw.

CLISSOLD, Peter, *Basic Seamanship*, Brown, Son & Ferguson, Glasgow. A text for beginners.

CLUNE, W. M., 'Optimum Track Ship Routing at FNWC Monterey', *Mariner's Weather Log*, vol. 19, No. 1, January 1975, U.S. National Oceanic and Atmospheric Administration.

COBB, G. (Editor), *Lecky's Wrinkles in Practical Navigation*, 23rd ed., George Philip & Son, London, 1956. The modern version of a classic long held in veneration by navigators around the world.

COCKCROFT, A. N., and J. N. F. LAMEIJER, *A Guide to the Collision Avoidance Rules*, Stanford Maritime, Ltd, London, 1976. A comprehensive explanation of the extensively-changed .972 Rules of the Road.

COHEN, Philip M., *Bathymetric Navigation and Charting*, U.S.N.I., 1970.

CORBET, A. G., see Burger, W., and A. G. Corbet.

COTTER, Charles, H., *A History of Nautical Astronomy*, Hollis & Carter, London, 1968.

COTTER, Charles H., *The Astronomical and Mathematical Foundations of Geography*, Hollis & Carter, London, 1966. An explanation of the mathematics and astronomy underlying navigation and geography.

COTTER, Charles H., *The Complete Coastal Navigator*, Hollis & Carter, London, 1964.

COTTER, Charles H., *The Complete Nautical Astronomer*, Hollis & Carter, London, 1969. A book for the serious student of astronavigation.

COTTER, Charles H., *The Elements of Navigation*, Pitman,

London, 1953.

COTTER, Charles H., *The Physical Geography of the Oceans*, Hollis & Carter, London, 1965. A concise introduction to oceanography for the general reader.

COTTER, Charles H., *The Principles and Practice of Radio Direction Finding*, Pitman, London, 1961. Written primarily for navigating officers preparing for British Ministry of Transport examinations.

COWDEN, D. J., see Croxton, F. E., and D. J. Cowden.

CRAIG, R. E., *Marine Physics*, Academic Press, London, 1973.

CREASE, J., 'The Origin of Ocean Currents', *J.N.*, **5**, 280, 1952.

CRONE, G. R., *Maps and their Makers*, Hutchinson, London, 1953. A treatise on the evolution of the nautical chart.

CROXTON, F. E., and D. J. COWDEN, *Applied General Statistics*, Prentice-Hall, New York, 1939.

CRUTCHER, H. L., and R. G. QUAYLE, *Mariners Worldwide Climatic Guide to Tropical Storms at Sea*, U.S. Naval Weather Service Command, G.P.O., 1974.

CYR, R. J., see Cestone, J. A., R. J. Cyr, and E. St. George, Jr.

DAY, A., 'Navigation and Hydrography', *J.N.*, **6**, 1, 1953.

DAY, Archibald, *The Admiralty Hydrographic Service 1795–1919*, H.M.S.O., 1967.

DEACON, G. E. R., 'Oceanographical Research and Navigation', *J.N.*, **4**, 276, 1951.

DEACON, G. E. R., 'Oceanography and Navigation', *J.N.*, **22**, 77, 1969.

DEACON, Margaret, *Scientists and the Sea 1650–1900; A Study of Marine Science*, Academic Press, London, 1971.

DEEBEL, W. R., see Baker, B. B., Jr., W. R. Deebel, and E. D. Geisenderfer.

DEETZ, Charles, *Cartography*, 2nd ed., U.S. Coast and Geodetic Survey Special Pub. No. 205, G.P.O., 1943. A treatise on map projections.

DEETZ, C., and O. S. ADAMS, *Elements of Map Projection*, 5th ed., U.S. Coast and Geodetic Survey

Special Pub. No. 68, G.P.O., 1945.

DEFANT, A., *Physical Oceanography*, Pergamon, New York, 1961.

DEMING, W. E., *Statistical Adjustment of Data*, John Wiley & Sons, New York, 1943.

DENNE, W., *Magnetic Compass Deviation and Correction*, Brown, Son & Ferguson, Glasgow, 1951.

DESOUTTER, D. M., *Small Boat Cruising*, John de Graff, Inc., New York, 1964.

DE VAUCOULEURS, G., see Rudaux, L., and G. De Vaucouleurs.

DEVEREUX, Frederick L., *Practical Navigation for the Yachtsman*, W. W. Norton and Co., New York.

DICKENS, D. A. G., 'The Lighthouse Services', *J.N.*, **24**, 165, 1971.

DIETRICH, Gunter, *General Oceanography*, John Wiley & Sons, New York, 1963.

DONN, W. L., *Meteorology*, 4th ed., McGraw–Hill, New York, 1975.

DOODSON, A. T., and H. D. WARBURG, *Admiralty Manual of Tides*, H.M.S.O., 1941.

DOVE, R. E., *Program Requirements for Short Count Integrated Doppler Satellite Navigation Solution*, Applied Physics Laboratory, The Johns Hopkins University, Laurel, Maryland, 1974.

DRAPER, Charles, Walter WRIGLEY, and John HOVORKA, *Inertial Guidance*, Pergamon Press, 1960. An introduction to inertial guidance.

DUGAN R. S., see Russell, H. N., R. S. Dugan, and J. Q. Stewart.

DUNCOMBE, R. L., and R. F. HAUPT, 'Time and Navigation', *Nav.*, **17**, 381, 1970.

DUNLAP, G. D., see Shufeldt, H. H., and G. D. Dunlap.

DUNN, G. E., and B. I. MILLER, *Atlantic Hurricanes*, Louisiana State University Press, 1960.

DUPIN, W. F., see Cima, N. E., and W. F. Dupin.

DUTTON, Benjamin, see Maloney, Elbert S.

DYER, A. G., 'Some Hazards to Submarine Navigation', *J.N.*, **28**, 156, 1975.

ELLIS, D. M., see Anderson, E. W., and D. M. Ellis.

EVERSON, John E., 'Navigational Requirements and Methods of Recreational Boatmen', *Nav.*, **12**, 306, 1965–1966.

FAIRBRIDGE, Rhodes W. (Editor), *The Encyclopedia of Oceanography*, Reinhold, New York, 1966.

FARWELL, R. F., see Bassett, Frank E., and Richard A. Smith.

FAURRE, P., *Navigation Inertielle Optimale et Filtrage Statistique*, Dunod, Paris, 1971. A treatise on inertial and hybrid navigation systems, including a lengthy discussion of statistical filtering methods of Wiener and Kalman. Primarily for engineers. Text in French.

FIORE, A. E., R. E. ANDERSON, and L. J. KAPANKA, 'Historical Approach to Marine Collision Avoidance', *Nav.*, **18**, 116, 1971.

FIRTH, Frank E. (Editor), *The Encyclopedia of Marine Resources*, Van Nostrand Reinhold, London, 1969.

FLAMMARION, Camille, *et al.*, *The Flammarion Book of Astronomy*, George Allen and Unwin, London, 1964. An English translation of the classic French book on popular astronomy.

FLEMING, R. H., see Sverdrup, H. U., M. W. Johnson, and R. H. Fleming.

FLETCHER, A., 'Astronomical Refraction at Low Altitudes in Marine Navigation', *J.N.*, **V**, 307, 1952.

FORBES, Eric G., *The Birth of Navigational Science*, National Maritime Museum, Greenwich, 1974. A short history of the 18th century solution of the problem of finding longitude at sea.

FORBES, Eric G., A. J. MEADOWS, and Derek HOWSE, *The Royal Observatory at Greenwich and Herstmonceux*, Taylor and Francis, Ltd., London, 1975. A comprehensive 3-volume account of the origins, history, buildings, and instruments of the British Royal Observatory.

FRANKEL, J. P., 'Polynesian Navigation', *Nav.*, **9**, 35, 1962.

FREIESLEBEN, H. C., *Geschichte der Navigation*, Franz Steiner Verlag, Wiesbaden. An excellent short history of navigation. Text in German.

FREIESLEBEN, H. C., *Navigation*, Matthiesen–Verlag, Hamburg, 1957. A standard text for German merchant and military navigators. Text in German.

FRENCH, John, *Electrical and Electronic Equipment for Yachts*, Adlard Coles, Ltd., London, 1973. A comprehensive general guide on electronics for yachtsmen.

FRENCH, John, *Small Craft Radar*, Stanford Maritime Ltd., London, 1977.

FRIED, Walter R., see Kayton, Myron, and Walter R. Fried (Editors).

FROST, A. (Reviser), *Practical Navigation for Second Mates*, Brown, Son & Ferguson, Glasgow.

GATTY, Harold, *Nature is Your Guide*, Collins, London, 1958. A discussion of finding one's way by utilizing to the utmost one's senses and whatever aids might be available.

GEISENDERFER, R. D., see Baker, B. B., Jr., W. R. Deebel, and R. D. Geisenderfer.

GLADWIN, Thomas, *East is a Big Bird*, Harvard University Press (distr. Oxford), 1970. An account of the traditional deep-sea canoe-voyaging still practised in the Carolines.

GOODWIN H. B., see Hall, W., and H. B. Goodwin (Editors).

GORDON, Robert B., 'The Attainment of Precision in Celestial Navigation', *J.N.*, **17**, 125, 1964.

GOULD, Rupert T., *John Harrison and his Timekeepers*, National Maritime Museum, Greenwich, 1968.

GOULD, Rupert T., *The Marine Chronometer*, The Holland Press, 1960.

GRANT, G. A. A., and J. KLINKERT, *The Ship's Compass*, 2nd ed., Routledge & Kegan Paul, London, 1970.

GRAY, W. M., *Tropical Cyclones Genesis in the Western North Pacific*, Environmental Prediction Research Facility, Monterey, California, Technical Paper, May 1975.

GREENHOOD, David, *Down to Earth: Mapping for Everybody*, Holiday House, New York, 1944.

GREGORY, P. J., 'Safety in the Dover Strait: a Progress Report', *J.N.*, **27**, 51, 1974.

GRIHAGNE, André, 'Vers les navires océaniques non conventionnels à 100 noeuds', *Navigation*, **XXVI**, 131, 1978, Institut Français de Navigation, Paris. Report of a conference at the French Marine Academy on 4 November 1977 relating to various non-conventional ocean-going craft operating at speeds of 100 knots. Text in French.

GROEN, P., *The Waters of the Sea*, Van Nostrand, London, 1967. A book on physical oceanography, including ice in the sea.

HAINES, Gregory, 'Navigation for the Fishing Industry', *J.N.*, **29**, 57, 1976.

HALL, J. S., *Radio Aids to Navigation*, M.I.T., Radiation Laboratory Series, McGraw–Hill, New York, 1947.

HALL, R. Glenn, 'Progress in Precision Timekeeping and Time Distribution', *Nav.*, **15**, 155, 1968.

HALL, W., and H. B. GOODWIN (Editors), *Inman Nautical Tables*, 1940.

HALL, W., and H. B. GOODWIN (Editors), *Raper's Practice of Navigation*, 20th ed., 1914.

HALTINER, G. J., and F. L. MARTIN, *Dynamical and Physical Meteorology*, McGraw–Hill, New York, 1957.

HAMMOND, G., 'Hovercraft Navigation', *J.N.*, **19**, 83, 1966.

HANSEN, L. F., revised by C. W. T. LAYTON, *Hansen's Improved Ex-Meridian Tables*, Brown, Son & Ferguson, Glasgow, 1954.

HARBORD, J. B., see Layton, C. W. T. (Editor).

HARDING, Edwin T., and William J. KOTSCH, *Heavy Weather Guide*, U.S.N.I., 1965. A discussion of the theory, origins, and habits of hurricanes and typhoons, and how to evade them.

HARRISON, A., 'Marine Radar Beacons', *J.N.*, **30**, 126, 1977.

HASLAM, D. W., 'The New Buoyage System', *J.N.*, **30**,

94, 1977. A description of IALA System A.

HAUPT, R. F., see Duncombe, R. L., and R. F. Haupt.

HEWSON, J. B., *A History of the Practice of Navigation*, Brown, Son & Ferguson, Glasgow, 1951.

HIGGINSON, John J., see Williams, Jerome, John J. Higginson, and John D. Rohrbough.

HILDER, Brett, 'Polynesian Navigational Stones', *Nav.*, **6**, 234, 1959.

HILL, H. O., and E. W. PAGET-TOMLINSON, *Instruments of Navigation*, H.M.S.O., 1958. A catalogue of the navigation instruments in the National Maritime Museum at Greenwich.

HIRAIWA, T., 'On the 95 percent Probability Circle of a Vessel's Position', *J.N.*, **20**, 258, 1967.

HISCOCK, Eric, *Cruising under Sail*, Oxford, 1965.

HISCOCK, Eric, *Voyaging under Sail*, Oxford, 1970.

HITCHINS, H. L., and W. E. MAY, *From Lodestone to Gyro-compass*, Hutchinson, 1952. An account of the history and uses of different kinds of compasses from early magnetic compasses to the sky compass using polarized light from the Sun to indicate direction in polar regions.

HOBBS, Richard R., *Marine Navigation*, I, *Piloting*, and II, *Celestial and Electronic*, U.S.N.I., 1974.

HOFFMAN, D., *Fuel Conservation and Heavy Weather Avoidance*, Webb Institute, Long Island, New York, May 8, 9, 1975.

HOGBEN, N., and F. E. LAMB, *Ocean Wave Statistics*, H.M.S.O., 1967. A digest of about a million wave observations over routes used by British vessels, excluding the North Pacific.

HOLDER, L. A., 'Computers and Navigation', *J.N.*, **25**, 192, 1972.

HOOD, P., *Observing the Heavens*, Oxford University Press, New York, 1951.

HOPKINS, F. N., see Norie J. W., edited by F. N. Hopkins.

HOSMER, G. L., *Geodesy*, 2nd ed., John Wiley & Sons, New York, 1930.

'Hovercraft Navigation', *J.N.*, **15,** 359, 1962. Six papers by various authors on different aspects of the subject.

HOVORKA, John, see Draper, Charles, Walter Wrigley, and John Hovorka.

HOWARD, Morton J., see Kritz, Jack, and Morton J. Howard.

HOWSE, Derek, see Forbes, Eric G., A. J. Meadows, and Derek Howse.

HOYLE, Fred, *Astronomy*, Macdonald & Co., London, 1962. A book on modern astronomy, but with extensive historical material.

HUSCHKE, Ralph E., *Glossary of Meteorology*, American Meteorological Society, Boston, 1959.

ILLINGWORTH, John H., *Offshore*, John de Graff, Inc., New York, 1963. A book on ocean racing.

INMAN, J., see Hall, W., and H. B. Goodwin (Editors).

JAMES, R. W., *Application of Wave Forecasts to Marine Navigation*, D.M.A.H.C. Special Pub. SP-1, G.P.O., July 1957.

JAMES, R. W., 'Dangerous Waves Along North Wall of the Gulf Stream', *Mariner's Weather Log*, vol. 18, No. 3, November 1974, U.S. National Oceanic and Atmospheric Administration.

JAMESON, A. H., and M. T. M. ORMSBY, *Elementary Surveying and Map Projection, Mathematical Geography*, vol. I, Pitman, London.

JOHNSON, G. C., *Practical Navigation for Second Mates*, Brown, Son & Ferguson, Glasgow. Originally by T. G. Jones. Solutions of practical navigation problems, with a minimum of explanatory material.

JOHNSON, M. W., see Sverdrup, H. U., M. W. Johnson, and R. H. Fleming.

JONES, Harold Spencer, *General Astronomy*, 4th ed., Longmans, New York, 1961.

JONES, Harold Spencer, 'The Development of Navigation', *J.N.*, **1,** 1, 1948.

JONES, Harold Spencer, 'The Earth's Magnetic Field', *J.N.*, **3,** 1, 1950.

JONES, Harold Spencer, 'Time and Frequency

Standards', *J.N.*, **2,** 1, 1949.

JONES, T. G., see Johnson, G. C.

KALS, W. S., *Practical Navigation*, Doubleday and Company, New York. An informal discussion of navigation from the viewpoint of the yachtsman.

KAPANKA, L. J., see Fiore, A. E., R. E. Anderson, and L. J. Kapanka.

KAYTON, Myron, and Walter R. FRIED (Editors), *Avionics Navigation Systems*, John Wiley & Sons, Inc., New York, 1969. A book on airborne navigation equipment, with considerable information on electronic systems used by mariners.

KEMP, Peter (Editor), *The Oxford Companion to Ships and the Sea*. Oxford University Press, 1977. A general encyclopedic guide to ships and the sea, including navigation, but excluding dinghies and oceanography.

KLINKERT, J., *Compass-Wise or getting to know your Compass*, Brown, Son & Ferguson, Glasgow, 1976.

KLINKERT, J., see, also, Grant, G. A. A., and J. Klinkert.

KLINKERT, J., and G. W. WHITE, *Nautical Calculations Explained*, Routledge and Kegan Paul, London, 1969. A book of some 300 calculations and exercises for students and navigating officers preparing for examinations.

KNIGHT, Austin M., see Noel, John V.

KNISKERN, Franklin E., 'Routing Ships Through Ice-Infested Areas', *Nav.*, **14,** 65, 1967.

KOCH, H. M., 'Radar for River Rhine Navigation', *J.N.*, **VIII,** 326, 1955.

KOTSCH, William J., *Weather for the Mariner*, 2nd ed., U.S.N.I., 1977.

KOTSCH, William J., see, also, Harding, Edwin T., and William J. Kotsch.

KRAUS, J. see Schnegelsberg, L., M. Berger, and J. Kraus.

KRITZ, Jack, and Morton J. HOWARD, 'Channel Navigation and Docking of Supertankers', *Nav.*, **16,** 3, 1969.

LAMB, F. E., see Hogben, N., and F. E. Lamb.

LAMEIJER, J. N. F., see Cockcroft, A. N., and J. N. F. Lameijer.

LARSSEN, H., 'The Use of Radar in the Ice-Breaker Service', *J.N.*, **2,** 315, 1949.

LAYTON, C. W. T. (Editor), *Harbord's Glossary of Navigation*, 4th ed., Brown, Son & Ferguson, Glasgow, 1938.

LAYTON, C. W. T., see also, Hansen, L. F., revised by C. W. T. Layton.

LECKY, G., see Cobb, G.

LEE, Clarence V., see Weems, Philip Van Horn, and Clarence V. Lee.

LEE, T. R., 'Submarine Navigation', *J.N.*, **21,** 480, 1968.

LE FORESTIER, F., 'Recent Advances in Maritime Surveillance and Control', *J.N.*, **30,** 69, 1977.

LEMONON, C., 'Applications de l'infrarouge à la navigation', *Navigation*, **XXI,** 32, 1973, Institut Français de Navigation, Paris. Report of a study relating to the application of infra-red to air and marine navigation. Text in French.

LE PAGE, L. S., and A. L. P. MILWRIGHT, 'Radar and Ice', *J.N.*, **VI,** 113, 1953.

LEWIS, David, 'Route Finding by Desert Aborigines in Australia', *J.N.*, **29,** 21, 1976.

LEWIS, David, *We, the Navigators*, Australian National University Press, 1972. A discussion of Polynesian navigation methods, from first-hand knowledge.

LIPSCOMBE, B. P., *Boat Owner's Guide to Coastwise Navigation*, Brown, Son & Ferguson, Glasgow.

LIZON, Andrzej, *Doppler Velocity Measurements of Ships*, *J.N.*, **20,** 151, 1967.

LOUZEAU, B., 'La Navigation des sous-marins nucléaires lanceurs d'engins', *Navigation*, **XXI,** 76, 1973, Institut Français de Navigation, Paris. A discussion of the navigation of nuclear submarines. Text in French.

LYNDS, B., see Struve, O., B. Lynds, and H. Pillans.

MACDONALD, Edwin A., *Polar Operations*, U.S.N.I., 1969, A treatise on the polar environment, ice breaking, voyage procedures, high-latitude navigation and seamanship, and wintering over.

MacLEAN, J. N., 'Marine Navigation in the Canadian Arctic', *J. N.*, **V**, 27, 1952.

MACMILLAN, D. H., see Russell, R. C. H., and D. H. Macmillan.

MAGINI, P., and J. BURROUGHS, 'Control of the Hydrofoil Ship', *J.N.*, **20**, 292, 1967.

MAINWARING, James, *An Introduction to the Study of Map Projections*, Macmillan, London, 1942.

MALING, D. H., *Coordinate Systems and Map Projections*, George Philip, London, 1973.

MALONEY, Elbert S., *Dutton's Navigation and Piloting*, 13th ed., U.S.N.I., 1978.

MALONEY, Elbert S., *Problems and Answers in Navigation and Piloting*, U.S.N.I., 1978.

MARA, Thomas D., 'Navigation Requirements and Design of a Control System for a Surface Effect Ship', *Nav.*, **16**, 151, 1969.

MARMER, H. A., *The Scope of Oceanography*, James Johnstone Memorial Volume, University Press of Liverpool, 1934.

MARMER, H. A., *The Tide*, Appleton, New York, 1926.

MARTIN, F. L., see Haltiner, G. J., and F. L. Martin.

MATTHEWS, G. V. T., *Bird Navigation*, 2nd ed., Cambridge University Press, London, 1968.

MATTHEWS, G. V. T., 'Navigation in Animals', *J.N.*, **22**, 118, 1969.

MAY, W. E., *A History of Marine Navigation*, G. T., Fontes & Co., Ltd., London, 1973.

MAY, W. E., *Compass Adjustment*, Hutchinson, London, 1951.

MAY W. E., 'The Birth of the Compass', *J.N.*, **2**, 259, 1949.

MAY, W. E., see, also, Hitchins, H. L., and W. E. May.

MAYALL, M. W., see Mayall, R. N., and M. W. Mayall.

MAYALL, R. N., and M. W. Mayall, *A Beginner's Guide to the Stars*, Putnam, New York, 1960.

MAYBOURN, R., 'Problems of Operating Large Ships in the Arctic', *J.N.*, **24**, 135, 1971.

McCLENCH, Donald, see Mixter, George W., edited by Donald McClench.

MEADOWS, A. J., see Forbes, Eric G., A. J. Meadows, and Derek Howse.

MERRIFIELD, F. G., *Ship Magnetism and the Magnetic Compass*, Pergamon Press, 1963. Intended primarily for officers preparing for British Ministry of Transport examinations.

MICHEL, Henri, *Traité de L'Astrolabe*, Gautier–Villars, Paris, 1947. Text in French.

MIDDLETON, W. E. K., and A. F. SPILHAUS, *Meteorological Instruments*, University of Toronto, Toronto, 1953.

MILLER, B. I., see Dunn, G. E., and B. I. Miller.

MILWRIGHT, A. L. P., see Le Page, L. S., and A. L. P. Milwright.

MITROPOULOS, E., *Avoidance of Collision at Sea*, published in Greece, 1975. Text in Greek.

MIXTER, George W., edited by Donald McClench, *Primer of Navigation*, 5th ed., D. Van Nostrand, Princeton, New Jersey, 1967. A complete textbook on marine navigation.

MOODY, Alton B, 'Celestial Fix–Internal or External', *Nav.*, **19**, 338, 1972–1973. Report of a study on the relative accuracy of positions within and outside the cocked hat when the bisectors of azimuth differences meet at a point outside the triangle.

MOODY, Alton B, 'Early Units of Measurement and the Nautical Mile', *J.N.*, **V**, 262, 1952.

MOODY, Alton B, 'Why Ships Ground', *Nav.*, **1**, 259, 1948. A discussion of navigational errors resulting in the stranding of ships.

MOORE, J. D. D., 'Special Problems in Polar Regions', *J.N.*, **IV**, 126, 1951.

MOSKOWITZ, Saul, 'From Simple Quadrant to Space Sextant', *Nav.*, **12**, 193, 1965. Survey and description of celestial data-acquisition instrumentation from earliest times to the date of the paper.

MOSKOWITZ, Saul, 'The Development of the Artificial

Horizon for Celestial Navigation', *Nav.*, **20**, 1, 1973.

MOSKOWITZ, Saul, 'The Method of Lunar Distances and Technological Advance', *Nav.*, **17**, 101, 1970. Summary of the development of astronavigation during the 18th century with emphasis on the search for a method of determining longitude at sea.

NEEDHAM, Joseph, see Taylor, E. G. R.

NEEDHAM, Joseph, *et al.*, *Science and Civilization in China*, Cambridge University Press, London. A monumental work in numerous volumes, covering various aspects of the subject, including navigation and related subjects.

NEUBERGER, Hans, *Introduction to Physical Meteorology*, Pennsylvania State University, State College, Pennsylvania, 1951.

NICHOLLS, see Brown, Charles H.

NIMITZ, Chester W., *et al.*, 'Typhoon Doctrine', *U.S. Naval Institute Proceedings*, **82**, 83, 1956, U.S.N.I.

NOEL, John V., *Knight's Modern Seamanship*, 15th ed., Van Nostrand Reinhold, London, 1972.

NORIE, J. W., edited by F. N. Hopkins, *Norie's Nautical Tables with Explanations of their Use*, rev. ed. Imray, Laurie, Norie and Wilson, London, 1963. Popular tables in publication since 1803.

OFFICER, C. B., *Introduction to the Theory of Sound Transmission*, McGraw–Hill, New York, 1958.

OLSON, L. B., *Olson's Small Boat Seamanship*, Van Nostrand, New York.

ORMSBY, M. T. M., see Jameson, A. H., and M. T. M. Ormsby.

OUDET, L., *Radar and Collision*, Hollis & Carter, London, 1960.

OUDET, L., 'The Ordering of Seaborne Traffic', *J.N.*, **22**, 57, 1969. A discussion of collision avoidance, with emphasis on traffic lanes.

PAGET-TOMLINSON, E. W., see Hill, H. O., and E. W. Paget-Tomlinson.

PARKER, J. B., see Anderson, E. W., and J. B. Parker.

PERRY, R. E., 'A Record of Radar Performance in Ice

Conditions', *J.N.*, **VI**, 74, 1953.

PÉTRY, Paul, see Blaise, Pierre, and Paul Pétry.

PETTERSSEN, Sverre, *Introduction to Meteorology*, 3rd ed., McGraw–Hill, New York, 1969.

PETZE, C. L., Jr., *The Evolution of Celestial Navigation*, Ideal Series, vol. 26, Motor Boating, New York, 1948.

PIERCE, J. A., and R. H. WOODWARD, *The Development of Long-range Hyperbolic Navigation in the United States*, Office of Naval Research Technical Report No. 620, Harvard University, Cambridge, Massachusetts, February 1971.

PILLANS, H., see Struve, O., B. Lynds, and H. Pillans.

PODMORE, J. C., *The Slide Rule for Sea and Air Navigation*, Brown, Son & Ferguson, Glasgow, 1957.

PRABONNEAU, P., et J. Barriac, 'Navigation des véhicules marins à plus de 50 noeuds', *Navigation*, **XXI**, 19, 1973, Institut Français de Navigation, Paris. Report of a study relating to the navigation of second-generation hydrofoils having totally immersed foils and speeds in excess of 50 knots. Text in French.

QUAYLE, R. G., see Crutcher, H. L., and R. G. Quayle.

QUILL, Humphrey, *John Harrison, the Man who found Longitude*, John Baker Publishers, London, 1966. The story of John Harrison and his development of the marine chronometer.

RAISZ, Erwin, *General Cartography*, McGraw–Hill, New York, 1938.

RANTZEN, M. J., *Little Ship Astro-Navigation*, Herbert Jenkins, London, 1952. A discussion of astronavigation for yachtsmen.

RAPER, H., see Hall, W., and H. B. Goodwin (Editors).

REED, Thomas, see Roberts, Charles (Editor).

RENARD, R. J., see Bowman, W. N., and R. J. Renard.

REYNOLDS, L. G. 'The Role of Lighting in Aids to Marine Navigation', *J.N.*, **30**, 108, 1977.

RICHEY, M. W., 'The Navigation of Small Craft', *J.N.*, **28**, 477, 1975.

RICHEY, M. W., see, also, Taylor, E. G. R., and M. W. Richey.

RITCHIE, G. S., *The Admiralty Chart*, Hollis & Carter, London, 1967. A discussion of British naval hydrography in the 19th century.

ROBERTS, Charles (Editor), *Reed's Ocean Navigator*, Thomas Reed Publications, 1969. A book of nautical tables, informative articles, and useful data.

ROBINSON, A. H. W., *Marine Cartography in Britain*, Leicester University Press, Leicester, England, 1961. A history of the sea chart to 1855.

ROHRBOUGH, John D., see Williams, Jerome, John J. Higginson, and John D. Rohrbough.

ROLAND, William F., *The Position Finder*, Geospace Engineering Co., Ottawá. A tabulation of data on a number of electronic navigation systems.

RUDAUX, L., and G. De Vaucouleurs, *Larousse Encyclopedia of Astronomy*, Prometheus, New York, 1959.

RUSSELL, H. N., R. S. DUGAN, and J. Q. STEWART, *Astronomy*, vol. I, *The Solar System*, rev. ed., 1945, vol. II, *Astrophysics and Stellar Astronomy*, 1938, Ginn, Boston.

RUSSELL, R. C. H., and D. H. MACMILLAN, *Waves and Tides*, Hutchinson, 1952.

SADLER, D. H., 'Astronomy and Navigation', *J.N.*, **22**, 71, 1969.

SADLER, D. H., 'Lunar Methods for "Longitude Without Time" ', *J. N.*, **31**, 244, 1978.

SADLER, D. H., *Man is not Lost*, H.M.S.O., 1968.

SADLER, D. H., 'Spheroidal Sailing and the Middle Latitude', *J.N.*, **IX**, 371, 1956.

SADLER, D. H., 'Tables for Astronomical Polar Navigation', *J.N.*, **2**, 9, 1949.

SADLER, D. H., 'The New System of Coordinated Universal Time', *J.N.*, **25**, 32, 1972.

SADLER, D. H., 'The Place of Astronomy in Navigation', *J.N.*, **IX**, 1, 1956.

ST GEORGE, E., Jr., see Cestone, J. A., and E. St. George, Jr.

SATOW, P. G., 'Meteorology and Navigation', *J.N.*, **V**, 203, 1952.

SATOW, P. G., 'Some Problems of Underwater Navigation', *J.N.*, **4**, 288, 1951.

SCHNEGELSBERG, L., M. BERGER, and J. KRAUS, *Handbuch für die Schiffsführung*, 2 vols., 5th ed., Springer-Verlag, 1956. A practical handbook for navigators. Text in German.

SCHUREMAN, Paul, *Manual of the Harmonic Analysis and Predictions of Tides*, rev. ed., U.S. Coast and Geodetic Survey Special Pub. No. 98, G.P.O., 1940.

SCHUREMAN, Paul, *Tide and Current Glossary*, rev. ed., U.S. National Ocean Survey, G.P.O., 1975.

SCHWARTZ, R. A., 'Coast Guard Vessel Traffic Systems: Present and Future', *Nav.*, **22**, 47, 1975.

SHUFELDT, H. H., *Slide Rule for the Mariner*, U.S.N.I., 1972.

SHUFELDT, H. H., *Using Electronic Calculators to Solve Problems in Navigation*, U.S.N.I., 1976. A supplement to *Slide Rule for Mariners*, by the same author.

SHUFELDT, H. H., and G. D. DUNLAP, *Piloting and Dead Reckoning*, U.S.N.I., 1970. An elementary text written primarily for yachtsmen.

SIMMONS, R. E. G., 'Winter Navigation through the Strait of Belle Isle', *J.N.*, **17**, 364, 1964.

SMITH, F. Graham, *Radio Astronomy*, Penguin Books, Ltd. (A Pelican Book), London, 1960.

SMITH, Humphrey M., 'Time Data and Navigation', *J.N.*, **25**, 11, 1972. A review of the relationship of uniform time systems to the precise astronomical observations that determine the irregularities of the Earth's rotation.

SMITH, Richard A., see Bassett, Frank E., and Richard A. Smith.

SPILHAUS, A. F., see Middleton, W. E. K., and A. F. Spilhaus.

SQUAIR, W. H., *Modern Chartwork*, Brown, Son & Ferguson, Glasgow, 1971.

STANSELL, T. A., Jr., 'Civil Marine Applications of the Global Positioning System', *Nav.*, **25**, 224, 1978.

STENBERG, T. R., 'Errors and Accuracy of Position,

LOP's, and Fixes', *Nav.*, **10**, 379, 1963–64.

STEWART, J. Q., see Russell, H. N., R. S. Dugan, and J. Q. Stewart.

STRATTON, Andrew, 'The Science and Technology of Navigation', *J.N.*, **22**, 1, 1969.

STRUVE, O., B. LYNDS, and H. PILLANS, *Elementary Astronomy*, Oxford University Press, New York, 1959.

SUMNER, Thomas, *A New and Accurate Method of Finding a Ship's Position at Sea*, 1843. An account of the discovery of the astronavigation position line.

SUSSKIND, Charles (Editor), *The Encyclopedia of Electronics*, Chapman & Hall, London, 1962.

SVERDRUP, H. U., M. W. JOHNSON, and R. H. FLEMING, *The Oceans*, Prentice–Hall, New York, 1942.

TANI, H., 'On the Stopping Distances of Giant Vessels', *J.N.*, **23**, 196, 1970.

TANNEHILL, I. R., *Hurricanes*, 9th ed., Princeton University Press, Princeton, New Jersey. 1956.

TANNEHILL, I. R., *Weather Around the World*, Princeton University Press, Princeton, New Jersey, 1951.

TAYLOR, E. G. R., *The Haven-Finding Art*, 2nd ed., Hollis & Carter, London, 1971. A history of navigation from Odysseus to Captain Cook, with an appendix by Joseph Needham on the history of navigation in China.

TAYLOR, E. G. R., *The Mathematical Practitioners of Hanoverian England*, Cambridge University Press, London, 1954. An account of the ideas, instruments, and methods of navigation and surveying between 1715 and 1840.

TAYLOR, E. G. R., *The Mathematical Practitioners of Tudor and Stuart England*, Cambridge University Press, London, 1955. An account of the ideas, instruments, and methods of navigation and surveying between 1485 and 1715, with biographical notes on the mathematical practitioners of the period.

TAYLOR, E. G. R., 'The Navigating Manual of Columbus', *J.N.*, **V**, 42, 1952.

TAYLOR, E. G. R., see, also, Bourne, William, edited by E. G. R. Taylor.

TAYLOR, E. G. R., and M. W. RICHEY, *The Geometrical Seaman*, Hollis & Carter, London, 1962. An illustrated work on early navigational instruments.

THOMAS, A. V., 'The Use of Compasses in High Latitudes', *J.N.*, **IV**, 135, 1951.

THROWER, Norman J. W., 'The Discovery of the Longitude', *Nav.*, **5**, 375, 1957–58. Observations on carrying timekeepers for determining longitude at sea, 1530–1770.

TUNNELL, G. A., 'Synoptic Ice Maps of the Meteorological Office', *J.N.*, **21**, 439, 1968.

URE, Charles W., *Simplified Sun Navigation*, Gosford, New South Wales, 1969. An elementary discussion of astronavigation using the Sun, intended primarily for yachtsmen.

URE, Charles W., *The Modern Sailor's Position Finder*, Gosford, New South Wales, 1967. An elementary book on navigation, intended primarily for the yachtsman or lifeboat navigator uncertain of his position at sea.

VASS, E. R., 'Omega Navigation System: Present Status and Plans 1977–1980', *Nav.*, **25**, 40, 1978.

VIDELO, D. A., and D. L. WRIGHT, 'Inertial Navigation for the Merchant Marine', *J.N.*, **23**, 221, 1970. The history and development of marine inertial systems from the gyro compass to complete inertial and integrated systems.

VON ARX, William S., 'Dead Reckoning by Surface Current Observation', *J.N.*, **IV**, 117, 1951.

VON ARX, William S., *Introduction to Physical Oceanography*, Addison–Wesley Publishing Co., 1962. A book for the serious student.

WALDO, Wayne M., see Carpenter, Max H., and Wayne M. Waldo.

WARBURG, H. D., see Doodson, A. T., and H. D. Warburg.

WARRINER, Ben, 'Yacht Navigation', *Nav.*, **16**, 37, 1969.

WATERS, D. W., *The Art of Navigation in England in Elizabethan and Early Stuart Times*, Hollis and Carter, London, and Yale University Press, New Haven,

Connecticut, 1958.

WATSON, D. W., and H. E. WRIGHT, *Radio Direction Finding*, Van Nostrand Reinhold, London, 1971. A non-mathematical survey of the theory, design, and applications of the major types of direction finding equipment.

WEEMS, Philip Van Horn, and Clarence V. LEE, *Marine Navigation*, 2nd ed., Weems System of Navigation, Annapolis, Maryland, 1958.

WENNINK, C. J. 'Ice and its Effect on Navigation in the Baltic Sea', *J.N.*, **18**, 336, 1965.

WHITE, G. W., see Klinkert, J., and G. W. White.

WILKES, Kenneth, *Ocean Yacht Navigator*, Nautical Publishing Co., London, 1975. Companion volume to *Practical Yacht Navigation* by the same author. The emphasis is on astronavigation.

WILKES, Kenneth, *Practical Yacht Navigation*, Nautical Publishing Co., London, 1973. Coastal navigation for small craft.

WILLIAMS, Jerome, John J. HIGGINSON, and John D. ROHRBOUGH, *Sea & Air*, 2nd ed., U.S.N.I., 1973. An introductory text presenting an integrated approach to the study of oceanography and meteorology.

WILLIS, Edward J., *The Methods of Modern Navigation*, D. Van Nostrand, New York, 1925. A mathematical approach to navigation.

WOODWARD, R. N., see Pierce, J. A., and R. H. Woodward.

Working Party of the (British) Institute of Navigation, 'The Accuracy of Astronomical Observations at Sea', *J.N.*, **X**, 223, 1957.

WRIGHT, D. L., see Videlo, D. A., and D. L. Wright.

WRIGHT, Frances W., *Particularized Navigation*, Cornell Maritime Press, Cambridge, Maryland, 1972. A packet of information useful for navigation in emergencies.

WRIGHT, Frances W., 'Selecting the Moon's Limb', *J.N.*, **V**, 141, 1952. Description of a method of determining the illuminated limb of the crescent or gibbous Moon.

WRIGHT, H. E., see Watson, D. W., and H. E. Wright.

WRIGHT, T. M. B., 'Simplified Methods of Position Fixing Using Earth Satellites', *J.N.*, **24,** 496, 1971.

WRIGLEY, Walter, see Draper, Charles, Walter Wrigley, and John Hovorka.

WROTH, L. C., *Some American Contributions to the Art of Navigation, 1519–1802*, John Carter Brown Library, Providence, Rhode Island, 1947.

WYLIE, F. J., 'Automation in Marine Navigation', *J.N.*, **XII,** 1, 1959.

WYLIE, F. J., *Choosing and Using Ship's Radar*, Hollis & Carter, London, 1969.

WYLIE, F. J., 'Marine Radar Automatic Plotting Display Philosophy', *J.N.*, **27,** 298, 1974.

WYLIE, F. J., 'Radar at Sea', *J.N.*, **22,** 29, 1969.

WYLIE, F. J., (Editor), *The Use of Radar at Sea*, 5th ed., Hollis & Carter, London, 1978.

WYLIE, F. J., 'The Case for Fully Automatic Plotting Radar', *J.N.*, **25,** 51, 1972.

WYLIE, Paul E., 'Middle Latitude Sailing When the Course Crosses the Equator', *Nav.*, **2,** 68, 1949.

APPENDIX B

Glossary

---

absolute motion. Motion relative to a fixed point.

acceleration error. The error resulting from change in velocity, particularly as such change causes deflection of the apparent vertical indicated by a bubble or pendulum sextant.

accuracy. The degree of conformity to truth.

advance. The distance a vessel travels in its initial direction in making a turn.

advanced (transferred) position line. A position line moved ahead to allow for the motion of the observer between the time of observation and the time to which the line is advanced.

age of the Moon. The elapsed time, usually expressed in days, since the last previous new Moon.

agonic line. A line connecting points of zero magnetic variation.

aid to navigation. A device external to a craft, constructed and maintained by man, to help navigators fix the positions of their craft or avoid danger.

air-temperature correction. The value applied to a sextant altitude to correct for non-standard air temperature.

alidade. A telescope mounted over a pelorus, compass repeater, or compass, for observing bearings.

almanac. A periodical publication of astronomical information of interest to navigators.

altitude. Angular distance, along a vertical circle, from the horizon.

altitude difference. *1.* Intercept. *2.* Difference in consecutive tabular entries of altitude.

altitude factor. The difference of altitude of an astronomical body at meridian transit and at a meridian angle of one minute of time.

amphidromic system. A tidal system based upon a rotating long-period or standing wave.

amplitude. *1*. Angular distance, along a parallel of altitude, clockwise or anticlockwise from the prime vertical. *2*. Maximum displacement of a wave or other periodic phenomenon from zero.

analog computer. A device that establishes a physical or electrical analogy to the physical problem to be solved.

angle of cut. The angle of intersection of two position lines.

apogee. An Earth satellite's orbital point farthest from the Earth.

apogee stream. Tidal stream associated with an apogee tide.

apogee tide. Tide occurring when the Moon is at apogee, characterized by less than average range.

apparent altitude. Sextant altitude corrected for reading errors and reference-level errors only.

apparent motion. Motion, especially of astronomical bodies, relative to a reference point which may itself be in motion.

apparent Sun. The real Sun that appears in the sky.

apparent time. Time based upon the rotation of the Earth relative to the apparent Sun.

apparent wind. Wind relative to a moving object such as a vessel.

arming. Tallow or other substance placed in a recess in the bottom of a sounding lead for obtaining a bottom sample.

artificial horizon. A device for indicating the horizontal.

assumed latitude. The latitude of an assumed position.

assumed longitude. The longitude of an assumed position.

assumed position. A position for which horizon system coordinates of an astronomical body are calculated.

astronavigation. Astronomical navigation; navigation involving observation of astronomical bodies.

astronomical triangle. The navigational triangle solved in sight reduction.

astronomical twilight. The period of incomplete darkness following Sunset or preceding Sunrise when the centre of the Sun is not more than 18° below the celestial horizon.

astro-tracker. A device that seeks and remains pointed toward an astronomical body.

atmospheric pressure correction. The value applied to a sextant altitude to correct for non-standard atmospheric pressure.

atmospherics. Radio noise caused by natural electrical discharges in the atmosphere.

atomic clock time. Time kept by a clock measuring the transitions of the caesium atom 133.

attenuation. Decrease in amplitude of a radiant energy signal with increasing distance of travel from its source.

augmentation. The increase in apparent semi-diameter of an astronomical body with increased altitude, because of reduced distance of the body from the observer.

autumnal equinox. That equinox at which the Sun crosses the celestial equator from north to south.

azimuth. Angular distance, along a parallel of altitude, clockwise from the principal vertical circle.

azimuth angle. Angular distance, along a parallel of altitude, clockwise or anticlockwise from the direction of the elevated pole, or occasionally from either this or the reciprocal direction, whichever is nearer.

azimuthal projection. Zenithal projection.

back angle. The altitude measured when a back sight is made.

back sight. An observation of an astronomical body made by facing *away* from the body.

bandwidth. The range of frequency required for transmission.

base line. A line of known length used as the datum for measurement of some quantity.

base line extension. The extension of a base line beyond a transmitter used with another for establishment of position lines.

bathymetric chart. A chart emphasizing depth of water.

bathymetric contour. Depth contour.

bathymetric navigation. Navigation by means of depth information.

beacon. *1.* Generally, anything serving as a mark to warn of danger or aid in position-fixing; specifically, a fixed navigational mark of importance secondary to a lighthouse or light tower. *2.* Radiobeacon.

beam width. The angular extent of a beam of radiant energy between some percentage of maximum signal strength.

bearing. The horizontal direction of one point from another.

bearing angle. Bearing reckoned from 0° at the reference direction clockwise or anticlockwise through 90° or 180°.

bearing compass. A portable hand-held magnetic compass intended primarily for measuring compass bearings.

bearing plate. Pelorus.

binnacle. The receptacle in which a compass is housed.

boat compass. A small magnetic compass mounted in a box for use in small marine craft.

bobbing a light. Changing height of eye to determine whether a light is at the geographical range.

bottom profile. A trace of depth of water *vs.* distance travelled or time.

bottom sample. A small portion of the material composing the ocean floor, brought up for inspection.

bow and beam bearings. Two bearings of the same object with the angle between the course line (over the ground) and the bearing line being 45° at the time of the first observation and 90° at the time of the second observation.

boxing the compass. Naming the compass points, and sometimes fractional points, in clockwise order.

buoy. A floating object, other than a lightship, anchored at an assigned location to serve as an aid to navigation.

cable. One-tenth nautical mile, or 185.2 metres, in British terminology; 720 feet (219.456 metres) in United States terminology.

calculated altitude. Altitude of an astronomical body as determined by calculation or equivalent means.

calculator. A relatively simple, portable computer.

can buoy. A buoy having its above-water portion in the shape of a cylinder.

cardinal system. A buoyage system in which the type and colour of a buoy relates to its position relative to an isolated obstruction.

carrier wave. A radio wave system carrying intelligence by modulation.

cathode ray tube. The picture tube of radar, television, etc.

celestial equator. The intersection of the plane of the Earth's equator and the celestial sphere.

celestial horizon. The celestial-sphere great circle midway between the zenith and nadir.

celestial meridian. A great circle through the celestial poles and the zenith.

celestial navigation. Astronavigation.

celestial pole. Either of the two points of intersection of the celestial sphere and the extension of the Earth's rotational axis.

celestial sphere. An imaginary sphere of great radius concentric with the Earth, and on which all astronomical bodies other than the Earth are imagined to be projected.

centicycle. One-hundredth of a cycle.

centilane. One-hundredth of a lane.

centimetric waves. Super high-frequency waves.

centre line. The locus of points equidistant from two reference points or lines.

centring error. The instrumental error resulting from inaccurate pivoting of a moving part.

chain. A group of related electronic transmitting stations producing a lattice.

character (of a light). Characteristics.

characteristics (of a light). The colour or colours and sequence and duration of light and dark periods assigned to a nagivational light to assist in its identification.

chart. A map intended primarily for navigation.

chart datum. The water level from which depths shown on a chart are reckoned.

chart projection. A map projection used for a chart.

chip log. A log consisting of a line and a device that remains essentially stationary in the water as the vessel moves.

chosen position. An assumed position consisting of an integral degree of latitude and a longitude selected so that the local hour angle is an integral degree.

chronograph. A timepiece producing a graphical record of elapsed time.

chronometer. A timepiece with a relatively uniform rate.

chronometer error. The difference between chronometer time and the correct time, usually Greenwich mean time.

chronometer rate. Change of chronometer error in unit time, generally expressed as seconds per day.

chronostat. A timepiece having a compensated balance wheel and a movement governed by transistors.

circle of equal altitude. An Earth-surface circle on every point of which the altitude of a specified astronomical body is identical at a given instant.

circle of visibility. A circle enclosing the area in which an object can or is expected to be visible.

circumpolar. Revolving about the elevated pole, without setting.

civil twilight. The period of incomplete darkness following Sunset or preceding Sunrise when the centre of the Sun is not more than 6° below the celestial horizon.

clearing angle. The maximum or minimum angle, as observed aboar a vessel, between two points a known distance apart; used to indicate the limit of safe approach to an off-lying obstruction.

clearing bearing. The limiting bearing of an object to ensure safe passage of an off-lying obstruction.

clearing circle. A circle indicating a clearing distance.

clearing distance. The limiting distance of an object to ensure safe passage of an obstruction.

clearing mark. A mark used for establishing a clearing bearing or clearing distance.

clearing sounding. The sounding identifying the contour marking the limit of safe navigation.

coastal refraction. Change in direction of travel of a radio wave as it enters an area of different conducting and reflecting properties, as when it crosses a coast line.

coasting. Proceeding along a coast sufficiently close to fix position periodically be means of landmarks or aids to navigation.

cocked hat. The triangle formed by three position lines, adjusted, if necessary, to a common time, that do not meet at one point.

collimation error. The errror of an optical instrument resulting from an offset of the line of sight.

comparing watch. A hack watch, particularly one having its error determined by comparison with a chronometer and then used for comparison with ship's clocks to determine their errors.

compass. An instrument for locating a horizontal reference direction.

compass adjustment. Neutralization of a craft's magnetic field at a magnetic compass.

compass card. That part of a compass having direction graduations.

compass compensation. Neutralization of the magnetic field, at a magnetic compass, established by a vessel's degaussing system.

compass correction. Compass adjustment and compass compensation.

compass correction card. Deviation card.

compass error. The difference between true north and compass north.

compass north. North as indicated by a magnetic compass.

compass point. One thirty-second of a circle, or $11\frac{1}{4}$ degrees.

compass rose. A graduated circle used for measurement of direction, as on a chart.

compasses. A device for drawing circles.

composite sailing. Modified great-circle sailing used to limit maximum latitude.

computed altitude. Calculated altitude.

computer. A device for performing mathematical calculations.

conformality. Correct representation of angles.

conic projection. A map projection in which the surface of a sphere or spheroid is conceived as developed on a secant or tangent cone or cones that are then flattened to form a plane.

conical buoy. A buoy having its above-water portion in the shape of a cone or truncated cone.

constant error. An error of unchanging magnitude and sign.

continuous waves. Waves of identical amplitude and frequency.

contour. A line connecting points of the same height or depth.

controlling depth. Minimum depth, below the chart datum, in a channel and its approaches, indicating the maximum draught of vessels that can use the area.

convergence of the meridians. The angle between two meridians.

conversion angle. The angle between the great circle and the rhumb line between two points.

coordinated universal time. A time approximating UT_2 used for uniformity of time signals.

Coriolis. An apparent force acting upon a mass in motion, because of rotation of the Earth, causing deflection to the right in the northern hemisphere and to the left in the southern hemisphere.

corner reflector. A device consisting of three mutually-perpendicular, conducting surfaces that return electromagnetic radiations toward their sources.

corrected sextant altitude. Observed altitude.

correcting. Application of a correction to remove an error, particularly variation, deviation, compass error, or gyro error.

course. The horizontal direction of travel of a craft.

course angle. Course reckoned from 0° at the reference direction clockwise or anticlockwise through 90° or 180°.

course line. *1.* A line extending in the direction of a course. *2.* A position line parallel to a course line (definition 1), or nearly so, providing an indication of course being made good over the ground.

craft. Any vessel or vehicle.

current. *1.* Fluid in motion. *2.* The total effect of all factors causing deviation from heading and the speed ordered.

cylindrical projection. A map projection in which the surface of a sphere or spheroid is conceived as developed on a tangent or secant cylinder that is then flattened to form a plane.

daily rate. The change in error of a timepiece per day.

danger angle. Clearing angle.

danger bearing. Clearing bearing.

danger circle. Clearing circle.

danger distance. Clearing distance.

danger mark. Clearing mark.

danger sounding. Clearing sounding.

daybeacon. An unlighted beacon.

daymark. An unlighted mark.

day's work. The daily routine of the navigation of a vessel at sea.

dead reckoning. Navigation based upon distance and direction travelled from a position of known coordinates.

decimetric waves. Ultra high-frequency waves.

deck log. The official record of navigational information and important events aboard a craft.

deck watch. Hack watch.

declination. Angular distance north or south of the celestial equator.

deep scattering layer. An assemblage of minute marine organisms, or larger zooplankton attracted to them, of sufficient density to produce a false reading by an echo sounder.

deep sea lead. A heavy sounding lead with a long lead line.

deep-water route. A traffic lane for the exclusive use of deep-draught vessels.

deflection of the vertical. Angular offset of the gravity vertical because of differences in the density and distribution of the material constituting the crust of the Earth.

deflector. A device for measuring the relative directive force of a magnetic compass on cardinal headings, for use in compass adjustment.

degaussing. Neutralization of the magnetic field of a vessel by means of direct-current electric coils permanently installed in the vessel.

demodulation. Recovery of a modulating wave from a modulated carrier wave.

departure. The east–west component of a rhumb line, expressed in linear units, usually nautical miles.

depressed pole. The celestial pole below the horizon.

depth contour. A line connecting points of the same depth.

deviation. The difference between magnetic north and compass north.

deviation card. A card on which a deviation table is recorded.

deviation coefficient. A deviation component having unique characteristics.

deviation table. A tabulation of deviation of a magnetic compass on various headings.

differential mode. A method of using an electronic navigation system by correcting readings for the difference between predicted and actual readings at a nearby position of known coordinates, to reduce error from anomalous propagation.

digital computer. A computer that solves mathematical

equations, providing numerical answers on a counter.

dip. The vertical angle between the horizontal and the line of sight to the visible horizon.

dip short. The vertical angle between the horizontal and the line of sight to a water line between the observer and his visible horizon.

direct wave. A wave of radiant energy arriving directly from its source without undergoing reflection or ionospheric refraction.

direction light. A narrow beam of light, usually flanked by sectors of different colours, intended as a leading light.

distance-finding station. A radiobeacon with a synchronized sound signal.

diurnal. Daily.

diurnal circle. The apparent daily path of an astronomical body.

diurnal inequality. The difference in height between two high tides or two low tides occurring at a place during a tidal day, or the difference in velocity between two flood strengths or two ebb strengths of a tidal stream during a tidal day.

diurnal stream. A tidal-stream system consisting of one flood stream and one ebb stream each tidal day.

diurnal tide. A tide system consisting of one high tide and one low tide each tidal day.

dividers. A device consisting, in its simple form, of two legs pivoted at one end and pointed at the other, used principally for measuring distance on a chart or plotting sheet.

Doppler effect. The change of frequency of arriving radiant energy when the distance between the source and the receiver or observer is changing.

Doppler sonar navigator. A dead-reckoning device that determines velocity and position of a vessel by measurement of the Doppler effect of transmitted and echo signals of ultrasonic energy in the water.

double tide. A high tide consisting of two maxima of nearly the same height, separated by a relatively slight depression (double high tide); or a low tide consisting of two minima separated by a relatively slight elevation (double low tide).

doubling the angle on the bow. Observation of two bearings on the same object with the angle between the course line (over the ground) and the bearing line at the time of the second observation being twice that at the time of the first observation.

draughting machine. A device that can be clamped to a chart desk or table and oriented to any desired direction, where it provides means for measuring directions, guiding a pencil in drawing straight lines, and moving its straight-edge arms without changing their orientation.

drift. Speed of a water current.

drift angle. The angle between lines extending in the directions of the heading and course.

ducting. *1*. The trapping of a radio wave between two discontinuities, particularly between the surface of the Earth and a layer of the atmosphere. *2*. Similar action of sound in the atmosphere or in water.

Dutchman's log. A log consisting of a floating object and means for timing its passage by a known length of the vessel.

easting. The eastward component of a craft's motion.

ebb stream. A tidal stream flowing away from land.

echo sounder. A device for determining depth of water by measuring the time interval between transmission of an acoustic signal and return of its echo from the ocean floor.

ecliptic. The apparent annual path of the Sun round the celestial sphere.

electromagnetic log. A log that determines vessel speed through the water by measurement of electromagnetic induction.

electronic navigation. Navigation involving the use of electronics.

elevated pole. The celestial pole above the horizon.

ephemeris (pl. ephemerides). A periodical publication of astronomical data of interest primarily to astronomers.

ephemeris time. A variation of mean time based upon the revolution of the Earth in its orbit.

equation of time. The difference between mean time and apparent time.

equator. The great circle midway between the geographical poles of the Earth.

equatorial projection. A map projection centred at the equator.

equatorial stream. Tidal stream associated with an equatorial tide.

equatorial tide. Tide occurring when the Moon is over the equator, characterized by minimum diurnal inequality.

equilibrium tide. A hypothetical tide consisting of the vector sum of the lunar and solar tides, assuming instant reaction of the water to tidal forces and absence of friction and the effect of intervening land.

equinoctial. Celestial equator.

equinoctial stream. Tidal stream associated with an equinoctial tide.

equinoctial tide. Tide occurring at the time of an equinox, when the Sun is over the equator, characterized by greater than average range of spring tide.

equinox. One of the two points of intersection of the ecliptic and the celestial equator.

error. The difference between an indicated value and the correct or true value.

establishment. Mean high water lunitidal interval.

estimated position. Any position, other than a dead reckoning position, established from incomplete data or data of questionable accuracy.

ex-meridian observation. An observation of the altitude of an astronomical body near the celestial meridian, for conversion to a meridian altitude.

extremely high frequency. Frequency of 30 to 300 GHz.

extremely low frequency. Frequency 1 to 3,000 Hz.

fading. Decrease in field strength of arriving radio signals because of changes in the transmission medium.

fathom. Six feet, or 1.8288 metres; a linear unit used for indicating depth.

first point of Aries. Vernal equinox.

fix. An accurate position determined relative to one or more external reference points.

flashing (light). Emitting light that is eclipsed at regular intervals, the duration of light being less than that of darkness.

Flinders bar. A bar of soft unmagnetized iron placed in a vertical position near a magnetic compass to correct for deviation caused by induced magnetism in vertical soft iron of the craft.

flood stream. A tidal stream flowing toward land.

form line. An approximate contour without a stated elevation.

gain (of an aerial). The increase in signal strength in the desired arc of transmission over the average in all directions if there were no directivity.

gain (of a receiver). Signal amplification given in a receiver.

Gaussian distribution. Probability and magnitude of random errors as indicated by a curve the ordinate of which represents probability and the abscissa represents magnitude, based upon a tabulation of the errors involved.

Gaussin error. Deviation of a magnetic compass resulting from transient induced magnetism in a vessel's structure after removal of the inducting force.

geographical mile. One minute of arc of the equator.

geographical plot. True plot.

geographical pole. Either intersection of the surface of the Earth and the Earth's axis of rotation.

geographical position. *1.* Sub-point. *2.* A position defined by geographical coordinates, usually latitude and longitude.

geographical range. The extreme distance at which an object can be expected to be seen at a given height of eye if limited only by the curvature of the Earth's surface.

geoid. The figure of the Earth as defined by mean sea level over the entire Earth.

geomagnetic meridian. A semi-great circle joining the geomagnetic poles.

geomagnetic pole. Either intersection of the surface of the Earth and the axis of a uniform geomagnetic field approximating the actual magnetic field of the Earth.

geomagnetism. Magnetism of the Earth.

geometric dilution of position. The decrease in accuracy of position in part of a coverage area because of the geometry of a family of position lines.

geometric projection. A map projection in which the surface of a sphere or spheroid is projected to a developable surface (one capable of being flattened without distortion) by means of projecting lines emanating from one point (including infinity).

geometrical horizon. The intersection of the celestial sphere and an infinite number of straight lines from the eye of the observer tangent to the surface of the Earth.

ghost. A radar echo returned by a discontinuity in the atmosphere or other non-apparent target.

giga-. A prefix meaning 1,000,000,000.

gnomonic projection. A geometric, zenithal map projection with the centre of the sphere or spheroid as the origin of the projecting lines.

goniometer. An instrument for measuring angles.

graduation error. Imperfection in the graduations of the scale of an instrument.

graticule. The network of lines representing parallels and meridians.

great circle. The intersection of the surface of a sphere with a plane through its centre.

great-circle chart. A chart on the gnomonic projection.

great-circle sailing. Solution of problems related to an arc of a great circle between two places.

Greenwich apparent time. Apparent time at the Greenwich meridian.

Greenwich hour angle. Angular distance, along a parallel of declination, west of the Greenwich celestial meridian.

Greenwich mean time. Mean time at the Greenwich meridian.

Greenwich sidereal time. Sidereal time at the Greenwich meridian.

grid. A family of parallel lines superimposed on a chart or plotting sheet to serve as a directional reference.

grid navigation. Navigation relating to a grid.

grid north. An arbitrary reference direction relative to a grid, especially one parallel, on the chart, to the prime meridian.

grid variation. The difference between grid north and magnetic north.

grivation. Grid variation.

ground log. A log consisting of a weight attached to a line, for measuring distance travelled over the ground.

ground wave. A radio wave following the curvature of the Earth because of interaction with the Earth.

gyro compass. A compass that uses one or more meridian-seeking gyroscopes as its directive element.

gyro error. The difference between true north and gyro north.

gyro north. North as indicated by a gyro compass.

hachures. Short lines, on a map or chart, extending along a slope, perpendicular to contours.

hack. Hack watch.

hack watch. A watch for timing astro observations, setting ship's clocks, and general purposes at sea.

half-tide level. The level midway between mean high water and mean low water.

hand lead. A light sounding lead with a short lead line.

hard iron. Magnetic material with high capability for retaining permanent magnetism.

hardware. The physical material constituting a computer, instrument, etc.

harmonic constituent. A sine wave representing one element of tide or tidal stream.

heading. Either the instantaneous (ship's head) or average (course steered) forward direction of the longitudinal axis of a craft.

heading angle. Heading reckoned from 0° at the reference direction clockwise or anticlockwise through 90° or 180°.

heading line. A line extending in the direction of a heading.

heeling error. The change in deviation of a magnetic compass when a vessel heels.

heeling magnet. A permanent magnet used to correct heeling error.

Hertz. One cycle per second; a unit for indicating frequency.

high frequency. Frequency of 3 to 30 MHz.

high tide. Maximum depth of water as a result of a rising tide.

high water. High tide.

homing. Navigating by maintaining constant some navigational coordinate.

horizon. That great circle of the celestial sphere midway between the zenith and nadir, or a line approximating this circle.

horizontal parallax. Geocentric parallax of an astronomical body on the horizon.

hour angle. Angular distance, along a parallel of declination, west of a reference celestial meridian or hour circle.

hour circle. A semi-great circle of the celestial sphere connecting the celestial poles and another fixed point on the surface of the sphere.

hydraulic stream. A tidal stream occurring in a channel or strait because of a difference in tide level at opposite ends.

hyperbolic position line. A position line all points of which have the same difference in distance from two points.

impeller-type log. A log that determines vessel speed relative to water by measurement of an electric current generated by a small propeller that is rotated by the relative motion of water as the vessel moves through it.

index error. The error in the reading of an instrument

resulting from a difference between the zero of the scale and the index when a zero reading should be indicated.

induced magnetism. Magnetism acquired by presence in a magnetic field.

inertial navigator. A dead-reckoning device that determines position, velocity, and heading of a craft by measurement and computer processing of accelerations since leaving a position of known coordinates.

inspection tables. Tables providing tabulated solutions of mathematical equations, particularly those relating to the navigational triangle.

instrument error. Inaccuracy of an instrument because of imperfections in its manufacture.

intercept. The difference between calculated and observed altitudes.

intercept terminal point. The foot of a perpendicular from an assumed position to an astro position line.

international nautical mile. The linear unit internationally accepted as the nautical mile; 1,852 metres.

interrogator. A radio transmitter that sends a signal to trigger a transponder.

ionosphere. Layers of ionized gas in the upper portion of the Earth's atmosphere.

irradiation. The apparent enlargement of a bright area observed adjacent to a darker area.

isogonic line. A line connecting points of equal magnetic variation.

isogriv. A line connecting points of equal grid variation.

isophase (light). Emitting light that is eclipsed at regular intervals, with light and dark periods of equal duration.

jamming. Intentional transmission or reradiation of radio signals to interfere with reception of desired signals by the intended receiver.

kilo-. A prefix meaning 1,000.

knot. One nautical mile per hour.

Lambert conformal projection. An orthomorphic map projection in which the surface of a sphere or spheroid is conceived as developed on a secant cone that intersects the sphere or spheroid at two standard parallels and is then flattened to form a plane.

land effect. Coastal refraction.

landfall. The first visual or radar contact with land approached from seaward.

landfall light. The first light to be seen by an observer approaching a coast from the open sea.

landmark. A conspicuous object on land, serving as an indicator for navigation or warning of a craft.

lane. A section of the coverage area of a phase-comparison navigation system in which there is a complete cycle of phase difference of two signals.

lane ambiguity. Duplication of phase difference in different lanes.

lane slippage. Loss of one or more units in the lane count of a phase-comparison navigation system.

laser. Acronym for *l*ight *a*mplification by *s*timulated *e*mission of *r*adiation; a device for producing a narrow, intense beam of light amplified and focused by an appropriate input signal.

laser log. A log that determines craft speed by measurement of the Doppler effect of transmitted and echo signals of a laser.

lateral system. A buoyage system in which the type, colour, and number (if any) of each buoy relate to its position relative to a channel traversed in a specified direction.

latitude. Angular distance north or south of the equator.

latitude factor. Change of latitude along a position line for unit change of longitude.

latitude line. A position line extending in an east–west direction, or nearly so.

lattice. The pattern formed by intersecting families of position lines.

lead. Sounding lead.

lead line. The line attached to a sounding lead.

leader cable. An energized cable the signals or magnetic field of which guides a suitably-equipped vessel along the route of the cable.

leading light(s). A direction light or transit, or range, lights marking a channel or safe route through dangers.

leading line. The line indicated by leading marks, or a leading light or lights, as a safe route.

leading marks. Marks constituting a transit, or range, marking a channel or safe route through dangers.

leeway. The leeward motion of a vessel caused by wind, expressed as an angle, speed, or distance.

light station. A place having structures and equipment for operating a major navigational light and any associated aids.

light tower. A tower established in a water area to exhibit a major navigational light.

light vessel. Lightship.

lighthouse. A distinctive structure exhibiting a major navigational light.

lights in line. Transit, or range, lights marking a boundary of a hazard or a lone point or line to be avoided.

lightship. A distinctively-marked vessel anchored at an assigned place to exhibit a major navigational light.

limb. The upper or lower half of the outer edge of an astronomical body.

line of position. Position line.

line of shoot. The direction in which a group of observed objects provides the greatest fixing accuracy.

line of soundings. A series of soundings measured as a vessel proceeds on its way, used as a means for determining the position of the vessel.

local apparent noon. The instant of upper transit of the apparent Sun.

local apparent time. Apparent time at a specified meridian.

local hour angle. Angular distance, along a parallel of declination, west of a specified celestial meridian.

local magnetic disturbance. Magnetic anomaly.

local mean time. Mean time at a specified meridian.

local sidereal time. Sidereal time at a specified meridian.

log. A device for measuring speed or distance travelled.

longitude. Angular distance, along a parallel, between the prime meridian and a specified meridian.

longitude factor. Change of longitude along a position line for unit change of latitude.

longitude line. A position line extending in a north–south direction, or nearly so.

loom. The glow of a light by reflection from particles in the atmosphere.

looming. Increase in the apparent elevation of an object by abnormal atmospheric refraction.

low frequency. Frequency of 30 to 300 kHz.

low tide. Minimum depth of water as a result of a falling tide.

low water. Low tide.

lower branch. That half of a celestial meridian through the nadir.

lower limb. The limb having the lesser altitude.

lower transit. The passage of an astronomical body across the lower branch of a celestial meridian.

loxodrome. An oblique rhumb line.

lubber line. The reference mark of a direction-indicating instrument, in line with the forward direction along the longitudinal axis of a craft.

luminous range. The extreme distance at which a light can be expected to be seen if there is no intervening obstruction.

lunar distance. The angle between the Moon and another astronomical body.

lunar month. One revolution of the Moon around the Earth.

lunitidal interval. The time interval between upper or lower transit of the Moon and the next high tide or low tide.

magnetic anomaly. A local departure from the normal pattern of the Earth's magnetic field.

magnetic compass. A compass that depends upon the magnetic field of the Earth for its directive force.

magnetic couple. The effect of a magnetic pole in attracting one end of the directive element of a magnetic compass and repelling the other end, tending to cause rotation of the directive element.

magnetic dip. The vertical angle between the horizontal and the line of force of the Earth's magnetic field.

magnetic equator. The line connecting all points of zero magnetic dip on the surface of the Earth.

magnetic field. The space in which magnetism exists.

magnetic inclination. Magnetic dip.

magnetic induction. The act or process by which material becomes magnetized when it is in a magnetic field.

magnetic latitude. The angle having a tangent half that of the magnetic dip.

magnetic line of force. A closed line in a magnetic field indicating the direction of magnetic force.

magnetic meridian. The horizontal component of a line of force of the Earth's magnetic field.

magnetic north. A horizontal reference direction identified as north along a magnetic meridian.

magnetic pole. *1.* A point on the surface of the Earth at which magnetic dip is 90°. *2.* Either of the two points of a magnet at which the magnetic force is greatest.

magnetic signature. The trace of the change in the Earth's magnetic field as a vessel passes over a point where the change is measured.

magnetic storm. Sudden ionospheric disturbance.

magnitude. Relative brightness of an astronomical body.

magnitude ratio. The ratio of relative brightness of two astronomical bodies differing in magnitude by 1.0: 2.512, the fifth root of 100.

map projection. A scheme for depicting all or part of the surface of a sphere or spheroid on a flat surface.

mark. *1.* A conspicuous object, structure, or light serving as an indicator for navigation or warning of a craft. *2.* Something attached to a lead line to indicate a specified length of the line.

master compass. A compass having repeaters.

master station. A transmitting station that controls the timing of transmissions from one or more related stations.

maximum usable frequency. The highest frequency at which sky waves can be received from a specified transmitting station.

mean latitude. The mean value of latitude along a rhumb line between two points, differing from middle latitude because of acceleration in convergence of the meridians with increasing latitude.

mean refraction correction. The correction applied to a sextant altitude to correct for refraction of the ray of light from an astronomical body.

mean sea level. The average level of the ocean.

mean Sun. A fictitious Sun conceived as moving eastward along the celestial equator at the average rate of the apparent Sun along the ecliptic.

mean time. Time based upon rotation of the Earth relative to the mean Sun.

measured distance. An accurately-measured and suitably-marked distance, usually one nautical mile, intended for measurement of vessel speed and calibration of logs.

medium frequency. Frequency of 300 to 3,000 kHz.

mega-. A prefix meaning 1,000,000.

Mercator projection. A cylindrical map projection having equal expansion of parallels and meridians.

Mercator sailing. Mathematical solution of a plot on a Mercator chart or plotting sheet.

meridian. A semi-great circle joining the geographical poles of the Earth.

meridian altitude. Altitude of an astronomical body on the celestial meridian.

meridian angle. Angular distance, along a parallel of declination, east or west of a specified celestial meridian.

meridian observation. Measurement of meridian altitude.

meridian passage. Meridian transit.

meridian sailing. Mathematical solution of problems of dead reckoning for motion along a meridian.

meridian transit. The passage of an astronomical body across a celestial meridian.

meridional difference. The algebraic difference of meridional parts of two parallels.

meridional parts. The length of a meridional arc between the equator and any given parallel on a Mercator chart, expressed in units of one minute of longitude at the equator.

meterological tide. Rise or fall of sea level caused by meteorological conditions.

meterological visibility. The greatest distance at which a black object of suitable size can be seen and identified against the horizon sky under standard conditions of threshold contrast.

microcomputer. A full-scale computer in miniature.

microsecond. One-millionth of a second.

microwaves. Waves shorter than one metre.

mid-latitude sailing. Middle-latitude sailing.

middle latitude. The latitude midway between two parallels.

middle-latitude sailing. Combined plane and parallel sailing with the use of middle latitude for interconversion of departure and longitude difference.

millimetric waves. Extremely high-frequency waves.

millisecond. One-thousandth of a second.

mixed stream. A tidal stream system having strong diurnal and semi-diurnal components.

mixed tide. A tidal system having strong diurnal and semi-diurnal components.

modulation. Variation of some characteristic of a radio wave, called a *carrier wave*, in accordance with instantaneous values of another wave, called the *modulating wave*.

most probable position. That point judged to represent most likely the actual position of a craft at any time.

multihop sky wave. A radio wave arriving after more than one refraction by the ionosphere, with reflection by the Earth's surface between refractions.

multipath. More than one path by which radiant energy travels from the transmitter to the receiver.

nadir. That point of the celestial sphere vertically below the observer.

name. The north or south designation of latitude, declination, and the celestial poles.

nanosecond. One-thousandth of a microsecond.

natural scale. A chart scale expressed as a fraction.

nautical astronomy. Navigational astronomy.

nautical chart. A chart intended for navigation afloat.

nautical mile. Generally, the length of one minute of arc of a great circle of the Earth. Specifically, the international nautical mile.

nautical twilight. The period of incomplete darkness following Sunset or preceding Sunrise when the centre of the sun is not more than 12° below the celestial horizon.

navaid. A navigational aid involving the use of radio.

navigation. The process of conducting a craft as it moves about its ways.

navigational aid. Any mark, instrument, electronic device, chart, publication, etc., of assistance in navigation.

navigational astronomy. That part of astronomy relating to astronavigation.

navigational triangle. The spherical triangle solved in sight reduction or great-circle sailing.

neap stream. Tidal stream associated with a neap tide.

neap tide. Tide occurring when the Moon is at first or third quarter, characterized by less than average range.

negative tide. A level of water lower than the tidal datum.

night effect. Disturbance of radio signals by variations in the ionosphere during the night, principally near the times of Sunrise and Sunset.

night order book. A notebook in which the Master of a vessel writes various memoranda and orders relating to the navigation of the vessel during the night, as a guide for deck watch officers.

noise. Unwanted stray signals of radiant energy.

nominal range. Luminous range in a homogeneous atmosphere with a meterological visibility of ten nautical miles.

normal distribution. Gaussian distribution.

northing. The northward component of a craft's motion.

null. Minimum or absence of signal in a directional pattern.

nun buoy. A buoy having its above-water portion in the shape of a cone or truncated cone.

nutation. Irregularities in precession of the equinoxes.

oblique projection. A map projection centred at some point or circle other than a pole or the equator.

observed altitude. Actual altitude of an astronomical body above the celestial horizon.

occulting (light). Emitting light that is eclipsed at regular intervals, the duration of light being greater than that of darkness.

octant. An optical instrument for measuring angles, primarily altitudes of astronomical bodies, and having a range of 90°.

orthographic projection. A geometric, zenithal map projection with infinity as the origin of projecting lines parallel to the axis through the point of tangency and its antipodal point.

orthomorphism. Correct representation of very small shapes.

outline chart. A plotting chart showing outlines of land areas.

parallactic angle. The navigational triangle angle at the astronomical body or destination.

parallax. Difference in apparent position of an object as viewed from different positions.

parallax in altitude. Geocentric parallax of an astronomical body at any specified altitude.

parallel. A circle of the Earth parallel to the plane of the equator.

parallel of altitude. A circle of the celestial sphere parallel to the plane of the celestial horizon.

parallel of declination. A circle of the celestial sphere parallel to the plane of the celestial equator.

parallel of latitude. Parallel.

parallel rulers. A device for transferring a direction or line to another position without change of direction.

parallel sailing. Mathematical solution of problems of dead reckoning for motion along a parallel.

pelorus. A device resembling a compass, but without a directive element, for observing bearings and azimuths.

perigee. An Earth satellite's orbital point nearest the Earth.

perigee stream. Tidal stream associated with a perigee tide.

perigee tide. Tide occurring when the Moon is at perigee, characterized by greater than average range.

period (of a light). The time interval of a complete cycle of characteristics.

periodic error. An inaccuracy that oscillates in magnitude.

personal error. A systematic error characteristic of an individual observer.

phantom bottom. A false bottom indicated by an echo sounder because of the presence of a deep scattering layer.

phase. The portion of completion of a cycle.

phase correction. The correction applied to a sextant altitude for phase of an astronomical body when the centre of the illuminated part of the body is observed.

picosecond. One-millionth of a microsecond.

pillar buoy. *1*. A buoy consisting of a tall central structure mounted on a broad, flat base. *2*. Skeleton buoy. *3*. Large Automatic Navigational Buoy, Lanby.

pilot chart. A chart presenting, principally in graphical form, accumulated meterological, oceanographic, magnetic, and miscellaneous information.

pilotage. *1*. The process of conducting a vessel through difficult waters. *2*. A pilot's fee.

pilotage waters. Areas in which pilotage is customarily used.

piloting. Pilotage.

Pitot-static log. A log determining vessel speed by measurement of dynamic water pressure by means of a Pitot tube.

Pitot tube. A double tube, one part being subject to both dynamic and static pressures, and the other part to static pressure only, for determining dynamic pressure.

plane sailing. Mathematical solution of problems of dead reckoning by considering the surface of the Earth to be a plane.

plotter. A device consisting of a protractor and one or more straight-edges to serve as guides for drawing lines in desired directions or for measuring directions of lines on a chart.

plotting chart. A chart showing a limited amount of information, intended primarily for plotting.

plotting sheet. A blank chart showing only the graticule and sometimes one or more compass roses.

point of departure. The last fix relative to land, as a vessel heads out to sea.

polar circle. The parallel (N. or S.) equal to the maximum co-declination of the Sun.

polar distance. Angular distance from a celestial pole.

polar motion. Wobbling motion of the geographical poles of the Earth, affecting measurement of universal time.

polar projection. A map projection centred at a geographical pole.

polarization (of radio waves). The direction of vibration.

polarization error. Night effect.

pole. Either of two opposite places or centres of force.

polyconic projection. A map projection in which the surface of a sphere or spheroid is conceived as developed on a series of tangent cones that are then flattened to form a plane.

position angle. Parallactic angle.

position fixing. Establishment of a craft's position by means of one or more external reference points.

position line. A line on which a craft is presumed to be located.

precalculated altitude. Altitude of an astronomical body calculated before it is observed, and altered by application of sextant altitude-corrections applied with reversed signs.

precession of the equinoxes. Conical motion of the Earth's rotational axis about the vertical to the plane of the ecliptic, caused by the attractive force of other bodies of the solar system on the equatorial bulge of the Earth, and resulting in a slow drift of the equinoxes and solstices.

precipitation static. Atmospherics associated with precipitation.

precision. The refinement to which a value is stated.

primary. An astronomical body around which another body revolves.

primary great circle. The great circle 90° from the poles of a system of spherical coordinates.

primary radar. Radar using reflections only.

prime meridian. The meridian from which longitude is reckoned.

prime vertical. Prime vertical circle.

prime vertical circle. The vertical circle through the east or west point of the horizon.

principal vertical circle. The vertical circle through the true north point of the horizon.

prismatic error. The error resulting from lack of parallelism of the two faces of an optical element.

proper motion. *1.* The component of motion of an astronomical body perpendicular to the line of sight. *2.* True motion of a craft, as contrasted with relative movement.

quadrant. An optical instrument for measuring angles, primarily altitudes of astronomical bodies, and having a range of 180°.

quadrantal correctors. Masses of soft iron placed near the magnetic compass to correct for quadrantal deviation.

quadrantal deviation. Deviation that changes sign in adjacent quadrants.

quadrantal error. An error that changes sign in adjacent quadrants.

quintant. An optical instrument for measuring angles, primarily altitudes of astronomical bodies, and having a range of 144°.

racon. Acronym for *ra*dar bea*con*; a radar transponder beacon that transmits a characteristic signal when triggered by radar.

radar. Acronym for *ra*dio *d*etection *a*nd *r*anging; a device for determining distance to an object by measuring the time interval between transmission of a beamed radio signal and return of an echo or a transmitted signal from a transponder.

radar beacon. A radiobeacon transmitting a characteristic signal on radar frequency, permitting a suitably-equipped craft to determine the bearing and in some cases the distance of the beacon from the craft.

radar horizon. Radio horizon of a radar aerial.

radar reflector. Corner reflector.

radar station. A coastal radar installation giving assistance to vessels upon request.

radial error. An uncertainty expressed as the radius of a circle enclosing some percentage of all errors.

radio astronomy. The science dealing with natural radiation at radio and thermal frequencies from extraterrestrial sources.

radio direction-finder. A device for determining the direction of arrival of radio signals by measuring the orientation of the wave front.

radio direction-finder station. An external station with a radio direction-finder and means of communicating the measured directions to the originators of the signals.

radio horizon. The line at which direct waves from a radio transmitting aerial become tangent the Earth's surface.

radio sextant. A device for measurement of the altitude and direction of a radio star.

radio spectrum. The range of electromagnetic radiation suitable for radio communication.

radio star. An extraterrestrial source of natural radiation at radio frequency.

radiobeacon. A radio station transmitting a characteristic signal to permit a suitably-equipped craft to determine its direction, distance, or position relative to the station.

radiodetermination. Determination of position, or obtaining information relating to position, by means of the propagation properties of radio waves.

radiolocation. Radiodetermination used for purposes other than navigation.

radionavigation. Radiodetermination used for navigation, including obstruction warning.

ramark. A radar beacon that transmits independently on radar frequency, providing means for a suitably-equipped craft to determine the direction of the beacon.

random error. An error unpredictable as to magnitude or sign.

range. *1.* Transit. *2.* The maximum distance at which a usable signal of radiant energy can be received.

range (of tide). The difference in height of high and low tides.

rate error. An inaccuracy that changes uniformly with change of some parameter.

rectangular distribution. Probability and magnitude of errors as indicated by a rectangle, the ordinate of which represents probability and the abscissa represents magnitude.

rectangular projection. A cylindrical map projection with uniform spacing of both parallels and meridians.

reduction of a sounding. Adjustment of a sounding to the corresponding value relative to the chart datum.

reduction to the meridian. Adjustment of an ex-meridian altitude to the equivalent meridian altitude.

reference station. A place for which full tidal or tidal current data are tabulated in United States tide or tidal current tables.

reflection. The return, back into the medium from which it approached, of radiant energy impinging on a surface of discontinuity.

reflection plotter. A device fitted over a radar scope to facilitate plotting for collision avoidance.

refraction. *1.* Change in direction of a wave front as a wave changes speed progressively along its length. *2.* Change in direction of a ray of radiant energy as it passes obliquely into a medium of different density.

relative accuracy. Difference in error of position of two craft using the same means of position determination.

relative azimuth. Azimuth using heading as the reference direction.

relative bearing. Bearing using heading as the reference direction.

relative movement. Apparent motion, especially with reference to motions of craft relative to one another.

relative plot. A plot of the movements of a craft relative to a reference point, particularly one in motion.

repeatable accuracy. Accuracy with which a craft can return to a position previously determined in the same manner.

repeater. A device for repetition of the indications of an instrument or device.

residual deviation. Deviation remaining after compass correction.

resolution. The separation, by radar or optics, of parts of an object or of multiple objects close together.

retentivity. The ability to retain magnetism after removal of the magnetizing force.

retired (transferred) position line. A position line moved back to allow for motion of the observer between the earlier time to which the line is retired and the time of observation.

reversing stream. A tidal stream flowing alternately in approximately reciprocal directions.

revolution. Motion of an astronomical body along its orbit.

revolver. Swinger.

rhumb line. A line on the surface of the Earth maintaining a constant angle with respect to all meridians.

right ascension. Angular distance, along a parallel of declination, east of the hour circle of the vernal equinox.

rise (of the tide). The height of a high-water reference level above the tidal datum.

rotary stream. A tidal stream changing its direction of flow progressively through 360° once or twice each tidal day.

rotation. Turning of an astronomical body about an axis within the body.

round of sights. A group of astronomical observations made over a short period of time, as during twilight.

rounding-off error. Inaccuracy resulting from reduction of the number of significant figures of a quantity.

running fix. A fix of which the position lines are not obtained simultaneously, or nearly so, but are adjusted to a common time.

rhythm. The sequence and duration of light and dark intervals of a light.

sailing directions. A book of descriptive material relating to coastal and offshore features, aids to navigation, facilities, and other information supplementing data shown on nautical charts.

sailings. Methods of solving various problems of dead reckoning by calculation.

sea-air temperature difference correction. The correction applied to a sextant altitude to correct for error in tabulated dip because of difference in the temperature of the water and air at their interface.

sea buoy. A buoy anchored outside an estuary, especially the outermost buoy marking the entrance.

sea mile. One minute of arc of a meridian.

sea position. The position of a craft determined by means of the course steered and the speed through the water; used when dead reckoning is relative to the ground.

sea return. Radar echoes reflected from the sea.

seamark. A conspicuous object in or near the water serving as an indicator or warning to vessels.

secondary port. A place for which British tide tables give tidal differences to be applied to the data for a stated standard port, or the four principal harmonic constituents, to determine the corresponding data at the secondary port.

secondary radar. Radar using return signals transmitted by a transponder triggered by signals from the radar.

secondary station. A slave station of the loran C system.

sector (of a light). The arc, defined by limiting bearings, in which a navigational light has designated characteristics or is obscured.

secular change. Long-term change in the Earth's magnetic field.

seiche. A long-period free oscillation of the water in an enclosed or semi-enclosed basin.

seismic sea wave. A tsunami caused by a submarine earthquake.

semi-circular deviation. Deviation that changes sign in opposite semi-circles.

semi-diameter. Half the angle, at the observer's eye, subtended by the visible disc of an astronomical body.

semi-diurnal stream. A tidal stream system consisting of two flood streams and two ebb streams each tidal day, with relatively little diurnal inequality.

semi-diurnal tide. A tide system consisting of two high tides and two low tides each tidal day, with relatively little diurnal inequality.

sense aerial. An aerial used to resolve ambiguity in a directional aerial.

sensible horizon. A small circle of the celestial sphere marking the intersection of a plane parallel to the plane of the celestial horizon, through the eye of the observer.

set. The direction toward which a water current flows.

sextant. A double-reflecting, optical instrument for measuring angles, primarily altitudes of astronomical bodies; particularly one having an arc of 60° (120° graduations).

sextant adjustment. The process of determining and removing or reducing the errors of a sextant.

sextant altitude. Altitude of an astronomical body as measured by a sextant.

ship's head. The instantaneous forward direction along the longitudinal axis of a vessel.

side error. The error in the reading of a marine sextant resulting from non-perpendicularity of the horizon glass to the frame.

sidereal. Of or pertaining to stars.

sidereal hour angle. Angular distance, along a parallel of declination, west of the hour circle of the vernal equinox.

sidereal time. Time based upon rotation of the Earth relative to the vernal equinox.

sight. A timed observation of the altitude, and sometimes also the azimuth, of an astronomical body for establishing a position line; or the data obtained by such observation.

sight reduction. The process of converting an astronomical observation or observations to position lines or the position of the observer.

sinking. Decrease in the apparent elevation of an object by subnormal atmospheric refraction.

skeleton buoy. A buoy consisting of a float surmounted by a small skeleton tower.

skip distance. The minimum distance from a transmitting aerial at which sky waves at a specified frequency can be received.

skip zone. The area between the maximum limit of reception of ground waves and the minimum limit of reception of sky waves, in which no signal is received.

sky wave. A radio wave arriving after being bent back toward Earth by refraction in the ionosphere.

slack water. Absence of flow of a tidal stream as it reverses its direction of flow.

slave station. A transmitting station controlled by another, called the *master station.*

small circle. The intersection of the surface of a sphere with a plane not through its centre.

soft iron. Magnetic material with low retentivity.

software. The instructions, collectively, to a digital computer.

solstice. One of the two points of the ecliptic farthest from the celestial equator.

solstitial stream. Tidal stream associated with a solstitial tide.

solstitial tide. Tide occurring at the time of a solstice, characterized by greater than average range of tropic tides.

sonar. Acronym for *s*ound *n*avigation *a*nd *r*anging; a device for determining distance off by measurement of the elapsed time from transmission of an acoustic signal in the water to return of an echo.

sounding. Depth of water or its measurement.

sounding lead. A weight attached to a lead line for sounding.

southing. The southward component of a craft's motion.

spar buoy. A buoy in the shape of a spar floating nearly vertically.

speed line. A position line perpendicular to a course line, or nearly so, providing an indication of speed being made good over the ground.

speedometer. A log that determines vessel speed by measurement of dynamic pressure of water against a strut protruding from the hull.

spillover. Reception of radio signals of a frequency different from that to which the receiver is tuned.

spring stream. Tidal stream associated with a spring tide.

spring tide. Tide occurring when the Moon is at new or full phase, characterized by greater than average range.

stable platform. A device designed to maintain its orientation with respect to the horizontal and a reference direction.

stadimeter. An instrument for determining the distance to an object by measurement of the angle subtended at the observer by a linear dimension of the object.

stage (or state) of the tide. Condition of the tide at any time.

stand (of the tide). Absence of change in water level at high tide or low tide.

standard compass. A magnetic compass designated as the standard reference for magnetic directions aboard a vessel.

standard parallel. A parallel of a map along which the

scale is the stated scale of the map.

standard port. A place for which full tidal or tidal-stream data are recorded in British tide tables.

standard time. The legal time at a place, usually that when summer time is not in effect.

star finder. A device using a map projection to facilitate identification of astronomical bodies.

star globe. A globe representing the celestial sphere, on which the positions of stars are shown.

static. Atmospherics.

station buoy. A small buoy marking the assigned station of a lightship or major buoy, to serve as a marker if the principal aid is off station or missing.

station pointer. A protractor having three arms, one fixed and two rotatable, used for locating the position of a craft from measured horizontal angles between charted objects.

statute mile. The land mile of 1,609.344 metres (5,280 feet).

stereographic projection. A geometric, zenithal map projection with the point antipodal to the point of tangency as the origin of projecting lines.

storm surge. Storm wave.

storm wave. A long wave, or crest of a wave, produced by wind and having the effect of a higher or lower than normal tide, particularly such a wave that overflows adjacent land with destructive effect.

strength (of a tidal stream). Maximum velocity.

sub point. That point on the Earth at which a specified point, usually an astronomical body, on the celestial sphere is in the zenith at a specified time.

subordinate station. A place for which United States tide or tidal current tables give tidal differences to be applied to the data for a stated *reference station* to determine the corresponding data at the subordinate station.

subpermanent magnetism. Magnetism that dissipates slowly over a relatively long period of time.

sudden ionospheric disturbance. Erratic change in the

ionosphere, associated with solar flares.

summer solstice. The solstice occupied by the Sun about June 21.

Sumner line. Generally, any astro position line. Specifically, such a line established by drawing a straight line through two points on the circle of equal altitude.

super high frequency. Frequency of 3 to 30 GHz.

swinger. A pair of horizontal angles between three objects measured at a point on a circle through the objects.

swinging ship. Placing a craft on various headings and determining deviation on each heading.

swinging the arc. The process of rotating a sextant about the line of sight to determine the vertical circle of the body.

System A. The buoyage system proposed by the International Association of Lighthouse Authorities (IALA) in 1976.

system accuracy. The accuracy of a navigation system exclusive of errors introduced by its users, geodesy, and cartography.

System B. A buoyage system similar to System A, considered for those countries preferring red to starboard for channel markings.

systematic error. An inaccuracy that follows some law by which it might be predicted.

taffrail log. A log consisting of a rotor turned by relative motion of water past it as it is towed by a vessel, with a suitable indicator to show distance travelled relative to the water.

taking departure. Establishing the best fix obtainable to serve as the origin for dead reckoning as one leaves land behind.

temperature–pressure correction. Combined air temperature–atmospheric pressure correction.

three-arm protractor. Station pointer.

tidal current. Tidal stream.

tidal cycle. A complete set of tidal conditions occurring between repetition of some periodic phenomenon, as during a tidal day.

tidal datum. A level of the sea used as a reference for indicating heights of tide.

tidal day. The period from a high tide to the corresponding high tide approximately one day later, averaging about 24 hours 50 minutes in length.

tidal stream. Water in essentially horizontal motion because of tidal forces.

tidal wave. Tide wave. The expression is popularly used incorrectly as the equivalent of tsunami or storm wave.

tide. The periodic rise and fall of the surface of the ocean.

tide staff. A vertical pole set in the ground and marked with graduations by which the height of the tide can be determined by visual observation.

tide wave. The crest and accompanying troughs (of water) created by tidal forces.

tide pole. Tide staff.

tilt error. The error introduced in the measurement of a direction or angle when the measurement plane differs from the wanted plane.

time diagram. A diagram on the plane of the celestial equator.

time sight. Observation of an astronomical body for determination of longitude by calculation of meridian angle and its comparison with Greenwich hour angle; and, by extension, the data.

time zone. An area in all parts of which the same zone time is kept.

topmark. A distinctive shape placed at the top of a buoy or beacon.

total drift. The total distance travelled by a water current over a specified period of time.

track. The path followed, or proposed or expected to be followed, by a craft or other moving entity, such as a storm centre; and, by extension, the direction of such a path.

track angle. The direction of a track reckoned from 0° at the reference direction clockwise or anticlockwise through 90° or 180°.

traffic lane. A designated area for one-way traffic.

transducer. A device that transforms energy from one form to another, as from electrical to acoustic.

transfer. The distance a vessel travels perpendicular to its initial direction of motion in making a turn.

transit. Two objects in line.

transmitting compass. A compass having means for transmitting its indications to other locations.

transponder. A combined receiver–transmitter that transmits a signal when triggered by an incoming signal.

transverse Mercator projection. A map projection constructed on the mercator principle with the cylinder tangent along a meridian.

traverse. A track consisting of multiple course lines.

traverse sailing. Mathematical solution for the resultant course and distance when there are multiple courses.

traverse table. A table of relative values of various parts of plane right triangles, for use in solving such triangles.

tropic stream. Tidal stream associated with a tropic tide.

tropic tide. Tide occurring when the Moon is at maximum declination, characterized by maximum diurnal inequality in range of the tide.

true altitude. Observed altitude.

true-motion radar. Radar having a display that moves with the motion of the vessel on which the radar is located, until reset, so that fixed objects remain stationary on the display.

true north. The direction of the north geographical pole.

true plot. A plot of the movements of a craft relative to the surface of the Earth.

true wind. Wind relative to the surface of the Earth.

tsunami. A gravity-wave system formed after a major short-duration disturbance of the surface of the ocean.

ultra high frequency. Frequency of 300 to 3,000 MHz.

uncorrecting. Conversion of a true direction to the equivalent magnetic, compass, or gyro direction, or a magnetic direction to the equivalent compass direction.

Uniform System. The buoyage system designed by a League of Nations subcommittee in 1936 to serve as a standard system for all countries.

universal time. A very close approximation of Greenwich mean time based upon rotation of the Earth, designated UT_0 as observed, UT_1 when a correction is applied for polar motion, and $UT°_2$ when an additional correction is applied for seasonal variation in the rotation rate of the Earth.

upper branch. That half of a celestial meridian through the zenith.

upper limb. The limb having the greater altitude.

upper transit. The passage of an astronomical body across the upper branch of a celestial meridian.

variation. The difference between true north and magnetic north.

velocity. *1.* Rate of motion in a designated direction. *2.* Speed of a tidal stream.

vernal equinox. That equinox at which the Sun crosses the celestial equator from south to north.

vertical circle. A semi-great circle joining the zenith and nadir.

very high frequency. Frequency of 30 to 300 MHz.

very low frequency. Frequency of 10 to 30 kHz.

visible horizon. The line where Earth and sky appear to meet.

watch error. The difference between watch time and the correct time, usually zone time.

watch rate. Change of watch error in unit time, generally expressed as seconds per day.

water position. Sea position.

weather routing. Determination of the most favourable route for a particular voyage, based upon predictions of weather, seas, ice, and ocean currents to be encountered and upon vessel characteristics and loading.

westing. The westward component of a craft's motion.

winter solstice. The solstice occupied by the Sun about December 22.

zenith. That point of the celestial sphere vertically overhead.

zenith distance. Angular distance from the zenith.

zenithal projection. A map projection in which the

surface of a sphere or spheroid is conceived as developed on a tangent or secant plane.

zone description. The number, with its sign, applied to zone time to convert it to the corresponding Greenwich mean time.

zone meridian. A reference meridian for zone time.

zone time. Mean time at a standard reference meridian whose time is kept throughout a designated area.

APPENDIX C

Abbreviations

A, amplitude, augmentation, away (intercept).

a, acceleration, altitude factor, assumed, equatorial radius of Earth, intercept.

a_0, first part of Polaris correction.

a_1, second part of Polaris correction.

a_2, third part of Polaris correction.

AA, the *Air Almanac.*

add'l, additional.

a **dec,** assumed declination.

AERO, aeronautical.

*a***L,** assumed latitude.

*a***Lo,** assumed longitude.

Alt, alternating (light).

alt, altitude.

Alt F Fl, alternating fixed and flashing (light).

Alt F Gp Fl, alternating fixed and group flashing (light).

Alt Fl, alternating flashing (light).

Alt Gp Fl, alternating group flashing (light).

Alt Occ, alternating occulting (light).

AM, amplitude modulation.

a.m., ante meridiem (before noon).

Amp, amplitude.

AP, assumed position.

App alt, apparent altitude.

ASF, additional secondary phase factor.

astro, astronomical, astronomical navigation.

AT, atomic clock time.

AU, astronomical unit.

Aug, augmentation.

Az, azimuth, azimuth angle.

*a*λ, assumed longitude.

B, atmospheric pressure correction, barometric (atmospheric) pressure, bearing, bearing angle, black, magnetic flux density.

b, polar radius of Earth.

Bn, beacon, bearing.

brg, bearing.

brng, bearing.

C, acceleration correction, Celsius, chronometer time, compass (direction), correction, course, course angle.

cab, cable(s).

CAS, collision avoidance system.

CB, compass bearing.

CC, chronometer correction, compass course.

CE, chronometer error, compass error.

cec, centicycle.

cel, centilane.

CH, compass heading.

CHY, chimney.

chron, chronometer.

cm, centimetre(s).

CMG, course made good.

Cn, course.

Co, course.

COG, course over the ground.

co-L, co-latitude.

conv., conversion.

corr, correction.

cos, cosine.

cot, cotangent.

CP, chosen position.

CPA, closest point of approach.

CRT, cathode ray tube.

C–S, contrary–same.

csc, cosecant.

ctr, centre.

CUP, cupola.

CW, continuous wave.

CZn, compass azimuth.

D, deviation, dip, distance, drift, drift angle, lunar distance.

D_V, distance from point of departure to vertex of great circle.

D_{VX}, distance along a great circle from its vertex to any designated point.

d, declination, difference, dip, distance, declination change in one hour.

dec, declination.

Dec Inc, declination increment.

deg, degree(s).

dep, departure.

dev, deviation.

DFS, distance finding station.

DG, degaussing.

diff, difference.

dist, distance.

d lat, latitude difference.

DLo, longitude difference.

DLo_V, longitude difference between point of departure and vertex of great circle.

DLo_{VX}, longitude difference between the vertex of a great circle and any designated point on the great circle.

d long, longitude difference.

DME, distance measuring equipment.

d mer parts, meridional difference.

DMP, meridional difference.

DR, dead reckoning, dead reckoning position.

Dr, drift, drift angle.

DRM, direction of relative movement.

Ds, dip short of the horizon.

ds, dip short of the horizon.

DSD, double second difference.

$d\lambda$, longitude difference.

E., east.

EHF, extremely high frequency.

E Int, equal interval (light).

ELF, extremely low frequency.

EM, electromagnetic.

EP, estimated position.

EPI, electronic position indicator.

EqSLW, equatorial spring low water.

EqT, equation of time.

ET, ephemeris time.

ETA, estimated time of arrival.

ETD, estimated time of departure.

F, Fahrenheit, fast, fixed (light), force, longitude factor, phase correction, total intensity of a magnetic field.

f, frequency, latitude factor, flattening or ellipticity.

F Fl, fixed and flashing (light).

F Gp Fl, fixed and group flashing (light).

Fl, flashing (light).

FM, frequency modulation.

fm, fathom(s).

FP, flagpole.

ft, foot, feet.

G, green, Greenwich, grid (direction), gyro (direction), upper branch of Greenwich celestial meridian.

g, gravity acceleration, lower branch of Greenwich celestial meridian.

GAT, Greenwich apparent time.

GB, grid bearing.

GC, great circle, grid course.

GDOP, geometric dilution of precision.

GE, gyro error.

GEM, ground effect machine.

GH, grid heading.

GHA, Greenwich hour angle.

GHz, gigaHertz.

GMT, Greenwich mean time.

GP, geographical position.

Gp Fl, group flashing (light).

Gp Occ, group occulting (light).

GPS, NAVSTAR Global Positioning System.

GRI, group repetition interval.

GST, Greenwich sidereal time.

GV, grid variation.

gyro, gyroscope, gyroscopic.

GZn, grid azimuth.

H, heading, height, horizontal intensity of Earth's

magnetic field, magnetic field intensity.

h, altitude, height, height of eye.

HA, hour angle.

ha, apparent altitude.

hav, haversine.

Hc, calculated altitude.

hdg, heading.

HE, heeling error, height of eye.

HF, high frequency.

HHW, higher high water.

HLW, higher low water.

Ho, observed (corrected sextant) altitude.

HP, horizontal parallax.

Hp, precalculated altitude.

hr(s), hour(s).

hs, sextant altitude.

ht, height.

HW, high water.

HWF & C, high water full and change.

Hz, Hertz.

I, instrument correction, magnetic dip.

IALA, International Association of Lighthouse Authorities.

IC, index correction.

IE, index error.

IMCO, Inter-Governmental Maritime Consultative Organization.

INS, inertial navigation system.

Int, intercept, interval.

I Qk Fl, interrupted quick flashing (light).

ISLW, Indian spring low water.

Iso, isophase (light).

ITP, intercept terminal point.

ITU, International Telecommunication Union.

J, irradiation correction.

K, knot(s).

kHz, kiloHertz.

km, kilometre(s).

kn, knot(s).

L, latitude, left, local.

L$_V$, latitude of vertex of great circle.

L$_X$, latitude of any designated point on a great circle.

l, latitude difference, logarithm, logarithmic.

LAN, local apparent noon.

LAT, local apparent time, lowest astronomical tide.

lat, latitude.

Ldg Lt, leading light.

LF, low frequency

LH, lighthouse.

LHA, local hour angle.

LHW, lower high water.

LL, lower limb.

LLW, lower low water.

Lm, middle latitude.

LMT, local mean time.

Lo, longitude.

log(s), logarithm(s), logarithmic.

long, longitude.

LOP, line of position.

LS, lightship.

LST, local sidereal time.

Lt, light.

Lt Ho, lighthouse.

LV, light vessel.

LW, low water.

M, intensity of magnetization, magnetic (direction), master station, meridional parts, million, nautical mile(s), upper branch of local celestial meridian.

m, mass, meridional difference, metre(s), lower branch of local celestial meridian.

mag, magnetic, magnitude.

max, maximum.

MB, magnetic bearing.

mb, millibar(s).

MC, magnetic course.

mer, meridian, meridional.

mer parts, meridional parts.

mer pass, meridian passage.

MF, medium frequency.
MH, magnetic heading.
MHHW, mean higher high water.
MHW, mean high water.
MHWS, mean high water springs.
MHz, megaHertz.
mi., mile(s), statute mile(s).
mid, middle.
min, minimum, minute(s).
mL, mean latitude.
m lat, mean latitude.
MLLW, mean lower low water.
MLLWS, mean lower low water springs.
MLW, mean low water.
MLWS, mean low water springs.
MON, monument.
MP, meridional parts.
MPP, most probable position.
Ms, microsecond(s).
ms, millisecond(s).
MSL, mean sea level.
MT, mean time.
MUF, maximum usable frequency.
MZn, magnetic azimuth.
N., north.
n, nautical, natural (trigonometric function).
NA, the *Nautical Almanac*.
Na, nadir.
naut., nautical.
NM, nautical mile(s).
n mi., nautical mile(s).
NNSS, United States Navy Navigational Satellite System.
ns, nanosecond(s).
obs alt, observed altitude.
Occ, occulting (light).
P, parallax, pole.
p, departure, polar distance, horizontal parallax of Venus.
PC, personal correction.

PCD, polar cap disturbance.
P in A, parallax in altitude.
PL, position line.
PM, pulse modulation.
p.m., post meridiem (afternoon).
Pn, north celestial pole, north pole.
PPI, plan position indicator.
PRR, pulse repetition rate.
Ps, south celestial pole, south pole.
ps, picosecond(s).
Pub., publication.
PV, prime vertical circle.
Qk Fl, quick flashing (light).
R, mean refraction correction, red, relative (direction), right.
RA, right ascension.
Ra, radar station.
RB, relative bearing.
R Bn, radiobeacon.
RDF, radio direction-finder, radio direction-finder station.
refr, refraction.
rel, relative.
rev, reversed.
RF, radio frequency.
R Fix, running fix.
RMS, root mean square.
R TR, radio tower.
RZn, relative azimuth.
S, sea–air temperature difference correction, set, slave station, slow, south, speed, sub point.
s, second(s).
SAR, search and rescue.
SD, semi-diameter.
SEC, sector (of light).
sec, secant, second(s).
SES, surface effect ship.
sext alt, sextant altitude.
SF, secondary phase factor.

SH, ship's head (heading).

SHA, sidereal hour angle.

SHF, super high frequency.

SI, international system of [metric] units.

SID, sudden ionospheric disturbance.

sin, sine.

S–L Fl, short–long flashing (light).

SMG, speed made good.

S/N, signal-to-noise ratio.

SOG, speed over the ground.

SP, sea position.

SRM, speed of relative movement.

SSB, single sideband transmission.

Sta, station.

st mi., statute mile(s).

T, air temperature correction, table, temperature, thousand, time, toward (intercept), true (direction).

t, meridian angle, time interval.

Tab, table, tabulated.

T alt, true altitude.

tan, tangent.

TB, temperature–pressure correction, true bearing.

TC, true course.

TcHHW, tropic higher high water.

TcLLW, tropic lower low water.

TCPA, time at closest point of approach.

temp, temperature.

T_G, ground-wave reception-time difference.

T_{GS}, ground-wave–sky-wave reception-time difference.

TH, true heading.

TR, tower, track, transmit–receive.

T_S, sky-wave reception-time difference.

T_{SG}, sky-wave–ground-wave reception-time difference.

TZn, true azimuth.

UHF, ultra high frequency.

UL, upper limb.

USMER, United States Flag Merchant Vessel Locator Filing System.

UT, universal time.

UTC, coordinated universal time.

UT_0, observed universal time.

UT_1, UT_0 corrected for polar motion.

UT_2, UT_1 corrected for Earth rotation rate variation.

V, variation, vertex.

v, excess of change of Greenwich hour angle in one hour over hourly change used in almanac increments table.

var, variation.

vel., velocity.

VHF, very high frequency.

VLF, very low frequency.

VOR, VHF omnirange.

W, watch time, west, white.

WE, watch error.

WP, water position.

X, parallactic angle, north component of horizontal intensity of Earth's magnetic field.

Y, east component of horizontal intensity of Earth's magnetic field, yellow.

yd(s), yard(s).

yr(s), year(s).

Z, azimuth angle, Coriolis correction, vertical intensity of Earth's magnetic field, zenith.

z, zenith distance.

ZD, zenith distance, zone description.

Zn, azimuth.

ZT, zone time.

α, conversion angle.

β, angle between lines of sight to top and bottom of an object or between two points, measured for determination of distance off.

Δ, difference in the value of a quantity for unit difference in a related value.

δ, latitude and velocity error of a gyro compass.

θ, angle between lines of sight to top of an object and the horizon.

λ, longitude, shielding factor, wave length (radiant energy).

λ_V, longitude of vertex of great circle.

λ_X, longitude of any designated point on a great circle.

μ, permeability.

μs, microsecond(s).

μ sec, microsecond(s).

σ, sigma.

ϕ, angle between lines of sight to the horizon and the water line of an object, magnetic flux.

χ, susceptibility.

APPENDIX D

Symbols

Positions

⌒ (British +) Dead reckoning position.
⊡ (British △) Estimated position.
⊙ Fix, assumed position, chosen position, most probable position, running fix.
△ Sea position.

Astronomical bodies

⊙ Sun
☽ Moon
♀ Venus
♂ Mars
♃ Jupiter
♄ Saturn
★ Star
⊙ ☽ Lower limb (Sun, Moon)
⊖ ☾ Centre (Sun, Moon)
⊙ ☽ Upper limb (Sun, Moon)

● New Moon
◑ Crescent Moon
◐ First quarter
◔ Gibbous Moon
○ Full Moon
◖ Gibbous Moon
◐ Third quarter
◕ Crescent Moon

Mathematics

+ Plus
− Minus
± Plus or minus
~ Algebraic difference

× Times
÷ Divided by
= Equals
> Greater than
< Less than

Miscellaneous

° Degree(s)

′ Minute(s) of arc

″ Second(s) of arc

♈ Vernal equinox

d Day(s)

h Hour(s)

m Minute(s) of time

s Second(s) of time

■ Does not rise

□ Does not set

//// Twilight all night

Index

734

INDEX

Amplitude, astronomical, 299
 of radio wave, 461
 of sound wave, 268
Anchoring, 584
Angle of cut, 32
Animal navigation, 632
Antenna, 474
 Adcock array, 485
 dipole, 474
 gain of, 476
 sense, 481
 Yagi, 476
Antennas, transmitting,
 positioning of, 516
Aphelion, 289
Apogee, 289
Apparent motion, 282
Aquino, Radler de, 419
Arctic sea smoke, 218
Arktika, Soviet icebreaker, 593
Astro observations at night, 578
Astrograph, 425
Astronavigation, defined, 280
Astronomical bodies,
 identification, 333ff
Astronomical triangle, 307
Astronomical unit, 282
Astro-tracker, 549
Atmospheric-pressure correction,
 383
Atmospheric pulling, 519
Atmospherics, 469
Attenuation of radio waves, 463
Augmentation, 384
Auroral zone, 514
Australian Institute of Navigation,
 The 85
Autopilot, 153
Azimuth, 299
 relative, 340
Azimuth angle, 299
 maximum, 304

Back sight, 347
Bandwidth, 473
Base line, of electronic navigation
 system, 501

of range finder, 145
Base line extension, 501
Bathymetric navigation, 256
Beacon, 68
 acoustic, 539, 614
 radar, 499
 (*See also* Radiobeacon, marine)
Bearing, 21
 clearing, 251
 danger, 251
 relative, 21
 turning, 584
Bearing angle, 22
Bearing plate, 135
Bearings, radio, 486
Beset, 596
Binary code, 529
Binnacle, 99
Bird navigation, 632
Blinking, 509
Blunder, 24
Bobbing a light, 265
Bore, tidal, 198
Bottom profile, 148
Bottom sample, 147
Bow and beam bearings, 246
Bowditch, Nathaniel, 401, 619
British Admiralty, 58, 59, 62, 66,
 72, 78, 79, 85, 209, 362, 525,
 619
British Standards Institution, 85,
 156, 157
Buoy, 68
 sea, 70
 station, 74
Buoyage, 69
 cardinal system, 69
 IALA System A, 70
 IALA System B, 72
 lateral system, 69
 Uniform System, 70
Bureau International de l'Heure,
 331

Cable (unit of distance), 23
Cable, coaxial, 477
Cable-laying vessels, 609

735